Supporting Self-Regulated Learning and Student Success in Online Courses

Danny Glick
University of California, Irvine, USA

Jeff Bergin
General Assembly, USA

Chi Chang
Michigan State University, USA

IGI Global
PUBLISHER of TIMELY KNOWLEDGE

A volume in the Advances in Educational Technologies and Instructional Design (AETID) Book Series

Published in the United States of America by
IGI Global
Information Science Reference (an imprint of IGI Global)
701 E. Chocolate Avenue
Hershey PA, USA 17033
Tel: 717-533-8845
Fax: 717-533-8661
E-mail: cust@igi-global.com
Web site: http://www.igi-global.com

Library of Congress Cataloging-in-Publication Data

Names: Glick, Danny, 1975- editor. | Bergin, Jeffrey, 1971- editor. | Chang, Chi, 1982- editor.
Title: Supporting self-regulated learning and student success in online courses / edited by Danny Glick, Jeffrey Bergin, Chi Chang.
Description: Hershey, PA : Information Science Reference, [2023] | Includes bibliographical references and index. | Summary: "With this in mind, this edited volume will examine current theoretical frameworks, research projects and empirical studies related to the design, implementation and evaluation of self-regulated learning models and SRL interventions in online courses, and discuss their implications for researchers, policymakers, instructional designers, and practitioners. This volume seeks to shed light on new instructional models which support self-regulated learning, and afford new ways of designing online instruction to promote self-regulation, including how to develop SRL interventions that improve student success, retention and engagement in online courses"-- Provided by publisher.
Identifiers: LCCN 2022041682 (print) | LCCN 2022041683 (ebook) | ISBN 9781668465004 (Hardcover) | ISBN 9781668465042 (Paperback) | ISBN 9781668465011 (eBook)
Subjects: LCSH: Self-culture--Case studies. | Motivation in education. | Academic achievement. | Distance education. | Web-based instruction. | Internet in education.
Classification: LCC LC32 .S89 2023 (print) | LCC LC32 (ebook) | DDC 371.33/4--dc23/eng/20220928
LC record available at https://lccn.loc.gov/2022041682
LC ebook record available at https://lccn.loc.gov/2022041683

This book is published in the IGI Global book series Advances in Educational Technologies and Instructional Design (AETID) (ISSN: 2326-8905; eISSN: 2326-8913)

British Cataloguing in Publication Data
A Cataloguing in Publication record for this book is available from the British Library.

All work contributed to this book is new, previously-unpublished material. The views expressed in this book are those of the authors, but not necessarily of the publisher.

For electronic access to this publication, please contact: eresources@igi-global.com.

Advances in Educational Technologies and Instructional Design (AETID) Book Series

Lawrence A. Tomei
Robert Morris University, USA

ISSN:2326-8905
EISSN:2326-8913

Mission

Education has undergone, and continues to undergo, immense changes in the way it is enacted and distributed to both child and adult learners. In modern education, the traditional classroom learning experience has evolved to include technological resources and to provide online classroom opportunities to students of all ages regardless of their geographical locations. From distance education, Massive-Open-Online-Courses (MOOCs), and electronic tablets in the classroom, technology is now an integral part of learning and is also affecting the way educators communicate information to students.

The **Advances in Educational Technologies & Instructional Design (AETID) Book Series** explores new research and theories for facilitating learning and improving educational performance utilizing technological processes and resources. The series examines technologies that can be integrated into K-12 classrooms to improve skills and learning abilities in all subjects including STEM education and language learning. Additionally, it studies the emergence of fully online classrooms for young and adult learners alike, and the communication and accountability challenges that can arise. Trending topics that are covered include adaptive learning, game-based learning, virtual school environments, and social media effects. School administrators, educators, academicians, researchers, and students will find this series to be an excellent resource for the effective design and implementation of learning technologies in their classes.

Coverage

- Hybrid Learning
- Classroom Response Systems
- Adaptive Learning
- Digital Divide in Education
- Higher Education Technologies
- Virtual School Environments
- Curriculum Development
- E-Learning
- Social Media Effects on Education
- Educational Telecommunications

IGI Global is currently accepting manuscripts for publication within this series. To submit a proposal for a volume in this series, please contact our Acquisition Editors at Acquisitions@igi-global.com or visit: http://www.igi-global.com/publish/.

The Advances in Educational Technologies and Instructional Design (AETID) Book Series (ISSN 2326-8905) is published by IGI Global, 701 E. Chocolate Avenue, Hershey, PA 17033-1240, USA, www.igi-global.com. This series is composed of titles available for purchase individually; each title is edited to be contextually exclusive from any other title within the series. For pricing and ordering information please visit http://www.igi-global.com/book-series/advances-educational-technologies-instructional-design/73678. Postmaster: Send all address changes to above address.

Titles in this Series

For a list of additional titles in this series, please visit: www.igi-global.com/book-series/advances-educational-technologies-instructional-design/73678

Handbook of Research on Scripting, Media Coverage, and Implementation of E-Learning Training in LMS Platforms
Mohamed Khaldi (Abdelmalek Essaadi University, Morocco)
Information Science Reference • © 2023 • 506pp • H/C (ISBN: 9781668476345) • US $285.00

Promoting Next-Generation Learning Environments Through CGScholar
Matthew Montebello (University of Malta, Malta)
Information Science Reference • © 2023 • 310pp • H/C (ISBN: 9781668451243) • US $215.00

Handbook of Research on Current Trends in Cybersecurity and Educational Technology
Remberto Jimenez (New Jersey City University, USA) and Veronica E. O'Neill (New Jersey City University, USA)
Information Science Reference • © 2023 • 482pp • H/C (ISBN: 9781668460924) • US $275.00

Multifaceted Analysis of Sustainable Strategies and Tactics in Education
Theresa Dell Neimann (Oregon State University, USA) Lynne L. Hindman (Oregon State University, USA) Elena Shliakhovchuk (The Polytechnic University of Valencia, Spain) Marian Moore (Austin Community College, USA) and Jonathan J. Felix (RMIT University, Vietnam)
Information Science Reference • © 2023 • 300pp • H/C (ISBN: 9781668460351) • US $215.00

Learning With Escape Rooms in Higher Education Online Environments
Alexandra Santamaría Urbieta (Universidad Internacional de La Rioja, Spain) and Elena Alcalde Peñalver (Universidad de Alcalá, Spain)
Information Science Reference • © 2023 • 356pp • H/C (ISBN: 9781668460818) • US $215.00

Handbook of Research on Learning in Language Classrooms Through ICT-Based Digital Technology
Rajest S. Suman (Bharath Institute of Higher Education and Research, India) Salvatore Moccia (EIT Digital Master School, Spain) Karthikeyan Chinnusamy (Veritas, USA) Bhopendra Singh (Amity University, Dubai, UAE) and R. Regin (SRM Institute of Science and Technology, India)
Information Science Reference • © 2023 • 359pp • H/C (ISBN: 9781668466827) • US $270.00

Handbook of Research on Shifting Paradigms of Disabilities in the Schooling System
Hlabathi Rebecca Maapola-Thobejane (University of South Africa, South Africa) and Mbulaheni Obert Maguvhe (University of South Africa, South Africa)
Information Science Reference • © 2023 • 435pp • H/C (ISBN: 9781668458006) • US $270.00

IGI Global
PUBLISHER of TIMELY KNOWLEDGE

701 East Chocolate Avenue, Hershey, PA 17033, USA
Tel: 717-533-8845 x100 • Fax: 717-533-8661
E-Mail: cust@igi-global.com • www.igi-global.com

Editorial Advisory Board

Table of Contents

Detailed Table of Contents

The author proposes a comprehensive process for applying established self-regulated learning models, strategies, scaffolding, and assessments to any online or blended program, course, or experience. The process draws upon the self-regulated learning model proposed by Barry J. Zimmerman, one of the leading self-regulated learning scholars, as well as contributions from a variety of self-regulated learning scholars, pedagogical researchers, and learning scientists. The chapter provides a step-by-step procedure for incorporating self-regulated learning strategies regardless of the reader's familiarity with online and blended learning, instructional design processes and principles, and self-regulated learning strategies and techniques.

Students today enjoy unprecedented freedom and autonomy to choose and manage what, when, where, and how they learn. However, many students squander these opportunities by embracing learning techniques that, at best, can help them attain short-term performance objectives but are relatively ineffective at fostering long-term learning and retention. This chapter describes research findings that highlight and address some of the most common misconceptions and cognitive biases that can impede or undermine self-regulated learning processes. The authors propose several research-based recommendations for addressing these misconceptions and biases in the design of self-regulated learning programs and curricula. These include integrating "desirable difficulties" in learning; instructing students about effective learning strategies along with common myths, misconceptions, and biases of learning; and tailoring interventions to improve critical social and emotional learning skills and mitigate relevant cognitive biases.

The perspective of self-directed and self-regulated learning as a generalized skill discounts the fact that a major driver of self-direction is an individual's motives centered on communities of practice. Effective design of learning experiences that foster agency, self-direction, and curiosity requires a clearer understanding of this relationship. Activity theory provides a helpful model for explaining the internal and external interactions of learning, both individually and within a community. Without this perspective, educators too often blame learners as failing to have self-regulation when in reality these learners are working under a different set of goals, roles, rules, or tools than those of the learning designer. Using this framework, this theoretical overview will demonstrate ways an immersive adult technology training academy helps support novices striving to enter technology-related careers, as they develop the identity, skills, and self-regulation of coding, data, and design professions.

Self-regulated learning (SRL) is a well-known concept within the field of online learning; however, tracking, interpreting, and scaffolding effective SRL strategies can be challenging. SRL encompasses complex and dynamic processes involved in monitoring and controlling the cognitive, motivational, and behavioral components of learning. Such processes include task interpretation, application of knowledge and strategies to solving that task, and monitoring the relative success of implementing a particular strategy. Metacognitive monitoring is a critical component of effective implementation of SRL. Without accurate monitoring, a learner doesn't have adequate information to know whether and how to adjust their learning choices. This chapter discusses two studies that explore how feedback valence influences learners' metacognitive perceptions of their performance and how those (mis)perceptions impact both their expectations for future success as well as SRL choices for a subsequent task.

The purpose of this chapter is to describe the development and impact of a digital tool that can be used to support students' self-regulated learning and metacognitive skills. The nature of online courses can restrict an instructor's ability to interact directly with their students. Digital courseware can help instructors connect with and support their online students in a different manner. A series of surveys were developed and digitally deployed to help students plan, monitor, and evaluate their progress toward goals. A multi-semester research study found that students enrolled in online classes who completed three or more surveys during the semester experienced better course performance compared to students who chose not to complete the surveys. Students who chose to complete less than three surveys performed comparably to their non-user peers. Students enrolled in hybrid or face-to-face classes tended to outperform their peers in online courses regardless of how many surveys they had completed.

Microsurveys are a powerful tool to gather data to enable improved learner self-regulation, which can contribute to improved learner outcomes. However, for microsurveys to be effective, researchers may need to refactor their research, design, and evaluation processes to address microsurvey creation, deployment, and optimization. This chapter considers how researchers may develop microsurveys by formulating a research base, developing initial designs, and then conducting formative evaluation for ongoing improvement.

The study aimed at exposing expressions of metacognitive knowledge and self-regulation among in-service teachers taking an online course, examining the changes they applied in the tasks they developed in the course and characterizing their perceptions regarding the online course design principles. Teachers' blogs were analyzed inductively, based on a metacognition and self-regulation rubric developed in this study, as well as on design principles for online learning environments. The findings indicate increased expressions of knowledge of the task, people, and strategies. However, obstacles regarding time management were mentioned. Teachers' perceptions analysis indicates that learning from and with peers, course organization, and making thinking visible were the most significant principles promoting their learning. It seems that the online course offered the teachers a constructive, supportive learning environment, enabling them to express their metacognition and self-regulation skills, as well as the insights they will consider when designing tasks in the future.

Digital education tools have revolutionized how learning solutions can be personalized for the benefit of all learners. When advances in technology are paired with knowledge of how individuals learn most effectively, more efficacious learning solutions can be developed. In this chapter, the authors contend that not only should learning science principles drive the technologies learners engage with, but combining these principles with the algorithms that personalize a learner's experience will greatly impact learning outcomes at scale. They offer a brief discussion of automation and self-regulation in educational technology, then provide an example of a novel learning solution that pairs personalization—through automated intelligence—with learning science principles to impact outcomes. A practical discussion of how to design and develop learning solutions for maximum impact is shared, as well as best practices for conducting validity and efficacy research to measure the extent to which intelligent self-regulation features are supporting learning outcomes.

Gamification is an active-learning approach commonly used in education to promote learner engagement. This chapter provides an overview of how gamified approaches can be applied to enable university students comprising of Generation Z and Y learners, to access authentic learning resources to self-regulate their learning in preparation for assessment. Methods and flexible strategies that can be incorporated into undergraduate and postgraduate education programs worldwide are provided. Three case studies illustrate the use of technology-enhanced weekly quizzes to optimise student engagement, knowledge retention, and academic performance. Key educational theories and practices that underpinned the case studies include social constructivism, disuse theory, and complexity theory alongside the use of scaffolding, chunking, flipped classroom, deliberate practice, and periodic revisitation. The chapter concludes with 12 pearls of wisdom to optimize leaner engagement using a gamified approach to enhance the students' ability to self-regulate their learning and achieve their learning goals.

This chapter focuses on a pilot project that utilized an artificial intelligence chatbot named the APABot to help 24 students from the Diploma in Psychology Studies apply APA (7th edition) style in their 400- to 500-word essay. This writing task was a requirement for Communication and Information Literacy, a fundamental subject for all first-year students in Temasek Polytechnic, Singapore. The four research questions were as follows: 1) How did the students respond to the APABot? 2) What strategies did the students use to learn from the APABot? 3) How did the APABot assist students to comply with the APA (7th edition) conventions in their writing? and 4) What were the characteristics of successful self-regulators using the APABot? Data from user logs, the number and types of errors, and a survey provided insights to the above questions.

Section 4
Self-Regulated Learning Across Contexts

Self-regulation is a core concept associated with the metacognitive, motivational, and emotional aspects of learning. The COVID-19 pandemic provides a large-scale setting to collect new empirical evidence to test this conceptual framework in an authentic online learning environment. By reference to 64,949 participants enrolled at 39 universities in China, the authors developed the Undergraduate Online Self-Regulated Learning Questionnaire and estimated the associations among self-regulation, motivation, emotion, and skill mastery with regard to online learning across different subgroups of a diverse student body. The results demonstrated that males, rural students, lower-division undergraduates, first-generation college students, SEAM majors, and students at elite universities reported significantly lower UOSL scores. After controlling for motivation and emotion, these gaps decreased substantially and become statistically nonsignificant. The findings highlight the critical role played by targeted interventions in the creation of a supportive online environment for disadvantaged subgroups.

Undergraduates who engage in high structure, high enrollment, active learning courses tend to perform best when they self-regulate their learning. Student self-regulated learning is encouraged by active learning designs that provide resources used to enact strategies and engage in planning, monitoring, and evaluation of one's learning processes. Some learners may need to "learn to learn" before these resources can be leveraged effectively. This chapter documents a scalable co-design and learning analytics project led by learning scientists and science, technology, engineering, and math (STEM) instructors who enhanced digital resources of large-lecture courses' learning management systems (LMSs). Students' course engagement produced data about self-regulated learning processes, affording feature engineering, prediction modeling and provision of timely support to students predicted to struggle. The authors report initial results through the lens of self-regulated learning theory and elaborate cases demonstrating institutionalization and replicability to research and regional institutions.

Online learning has been recognized as a promising approach to improve learning outcomes in developing

Preface

Online and blended learning have been growing in both popularity and practice over the past thirty years, with a drastic acceleration since the onset of the COVID-19 pandemic (Ginder, Kelly-Reid, & Mann, 2019; National Student Clearinghouse Research Center, 2022; Seaman, Allen, & Seaman, 2018; Xu & Xu, 2019).While online education has traditionally been viewed as an alternative pathway for nontraditional students seeking higher education opportunities, the emergence of the COVID-19 pandemic has forced students and educators across all levels of education to rapidly adapt to online learning. The pandemic has created the largest disruption of education systems in history, affecting nearly 1.6 billion learners in more than 190 countries, forcing K-20 education to shift to online learning (United Nations, 2020). Today, learners engage in online or blended learning in primary, secondary, post-secondary, workforce training, and workplace learning like never before in modern history.

Concomitant with the boom in online learning are escalating concerns about academic accountability, specifically with respect to student outcomes as measured by persistence and success. These concerns emerge from research indicating that dropout rates in online courses are significantly higher than in traditional brick-and-mortar learning environments (Soffer & Cohen, 2019). A 2019 report by Xu and Xu found that online students are up to 15 percent more likely to drop out than are students in face-to-face classes at community colleges in North America (Xu & Xu, 2019). This finding is very problematic, as lower retention rates among online students have been connected to overall lack of academic success in higher education (Xu & Jaggars, 2011). Xu and Jaggars' study points to the importance of online course success, particularly in view of evidence suggesting that failing online college courses early in one's college career may impede progression towards graduation (Xu & Jaggars, 2011).

While online learning is growing in popularity, many students struggle in such settings, especially students lacking certain personal attributes - such as being goal-oriented and self-disciplined - that are essential for online success. Learners need to be able to navigate, engage, and persist in such environments with more autonomy and self-directedness than was otherwise needed in traditional brick-and-mortar learning environments. This, in turn, requires learners to adopt, practice, and internalize self-regulated learning strategies. Students who self-regulate are more likely to improve their academic performance, find value in their learning process, and continue to be effective lifelong learners (Zimmerman, 2002). However, online students often struggle to self-regulate, which may contribute to lower academic performance. Likewise, less experienced online teachers who are in the process of implementing—or have implemented—a shift from in-person to distance learning may struggle to enable their students to employ effective self-regulation strategies.

While self-regulation strategies - and the models that underpin them - have been the subject of considerable research and publication, their direct application to online and blended learning remains nascent but quickly evolving. To put it plainly, while both self- regulated learning and blended learning have been the focus of increased research, far less research has brought these two concepts together, critical and complimentary as they are. This book addresses a number of important considerations related to learner self-regulation in online and blended environments. The literature indicates that self-regulation is indeed an effective practice for enhancing student success, engagement and retention among students. While it is closely tied to motivation, emotion, and skill mastery, the nature of these relationships remain elusive. Indeed, the very notion of self-regulation is often surrounded by misconceptions, myths, and biases that impede the adoption or implementation of successful practices.

Technology is opening up the concept of self-regulated learning in exciting and innovative ways. Increasingly, learning technologists are able to invoke self-regulated learning strategies in their platform, feature, and AI designs. For example, AI can be leveraged to develop algorithms that can automate and personalize self-regulation at scale and can enable technologies, such as chatbots, that can help learners to self-regulate in a variety of courses. Active learning designs can foster self-regulated learning and inform the development of technologies that enable it at scale, including learning platform features, predictive modeling, and targeted support. Gamification can both be informed by self-regulated learning and promote self-regulated learning in ways that are based on a host of learning science and pedagogical principles. And self-regulated learning methods provide an opportunity to address the dropout rates and boost student success in self-paced Massive Open Online Courses (MOOCs) through risk detection and improved design.

Increased awareness of self-regulated learning is enabling learning designers and instructors to adopt simple processes to begin to implement self-regulated learning strategies in their programs, courses, and pedagogies. Common learning technologies, such as LMSs and course authoring systems, enable instructors to more readily develop and facilitate online courses in ways that are aligned with self-regulated learning. Simple tools that can foster self-regulation, especially with students at a distance from their instructors, need to be deployed to help learners plan, monitor, and evaluate their own progress. Yet, adherents would do well to consider philosophical issues such as the degree to which self-regulation is a skill that learners can and should acquire or the result of being in a community of practice that fosters their own motivation, agency, self-direction, and curiosity.

Most importantly, learners themselves need encouragement and opportunities in their earliest online courses to practice, embrace, and benefit from self-regulated learning strategies and resources. This includes practice with metacognitive monitoring – based in part on learner perceptions and the feedback that informs those perceptions – which is a critical component of both learner expectations and choices. Being able to successfully think about one's thinking, learning, and performance is of course foundational to the very concept of self regulation.

ORGANIZATION OF THE BOOK

This book examines self-regulated learning through a variety of lenses informed by applied, empirical, and theoretical scholarship provided by contributors from academia, industry, and consulting from countries as diverse as Australia, China, Israel, Singapore, and the United States in settings as varied as primary, secondary, post-secondary, and higher education including workforce and workplace learning. The authors featured in this volume possess experience and expertise in disciplines as wide-ranging as Assessment and Measurement, Learning Science and Design, Education Policy and Research, Educational Publishing and Technology, Artificial Intelligence and Learning Analytics, Online and Blended Learning Modalities, Computer Science and Engineering, Gamification, Student Success, and Health and Medical Education.

The book has 15 chapters organized into four sections. Section 1, "Contemporary and Future Perspectives on Self-Regulated Learning" (Chapters 1-3), focuses on processes for applying self-regulated learning constructs to online or blended learning; the most common misconceptions, biases, and illusions pertaining to self-regulated learning; and the degree to which self-regulation is a skill or a feature of a community of practice. Section 2, "Metacognitive Feedback and Assessment" (Chapters 4-7), focuses on metacognitive monitoring and tools as key elements of online and blended learning experiences and their implementation. Section 3, "Learning Technologies and Pedagogies for Promoting Self-Regulated Learning" (Chapters 8-10), focuses on the importance of using learning science principles to inform algorithms to drive learning outcomes at scale; the possibility of using gamification to access authentic learning resources to self-regulate and prepare for assessments; and the development of AI chatbots to foster self-regulation. Finally, Section 4, "Self-Regulated Learning Across Contexts" (Chapters 11-15), focuses on the associations between self-regulation, motivation, emotion, and skill mastery; the relationship between self-regulated learning and active learning designs; the relationship between SRL learning processes, metacognition and student retention within the context of developing countries; the practices aimed at improving students' self-regulation of online learning; and the benefits of self-regulated learning techniques for adult learners taking transitional studies courses.

Following is a brief description of each of the chapters:

Section 1: Contemporary and Future Perspectives on Self-Regulated Learning

Chapter 1, "Promoting Learner Self-Regulation in Blended Learning: A Process for Systematic Application," presents a comprehensive process for applying established self-regulated learning models, strategies, scaffolding and assessments to any online or blended program, course or experience. The process draws upon the self-regulated learning model proposed by Barry J. Zimmerman as well as contributions from a variety of self-regulated learning scholars, pedagogical researchers, and learning scientists. The chapter provides a step-by-step procedure for incorporating self-regulated learning strategies regardless of the reader's familiarity with online and blended learning, instructional design processes and principles, and self-regulated learning strategies and techniques.

Chapter 2, "When Learning Is Too Good to Be True: Addressing Common Myths, Misrepresentations, and Misconceptions Through the Science of Self-Regulation," examines some of the most common misconceptions of self-regulated learning, as well as the cognitive biases and illusions that underlie them. The authors offer several research-based recommendations for addressing these misconceptions and biases in the design of self-regulated learning programs and curricula, such as instructing students about effective learning strategies along with common myths, misconceptions, and biases of learning; integrating "desirable difficulties" in learning; and emphasizing critical social and emotional learning skills to mitigate relevant cognitive biases.

Chapter 3, "Self-Directed Learning Is a Social Activity (and Not a Generalized Skill)," refutes the notion that self-directed and self-regulated learning as a generalized skill, which discounts the fact that a major driver of self-direction is an individual's motives centered on communities of practice. The author argues that effective design of learning experiences that foster agency, self-direction, and curiosity requires a clearer understanding of this relationship. The author suggests that activity theory provides a helpful model for explaining learning interactions, both individually and within a community and that without this perspective, educators mistake learners as failing to self-regulate, when in fact, these learners are working under different goals, roles, rules or tools than those of the learning designer.

Section 2: Metacognitive Feedback and Assessment

Chapter 4, "Perception as Reality: Perceived Performance Impacts Expectancies, Values, and Self-Regulated Choices," focuses on metacognitive monitoring as a critical component of effective implementation of SRL. The authors assert that without accurate monitoring a learner doesn't have adequate information to know whether and how to adjust their learning choices. They discuss two studies that explore how feedback valence influences learners' metacognitive perceptions of their performance, and how those (mis)perceptions impact both their expectations for future success as well as SRL choices for a subsequent task.

Chapter 5, "The Implementation and Impact of a Self-Regulated Learning Survey on Student Outcomes," describes the development and impact of a digital tool intended to support students' self-regulated learning and metacognitive skills. This included a series of surveys that were developed and digitally deployed to help students plan, monitor, and evaluate their progress toward goals. The researchers found that students enrolled in online classes who completed three or more surveys during the semester experienced better course performance compared to students who chose not to complete the surveys. Students who chose to complete less than three Surveys performed comparably to their non-user peers. Students enrolled in hybrid or face-to-face classes tended to outperform their peers in online courses regardless of how many surveys completed.

Chapter 6, "Supporting Student Self-Regulation: Designing and Deploying Effective Microsurveys and Warning Systems to Help Learners Help Themselves," considers how researchers may develop microsurveys by formulating a research base, developing initial designs, and then conducting formative evaluation for ongoing improvement. The chapter focuses on initial and iterative design issues, such as microsurvey creation and modification, microsurvey formats and usability, microsurvey deployment protocols (such as first occurrence, frequency, and deployment tiers) and microsurvey transparency within the context of self-regulated learning.

Chapter 7, "Metacognitive Knowledge and Self-Regulation of In-Service Teachers in an Online Learning Environment," focuses on exposing expressions of metacognitive knowledge and self-regulation among in-service teachers taking an online course. The authors examine changes applied in the lessons they developed and characterize their perceptions regarding online course design principles. They found increased expressions of knowledge of the task, people and strategies, as well as obstacles regarding time management. They assert that teachers' perceptions indicate that learning from and with peers, course organization, and making thinking visible were the most significant principles promoting their learning. The online course offered the teachers a constructive and supportive learning environment which enabled them to express their metacognition and self-regulation skills, and insights for future lessons.

Section 3: Learning Technologies and Pedagogies for Promoting Self-Regulated Learning

Chapter 8, "Intelligent Self-Regulation: Bridging AI and Learning Science to Support Student Success," asserts that not only should learning science principles drive the technologies learners engage with, but combining these principles with the algorithms that personalize a learner's experience will greatly impact learning outcomes at scale. The authors discuss the automation and self-regulation in educational technology and provide an example of a novel learning solution that pairs personalization—through automated intelligence—with learning science principles to impact outcomes. A practical discussion of how to design and develop learning solutions for maximum impact is shared, as well as best practices for conducting validity and efficacy research to measure the extent to which intelligent self-regulation features are supporting learning outcomes.

Chapter 9, "Re-Imagining Health and Medicine Education: Implementing a Mobile-Based Gamification App for Improved Affective Learner Engagement," examines how gamification enables university students to access authentic learning resources to self-regulate their learning in preparation for assessment and provide methods and strategies that can be incorporated into undergraduate and postgraduate education programs. The authors provide case studies that illustrate the use of technology-enhanced quizzes to optimize student engagement, knowledge retention, and academic performance based on social constructivism, disuse theory, and complexity theory alongside the use of scaffolding, chunking, flipped classroom, deliberate practice, and periodic revisitation. The chapter concludes with twelve strategies to optimize learner engagement and self-regulation using gamification.

Chapter 10, "AI Chatbot to Assist Students Applying APA (7th Edition) Style in Their Academic Writing in a Polytechnic in Singapore," focuses on a research project that utilized an Artificial Intelligent Chatbot, named the APABot, to help 24 students from the Diploma in Psychology Studies apply APA (7th edition) style in a 400-to-500-word essay to achieve a requirement for Communication and Information Literacy course required by Temasek Polytechnic in Singapore. Data from user logs, the number and types of errors, and a survey provided insights how students responded to this intervention, the strategies they learned, their compliance with writing conventions, and the characteristics of successful self-regulation.

Section 4: Self-Regulated Learning Across Contexts

Chapter 11, "Self-Regulation, Motivation, Emotion, and Skill Mastery of Online Learning: New Evidence From a Survey During COVID-19," examines the associations between self-regulation, motivation, emotion, and skill mastery of online learning across different subgroups in a diverse student body. The authors developed the Undergraduate Online Self-Regulated Learning (USOL) Questionnaire and gathered empirical evidence from 64,949 participants enrolled at 39 universities of China in authentic online learning environments. They found that males, rural students, lower division of undergraduates, first-generation college students, SEAM majors, and students at elite universities reported significantly lower UOSL scores. After controlling motivation and emotion, these gaps have shrunk substantially and become statistically insignificant. The findings highlight the critical role of the targeted interventions to create a supportive online environment for specific subgroup of learners.

Chapter 12, "Development, Sustainment, and Scaling of Self-Regulated Learning Analytics: Prediction Modeling and Digital Student Success Initiatives in University Contexts," examines the relationship between self-regulated learning and active learning designs that provide resources that can be used to engage in planning, monitoring, and evaluating one's learning processes. The authors document a scalable co-design and learning analytics project led by learning scientists and science, technology, engineering, and math (STEM) instructors, who enhanced digital resources of large-lecture courses' learning management system (LMS). Leveraging course engagement data, the researchers analyzed self-regulated learning processes that enabled feature engineering, prediction modeling and targeted support for struggling students.

Chapter 13, "Using Written Responses to Reflection Questions to Improve Online Student Retention: A Text Analysis Approach," examines whether persistence and achievement in online courses are affected by evidence of reflection found in Latino students' responses to open-ended questions. The results suggest that traces of SRL learning behaviors and metacognitive processes may prove effective in identifying at-risk students in developing countries – a previously understudied context. The chapter provides guidance on how to identify at-risk students in developing countries by analyzing student responses to open-ended questions using automated text analysis techniques.

Chapter 14, "Developing Students' Self-Regulation Skills Within and Outside Academic Modules," examines practices aimed at improving students' self-regulation of online learning. They describe initial learning experiences in online, self-paced courses in mathematics, physics and chemistry that provide students opportunities to embrace the 'norm' of self-paced, self-directed online learning and to encourage them to develop self-regulation skills by self-assessing and accessing learning resources based on their identified needs. The researchers developed an intervention based on Zimmerman's self-regulated learning model, guiding students to plan, monitor and adjust their learning plans; and leverage coaching sessions to facilitate implementation.

Chapter 15, "Teaching Students to Be Students: Facilitating Self-Regulated Learning in Transitional Studies," focuses on the benefits of self-regulated learning techniques for adult learners taking transitional studies courses. The chapter addresses the advances in educational technology, including learning management systems and numerous interactive learning tools, that have made it easier for subject matter experts, or SMEs, to design courses in which students learn key topics with minimal instructor intervention, and how this provides tools to allow the instructor to facilitate learning more effectively.

Clearly, this volume represents a wide variety of views on self-regulated learning from authors in both academia and industry, including assertions based on the research expertise and anecdotal experience of the authors. It is worth noting that these views may not necessarily reflect the practices or opinions of their current institutional or organizational affiliation.

CONCLUSION

Supporting Self-Regulated Learning and Student Success in Online Courses examines current theoretical frameworks, research projects, and empirical studies related to the design, implementation, and evaluation of self-regulated learning models and interventions in online courses and discusses their implications. Covering key topics such as online course design, student retention, and learning support, this reference work is ideal for administrators, policymakers, researchers, academicians, practitioners, scholars, instructors, and students.

This book is both important and timely given both the preponderance of online and blended learning experiences and the expectations that learning will necessarily become a lifelong pursuit in a rapidly evolving information age. As online and blended learning continue to evolve, improve, and gain acceptance (sometimes urgently), learners need to be equipped with the skills to succeed in these environments. This requires institutions to develop policies, practices, and professional development that support successful self-regulation; program designers, learning designers, and instructors to approach student success from the angle of self-regulation; and technologists to develop platforms, capabilities, and algorithms that support self-regulation. Most importantly, this requires learners to internalize metacognition and self-regulation independently, in communities, and in ways that tap into their motivation, agency, and overall wellbeing.

Danny Glick
University of California, Irvine, USA

Jeff Bergin
General Assembly, USA

Chi Chang
Michigan State University, USA

REFERENCES

Ginder, S. A., Kelly-Reid, J. E., & Mann, F. B. (2019). Enrollment and employees in postsecondary institutions, fall 2017; and financial statistics and academic libraries, fall 2017. U.S. Department of Education, National Center for Education Statistics. https://nces.ed.gov/pubs2019/2019021REV.pdf

National Student Clearinghouse Research Center. (2022). *Overview: Spring 2022 enrollment estimates.* https://nscresearchcenter.org/stay-informed/

Seaman, J. E., Allen, I. E., & Seaman, J. (2018). *Grade increase: tracking distance education in the United States.* Babson Survey Research Group. https://www.bayviewanalytics.com/reports/gradeincrease.pdf

Soffer, T., & Cohen, A. (2019). Students' engagement characteristics predict success and completion of online courses. *Journal of Computer Assisted Learning*, *35*(3), 378–389. doi:10.1111/jcal.12340

United Nations. (2020). *Policy Brief: Education during COVID-19 and beyond.* https://unsdg.un.org/resources/policy-brief-education-during-covid-19-and-beyond

Xu, D., & Jaggars, S. S. (2011). *Online and hybrid course enrollment and performance in Washington state community and technical colleges.* CCRC working paper no. 31. Community College Research Center, Columbia University.

Xu, D., & Xu, Y. (2019). *The promises and limits of online higher education: Understanding how distance education affects access, cost, and quality.* American Enterprise Institute. https://www.aei.org/research-products/report/the-promises-and-limits-of-online-higher-education

Zimmerman, B. J. (2002). Becoming a self-regulated learner: An overview. *Theory into Practice*, *41*(2), 64–72. doi:10.120715430421tip4102_2

Section 1

Contemporary and Future Perspectives on Self-Regulated Learning

Chapter 1
Promoting Learner Self-Regulation in Blended Learning:
A Process for Systematic Application

Jeff Bergin
General Assembly, USA

ABSTRACT

The author proposes a comprehensive process for applying established self-regulated learning models, strategies, scaffolding, and assessments to any online or blended program, course, or experience. The process draws upon the self-regulated learning model proposed by Barry J. Zimmerman, one of the leading self-regulated learning scholars, as well as contributions from a variety of self-regulated learning scholars, pedagogical researchers, and learning scientists. The chapter provides a step-by-step procedure for incorporating self-regulated learning strategies regardless of the reader's familiarity with online and blended learning, instructional design processes and principles, and self-regulated learning strategies and techniques.

INTRODUCTION

The COVID-19 pandemic and associated shelter-in-place, social distancing and quarantine efforts accelerated the already rapid shift from traditional, face-to-face education to online and blended learning. According to research from the U.S. Census Bureau, 93% of all learners received some kind of online instruction during the pandemic (McElrath, 2020). Engaging in online and blended learning necessarily requires students to be, at a minimum, more self-directed. Fortunately, abundant research on learner self-regulation exists; the past three decades have provided growing research on self-regulated learning (SRL), including at least three meta-analyses (Dignath & Büttner, 2008; Dignath et al., 2008; Sitzmann & Ely, 2011) and a critical review (Panadero, 2017).

Similarly, the growth in online and blended learning over that same time has resulted in decades of research including meta-analyses that show that blended learning can be even more effective than traditional learning alone. This is attributed to the possibility that blended learning involves additional

DOI: 10.4018/978-1-6684-6500-4.ch001

learning time, instructional resources, and course elements (Means et al., 2013). Incidentally, this points to the superior instructional and learning design that blended experiences often undergo through the thoughtful process of instructional systems design and learning experience design. Therefore, blended learning design is an outstanding opportunity to improve the overall quality of a program, course, or experience and, therefore, an opportune moment to enhance the experience with a systematically designed and implemented SRL strategy.

While both SRL and blended learning have been the focus of increased research, little attention has been paid to the process of designing, implementing, assessing, evaluating, and improving SRL strategies and elements within blended program design, pedagogical practices, and student success services. And while learners are increasingly trained to adopt their own self-regulation strategies, they are often reluctant or unprepared to adopt these strategies in actual practice (Foerst et al., 2017). Therefore, it is incumbent upon instructional designers, educational technologists, and instructors to integrate these strategies thoughtfully and strategically into all aspects of their learning experiences.

This chapter proposes a design, implementation, and evaluation process that can be applied to any online or blended program, course or experience. The process draws upon the SRL model proposed by Barry J. Zimmerman, one of the leading SRL scholars, as well as contributions from a variety of SRL scholars and researchers. The process for systematic application presented in this chapter is proposed by the author, but the self-regulated learning model and strategies are those derived by Zimmerman and other scholars. These models and strategies are, arguably, more important than the application process itself; the process is simply intended to help instructors and instructional designers thoughtfully (and systematically) integrate SRL strategies into a variety of learning experiences.

The process provides a step-by-step procedure for incorporating SRL strategies regardless of a reader's familiarity with online and blended learning, instructional design processes and principles, and SRL strategies and techniques. The process begins by analyzing learners' self-regulation experience, then considering the intended learner outcomes and learning objectives and the ways in which these are delivered, and then facilitates the incorporation of SRL phases, strategies, and scaffolding. It then introduces ideas for implementation, assessment, evaluation and ongoing optimization. The chapter concludes with three short samples that illustrate how SRL can be applied to programs, courses, and shorter experiences. The process is intended to provide practitioners with a practical overview to facilitate more thoughtful and evidence-based approaches to self-regulation as a fundamental part of the design process. By applying this process, instructors and instructional designers can integrate SRL principles into all aspects of their online and blended learning experiences. As with many processes, using every element could be overwhelming, time consuming, and ultimately yield an over-architected experience. It may make more sense for each reader to select those areas that seem best aligned to their context and needs, experimenting to reach a combination of approaches that best serve their learners and intended outcomes.

BACKGROUND

Learning has never been in greater demand than it is today. The ongoing shift to a knowledge economy and the lengthened lifespan in western countries – with skills rapidly evolving – has created an environment in which learning is a skill needed to acquire new skills (Weiss, 2020; World Bank, 2003). On top of these macro demands, the nature of learning itself is changing. For example, lifelong learning may not include traditional higher education, or it may go beyond traditional higher education to include the ongoing acquisition of specific skills through online platforms and other shortform learning programs. Learning needs to become more accessible, more equitable, and more inclusive. Learning need not be bound by one's proximity to a place of learning; blocked by physical or learning disabilities; limited by a lack of finances, resources, and support; or unattainable due to a perceived lack of linguistic skills, prior knowledge, or ability. Learning is, increasingly, becoming more accessible – and shifting to online and blended models has enabled this access (Study International, 2017).

Yet, while learning is becoming both more necessary, more ubiquitous, and more accessible, learners often lack an understanding or desire about how to improve their own learning skills and adopt learning strategies (Foerst et al., 2017). Thus, learners remain largely reliant upon the quality of instruction they receive. This is increasingly problematic in a world in which instruction itself is increasingly delivered in online and blended formats – formats in which learners need to be able to manage and monitor their own learning effectively. Not surprisingly, students report finding online learning more challenging than traditional learning – especially when it hasn't been intentionally designed. In one such study, 60% of students found information processing to be more difficult online (Corman et al., 2020). In another study, only 41% of students reported feeling mentally and physically prepared for online learning (Baticulon et al., 2021). Clearly, learners need help regulating their learning in online and blended environments.

SRL meets this imperative. SRL is the practice of managing and monitoring one's learning. According to Zimmerman, SRL is "The degree to which students are metacognitively, motivationally, and behaviorally active participants in their own learning processes" (2013, p.137). SRL is related to the concept of metacognition. Metacognition involves being aware of one's cognition and being able to regulate it (Sperling et al., 2004). It's generally accepted that, "Knowledge of cognition refers to how much learners understand about their own memories and the way they learn. Regulation of cognition refers to how well learners can regulate their own memory and learning" (Sperling et al., 2004, p.118). When learners think about what they are about to learn; think about how they are studying; and think about what they have just learned, they are using their metacognitive skills. By engaging in these types of processes, they are beginning to regulate their own learning.

In an education paradigm in which learners often negotiate their own learning through the practice of instruction, does the notion of self-regulation actually work? Researchers have overwhelmingly found that SRL improves learning performance ((Dignath and Büttner 2008; Dignath et al., 2008; Hattie et al., 1996; Richardson et al., 2012; Sitzmann and Ely, 2011; Theobald, 2021). Although there remains debate about its overall long-term benefit, which strategies are most effective for which learner populations, and the nature of the relationship between SRL and academic achievement markers, such as GPA (Cetin, 2015; de Boer, H. et al., 2018; Sitzmann and Ely, 2011).

Despite the strong evidence base, SRL may not actually help learners learn. Not because it doesn't work; but rather because learners don't know how to self-regulate and instructors and instructional designers may not be applying SRL strategies and practices effectively into their course designs, pedagogies, and into the support services that enable student success (Foerst et al., 2017). Herein lies a central irony: to help learners learn within a domain, instructors and instructional designers need to help them learn *how to* learn.

To be effective, self-regulation strategies need to be systematically applied to a learning experience. This requires instructors and instructional designers to understand SRL models and strategies and to incorporate the elements of these into their learning designs, pedagogical practices, and even into the services with which learners come into contact throughout their learning experience. This, in turn, requires instructors and instructional designers to better understand their learners, the outcomes that they expect these learners to achieve, and how to assess the degree to which SRL strategies are improving these outcomes.

A PROCESS FOR THE SYSTEMATIC APPLICATION OF SRL

The effective implementation of SRL strategies doesn't happen by randomly incorporating a learning strategy or metacognitive technique within a learning experience. Rather, self-regulation is enhanced through the systematic design of SRL strategies and techniques in a learning experience - based, in large part, on an analysis of the learner population, the intended outcomes and objectives and how these will be delivered, and the best self-regulation strategies as well as the scaffolding needed at specific timepoints to enable those strategies to be adopted and used autonomously by learners.

Importantly, this process integrates SRL strategy instruction into the design and delivery of a particular learning experience, rather than treating SRL as a separate instructional or learning activity. There are three reasons for this intentional integration. First, to get learners to practice using these strategies in actual, authentic practice (Foerst et al., 2017). Second, to tie these strategies to legitimate learning goals, self-monitoring, and experiences (Guo, 2022; Papies and Aarts, 2016; Perry & Martin, 2016). Third, because research indicates that effective strategy use should be in context using tasks within the target content domain (Hattie et al., 1996). Taken together, it makes more sense to integrate SRL strategies into a learning experience than to train learners in these strategies in isolation.

To achieve this aim, this chapter presents a process for the systematic application of SRL strategies (see Table 1). This process takes instructors and instructional designers through a thorough design process beginning with an analysis of their learners current SRL understanding, followed by an analysis of intended outcomes and, importantly, the ways in which those outcomes are delivered through course design, pedagogy, and support; followed then by the adoption of self-regulation strategies and techniques. The process then encourages instructors and instructional designers to consider the scaffolding needed to support these strategies and techniques and the best practices for implementing them with fidelity. The process concludes with recommendations for assessment, evaluation, and ongoing optimization. In short, this process enables instructors and instructional designers to establish the intensity, architecture, strategies and scaffolding needed, as well as the practices for implementation, assessment, and evaluation. The next section walks through each step in this process.

Analyze Learner Attributes

The first step in developing a SRL approach is considering the SRL skills, habits, and aptitudes of the learners – especially relative to domain or subject matter. Naturally, learners may be proficient self-regulators in some areas but poor self-regulators in others. In a blended learning environment, analyzing learner attributes may include their ability to self-regulate in a partially virtual or remote environment. The following considerations may help instructors and instructional designers determine the self-regulatory experience of learners: their intrinsic motivation level, prior knowledge, and familiarity with SRL strategies.

- **Intrinsic Motivation:** Learners who are interested in a program, course or learning experience and highly intrinsically motivated may already possess – even if informally – SRL skills by the

Table 1. An evidence-based process for supporting learner self-regulation in blended learning experiences

Step	Guiding Question	Consideration	Establishes
Step 1: Analyze learner attributes	How well can learners already self-regulate?	Intrinsic motivation Prior knowledge SRL experience	Intensity of the SRL interventions
Step 2: Determine outcome and objective delivery	What are the intended learner outcomes and learning objectives, how will they be delivered, and how can they be enhanced by SRL strategies?	Program design Pedagogical practices Support services	Architecture of the SRL strategies
Step 3: Select strategies for SRL	What SRL techniques will best support learning?	SRL models SRL categories	Techniques incorporated into the SRL strategies
Step 4: Establish scaffolding needed by level	How much scaffolding is needed at certain points in the learning experience?	Learner progress through stages of SRL development	Scaffolding provided for SRL at the beginning, middle and end of the program, course or learning experience
Step 5: Implement with fidelity	How can instructors successfully implement a learning experience that is enhanced by SRL?	Managing Cognitive Load Making SRL Explicit Enabling Autonomy and Automaticity	Practices for implementing SRL in the program, course, or learning experience
Step 6: Provide meaningful assessments	How can SRL strategies be assessed?	Directly Assessing Self-regulation Skills Drawing Indirect Inferences from Academic Performance Assessing Student Affect	Multiple measures that assess skills, performance, and affect
Step 7: Evaluate and optimize the experience	How can a program, course, or experience that is enhanced by SRL be evaluated and improved?	Impact on Learner Outcomes Impact on Learning Objectives Impact on Learners	Methodology to evaluate the impact of the SRL and how it can be optimized for ongoing improvement

very nature of their own contemplation of a subject, desire to learn or practice a subject, and reflection on their own performance (Pintrich, 2000). Indeed, some SRL dimensions that are related to motivation – such as goal level and self-efficacy – are more closely related to learning (Sitzmann & Ely, 2011). These skills may not be well-honed, but the raw material that exists may enable instructors and instructional designers to "short cut" their approach to SRL. Ways to establish the level of learners' intrinsic motivation is to understand whether a learning experience is directly related to their personal interests, whether it is a required or elective course, and whether it is tied to learners' personal or professional goals.

- **Prior Knowledge:** Learners who possess more prior knowledge in a particular subject – in particular those learners who are further along the path from novice to expert – may already understand how to regulate their learning in that domain and therefore require less support during task performance (Yang et al., 2018). For example, they may be better able to manage their time and resources, better able to monitor their own performance during a task or procedure, and better able to judge their own performance than peers with less prior knowledge or expertise. At minimum, learners with more prior knowledge may be able to adopt SRL strategies with less demands on cognitive load.

- **SRL Experience:** Learners who have received prior training in SRL or metacognitive techniques may already incorporate some of these strategies into their own learning. If not, they may be better positioned to reconsider these strategies through fresh instruction. For a more accurate indicator of learner self-regulation skill, consider implementing a scale, inventory, or assessment. Several such tools have been developed to better assess learner self-regulation. These include the Academic SRL Scale (A-SRL-S), Motivated Strategies for Learning Questionnaire (MSQL), Learning and Study Strategies Inventory (LASSI), and Learning Strategy Scale (LSS).
    - Academic SRL Scale (A-SRL-S). This scale was based on responses from 1454 college students on eight protocols, which in turn were based on six SRL contexts. In sum, 111 items were generated and classified according to 14 categories (Magno, 2010).
    - Motivated Strategies for Learning Questionnaire (MSQL). This self-report instrument was developed to assess college students' motivation and use of learning strategies for a college course, based on a cognitive view of motivation and learning strategies. It includes two sections: a motivation section and a learning strategies section. There are 81 items on the 1991 version of the MSLQ. The motivation section contains 31 items that assess learners' goals, beliefs about their skill to succeed, and anxiety about tests. The learning strategy section contains 31 items regarding learners' use of cognitive and metacognitive strategies, as well as 19 items concerning learner resource management (Pintrich et al., 1991).
    - Learning Attitude and Study Strategies Inventory (LASSI). This is a 10-scale, 60-item assessment of learners' understanding and use of learning strategies focusing on motivations, attitudes, and behaviors related to successful postsecondary and professional education that can be demonstrably altered through interventions such as learning strategies and self-regulated study courses and programs (Weinstein et al., 2016).
    - Learning Strategy Scale (LSS). This five-factor scale is based on the Learning Attitude and Study Strategies Inventory (LASSI). The five factors of this scale cover elaboration, comprehension monitoring, organizational, affective, and rehearsal strategies (Guven, 2008).

Determine Outcome and Objective Delivery

The second step in the process is considering the intended learning objectives and learner outcomes for the learning experience and the ways in which these will be delivered through program design, pedagogical practices, and support services. By pairing objective and outcome analysis with the delivery methods for achieving these objectives and outcomes, the process encourages instructors and instructional designers to keep objectives and outcomes central to their SRL approach and to revisit the alignment between these important goals and the design, implementation, and support for an experience.

- **Program Design:** When considering incorporating SRL into instructional design, one of the first decisions that instructional designers and instructors need to make is the locus of the intervention. There are four potential areas of focus: a) at the curricular level b) at the course level c) at the modular level and d) at the assignment or assessment level. Each of these levels, in turn, is driven by objectives and outcomes that can guide the placement of SRL components.
    - Curriculum Level. The curricular or programmatic level is the highest level for incorporating SRL strategies. By incorporating SRL at the curricular level, learners are better able to monitor, manage, and improve their performance across a set of courses in the interest of

enhancing their learning across an entire program or degree. Instructional designers may incorporate SRL strategies to enhance curricular objectives and outcomes, such as those that spiral throughout a curriculum; support curricular elements, such as capstone experiences; and draw connections among courses, such as those that are prerequisites or corequisites.

  - Course Level. The course level is the second highest level for incorporating SRL strategies. By incorporating SRL at the course level, learners are better able to monitor, manage, and improve their performance within a course. Instructors and instructional designers may incorporate SRL strategies to enhance important learning objectives, including both foundational and higher order objectives; enhance specific course elements, such as labs, projects, and collaborative work; and draw connections among course concepts.
  - Modular Level. The modular level is the third highest level for incorporating SRL strategies. By incorporating SRL at the modular level, learners are better able to monitor, manage, and improve their performance within a module, unit, lesson, or topic. Instructors and instructional designers may incorporate SRL strategies to enhance primary and secondary learning objectives, including those that learners may typically find more difficult; enhance specific modular elements, such as knowledge acquisition, applied practice, and procedures; and draw connections among conceptual, declarative, and procedural knowledge.
  - Assignment and Assessment Level. The assignment or assessment level is a "finer grain" level for incorporating SRL strategies. By incorporating SRL at the individual assignment or assessment level, learners are better able to monitor, manage, and improve their performance within one assignment or on one assessment – down to the individual task or assessment item level. Instructors and instructional designers may incorporate SRL strategies to enhance discrete learning objectives; enhance task performance, including performance on an individual learning or assessment task; and draw connections among distinct knowledge components.
- **Pedagogical Practices:** Applying SRL strategies to program design may achieve a foundational level of integration but may not be fully interwoven into the learning experience until it is fully present in disciplinary pedagogies, cognitive engagement, and the digital design.
  - Disciplinary Pedagogies. Disciplinary pedagogies are the practices – often handed down from instructors to future instructors – that are commonplace within a discipline or domain (Gurung, 2009). These, for example, are the labs used in science instruction, the case studies used in business courses, and the writing process used in composition courses. These pedagogical practices are important opportunities to incorporate SRL techniques that may be missed due to the habitual nature of teaching in these disciplinary ways.
  - Cognitive Engagement. Cognitive engagement is the degree to which learners are expected to actively engage in the learning experience. According to Michelene Chi and Ruth Wylie, there are four levels of cognitive engagement: passive, active, constructive, and interactive (2014). Chi asserts that learning performance is higher when learners are more cognitively engaged; that is, for more active, constructive, and interactive experiences, respectively. SRL strategies may enhance each level of engagement and may make learning a more engaging process (Hadwin et al., 2011).
  - Digital Design. The digital design is the way in which blended learning environments and tools – such as learning management systems, synchronous video conferencing tools, and educational technologies – are organized and constructed to support usability, accessibility,

and learning. The general usability of these resources directly affects learner interactions and satisfaction in the digital environment (Gunesekera et al., 2019). Furthermore, these environments can help instructors and instructional designers make SRL techniques and strategies visible to learners and well-integrated into the learning experience.

- **Support Services:** While program design and pedagogical practices are two obvious loci for SRL strategies, there are other important interactions that may be considered outside of the curriculum or course. Namely, these include student success services that tend to fall into three categories: a) coaching, b) academic support and c) experiential programs. While these may seem beyond the scope of traditional teaching and learning, they play an important role that SRL strategies can enhance.
    - Coaching. Coaching services can include enrollment advising, career coaching, and success mentoring. Traditionally, these are not always considered part of the learning experience itself or the loci for learning. However, by incorporating SRL strategies into these interactions, they can not only become more deeply integrated into the learning experience, but they can better *support* the learning experience. By incorporating SRL into coaching interactions, learners are better able to leverage these interactions to monitor, manage, and improve their performance through programs or courses. Instructional designers may incorporate SRL strategies into coaching interactions by encouraging learners to practice SRL strategies ahead of, during, and after each of these exchanges.
    - Academic Support. Academic support services can include professional tutoring, skills workshops, and library services such as research support. Like coaching services, these may not be well-integrated into the learning experience. However, by incorporating SRL strategies into these types of academic support activities, their effectiveness can be amplified. Instructional designers may incorporate SRL strategies into academic support services by encouraging learners to practice SRL strategies that connect these practices to other aspects of the learning experience.
    - Experiential and Ancillary Programs. Experiential programs, such as internships, externships, and other work-study programs, are an important part of many programs. These programs benefit from reflection (Perry and Martin, 2016); they may also benefit from other self-regulation techniques. Instructional designers may incorporate SRL strategies into these experiential programs by encouraging learners to practice a variety of self-regulation techniques not only at the beginning and end of the program, but on a more regular cadence throughout the duration.

In a blended learning environment, determining outcomes and objectives and their associated delivery may include considering how blended technologies – such as video conferencing, threaded discussions, and communication tools – may better drive learning objectives and learner outcomes. Using these tools to further support SRL strategies, and building both into the program design, pedagogical practices, and support services, provides a great opportunity to enhance learning objectives and learner outcomes.

Select Strategies for SRL

There are numerous SRL strategies that learners can be instructed to employ. While a full review of all strategies is outside the scope of this chapter, Panadero (2017) provides an overview of the main SRL models. For the purposes of simplicity, the process focuses on one of the most respected and established models and categorizations: Zimmerman's Cyclical Model and a categorization also advanced by Zimmerman consisting of 15 SRL behaviors (Panadero & Alonso-Tapia, 2014; Zimmerman, 2013). Together, these provide a simple yet robust way for instructors and instructional designers to ensure that they are adopting all phases of a strong SRL model and incorporating SRL strategies that can subsequently evolve into more sophisticated learning designs.

- **SRL Models:** According to Ernesto Panadero (2017) there are several dominant models: Zimmerman, Boekaerts, Winne, Pintrich, Efklides and Hadwin, Järvelä, and Miller. Zimmerman's Cyclical model – which he advanced in 2000 and then revised in 2009 – is presented here due to its foundational acceptance within the field as well as its relatively easy application. Once practitioners gain familiarity with these foundational SRL techniques, they may choose to go beyond this model. Zimmerman's model is divided into three phases: the forethought phase, the performance phase, and the self-reflection phase. Simply by focusing on incorporating each of these three phases, instructors and instructional designers can begin to build the foundation for a strong SRL environment into their programs, courses, and learning experiences.
    - Forethought Phase. The Forethought Phase includes Task Analysis and Self-Motivation Beliefs. Task Analysis includes goal setting and strategic planning. Self-Motivation Beliefs include self-efficacy, outcome expectations, task interest/value, and goal orientation (Panadero & Alonso-Tapia, 2014). In general, forethought includes analyzing the learning task that lies ahead and contemplating how to go about it, how much time to spend on it, and what resources are needed to complete it. Forethought also includes considering one's own motivations and beliefs. This includes asking oneself how performing or accomplishing a learning task will help achieve goals or advance one's beliefs about one's abilities and aptitudes.
    - Performance Phase. The Performance Phase includes Self-Control and Self-Observation. Self-Control includes task strategies, self-instruction, imagery, time management, environmental structuring, help-seeking, interest incentives, and self-consequences. Self-Observation includes metacognitive monitoring and self-recording (Panadero & Alonso-Tapia, 2014). In general, performance includes exercising self-control over a learning task to enable the focus, effort, and persistence to complete it. Performance also includes observing oneself and monitoring one's progress and success. This includes asking oneself how one is doing and what adjustments one needs to make. Self-monitoring has been shown to improve learner performance (Guo, 2022).
    - Self-Reflection Phase. The Self-Reflection Phase includes Self-Judgment and Self-Reaction. Self-Judgment includes self-evaluation and causal attribution. Self-Reaction includes self-satisfaction/affect and adaptive/defensive (Panadero & Alonso-Tapia, 2014). In general, reflection includes considering one's reaction to one's performance. This includes asking oneself how one's performance made one feel and how those feelings may have affected the performance itself.
- **SRL Categories:** Numerous researchers, including Hattie, Biggs and Purdie (1996), Ergen and Kanadli (2017), and Theobald (2021) have offered categorization schemes for SRL strategies (often to establish the effectiveness of strategies within categories). Zimmerman (2013) indicates fifteen types of SRL categories (excerpted below in Table 2). Selecting among these categories

(as well as those provided by other researchers, including those indicated in the scales referenced above) can be helpful for instructors and instructional designers as they design and implement programs, courses, and experiences enhanced by SRL strategies.

Table 2. Zimmerman's SRL categories

Category of Strategy	Definition
1. Self-evaluation	Statements indicating student-initiated evaluations of the quality or progress of their work, e.g., "I check over my work to make sure I did it correct."
2. Organizing and transforming	Statements indicating student initiated overt or covert rearrangement of instructional materials to improve learning, e.g., "I make an outline before I write my paper."
3. Goal setting and planning	Statements indicating student-initiated setting of educational goals or subgoals and planning for sequencing, timing, and completing activities related to those goals, e.g., "First I start studying 2 weeks before exams, and I pace myself."
4. Seeking information	Statements indicating student-initiated efforts to secure further task information from nonsocial sources when undertaking an assignment, e.g., "Before beginning to write the paper, I go to the library to get as much information as possible concerning the topic."
5. Keeping records and monitoring	Statements indicating student-initiated efforts to record events or results, e.g., "I took notes of the class discussion." "I kept a list of the words I got wrong."
6. Environmental structuring	Statements indicating student-initiated efforts to select or arrange the physical setting to make learning easier, e.g., "I isolate myself from anything that distracts me." "I turned off the radio so I can concentrate on what I am doing."
7. Self-consequences	Statements indicating student arrangement or imagination of rewards or punishment for success or failure, e.g., "If I do well on a test, I treat myself to a movie."
8. Rehearsing and memorizing	Statements indicating student-initiated effort to memorize material by overt or covert practice, e.g., "In preparing for a math test, I keep writing the formula down until I remember it."
9 - 11. Seeking social assistance	Statements indicating student initiated to solicit help from peers (9), teachers (10), and adults (11), e.g., "If I have problems with math assignments, I ask a friend to help."
12 -14. Reviewing records	Statements indicating student-initiated efforts to reread tests (12), notes (13), or textbooks (14), to prepare for class or further testing, e.g., "When preparing for a test, I review my notes."
15. Other	Statements indicating learning behavior that is initiated by other persons such as teachers or parents, and all unclear verbal responses, e.g., "I just do what the teachers say."

Source: (Zimmerman, 2013, p. 138)

In a blended learning environment, adopting a SRL model and selecting specific strategies for SRL may include considering the specific blended format of the course. For example, in blended formats that rely on a flipped classroom approach, learners need to prepare online for activities that happen in traditional settings. Such preparation is an opportune moment for SRL skills. Alternatively, in blended formats that are primarily asynchronous, seeking social assistance from instructors and tutors may be a more important and effective strategy for learners who may otherwise feel more isolated.

Establish Scaffolding Needed by Level

Becoming fluent in SRL strategies takes effort and time. This process, according to Zimmerman, takes learners from one level to the next. According to Zimmerman's Multilevel Model, learners progress through four stages of self-regulation: observation, emulation, self-control and finally self-regulation

(Zimmerman, 2013). Zimmerman believes that the first two levels include a social component while the last two levels are more self-focused (Zimmerman, 2013). Keeping this model in mind, it's important to consider what scaffolding learners may need to move along this journey – both in terms of expert support and sufficient "time" along a learning journey. For example, strategies presented in the early part of an experience can be modeled; whereas in the mid stages of an experience, strategies may be nudged and in the latest stages of an experience strategies may be prompted entirely by the learner who has gained some level of independent control or regulation. Zimmerman's four levels are as follows.

- **Observation**: At the first level, learners observe a skill being modeled and are motivated by vicarious reinforcement. According to Zimmerman, "To acquire a skill at an observational level, a student must carefully watch a social model learn or perform" (2013, p.140).
- **Emulation:** At the second level, learners emulate a skill being performed and receive social feedback. According to Zimmerman, "To acquire skill at second or emulation level, a learner must duplicate the general form of a model's response on a correspondent task" (2013, p.140).
- **Self-control**: At the third level, learners begin to exhibit self-control. According to Zimmerman, "Attainment of a self-controlled level of self-regulatory skill occurs when learners master the use of a skill in structured settings outside the presence of models, such as when a pianist can play scales fluidly in the major and minor keys" (2013, p.140).
- **Self-regulation**: At the fourth level, learners are able to independently self-regulate. According to Zimmerman, "A self-regulated level of task skill is achieved when learners can systematically adapt their performance to changing personal and contextual conditions that are present in naturalistic settings but not in practice settings" (2013, p.141).

In a blended learning environment, providing scaffolding by learner or cohort level may be done through posted instructions, sample assignments, and discussion prompts. The nature of the scaffolding may vary over time from the beginning to the end of the program, course, or experience such that it starts off with an explanation and worked examples of strategies in use and tapers off as learners become more proficient in applying the strategies as the experience progresses.

Implement With Fidelity

Once instructors and instructional designers have considered the right model elements, strategies, and scaffolding-by-level, they can turn their attention toward the proper implementation of a program, course, or experience enhanced by SRL. There are three considerations for implementing SRL strategies: a) managing cognitive load, b) making the strategies explicit, and c) enabling learner autonomy and automaticity.

- **Managing Cognitive Load:** Incorporating SRL strategies into a learning experience can add to the overall cognitive load (Seufert, 2018). For example, attempting a new learning task *while* thinking about your performance on that task can, in fact, add to the burden that already exists from learning alone. There are three types of cognitive load: intrinsic, extraneous, and germane. Intrinsic cognitive load is the inherent level of difficulty of a concept or learning objective. Extraneous cognitive load refers to the cognitive resources required to process information unrelated to learning itself, such as navigating the presentation of content. Germane cognitive load is the cognitive resources required to integrate new information into memory (Sweller, 2010). When incorporating SRL strategies, instructors and instructional designers should carefully consider the intrinsic cognitive load, reduce any additional extraneous cognitive load, and use SRL strategies to enhance the germane cognitive load. This may mean foregoing SRL during acute lab-based work, for example, where adding to the intrinsic cognitive load may introduce safety risks into a procedure. Or this may mean minimizing other extraneous cognitive load elements – such as noise, disorganization, or unclear instructions – from a learning experience. Enhancing the germane cognitive load can be accomplished by carefully considering which learning tasks are enhanced by SRL strategies, especially during the performance phase. According to Tina Seufert, "When learners plan their learning activities and invest effort to do so, we can see this effort as germane for planning." Seufert continues, "With respect to planning there is nevertheless one instructional means that can be seen as prompts for planning, the above-mentioned implementation intentions. They explicitly address the phase of initiating a learning activity by forming concrete if-then-plans and thus can be seen as prompts for planning" (2018, p.121).

- **Making SRL Explicit:** Learners – especially novice learners or learners without training in SRL techniques – benefit from explicit instruction on how and when to apply self-regulation strategies. Indeed, researchers have discovered that most SRL instruction is implicit, despite also finding that explicit instruction is associated with a gain in performance (Kistner et al., 2010). Being explicit means incorporating these instructions into the directions that are provided for assignments, assessments, and even classroom or "zoom room" activities. Being explicit may also mean providing time for learners to practice these SRL skills and, initially, modeling, discussing, and debriefing the use of these strategies.
- **Enabling Autonomy and Automaticity:** For students to use SRL strategies autonomously and for them to eventually become automatic, self-regulation techniques need to be used habitually and adopted in the pursuit of goals (Corno, 2011; Papies and Aarts, 2016). This can be accomplished by providing an explanation for the strategies in a course syllabus and noting them in other organizational tools, such as the learning management system folder structure, calendar, or other pacing tools. Building SRL strategies into these documents and environments will enable learners to understand their value and see them in places that they frequent as part of the overall learning experience. Learners are also more likely to adopt SRL strategies if they have a mindset in which they believe that their performance can be improved through effort; thus, encouraging this mindset may yield a higher level of SRL strategy engagement (Yan et al., 2014).

In a blended learning environment, implementing SRL with fidelity may include reducing the cognitive load of the interface and digital materials by ensuring that they are well structured, properly labeled, and easy to navigate and use. Implementation may also involve providing explicit instruction on how to apply SRL strategies and samples of strategies being modeled. And, repeating the use of specific strategies over time – such as preparing their learning environment – may help learners internalize these as habits of mind.

Provide Meaningful Assessments

When implementing SRL learning strategies, it's important to understand how well learners are developing their self-regulatory skills. Assessing self-regulatory skills may take several forms: directly assessing self-regulation skills, drawing inferences from academic performance, considering student engagement, confidence, and satisfaction.

- **Directly Assessing Self-regulation Skills:** Directly assessing SRL skills entails developing learning objectives specifically related to SRL – in addition to content objectives – and then developing and aligning assessments to these objectives. The benefit of this approach is that it provides substantial data on how well learners are self-regulating. However, these types of assessments may be beyond the typical scope of a program, course, or experience; indeed, this may feel a bit heavy handed for many instructors and instructional designers – and learners. An alternate approach is to administer the SRL scale mentioned previously at both the beginning and end of a course to understand how students may have improved their self-regulation skills during the course.
- **Drawing Indirect Inferences from Academic Performance:** According to researchers, SRL improves academic performance (Dignath and Büttner 2008; Dignath et al., 2008; Hattie et al., 1996; Richardson et al., 2012; Sitzmann and Ely, 2011; Theobald, 2021). Therefore, one way of indirectly assessing the effectiveness of SRL strategies is by comparing learner performance in courses that employ these strategies to learner performance in courses that don't incorporate them. Any improvement in performance, assessment scores, or final grades could be inferred to have been the result of SRL strategies – assuming that all other things, including learner population attributes, are held steady. At best, this would be a correlational data point, indicating that there is a potential correlation between SRL and improved performance, not that there is direct causality.
- **Assessing Student Affect**: It is also important to consider the role that SRL strategies may have on students' affect (Efklides, 2011). Does exercising increased control over their learning enable students to feel more motivated, confident, and satisfied? It may be worth implementing a simple measure to understand student affect, including adding confidence measures to assessments, adding items to end-of-term satisfaction surveys, or by directly asking students to reflect on their experience and share their feelings in a paragraph or discussion. This kind of qualitative research can then be triangulated against direct measures of self-regulation and indirect measures of student performance for a more holistic view of the efficacy of the SRL strategy instruction.

In a blended learning environment, providing assessments may need to be done using quizzes, assessments, and survey tools. These tools may enable greater flexibility and expediency in assessment; for example, micro surveys can check learner affect immediately after SRL strategies have been put into practice.

Evaluate and Optimize the Experience

At the end of a learning experience, instructors may evaluate the efficacy of the self-regulation techniques that they incorporated. This may be done by considering the impact that the inclusion of these techniques had on learner outcomes, learning objectives, and learners themselves. By looking at these data points, instructors can make wise decisions about how to improve and optimize their SRL implementations over time.

- **Impact on Learner Outcomes:** Upon completion of a program, course, or experience that incorporates SRL strategies, instructors and instructional designers may evaluate the effect of the strategies on any outcomes of interest. These may include academic performance, persistence through completion, and potential lagging outcomes, such as skill transfer, employment, or advancement. The central question is: what impact did the SRL strategies have on these outcomes? This is followed closely by a second question: how might the impact be amplified for an even stronger impact in the future? Together, the answers to these questions will inform how the strategies need to be optimized in future programs, courses, or experiences.

- **Impact on Learning Objectives:** In addition to examining the impact the SRL strategies may have on higher-order outcomes, instructors and instructional designers may evaluate the effect of the strategies on finer-grain learning objectives. These may include primary and ancillary objectives that guide the assessments and instruction for a program, course, or experience. The central questions are what impact SRL strategies had on any performance measures for these objectives, including assessments, assignments, and projects. Specifically: did the techniques improve student performance – in particular on difficult objectives? The answers to these questions will guide how instructors and instructional designers tweak the SRL strategy instruction to better enhance performance-against-objectives in the future.
- **Impact on Learners:** In addition to examining the impact on outcomes and objectives, instructors and instructional designers may wish to evaluate the impact of SRL strategies on learner self-efficacy, mindsets, and attitudes. The central questions here are: what impact did SRL strategies have on learners' feelings about their own learning abilities? Did these strategies enable them to feel and behave more strategically, manage their time more appropriately and apply their learning resources more effectively? And did these behaviors enable students to stay engaged, keep pace, and collaborate more productively? Answering these questions enables instructors and instructional designers to evolve their approaches to ensure that these strategies are ultimately proving beneficial for all learners.

In a blended learning environment, evaluating and optimizing the experience requires adjusting a course template and the associated learning materials. Planning for this revision work is a necessary and important logistical step, with revisions happening at logical timepoints in a program or at the conclusion of a course or learning experience.

SAMPLE PROCESSES

The following three examples illustrate how the process may be applied to programs, courses, and projects. These are theoretical examples only that are intended to help readers better understand how all aspects of the process come together in a particular design context.

FUTURE RESEARCH DIRECTIONS

It would be beneficial to direct future research to the efficacy of blended learning experiences that are enhanced by approaches, as outlined in the last section, of specific SRL designs. By better understanding the efficacy of these program design, pedagogical, and student success implementations, instructors and instructional designers can increasingly adopt highly efficacious models.

Table 3. Sample A: Enhancing a program with SRL strategies

Program: Micro-credential That Includes a Total of Six Courses	
Step 1: Analyze Learner Attributes	• Learners possess a high awareness of self-regulation strategies and an interest in using these strategies
Step 2: Determine Outcome and Objective Delivery	• Learner outcomes are primarily achieved through program design, with a asynchronous learning and limited support services
Step 3: Select Strategies for SRL	• Each course includes forethought, performance monitoring, and self-reflection strategies • Strategies include self-evaluation and goal setting at the beginning of each course, information seeking and recording keeping during learning activities, and reflection essays at the end of each course
Step 4: Establish Scaffolding Needed by Level	• Scaffolding includes instructions for all courses as well as a detailed sample of all self-regulation activities for the first course
Step 5: Implement with Fidelity	• Implementation includes explicit instructions to incorporate the strategies; a user-tested digital environment to reduce extraneous cognitive load; and repetition to build habits
Step 6: Provide Meaningful Assessments	• While there is no SRL-specific assessment, there is a comparison of cohort performance to prior, non-SRL cohorts
Step 7: Evaluate and Optimize the Experience	• Performance data and student satisfaction data are gathered and used to inform SRL modifications, including the peer-review of reflection essays

CONCLUSION

Learning is an in-demand skill that is both highly necessary in a knowledge-based society and becoming increasingly managed by learners themselves – particularly important in online, blended, and hybrid learning environments. SRL strategies enable learners to monitor, manage, and improve their own learning; however, they need to be systematically applied to the learning experience to enable both learner adoption and learning performance improvement. This requires instructors and instructional designers to understand SRL models and strategies and to incorporate the elements of these into program design,

Table 4. Sample B: Enhancing a course with SRL strategies

Course: A Single Course Offered Over 16 Weeks	
Step 1: Analyze Learner Attributes	• Learners possess a medium awareness of self-regulation strategies and a relatively low interest in using these strategies
Step 2: Determine Outcome and Objective Delivery	• Learning objectives are primarily achieved through a mix of course design, pedagogy, and support services including tutoring
Step 3: Select Strategies for SRL	• The course includes forethought, performance monitoring, and self-reflection strategies for each unit • Strategies include organizing materials, monitoring performance during practice exercises, and seeking social assistance from tutors
Step 4: Establish Scaffolding Needed by Level	• Scaffolding includes explicit instructions to incorporate the strategies and modeling self-monitoring and assistance seeking
Step 5: Implement with Fidelity	• Implementation includes minimizing extraneous cognitive load during practice activities through environmental structuring and explicit instructions around learner self-monitoring and self-evaluation
Step 6: Provide Meaningful Assessments	• Assessment includes a self-reported performance monitoring rating during each practice exercise as well as self-reported performance-monitoring rating after sessions spent with tutors
Step 7: Evaluate and Optimize the Experience	• Performance data and tutor feedback are gathered and used to modify the approach to tutoring, including a greater focus on pre-tutoring preparation and post-tutoring reflection

Table 5. Sample C: Enhancing a project with SRL strategies

Project: A Capstone Project	
Step 1: Analyze Learner Attributes	• Learners possess a low awareness of SRL strategies and, therefore, an uncertain interest in using them
Step 2: Determine Outcome and Objective Delivery	• Learning objectives are primarily delivered through a collaborative capstone project with limited instructor involvement
Step 3: Select Strategies for SRL	• The capstone includes forethought, performance monitoring, and self-reflection strategies for the entire project • Strategies include a detailed goal setting and planning (proposal for project, timeline), ongoing self-assessments to check progress and performance, and a self-reflection essay
Step 4: Establish Scaffolding Needed by Level	• Scaffolding includes explicit instructions to incorporate the strategies and samples of goal setting, planning, self-assessments and self-reflections collected and shared from prior learners with their consent
Step 5: Implement with Fidelity	• Implementation includes explicit explanations of the personal, professional, and academic value of SRL strategies as well as self-assessments instead of self-monitoring to reduce extrinsic cognitive load
Step 6: Provide Meaningful Assessments	• Assessment includes delivering an SRL instrument as a pre- and post-assessment based upon published instruments
Step 7: Evaluate and Optimize the Experience	• Performance data and student satisfaction data are gathered and analyzed, resulting in the addition of additional self-regulation strategies, including self-consequences

pedagogical practices, and the support services with which learners come into contact throughout a learning experience.

This chapter provides a process for the systematic design and implementation of a blended program, course, or experience that is enhanced by including SRL strategies. This process provides steps that begin with an understanding of learners current SRL habits, followed by an analysis of intended outcomes and objectives and the ways in which these are delivered through course design, pedagogy, and support; followed by the adoption of self-regulation models and strategies. This process enables instructors and instructional designers to establish the intensity, architecture, strategies and scaffolding needed to design and implement a learning experience rooted in SRL.

This chapter also proposes three considerations for implementing SRL that include managing cognitive load, making SRL explicit, and enabling autonomy and automaticity. It concludes by providing recommendations for assessment, evaluation, and optimization. Taken as a whole, this process may enable instructors and instructional designers to thoughtfully and systematically design, implement, and evaluate SRL strategies for their learners' immediate academic improvement and lifelong learning.

REFERENCES

Baticulon, R., Sy, J., Alberto, N., Baron, M., Mabulay, R., Rizada, L., Tiu, C., Clarion, C., & Reyes, J. (2021). Barriers to online learning in the time of COVID-19: A national survey of medical students in the Philippines. *Medical Science Educator, 31*(2), 615–628. doi:10.100740670-021-01231-z PMID:33649712

Cetin, B. (2015). Academic motivation and self-regulated learning in predicting academic achievement in college. *Journal of International Education Research, 11*(2), 95-106.

Chi, M., & Wylie, R. (2014). The ICAP Framework: linking cognitive engagement to active learning outcomes. *Educational Psychologist, 49*(4), 219-243.

Corman, C., Tiru, L., Mesesan-Schmitz, L., Stanciu, C., & Bularca, M. (2020). Online teaching and learning in higher education during the Coronavirus pandemic: Students' perspective. *Sustainability, 20*, 24.

Corno, L. (2011). *Studying self-regulation habits. Handbook of self-regulation of learning and performance*. Routledge.

de Boer, H., Donker, A. S., Kostons, D. D. N. M., & van der Werf, G. P. C. (2018). Long-term effects of metacognitive strategy instruction on student academic performance: A meta-analysis. *Educational Research Review, 24*, 98–115. doi:10.1016/j.edurev.2018.03.002

Dignath, C., & Büttner, G. (2008). Components of fostering self-regulated learning among students. a meta-analysis on intervention studies at primary and secondary school level. *Metacognition and Learning, 3*(3), 231–264. doi:10.100711409-008-9029-x

Dignath, C., Büttner, G., & Langfeldt, H. (2008). How can primary school students learn self-regulated learning strategies most effectively? A meta-analysis on self-regulation training programmes. *Educational Research Review, 3*(2), 101–129. doi:10.1016/j.edurev.2008.02.003

Efklides, A. (2011). Interactions of metacognition with motivation and affect in self-regulated learning: The MASRL model. *Educational Psychology, 46*(1), 6–25. doi:10.1080/00461520.2011.538645

Ergen, B., & Sedat, K. (2017). The effect of self-regulated learning strategies on academic achievement: A meta-analysis study. *Eurasian Journal of Educational Research, 69*(69), 55–74. doi:10.14689/ejer.2017.69.4

Foerst, N., Klug, J., Jostl, G., Spiel, C., & Schober, B. (2017). Knowledge vs. action: Discrepancies in university students' knowledge about and self-reported use of self-regulated learning strategies. *Frontiers in Psychology, 8*, 27. doi:10.3389/fpsyg.2017.01288 PMID:28798713

Gunesekera, A., Bao, Y., & Kibelloh, M. (2019). The role of usability on e-learning user interactions and satisfaction: A literature review. *Journal of Systems and Information Technology, 21*(3), 368–394. doi:10.1108/JSIT-02-2019-0024

Guo, L. (2022). The effects of self-monitoring on strategy use and academic performance: A meta-analysis. *International Journal of Educational Research, 112*, 112. doi:10.1016/j.ijer.2022.101939

Gurung, R., & Chick, N. (Eds.). (2009). *Exploring Signature Pedagogies: Approaches to Teaching Disciplinary Habits of Mind*. Stylus Publishing.

Guven, M. (2008). Development of learning strategy scale: Study of validation and reliability. *World Applied Sciences Journal, 4*(1), 31–36.

Hadwin, A., Järvelä, S., & Miller, M. (2011). Self-regulated, co-regulated, and socially shared regulation of learning. In B. J. Zimmerman & D. H. Schunk (Eds.), *Handbook of Self-Regulation of Learning and Performance* (pp. 65–84). Routledge.

Hattie, J., Biggs, J., & Purdie, N. (1996). Effects of learning skills interventions on student learning: A meta-analysis. *Review of Educational Research, 66*(2), 99–136. doi:10.3102/00346543066002099

Kistner, S., Rakoczy, K., Otto, B., & Dignath, C. (2010). Promotion of self-regulated learning in classrooms: Investigating frequency, quality, and consequences for student performance. *Metacognition and Learning, 5*(2), 157–171. doi:10.100711409-010-9055-3

Magno, C. (2010). Assessing academic self-regulated learning among Filipino college students: The factor structure and item fit. *The International Journal of Educational and Psychological Assessment, 5*, 61–76.

McElrath, K. (2020). *Nearly 93% of households with school age children report some form of distance learning during Covid 19. In Schooling During the Covid-19 Pandemic.* U.S. Census Bureau.

Means, B., Toyama, Y., Murphy, R., & Baki, M. (2013). The effectiveness of online and blended learning: A meta-analysis of the empirical literature. *Teachers College Record, 115*(3), 1–47. doi:10.1177/016146811311500307

Panadero, E. (2017). A review of self-regulated learning: Six models and four directions for research. *Frontiers in Psychology, 8*, 28. doi:10.3389/fpsyg.2017.00422 PMID:28503157

Panadero, E., & Alonso-Tapia, J. (2014). How do students self-regulate? Review of Zimmerman's cyclical model of self-regulated learning. *Anales de Psicología, 30*, 450–462.

Papies, E., & Aarts, H. (2016). Automatic self-regulation: from habit to goal pursuit. In K. D. Vohs & R. F. Baumeister (Eds.), *Handbook of Self-Regulation: Research, Theory, and Applications.* Guilford Press.

Perry, S. & Martin, R. (2016) Authentic reflection for experiential learning at international schools. *International Journal of Research on Service-Learning and Community Engagement, 4*(1), 53-68.

Pintrich, P. (2000). The role of goal orientation in self-regulated learning. In M. Boekaerts, P. R. Pintrich, & M. Zeidner (Eds.), *s), Handbook of Self-Regulation* (pp. 452–502). Academic Press. doi:10.1016/B978-012109890-2/50043-3

Pintrich, P., Smith, D., Garcia, T., & McKeachie, W. (1991). *A manual for the use of the motivated strategies for learning questionnaire (MSQL).* National Center for research to Improve Post-secondary Teaching and Learning. Ann Arbor: MI: The Regents of the University of Michigan. Technical Report No. NCRIPTAL-91-B-004.

Richardson, M., Abraham, C., & Bond, R. (2012). Psychological correlates of university students' academic performance: A systematic review and meta-analysis. *Psychological Bulletin, 138*(2), 353–387. doi:10.1037/a0026838 PMID:22352812

Seufert, T. (2018). The interplay between self-regulation in learning and cognitive load. *Educational Research Review, 24*, 116–129. doi:10.1016/j.edurev.2018.03.004

Sitzmann, T., & Ely, K. (2011). A meta-analysis of self-regulated learning in work-related training and educational attainment: What we know and where we need to go. *Psychological Bulletin, 137*(3), 421–442. doi:10.1037/a0022777 PMID:21401218

Sperling, R., Howard, B., Staley, R., & DuBois, N. (2004). Metacognition and self-regulated learning Constructs. *Educational Research and Evaluation, 10*(2), 117–139. doi:10.1076/edre.10.2.117.27905

Study International. (2017). Edtech and online learning are making higher education more accessible. *Online (Bergheim).*

Sweller, J. (2010). Element interactivity and intrinsic, extraneous, and germane cognitive load. *Educational Psychology Review, 22*(2), 123–138. doi:10.100710648-010-9128-5

Theobald, M. (2021). Self-regulated learning training programs enhance university students' academic performance, self-regulated learning strategies, and motivation: A meta-analysis. *Contemporary Educational Psychology, 66*, 1. doi:10.1016/j.cedpsych.2021.101976

Weinstein, C., Palmer, D., & Acee, T. (2016). *LASSI user's manual: learning and study strategies inventory* (3rd ed.). H&H Publishing Company.

Weiss, M. (2020). *Long Life Learning: Preparing for Jobs that Don't Even Exist Yet.* Wiley.

World Bank. (2003). *Lifelong Learning in the Global Knowledge Economy: Challenges for Developing Countries.* Author.

Yan, V., Thai, K., & Bjork, R. (2014). Habits and beliefs that guide self-regulated learning: Do they vary with mindset? *Journal of Applied Research in Memory and Cognition, 3*(3), 123. doi:10.1037/h0101799

Yang, T., Chen, M. C., & Chen, S. (2018). The influences of self-regulated learning support and prior knowledge on improving learning performance. *Computers & Education, 126*, 37–52. doi:10.1016/j.compedu.2018.06.025

Zimmerman, B. (2000). Attaining self-regulation: a social cognitive perspective. In M. Boekaerts, P. R. Pintrich, & M. Zeidner (Eds.), *s), Handbook of Self-Regulation* (pp. 13–40). Academic Press. doi:10.1016/B978-012109890-2/50031-7

Zimmerman, B. (2013). From cognitive modeling to self-regulation: A social cognitive career path. *Educational Psychologist, 48*(3), 135–147. doi:10.1080/00461520.2013.794676

ADDITIONAL READING

Diamond, R. (1998). *Designing and Assessing Courses and Curricula: A Practical Guide.* Jossey-Bass.

Horn, M., & Staker, H. (2015). *Blended: using disruptive innovation to improve schools.* Jossey-Bass.

Huba, M., & Freed, J. (2000). *Learner-centered assessment on college campuses: shifting the focus from teaching to learning.* Allyn & Bacon.

McDonald, J. K., & West, R. E. (2021). *Design for Learning: Principles, Processes, and Praxis* (1st ed.). EdTech Books.

Schunk, D., & Greene, J. (Eds.). (2017). *Handbook of self-regulation of learning and performance.* Routledge. doi:10.4324/9781315697048

Tucker, C. (2022). *The complete guide to blended learning: activating agency, differentiation, community, and inquiry for students*. Solution Tree Press.

Tucker, C., Wycoff, T., & Green, J. (2016). *Blended learning in action: A practical guide toward sustainable change*. Corwin Teaching Essentials.

Weimer, M. (2013). *Learner-centered teaching: five key changes to practice*. Jossey-Bass.

KEY TERMS AND DEFINITIONS

Blended Learning: Learning experiences that incorporate technology into onground or instructor-led learning that enables learners to work remotely or independently.

Cognitive Engagement: The degree to which learners are expected to actively engage in the learning experience.

Disciplinary Pedagogies: Teaching practices that are commonplace within a discipline or domain.

Metacognition: Thinking about one's learning, strategies, and performance.

Online Learning: Learning experiences that are conducted entirely online.

Self-Regulated Learning: Strategies that learners employ to monitor and manage their own learning.

Support Services: Student success services including coaching, academic support and experiential program delivery.

Chapter 2
When Learning Is Too Good to Be True:
Addressing Common Myths, Misrepresentations, and Misconceptions to Foster Self-Regulated Learning

Franklin M. Zaromb
National Authority for Measurement and Evaluation in Education, Israel

Richard D. Roberts
Research & Assessment Design (RAD) Science Solution, USA

ABSTRACT

Students today enjoy unprecedented freedom and autonomy to choose and manage what, when, where, and how they learn. However, many students squander these opportunities by embracing learning techniques that, at best, can help them attain short-term performance objectives but are relatively ineffective at fostering long-term learning and retention. This chapter describes research findings that highlight and address some of the most common misconceptions and cognitive biases that can impede or undermine self-regulated learning processes. The authors propose several research-based recommendations for addressing these misconceptions and biases in the design of self-regulated learning programs and curricula. These include integrating "desirable difficulties" in learning; instructing students about effective learning strategies along with common myths, misconceptions, and biases of learning; and tailoring interventions to improve critical social and emotional learning skills and mitigate relevant cognitive biases.

Conditions of learning that make performance improve rapidly often fail to support long-term learning and transfer, whereas conditions that create challenges and slow the rate of apparent learning often optimize long-term retention and transfer (Bjork & Bjork, 2011).

DOI: 10.4018/978-1-6684-6500-4.ch002

INTRODUCTION

Recent years have witnessed extraordinary technological advances that have provided students and teachers throughout the world with a rich and rapidly expanding menu of relatively inexpensive, and often free, educational resources for both learning and instruction. With the rise and proliferation of Massive Open Online Courses (MOOCs), mobile educational apps, social media, virtual reality, and blended learning environments, people today enjoy unprecedented freedom and autonomy to choose and manage what, when, where, and how they learn. However, with such freedom and autonomy come the responsibilities and challenges of making informed judgments and decisions. What programs and learning strategies would best address each person's educational needs? How should they manage their learning activities? And on what criteria and metrics should they base these decisions?

The challenge of attempting to answer this loaded set of questions is manifold. For example, one must have adequate information about the quality and utility of the educational resource options under consideration. But such information may be difficult or even impossible to obtain for the smartest of users, the best practitioner, or even the most accomplished of scientists. Private companies and educational institutions seldom evaluate the efficacy of their programs, possibly because they do not consider it to be critical to their business model. Or if it is, rigorous evaluation studies come with a hefty price tag.

There are resources like the What Works Clearing House (https://ies.ed.gov/ncee/wwc/) from which some of this information can be gleaned (usually from those organizations bold enough to be evaluated by such rigorous standards). In so doing, one likely is disappointed by the small number of interventions that have strong proof of efficacy. With over 1,000 interventions in the database, and nearly 12,000 studies variously meant to support these programs, less than 2% of studies provide strong support for the claims aligned to these interventions. Table 1 provides a breakdown of many types of interventions in different domains that have been provided to this independent body for evaluation and how many have strong, moderate, or no/indeterminate evidence for efficacy.

Beyond this noteworthy challenge, one must have comprehensive, holistic knowledge about one's current knowledge, skills, and abilities (KSAs) and to what extent a particular type of educational resource in question would be a good fit. It is likely no person has the expert knowledge and objective self-insight required to take full advantage of the freedom and autonomy in education that modern society brings us with so very many of its seemingly reasonable, but not necessarily evidentiary, options. Unfortunately, not all resources are created equally, and there are a sub-set that may violate the educational mantra, "to do no harm".

Nevertheless, to the extent that one must attempt to make the best learning decisions under conditions of uncertainty and limited knowledge, there is yet another challenge, which is that when left to their own devices, people who wish to learn (i.e., students, so defined) tend to rely on common misconceptions and cognitive biases, which lead them to embrace ineffective or even counterproductive learning strategies (Bjork, Dunlosky, & Kornell, 2013). These include "cramming" (i.e., rereading or massing studying of to-be-learned materials), studying in the same setting or context, studying only until one reaches a target level of performance, highlighting or underlining during study, using keyword mnemonics and imagery for text. In addition, people may choose ineffective learning strategies, because they harbor misconceptions about how the human mind encodes information (e.g., Kornell, 2012; Simons & Chabris, 2011, 2012) or are influenced by cognitive biases that foster illusions of learning mastery (e.g., Koriat et al., 2004; Kornell et al., 2011; Rhodes & Castel, 2008, 2009).

Table 1. Summary of findings around all educational interventions submitted to the What Works Clearing House for evaluation of efficacy (https://ies.ed.gov/ncee/wwc/)

Domain	Strong Evidence	Moderate Evidence	No/ Indeterminant Evidence	Total
Literacy Interventions	51 (1.1%)	68 (1.5%)	4,537 (97.5%)	4,656
Mathematics Interventions	35 (2.3%)	47 (3.2%)	1,412 (94.5%)	1,494
Science Interventions	9 (6.6%)	14 (10.4%)	112 (83.0%)	135
Behavioral Interventions	10 (0.6%)	21 (1.3%)	1,577 (98.1%)	1,608
English Learner Interventions	4 (1.4%)	8 (2.6%)	290 (96.0%)	302
Post-Secondary Interventions	67 (6.2%)	76 (7.1%)	934 (86.7%)	1,077
K-12 Interventions	85 (1.0%)	139 (1.6%)	8,299 (97.4%)	8,523
All Interventions*	219 (1.9%)	305 (2.6%)	11,139 (95.5%)	11,663

* Some studies fall into one or more categories of intervention, such that this final column is not simply the sum of all previous rows.

This state of affairs poses obvious dilemmas for self-regulated learning, whereby students proactively engage in a cyclical, multi-faceted process of consciously planning and setting learning goals, monitoring their performance, and reflecting on the learning outcome (e.g., Efklides, 2011; Zimmerman & Moylan, 2009). In this chapter, we describe findings from laboratory, classroom, and large online studies that highlight and address some of the most common misconceptions and cognitive biases that can impede, or even undermine, self-regulated learning throughout the cyclical process. We conclude by offering several research-based recommendations for learners, instructors, and/or learning content designers and creators to address these misconceptions and biases to help foster self-regulated learning.

Fleeting Rewards of "Cramming"

Bjork and colleagues (2013) argue that one reason why people might decide to adopt ineffective learning strategies is that that they tend to confuse "performance" with "learning". Performance, in an academic or workforce context, is an expression of knowledge or task behavior that one can directly and immediately perceive or observe. Learning represents an enduring, latent change in one's knowledge, understanding, or skill level that may not be directly perceptible or observable. This contrast is important, because people often view their current performance as evidence of whether they achieved their learning goals. While some learning techniques may help people achieve good short-term performance measures, they are poor at fostering long-term learning and retention. Thus, the use of such techniques to achieve short-term performance goals can engender illusions of learning and skill mastery. Educational courses and applications may reinforce such perceptions by rewarding immediate performance and instilling in learners a false sense of confidence that they have mastered subject matter or skills. However, rigorous research studies have shown that a person's current performance can be a poor indicator of what they have learned (e.g., Soderstrom & Bjork, 2015).

One misconception that is widely held by students poignantly highlights the contrast between short-term performance and long-term learning and retention. It is the misguided belief that repeated study or rereading of to-be-learned material just prior to taking a criterial test (e.g., "cramming") is an effective learning strategy (e.g., Ekuni et al., 2022; Hartwig & Dunlosky, 2012; Yan, Thai, & Bjork, 2014). In a highly influential experiment, Roediger and Karpicke (2006) asked several groups of students to learn and attempt to recall a short text. One group was asked to learn the text by rereading it repeatedly over 20 minutes. A second group was asked to reread the text over 15 minutes and then tested on their recall of the text whereby they were given 5 minutes to "retrieve" the information by writing down as much of the text as they could recall with no assistance. A third group had only 5 minutes to read the text, then were given a 15-minute memory test to retrieve as much as they could recall.

How well did these students think they learned the material? Not surprisingly, students who had the task of repeatedly reading the text over 20 minutes (i.e., the "re-readers") predicted that they would remember the text better a week later than students who were challenged to practice retrieving information for 15 minutes by writing it down. Indeed, re-reading is one of the most widely-adopted techniques by students in self-regulated study (Carrier, 2000; Ekuni et al., 2022; Hartwig & Dunlosky, 2012; Karpicke, Butler, & Roediger, 2009; Kornell & Bjork, 2007; Wissman, Rawson, & Pyc, 2012; Yan, Thai, & Bjork, 2014). In a survey of undergraduates at an elite US university, Karpicke and colleagues (2009) even found that re-reading was the most frequently listed study technique. By contrast, only 11% of students surveyed reported using self-testing, or what is also referred to as retrieval practice. A few studies have asked people to directly compare these techniques, and they showed that most students and close to the majority of teachers view re-reading as more beneficial than retrieval practice for learning (Firth, 2018; Kornell & Bjork, 2007; McCabe, 2011; Morehead, Rhodes, & DeLozier, 2016).

Returning to the experiment, in order to assess students' learning of the text, Roediger and Karpicke (2006) gave half of the students a final test five minutes later in which they were asked to write down as much of the text as they could recall. The remaining students were given the same final test one week later. The students were also asked to predict how well they would do on the test. It turns out the re-readers successfully predicted they would do better, at least on the final test that was taken only 5 minutes after the reading task. However, contrary to their own learning predictions, students who practiced retrieval performed much better on the final test given one week later than the group that repeatedly read the text alone.

Retrieval practice produced less forgetting over a one-week delay even though it made initial learning worse in the short term. In this case, re-reading was akin to cramming right before a final exam – it likely helped make the words of the text appear to be right at students' fingertips and therefore easier to immediately recall. However, the information that was "crammed" right before the immediate test was also more rapidly forgotten by the final delayed recall test. And so why do learners often prefer this ineffective strategy over more effective strategies? One answer is poor planning – students opt to study for whatever exam is scheduled sooner, often waiting for the last minute when there is little choice or time but to cram (Hartwig & Dunlosky, 2012; Kornell & Bjork, 2007), and despite having good intentions to begin studying sooner (Blasiman, Dunlosky, & Rawson, 2017). Yet, the fact that cramming does help students quickly prepare for and perform well on immediate tests might also explain why students and teachers may have difficulty discovering the factors that lead to good long-term learning, because it is easier for them to recognize and concentrate on what facilitates good short-term performance (Hartwig & Dunlosky, 2012; Roediger & Pyc, 2012).

Counterintuitive Benefits of Retrieval Practice

While students and teachers may see utility in retrieval practice for identifying gaps in knowledge or comprehension, they generally do not consider it to be an effective learning strategy, in and of itself (Kornell & Son, 2009; McCabe, 2011). And yet a sizable body of scientific research dating back over a century shows it is more effective in improving learners' long-term retention than re-reading (Carrier & Pashler, 1992; Gates, 1917; Kühn, 1914; for reviews, see Roediger & Karpicke, 2006; and Rowland, 2014). This finding, known as the retrieval practice or testing effect, has been demonstrated using a wide range of subject materials; types of tests; in both laboratory and classroom settings; as well as in different student populations (e.g., Adesope, Trevisan, & Sundararajan, 2017; Agarwal, Nunes, & Blunt, 2021; Butler et al., 2014; Butler & Roediger, 2007; Gates, 1917; Kang, McDermott, & Roediger, 2007; Karpicke, 2012; Karpicke & Blunt, 2011; Larsen et al., 2013; McDermott et al., 2014; Roediger & Karpicke, 2006; Rowland, 2014; Spitzer, 1939). More recent research has further demonstrated that retrieval practice can help learners mentally organize information, learn complex concepts, transfer knowledge to related situations, and even learn new information as compared to rereading or using other recommended study techniques, such as concept mapping (Blunt & Karpicke, 2014; Congleton & Rajaram, 2012; Karpicke & Blunt, 2011; Pastötter & Bäuml, 2014; Zaromb & Roediger, 2010).

The benefit of retrieval practice on long-term retention is counterintuitive when one considers that rereading typically provides students with more exposure to the to-be-learned information than retrieval practice. For example, in the Roediger and Karpicke (2006) study, students could not recall all the information during the retrieval practice periods, nor were they provided with feedback afterwards. However, in the re-reading periods, 100% of the information was represented to the students. When learners further take the opportunity to review what information they remembered correctly or incorrectly, and what they failed to remember at all, the long-term learning advantages of retrieval practice can be quite large and robust (e.g., Butler, 2010; Butler, Karpicke, & Roediger, 2008). Another reason the retrieval practice effect may seem counterintuitive is that it is slower and more difficult to reach desired performance levels through retrieval practice as compared to repeated study, and people tend to predict that they will better remember information that is acquired more quickly and easily (e.g., Kornell et al., 2011).

Why is retrieval practice such an effective method for fostering long-term learning and retention of information and skills? While scientists have yet to reach a consensus, there are several types of theoretical explanations that have been proposed. One is that retrieval practice *indirectly* enhances learning and retention by functioning as an assessment and providing feedback to students regarding what they have already successfully learned and where they should best concentrate their efforts during subsequent study attempts (Roediger & Karpicke, 2006). The majority of theoretical explanations, however, have proposed cognitive mechanisms for how the retrieval of information *directly* enhances its long-term learning and retention. For example, Carpenter (2009, 2011) and Pyc and Rawson (2010, 2012) argue that engaging in retrieval practice produces an elaboration of the target information searched in memory through the activation of associated semantic information. Let's say a person studies the pair of words "BIRD – EAGLE" and subsequently engages in retrieval practice by attempting to recall the pair-associate when given the cue word "BIRD - ?". According to this theory, retrieval practice may activate related concepts (e.g., sparrow, crow, blue jay) along with the target (eagle), and so during a later recall test, the activation of these semantically-related concepts may serve as additional retrieval cues to facilitate recall of the correct target. According to other theories, retrieval practice enhances the number of retrieval routes that are able to be effectively utilized at a later test (e.g., Bjork, 1975; McDaniel & Masson, 1985); processing of item-specific and relational information (e.g., Karpicke & Zaromb, 2010; Peterson & Mulligan, 2013); or mental organization of retrieval schemas (Zaromb & Roediger, 2010; for a review and account of these and additional theories, see Rowland, 2014).

Learning, Fast and Slow

The contrast between the fleeting short-term benefits of rereading and the more gradual, longer-term benefits of retrieval practice for learning and retention are reflected in studies and comparisons of other types of "quick and easy" vs. "slow and difficult" strategies. For example, just as students tend to prefer rereading over retrieval practice, they also tend to prefer "cramming" or massing their study periods together in close succession over spacing them out over extended intervals of time (e.g., McCabe, 2011). Likewise, once students have learned something, they see no need or benefit to "overlearning" it (e.g., Kornell & Bjork, 2007; Hartwig & Dunlosky, 2012). Overall, the extant research on beliefs about learning confirm that most students (and many teachers) embrace strategies, such as rereading, that boost short-term performance but do not necessarily foster long-term learning and retention. By contrast, they often underestimate or fail to recognize the value of more difficult, slower learning strategies in fostering long-term learning and retention (e.g., Hartwig & Dunlosky 2012; Kornell, 2009; McCabe, 2011). We now turn to summarize some of the research findings showing the relative advantages of these "slower and more difficult" learning strategies over the "quicker and easier" techniques.

Massed vs. Distributed Learning

Will students learn and retain more if they study a given topic for 60 minutes each school day, rather than for five hours all on one day? Hundreds of experiments in verbal learning (e.g., syllables, words, prose) dating back to the classic work of Ebbinghaus (1885/1964) have addressed this question by demonstrating the "spacing effect". This is the finding that spacing periods of study renders verbal material more resistant to long-term forgetting than massing the study periods, while massed study typically produces better short-term recall performance (Cepeda et al., 2006; Dempster, 1988). Most of these experiments were conducted using relatively simple verbal materials, such as single words or word pairs. For example, in one experiment reported by Bloom and Shuell (1981), high school students were asked to study pairs of English-French vocabulary (e.g., lawyer - l'avocat) for either 30 minutes on a single day or distributed over three consecutive days (10 minutes of study per day). Performance on a recall test administered immediately following the 30-minute study period for the first group and the last 10-minute study period of the second group was similar for both groups. However, when a recall test was administered one week later, students who distributed their study over three consecutive days remembered more vocabulary than those who had massed their study.

The spacing effect is quite robust and has been shown to generalize across age groups (e.g., Balota, Duchek, & Paullin, 1989), complexity of verbal materials (e.g., Rawson & Kintsch, 2005), and types of concepts or subject matter (Carlson & Yaure, 1990; Kang & Pashler, 2012; Kornell & Bjork, 2008; Kornell et al., 2010; Rohrer, Dedrick, & Burgess, 2014; Rohrer & Taylor, 2007; Taylor & Rohrer, 2010). Similar effects of massed versus distributed practice have also been reported in the study of motor skill learning, such as typing, playing sports, or playing musical instruments (e.g., Abushanab & Bishara, 2013; Baddeley & Longman, 1978; Hall, Domingues, & Cavazos, 1994; Shea & Morgan, 1979). The benefits of distributed study and practice on learning and long-term retention are not self-evident and may not be discernible to students and teachers alike, because they can be overshadowed by the immediate, short-term performance advantage of massed study, or cramming.

Learning in the Same vs. Variable Contexts

When one is studying subject matter in school in preparation for a final exam, is it better to study the course materials in the same room under the exact same conditions (e.g., quiet setting, comfortable temperature, same time of day or night)? Or is it better to study the same materials in varied locations under different study conditions? Not sure of the answer? Let's pose a similar question whose answer may seem more intuitive. Suppose you are trying to improve your basketball free-throw shot. Is it better to only practice shooting free throws, or is it better to practice shooting from a variety of different locations and distances from the basket, even if they do not include shooting from the free-throw line? Intuition or common sense would suggest that one should practice shooting from the free-throw line. After all, that is precisely the skill that one is trying to improve.

Contrary to such intuitions, research studies have shown that studying or practicing under varied conditions fosters better long-term learning and retention of information and skills. For example, in one famous study, students at the University of Michigan were asked to study a list of words in one of two campus locations. Several hours later, half of the students restudied the list in the same location, while the other half restudied the list in the other location. A few hours later, all students were given a final test on their memory for the list of words in a new location on campus. Interestingly, the students who studied in different locations during the two study sessions recalled 21% more words than those who only studied in the same room (Smith, Glenberg, & R. A. Bjork, 1978). This finding that varying one's physical study environment bolsters retention was replicated using both similar study materials as well as more complex materials and substantially longer retention intervals (Glenberg,1979; Smith, 1982; Smith & Rothkopf, 1984).

Studies of motor-learning skills, including basketball shooting, have reported similar findings (e.g., Kerr & Booth, 1978; Landin, Hebert, & Fairweather, 1993; Green, Whitehead, & Sugden, 1995). For example, returning to the question of how to best learn to shoot a free throw, Landin and colleagues (1993) had two groups of participants practice shooting a basketball over a three-day period. One group practiced shooting only free throws, while a second group practiced shooting free throws as well as shooting from shorter and longer distances from the basket. Both groups practiced the same total number of shots. Three days later, the participants were asked to shoot ten free throws from the free-throw line. The counterintuitive finding was that participants who practiced shooting from multiple distances in relation to the basket successfully shot more free throws than those who only practiced shooting free throws at the fixed distance.

Learning to Criteria vs. Overlearning

Imagine that you are a professional singer, and you are scheduled to perform in front of an audience of several thousand concertgoers in two weeks. During your rehearsal today you sang all of the concert pieces without any mistakes and you already feel "concert ready." Will you decide not to rehearse any further for the next two weeks, or would you still have rehearsals right up until the day of the performance? In singing and other performing arts, the common practice is to continue rehearsing for a performance even after one has learned the piece(s) to the desired performance criteria. Athletes also generally continue to practice right up until a game or tournament even if they had already achieved a target performance level at some earlier point in time.

In most academic settings, however, such a strategy appears to be inefficient and unnecessary. If one has learned some new information in class and can accurately recall and explain what was learned right at the end of class, why should you spend additional time continuing to review the information that already seems known? The answer suggested by numerous experiments dating back to Ebbinghaus's (1885/1964) famous study is that the practice of "overlearning" or "successive relearning" can be a quite potent technique for improving the long-term retention of information and skills (e.g., Gilbert, 1957; Krueger, 1929; Postman, 1962). In a recent experiment, Rawson and colleagues (2018) asked college students to study a list of English-Lithuanian word pairs (e.g., cake - pyragas). They were then given a cued recall test whereby they were presented with one word from each pair and had to recall the corresponding paired associate (e.g., pyragas - ?). Each time students did not recall the correct paired associate they were shown the correct response. Students continued to attempt to recall each word pair until they recalled each word pair either one or three times correctly.

One week later, students were asked to "relearn" the word pairs by taking a cued-recall test until they correctly recalled each pair once. The same relearning procedure was repeated over the course of the following 3 weeks, one relearning session per week. While this procedure already incorporates both retrieval practice and spaced practice, what is unique about successive relearning is the requirement to reach 100% recall accuracy by the end of each session. Rawson and colleagues (2018) found that initial recall performance increased substantially from each relearning session to the next, suggesting that each session of successive relearning improved retention of the word pairs even though students could recall them with 100% accuracy by the end of each session. Additional studies conducted using more complex materials and in classroom settings have also shown dramatic, incremental improvements in learning and retention with successive relearning (Higham et al., 2022; Janes et al., 2020; Rawson, Dunlosky, & Sciartelli, 2013; for a recent review, see Rawson & Dunlosky, 2022).

The tendency for people to embrace quick and easy learning strategies poses a serious challenge for self-regulated learning. Since these techniques may help students achieve their desired short-term performance objectives, their attempts to monitor and evaluate performance may only serve to reinforce the misconception that these are effective learning techniques. They may become overconfident in their mastery of the to-be-learned domain and quit studying or practicing it too early. They may also become overconfident in their self-efficacy to apply these techniques to learn new knowledge and skills.

Additional Misconceptions of Learning

Many students harbor misconceptions about how the human mind encodes information that may lead them to embrace ineffective learning techniques. For example, several surveys have indicated that the majority of people believe that memory "works like a video camera, accurately recording the events we see and hear so that we can review and inspect them later" (Simons & Chabris, 2011, 2012). Consistent with these findings, other experimental studies have shown that people tend to exhibit a "stability bias" – the tendency to believe that their memory for newly learned information will remain stable and not be forgotten in the future (e.g., Koriat et al., 2004; Kornell, 2012).

There remains a slew of additional learning strategies that students frequently report using and are featured in teachers' educational psychology textbooks and courses that lack a sufficient evidentiary base for their utility (e.g., Dunlosky et al., 2013; Snowman, 1986; Sternberg & Williams, 2010). Space precludes a detailed discussion of each of these approaches, but we will provide a brief exposition of a selection, focusing on techniques that students can implement by themselves with little or no external assistance, and are, therefore, suitable for self-regulated learning contexts. At best each of these techniques appears to have marginal utility, and in certain instances (all other things being equal) they may result in negative effects (for an in-depth review of these techniques, see Dunlosky et al., 2013).

Highlighting and Underlining

Defined as marking potentially important portions of to-be-learned materials while reading. It is simple and quick, and again probably makes students feel like they are engaged in the learning process. Across a range of studies, highlighting and underlining has failed to help military trainees, English language learners, K-12 regular and remedial students, as well as university undergraduates (e.g., Nist & Hogrebe, 1987). Underlining has regularly been shown to be ineffective regardless of text length and topic, with some evidence suggesting it may even hurt performance (e.g., Dunlosky et al., 2013). For example, one study found that underlining reduced student's ability to draw inferences from a textbook, with underlining plausibly drawing attention to individual items rather than to connections across items (in essence, working against several effective learning strategies like elaboration) (see Petersen, 1992).

Keyword Mnemonics

This approach uses keywords and mental imagery to associate verbal materials. For example, if you are teaching a student the meaning of the word "assail," you could use "sailboat" as the keyword to associate the new word with. Students can think of a sailboat crashing into someone to remember that "assail" means to attack someone with words, actions, or deeds. There is some research to suggest keyword mnemonics do seem to help in improving foreign-language acquisition, word definitions and scientific terminology, but the effects are not especially robust (Dunlosky et al., 2013). In addition, the effort involved in generating keywords may not be an especially efficient use of the student's time; thus, keyword mnemonics tends to behave poorly if put up against other learning strategies in experimental studies (see e.g., Fritz et al., 2007).

Imagery for Text

This procedure has the student attempting to form mental images of text materials while reading or listening. Research has revealed a patchwork of inconsistent results. While studies have found that this strategy may be somewhat effective when used with image-friendly texts, its usefulness outside this specific instantiation is uncertain, and again requires conscious effort the student likely could be expending more efficiently using alternative strategies (see e.g., De Beni & Moè, 2003).

Summarization

In summarization, students identify a text's main points, in the process attempting to exclude unimportant material. Whether it works is difficult to answer, as it has been implemented in a host of different ways and spurned a number of fairly well-respected training resources. But there are many unknowns tied to this approach. It is unknown, for example, whether summarizing small pieces of a text or large chunks of it works better or whether the length, readability, or organization of the material to be summarized plays a meaningful role (Dunlosky et al., 2013). Nevertheless, even in experimental studies where summarizing did not show a significant learning advantage over control study conditions (e.g., simply reading the to-be-learned materials), higher quality summaries were associated with better learning measures (e.g., Bednall & Kehoe, 2011).

How Cognitive Biases Contribute to Conceptions of Self-Regulated Learning

Cognitive heuristics and biases likely also underlie students' tendencies to prefer ineffective learning strategies. Social scientists have long grappled with questions about how intuitive processes affect human judgment and decision making. Building on the work of pioneering researchers such as Meehl (1954) and Simon (1957), Tversky and Kahneman (1974) proposed that people often rely on mental shortcuts, known as heuristics, which help them make judgments quickly, efficiently, and, usually, accurately. Although heuristics are usually adaptive, they sometimes cause people to make irrational judgments and decisions. For example, people who drive instead of fly because instances of plane crashes from news reports come to mind easily can be said to be making an irrational decision, because, statistically, flying is safer than driving. In such instances, we can say that the "availability" heuristic (Tversky & Kahneman, 1974), the tendency to judge what comes to mind most easily as most frequent, likely, and typical has biased the decision.

Researchers have identified two families of cognitive processes that provide a useful way of understanding a wide variety of heuristics and biases (Kahneman, 2011; Sloman, 2002; Stanovich & West, 2000; Thaler & Sunstein, 2009). This dual-process model distinguishes System 1, or intuitive, and System 2, or reflective, thinking. System 1 thinking includes automatic mental processes and affective reactions that occur quickly and effortlessly, often without conscious attention or even awareness. Heuristics are generally associated with System 1 thinking (Evans, 2003). This type of thinking underlies routine, well-learned activities without having to consciously focus attention on the steps required to perform those activities. By contrast, System 2 thinking occurs more slowly and involves conscious, effortful mental deliberation. Humans engage in System 2 thinking when learning how to perform new and challenging tasks or when attempting to solve complex problems that require rule-based reasoning strategies. Furthermore, while the two systems are always active, judgments made by System 1 can at times be overridden by System 2. Heuristics are usually considered adaptive, because they tend to work well most of the time and they may be necessary when decisions must be made quickly with limited information under conditions of uncertainty.

Numerous studies have documented the existence and operation of dozens of heuristics in a wide variety of judgment and decision-making paradigms and contexts (e.g., Gigerenzer & Gaissmaier, 2011; Gigerenzer, Todd, & the ABC Research Group, 1999; Kahneman & Frederick, 2002; Shah & Oppenheimer, 2008, 2009). Ironically, despite their widely recognized prevalence and influence on behavior, heuristics are still elusive because individuals are, by-in-large, unaware of the mental processes that underlie their own judgments and decisions (e.g., Nisbett & Wilson, 1977). Likewise, research studies examining how students monitor their learning activities have shown that metacognitive judgments of learning and knowing are influenced by heuristics that can often foster illusions of learning mastery (Castel, McCabe, & Roediger, 2007; Finn & Tauber, 2015; Jacoby, Kelley, & Dywan, 1989; Kelley & Jacoby, 1996; Kornell et al., 2011; Rhodes & Castel, 2008, 2009).

For example, when being taught new subject matter for a course, students may suddenly feel confident that they have learned the material well if they feel that the information is relatively easy to process and comprehend. In one striking demonstration of this phenomenon, Carpenter and colleagues (2013) presented college students with one of two videos of an instructor explaining a scientific concept that differed in presentation fluency. In one version the instructor stood upright and spoke fluidly without relying on lecture notes, whereas in the alternate version the instructor looked away from the students and spoke haltingly. Although the fluency of the presentation did not influence how much information students learned from the lecture, students who viewed the fluent presentation predicted that they would remember much more information from the lecture than students who viewed the disfluent presentation.

In addition, when new information is fresh in their minds, students may use the availability heuristic to mistakenly determine that they know the material well and will not need to review it in the future. As discussed earlier, if given an immediate test of their knowledge and comprehension of the material, these students may interpret their high performance as further corroboration of their learning mastery, and a stability bias may lead them to mistakenly believe that their current performance level will endure long term.

The pervasive influence of cognitive heuristics and biases on human decision making poses another dilemma for self-regulated learning. Current models of self-regulated learning assume that self-regulated learning requires conscious planning, monitoring, and control of one's learning behavior (Panadero, 2017; Wirth et al., 2020), and yet people may not even be consciously aware of the extent to which heuristics and biases guide their learning decisions and behaviors. It is unclear how students can adequately monitor and evaluate the quality and quantity of their learning if some of the heuristics underlying their learning decisions are beyond conscious inspection or control.

RECOMMENDATIONS

Up until this point, we have discussed some of the common misconceptions and biases that can impede or derail self-regulated learning. Table 2 below lists many of the learning techniques discussed earlier and identifies which ones have been shown to be:

1. Effective in fostering long-term learning and retention of information and skills.
2. Show mixed or indeterminate effects.
3. Appear, based on available evidence, to be relatively ineffective, problematic, or lack solid evidentiary support.

The emphasis here is on what strategies can help foster long-term learning and retention of information and skills rather than on achieving short-term performance objectives. If the focus were on short-term objectives, it would be necessary to flip some of the classifications, because some of the techniques, such as rereading and massed practice, often result in higher performance on short-term learning measures.

Table 2. List of common learning strategies that have demonstrated moderate or strong effects; weak or no effects; or showed mixed or indeterminate effects on fostering long-term learning and retention

Moderate/Strong	Mixed/Indeterminate	Weak/Ineffective
Retrieval Practice	Imagery for Text	Rereading
Distributed Practice	Summarization	Massed Practice
Variable Context Learning		Same Context Learning
Overlearning/Successive Relearning		Practicing until Target Performance Achieved
Interleaving		Highlighting and Under-lining
Concrete Examples		Keyword Mnemonics
Elaboration		
Dual Coding		

The fact that that "low utility" strategies can still help learners achieve their short-term performance objectives is likely one reason why many of the listed techniques that appear to be ineffective or show mixed or indeterminate effects are among the techniques most frequently used by students and encouraged by teachers (e.g., Roediger & Pyc, 2012). We now turn to discussing several research-based recommendations for addressing common misconceptions and biases and designing curricula and programs for fostering self-regulated learning.

Teaching "Desirable Difficulties" in Learning

As Bjork and colleagues (e.g., Bjork, 1994; Bjork & Bjork, 2011; Bjork et al., 2013) argue, techniques such as retrieval practice and distributed practice are more difficult for learners in that they tend to slow learning and impair performance relative to their rivals, rereading and massed practice. Nevertheless, these techniques are more desirable because they foster better long-term learning and retention of information and skills. Therefore, self-regulated learning programs and curricula should incorporate techniques that present "desirable difficulties" in learning. Fortunately, there are already a number of online tools that enable students and educators to incorporate retrieval practice, interleaving, spaced practice, and successive relearning both in and outside of classroom settings (see https://www.retrievalpractice.org/strategies/2019/6/19/tech for examples and brief descriptions of such tools).

Self-regulated learning programs and curricula could also benefit from providing explicit instruction about the benefits of incorporating desirable learning difficulties along with the limited utility of more popular, "quick and easy" learning strategies. Surveys of college students have confirmed that most students do not use study strategies that were taught to them by others (Hartwig & Dunlosky, 2012; Kornell & Bjork, 2007), suggesting that students, by and large, rely on their own experiences and intuitions to determine what study strategies work best for them. Often academic and workforce training programs and institutions deliver educational content while providing little or no instruction or guidance regarding how to best learn it – that is, they seem to assume that students already know how to study the material. One should, therefore, not assume that students have been previously taught about effective learning strategies, and while it may never be too late to learn such strategies, the earlier in one's education they are inculcated the better. Moreover, and at the risk of stating what might now seem obvious, instruction about "desirable difficulties" in learning should itself embody those techniques so as to potentially further enhance their long-term adoption, and not doing so would be hypocritical.

With some of these aims in mind, a team of researchers in the Netherlands recently developed a learning strategy intervention that consists of three two-hour sessions designed to enhance students' awareness of, reflection on, and practice implementing effective learning strategies and desirable difficulties (Biwer et al., 2020). Each session is conducted with a small group of students and an instructor and is scheduled over the course of several weeks. During the first session, students are asked to discuss the learning techniques they use and how effective they believe they are, and then they are given instruction about and empirical evidence supporting the utility of particular techniques, including desirable difficulties. In the second session, students are asked to complete a questionnaire about their academic goal orientation and set goals for practicing effective learning strategies. For the final session, students are asked to practice different effective learning strategies using materials from their own academic courses. While the program is still in its infancy, preliminary observations and data from both students and instructors look promising, but they also underscore some of the challenges of implementing desirable difficulties in practice. For example, students were hesitant to abandon learning techniques such as rereading and cramming that they believed worked well for them up until that point in favor of new strategies they were uncertain would work for them.

Expanding the Self-Regulated Learning Toolkit

Aside from the methods discussed up to this point, there is a growing body of research supporting the utility of other little known learning techniques that could also be incorporated into the self-regulated learning toolkit. These include:

Interleaving

The scientific evidence suggests that students learn more when they can switch between different topics, or even procedures within the same topic area (Kang & Pashler, 2012; Mayfield & Chase, 2002). For example, in mathematics, students learn more when they solve many different types of problems during practice rather than solving the same type of problem repetitively. Doing mathematics in this way helps students learn the similarities and differences between distinct ideas and concepts.

Concrete Examples

Research shows that multiple examples of the same idea, especially with different surface details, help students understand the true idea the example is intending to illustrate (Paivio, Walsh, & Bons, 1984). This is because novices tend to remember surface details, not abstract ones. As for other strategies, there is multiple information on examples of this strategy in practice and ways it can be used to enhance performance.

Elaboration

This strategy involves the student asking "how" and "why" questions about a specific topic, and then trying to find the answers to these questions. Research has demonstrated consistently that the act of trying to describe and explain how and why things work helps students understand and learn more efficiently (Donoghue & Hattie, 2021; Dunlosky et al., 2013).

Dual-Coding

Research suggests that another efficacious learning strategy has students combining verbal representations of information (words) with visual representations of information (pictures/diagrams) (Meyer & Anderson, 1992). This technique is not the same as imagery for text discussed earlier. Where visual imagery simply requires students to encode a visual representation of to-be-learned information, dual coding requires students to encode the same information in two different formats and to mentally combine the representations by developing a conceptual understanding of how the two representations are related.

We would also venture to recommend a couple of, as yet, relatively unexplored directions for expanding the self-regulated learning toolkit. As we discuss below, these include examining whether social and emotional learning (SEL) skills and cognitive bias mitigation interventions can facilitate the effective utilization of desirable difficulties in learning to foster self-regulated learning.

Critical Role of SEL Skills in Self-Regulated Learning

For individuals who primarily use and believe in the effectiveness of "quick and easy" learning techniques that have marginal utility, it may be especially challenging to replace these habits with slower, more difficult learning strategies (Biwer et al., 2020; Zepeda, Martin, & Butler, 2020).

While some very popular educational apps successfully incorporate some desirable difficulties in learning, such as retrieval practice, distributed practice, and successive relearning, they rely primarily on a repertoire of behavioral nudging techniques (e.g., gamification and external rewards) to promote their use, and it appears unclear how effective such tactics are at fostering self-regulated learning (Shortt et al., 2021). Indeed, once the novelty of the gamification and rewards fades, learners must find new sources of motivation, interest, and inspiration to continue learning through a particular MOOC or application (e.g., Alamri & Higham, 2022). Indeed, since their inception, MOOCs and other self-directed learning programs have suffered from low rates of long-term student participation and engagement (e.g., Reich & Ruipérz-Valiente, 2021).

Why might that be? One possibility is that students soon find that the course material exceeds their level of knowledge and ability and cannot continue with the program. However, previous research on factors associated with student retention in 4-year university programs has suggested that measures of cognitive ability (e.g., GPA, SAT scores) per se are not too highly correlated with students' retention, while non-cognitive factors, such as conscientiousness (i.e., work ethic), are significant predictors of student retention (Caviglia-Harris & Maier, 2020).

Plausibly, we suspect that work ethic and other SEL skills (see Roberts, Martin, & Olaru, 2015, for a review) are all the more important both for retention and learning in less-structured self-regulated learning contexts. Indeed, to become a mature, sophisticated, independent learner, one must demonstrate high levels of the following three SEL skills:

Conscientiousness/Work Ethic

To successfully adopt more difficult learning techniques, such as distributed practice and successive relearning on a regular basis for extended periods of time, students must have good time management skills, awareness of goal-setting strategies, and self-discipline. Even when learners see that they have achieved their performance targets, they should resist thinking that they have already achieved their learning goals and can now move onto something new. They need to persist with established short and long-term goals and have a long-term learning plan.

Emotional Stability

It is important for students to be able to cope with the frustrations and disappointments that come with using slower and more difficult learning techniques. Learners who regularly use these techniques will likely make many mistakes and see poor short-term performance. They may be quickly discouraged by their slow learning progress. Emotional stability is critical to helping learners become emotionally resilient in the face of all of the types of frustrations and disappointments they will likely experience.

Openness/Curiosity

It is important for students to be willing to embrace new learning techniques and continue to expand and deepen one's knowledge and skills in a particular domain. Individuals who are high in openness/curiosity are willing to question their current knowledge and beliefs and are open to considering alternative points of view and trying out new approaches.

SEL interventions may be critical to helping students become more mature, sophisticated learners, as changing one's learning habits and embracing more challenging, gradual learning strategies may require that students improve their SEL skills (but see also Zepeda, Martin, & Butler, 2020, who propose additional motivational strategies for adopting desirable difficulties in learning). There is an emerging literature supporting the importance of these noncognitive skills to self-regulated learning, a topic that might, in its own right, fill a chapter. For example, Bruso, Stefaniak, and Bol's (2020) findings highlight the need for effective time management as an important self-regulation strategy and various Openness and Emotional Stability manipulations for those lacking in motivation. Notably, where once such noncognitive skills were thought to be "set like plaster", the scientific evidence now suggests they are perhaps more amenable to interventions than typical cognitive skills (see Roberts, Martin, & Olaru, 2015).

Mitigating Cognitive Biases to Foster Self-Regulated Learning

Last, self-regulated learning programs and curricula may benefit from explicitly instructing students about the types of cognitive biases that can impede their learning progress. For instance, as discussed earlier, students tend to think that new information that they read or understood more quickly and fluently will be remembered better in the long term than information that required more time and mental effort to read or understand (Kornell et al., 2011; Rhodes & Castel, 2008, 2009). Similarly, many students exhibit "stability bias" – the tendency to believe that what one currently knows will be remembered just as well into the future (Koriat et al., 2004; Kornell, 2012). Such subjective experiences can create a powerful illusion of learning for students and, therefore, providing students with explicit instruction about such biases may help them better recognize and mitigate their own susceptibility to them. Researchers have suggested additional techniques for mitigating some of these cognitive biases, such as asking students as they are learning to slow down, think more carefully, and consider other potential factors that may influence their learning aside from subjective perceptions of cognitive fluency (Finn & Tauber, 2015; Larrick, 2004). Another mitigation technique is to ask people to think deliberatively about how one's long-term learning could be impacted by choosing alternative learning strategies (Fischhoff, 1982; Koriat et al., 1980; although see Larrick, 2004, for examples of how this mitigation technique can also backfire).

CONCLUSION

A troubling irony of education in today's modern society is that while students have unprecedented freedom and autonomy to choose and manage what, when, where, and how they learn, they generally do not take good advantage of this freedom and autonomy, because they often, absent of knowledge, use relatively ineffective learning strategies. Preferred strategies such as rereading, highlighting/underlining, and massed study are "quick" and "easy" to implement, not only in a logistical sense, but also because they can produce rapid acquisition of information and skills to attain short-term performance objectives (e.g., cramming right before a test). However, these same strategies have marginal utility for fostering long-term learning and retention. By contrast, a sizeable body of research conducted in both laboratories and educational settings have identified learning strategies, such as retrieval practice, distributed practice, and successive relearning that can be quite effective at enhancing long-term learning and retention of new information and skills. It appears counterintuitive to most students and many teachers that these techniques would be effective as learning strategies, because they are "slow" and "difficult" to implement in that they require more time and effort and appear to impede the rate of acquisition. As such, they represent "desirable difficulties" in learning.

Student preferences for quick and easy study techniques over embracing "desirable difficulties" in learning is not surprising considering some of the common myths, misconceptions, and biases that influence students' learning decisions. These include mistakenly believing that the mind can instantaneously record and store new information like a camera (i.e., once the information has been captured, it's always available and can be easily recalled), or that newly acquired information that is fresh in one's mind, easily read, or readily comprehensible will be remembered for the long term. They can lull students into mistakenly believing that they have mastered learning a new subject or skill and no longer need to further study or practice it.

To help remedy this state of affairs, designers of self-regulated learning programs and curricula should strongly consider incorporating "desirable difficulties" in learning. Although there is already a sizeable body of scientific evidence supporting the efficacy of the slow and difficult learning strategies discussed in the chapter, more research is still needed to investigate the optimal conditions for their operationalization in educational settings, especially in online and blended learning environments. Considering that many students are not formally taught about effective learning strategies, we further recommend instructing students about both effective and ineffective learning techniques, preferably in a manner that is itself consistent with effective learning principles.

Nevertheless, we suspect that fully embracing slower and more difficult learning techniques is much easier said than done, and that when push comes to shove many students will default to doing whatever seems to work best just to get by in their studies and achieve their short-term performance objectives (i.e., get a passing or good test score). For example, many students may simply not have adequate time-management skills to implement a distributed learning schedule, despite having good intentions to follow one. It would, therefore, seem logical that in order to be truly effective and foster long-term learning and retention, self-regulated learning programs should also target those SEL skills and cognitive biases that are most critical to replacing poor study habits with more effective learning techniques and long-term habits. Admittedly, these claims are speculative and future research should also address the question of how students' learning strategies relate to SEL skills and cognitive biases and how interventions can be tailored to support students' adoption and utilization of effective learning strategies.

REFERENCES

Abushanab, B., & Bishara, A. J. (2013). Memory and metacognition for piano melodies: Illusory advantages of fixed- over random-order practice. *Memory & Cognition*, *41*(6), 928–937. doi:10.375813421-013-0311-z PMID:23508339

Adesope, O. O., Trevisan, D. A., & Sundararajan, N. (2017). Rethinking the use of tests: A meta-analysis of practice testing. *Review of Educational Research*, *87*(3), 659–701. doi:10.3102/0034654316689306

Agarwal, P. K., Bain, P. M., & Chamberlain, R. W. (2012). The value of applied research: Retrieval practice improves classroom learning and recommendations from a teacher, a principal, and a scientist. *Educational Psychology Review*, *24*(3), 437–448. doi:10.100710648-012-9210-2

Agarwal, P. K., D'Antonio, L., Roediger, H. L. III, McDermott, K. B., & McDaniel, M. A. (2014). Classroom-based programs of retrieval practice reduce middle school and high school students' test anxiety. *Journal of Applied Research in Memory and Cognition*, *3*(3), 131–139. doi:10.1016/j.jarmac.2014.07.002

Agarwal, P. K., Nunes, L. D., & Blunt, J. R. (2021). Retrieval practice consistently benefits student learning: A systematic review of applied research in schools and classrooms. *Educational Psychology Review*, *33*(4), 1409–1453. doi:10.100710648-021-09595-9

Alamri, A., & Higham, P. A. (2022). The dark side of corrective feedback: Controlled and automatic influences of retrieval practice. *Journal of Experimental Psychology. Learning, Memory, and Cognition*, *48*(5), 752–768. doi:10.1037/xlm0001138 PMID:35389700

Baddeley, A. D., & Longman, D. J. A. (1978). The influence of length and frequency of training session on the rate of learning to type. *Ergonomics*, *21*(8), 627–635. doi:10.1080/00140137808931764

Balota, D. A., Duchek, J. M., & Paullin, R. (1989). Age-related differences in the impact of spacing, lag, and retention interval. *Psychology and Aging*, *4*(1), 3–9. doi:10.1037/0882-7974.4.1.3 PMID:2803609

Bednall, T. C., & Kehoe, E. J. (2011). Effects of self-regulatory instructional aids on self-directed study. *Instructional Science*, *39*(2), 205–226. doi:10.100711251-009-9125-6

Biwer, F., de Bruin, A. B., Schreurs, S., & oude Egbrink, M. G. A. (2020). Future steps in teaching desirably difficult learning strategies: Reflections from the Study Smart program. *Journal of Applied Research in Memory and Cognition*, *9*(4), 439–446. doi:10.1016/j.jarmac.2020.07.006

Bjork, E. L., & Bjork, R. A. (2011). Making things hard on yourself, but in a good way: Creating desirable difficulties to enhance learning. *Psychology and the real world: Essays illustrating fundamental contributions to society, 2*, 59-68.

Bjork, R. A. (1975). Retrieval as a memory modifier: An interpretation of negative recency and related phenomena. In R.L. Solso (Ed.), *Information Processing and Cognition: The Loyola Symposium* (pp. 123–144). Hillsdale, NJ: Erlbaum.

Bjork, R. A. (1994). Memory and metamemory considerations in the training of human beings. In J. Metcalfe & A. Shimamura (Eds.), *Metacognition: Knowing about knowing* (pp. 185–205). MIT Press.

Bjork, R. A., Dunlosky, J., & Kornell, N. (2013). Self-regulated learning: Beliefs, techniques, and illusions. *Annual Review of Psychology, 64*(1), 417–444. doi:10.1146/annurev-psych-113011-143823 PMID:23020639

Blasiman, R. N., Dunlosky, J., & Rawson, K. A. (2017). The what, how much, and when of study strategies: Comparing intended versus actual study behaviour. *Memory (Hove, England), 25*(6), 784–792. doi:10.1080/09658211.2016.1221974 PMID:27561889

Bloom, K. C., & Shuell, T. J. (1981). Effects of massed and distributed practice on the learning and retention of second-language vocabulary. *The Journal of Educational Research, 74*(4), 245–248. doi:10.1080/00220671.1981.10885317

Blunt, J. R., & Karpicke, J. D. (2014). Learning with retrieval-based concept mapping. *Journal of Educational Psychology, 106*(3), 849–858. doi:10.1037/a0035934

Bruso, J., Stefaniak, J., & Bol, L. (2020). An examination of personality traits as a predictor of the use of self-regulated learning strategies and considerations for online instruction. *Educational Technology Research and Development, 68*(5), 2659–2683. doi:10.100711423-020-09797-y

Butler, A. C. (2010). Repeated testing produces superior transfer of learning relative to repeated studying. *Journal of Experimental Psychology. Learning, Memory, and Cognition, 36*(5), 1118–1133. doi:10.1037/a0019902 PMID:20804289

Butler, A. C., Karpicke, J. D., & Roediger, H. L. III. (2008). Correcting a metacognitive error: Feedback increases retention of low-confidence correct responses. *Journal of Experimental Psychology. Learning, Memory, and Cognition, 34*(4), 918–928. doi:10.1037/0278-7393.34.4.918 PMID:18605878

Butler, A. C., Marsh, E. J., Slavinsky, J. P., & Baraniuk, R. G. (2014). Integrating cognitive science and technology improves learning in a STEM classroom. *Educational Psychology Review, 26*(2), 331–340. doi:10.100710648-014-9256-4

Butler, A. C., & Roediger, H. L. III. (2007). Testing improves long-term retention in a simulated classroom setting. *The European Journal of Cognitive Psychology, 19*(4-5), 514–527. doi:10.1080/09541440701326097

Carlson, R. A., & Yaure, R. G. (1990). Practice schedules and the use of component skills in problem solving. *Journal of Experimental Psychology. Learning, Memory, and Cognition, 15*(3), 484–496. doi:10.1037/0278-7393.16.3.484

Carpenter, S. K. (2009). Cue strength as a moderator of the testing effect: The benefits of elaborative retrieval. *Journal of Experimental Psychology. Learning, Memory, and Cognition*, *35*(6), 1563–1569. doi:10.1037/a0017021 PMID:19857026

Carpenter, S. K. (2011). Semantic information activated during retrieval contributes to later retention: Support for the mediator effectiveness hypothesis of the testing effect. *Journal of Experimental Psychology. Learning, Memory, and Cognition*, *37*(6), 1547–1552. doi:10.1037/a0024140 PMID:21707217

Carpenter, S. K., Wilford, M. M., Kornell, N., & Mullaney, K. M. (2013). Appearances can be deceiving: Instructor fluency increases perceptions of learning without increasing actual learning. *Psychonomic Bulletin & Review*, *20*(6), 1350–1356. doi:10.375813423-013-0442-z PMID:23645413

Carrier, L. M. (2003). College students' choices of study strategies. *Perceptual and Motor Skills*, *96*(1), 54–56. doi:10.2466/pms.2003.96.1.54 PMID:12705510

Carrier, M., & Pashler, H. (1992). The influence of retrieval on retention. *Memory & Cognition*, *20*(6), 633–642. doi:10.3758/BF03202713 PMID:1435266

Castel, A. D., McCabe, D. P., & Roediger, H. L. (2007). Illusions of competence and overestimation of associative memory for identical items: Evidence from judgments of learning. *Psychonomic Bulletin & Review*, *14*(1), 107–111. doi:10.3758/BF03194036 PMID:17546739

Caviglia-Harris, J., & Maier, K. (2020). It's not all in their heads: The differing role of cognitive factors and non-cognitive traits in undergraduate success. *Education Economics*, *28*(3), 245–262. doi:10.1080/09645292.2020.1729702

Cepeda, N. J., Pashler, H., Vul, E., Wixted, J. T., & Rohrer, D. (2006). Distributed practice in verbal recall tasks: A review and quantitative synthesis. *Psychological Bulletin*, *132*(3), 354–380. doi:10.1037/0033-2909.132.3.354 PMID:16719566

Congleton, A., & Rajaram, S. (2012). The origin of the interaction between learning method and delay in the testing effect: The roles of processing and conceptual retrieval organization. *Memory & Cognition*, *40*(4), 528–539. doi:10.375813421-011-0168-y PMID:22160872

De Beni, R., & Moè, A. (2003). Presentation modality effects in studying passages. Are mental images always effective? *Applied Cognitive Psychology*, *17*(3), 309–324. doi:10.1002/acp.867

Dempster, F. N. (1988). The spacing effect: A case study in the failure to apply the results of psychological research. *The American Psychologist*, *43*(8), 627–634. doi:10.1037/0003-066X.43.8.627

Donoghue, G. M., & Hattie, J. A. (2021). A meta-analysis of ten learning techniques. In *Frontiers in Education* (p. 48). Frontiers.

Dunlosky, J. (2013). Strengthening the student toolbox: Study strategies to boost learning. *American Educator*, *37*(3), 12–21.

Dunlosky, J., Rawson, K. A., Marsh, E. J., Nathan, M. J., & Willingham, D. T. (2013). Improving students' learning with effective learning techniques: Promising directions from cognitive and educational psychology. *Psychological Science in the Public Interest*, *14*(1), 4–58. doi:10.1177/1529100612453266 PMID:26173288

Ebbinghaus, H. (1995). *Memory: A contribution to experimental psychology* (H. A. Ruger & C. E. Bussenius, Trans.). Dover. (Original work published 1964)

Efklides, A. (2011). Interactions of metacognition with motivation and affect in self-regulated learning: The MASRL model. *Educational Psychology, 46*(1), 6–25. doi:10.1080/00461520.2011.538645

Ekuni, R., de Souza, B. M. N., Agarwal, P. K., & Pompeia, S. (2022). A conceptual replication of survey research on study strategies in a diverse, non-WEIRD student population. *Scholarship of Teaching and Learning in Psychology, 8*(1), 1–14. doi:10.1037tl0000191

Finn, B., & Tauber, S. K. (2015). When confidence is not a signal of knowing: How students' experiences and beliefs about Processing Fluency Can Lead to Miscalibrated Confidence. *Educational Psychology Review, 27*(4), 567–586. doi:10.100710648-015-9313-7

Firth, J. (2018). Teachers' beliefs about memory: What are the implications for in-service teacher education? *Psychology of Education Review, 42*(2), 15–22. doi:10.53841/bpsper.2018.42.2.15

Fischhoff, B. (1982). Debiasing. In D. Kahneman, P. Slovic, & A. Tversky (Eds.), *Judgment under uncertainty: heuristics and biases* (pp. 422–444). Cambridge University Press. doi:10.1017/CBO9780511809477.032

Fritz, C. O., Morris, P. E., Acton, M., Voelkel, A. R., & Etkind, R. (2007). Comparing and combining retrieval practice and the key-word mnemonic for foreign vocabulary learning. *Applied Cognitive Psychology, 21*(4), 499–526. doi:10.1002/acp.1287

Gates, A. I. (1917). Recitation as a factor in memorizing. *Archives de Psychologie, 6*, 1–104.

Gigerenzer, G., & Gaissmaier, W. (2011). Heuristic decision making. *Annual Review of Psychology, 62*(1), 451–482. doi:10.1146/annurev-psych-120709-145346 PMID:21126183

Gigerenzer, G., & Todd, P. M.ABC Research Group. (1999). *Simple heuristics that make us smart.* Oxford University Press.

Gilbert, T. F. (1957). Overlearning and the retention of meaningful prose. *The Journal of General Psychology, 56*(2), 281–289. doi:10.1080/00221309.1957.9920339 PMID:13429005

Glenberg, A. M. (1979). Component-levels theory of the effects of spacing of repetitions on recall and recognition. *Memory & Cognition, 7*(2), 95–112. doi:10.3758/BF03197590 PMID:459836

Green, D. P., Whitehead, J., & Sugden, D. A. (1995). Practice variability and transfer of a racket skill. *Perceptual and Motor Skills, 81*(3, suppl), 1275–1281. doi:10.2466/pms.1995.81.3f.1275 PMID:8684925

Hall, K. G., Domingues, D. A., & Cavazos, R. (1994). Contextual interference effects with skilled baseball players. *Perceptual and Motor Skills, 78*(3), 835–841. doi:10.1177/003151259407800331 PMID:8084699

Hartwig, M. K., & Dunlosky, J. (2012). Study strategies of college students: Are self-testing and scheduling related to achievement? *Psychonomic Bulletin & Review, 19*(1), 126–134. doi:10.375813423-011-0181-y PMID:22083626

Higham, P. A., Zengel, B., Bartlett, L. K., & Hadwin, J. A. (2022). The benefits of successive relearning on multiple learning outcomes. *Journal of Educational Psychology, 114*(5), 928–944. doi:10.1037/edu0000693

Jacoby, L. L., Kelley, C. M., & Dywan, J. (1989). Memory attributions. Varieties of memory and consciousness. *Essays in Honour of Endel Tulving, 391*, 422.

Janes, J. L., Dunlosky, J., Rawson, K. A., & Jasnow, A. (2020). Successive relearning improves performance on a high-stakes exam in a difficult biopsychology course. *Applied Cognitive Psychology, 34*(5), 1118–1132. doi:10.1002/acp.3699

Kahneman, D. (2011). *Thinking, fast and slow*. Macmillan.

Kahneman, D., & Frederick, S. (2002). Representativeness revisited: Attribute substitution in intuitive judgment. In T. Gilovich, D. Griffin, & D. Kahneman (Eds.), *Heuristics and biases: The psychology of intuitive judgment* (pp. 49–81). Cambridge University Press. doi:10.1017/CBO9780511808098.004

Kang, S. H. K., McDermott, K. B., & Roediger, H. L. III. (2007). Test format and corrective feedback modify the effect of testing on long-term retention. *The European Journal of Cognitive Psychology, 19*(4-5), 528–558. doi:10.1080/09541440601056620

Kang, S. H. K., & Pashler, H. (2012). Learning painting styles: Spacing is advantageous when it promotes discriminative contrast. *Applied Cognitive Psychology, 26*(1), 97–103. doi:10.1002/acp.1801

Karpicke, J. D. (2012). Retrieval-based learning: Active retrieval promotes meaningful learning. *Current Directions in Psychological Science, 21*(3), 157–163. doi:10.1177/0963721412443552

Karpicke, J. D., & Blunt, J. R. (2011). Retrieval practice produces more learning than elaborative studying with concept mapping. *Science, 331*(February), 772–775. doi:10.1126cience.1199327 PMID:21252317

Karpicke, J. D., Butler, A. C., & Roediger, H. L. III. (2009). Metacognitive strategies in student learning: Do students practice retrieval when they study on their own? *Memory (Hove, England), 17*(4), 471–479. doi:10.1080/09658210802647009 PMID:19358016

Karpicke, J. D., & Zaromb, F. M. (2010). Retrieval mode distinguishes the testing effect from the generation effect. *Journal of Memory and Language, 62*(3), 227–239. doi:10.1016/j.jml.2009.11.010

Kelley, C. M., & Jacoby, L. L. (1996). Adult egocentrism: Subjective experience versus analytic bases for judgment. *Journal of Memory and Language, 35*(2), 157–175. doi:10.1006/jmla.1996.0009

Kerr, R., & Booth, B. (1978). Specific and varied practice of motor skill. *Perceptual and Motor Skills, 46*(2), 395–401. doi:10.1177/003151257804600201 PMID:662537

Koriat, A., Bjork, R. A., Sheffer, L., & Bar, S. K. (2004). Predicting one's own forgetting: The role of experience-based and theory-based processes. *Journal of Experimental Psychology. General, 133*(4), 643–656. doi:10.1037/0096-3445.133.4.643 PMID:15584811

Koriat, A., Lichtenstein, S., & Fischhoff, B. (1980). Reasons for confidence. *Journal of Experimental Psychology. Human Learning and Memory, 6*(2), 107–118. doi:10.1037/0278-7393.6.2.107

Kornell, N. (2009). Optimising learning using flashcards: Spacing is more effective than cramming. *Applied Cognitive Psychology*, *23*(9), 1297–1317. doi:10.1002/acp.1537

Kornell, N. (2012). A stability bias in human memory. In N. M. Seel (Ed.), *Encyclopedia of the sciences of learning* (pp. 4–7). Springer. doi:10.1007/978-1-4419-1428-6_1683

Kornell, N., & Bjork, R. A. (2007). The promise and perils of self-regulated study. *Psychonomic Bulletin & Review*, *14*(2), 219–224. doi:10.3758/BF03194055 PMID:17694904

Kornell, N., & Bjork, R. A. (2008). Optimizing self-regulated study: The benefits-and costs-of dropping flashcards. *Memory (Hove, England)*, *16*(2), 125–136. doi:10.1080/09658210701763899 PMID:18286417

Kornell, N., Castel, A. D., Eich, T. S., & Bjork, R. A. (2010). Spacing as the friend of both memory and induction in young and older adults. *Psychology and Aging*, *25*(2), 498–503. doi:10.1037/a0017807 PMID:20545435

Kornell, N., Rhodes, M. G., Castel, A. D., & Tauber, S. K. (2011). The ease-of-processing heuristic and the stability bias: Dissociating memory, memory beliefs, and memory judgments. *Psychological Science*, *22*(6), 787–794. doi:10.1177/0956797611407929 PMID:21551341

Kornell, N., & Son, L. K. (2009). Learners' choices and beliefs about self-testing. *Memory (Hove, England)*, *17*(5), 493–501. doi:10.1080/09658210902832915 PMID:19468957

Krueger, W. C. F. (1929). The effect of overlearning on retention. *Journal of Experimental Psychology*, *12*(1), 71–78. doi:10.1037/h0072036

Kühn, A. (1914). Über einprägung durch lesen und durch rezitieren. *Zeitschrift für Psychologie mit Zeitschrift für Angewandte Psychologie*, *68*, 396–481.

Landin, D. K., Hebert, E. P., & Fairweather, M. (1993). The effects of variable practice on the performance of a basketball skill. *Research Quarterly for Exercise and Sport*, *64*(2), 232–237. doi:10.1080/02701367.1993.10608803 PMID:8341849

Larrick, R. P. (2004). Debiasing. In D. J. Koehler & N. Harvey (Eds.), *Blackwell handbook of judgment and decision making* (pp. 316–337). Blackwell Publishing. doi:10.1002/9780470752937.ch16

Larsen, D. P., Butler, A. C., Lawson, A. L., & Roediger, H. L. III. (2013). The importance of seeing the patient: Test-enhanced learning with standardized patients and written tests improves clinical application of knowledge. *Advances in Health Sciences Education: Theory and Practice*, *18*(3), 409–425. doi:10.100710459-012-9379-7 PMID:22618856

Mayfield, K. H., & Chase, P. N. (2002). The effects of cumulative practice on mathematics problem solving. *Journal of Applied Behavior Analysis*, *35*(2), 105–123. doi:10.1901/jaba.2002.35-105 PMID:12102132

McCabe, J. (2011). Metacognitive awareness of learning strategies in undergraduates. *Memory & Cognition*, *39*(3), 462–476. doi:10.375813421-010-0035-2 PMID:21264604

McDaniel, M. A., & Masson, M. E. (1985). Altering memory representations through retrieval. *Journal of Experimental Psychology. Learning, Memory, and Cognition*, *11*(2), 371–385. doi:10.1037/0278-7393.11.2.371

McDermott, K. B., Agarwal, P. K., D'Antonio, L., Roediger, H. L., & McDaniel, M. A. (2014). Both multiple-choice and short-answer quizzes enhance later exam performance in middle and high school classes. *Journal of Experimental Psychology. Applied*, *20*(1), 3–21. doi:10.1037/xap0000004 PMID:24274234

Meehl, P. E. (1954). *Clinical versus statistical prediction: A theoretical analysis and a review of the evidence*. University of Minnesota. doi:10.1037/11281-000

Morehead, K., Rhodes, M. G., & DeLozier, S. (2016). Instructor and student knowledge of study strategies. *Memory (Hove, England)*, *24*(2), 257–271. doi:10.1080/09658211.2014.1001992 PMID:25625188

Nisbett, R. E., & Wilson, T. D. (1977). Telling more than we can know: Verbal reports on mental processes. *Psychological Review*, *84*(3), 231–259. doi:10.1037/0033-295X.84.3.231

Nist, S. L., & Hogrebe, M. C. (1987). The role of underlining and annotating in remembering textual information. *Reading Research and Instruction*, *27*(1), 12–25. doi:10.1080/19388078709557922

Paivio, A., Walsh, M., & Bons, T. (1994). Concreteness effects on memory: When and why? *Journal of Experimental Psychology. Learning, Memory, and Cognition*, *20*(5), 1196–1204. doi:10.1037/0278-7393.20.5.1196

Panadero, E. (2017). A review of self-regulated learning: Six models and four directions for research. *Frontiers in Psychology*, *8*, 422. doi:10.3389/fpsyg.2017.00422 PMID:28503157

Pastötter, B., & Bäuml, K. H. T. (2014). Retrieval practice enhances new learning: The forward effect of testing. *Frontiers in Psychology*, 286. PMID:24772101

Peterson, D. J., & Mulligan, N. W. (2013). The negative testing effect and multifactor account. *Journal of Experimental Psychology. Learning, Memory, and Cognition*, *39*(4), 1287–1293. doi:10.1037/a0031337 PMID:23421505

Peterson, S. E. (1992). The cognitive functions of underlining as a study technique. *Reading Research and Instruction*, *31*(2), 49–56. doi:10.1080/19388079209558078

Postman, L. (1962). Retention as a function of degree of overlearning. *Science*, *135*(3504), 666–667. doi:10.1126cience.135.3504.666 PMID:14037399

Pyc, M. A., & Rawson, K. A. (2010). Why testing improves memory: Mediator effectiveness hypothesis. *Science*, *330*(6002), 335–335. doi:10.1126cience.1191465 PMID:20947756

Pyc, M. A., & Rawson, K. A. (2012). Why is test–restudy practice beneficial for memory? An evaluation of the mediator shift hypothesis. *Journal of Experimental Psychology. Learning, Memory, and Cognition*, *38*(3), 737–746. doi:10.1037/a0026166 PMID:22060276

Rawson, K. A., & Dunlosky, J. (2022). Successive relearning: An underexplored but potent technique for obtaining and maintaining knowledge. *Current Directions in Psychological Science*, *31*(4), 362–368. doi:10.1177/09637214221100484

Rawson, K. A., Dunlosky, J., & Sciartelli, S. M. (2013). The power of successive relearning: Improving performance on course exams and long-term retention. *Educational Psychology Review*, *25*(4), 523–548. doi:10.100710648-013-9240-4

Reich, J., & Ruipérez-Valiente, J. A. (2019). The MOOC pivot. *Science, 363*(6423), 130–131. doi:10.1126cience.aav7958 PMID:30630920

Rhodes, M. G., & Castel, A. D. (2008). Memory predictions are influenced by perceptual information: Evidence for metacognitive illusions. *Journal of Experimental Psychology. General, 137*(4), 615–625. doi:10.1037/a0013684 PMID:18999356

Rhodes, M. G., & Castel, A. D. (2009). Metacognitive illusions for auditory information: Effects on monitoring and control. *Psychonomic Bulletin & Review, 16*(3), 550–554. doi:10.3758/PBR.16.3.550 PMID:19451383

Roberts, R. D., Martin, J. E., & Olaru, G. (2015). *A Rosetta stone for noncognitive skills: Understanding, assessing, and enhancing noncognitive skills in primary and secondary education*. Academic Press.

Roediger, H. L. III, & Karpicke, J. D. (2006). The power of testing memory: Basic research and implications for educational practice. *Perspectives on Psychological Science, 1*(3), 181–210. doi:10.1111/j.1745-6916.2006.00012.x PMID:26151629

Roediger, H. L., & Pyc, M. A. (2012). Inexpensive techniques to improve education: Applying cognitive psychology to enhance educational practice. *Journal of Applied Research in Memory and Cognition, 1*(4), 242–248. doi:10.1016/j.jarmac.2012.09.002

Rohrer, D., Dedrick, R. F., & Burgess, K. (2014). The benefit of interleaved mathematics practice is not limited to superficially similar kinds of problems. *Psychonomic Bulletin & Review, 21*(5), 1323–1330. doi:10.375813423-014-0588-3 PMID:24578089

Rohrer, D., & Pashler, H. (2010). Recent research on human learning challenges conventional instructional strategies. *Educational Researcher, 39*(5), 406–412. doi:10.3102/0013189X10374770

Rohrer, D., & Taylor, K. (2007). The shuffling of mathematics problems improves learning. *Instructional Science, 35*(6), 481–498. doi:10.100711251-007-9015-8

Rowland, C. A. (2014). The effect of testing versus re-study on retention: A meta-analytic review of the testing effect. *Psychological Bulletin, 140*(6), 1–32. doi:10.1037/a0037559 PMID:25150680

Shah, A. K., & Oppenheimer, D. M. (2008). Heuristics made easy: An effort-reduction framework. *Psychological Bulletin, 134*(2), 207–222. doi:10.1037/0033-2909.134.2.207 PMID:18298269

Shah, A. K., & Oppenheimer, D. M. (2009). The path of least resistance: Using easy-to-access information. *Current Directions in Psychological Science, 18*(4), 232–236. doi:10.1111/j.1467-8721.2009.01642.x

Shea, J. B., & Morgan, R. L. (1979). Contextual interference effects on the acquisition, retention, and transfer of a motor skill. *Journal of Experimental Psychology. Human Learning and Memory, 5*(2), 179–187. doi:10.1037/0278-7393.5.2.179

Shortt, M., Tilak, S., Kuznetcova, I., Martens, B., & Akinkuolie, B. (2021). Gamification in mobile-assisted language learning: A systematic review of Duolingo literature from public release of 2012 to early 2020. *Computer Assisted Language Learning*, 1–38. Advance online publication. doi:10.1080/09588221.2021.1933540

Simon, H. A. (1957). *Models of man: Social and rational.* Wiley.

Simons, D. J., & Chabris, C. F. (2011). What people believe about how memory works: A representative survey of the US population. *PLoS One*, *6*(8), e22757. doi:10.1371/journal.pone.0022757 PMID:21826204

Simons, D. J., & Chabris, C. F. (2012). Common (mis) beliefs about memory: A replication and comparison of telephone and Mechanical Turk survey methods. *PLoS One*, *7*(12), e51876. doi:10.1371/journal.pone.0051876 PMID:23272183

Sloman, S. A. (2002). Two systems of reasoning. In T. Gilovich, D. Griffin, & D. Kahneman (Eds.), *Heuristics and biases: The psychology of intuitive judgment* (pp. 379–396). Cambridge University Press. doi:10.1017/CBO9780511808098.024

Smith, S. M. (1982). Enhancement of recall using multiple environmental contexts during learning. *Memory & Cognition*, *10*(5), 405–412. doi:10.3758/BF03197642 PMID:7176900

Smith, S. M., Glenberg, A., & Bjork, R. A. (1978). Environmental context and human memory. *Memory & Cognition*, *6*(4), 342–353. doi:10.3758/BF03197465

Smith, S. M., & Rothkopf, E. Z. (1984). Contextual enrichment and distribution of practice in the classroom. *Cognition and Instruction*, *1*(3), 341–358. doi:10.12071532690xci0103_4

Snowman, J. (1986). Learning tactics and strategies. In G. D. Phye & T. Andre (Eds.), *Cognitive classroom learning: Understanding, thinking, and problem solving* (pp. 243–275). Academic Press.

Soderstrom, N. C., & Bjork, R. A. (2015). Learning versus performance: An integrative review. *Perspectives on Psychological Science*, *10*(2), 176–199. doi:10.1177/1745691615569000 PMID:25910388

Spitzer, H. F. (1939). Studies in retention. *Journal of Educational Psychology*, *30*(9), 641–656. doi:10.1037/h0063404

St. Evans, J. S. B. (2003). In two minds: Dual-process accounts of reasoning. *Trends in Cognitive Sciences*, *7*(10), 454–459. doi:10.1016/j.tics.2003.08.012 PMID:14550493

Stanovich, K. E., & West, R. F. (2000). Individual differences in reasoning: Implications for the rationality debate? *Behavioral and Brain Sciences*, *23*(5), 645–665. doi:10.1017/S0140525X00003435 PMID:11301544

Sternberg, R. J., & Williams, W. M. (2010). *Educational psychology* (2nd ed.). Pearson.

Taylor, K., & Rohrer, D. (2010). The effects of interleaved practice. *Applied Cognitive Psychology*, *24*(6), 837–848. doi:10.1002/acp.1598

Thaler, R. H., & Sunstein, C. R. (2009). *Nudge: Improving decisions about health, wealth, and happiness*. Penguin.

Tversky, A., & Kahneman, D. (1974). Judgment under uncertainty: Heuristics and biases (Biases in judgments reveal some heuristics of thinking under uncertainty). *Science*, *185*(4157), 1124–1131. doi:10.1126cience.185.4157.1124 PMID:17835457

Wirth, J., Stebner, F., Trypke, M., Schuster, C., & Leutner, D. (2020). An interactive layers model of self-regulated learning and cognitive load. *Educational Psychology Review*, *32*(4), 1127–1149. doi:10.100710648-020-09568-4

Wissman, K. T., Rawson, K. A., & Pyc, M. A. (2012). How and when do students use flashcards. *Memory (Hove, England)*, *20*(6), 568–579. doi:10.1080/09658211.2012.687052 PMID:22671698

Yan, V. X., Thai, K. P., & Bjork, R. A. (2014). Habits and beliefs that guide self-regulated learning: Do they vary with mindset? *Journal of Applied Research in Memory and Cognition*, *3*(3), 140–152. doi:10.1037/h0101799

Zaromb, F. M., & Roediger, H. L. (2010). The testing effect in free recall is associated with enhanced organizational processes. *Memory & Cognition*, *38*(8), 995–1008. doi:10.3758/MC.38.8.995 PMID:21156864

Zepeda, C. D., Martin, R. S., & Butler, A. C. (2020). Motivational strategies to engage learners in desirable difficulties. *Journal of Applied Research in Memory and Cognition*, *9*(4), 468–474. doi:10.1016/j.jarmac.2020.08.007

Zimmerman, B. J., & Moylan, A. R. (2009). Self-regulation: where metacognition and motivation intersect. In D. J. Hacker, J. Dunlosky, & A. C. Graesser (Eds.), *Handbook of Metacognition in Education* (pp. 299–315). Routledge.

ADDITIONAL READING

Agarwal, P. K., & Bain, P. M. (2019). *Powerful teaching: Unleash the science of learning*. John Wiley & Sons. doi:10.1002/9781119549031

Bjork, R. A., & Bjork, E. L. (2020). Desirable difficulties in theory and practice. *Journal of Applied Research in Memory and Cognition*, *9*(4), 475–479. doi:10.1016/j.jarmac.2020.09.003

Brown, P. C., Roediger, H. L. III, & McDaniel, M. A. (2014). *Make it stick: The science of successful learning*. Harvard University Press.

Burrus, J., Mattern, K., Naemi, B. D., & Roberts, R. D. (Eds.). (2017). *Building better students: Preparation for the workforce*. Oxford University Press. doi:10.1093/acprof:oso/9780199373222.001.0001

Jones, K. (2020). *Retrieval Practice: Research & Resources for every classroom*. John Catt Educational.

Oakley, B., Sejnowski, T., & McConville, A. (2018). *Learning how to learn: How to succeed in school without spending all your time studying; a guide for kids and teens*. Penguin.

Oakley, B., & Sejnowski, T. J. (2021). *Uncommon sense teaching: Practical insights in brain science to help students learn*. Penguin.

Smith, M., & Firth, J. (2018). *Psychology in the classroom: A teacher's guide to what works*. Routledge. doi:10.4324/9781315163420

KEY TERMS AND DEFINITIONS

Cognitive Bias: Deviation from normative or rational judgment and decision-making stemming from maladaptive heuristic thinking.

Learning: Enduring, latent change in a person's knowledge, understanding, or skill level that may not be directly perceptible or observable.

Learning Misconception: Erroneous understanding or false belief regarding the factors or strategies that foster learning.

Long-Term Retention: Capacity to remember information after a relatively long period of time has passed since the information was acquired.

Performance: Expression of a person's knowledge or task behavior that can be directly and immediately perceived or observed.

Retrieval Practice: Learning strategy that involves attempting to remember to-be-learned information.

Social and Emotional Learning Skills: Combination of a person's unique systems of thinking, patterns of emotions, and sets of behaviors that characterize his or her personality.

Chapter 3
Self-Directed Learning Is a Social Activity (and Not a Generalized Skill)

David S. Porcaro
Insight Partners, USA

ABSTRACT

The perspective of self-directed and self-regulated learning as a generalized skill discounts the fact that a major driver of self-direction is an individual's motives centered on communities of practice. Effective design of learning experiences that foster agency, self-direction, and curiosity requires a clearer understanding of this relationship. Activity theory provides a helpful model for explaining the internal and external interactions of learning, both individually and within a community. Without this perspective, educators too often blame learners as failing to have self-regulation when in reality these learners are working under a different set of goals, roles, rules, or tools than those of the learning designer. Using this framework, this theoretical overview will demonstrate ways an immersive adult technology training academy helps support novices striving to enter technology-related careers, as they develop the identity, skills, and self-regulation of coding, data, and design professions.

INTRODUCTION

This chapter's exploration begins with the premise that self-directed learning *is* the ultimate goal of education. Ideally, adults set goals for their lifelong learning, and make choices to follow and evaluate the effectiveness of different learning pathways, surround themselves with communities of practice, connect to peers and mentors, and apply their learning in a variety of contexts that expand throughout their lives. Self-directed learning, then, is the agentic development and exercise of learning goals.

In essence, this self-direction is what separates adult learning from other forms of formal education, including primary and secondary education. For the most part, adults choose what and how they learn, and are motivated (sometimes for social or economic reasons) to pursue different learning and development paths (Knowles, 1975). Children, on the other hand, are often compelled to learn how to divide

DOI: 10.4018/978-1-6684-6500-4.ch003

mixed numbers, recall dates of battles, verbalize the spelling of rare words, or other tasks that they did not choose, and neither have much use in most of their day-to-day interactions or are connected to their own short and long-term learning or life goals.

Within the larger and more external concept of self-directed learning is the related subconcept of self-regulated learning (SRL; see Linkous, 2021; Neelen & Kirschner, 2020). Self-regulated learning includes the mechanisms that drive someone to start, persist or put in the mental effort (Clark & Saxberg, 2018) needed to learn and perform toward their goals.

Since the 1980s, researchers have been investigating how SRL leads to academic outcomes (Schunk & Greene, 2018b). Since that time, many educators have developed the perspective that SRL is a concept they have or don't (see, Kirwan et al., 2014), and that can be measured with tools like LASSI (Weinstein et al., 2016), MSLQ (Pintrich & Others, 1991), etc. and that can be developed (or not). Through the subsequent generations, a more dynamic, two-way relationship between learning achievement and self-regulated learning has developed, leading to a better understanding of the more complex nature of SRL development.

While this dynamic and reciprocal relationship between SRL operations and achievement outcomes was a welcome development of the 2000s, this approach is insufficient in one major aspect. Self-directed learning is not a generalizable, self-standing skill that one has or does not have. It's rather a highly community-, discipline-, and even context- dependent collection of constructs (Merrienboer, 1997). Much like the attention paid to grit, the more one looks for a single stable construct, the less there is to see (Credé et al., 2017).

SRL is an extremely complex subject, and much has been said about it. In fact, SRL is in essence an overarching theory of learning that actually encompasses many subsystems of learning, including motivation, cognition, behavior, affect, social interactions, performance and culture (see Panadero, 2017). It is *not* the intention of this chapter to recreate that work.

The reader who wants a recent and more in-depth overview of many of the concepts discussed here may refer to Schunk and Greene's (2018) second edition of the *Handbook of Self-Regulation of Learning and Performance* (Schunk & Greene, 2018a). In an attempt for breadth, this chapter may leave many of the details of the key concepts, relationships, and theories underdeveloped or even unstated. This chapter builds off this strong framework of SRL to layer on the additional insights of Activity Theory (also referred to as Cultural-Historical Activity Theory; Engeström, 1999) to demonstrate how one can better understand how learners exercise agency to navigate complex community relationships and activity systems in their attempts to self-regulate their learning.

This chapter concludes with the design of a blended (online, virtual, and in some cases face-to-face) adult technical training academy (commonly referred to as a coding bootcamp) as an example of how learners develop self-regulation in their learning while becoming practitioners and members of a community of practice.

A SOCIAL COGNITIVE THEORY OF SELF-REGULATED LEARNING

In their chapter in the *Handbook of Self-Regulation of Learning and Performance*, Schunk and Greene outline a unifying theory of SRL building off Zimmerman's sub-functions of SRL. There are three major parts of their overview that are foundational for understanding SRL.

The Cyclical Nature of Learning

Schunk and Greene highlight that learning is a continual process of individuals taking agentic action in a process of forethought, performance, and reflection. In other words, individuals have in their mind some goal, they plan a mental model of how to reach that goal, they act out that model as well as they can (or in some cases choose to meet their goals by *not* acting), then they take in feedback to refine their model or goal. And then repeat–over and over and over and over. It's not complicated; it's basically what engineers would call a closed feedback system. But repeated over trillions (or more?) of micro interactions, these models can become robust schemas and automated operations that can create very complex thoughts, behaviors, predictions, and beliefs. (As a side note, this process is not that different from those at the foundation of reinforcement learning and other artificial intelligence fields, and some of the massive improvements in artificial intelligence over the past few years has been largely due to our ability to better model with larger dimensionality and closer approximation, to better define and reward goal success, to create and utilize better sensors and instruments to determine approximation to goals, and to iterate on this feedback cycle at massive scale).

This learning feedback process is complicated by the fact that one does not work alone in this environment. There are others one interacts with who think and live in contradictory ways. And furthermore, one's goals are not always one's own to create. Goals may be imposed on learners, selected by learners, as well as created from learners (Bandura, 1986). The synergistic and contradictory interplay between these interactions creates complex and often unpredictable learning and performance environments. (Again, as a side note, much of the work on multi-agent reinforcement models can shed some light on the complexity that occurs when one introduces multiple goals and actors, as well as introduces game theory concepts in competitive, cooperative and mixed-sum settings. See for instance, how the challenges of defining reward functions can lead agents to create unexpected actions that don't meet the designers' goals (Hofstätter, 2021)).

The Sub-Functions of Self-Regulation

This feedback system is made more rich when layered with the top the sub-functions of self-regulation. Zimmerman (2000) introduced a model of self-regulation that includes components of self-observation, self-evaluation, and self-reaction, that when applied during each of the 3 phases of action (goal setting plus modeling, acting, and reflecting), produce a variety of concepts including monitoring, strategy use, task analysis, motivation and beliefs, assessment and self-reaction.

These sub-functions implicate a number of well-known concepts in education (what Stafford-Brizard, 2016, calls the Building Blocks for Learning), such as self-awareness (including metacognition), self-concept (including self-efficacy), executive functions (including working memory, inhibitory control and task-switching flexibility), goal orientation, outcome expectation and value (including relevancy and performance standards), affect control and stress-management (both positive and self-handicapping behaviors (Schwinger et al., 2014)), social relationships (including help-seeking behavior), attribution (including growth mindset) and many more behavioral and cognitive constructs.

Development of Self-Regulatory Competence

While Zimmerman's model as described provides a better understanding of what SRL is, it does little to explain how exactly people develop these attributes in helpful or harmful ways. While these components are useful to learning, every educator ultimately wants to know how to help learners develop self-regulatory competence across these components. Building off an earlier model (Schunk and Zimmerman (Schunk & Zimmerman, 1997) for developing self-regulatory competence, Schunk and Greene (2018b) point out that competence grows through observation, emulation, self-control and self-regulation. In other words, using the terms of Vygotsky, learners develop skills in the components of SRL by interacting (even if separated in time or space) with more knowledgeable peers (including coping models who describe their own efforts and successes in similar situations, see Pajares, 2006), observing their actions, practicing them in a zone of proximal development, and receiving feedback until they become internalized and automatized. While some learning can be done independently through observation of activity in the world alone, it's done most often with others (even if mediated through text, tools or symbols).

Working within these dynamic situations, learners not only develop internal mental models, but they continuously shape their interactions with others. Through repeated interactions (or what game theorists call repeated games), individuals improve in their ability to make their goals explicit and verbalizable, they turn to others for accountability, inspiration or help, and they shape their own environment with tools (like notetaking or timers), contexts (such as quiet study areas) or rewards (self-rewards or externally imposed rewards like grades or achievements) that help them reach their goals consistently. In other words, they create habits, strategies, frameworks, and networks, and seek help through relationships that enable them to reach goals with greater fluency and automaticity.

Losing SRL in Transfer

While Schunk and Greene's model helps to unify many constructs in learning, it falls short of fully integrating the community-based and contextually driven nature of each and every learning interaction and social group a person may encounter. Like most aspects of learning, transfer is a tricky devil (Bransford & Schwartz, 1999). Developing self-efficacy in math does not generalize to English writing. Developing stress management in one learning environment with one teacher, may not translate well in another room in the building or online context each with their own triggering objects, inputs or people. Value and motivation in one task or field of study does not automatically transfer to another. Many learners are better at self-regulating and self-directing learning when motivated in a task, but struggle when they either don't value the task or believe they won't succeed at the task. In essence, they develop self-regulation in one domain at a time.

But what about those learners who seem to do well in any subject? They get good grades in all disciplines, are highly motivated, and like Midas, seem to turn anything they touch into gold? Are there not people who are just "high achievers" or somehow possess some gift that enables them to self-direct in any space?

There are two problematic realities to these situations. First, these learners may have actually learned to self-regulate in a highly confined and highly artificial setting: school (for a better look at how school settings rarely mimic the practices of the disciplines, see Mehta & Fine, 2019). In fact, some may have developed automaticity, value, motivation, strategies, schemas, social networks, etc. that only work in one school setting and don't transfer well to others. For instance, students who do well in elementary school may struggle in the highly social and less-structured setting of secondary school, or students who managed well in secondary school may struggle to manage in the more self-directed world of higher education. Never mind the number of cases of people who excel in structured academic settings, but struggle in applied work settings.

Second, what many researchers have identified as the behaviors, values, norms, beliefs, and tools of highly successful self-regulated learners in academic settings, may actually be the values and norms of the elite white class from which many researchers belong (or have become enculturated into). What many call "merit" may actually be a set of privileged values of a single class and worldview, thus highly restricting the acceptance of people or behaviors of those who are actually great at self-regulating within the values and practices of a different community (see, Bills, 2019). Thus, better tools are needed to separate the influence of culture, power structure, and hegemony from the issues of self-regulation, cognition and learner agency.

ACTIVITY THEORY ENTERS SELF-DIRECTED LEARNING

While many educators turn readily to the theories of Vygotsky to understand the socio-cultural interactions of learners, they often neglect the Activity Theory traditions of his colleagues and followers, including Leontiev, Rubinshtein, and others (Mironenko, 2013) which developed for decades in Russian until Engeström (1999) introduced the learning sciences to what is often called Cultural Historical Activity Theory. While many are familiar with Activity Theory, it has been used more frequently to provide academic analysis of particular case studies, and it is rarely used as a foundation for instructional design decision making (though ironically, it's the foundation of a lot of interaction design practices and theories; see Kaptelinin, N.D.).

Activity theory posits that life can be described through activity, or the interaction between an agent and the world. The agent (or subject) acts on objects in the world. These objects can be physical artifacts or mental concepts and ideas. The driving needs of the subject become unverbalized motives, and as those motives are externalized, they become goals. Just as with Zimmerman's three-part feedback model of Self-Regulation, motives shape the internal models hypothesized to reach those goals, which drive actions on objects based on those models, which then lead to feedback and reflection based on activities, which are internalized and reshaped into models. When those activities are so internalized that they become automatic and unconscious, they become operations. Through interaction in the world, a person's mental objects expand and create meaning. Their goals and internal models are transformed by their interaction with the world. Their models and operations become more automatic (allowing them to process more and larger internal objects such as schemas, concepts, models and procedures). Or, in other words, they learn. Thus, the seemingly inseparable interaction of internal and external is mediated through activity.

Activity also exists at several levels. For instance, much of the SRL research talks about the planning someone undertakes *before* engaging in some external performance. A learner may think about an upcoming math assignment, and as they think about it, they feel nervous (an affective response) and solidify their thinking that they are not good at math (impacting their self-efficacy). They get overwhelmed (another affective response) and thus decide to not study any more but find something more pleasant for them, like texting their friends, which makes them less prepared for the assignment, impacting their academic outcomes.

Zimmerman (2000) and others would call this all "pre-activity." But instead of happening before an activity, activity theory would consider these multiple micro-cycles of activity. A learner is acting internally, impacting the object of self-concept, even changing their physical state through affective regulation and thought perseveration, leading them to act by *not acting* on their studying tasks, but instead engaging in other desirable (to them in the moment) activities. Furthermore, much of this was done to meet a proximal and short-term motive (feeling pleasant) rather than exercising impulse control to meet a more distal and longer-term goal (doing well on the assignment). Each of these dynamic actions worked in cyclical and multi-directional fashion, both internally and externally, impacting the learner as well as the environment around them. Furthermore, the learner may never have externalized either the motives (feeling pleasant in the short term) or the operations (self-talk or self-concept modification), but they were happening. If the learner had developed metacognitive strategies, they may have been able to externalize some of those motives and operations, and could possibly have enacted other automatic actions (habits) or have engaged in helpful behaviors (strategies) that would help them achieve their long-term goal of academic success.

In a simple setting, with very basic needs, this process is highly effective. However, individuals are polymotivated. As the fictional learner above demonstrated, the need to feel good right now was in direct competition with the need to perform well on the activity to please others or even to feel good later or the need to master some knowledge or skill to achieve their goals. Sometimes, in the process of translating nonverbal motives into verbalized goals, learners struggle to articulate what they really want or need (think back to all those times when one may have said to oneself, "I just don't feel right about this but I can't really explain why" or "I know I need to be doing something different right now, but I just don't know what"). Additionally, one's ability to observe and receive feedback from an activity is highly dependent on the models created (see for instance Kuhn's (1962) description of how paradigms shape observation). One can only see what one knows, and as internal objects expand, standards of what good looks like increases, and the ability to observe and perceive feedback expands. So the feedback received and the ability to internalize it into signs, models, or other internal objects is limited by the objects already internalized. In the process of automating operations, one may have created misconceptions, poorly formed theories, or self-limiting internal self-concepts. For instance, if internal models include misconceptions, fixed mindset, an external attribution model, stereotype-threat informed self-efficacy models, or self-harming stress management behaviors, then continued cycles of interaction in a learning environment will further solidify those internal models and take learners further from their goals.

Adding Others Increases Complexity Exponentially

Activity Theory's power is in its ability to explain complex communities of individuals all acting on the world *and each other*. Shared goals combine multiple individuals into an activity space. But the ability for two or more individuals to align their goals with each other, synchronize them across multiple internal motives, externalize their mental models in a way that each person in a community perceives, comprehends, and shares, and then act on the objects of the world in a way that produces the shared goals is not only complex, but it also *requires* tools.

Tools (or "signs" when they are non-physical) are mediating objects created by individuals to expand their own internal processing. For instance, when cognition is distributed by offloading short-term memory through writing (see Hutchins, 2006) one uses language, script, words, and physical objects like pens and notebooks or computers to greatly expand their cognitive abilities. As external objects, tools allow learners to mediate interactions with others. Tools can be physical, mental, conceptual, symbolic, or digital. One famous tool Vygotsky spent much of his focus on was language. The ability to use physical and vocal symbols to represent internal ideas enabled highly complex activities to be coordinated and allowed the activity space to expand (thus writing and complex societies usually developed together anciently). Other tools and signs such as representations of concepts and models, stories, and physical tools have expanded to such complicated levels that digital tools, data visualizations, mathematical representations, scientific paradigms, etc. can be used to combine people into highly complex shared communities of practice. As digital tools proliferate in education settings, it's important to remember that tools are, by their very definition, goal- and community- bound. There is no such thing as a neutral tool, but tools reflect the goals and beliefs of those who designed them.

As societies and communities have grown, individuals have taken on specialized activity and behavioral roles, allowing for even more complicated goal realization. For instance, early hunter gatherers divided and specialized their labor, allowing some individuals to beat out rabbits from bushes while others caught them in nets (Leont'ev, 2009). Through alignment of long-term goals (catching more food for a village), these communities learned to subsume immediate and personal needs (catching a rabbit in one's net *right now*) for seemingly conflicting goals (the seemingly irrational act of chasing away a rabbit now so one can eat more *later*).

Roles are the ways communities interact with objects. Some roles are more central to the community and have a bigger impact on the collective goals and activities of the community, while others are more peripheral (Lave & Wenger, 1991). Authority conferred by position in the community shapes the agency of individuals. Often those in the center are able to define rules that constrain the kinds of activities that are considered valued to the community or to individuals. Those with central roles define the rules or epistemic practices (or actions/behaviors) of that community and strive to get others to adopt them as well. These rules become the way communities interact with subjects. Thus, a community can be simply described through its **goals, roles, rules** and **tools**, or in other words a cultural system.

Since each individual is an agent of their own motives, they are not simply passive recipients of the goals, roles, rules or tools of others imposed on them in a deterministic fashion. As self-directed agents they can *adopt, adapt* or *reject* the goals, roles, rules, or tools of the systems they personally identify with. They can change how they use story and language, they can center their own position in the community (or decenter others), they can modify the physical or digital tools of the community through workarounds or hacks they create, they can reject the theories or practices of the community and push back against the rules that guide them, or they can change their own internal goals or advocate to change the goals of the community. They can act on the object of the community, just as the community shapes their internal mental objects.

In fact, they can choose to further engage in the community, deepening their identity and sense of belonging in that community by adopting its culture. Or they can try to get the community to change by adapting it to something new. Or they can reject the community outright and start their own communities and recruit others to join them.

Multiple communities and activity spaces overlap not only in the same physical space, but in the same person. Communities and activity systems can be hierarchical, contradictory, or synchronistic. A person can belong to a community of scientists, a community in a virtual or real classroom within the community of a virtual or traditional school, a family or cultural community, a community of fans of a movie or band, or a sub community of users of a particular app or computer program, or practitioners within a similar role or industry. Each of these competing activity spaces exists in one person, and they are constantly navigating the goals, roles, rules and tools of those spaces.

So, for example, when a student is asked to use the language or follow the behavioral norms of a culturally white school community of practice, they may reject that community, not wanting to be shamed by their peers for being what their peers may deride as being "too intelligent" or too aligned to the values of the hegemonic culture (Brown, 2011). While some in the community (for instance teachers and administrators, parents, or even other students) may value these practices as highly connected to their own goals and activities, particular students may not. Those in the center of their classroom community (teachers) may then label a student misaligned to the values of the classroom community as a troublemaker and act in ways that drive the student further from wanting to engage in that community (Okonofua & Eberhardt, 2015).

All the while, someone would label that student as not having self-regulated learning, when in fact, that individual is fully regulating across *multiple* learning states, and constantly learning by expanding internal concepts and operations, even if they are not aligned with what the teacher, or the state, or the assessment provider believes they should know and do and be. Another classroom in the same institution could be more inclusive and pluralistic, building on the assets and identities the student holds, and in that way can create a more robust, expansive, and welcoming learning community (Cheryan et al., 2009; Lewis et al., 2016; Walton et al., 2012).

Measuring SRL in a Dynamic and Complex System

The key to understanding how or why an agent acts in a complex activity system is to understand that person's motives. What draws someone to want to be a part of an activity system? Or, in other words, what drives someone to identify with one community of practice rather than reject it?

Ultimately, the building blocks and sub-functions of SRL provide a useful tool (in a truly activity theory sense of the word) for helping visualize learners' internal states, while also understanding their motivations. As one understands *in each activity space* or in *each community of practice* how confident a learner is at performing successfully an activity or task (e.g., their self-efficacy, their prior knowledge, their tenacity and resilience) **plus** how much they identify with that community (e.g., their sense of belonging, the value and relevance they place on the norms and practices of that community, their attachment to people in the community, and their goal orientation) **plus** their ability to perform the task (e.g., their agency, their roles and rules in the community, and their physical, social, and mental abilities to do *that task*) the more they'll be able to assess that student's motivation *in that context and setting*. Since each of those variables changes in each setting or even for each task, a dynamic and context-specific assessment is necessary.

Thus, a single measure of SRL is not possible, even if it were a complex, multi-dimensional measure of the subcomponents of self-regulation, because each concept is dynamic, changeable, and context or activity-system dependent. New measurement tools are required that externalize the internal and make visible the self-regulation sub-functions of a learner. *The Handbook of Self-Regulation of Learning and Performance* devotes a whole section to these tools, including self-reports (Wolters & Won, 2017), think aloud protocols (Greene et al., 2017), microanalytic methods (Cleary & Callan, 2017), in-depth case studies (Butler & Cartier, 2017), trace data (Bernacki, 2017) and data mining techniques (Biswas et al., 2017). As more learning interactions occur in digital spaces (including increased video conferencing and computer-mediated learning during the COVID-19 pandemic) our sensors for collecting, analyzing and interpreting the activities of communities and the subcomponents of self-regulated learning *in situ* expand tremendously.

The more tools used and valued as communities of practice, the more they can help align the goals and behaviors of learners in that community. As with other tools, assessment methods and instruments help align parties in an activity system by making the goals visible, exposing the roles and rules of the system (including where power structures lie), and providing insight to a learner to reflect on as they internalize their own goals and evaluate progress toward them. This helps them feel more confident about succeeding in future actions and helps them make decisions about their identity and motivations within a community. By making the gaps between goal and performance visible, others in the community can help co-regulate (Hadwin et al., 2018) the learning of the community by intervening with tools (like languages, concepts, symbols, or physical objects) to support the learner in reaching the community goals and expanding the learners' internal objects; or in other words "teaching" others.

Within communities, a collective sense of the standards of what good performance looks like is extremely important for shared meaning making and alignment. By setting standards of good performance, either by displaying actions and behaviors that show excellence, by setting levels of expected performance for different roles, by displaying expected competencies, or by giving corrective and epistemic feedback (Neelen & Kirschner, 2020) to learners, communities help learners internalize their standards. And as learners perform well in a highly scaffolded setting, and gain confidence in their ability to meet the standards, they internalize and expand their own internal standards.

In other words, by giving learners, teachers, administrators, parents, and other educators explicit concepts, tools, principles, models and strategies for learning, along with varied feedback, data, reports, and exemplars, they may become "mini-learning scientists" of their own learning environments, creating their own hypotheses of what will get them to their learning goals. They then can conduct micro experiments by acting on those hypotheses, collecting evidence of how and whether their behaviors led to their goals, reflecting on that evidence, and refining their hypotheses and mental models.

It is important to remember the agency of the learner in the methods used to visualize self-regulated learning. As with every other tool, a learner (or even a community) can adopt, adapt or reject the tools and technologies of others when the goals that shaped the tool don't align with their own. In other words, measures of self-regulated learning created by academic elites, representing a privileged worldview or particular set of norms and values, may have much less usefulness to a community that doesn't share those norms, mental models, goals, or values than a measure or research methodology co-created *with* the community (rather than done to the community). For this reason, Engeström (2009) believes even dynamic and human-centered research methodologies like design-based research, while a helpful step forward from objectivist models of research, evaluation and measurement, are limited by the fact that they still assume the primacy of the goals of the researchers, not the communities of learners and practitioners. Instead, he advocates for more participatory research methods, like Change Laboratories (Engeström, 2011) that are community driven, community interpreted, and community actioned on.

Automaticity and Resource Constraints

Since Activity Theory was built on the foundation of Vygotsky's socio-cultural learning theory, the process of learning and internalizing through the zone of proximal development is deeply tied to activity. Layering on the process of internalizing through observation, emulation, control, and automation (or "appropriation" in Vygotskian terms) to each and every subcomponent within an activity space, there is a model for analyzing very complex systems.

As with any complex system, the ability of the cognitive system to meet its goals (without breaking down under cognitive load) lies in the ability to automate and optimize subsystems. Learning takes energy, and our mental workbench of working memory can only accommodate so much cognitive load at one time. Furthermore, some learners have physical or cognitive limitations to how much they can support in working memory at any given time. Any subsystem of self-regulation that requires mental attention means less energy or cognitive focus available to other parts of the system.

In other words, an individual comes into an activity space with a set amount of resources based on their most recent prior state (Markov chains anyone?). Their ability to succeed at a task is driven by their prior knowledge and how well that has been internalized and automatized, the size, shape and accuracy of their internalized schemas or concepts, their proficiency with tools (including language and procedures), their physical/biological/chemical ability to manage working memory or control emotions, the importance they place on the goal, their sense of belonging or sense of threat in the learning space, their psychological safety and willingness to take risks, their role within the community including the social capital they have at their disposal, their most recent affective state, how tired they are in the moment or how recently they ate, the network of people they can turn to for help, etc. The extent to which these are automated, or the extent to which they consume limited cognitive load or mental energy will greatly impact their success.

For instance, if a learner has not automated their sense of belonging, they will spend most of their cognitive resources on observing and monitoring threats, including stereotype threat (Barber, 2020; Schmader & Johns, 2003). If they haven't automated key prerequisite knowledge for the task, they will spend cognitive resources recalling facts rather than fluently bringing them to attention. If they have not automated the use of a tool (such as the program used to deliver online learning), they will spend cognitive resources navigating their way through the task. If they haven't automated navigating the social structures of the learning environment or have control over their basic living needs such as housing or childcare or financial stability, they will not have the space to learn. They will rather be thinking about caregiving, working to earn money, housing issues, or other distractions to learning activities. In fact, if they see their primary identity as a caregiver or financial provider, and they believe that time spent studying competes with their primary identity, they may place little value on the roles and rules of a learning setting. They will likely see little value in turning assignments in on time, or they may be content with a lower standard of completion (a lower but passing mark) than may be expected by others more central to the community (teachers, administrators, etc.).

For those who have automated many of these components or subsystems - for instance because they have the privilege of a stable family and home environment, or time to devote to learning without distractions of additional work, or financial resources to engage in activities that center them in a community or enable them more opportunities to practice and receive feedback, or a highly rich network or social capital to draw on (Chetty et al., 2022), highly capable physical abilities such as working memory, task switching flexibility, or even motor ability, etc. - they will have subconsciously converted those components to automated operations. As such, their automaticity of these components of self-regulation within a community will make them less prone to conscious scrutiny (the basis of the expert blind spot, see Nathan et al., 2001), and those with the most resources will have the most limited ability to reflect on them or verbalize their impact on their performance. In other words, it's no wonder that little attention has been paid to the role of tools, rules and roles in SRL, since many of these aspects have become automatized to invisibility by most researchers in the field. Unfortunately for the field of SRL, many of those same highly resourced individuals are the ones who are defining the standards of SRL, academic performance, or the practices of many communities of practice. Thus, they are defining goals, roles, rules and tools that are unattainable and alienating for many within the communities they are trying to serve.

MOVING FROM THEORY TO PRACTICE: TRAINING ADULTS TO BECOME CODERS

While applying activity theory to recent dynamic and multi-faceted models of self-regulated and self-directed learning provides a more comprehensive and accurate framework for understanding the complex relationships of individuals learning in society, its complexity makes it difficult to apply. Hence most practitioners crave a single test they can give students to know whether they are self-regulated or not, and a single recipe for developing SRL in students who "lack" it. Crave they will until the end of time, such a tool will not help them meet their goals.

While an activity theory-based model of self-regulated learning is *complex*, it doesn't have to be *complicated.* The following example examines how a learning environment can be designed to create self-regulated learners in the adult technical training space, namely coding bootcamps.

Bootcamp students travel along a journey that is shaping their identity as a coder, data scientist, designer, etc. From the moment they begin that journey, including their interactions with the website, talking to admissions personnel, engaging in online admissions screening, or completing online pre-work, they are constantly measuring their goals against the standards and values of the field. They are looking for cues of whether they belong, either because they have the right core knowledge, prior experience, or cultural alignment.

For the learning or product designer, this requires intentionally attending to the goals, roles, rules, and tools of that learning environment. Are there others in their learning community that this technology striver can relate to, that may look like them, or have similar life experiences? Are there peer mentors they can relate to, who are a few steps further along in the program and can provide "coping mentorship" and inspiration (Pajares, 2006)? These questions drive decisions such as whom to hire as instructors, how to train and develop those instructors, what tools are used to communicate between students and what emojis, gifs, jokes, or other symbols are used in virtual learning spaces, how video is used to expose students to others they may feel a connection to, how often students interact with peers formally and informally (including how in-person meet-up spaces are designed), and how alumni and inspirational community members connect through guest lectures, lunch-and-learners, ask-me-anything sessions, or other community events.

Every aspect of the experience needs to be intentionally built to create a sense of belonging, foster relationships, and build learners' confidence to take risks. Those further along in their journey (such as instructors, Teaching Assistants, and other instructional staff) should be explicit about the norms and practices of the community, discussing not only how they implement a particular tool in their work, but why, and what alternatives might exist. Good instructors discuss the challenges they have had in learning a process, tool or technology, and mistakes they made in that journey, normalizing risk, failure, and growth. Because instructors are practitioners in their field, they can give case studies of how these practices are applied in context, and how the roles and rules of the context defined their use.

As learners practice not only the theory and tools of the tech field–for instance what is recursion in coding or how to use the pandas framework in python–they get to "play the whole game at the junior level" (Perkins, 2009). As they practice the behaviors and roles and rules of the field–for instance, forking a shared code from a GitHub repository, engaging in code review with a peer or instructor, and getting their code approved and applied to production–they start to internalize the norms and practices of the field. Assignments are designed explicitly to recreate job-aligned tasks, rather than focus on accumulating knowledge or generalized theories, as is still quite common in many higher education classrooms even in computer science. Applying an instructional design model for building complex adult learning such as the 4C/ID model (Van Merriënboer et al., 2002), curriculum designers can create repeatable and scaffolded projects with just-in-time practice on learning task sub-components that need automation (such as coding challenges or terminology fluency drills), purposeful supportive instruction (such as stand-alone pre-recorded lectures on key concepts needed to complete the project), and actionable procedural support (such as job aides of common JavaScript syntax).

Within this context of projects, students also learn to exercise increased levels of autonomy. Allowing them flexibility to choose their own data sets, use cases, tools or frameworks to meet the requirements of the assignment, students further develop their self-directed learning skills. They self-organize support networks and choose the roles they will act out within learning environments and on specific projects. Through their interactions with different types of instructional support (teaching assistants, instructional associates, and lead instructors), they start to develop relationships with different kinds of instructional mentors, and learn to create relationships with them that are separate from those they develop with direct managers in their jobs.

Instructors can also model the processes they take in regulating their own learning. Instructors model how they learn new coding languages, which blogs they turn to when they need to learn new techniques, how they ask for help on StackOverflow or other online communities, and how to read documentation for an API, library, or new tool. They can also discuss how they use books or asynchronous learning platforms to continually learn and expand their toolsets and skills.

They also make explicit the values and norms of the field. They discuss ethics openly, including how different parts of the community value code commenting, reuse of code, participation in open-source software, the use of data and AI, or other values. And they allow learners to shape and adopt those values and practices, aligning them to their own values and the communities they intend to work within.

Instructors and learning designers also set the standard of what good looks like. Through digital libraries of case studies, exemplar projects, demonstrations such as code-alongs, or libraries of past student products, instructors can demonstrate not only the standards of the community, but also help visualize the learning objectives of the course. As Mehta and Fine (2019) noted when they examined a project-based learning school in the southwestern United States, the past students' projects hanging on the walls of the school were a tangible demonstration to new students of what students there would learn and do. This can be replicated in a self-paced or blended learning environment as well through exemplar libraries and course overviews or marketing materials.

The instructors, including more junior instructional staff, can provide consistent feedback to learners as they practice taking on their new roles. The benefit of a scaffolded learning environment like a virtual, online, or in-person training setting, as compared with on-the-job learning, is the ability to practice and take risks more frequently, since the consequences are lower. As with all scaffolding in the zone of proximal development, the balance is between fidelity to the work environment and risk. Many learning environments skew too heavily on minimizing risk with "throw away" projects that don't accurately simulate the goals, roles, rules, and tools of the actual work environment. Consequently, students struggle to transfer what they learn in the new applied work environments. Balancing real world tasks with the ability to give corrective (i.e., the hows of certain actions) as well as epistemic (i.e., the whys of certain action) feedback (Neelen & Kirschner, 2020) gives students the ability to internalize and automate skills and knowledge, while strengthening their confidence.

Furthermore, scaffolding may come in strong supportive structures, especially at the beginning of the program. Student success teams support everything from stress management and time management issues, to ensuring students come with the resources to focus entirely during their study on practice and learning through helping students apply for grants for childcare, housing assistance, or other services. Government and employer-funded programs where students earn an income during training, such as apprenticeships, internal reskilling, and hire-train-deploy models further enable students to free cognitive resources up from worrying about how learners will provide financial support to themselves and their families. As these various aspects of self-regulation become automated, or operationalized, they can be faded, or reduced in intensity or frequency.

Additionally, there is explicit instruction and practice in building a professional identity. As students work with career coaches, they learn to create a portfolio to show to future employers, learn the practices and expectations of interviews and technical assessments, and how to present resumes and online profiles in ways that employers and others with central roles in the community of practice value. They also learn the norms of working environments, such as dress and communication expectations in different communities or work environments, and how to work in a shared professional workspace or remote work environment. Too often, these "soft skills" are assumed to be self-evident, and especially when culturally defined, no explicit attention is paid to making them transparent or the topic of instruction and discussion. Students can then choose to adapt, adopt, or reject those norms and practices, and seek out the communities, employers and peer networks of those who share their values and practices, or work to change business expectations and practices to be more diverse, equitable and inclusive.

CONCLUSION

As the insights from activity theory are layered onto the current understanding of self-regulated learning, the view of SRL and self-directed learning development becomes more clear. Rather than a unified trait that develops (no-matter how dynamically or reciprocally) along a single continuum, self-regulated and self-directed learning is a highly context-, activity-, and community-centered concept. Some may believe adding this layer overcomplicates the understanding of SRL, perhaps to a point of uselessness. However, by *not* including and making explicit the layer of activity/community, with its goals, roles, rules, and tools, and the centrality of individual agency to adopt, adopt, or reject the cultural systems of adjacent or overlapping communities, one may over-index on those who have learned to play the game of school, or those who have automated many of the social, environmental, and power-related aspects of learning, to the point of invisibility. Society too often blames underrepresented groups for misinterpreted deficits they bring to the learning environment, especially a lack of motivation and engagement, rather than turning the mirror of activity on the goals, roles, rules and tools, and their effectiveness within overlapping contexts and communities. It is critical to be more reflective about the role that the learning science and research community plays in defining what "good learning" is and which community that standard is centered on.

By understanding how motives and the more verbally explicit goals drive motivation, belonging, and identity, and by better analyzing and interrogating the contribution of social aspects of roles, rules, and tools on the culture, norms, values and practices of a community, it is possible to more consciously adopt and adapt the many tools of different communities. This includes the interventions, assessments, research studies, standards and study results that the learning science community is actively building. As one better understands the ways individuals move into the center of those communities and navigate the many zones of proximal development across many elements of self-regulated learning in many domains, they can have more explicit conversations about *whose* values are elevated in different spaces and why, and give students more agency to adapt, adopt, or reject those beliefs as they shape existing communities and build new ones. Rather than creating an intervention believed to be most effective for developing self-regulation in learning (for instance a digital tool, a curriculum, a dashboard, or a metric) and then struggling to scale it universally, efforts can be made to create more flexible, dynamic, community-driven, and agentic tools for different communities and activities.

REFERENCES

Bandura, A. (1986). *Social foundations of thought and action: A social cognitive theory*. Prentice-Hall.

Barber, S. J. (2020). The applied implications of age-based stereotype threat for older adults. *Journal of Applied Research in Memory and Cognition*, *9*(3), 274–285. doi:10.1016/j.jarmac.2020.05.002 PMID:36032188

Bernacki, M. L. (2017). Examining the cyclical, loosely sequenced, and contingent features of self-regulated learning: Trace data and their analysis. In *Handbook of Self-Regulation of Learning and Performance* (2nd ed.). Routledge. doi:10.4324/9781315697048-24

Bills, D. B. (2019). The problem of meritocracy: The belief in achievement, credentials and justice. *Research Handbook on the Sociology of Education*, 88–105.

Biswas, G., Baker, R. S., & Paquette, L. (2017). Data mining methods for assessing self-regulated learning. In *Handbook of Self-Regulation of Learning and Performance* (2nd ed.). Routledge. doi:10.4324/9781315697048-25

Bransford, J. D., & Schwartz, D. L. (1999). Rethinking Transfer: A Simple Proposal with Multiple Implications. *Review of Research in Education*, *24*, 61. doi:10.2307/1167267

Brown, B. A. (2011). Isn't That Just Good Teaching? Disaggregate Instruction and the Language Identity Dilemma. *Journal of Science Teacher Education*, *22*(8), 679–704. doi:10.100710972-011-9256-x

Butler, D. L., & Cartier, S. C. (2017). Advancing Research and Practice about Self-Regulated Learning: The Promise of In-Depth Case Study Methodologies. In *Handbook of Self-Regulation of Learning and Performance* (2nd ed.). Routledge. doi:10.4324/9781315697048-23

Cheryan, S., Plaut, V. C., Davies, P. G., & Steele, C. M. (2009). Ambient belonging: How stereotypical cues impact gender participation in computer science. *Journal of Personality and Social Psychology*, *97*(6), 1045–1060. doi:10.1037/a0016239 PMID:19968418

Chetty, R., Jackson, M. O., Kuchler, T., Stroebel, J., Hendren, N., Fluegge, R. B., Gong, S., Gonzalez, F., Grondin, A., Jacob, M., Johnston, D., Koenen, M., Laguna-Muggenburg, E., Mudekereza, F., Rutter, T., Thor, N., Townsend, W., Zhang, R., Bailey, M., ... Wernerfelt, N. (2022). Social capital II: Determinants of economic connectedness. *Nature, 608*(7921), 7921. Advance online publication. doi:10.103841586-022-04997-3 PMID:35915343

Clark, R., & Saxberg, B. (2018). Engineering Motivation Using the Belief-Expectancy-Control Framework. *Interdisciplinary Education and Psychology, 2*. Advance online publication. doi:10.31532/InterdiscipEducPsychol.2.1.004

Cleary, T. J., & Callan, G. L. (2017). Assessing Self-Regulated Learning Using Microanalytic Methods. In *Handbook of Self-Regulation of Learning and Performance* (2nd ed.). Routledge. doi:10.4324/9781315697048-22

Credé, M., Tynan, M. C., & Harms, P. D. (2017). Much ado about grit: A meta-analytic synthesis of the grit literature. *Journal of Personality and Social Psychology, 113*(3), 492–511. doi:10.1037/pspp0000102 PMID:27845531

Engeström, Y. (1999). Activity theory and individual and social transformation. In R. Miettinen & R. L. Punamäki-Gitai (Eds.), *Perspectives on activity theory*. Cambridge University Press. doi:10.1017/CBO9780511812774.003

Engeström, Y. (2009). The Future of Activity Theory: A Rough Draft. In A. Sannino, H. Daniels, & K. D. Gutierrez (Eds.), *Learning and Expanding with Activity Theory* (pp. 303–328). Cambridge University Press. doi:10.1017/CBO9780511809989.020

Engeström, Y. (2011). From design experiments to formative interventions. *Theory & Psychology, 21*(5), 598–628. doi:10.1177/0959354311419252

General Assembly. (2020). *Student Outcomes Report: GA's Full-Time Program Data: Jan. 1, 2019-Dec. 31, 2019*. https://generalassemb.ly/sites/default/files/2021-08/GA_OutcomesReport_19_8.5.21.pdf

Greene, J. A., Deekens, V. M., Copeland, D. Z., & Yu, S. (2017). Capturing and Modeling Self-Regulated Learning Using Think-Aloud Protocols. In *Handbook of Self-Regulation of Learning and Performance* (2nd ed.). Routledge. doi:10.4324/9781315697048-21

Hadwin, A., Järvelä, S., & Miller, M. (2018). Self-regulation, co-regulation, and shared regulation in collaborative learning environments. In Handbook of self-regulation of learning and performance, 2nd ed (pp. 83–106). Routledge/Taylor & Francis Group.

Hofstätter, F. (2021, November 16). *How learning reward functions can go wrong*. Medium. https://towardsdatascience.com/how-learning-reward-functions-can-go-wrong-6e794e42f4fc

Hutchins, E. (2006). Cognition in the wild. MIT Press.

Kirwan, J. R., Lounsbury, J. W., & Gibson, L. W. (2014). An Examination of Learner Self-Direction in Relation to the Big Five and Narrow Personality Traits. *SAGE Open*, *4*(2), 2158244014534857. doi:10.1177/2158244014534857

Knowles, M. S. (1975). *Self-Directed Learning: A Guide for Learners and Teachers*. Academic Press.

Kuhn, T. S. (1962). *The structure of scientific revolutions*. University Of Chicago Press.

Lave, J., & Wenger, E. (1991). *Situated learning*. Cambridge University Press. doi:10.1017/CBO9780511815355

Leont'ev, A. N. (2009). *The Development of Mind: Selected works of Aleksei Nikolaevich Leontyev*. Academic Press.

Lewis, K. L., Stout, J. G., Pollock, S. J., Finkelstein, N. D., & Ito, T. A. (2016). Fitting in or opting out: A review of key social-psychological factors influencing a sense of belonging for women in physics. *Physical Review. Physics Education Research*, *12*(2), 020110. doi:10.1103/PhysRevPhysEducRes.12.020110

Linkous, H. M. (2021). Self-Directed Learning and Self-Regulated Learning: What's the Difference? A Literature Analysis. *American Association for Adult and Continuing Education 2020 Conference*.

Mehta, J., & Fine, S. (2019). *In Search of Deeper Learning—Jal Mehta, Sarah Fine*. Harvard University Press. https://www.hup.harvard.edu/catalog.php?isbn=9780674988392

Mironenko, I. (2013). Concerning Interpretations of Activity Theory. *Integrative Psychological & Behavioral Science*, *47*(3), 376–393. Advance online publication. doi:10.100712124-013-9231-5 PMID:23512520

Nathan, M. J., Koedinger, K. R., & Alibali, M. W. (2001). *Expert blind spot: When content knowledge eclipses pedagogical content knowledge*. Paper presented at the Annual Meeting of the American Educational Research Association.

Neelen, M., & Kirschner, P. A. (2020). *Evidence-Informed Learning Design*. Kogan Page. https://www.koganpage.com/product/evidence-informed-learning-design-9781789661415

Okonofua, J. A., & Eberhardt, J. L. (2015). Two strikes: Race and the disciplining of young students. *Psychological Science*, *26*(5), 617–624. doi:10.1177/0956797615570365 PMID:25854276

Pajares, F. (2006). Self-efficacy during childhood and adolescence: Implications for Teachers and Parents. In *Adolescence and education: Self-efficacy beliefs of adolescents* (Vol. 5, pp. 339–367). Information Age Publishing.

Panadero, E. (2017). A Review of Self-regulated Learning: Six Models and Four Directions for Research. *Frontiers in Psychology*, *8*, 422. Advance online publication. doi:10.3389/fpsyg.2017.00422 PMID:28503157

Perkins, D. N. (2009). *Making learning whole: How seven principles of teaching can transform education* (1st ed.). Jossey-Bass.

Pintrich, P. R. (2000). The role of goal orientation in self-regulated learning. In *Handbook of self-regulation* (pp. 451–502). Academic Press. doi:10.1016/B978-012109890-2/50043-3

Pintrich, P. R., & Others, A. (1991). *A Manual for the Use of the Motivated Strategies for Learning Questionnaire (MSLQ)*. https://eric.ed.gov/?id=ED338122

Schmader, T., & Johns, M. (2003). Converging evidence that stereotype threat reduces working memory capacity. *Journal of Personality and Social Psychology*, *85*(3), 440–452. doi:10.1037/0022-3514.85.3.440 PMID:14498781

Schunk, D. H., & Greene, J. A. (Eds.). (2018a). *Handbook of Self-Regulation of Learning and Performance* (2nd ed.). Routledge. https://www.routledge.com/Handbook-of-Self-Regulation-of-Learning-and-Performance/Schunk-Greene/p/book/9781138903197

Schunk, D. H., & Greene, J. A. (2018b). Historical, contemporary, and future perspectives on self-regulated learning and performance. In Handbook of self-regulation of learning and performance (2nd ed., pp. 1–15). Routledge/Taylor & Francis Group.

Schunk, D. H., & Zimmerman, B. J. (1997). Social origins of self-regulatory competence. *Educational Psychologist*, *32*(4), 195–208. doi:10.120715326985ep3204_1

Schwinger, M., Wirthwein, L., Lemmer, G., & Steinmayr, R. (2014). Academic self-handicapping and achievement: A meta-analysis. *Journal of Educational Psychology*, *106*(3), 744–761. doi:10.1037/a0035832

Soegaard, M., & Dam, R. F. (2012). *The encyclopedia of human-computer interaction*. Academic Press.

Stafford-Brizard, K. B. (2016). *Building blocks for learning: A framework for comprehensive student development.* Turnaround for Children. https://turnaroundusa.org/wp-content/uploads/2016/03/Turnaround-for-Children-Building-Blocks-for-Learningx-2.pdf

Van Merriënboer, J. J., Clark, R. E., & De Croock, M. B. (2002). Blueprints for complex learning: The 4C/ID-model. *Educational Technology Research and Development*, *50*(2), 39–61. doi:10.1007/BF02504993

van Merrienboer, J. J. G. (1997). *Training complex cognitive skills: A four-component instructional design model for technical training*. Educational Technology Publications. https://research.utwente.nl/en/publications/training-complex-cognitive-skills-a-four-component-instructional-

Walton, G. M., Cohen, G. L., Cwir, D., & Spencer, S. J. (2012). Mere belonging: The power of social connections. *Journal of Personality and Social Psychology*, *102*(3), 513–532. doi:10.1037/a0025731 PMID:22023711

Weinstein, C. E., Palmer, D. R., & Acee, T. W. (2016). LASSI user's manual: Learning and study strategies. H&H.

Wolters, C. A., & Won, S. (2017). Validity and the Use of Self-Report Questionnaires to Assess Self-Regulated Learning. In *Handbook of Self-Regulation of Learning and Performance* (2nd ed.). Routledge. doi:10.4324/9781315697048-20

Zimmerman, B. J. (2000). Attaining Self-Regulation. In M. Boekaerts, P. Pintrich, & M. Zeidner (Eds.), *Handbook of Self-Regulation* (pp. 13–39). Elsevier. doi:10.1016/B978-012109890-2/50031-7

ADDITIONAL READING

Engeström, Y. (1999). Activity theory and individual and social transformation. In R. Miettinen & R. L. Punamäki-Gitai (Eds.), *Perspectives on activity theory*. Cambridge University Press. doi:10.1017/CBO9780511812774.003

Engeström, Y. (2009). The future of activity theory: a rough draft. In A. Sannino, H. Daniels, & K. D. Gutierrez (Eds.), *Learning and expanding with activity theory* (pp. 303–328). Cambridge University Press. doi:10.1017/CBO9780511809989.020

Panadero, E. (2017). A review of self-regulated learning: Six models and four directions for research. *Frontiers in Psychology*, *8*, 422. Advance online publication. doi:10.3389/fpsyg.2017.00422 PMID:28503157

Schunk, D. H., & Greene, J. A. (2018b). Historical, contemporary, and future perspectives on self-regulated learning and performance. In Handbook of self-regulation of learning and performance, 2nd ed (pp. 1–15). Routledge/Taylor & Francis Group.

Schunk, D. H., & Zimmerman, B. J. (1997). Social origins of self-regulatory competence. *Educational Psychologist*, *32*(4), 195–208. doi:10.120715326985ep3204_1

KEY TERMS AND DEFINITIONS

Community: An activity system of individual agents who share a common goal, such as a community of practice, a cultural or location-based community, or a sub-community within a field, practitioners, etc. For instance, a community of Python using data analysts in the Euro-American finance industry.

Goals: The verbalized intentions of an individual agent. Communities are formed when individuals share goals with others in a community. While goals are relatively stable over time, they can change as objects expand through activity or competing motives are prioritized.

Motives: Unverbalized intentions and values of individual agents. Even within an individual, motives may conflict with each other, and longer-term goals may require deprioritizing immediate motives.

Operations: The automatic and internalized activities of individuals, often expressed as long-term memory. As operations become more automatic, they can become non-conscious.

Roles: The expected place and behaviors of individuals within a community. These may be formalized and hierarchical, or informal and unstated. Individuals with more central roles in a community hold power to define and enforce community rules. Roles are constantly in flux in a community and an individual can act out different roles in different communities.

Rules: The norms and expected behaviors of a community or activity system, both formalized and spoken, or unexpressed. One of the major learning goals of communities is to enculturate individuals to the rules of a community, which are constantly in flux as individuals exercise agency and adapt or create goals, roles, and tools.

Tools: Tools are mediating objects (e.g., physical or digital) designed to support efficiency in the behaviors/activities that contribute to shared goals. Tools that are non-physical, such as language, story, or symbols, are called signs. The introduction or alteration of tools can change the goals, roles and rules of a community.

Section 2

Metacognitive Feedback and Assessment

Chapter 4
Perception as Reality:
Perceived Performance Impacts Expectancies, Values, and Self-Regulated Choices

Bridgid Finn
Educational Testing Service, USA

G. Tanner Jackson
Educational Testing Service, USA

Delano Hebert
Friends School, USA

ABSTRACT

Self-regulated learning (SRL) is a well-known concept within the field of online learning; however, tracking, interpreting, and scaffolding effective SRL strategies can be challenging. SRL encompasses complex and dynamic processes involved in monitoring and controlling the cognitive, motivational, and behavioral components of learning. Such processes include task interpretation, application of knowledge and strategies to solving that task, and monitoring the relative success of implementing a particular strategy. Metacognitive monitoring is a critical component of effective implementation of SRL. Without accurate monitoring, a learner doesn't have adequate information to know whether and how to adjust their learning choices. This chapter discusses two studies that explore how feedback valence influences learners' metacognitive perceptions of their performance and how those (mis)perceptions impact both their expectations for future success as well as SRL choices for a subsequent task.

INTRODUCTION

Self-regulated learning (SRL) is considered key to student success across a wide range of student learning contexts (e.g., Dent & Koenka, 2016; Donker, De Boer, Kostons, Van Ewijk, & van der Werf, 2014;

DOI: 10.4018/978-1-6684-6500-4.ch004

Pintrich, 2000). SRL is a broad conceptual term used to encompass the multivariate cognitive, affective, and motivational processes that underlie students' dynamic learning behaviors. Key models of SRL (see e.g., Panadero, 2017 for an overview) emphasize the importance of distinct SRL cognitive and affective mechanisms and behaviors such as metacognitive processes, goal setting, and emotion and motivation regulation. In general, however, there is agreement across frameworks that the learner is an active participant in the strategic control of their own knowledge and skills and that SRL has an important impact on student achievement.

Much of the educational research on SRL has examined the relationship between students' SRL capacities and strategies with their achievement outcomes (e.g., Dent & Koenka, 2016), and on the efficacy of a variety of SRL training interventions (e.g., Jansen, Van Leeuwen, Janssen, Jak & Kester, 2019) with metacognitive processes often a key construct of interest. Like SRL, metacognition can be broadly construed—encompassing numerous regulatory behaviors that rely on monitoring and control of current and prior knowledge, adaptive deployment of learning and planning strategies, and goal setting and revision. The deployment of the constellation of metacognitive processes that are involved in SRL show individual differences that relate to academic performance (e.g., Winne, 1996).

From a cognitive perspective, metacognitive evaluations of what one knows, of recent performance outcomes, or of the current rate of learning are directly linked to metacognitive control processes (e.g., Nelson & Narens, 1990). Because metacognitive monitoring directly influences regulatory behaviors (e.g., Metcalfe & Finn, 2008), the accuracy of those evaluations is critical. The accuracy of metacognitive monitoring relates to the kinds of cues that people use to evaluate their knowing (e.g., Koriat, 1997). Monitoring can be subject to systematic biases when learners rely on cues that are not diagnostic of actual learning (e.g., Finn & Tauber, 2015).

The learning context has an important influence on the cues that are available for learners to evaluate their ongoing cognition. For example, when information is presented in such a way that it feels more fluently processed (e.g., large versus small font, louder versus quieter) people evaluate that their learning as better than when it feels less fluently processed even though perceptual fluency doesn't impact actual learning. (e.g., Murphy, Huckins, Rhodes & Castel, 2022). We present two studies that manipulated features of the design of the learning task to investigate how they would influence students' metacognition about their performance and as a result their regulatory choices about the difficulty of their next task.

We chose to investigate feedback valence and autonomy as our design features of interest because as learning has increasingly become more digitally mediated in the classroom and in online and blended learning environments, educators and assessment developers have been utilizing games as a medium to support learning and assessment. Feedback valence and autonomy are two commonly used game features. The gamification of learning or assessment involves designing or adding game elements (such as points, feedback, interactive mechanics, and graphics) into a digital assessment or a learning task. Gamification is used in educational contexts because it is thought to increase student motivation and engagement (e.g., Gee, 2003; Prensky, 2001; Shute & Ke, 2012), which may positively benefit learning and assessment performance. Though some research has explored the impact of gamification in learning and instruction (e.g., Kapp, 2012) there is considerably less research on how gamification influences assessment behaviors and performance. In the current study we explored how two different features—feedback valence and autonomy-- influenced students' performance, metacognitive evaluations of their own performance, and choices about task difficulty on a subsequent task.

Feedback

Feedback provides learners with information regarding their performance on a task and can exert a powerful impact on learning and performance (Hattie, 2012; Kluger & DeNisi, 1998; Mertens, Finn, & Lindner, in press). Learners use the information provided in feedback to regulate their learning, by adjusting their attention, effort, behaviors, and strategies. According to the Feedback Intervention theory, (Kluger & DeNisi, 1996) a prominent theory relating feedback to self-regulatory behaviors, people use feedback to regulate their learning behavior to reach task goals or standards. For example, upon receiving feedback that an answer was incorrect, a person may subsequently invest more effort on the task, which can positively benefit their performance and get them closer to a desired learning goal (Hattie & Timperley, 2007).

A large body of research has explored what methods of presenting feedback provide the best outcomes for learning. There is consensus that feedback that provides the correct response is more effective than feedback that only tells the learner whether they are right or wrong (Fazio, Heulser, Johnson & Marsh, 2010; Mertens, et al., in press; Pashler, Cepeda, Wixted, & Rohrer, 2005). Several meta-analyses have converged on the finding that elaborated feedback- or feedback that provides actionable information to guide error correction, tends to yield better learning outcomes than simpler feedback methods. There is a caveat to this finding, however: the content of the elaboration should not be too complex or overly detailed, otherwise the learner will not know how to regulate their behavior to correct their errors (Bangert-Drowns, Kulik, Kulik, & Morgan, 1991; Mertens et al., in press; Kluger & DeNisi, 1996; Kulhavy, White, Topp, Chan, & Adams, 1985; Shute, 2008; Van der Kleij, Feskens, & Eggen, 2015).

Feedback can also have a potent impact on a learner's emotional (Mory, 2013; Shute, 2008) and motivational states (Cerasoli, Nicklin, & Ford, 2014; Fong, Patall, Vasquez & Stautberg, 2019; Hattie & Timperley, 2007; Koenka & Anderman, 2019; Mishra, 2006), both of which exert indirect effects on learning outcomes. The effect of feedback on motivation depends on a range of features embedded in the feedback message that goes beyond the corrective informational content. Factors such as feedback valence, how the feedback is implemented in the learning environment, and how it is interpreted by the learner all influence whether feedback is effective as a motivator (e.g., Burgers, Eden, van Engelenburg, & Buningh, 2015; Kluger & DeNisi, 1996; Lipkus & Klein, 2006). For example, when students are given feedback in the form of written comments as compared to a letter or numeric grade only, they tend to have more confidence and feel more interested in the academic domain (Butler, 1987; Koenka, Linnenbrink-Garcia, Moshontz, Atkinson, Sanchez, & Cooper, 2021).

In the current chapter, we explore the effects of feedback valence on students' motivation and regulatory choices. Much of the research on this topic has explored how positive and negative feedback presented at the end of a task, summarizing overall task performance, influences student motivation and upcoming task choices. In the studies presented here we extend this work to explore how item-level feedback influenced a number of key drivers of student outcomes including within-task performance, metacognitive evaluations of perceived performance, expectancies and values related to completing a similar task, as well as regulatory choices regarding the choice of difficulty of the next task. Below we provide a brief review of the relevant research on feedback valence.

Links Between Feedback Valence, Motivation, and Self-Regulation

Motivation is an important driver of the academic choices that people make (Eccles-Parsons, 1983; Eccles & Wigfield, 2020), and can be influenced by feedback valence. Positive feedback, which highlights correctness about one's performance, is associated with increased enjoyment, perceived competence, self-efficacy beliefs, and intrinsic motivation (Bernacki, Nokes-Malach, & Aleven, 2015; Burgers, et al., 2015; Kuklick & Lindner, 2021) all of which can result in better learning outcomes (See Mertens et al., in press for a review). Negative feedback, which highlights errors, points the learner toward gaps between their current performance and a desired goal. Negative feedback can decrease intrinsic motivation (Fong et al., 2019) and expectancies of future success on similar tasks (e.g., Kuklick & Lindner, 2021). However, negative feedback can also propel participants to invest more effort to improve their performance as a way of attempting to increase their competence beliefs related to the task (Burgers et al., 2015; Vallerand & Reid, 1988).

Burgers et al., investigated the role of positive and negative feedback in a game based educational task on participant's intrinsic motivation and their willingness to play the game again. They used Self Determination Theory (SDT) as a framework to guide their investigations on the impact of feedback valence on intrinsic motivation (Deci & Ryan, 1985, Ryan & Deci, 2000). SDT proposes that people are motivated to pursue activities that provide them with a sense of pleasure and satisfaction, even in the absence of external rewards. In their study, participants played a visuospatial memory matching task. At the end of the matching task, participants were given feedback related to their time completing the task. In the positive feedback conditions, participants were told that they had completed the task faster, and negative feedback condition that they had completed the task slower, than the optimal time or when compared to peers in their age group. Their findings showed that people given positive feedback had more positive attitudes toward feedback, perceived themselves as more competent, and had higher intrinsic motivation related to the game than participants given negative feedback.

Burgers et al. also showed that feedback valence was related to participant's regulatory choices about whether to play the game again. Participants who received negative feedback were *more* likely to play the game again than participants who received positive feedback. The researchers concluded that people who perceived themselves as having lower task competence were more likely to choose to play the game again. They argued that reductions to perceived competence can, in some scenarios, make the learner want to immediately engage with the task again to restore their need for competence.

Feedback valence has also been shown to influence students' choice of task difficulty. Similar to the findings of Burgers et al., Reinecke et al. (2012) also found that a feedback manipulation that reduced perceived competence without reducing actual performance led participants to want to complete the task again. Critically, however, participants in their study chose to repeat the task at a lower difficulty level. In a related study, Krenn, Würth, S., & Hergovich. (2013) manipulated the valence of the feedback that participants were given as they performed a series of cognitive tasks. The researchers found that when participants had received positive feedback, they were more likely to increase the difficulty of their next task. In contrast, participants who received negative feedback were more likely to decrease the difficulty.

Autonomy of Choice

The study design also enabled us to evaluate the effects of autonomy on students' expectancies and values. Autonomy, or the freedom to choose one's own courses of action, has also been linked to positive outcomes in education. In an educational context, allowances for autonomy typically enable the learner to self-direct their learning, for instance by choosing their own learning tasks. Students who take initiative for their own learning tend to learn more than those who engage in passive, or reactive learning (Knowles, 1975; Morris, 2019). For example, one study found that students in self-directed learning programs showed greater interest in the content and greater conceptual learning than those in a more controlled learning setting. In addition, students in the self-directed setting showed improved retention of information they had previously learned (Grolnick & Ryan, 1987).

Autonomy is thought to benefit learning by increasing intrinsic motivation, which is often more influential in learning contexts than is extrinsic motivation (Deci, Koestner & Ryan, 2001; Deci & Ryan, 1985; Dickinson, 1995; Hennessey, Moran). For example, researchers have shown that learning for one's own sake (i.e., an intrinsic interest) leads to higher motivation than trying to obtain an external reward (an extrinsic motivator), and that learning goals tend to outweigh performance goals in terms of motivation, because of their association with an internal benefit rather than an external performance level (Deci & Ryan, 1985; Dweck, 1986). When engaged in self-directed learning, students may be more motivated than those simply doing as prescribed by a lesson plan or teacher. Increased motivation may lead to higher engagement with the task, and potentially higher levels of learning (Dickinson, 1995).

Autonomy has been used in many ways in educational game research (e.g., Ferguson, van den Broek, & van Oostendorp, 2020). For example, while not directly related to our design, a study by Kinzer et al. (2012) found that giving players of an educational game a choice of which avatar would serve as their instructional guide over the course of the game led to higher increases in learning (post-test results minus pre-test results) when compared to those who were assigned an avatar (Kinzer et al., 2012). Those with a choice of avatar also noted a significantly higher desire to continue playing the game on a post-task survey than those without a choice, suggesting that there were motivational effects of autonomy.

We evaluated whether autonomy in the choice of task difficulty would have similarly positive effects. In Experiment 2, we investigated how autonomy, implemented as choice of difficulty on a second game play, influenced motivation. We expected to see differences in performance for groups that did and did not have a choice in task difficulty ("free-choice" and "no-choice", respectively), as we anticipated that there would be ability-based-self-selection into the more or less difficult versions in a free-choice condition, whereas higher and lower performers would be randomly distributed into the more and less difficult versions in the no-choice condition. Our primary interest, therefore, was in how the opportunity to choose the difficulty of the next game-based assessment would influence motivational measures.

CURRENT STUDIES

This chapter presents two experiments that explored how positive and negative feedback influenced students' motivation and performance during a game-based mathematics task. In both experiments, participants completed math tasks targeting their understanding of linear functions and basic algebra. We investigated the effects of positive and negative feedback on performance, perceived performance, measures of motivation, and self-regulatory behavior (as measured by choice of difficulty on a subsequent task).

In Experiment 1 we focused on how positive and negative feedback influenced participants within task performance and their expectancies and values related to the task. We manipulated the valence of the feedback participants were given during the task by varying the points that were awarded for correct responses or that were lost for incorrect responses. We evaluated whether an emphasis on correct as compared to incorrect responses would influence participants' within-game performance and self-reported motivation.

We evaluated two competing hypotheses about feedback's overall influence on performance. On the one hand, both positive and negative feedback can provide students with insight into their performance which may affect or even improve within-task self-regulatory behaviors resulting in superior performance (McNamara, Jackson, & Graesser, 2010). On the other hand, the type of point-based feedback we employed may provide insufficient information for learners to self-regulate their performance. If so, we would not expect to see an overall effect of feedback on task 1 performance.

With respect to the effect of our manipulation on participant's motivation, we hypothesized that feedback emphasizing incorrect responses, in which participants lost points when they answered an item incorrectly, would have a greater negative influence on participant's motivation as compared to feedback that emphasized correct responses, in which participants gained points for answering an item correctly.

We utilized a modified version of the Eccles and Wigfield expectancy-value measure (Eccles & Wigfield, 2020) to evaluate the effect of feedback condition on motivation measures specifically as they related to math. Eccles and Wigfield's (2020; Wigfield & Eccles, 2000) situated expectancy-value theory proposes that expectancies for success (i.e., beliefs about how well one thinks that they will do on an upcoming task or activity) and subjective task values (i.e., the incentives or reasons for engaging in different activities) are the most proximal predictors of performance and choice. The four components of task value are interest or *intrinsic value,* or how enjoyable one finds a task or activity to be, *attainment value* or how important the activity is and how well it fits in with one's identity, *utility value* or how useful the activity is, and *cost* or what one has to give up to do a certain activity (e.g., sacrificing time on TikTok to do one's homework).

Participants rated their expectations of future success on a similar mathematics task, their positive value (attainment value, intrinsic value, and utility value), and negative value, or perceived costs associated with playing the game (e.g., feelings of difficulty and discomfort). If feedback emphasizing player's errors had a stronger negative impact on math motivation, we might find lower self-efficacy ratings (i.e., expectations of future success), lower positive value ratings, and increased perceived costs in the conditions emphasizing incorrect as compared to correct responses. It was also possible that the negative feedback conditions that emphasized incorrect responses would have a greater influence on particular motivational constructs (i.e., cost but not positive task value) than positive feedback conditions emphasizing correct responses. For example, feedback emphasizing incorrect responses may increase the perceived costs associated with playing the game but may not differentially impact one's self-efficacy about the math task relative to feedback emphasizing correct responses. These predictions were informed by research on loss aversion, which refers to the phenomenon that people prefer to avoid losses than procure a comparable gain. That is, "losses loom larger than gains" (Kahneman & Tversky, 1979, p. 279). It was possible, therefore, that the more negative feedback conditions (greater emphasis on incorrect) would show the lowest expectancies and values.

EXPERIMENT 1

Method

Participants

Data were collected from 756 adult participants. Of these 756 participants, 85 either did not complete the experiment or restarted the experiment (after failing to complete the first task) at least twice, leaving a total of 671 participants for analysis (72% of whom described themselves as Caucasian or White, 9% as Black, 5% as Asian, 3% as Hispanic/Latinx, and 11% as Other). The number of participants per condition are reported in Table 1. Participants were recruited from Amazon's Mechanical Turk (MTurk) online survey program. (For a review of the psychological properties of samples obtained through MTurk, see e.g., Paolacci et al., 2014). Participation was restricted to those with an IP address in the United States and with a 90% or better completion rate in their history as MTurk workers. In this and in the following experiments, MTurk participants were paid $10 for completing the experiment, which took approximately 60 minutes of their time. Participants were treated following American Psychological Association ethical guidelines in all experiments.

Design

Experiment 1 included 7 feedback conditions which are listed in Table 1.

Materials

Math Task

Participants completed a 30-item game-based math task called Robot Sorter, which targets the mathematical concept of linear functions. The goal of the task is to sort mathematical statements that agree with a mathematical claim (see Figure 1). As participants completed the task, they were given feedback for correct and incorrect responses. A pleasant tone played for correct responses, and a distinct, dissonant sound played for incorrect responses. This tone co-occurred with a change in score, displayed in the top right corner of the screen, which increased, decreased, or did not change for correct and incorrect responses according to the different feedback conditions. There were two limited feedback conditions (no tone + no score, and no score), in which one or both feedback systems were disabled. The "No Score" condition still contained the auditory feedback, while the "No Feedback" condition contained neither the score nor the sounds. The remaining conditions used both auditory and point-based feedback and differed only in the increments of points gained/lost for correct and incorrect responses.

Questionnaires

Participants completed a modified version of the Expectancy-Value questionnaire (Eccles & Wigfield, 2020). The survey questions can be found in the Supplementary Materials (osf.io/a83sm). The 11item expectancy-value questionnaire measured participants expectancies and values related to the math task they had just completed. According to Eccles and colleagues (Eccles & Wigfield, 2020; Wigfield & Eccles, 2000) expectancies are beliefs about how well one thinks they will do on an upcoming task or activity and are closely related to people's assessments of their own ability in the task domain (i.e., their ability self-concept). Subjective task values are the incentives or reasons that individuals have for engaging in different activities. The researchers distinguish between three positive components of value (i.e., interest/enjoyment, perceived importance, and perceived utility) and one negative component (i.e., the perceived costs of engaging in the task; e.g., having to work really hard to complete a math problem). Separate scores were created for positive task values, perceived costs, and expectancies by averaging participants responses to the 6 positive task value items, 3 cost items, and 2 expectancy items.

Participants also answered general demographic questions about their background, and a math attitudes questionnaire adapted from Linnenbrink-Garcia, et al., (2010) which included questions about the extent to which they found the material engaging, to have grabbed their attention, and to be interesting and valuable.

Procedure

Participants completed the tasks and surveys from their own computer and were removed from the study if they stopped actively participating for 10 minutes. After reading task instructions, participants completed a practice item before starting the task. During the task, participants were presented with 30 math statements. For each statement, they had to decide whether it agreed or disagreed with a presented claim. After each decision, participants were given feedback according to the feedback condition they had been randomly assigned to (see Table 1). After both math tasks, participants completed the questionnaires, after which time they were debriefed and thanked for their participation.

Results

Math Task Performance

Overall, participants chose the correct option in Robot Sorter 79.49% (SD = 1.36) of the time, with performance ranging from 30-100% correct. As can be seen in Figure 2 and in the ANOVA results presented in Table 2, participants' proportion of correct responses on the Robot Sorter task did not vary by condition. That is, the feedback manipulation did not impact participants' task performance. Because conditions differed in terms of the points awarded or lost based on the correctness of the response, the score that participants were shown in the task varied widely by condition. Figure 2 shows both proportion correct and the total points that participants had received by the end of the task.

Expectancy-Value Measures

Participants positive task values, perceived costs, and expectancies for each feedback condition are presented in Table 3. A MANOVA (See Table 4) was computed for the expectancy value measures, positive task value, cost, and expectancies, with feedback as the independent variable (Pillai's Trace = .061, F(1977) = 1.95, p<.006). There were no significant differences between feedback conditions for positive task values. A main effect of feedback condition was found for costs. As can be seen in Table 3, the highest costs were associated with the +0 -10 condition (the most extreme negative condition). However, the lowest costs were not associated with what we considered the most extreme positive feedback condition—the condition that only emphasized correct responses (i.e., the +10 -0 condition). Rather the lowest costs were found for the +10 -5 condition, in which points were gained for correct responses and lost for incorrect responses, with relatively more points gained for corrects than lost for incorrect.

In general, pairwise comparisons showed that the conditions that emphasized incorrect responses (higher penalty for incorrect response than reward for correct response) had costs than conditions that emphasized correctness. Additionally, having no feedback whatsoever was associated with higher costs than the conditions that provided positive feedback. Pairwise results (In this, and in analyses that follow, post-hoc comparisons were conducted using Tukey's HSD) for each comparison are displayed in Table 5.

There was also a main effect of feedback condition on participants' expectancies. In general, those in the most negative feedback condition (+0 -10) had significantly lower expectancies of future success than participants in the feedback conditions which highlighted correct responses. The pairwise tests for each comparison are displayed in Table 6.

Math Attitudes Questionnaire

The post-task survey also asked participants about their interest and implicit value in mathematics. A Univariate ANOVA indicated that these survey responses did not differ by feedback condition ($F(6, 664) = 2.02$, $p = .061$, $\eta_p^2 = .018$) and will not be discussed further.

Discussion

Experiment 1

Although performance on the math task did not differ across the feedback conditions, we did find that emphasizing correct and incorrect responses had different effects on expectancies and costs. Expectancies were higher for participants in the emphasize corrects conditions than those in the emphasize incorrect conditions, whereas the perceived cost of completing the math task was significantly higher for the conditions that emphasized incorrect responses or gave no, or limited feedback. Positive value was not associated with any major differences by feedback condition. The differences in expectancies and costs occurred despite equivalent performance across all conditions. The findings suggest that apart from actual performance, task experience is influences by feedback valence, which impacts motivation.

The differences in expectancies and values across the feedback conditions also revealed which of the point-based systems had the strongest influence on these motivational measures. Not surprisingly, the +0 -10 condition (the most extreme negative condition) was associated with the highest perceived costs, and the lowest positive task value and expectancies. In contrast, the +10 -5 condition had the lowest perceived costs, and highest positive value and expectancies. This result suggests that participants positively valued a balance of positive and negative feedback as opposed to only receiving positive (or negative) feedback. The most extreme positive feedback condition, +10 -0 condition did not significantly differ in perceived costs or expectancies when compared to the limited feedback conditions.

In sum, Experiment 1 confirmed that positive and negative within task feedback affected expectancies and costs related to completing the math task. Despite showing equivalent performance, participants in the limited and negative-focused feedback conditions reported higher costs from completing the task, and lower expectations of future success than those in the other conditions. In Experiment 2 we extended these findings by exploring whether these differences in cost and expectancies would influence self-regulatory behaviors.

Experiment 2

The main goals of Experiment 2 were to replicate the findings of feedback valence on expectancies and values, and to determine whether positive and negative feedback would impact participants' perceptions of their own performance and their self-regulatory behaviors. We expected to replicate the findings of Experiment 1 showing that despite equivalent performance for the two feedback conditions, negative feedback would be related to lower expectancies and higher costs than would positive feedback. We sought to extend the findings of Experiment 1 by investigating whether feedback valence influenced participants' perceptions of their overall accuracy (despite there being no differences in actual accuracy). We also investigated whether the feedback manipulation would influence regulatory behaviors by exploring participants' choice to increase or decrease the difficulty of a second math task. Previous research has shown that when participants received positive feedback, they were more likely to increase the difficulty of their next task (e.g., Krenn et al, 2013; Reinecke et al., 2012). Thus, we predicted that participants in the positive feedback condition would be more likely to choose to increase the difficulty of their next task than participants in the negative feedback condition.

A secondary goal of Experiment 2 was to evaluate how the opportunity to choose task difficulty, influenced performance and motivation on the second task.

On the second math task half of the participants were assigned to a difficulty condition (easier or more difficult than the first task), and half were able to choose the difficulty of the task. Feedback condition (negative or positive) remained constant across both tasks. Thus, in addition to investigating whether the feedback condition influenced participants' choice of difficulty for their second math task, we were also able to explore the extent to which the opportunity to choose task difficulty influenced task 2 performance, perceived performance, and expectancies and values. The primary dependent measures of interest in Experiment 2 were participants' ratings of perceived performance on task 1 and 2, expectancy value measures on task 1 and 2, and choice of difficulty on task 2 (for those who had such a choice).

Methodology

Participants

Data were collected from 600 participants recruited from Amazon Mechanical Turk. Of these 600, 69 either did not complete all parts of the study or started the study more than once. These participants' data were removed, leaving 531 participants, with between 80 – 99 participants in each condition. The participants self-identified as 75% white, 7% African American, 6% Hispanic or Latinx, 6% Asian, and 6% other.

Design

Experiment 2 was a 2 (feedback: positive vs. negative) x 2 (choice: free choice vs. no choice) x 2 (task 2 difficulty: easier vs. more difficult than task 1) mixed-measures design (see Figure 3). Participants were randomly assigned to one of the six conditions shown in Table 7. Half of these were the positive feedback condition (+10 for correct, -5 for incorrect), while the other half was the negative feedback condition (+0 for correct, -10 for incorrect). On task 1, all participants completed the same version of Robot Sorter, with either positive or negative feedback, provided an evaluation of their perceived performance, and completed an expectancy value questionnaire, which was the same as used in the Experiment 1. On the second task, half of the participants in each feedback condition were assigned to the no choice condition and half in each condition were assigned to the free choice condition. Of the participants assigned to the no choice condition, half were assigned a more difficult version of Robot Sorter, and half were assigned an easier version. After removing participants who did not complete the tasks, there were 276 participants in the negative feedback condition, and 255 participants in the positive feedback condition. Among these 531 remaining participants, 181 were randomly assigned to the free choice condition, while the remaining 350 assigned to the no choice condition were randomly assigned to either the easier condition (N=181) or the more difficult condition ($N = 169$) for task 2.

Materials

Math Tasks

The first math task participants completed was identical to that used in Experiment 1. The second task was similar to the first task, except that the items were either easier or more difficult than those used on the first task. The new items were created by modifying the original items by including more variables in the expression and using both positive and negative numbers to make them more difficult, or by including fewer variables in the expression and no negative numbers to make them easier. On both tasks, participants answered 30 items about whether each statement agreed with the presented claim.

Questionnaires

After each task participants indicated what percentage of their responses that they thought they answered correctly and completed an expectancy-value questionnaire. After completing both math tasks and questionnaires participants answered a set of demographic questions, and provided information about their technology usage, familiarity with educational games, and attitudes about math.

Procedure

Participants started the experiment by reading the task instructions. They completed the first task and answered the mid-task-questionnaire items. At the start of the second task, participants were given instructions that differed depending on their assigned experimental condition. Participants in the free choice condition were instructed that they were going to complete the math task again, but with new questions, and that they would have the option to choose either an easier version, or a more difficult version of the task. Those in the no choice condition were told that they had been assigned to an easier or to a more difficult version of the task. After completing their second task all groups completed the post-task questionnaires.

Results

Task 1: Actual and Perceived Performance

An independent samples *t*-test was conducted and revealed no significant differences on performance by feedback condition ($t(529) = 1.457, p = .146$), replicating the findings of Experiment 1. Overall participants answered 79.62% correct (*SD* 13.34%), with performance ranging from 30-100% correct. While feedback condition did not have an effect on actual performance, participants in the positive feedback condition gave higher estimates of their own performance (M = 75.65% correct, SD = 17.16%, range: 33-100%) than those in the negative feedback condition (M = 52.03% correct, SD = 3.34%, range: 30-100%), $t(529)$ = 1.92, $p < .001$. Figure 4 shows mean perceived and actual performance for each feedback condition.

In addition to the finding of a difference between feedback conditions in perceived performance, we were also interested in whether participants' metacognitive accuracy of perceived performance was influenced by feedback. We evaluated metacognitive calibration as a measure of metacognitive accuracy. Calibration is the difference between participants' average ratings of the perceived percentage of items that they answered correctly minus the average of percentage of actual correct responses. Results indicated that participants who had received positive feedback were more calibrated (M = -4.85%, SD = 13.85%, range: -77 – 35%) than those in the negative feedback condition, who showed substantial under confidence in their performance (M = -26.79%, SD = 24.47%, range: -90 – 33%), $t(529)$ = 12.58, $p < .001$.

Task 1: Expectancy Value Measures

As in Experiment 1, a MANOVA was computed for the expectancy value measures, positive task value, cost, and expectancies, with feedback as the independent variable. The MANOVA revealed a significant effect of feedback on positive value, costs, and expectancies (Pillai's Trace = .087, $F(526)$ = 16.73, $p<.001$). (See Table 8). Table 9 shows the average values of participants' ratings for the three expectancy value measures, split by feedback condition. All three measures showed significant differences by condition, indicating that feedback had a potent effect on participants' game experiences, with the positive feedback condition producing more positive expectancies and values than the negative feedback condition.

Choice of Difficulty for Task 2

A primary question of interest was whether the feedback condition would affect participants' choice of difficulty on task 2 (for those who had a choice). Table 10 shows the breakdown of participants' choice by feedback condition. Of the 181 participants in the free choice condition, 90 were given positive feedback, and 91 were given negative feedback. There was not a statistically significant difference between feedback conditions on choice of difficulty. In both the positive and negative feedback conditions, people chose the easier version of the task roughly 75% of the time.

What factor, or factors did play a role in determining participants' choice of difficulty in task 2? To answer this question, binary logistic regression was employed to predict the probability of participants selecting the difficult version of task 2. The predictors were feedback condition, participants' perceived performance on task 1[1], and averages for the expectancy value measures (cost, positive task value, and expectancies). A test of the full model versus a model with only the intercept was statistically significant, $\chi^2(5, df = 2) = 18.398$, $p = .002$. The model was able to correctly classify 95.6% of those who self-selected into the easier version, and 13.3% of those who self-selected into the difficult version, for an overall success rate of 75.1%.

Table 11 shows the logistic regression coefficients, Wald test, and odds ratio for each of the predictors. Using a .05 criterion of statistical significance, only expectancies of future success had a significant partial effect, which indicated that expectancies were the sole predictor in the model for participants' choice of difficulty. The odds ratio for expectancies of future success revealed that for every one-point increase in the 6-point scale, the participant was 1.728 times more likely to choose the difficult version for task 2. In sum, the findings indicated that participants' expectancies for future success were the strongest predictor of whether they chose the easier or the more difficult version of the task.

As we saw in previous analyses, expectancies were related to feedback conditions. This pattern suggested that there may be a mediated relationship between feedback and choice of difficulty through expectancies of future success. To investigate, a path analysis was conducted (Figure 5) with feedback, perceived performance, and expectancies as predictors for the choice of difficulty. The sequence of the path was ordered by when each measure was taken. For example, feedback was present in task 1, ratings of perceived performance occurred just after task 1, ratings of expectations of future success occurred after ratings of perceived performance and just before selecting difficulty level for task 2. The model showed acceptable model fit[2]; RMSEA = .052; CFI = .986; TLI = .959; SRMSR = .039.

Figure 5 displays the path analysis and the associated standardized coefficients for each direct and indirect effect. Mediation analyses indicated that there was a significant specific indirect effect of feedback on expectancies through perceived performance, β = .392, *SE* = .132, *p* = .003, while the direct effect of feedback on expectancies (when controlling for perceived performance) was not significant, β = -.102, *SE* = .249, *p* = .683. This pattern indicated a complete mediation of the relationship between feedback and expectancies by perceived performance. The specific indirect effect of feedback on choice of difficulty through expectancies only was not significant, β = -.041, *SE* = .098, *p* = .674. However, when including perceived performance, as well as expectancies (i.e., the entire model displayed in Figure 5), the specific indirect effect of feedback on choice of difficulty was significant β = .159, *SE* = .07, *p* = .023. The results of this path analysis suggested that feedback impacted expectations of future success through perceived performance, and it was through this mediated relationship that feedback influenced choice of difficulty; That is, feedback influenced participants' beliefs about their own performance, which in turn affected their expectations of future success, which ultimately influenced their subsequent choice of difficulty for their second math task.

Task 2: Performance

An ANOVA evaluated the effect of feedback, choice, and difficulty on task 2 performance (See Table 12). A significant interaction between choice and difficulty revealed that our manipulations were successful. Feedback did not significantly impact task 2 performance. There was not a significant 3-way interaction between feedback, choice, and difficulty. Pairwise comparisons for the 2-way interaction between choice and difficulty on performance, perceived performance, and accuracy of the self-evaluation are displayed in Table 13. On average, the no choice condition was associated with greater differences in performance between the easier and more difficult versions, than was the free choice condition.

Table 14 displays the means and standard errors for actual and perceived performance, and accuracy of these ratings, split by choice condition and difficulty. As can be seen in Table 14, performance in the free choice difficult condition was higher than performance in the no-choice difficult condition, which reflects ability-based self-selection into the more difficult version in the free choice condition. In contrast, performance in the no-choice easy condition was higher than in the free-choice easy condition, which reflects the random assignment of participants in the no-choice group. That is, the easy task in the no-choice condition included high and low performers, as compared to the easy task in the free choice condition, which included the lower performers who self-selected, the easier version of the task.

Task 2: Perceived Performance

A separate ANOVA was computed to measure the effect of feedback, choice, and difficulty on perceived performance for task 2. See Table 12. There was not a significant 3-way interaction between feedback, choice, and difficulty as was found with actual performance. However, there was a significant interaction between choice and difficulty, which is in line with the finding of a significant interaction between choice and difficulty on actual performance. Perceived performance was significantly lower for participants in the no-choice difficult condition than either the no-choice easy, or free-choice difficult conditions. People who were randomly assigned to the difficult condition in the no-choice condition had lower perceived performance than those in the free-choice condition who self-selected into the difficult condition. These were the only significant differences between groups for perceived performance (See Table 13). Feedback had a significant main effect on perceived performance with higher perceived performance in the positive feedback condition as compared to the negative feedback condition.

A third ANOVA evaluated metacognitive accuracy as measured as the difference between participants' perceived and actual performance on task 2. See Table 12. Once again, there was not a significant 3-way interaction between feedback, choice, and difficulty on the accuracy of participants' self-evaluations. However, there was a significant interaction between feedback and choice condition. Table 15 displays the means and standard errors for metacognitive accuracy for the feedback by choice conditions. As with task 1, participants who received positive feedback were on average more accurate about their performance than those with negative feedback. Participants who were not able to choose their task difficulty and who had received negative feedback showed the greatest difference between perceived and actual performance.

Task 2: Expectancy-Value Measures

A MANOVA was conducted for the three subcomponents of expectancy-value: positive value, cost, and expectancies of future success. Means and standard errors for these measures are displayed in Table 16. The MANOVA demonstrated that there was a significant main effect of feedback on positive value, cost and expectancies (Pillai's Trace = .066, $F(527) = 12.43$, $p<.001$). The MANOVA also revealed a significant interaction between choice condition and task difficulty on cost and expectancies, but not positive value. Finally, a significant three-way interaction between feedback, choice, and difficulty was found for cost, but not for expectancies, or positive value.

The post-hoc tests found that only those in the negative feedback condition who were assigned (i.e., no choice condition) to the difficult version, and those in the negative feedback condition who chose the easier version had significantly higher ratings of cost than others ($ps<.001$).

To further our understanding of the interaction between feedback, choice, and difficulty on cost ratings, two separate ANOVAs, one for each feedback condition, were conducted. See Table 17. The ANOVA for positive feedback showed no significant interaction between choice and difficulty on cost, while the interaction between choice and difficulty on cost for those in the negative feedback condition was significant.

In sum, positive feedback was associated with uniformly lower costs. Moreover, choice and difficulty had no effect on the perceived costs for participants who received positive feedback. However, for those who received negative feedback, choice and difficulty played a substantial role in perceived costs. In the negative feedback condition, if one chose the more difficult version of the task, cost ratings were no different than the uniformly low costs of those with positive feedback. This was likely because higher performers were more likely to choose the difficult version in the negative feedback condition. Those who received negative feedback and then chose the easier version of the task (lower performers) showed higher costs than their counterparts who received positive feedback. Having no choice of task difficulty in the negative feedback condition led to relatively medium cost ratings when assigned to the easier difficulty (i.e., no significant differences in the post-hoc comparisons). However, being assigned to the more difficult version of the task in the negative feedback condition led to the highest ratings of cost across groups. The no-choice – difficult group showed significantly higher cost ratings than every group aside from those who self-selected into the easier difficulty with negative feedback.

DISCUSSION

Experiment 1 demonstrated that feedback valence influenced participants' motivation (measured by expectancy-value ratings). Namely, feedback conditions that focused on emphasizing gains led to a more positive experience for the player and higher expectancies and lower costs than those of players who had received feedback with a negative emphasis or had received no feedback at all. Experiment 2 sought to extend the results of Experiment 1 by examining how positive and negative feedback conditions influenced participants' perceptions of their performance, and their choice of difficulty on a second math task. Experiment 2 also investigated how autonomy (choice of task difficulty) and difficulty itself affected motivation, and whether these variables interacted with feedback valence.

The results from Experiment 2 indicated that feedback valence influenced how well participants believed they performed during the first task, with negative feedback related to lower perceived performance, and greater under confidence. Perceived performance influenced expectancies of how well participants believed they would perform in the future, and as a result, influenced their choice of difficulty for their second task (for those assigned to the free choice condition). This relationship suggests an indirect (though still significant) effect of feedback valence on self-regulatory behaviors, through an influence on their perceptions of how well they did, and how well they believed they would perform in the future. The findings suggest that manipulations that increase the likelihood of students selecting the more challenging set of items for a future math task may be beneficial in helping them to increase their mastery of math content over time.

Experiment 2 also investigated whether autonomy (choice of difficulty) influenced performance and motivational measures. The results demonstrated a significant interaction effect of choice condition and difficulty in task 2 on both actual and perceived performance. In terms of actual performance, in the free choice condition, lower performing individuals tended to self-select into the easier version of the task, while higher performers were more likely to self-select into the difficult version. In contrast, in the no choice condition, higher and lower performers were randomly assigned to the easier and more difficult versions of the task. Not surprisingly this resulted in higher performance on the difficult version of the task in the free choice condition than in the no choice condition (79% vs 72%, respectively). On the easy version of the task, performance was lower in the free choice group than the no choice group (80% vs 83%, respectively), likely due fewer higher performers self-selecting the easier version of the task in the free choice condition.

We evaluated how feedback valence and autonomy influenced motivational constructs, using the expectancy-value framework to measure expectancies of future success, and positive and perceived costs. Participants' expectancies were significantly impacted by feedback valence, opportunity to choose task difficulty, and task difficulty. Negative feedback led to lower expectations of future success, when compared to positive feedback. A significant interaction between choice condition and difficulty on expectancy ratings was due, most likely, to participants who had self-selected into the difficult version for task 2, and who showed a much higher expectation of future success than the other three choice by difficulty groups. This pattern supports the finding that expectancy ratings following task 1 were predictive of task 2 difficulty selections.

The effects of feedback on positive task value, which corresponds to how interesting and important one finds the material in the task, showed inconsistent effects. While the feedback condition in task 1 influenced positive value ratings, there was only a marginal effect of feedback on positive value ratings following task 2 (when both autonomy and difficulty manipulations were also present).

Finally, a three-way interaction was found to be significant for the effect of feedback, choice, and difficulty on cost. To investigate the source of the interaction, separate ANOVAs for the positive and negative feedback conditions were conducted. In the positive feedback condition, there was not a significant interaction between choice and difficulty on cost. Positive feedback was associated with uniformly low costs, regardless of choice condition and difficulty. The similarity of cost ratings in the positive feedback condition suggests that positive feedback may have shielded against the negative costs associated with being assigned to the difficult task condition.

In the negative feedback condition, there was a significant interaction between choice and difficulty on cost. Participants in the no choice, difficult group showed the highest ratings of cost, whereas participants in the free choice condition who chose to play the more difficult version of the task, had the lowest cost ratings. Thus, negative feedback amplified the negative costs associated with being assigned to the difficult task condition. There were no significant differences between ratings of cost for players who did or did not choose the easy version of the task.

Choosing the difficult version of the task (regardless of feedback condition) was associated with higher perceived performance and higher self-efficacy. Thus, those who self-selected into the difficult version of the task were protected from the high motivational costs of receiving negative feedback. The results of the path analysis indicated that choosing the difficult version was dependent on having high expectancies, which in turn were dependent on high perceived performance. Through the path analysis, we showed that feedback valence can influence this relationship by affecting both expectancies and perceived performance.

The results from both experiments imply that feedback manipulation can greatly impact the player's motivation – specifically their self-efficacy for similar future tasks and the negative costs associated with playing the task. Indirectly, manipulating feedback also influenced self-regulatory behaviors, here specifically by influencing whether participants increased the difficulty on a second math task. Additionally, giving participants the opportunity to make choices about difficulty of the task reduced the costs associated with performing that task. This may be particularly important in domains such as mathematics, in which students might automatically feel some level of discomfort for the domain itself, and in which tasks that allow autonomy of choice can improve students' motivation.

LIMITATIONS AND FUTURE DIRECTIONS

This study was conducted using points-based feedback and did not give participants rich or detailed information about how to improve their performance. In addition, the task held no stakes for the participant, thus choosing the difficult version in task 2 carried no inherent risk, other than potentially greater effort. Furthermore, the participants in this study were recruited from Amazon.com's crowdsourcing platform, Mturk, did not have a background in math, and were significantly older (18+) than the target population for learning linear functions (middle school students). This was primarily a convenience sample, as this population is readily available and can support large sample sizes in a short time period. While it is clear that positive feedback leads to better motivational outcomes in adults, future research needs to evaluate whether the same pattern is evident in young students and in other types of learning contexts.

For example, future research should also explore the role that features such as feedback valence and opportunities for choice transfer beyond gamified learning contexts and into in person, blended, and online learning scenarios. For example, in blended learning scenarios, students engage with both digital and face to face instruction. Does feedback valence have a similar impact on student confidence when delivered digitally as compared to face to face? How might more positive feedback in a digital scenario and more negatively valence feedback in a face-to-face scenario (or vice versa) influence students' preferences for the kinds of contexts in which they prefer to learn?

CONCLUSION

Understanding how to improve motivation is paramount to developing valid assessments and engaging digital learning environments. Without motivated learners and test takers, there is no assurance that the performance represented in a task is indicative of that students' ability (e.g., Finn, 2015). Game-based assessments (GBAs) have sought to tackle this problem in many ways, including making the act of taking a test more enjoyable, more engaging, and by representing problems in unique formats. These findings suggest that implementing some immediate form of positive feedback (like real-time gains to a learner's score) may reduce perceived costs and discomfort, increase test-taker motivation, and ultimately have (indirect) impacts of self-regulatory learning behaviors.

REFERENCES

Bangert-Drowns, R. L., Kulik, C. L. C., Kulik, J. A., & Morgan, M. (1991). The instructional effect of feedback in test-like events. *Review of Educational Research, 61*(2), 213–238. doi:10.3102/00346543061002213

Bentler, P. M. (1990). Comparative fit indexes in structural models. *Psychological Bulletin, 107*(2), 238–246. doi:10.1037/0033-2909.107.2.238 PMID:2320703

Bernacki, M. L., Nokes-Malach, T. J., & Aleven, V. (2015). Examining self-efficacy during learning: Variability and relations to behavior, performance, and learning. *Metacognition and Learning, 10*(1), 99–117. doi:10.100711409-014-9127-x

Browne, M. W., & Cudeck, R. (1993). Alternative ways of assessing model fit. In K. A. Bollen & J. S. Long (Eds.), *Testing structural equation models* (pp. 111–135). Sage.

Burgers, C., Eden, A., van Engelenburg, M. D., & Buningh, S. (2015). How feedback boosts motivation and play in a brain-training game. *Computers in Human Behavior*, *48*, 94–103. doi:10.1016/j.chb.2015.01.038

Butler, R. (1987). Task-involving and ego-involving properties of evaluation: Effects of different feedback conditions on motivational perceptions, interest, and performance. *Journal of Educational Psychology*, *79*(4), 474–482. doi:10.1037/0022-0663.79.4.474

Cerasoli, C. P., Nicklin, J. M., & Ford, M. T. (2014). Intrinsic motivation and extrinsic incentives jointly predict performance: A 40-year meta-analysis. *Psychological Bulletin*, *140*(4), 98. doi:10.1037/a0035661 PMID:24491020

Deci, E. L., Koestner, R., & Ryan, R. M. (2001). Extrinsic rewards and intrinsic motivation in education: Reconsidered once again. *Review of Educational Research*, *71*(1), 1–27. doi:10.3102/00346543071001001

Deci, E. L., & Ryan, R. M. (1985). *Intrinsic Motivation and Self Determination in Human Behaviour*. Plenum Press. doi:10.1007/978-1-4899-2271-7

Dent, A. L., & Koenka, A. C. (2016). The relation between self-regulated learning and academic achievement across childhood and adolescence: A meta-analysis. *Educational Psychology Review*, *28*(3), 425–474. doi:10.100710648-015-9320-8

Dickinson, L. (1995). Autonomy and motivation a literature review. *System*, *23*(2), 165–174. doi:10.1016/0346-251X(95)00005-5

Donker, A. S., De Boer, H., Kostons, D., Van Ewijk, C. D., & van der Werf, M. P. (2014). Effectiveness of learning strategy instruction on academic performance: A meta-analysis. *Educational Research Review*, *11*, 1–26. doi:10.1016/j.edurev.2013.11.002

Dweck, C. S. (1986). Motivational processes affecting learning. *The American Psychologist*, *41*(10), 1040–1048. doi:10.1037/0003-066X.41.10.1040

Eccles, J. S., & Wigfield, A. (2020). From expectancy-value theory to situated expectancy-value theory: A developmental, social cognitive, and sociocultural perspective on motivation. *Contemporary Educational Psychology*, *61*, 101859. doi:10.1016/j.cedpsych.2020.101859

Eccles-Parsons, J. S. (1983). Expectancies, values, and academic behaviors. In J. T. Spence (Ed.), *Achievement and Achievement Motivations* (pp. 75–121). W. H. Freeman & Co.

Fazio, L. K., Huelser, B. J., Johnson, A., & Marsh, E. J. (2010). Receiving right/wrong feedback: Consequences for learning. *Memory (Hove, England)*, *18*(3), 335–35. doi:10.1080/09658211003652491 PMID:20408043

Ferguson, C., Van den Broek, E. L., & Van Oostendorp, H. (2020). On the role of interaction mode and story structure in virtual reality serious games. *Computers & Education*, *143*, 103671. doi:10.1016/j.compedu.2019.103671

Finn, B. (2015). Measuring motivation in low stakes assessment. Educational Testing Service, ETS RR-15-19. doi:10.1002/ets2.12067

Finn, B., & Tauber, S. K. (2015). When confidence is not a signal of knowing: How students' experiences and beliefs about processing fluency can lead to miscalibrated confidence. *Educational Psychology Review*, *27*(4), 567–586. doi:10.100710648-015-9313-7

Fong, C. J., Patall, E. A., Vasquez, A. C., & Stautberg, S. (2019). A meta-analysis of negative feedback on intrinsic motivation. *Educational Psychology Review*, *31*(1), 121–162. doi:10.100710648-018-9446-6

Gee, J. P. (2003). What video games have to teach us about learning and literacy. *Computers in Entertainment*, *1*(1), 20–22. doi:10.1145/950566.950595

Grolnick, W. S., & Ryan, R. M. (1987). Autonomy in children's learning: An experimental and individual difference investigation. *Journal of Personality and Social Psychology*, *52*(5), 89. doi:10.1037/0022-3514.52.5.890 PMID:3585701

Hattie, J. (2012). *Visible learning for teachers: Maximizing impact on learning*. Routledge. doi:10.4324/9780203181522

Hattie, J., & Timperley, H. (2007). The power of feedback. *Review of Educational Research*, *77*(1), 81–112. doi:10.3102/003465430298487

Hu, L. T., & Bentler, P. M. (1998). Fit indices in covariance structure modeling: Sensitivity to underparameterized model misspecification. *Psychological Methods*, *3*(4), 424–453. doi:10.1037/1082-989X.3.4.424

Jansen, R. S., Van Leeuwen, A., Janssen, J., Jak, S., & Kester, L. (2019). Self-regulated learning partially mediates the effect of self-regulated learning interventions on achievement in higher education: A meta-analysis. *Educational Research Review*, *28*, 100292. doi:10.1016/j.edurev.2019.100292

Kahneman, D., & Tversky, A. (1979). Prospect theory: An analysis of decision under risk. *Econometrica*, *47*(2), 263. doi:10.2307/1914185

Kapp, K. M. (2012). *The gamification of learning and instruction: game-based methods and strategies for training and education*. John Wiley & Sons.

Kinzer, C., Hoffman, D., Turkay, S., Gunbas, N., Chantes, P., Dvorkin, T., & Chaiwinij, A. (2012). The impact of choice and feedback on learning, motivation, and performance in an educational video game. In *Proceedings of the games, learning, and society conference* (Vol. 2, pp. 175-181). ETC.

Kluger, A. N., & DeNisi, A. (1996). The effects of feedback interventions on performance: A historical review, a meta-analysis, and a preliminary feedback intervention theory. *Psychological Bulletin*, *119*(2), 254–284. doi:10.1037/0033-2909.119.2.254

Kluger, A. N., & DeNisi, A. (1998). Feedback interventions: Toward the understanding of a double-edged sword. *Current Directions in Psychological Science*, *7*(3), 67–72. doi:10.1111/1467-8721.ep10772989

Knowles, M. S. (1975). Self-directed learning: A guide for learners and teachers (Vol. 2). Association Press.

Koenka, A. C., & Anderman, E. M. (2019). Personalized feedback as a strategy for improving motivation and performance among middle school students. *Middle School Journal*, *50*(5), 15–22. doi:10.1080/00940771.2019.1674768

Koenka, A. C., Linnenbrink-Garcia, L., Moshontz, H., Atkinson, K. M., Sanchez, C. E., & Cooper, H. (2021). A meta-analysis on the impact of grades and comments on academic motivation and achievement: A case for written feedback. *Educational Psychology*, *41*(7), 922–947. doi:10.1080/01443410.2019.1659939

Koriat, A. (1997). Monitoring one's own knowledge during study: A cue-utilization approach to judgments of learning. *Journal of Experimental Psychology. General*, *126*(4), 349–370. doi:10.1037/0096-3445.126.4.349

Krenn, B., Würth, S., & Hergovich, A. (2013). The impact of feedback on goal setting and task performance. *Swiss Journal of Psychology*, *2*(2), 79–89. doi:10.1024/1421-0185/a000101

Kuklick, L., & Lindner, M. A. (2021). Computer-based knowledge of results feedback in different delivery modes: Effects on performance, motivation, and achievement emotions. *Contemporary Educational Psychology*, *67*, 102001. doi:10.1016/j.cedpsych.2021.102001

Kulhavy, R. W., White, M. T., Topp, B. W., Chan, A. L., & Adams, J. (1985). Feedback complexity and corrective efficiency. *Contemporary Educational Psychology*, *10*(3), 285–291. doi:10.1016/0361-476X(85)90025-6

Linnenbrink-Garcia, L., Durik, A. M., Conley, A. M., Barron, K. E., Tauer, J. M., Karabenick, S. A., & Harackiewicz, J. M. (2010). Measuring situational interest in academic domains. *Educational and Psychological Measurement*, *70*(4), 647–671. doi:10.1177/0013164409355699

Lipkus, I. M., & Klein, W. M. (2006). Effects of communicating social comparison information on risk perceptions for colorectal cancer. *Journal of Health Communication*, *11*(4), 391–407. doi:10.1080/10810730600671870 PMID:16720537

McNamara, D. S., Jackson, G. T., & Graesser, A. (2010). Intelligent tutoring and games (ITaG). In *Gaming for classroom-based learning: Digital role playing as a motivator of study* (pp. 44–65). IGI Global. doi:10.4018/978-1-61520-713-8.ch003

Mertens, U., Finn, B., & Lindner, M. (2022, November). Effects of computer-based feedback on lower and higher order learning outcomes: A network meta-analysis. *Journal of Educational Psychology*, *114*(8), 1743–1772. doi:10.1037/edu0000764

Metcalfe, J., & Finn, B. (2008). Evidence that judgments of learning are causally related to study choice. *Psychonomic Bulletin & Review*, *15*(1), 174–179. doi:10.3758/PBR.15.1.174 PMID:18605499

Morris, T. H. (2019). Self-directed learning: A fundamental competence in a rapidly changing world. *International Review of Education*, *65*(4), 633–653. doi:10.100711159-019-09793-2

Mory, E. H. (2013). Feedback research revisited. In *Handbook of research on educational communications and technology* (pp. 738–776). Routledge.

Murphy, D. H., Huckins, S. C., Rhodes, M. G., & Castel, A. D. (2022). The effect of perceptual processing fluency and value on metacognition and remembering. *Psychonomic Bulletin & Review, 29*(3), 910–921. doi:10.375813423-021-02030-8 PMID:34846689

Nelson, T. O., & Narens, L. (1990). Metamemory: A theoretical frame-work and new findings. *Psychology of Learning and Motivation, 26*, 125–141. doi:10.1016/S0079-7421(08)60053-5

Panadero, E. (2017). A review of self-regulated learning: Six models and four directions for research. *Frontiers in Psychology, 8*, 422. doi:10.3389/fpsyg.2017.00422 PMID:28503157

Paolacci, G., & Chandler, J. (2014). Inside the Turk: Understanding Mechanical Turk as a participant pool. *Current Directions in Psychological Science, 23*(3), 184–188. doi:10.1177/0963721414531598

Pashler, H., Cepeda, N. J., Wixted, J. T., & Rohrer, D. (2005). When does feedback facilitate learning of words? *Journal of Experimental Psychology. Learning, Memory, and Cognition, 31*(1), 3–8. doi:10.1037/0278-7393.31.1.3 PMID:15641900

Pintrich, P. R. (2000). The role of goal orientation in self-regulated learning. In *Handbook of self-regulation* (pp. 451–502). Academic Pres. doi:10.1016/B978-012109890-2/50043-3

Prensky, M. (2001). Digital natives, digital immigrants, part 1. *On the Horizon, 9*(5), 1–6. doi:10.1108/10748120110424816

Reinecke, L., Tamborini, R., Grizzard, M., Lewis, R., Eden, A., & Bowman, D. N. (2012). Characterizing mood management as need satisfaction: The effects of intrinsic needs on selective exposure and mood repair. *Journal of Communication, 62*(3), 437–453. doi:10.1111/j.1460-2466.2012.01649.x

Ryan, R. M., & Deci, E. L. (2000). Self-determination theory and the facilitation of intrinsic motivation, social development, and well-being. *The American Psychologist, 55*(1), 68–78. doi:10.1037/0003-066X.55.1.68 PMID:11392867

Shute, V. J. (2008). Focus on formative feedback. *Review of Educational Research, 78*(1), 153–189. doi:10.3102/0034654307313795

Shute, V. J., & Ke, F. (2012). Games, learning, and assessment. In *Assessment in game-based learning* (pp. 43–58). Springer. doi:10.1007/978-1-4614-3546-4_4

Tucker, L. R., & Lewis, C. (1973). A reliability coefficient for maximum likelihood factor analysis. *Psychometrika, 38*(1), 1–1. doi:10.1007/BF02291170

Vallerand, R. J., & Reid, G. (1988). On the relative effects of positive and negative verbal feedback on males' and females' intrinsic motivation. *Canadian Journal of Behavioural Science/Revue Canadienne des Sciences du Comportement, 20*(3), 239.

Van der Kleij, F. M., Feskens, R. C., & Eggen, T. J. (2015). Effects of feedback in a computer-based learning environment on students' learning outcomes: A meta-analysis. *Review of Educational Research, 85*(4), 475–511. doi:10.3102/0034654314564881

Wigfield, A., & Eccles, J. S. (2000). Expectancy–value theory of achievement motivation. *Contemporary Educational Psychology, 25*(1), 68–81. doi:10.1006/ceps.1999.1015 PMID:10620382

Winne, P. H. (1996). A metacognitive view of individual differences in self-regulated learning. *Learning and Individual Differences*, *8*(4), 327–353. doi:10.1016/S1041-6080(96)90022-9

ADDITIONAL READING

Brandmo, C., Panadero, E., & Hopfenbeck, T. N. (2020). Bridging classroom assessment and self-regulated learning. *Assessment in Education: Principles, Policy & Practice*, *27*(4), 319–331. doi:10.1080/0969594X.2020.1803589

Broadbent, J., Panadero, E., Lodge, J. M., & Barba, P. D. (2020). Technologies to enhance self-regulated learning in online and computer-mediated learning environments. In *Handbook of research in educational communications and technology* (pp. 37–52). Springer. doi:10.1007/978-3-030-36119-8_3

Eccles, J. S., & Wigfield, A. (2020). From expectancy-value theory to situated expectancy-value theory: A developmental, social cognitive, and sociocultural perspective on motivation. *Contemporary Educational Psychology*, *61*, 101859. doi:10.1016/j.cedpsych.2020.101859

Kinzer, C., Hoffman, D., Turkay, S., Gunbas, N., Chantes, P., Dvorkin, T., & Chaiwinij, A. (2012). The impact of choice and feedback on learning, motivation, and performance in an educational video game. In *Proceedings of the games, learning, and society conference* (Vol. 2, pp. 175-181). ETC.

Koskinen, A., McMullen, J., Ninaus, M., & Kiili, K. (2022). Does the emotional design of scaffolds enhance learning and motivational outcomes in game-based learning? *Journal of Computer Assisted Learning*.

Sailer, M., & Homner, L. (2020). The gamification of learning: A meta-analysis. *Educational Psychology Review*, *32*(1), 77–112. doi:10.100710648-019-09498-w

Schunk, D. H., & Zimmerman, B. J. (Eds.). (2012). *Motivation and self-regulated learning: Theory, research, and applications*. Routledge. doi:10.4324/9780203831076

Shute, V. J., & Ke, F. (2012). Games, learning, and assessment. In *Assessment in game-based learning* (pp. 43–58). Springer. doi:10.1007/978-1-4614-3546-4_4

KEY TERMS AND DEFINITIONS

Autonomy: A person's belief that they can control their own actions and choices.

Expectancy-Value Theory: A theory that describes how a learner's motivation is determined by how much they value a goal or task and whether they expect to succeed at it.

Feedback: Information regarding a learner's strategies and performance on a task.

Gamification: Designing or adding game elements (such as points, feedback, interactive mechanics, and graphics) into a digital assessment or a learning task.

Metacognition: The monitoring and control of one's own cognition.

Self-Regulated Learning: A broad conceptual term used to encompass the multivariate cognitive, affective, and motivational processes that underlie students' dynamic learning behaviors.

Valence: The extent to which a stimulus elicits positive or negative emotions.

ENDNOTES

1 Participants were never told the actual percentage of items they got correct, and their final in-game score displayed to them was determined by feedback condition. Perceived performance was the percentage of items they believed they got correct (as reported by them in the mid-survey).

2 Traditional overall goodness-of-fit indices (Hu & Bentler, 1998) *RMSEA*: Root Mean Squared Error of Approximation (Browne & Cudeck, 1993) *CFI*: Comparative Fit Index (Bentler, 1990) *TLI*: Tucker-Lewis Index (Tucker & Lewis, 1973) *SRMSR*: Standardized Root Mean Squared Residual (Browne & Cudeck, 1993)

APPENDIX 1: TABLES

Table 1. Feedback Conditions in Experiment 1

Feedback Type	Feedback Conditions	*N*
Limited Feedback	No Feedback No Score (auditory feedback remains)	96 99
Emphasis on Incorrect Responses	+0 for correct response, -10 for incorrect +5 for correct response, -10 for incorrect	100 96
Emphasis on Correct Responses	+10 for correct response, -0 for incorrect +10 for correct response, -5 for incorrect	95 94
Equivalent	+10 for correct response, -10 for incorrect	97

Table 2. Univariate ANOVA of the Effects of Feedback Condition on Math Task Performance in Experiment 1

Predictor	Sum of Squares	df	Mean Square	F	p	Partial η2
Intercept	423.963	1	423.963	22757.237	<.001	.972
Feedback Condition	.177	6	.030	1.588	.148	.014
Error	12.37	664	.019			
Total	436.635	671				

Table 3. Expectancy Value Measures by Feedback Condition in Experiment 1

Feedback Condition	Positive Value	Perceived Cost	Expectancies
No Feedback	4.14 (.10)	2.58 (.11)	4.17 (.12)
No Score	4.33 (.09)	2.45 (.11)	4.38 (.11)
+0_-10	4.09 (.10)	2.88 (.11)	3.95 (.12)
+5_-10	4.15 (.10)	2.41 (.11)	4.20 (.12)
+10_-10	4.34 (.10)	2.22 (.11)	4.48 (.12)
+10_-5	4.32 (.10)	2.10 (.11)	4.67 (.12)
+10_-0	4.24 (.10)	2.38 (.11)	4.42 (.12)
Overall	4.23 (.04)	2.43 (.04)	4.32 (.04)
Range	1-6	1-6	1-6

Note. Values displayed are means across all participants in each condition, with the standard error depicted in parentheses.

Table 4. Summary Table of One-Way MANOVA for Feedback Condition on Expectancies and Values in Experiment 1

Source	Dependent Variable	Sum of Squares	df	Mean Square	F	p	Partial η2
Feedback Condition	Positive Value	6.402	6	1.067	1.263	.272	.011
	Perceived Costs	37.119	6	6.187	5.475	<.001	.048
	Expectancies	31.423	6	5.237	4.1	<.001	.036
Error	Positive Value	552.347	654	.845			
	Perceived Costs	739.065	654	1.13			
	Expectancies	835.294	654	1.277			

*Table 5. Pairwise Comparisons of Perceived Costs in Each Feedback Condition, Based on Estimated Marginal Means. * Indicates Significance at p<.05*

Feedback Condition	Contrast	Mean Difference	*S.E.*	Sig (*p*)
+0 -10	+10 -0	.500*	.157	.031
	+10 -10	.661*	.156	.001
	+10 -5	.779*	.157	<.001
	+5 -10	.477*	.156	.048
	No Feedback	.308	.156	1.00
	No Score	.435	.155	.106
+10 -0	+10 -10	.161	.156	1.00
	+10 -5	.279	.157	1.00
	+5 -10	-.023	.156	1.00
	No Feedback	-.192	.156	1.00
	No Score	-.065	.155	1.00
+10 - 10	+10 -5	.118	.156	1.00
	+5 -10	-.184	.155	1.00
	No Feedback	-.353	.155	.491
	No Score	-.226	.154	1.00
+10 -5	+5 -10	-.302	.156	1.00
	No Feedback	-.471	.157	.057
	No Score	-.344	.155	.566
+5 - 10	No Feedback	-.169	.155	1.00
	No Score	-.042	.154	1.00
No Feedback	No Score	.128	.154	1.00

*Table 6. Pairwise Comparisons of Expectancies in Each Feedback Condition, Based on Estimated Marginal Means. * Indicates Significance at p<.05*

Feedback Condition	Contrast	Mean Difference	*S.E.*	Sig (*p*)
+0 -10	+10 -0	-.469*	.165	.005
	+10 -10	-.538*	.164	.001
	+10 -5	-.718*	.165	<.001
	+5 -10	-.251	.164	.127
	No Feedback	-.227	.165	.169
	No Score	-.437*	.163	.008
+10 -0	+10 -10	-.069	.164	.676
	+10 -5	-.249	.165	.131
	+5 -10	.218	.164	.184
	No Feedback	.242	.164	.141
	No Score	.032	.163	.844
+10 - 10	+10 -5	-.181	.164	.273
	+5 -10	.286	.164	.080
	No Feedback	.311	.164	.059
	No Score	.101	.162	.536
+10 -5	+5 -10	.467*	.164	.005
	No Feedback	.491*	.165	.003
	No Score	.281	.163	.085
+5 - 10	No Feedback	.024	.164	.883
	No Score	-.186	.162	.252
No Feedback	No Score	-.21	.163	.197

Table 7. Feedback, Autonomy, and Task Difficulty Conditions in Experiment 2

Feedback Condition	Autonomy Condition	Math Task Difficulty	Sample Size
Positive	No choice	Easy	82
Positive	No choice	Difficult	83
Negative	No choice	Easy	99
Negative	No choice	Difficult	86
Positive	Free choice	--	90
Negative	Free choice	--	91

Table 8. Summary Table of One-Way MANOVA for Feedback Condition on Expectancies and Values in Task 1 and Task 2, Experiment 2

Task	Source	Dependent Variable	Sum of Squares	df	F	p	Partial η2
Task 1	Feedback Condition	Positive Value	5.341	1	6.147	.013	.012
		Perceived Costs	56.318	1	46.416	<.001	.081
		Expectancies	29.823	1	25.344	<.001	.046
	Error	Positive Value	458.793	528			
		Perceived Costs	64.645	528			
		Expectancies	621.313	528			
Task 2	Feedback Condition	Positive Value	3.988	1	3.796	.052	.007
		Perceived Costs	19.286	1	15.713	<.001	.029
		Expectancies	18.406	1	14.153	<.001	.026
	Choice Condition	Positive Value	.127	1	.121	.728	.000
		Perceived Costs	5.594	1	4.558	.033	.009
		Expectancies	6.523	1	5.016	.026	.009
	Task Difficulty	Positive Value	.281	1	.268	.605	.001
		Perceived Costs	.022	1	.018	.893	.000
		Expectancies	1.516	1	1.166	.281	.002
	Feedback Condition x Choice Condition	Positive Value	.158	1	.150	.698	.000
		Perceived Costs	3.073	1	2.504	.114	.005
		Expectancies	2.219	1	1.706	.192	.003
	Feedback Condition x Task Difficulty	Positive Value	.091	1	.087	.769	.000
		Perceived Costs	.141	1	.115	.735	.000
		Expectancies	.093	1	.071	.789	.000
	Choice Condition x Task Difficulty	Positive Value	.935	1	.890	.346	.002
		Perceived Costs	8.649	1	7.047	.008	.013
		Expectancies	15.389	1	11.833	.001	.022
	Feedback Condition x Choice Condition x Task Difficulty	Positive Value	1.667	1	1.587	.208	.003
		Perceived Costs	8.333	1	6.790	.009	.013
		Expectancies	1.557	1	1.197	.274	.002
Error		Positive Value	549.402	523			
		Perceived Costs	641.928	523			
		Expectancies	68.144	523			

Table 9. Expectancy Value Measures, Task 1, Experiment 2

Feedback Condition	Positive Value	Cost	Expectancies
Negative	4.25 (.06)	2.74 (.07)	4.14 (.07)
Positive	4.45 (.06)	2.09 (.07)	4.62 (.07)

Note: Values displayed are estimated marginal means across all participants in each condition, with the Standard Errors depicted in parentheses.

Table 10. Number of Free-Choice Participants in the Positive or Negative Feedback Condition Who Chose the Easier or More Difficult Task for Task 2

Feedback Condition	Easy	Difficult	Total
Negative	68	23	91
Positive	68	22	90

Table 11. Regression Coefficients for Choice of Difficulty, Experiment 2

Predictor	*B*	*S.E.*	Wald χ^2	*p*	Odds Ratio
Feedback	-.427	.391	1.193	.275	1.532
Task 1 Perceived Performance	.008	.010	.727	.394	1.008
Task 1 Positive Task Value	-.044	.035	1.559	.212	.769
Task 1 Cost	-.116	.074	2.444	.118	.706
Task 1 Expectancies	.273	.120	5.193	.023	1.728
Constant	-2.056	1.560	1.738	.187	.128

Table 12. Univariate ANOVA of the Effects of Feedback Condition, Choice Condition, and Task Difficulty on Math Task 2 Performance, and Perceived Performance

Dependent Measure	Predictor	Sum of Squares	df	Mean Square	F	p	Partial η2
Performance							
	Intercept	244.04	1	244.040	13842.437	<.001	.964
	Feedback Condition	.054	1	.054	3.083	.080	.006
	Choice Condition	.046	1	.046	2.614	.107	.005
	Task Difficulty	.356	1	.356	2.203	<.001	.037
	Feedback Condition x Choice Condition	.014	1	.014	.769	.381	.001
	Feedback Condition x Task Difficulty	.002	1	.002	.105	.746	.000
	Choice Condition x Task Difficulty	.265	1	.265	15.006	<.001	.028
	Feedback Condition x Choice Condition x Task Difficulty	.001	1	.001	.053	.818	.000
	Error	9.22	523	.018			
	Total	341.701	531				
Perceived Performance							
	Intercept	1621465.300	1	1621465.3	2543.116	<.001	.829
	Feedback Condition	29108.232	1	29108.232	45.654	<.001	.080
	Choice Condition	4697.613	1	4697.613	7.368	.007	.014
	Task Difficulty	4685.432	1	4685.432	7.349	.007	.014
	Feedback Condition x Choice Condition	1063.841	1	1063.841	1.669	.197	.003
	Feedback Condition x Task Difficulty	115.338	1	115.338	.181	.671	.000
	Choice Condition x Task Difficulty	7428.617	1	7428.617	11.651	.001	.022
	Feedback Condition x Choice Condition x Task Difficulty	608.965	1	608.965	.955	.329	.002
	Error	333459.546	523	637.59			
	Total	2518825	531				
Metacognitive Accuracy							
	Intercept	8.341	1	8.341	222.909	<.001	8.341
	Feedback Condition	2.170	1	2.170	57.983	<.001	2.170
	Choice Condition	.222	1	.222	5.922	.015	.222
	Task Difficulty	.008	1	.008	.206	.650	.008
	Feedback Condition x Choice Condition	.196	1	.196	5.234	.023	.196
	Feedback Condition x Task Difficulty	.023	1	.023	.605	.437	.023
	Choice Condition x Task Difficulty	.121	1	.121	3.228	.073	.121
	Feedback Condition x Choice Condition x Task Difficulty	.077	1	.077	2.056	.152	.077
	Error	19.570	523	.037			19.570
	Total	37.492	531				37.492

Table 13. Differences in Performance Outcomes by Choice Condition and Task Difficulty, Experiment 2

Dependent Variable			Mean Difference	SE	p
Task 2 Performance	No Choice Difficult	No Choice Easy	-.112	.014	<.001
	No Choice Difficult	Free Choice Difficult	-.074	.022	.001
	No Choice Easy	Free Choice Easy	.030	.015	.048
	Free Choice Easy	Free Choice Difficult	-.009	.023	.699
Task 2 Perceived Performance	No Choice Difficult	No Choice Easy	-14.966	2.880	<.001
	No Choice Difficult	Free Choice Difficult	-15.760	4.517	.001
	No Choice Easy	Free Choice Easy	.888	3.056	.772
	Free Choice Easy	Free Choice Difficult	1.682	4.631	.717
Metacognitive Accuracy	No Choice Difficult	No Choice Easy	-.037	.023	.099
	No Choice Difficult	Free Choice Difficult	-.084	.036	.018
	No Choice Easy	Free Choice Easy	.026	.036	.482
	Free Choice Easy	Free Choice Difficult	.026	.036	.482

Table 14. Perceived Performance, Actual Performance and Metacognitive Accuracy (Perceived – Actual Performance) by Choice Condition and Task 2 Difficulty

Choice	Task Difficulty	Perceived	Actual	Metacognitive Accuracy
No Choice	Easy	67.98 (1.97)	83.65 (.84)	-15.67 (1.59)
	Difficult	53.02 (2.23)	72.43 (1.16)	-19.41 (1.71)
Free Choice	Easy	67.10 (2.19)	8.66 (1.13)	-13.57 (1.77)
	Difficult	68.78 (3.62)	79.78 (2.05)	-11.00 (2.46)

Note: Values displayed are the means with standard errors depicted in parentheses.

Table 15. Metacognitive Accuracy (Perceived – Actual Performance) by Feedback and Choice Condition, Experiment 2

Feedback	Choice	Metacognitive Accuracy
Negative	No Choice	-26.73 (1.02)
	Free Choice	-17.47 (.90)
Positive	No Choice	-7.31 (.63)
	Free Choice	-7.03 (.72)

Note: Values displayed are participant means with standard errors depicted in parentheses.

Table 16. Expectancy Value Measures for Task 2 by Feedback, Choice, and Difficulty Conditions

Feedback	Choice	Difficulty	Positive Value	Cost	Expectancies
Negative	No Choice	Easy	4.30 (.10)	2.50 (.11)	4.22 (.12)
		Difficult	4.04 (.11)	3.07 (.12)	3.85 (.12)
	Free Choice	Easy	4.14 (.12)	2.67 (.13)	4.10 (.14)
		Difficult	4.35 (.21)	2.06 (.23)	4.78 (.24)
Positive	No Choice	Easy	4.44 (.11)	2.13 (.12)	4.71 (.13)
		Difficult	4.39 (.11)	2.19 (.12)	4.53 (.13)
	Free Choice	Easy	4.47 (.12)	2.07 (.13)	4.54 (.14)
		Difficult	4.35 (.22)	2.12 (.24)	4.91 (.24)

Note: Values displayed are the estimated marginal means with standard errors depicted in parentheses.

Table 17. ANOVAS for Cost Split by Feedback Condition

Feedback Condition	Predictor	Sum of Squares	df	Mean Square	F	p	Partial η2
Negative							
	Intercept	1325.956	1	1325.956	897.493	<.001	.767
	Choice Condition	8.718	1	8.718	5.901	.016	.021
	Task Difficulty	.027	1	.027	.018	.894	.000
	Choice Condition x Task Difficulty	17.459	1	17.459	11.817	.001	.042
	Error	401.853	272	1.477			
	Total	241.889	276				
Positive							
	Intercept	858.742	1	858.742	897.818	<.001	.782
	Choice Condition	.182	1	.182	.191	.663	.001
	Task Difficulty	.134	1	.134	.140	.708	.001
	Choice Condition x Task Difficulty	.001	1	.001	.001	.969	.000
	Error	24.076	251	.956			
	Total	1401.111	255				

APPENDIX 2: FIGURES

Figure 1. Screenshot of Robot Sorter

Note. During the task, a small robot is shown with a mathematical statement in a speech bubble over its head. The robot moves along a conveyer belt, and the player selects whether the robot should continue to the upper or lower belt. The directional choice indicates whether the mathematics statement shown above the robot's head is in agreement or disagreement with the mathematics claim shown in the lower left-hand corner. Example statements and claims are included in the Supplementary Materials. During the game, players made 30 agree/disagree decisions for mathematics items involving linear functions and algebra.

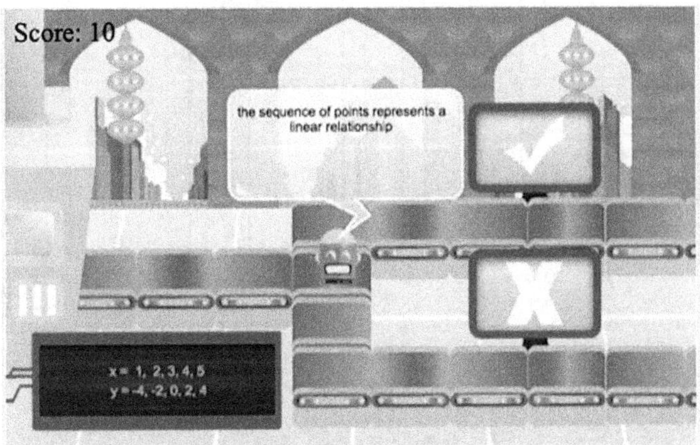

Figure 2. Proportion Correct (Top) and Point Total (Bottom) for Each Point-based Feedback Condition in Experiment 1. Error bars depict standard error of the mean.

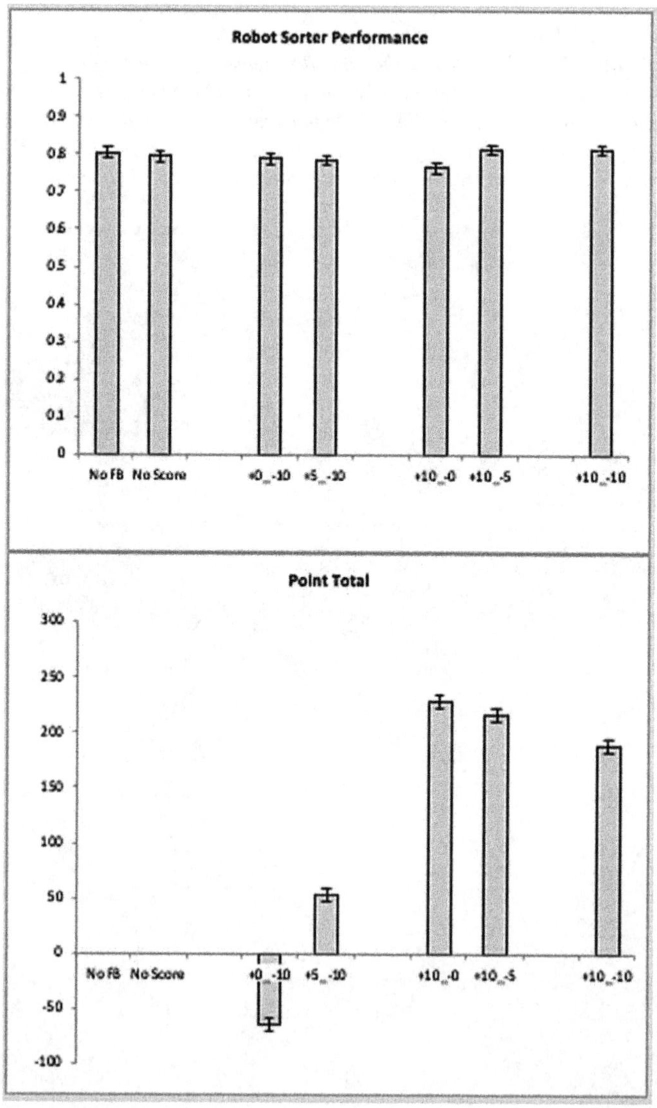

Figure 3. Experiment 2 Design.

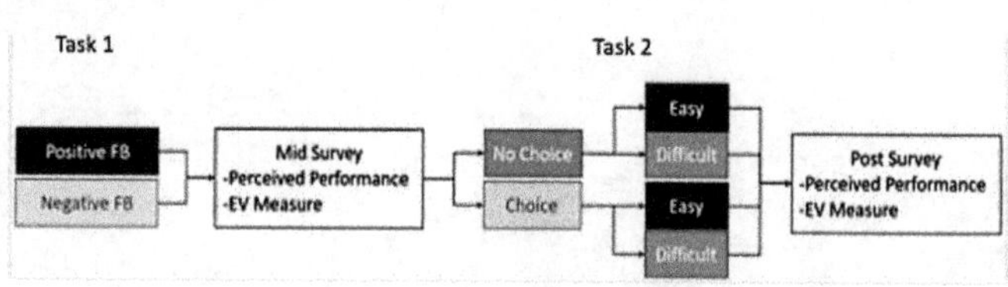

Figure 4. Comparison of Actual and Perceived Performance on Task 1 by Feedback Condition in Experiment 2. Error Bars Depict Standard Error of the Mean.

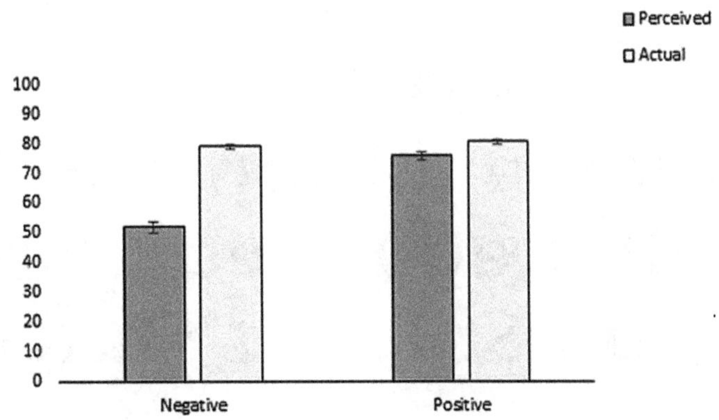

Figure 5. Path Analysis Diagram.

*Note: Dashed lines indicated indirect effects, solid lines are direct effects. Values displayed are the standardized path coefficients, S.E. in parentheses, * p < .05, ** p < .01.*

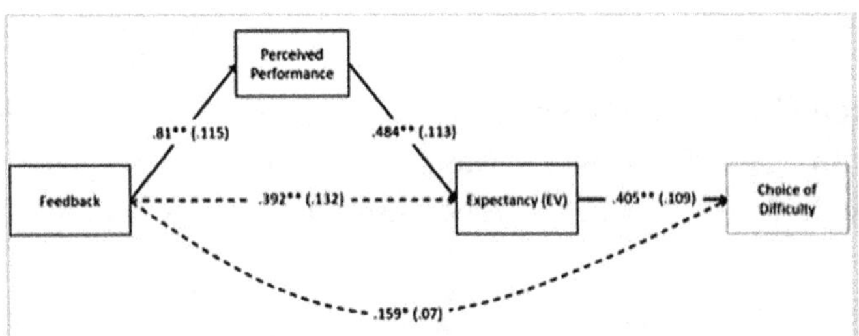

Chapter 5
The Implementation and Impact of a Self-Regulated Learning Survey on Student Outcomes

Marcy Baughman
Macmillan Learning, USA

Guido G. Gatti
Macmillan Learning, USA

Kelly Boden
Macmillan Learning, USA

ABSTRACT

The purpose of this chapter is to describe the development and impact of a digital tool that can be used to support students' self-regulated learning and metacognitive skills. The nature of online courses can restrict an instructor's ability to interact directly with their students. Digital courseware can help instructors connect with and support their online students in a different manner. A series of surveys were developed and digitally deployed to help students plan, monitor, and evaluate their progress toward goals. A multi-semester research study found that students enrolled in online classes who completed three or more surveys during the semester experienced better course performance compared to students who chose not to complete the surveys. Students who chose to complete less than three surveys performed comparably to their non-user peers. Students enrolled in hybrid or face-to-face classes tended to outperform their peers in online courses regardless of how many surveys they had completed.

INTRODUCTION

The educational "classroom" has shifted continuously over the past several decades. Before the introduction of educational technology in the classroom, instruction primarily took place in a physical classroom with a focus on specific learning objectives. Direct instruction was a popular teaching pedagogy, and

DOI: 10.4018/978-1-6684-6500-4.ch005

the concept of holistic instruction was less known. The introduction of educational technology in the classroom offered greater opportunities for educational pedagogies to evolve (Garrison & Vaughan, 2008; Rogers, 2004).

Incorporating technology into a higher education course has been found to increase engagement (Chiu, 2021), intrinsic motivation (Alamri et al., 2020), as well as competence and relatedness (Bombaerts & Nickel, 2017). Technology also enables access to instructional content outside the classroom environment, facilitating fully online and hybrid instruction. One of the benefits of online courses is the *potential* for greater educational access and equity across students (Iyer et al., 2022; Lambert, 2020; Tate & Warschauer, 2022). However, the nature of online courses can also restrict an instructor's ability to interact directly with their students in order to identify gaps in knowledge or skills, opportunities for growth, and thus the ability to personalize instruction (Wright, 2014). This has opened an opportunity for using digital courseware to help instructors connect with, understand, and support their online students in a different manner by providing both cognitive and non-cognitive support.

To facilitate this type of instructor to student interaction and support, a courseware research team developed and tested an online resource aimed at increasing students' self-regulated learning skills, particularly their metacognition. Metacognition represents an awareness of one's own knowledge. When students practice metacognition, they are able to monitor and control their thinking processes (Meichenbaum, 1985; Nelson & Naren, 1990). Being metacognitive can help students self-regulate their own learning more effectively by performing activities like setting goals, using appropriate strategies, retrieving related knowledge, and self-regulating their own learning behavior. The developed online resource not only allowed students to think metacognitively, but it also allowed instructors to better understand students' goals, backgrounds, and learning strategies in order to provide needed instructional support.

The authors begin by giving a brief overview of self-regulated learning and metacognition as these are the foundational theories used to develop the resources. Then, the authors describe interventions and methods that have been identified as successful in improving students' metacognition within previous research. Finally, the authors describe the current resource's process of development before presenting results for how these resources improved student outcomes.

BACKGROUND

Self-Regulated Learning and Metacognition

In order to be successful in college courses, students need to adapt their problem-solving behaviors to different academic tasks, environments, and feedback. This ability has been referred to as self-regulated learning (SRL) and includes a set of interrelated cognitive and motivational skills that control learning (Boekaerts & Corno, 2005; Zimmerman & Schunk, 2001, 2018). In order to be a self-regulated learner, a student must engage in multiple processes including setting learning goals, attending and engaging in instruction, use effective strategies to store needed information, be able to retrieve needed information, establish and maintain a productive study environment, use available resources effectively, monitor performance and learning, manage time, evaluate and reflect on learning and performance outcomes, and seek help and resources when needed (Schunk & Ertmer, 2000). This requires cognitive strategies, metacognitive skills, and motivation to interact with one another in determining learning outcomes.

Metacognition is our thinking about our own thinking. It is our knowledge and self-awareness of our own cognitive processes and behaviors (Dinsmore et al., 2008; Nelson & Naren, 1990). Metacognition requires students to engage in both monitoring and control during learning in order to reflect on their cognitive processes and knowledge, and select appropriate actions/strategies (Nelson & Naren, 1990). Metacognition has been theorized to include three basic skills/phases during learning: planning, monitoring, and evaluation (Zimmerman & Campillo, 2003). Planning occurs when the learner sets goals for the task, identifies the task components and critical features, and plans strategies accordingly. Monitoring occurs as the learner tracks their current state during the task, monitoring their progress towards their goals. Evaluating occurs when the learner assesses their solutions and whether their goals have been satisfied, reviewing the strategies used and making adjustments as needed. This is a cyclical process that, depending on the given learning task, can cycle through all phases multiple times, adjusting along the way. Advanced metacognitive learners are able to self-regulate, sustaining their self-awareness and engagement throughout the cycle while building their knowledge. Many college students struggle with this sustained self-awareness and engagement, particularly in today's online learning environments (Winters et al., 2008).

This lack of self-awareness can lead to misjudgments of knowledge. Previous research has found students are frequently inaccurate in their judgments of their own learning, often being overconfident in their accuracy on a task or knowledge of a topic (Schraw, 2009; Valdez, 2013). This inaccuracy, often referred to as metacognitive monitoring accuracy, has been found to be negatively related to academic achievement outcomes including exam performance and course grades (Nietfeld, 2005; Valdez, 2013). Furthermore, beyond simply being inaccurate in their monitoring accuracy, students often don't select appropriate study strategies for a given task or their current knowledge of a topic. For example, students often opt to reread class materials and cram studying right before an exam, which has been shown to be ineffective, rather than employing more successful strategies (i.e., self-testing) over spaced study sessions (Delaney et al., 2010).

Self-Regulated Learning Interventions

Multiple interventions have been implemented previously, all aimed at increasing students' self-regulated learning and metacognitive skills. Some interventions have tried to prompt students to think metacognitively *during* learning (e.g., Aleven & Koedinger, 2002; Zepeda et al., 2015), others have tried to directly instruct students on self-regulated learning (SRL) and metacognitive strategies (Bernacki et al., 2020; Patterson et al., 2014), while others have had students reflect on their own learning and strategy use *after* learning (e.g., Broadbent, 2020; Stanton et al., 2015). For the purposes of this chapter, the researchers will focus on interventions that directly instruct on SRL and metacognition, as well as have students reflect, after learning.

Direct instruction interventions have been incorporated into content-area courses (i.e., intro biology), as well as their own stand-alone courses (Bernacki et al., 2020; Cogliano et al., 2020; Hudesman et al., 2013; Patterson et al., 2014). As such, there are variations in the length and depth of information included across direct instruction interventions. However, directly instructing students on specific strategies (i.e., retrieval practice) and their associated benefits are common practice across these types of interventions. Self-reflection interventions have utilized surveys, typically given right before or after an exam, which give a mix of likert scale and open-ended questions that have students reflect on study strategies, goals, and future changes (e.g., Colthorpe et al., 2015). Another common type of self-reflection intervention are exam wrappers, which are always given after an exam and include similar questions as survey interventions, but also have students go through a graded exam, reflecting on possible missteps and improvements for future exams (e.g., Carpenter et al., 2020). Finally, another more intensive type of self-reflection intervention are daily diaries, which are not necessarily tied to an exam but give similar questions as the surveys but are given at least once a day over the course of a week or two (e.g., Dorrenbacher & Perels, 2016).

All of the above intervention types have been related to positive student outcomes including exam performance, course grade, GPA, college enrollment, graduation, as well as self-reported metacognition (Dinsmore et al., 2008; Donker et al., 2014; Ellis et al., 2014; Theobald, 2021; Zepeda et al., 2015). As such, a resource that includes both direct instruction on self-regulated learning and metacognitive strategies and their benefits, as well as opportunities to reflect on previous and future learning and strategy use, appears to have promising potential for positively impacting students' learning outcomes. Furthermore, providing this information to instructors allows them to better understand their students' goals and strategy use in order to better connect with and support students.

Current Work

Goal Setting and Reflection Surveys Description

To help support students' self-regulated learning and metacognitive skills within an online learning environment, our research team developed a self-regulated learning tool called Goal Setting and Reflection Surveys (called Surveys hereafter). The Surveys were incorporated into a digital full course solution called Achieve. The Surveys incorporated support and instruction for the three phases of metacognition: planning (goal setting & strategic planning), monitoring (self-instruction, attention focusing, & help-seeking), and evaluating (self-evaluation & causal attribution).

The Surveys consist of five surveys to support self-regulated learning. At the beginning of the semester, an introductory survey asks students to: consider their goals for the class, to think about how they plan to manage their time, and to identify learning strategies they plan to use. Each strategy category includes a short description of what it is, and why it's beneficial before students select the strategies they plan to use. For example, one section of strategies is under the category of "Spacing" and includes the following description:

"Learning happens over time, not all at once. Research has shown memory benefits from spacing studying/review sessions over time rather than trying to "cram" right before a test. Our brains take time to consolidate information into long-term memory and therefore we're better able to recall information and concepts if we learn them in multiple, spread-out sessions."

Questions are a blend of multiple choice and a few short-written responses. Instructors can learn about students' majors, goals for the course, background information, and what they hope to learn from the class. It can also act as a baseline to measure student progress.

Four checkpoint surveys then act as progress checks throughout the semester. Each checkpoint survey includes questions to: encourage students to reflect on the strategies they are using and their effectiveness, support making informed decisions about changes to make, and to measure their progress toward goals.

Instructors can access a report of Survey responses that provides insight into how their class is doing beyond their grades and gives insight into specific areas where students may be struggling so that instruction can be remediated, or interventions prescribed. The reports are not prescriptive, instead instructors choose how to use the information provided in the reports.

METHODOLOGY

Macmillan Learning funded a series of research studies, across semesters, to examine the impact of using the Surveys on student course performance. Our theory, given previous research indicating self-reflection interventions were positively related to course grade, was that usage of the Surveys would improve student course performance. The studies began in fall 2019 and were repeated the subsequent four semesters with different cohorts of instructors and/or students. The authors of this report were also the researchers conducting these studies.

The Surveys were still in beta format for the fall 2019 and spring 2020 semesters and usage was very low. However, these semesters are included in the overall analyses for two reasons; the low usage during these semesters enabled the researchers to contrast usage compared to non-usage, and this study allowed natural variation of implementation. The natural variation of implementation meant that the Surveys were available, and instructors made their own choices about whether to use or not, and also how many Surveys to implement if they chose to use them.

At the conception of the research studies, the researchers were not focused on comparing the outcomes of students enrolled in online courses compared to face-to-face courses. During the first semester of research (fall 2019), nearly all of the study participants were enrolled in face-to-face courses. When the COVID 19 pandemic occurred in spring 2020, all study participants had to abruptly transition to online classes in March 2020. The majority of study participants began the spring 2020 semester in face-to-face classes. The researchers had to minimize data collection events within that semester in response to instructor and student feedback that they were overwhelmed with transitioning so quickly from face-to-face to virtual courses. In addition, many instructors reported that they were not implementing their "typical" course for the remainder of the spring 2020 semester as they navigated trying to complete the disrupted semester. Ultimately, the researchers were not able to collect any data beyond March 2020 for more than half of the study sample. Data that was available on Survey usage from the beginning of the spring 2020 semester is included in the overall analyses of usage.

However, an opportunity to conduct a natural experiment arose from the COVID 19 pandemic. The researchers realized there were two semesters with instruction exclusively online (fall 2020 and spring 2021) and two semesters (fall 2021 and spring 2022) with less than half of the instruction exclusively online as students returned to campus. The majority of study participants in fall 2020 and spring 2021 were enrolled in either completely online or hybrid courses. While the researchers were not able to randomize the modality of instruction, it was possible to compare the outcomes between these two semester pairs.

The researchers first present the results of the entire study sample across semesters, and then explore the results by semester to examine differences in student outcomes by instructional modality.

Table 1. Number of Institutions, Instructors and Courses by Semester

Semester	Institutions	Instructors	Courses
Fall 2019	49	58	81
Spring 2020**	32	42	44
Fall 2020	26	29	68
Spring 2021*	16	16	27
Fall 2021	38	45	72
Total Unique	115	136	292

Note. Some instructors and institutions participated in multiple semesters of the study.

* Denotes only Psychology courses participated in this semester of the study.

** The pandemic occurred mid-spring 2020 semester and the majority of end of semester data collection was lost due to instructor and student disruption of normal educational experience.

Table 2. Number of Two Year/Four Year, Public/Private Institutions, by Semester and State

Semester	2yr Public	4yr Public	4yr Private	Number of States
Fall 2019	36	28	17	18
Spring 2020	15	17	12	14
Fall 2020	42	25	1	18
Spring 2021	14	9	4	13 + Canada
Fall 2021	8	49	15	22 + Canada
Total	115	128	49	32 + Canada

Study Sample

Data collection methods were replicated across each study, enabling the sample to be combined across semesters. The final study sample included 136 unique instructors, teaching 292 courses, in eight subject areas (chemistry, biochemistry, biology, calculus, precalculus, psychology, economics, English), from

Table 3. Course Size by Semester

Semester	Course Size		
	Small	Medium	Large
Fall 2019	22	49	6
Spring 2020**	15	27	1
Fall 2020	18	44	6
Spring 2021*	5	19	3
Fall 2021	14	48	10
Total	74	192	26

Note: Small courses have 20 or fewer students, while large courses have 100 or more students.

Table 4. Institution Size by Semester

Semester	Institution Size		
	Small	Medium	Large
Fall 2019	24	16	41
Spring 2020**	10	16	18
Fall 2020	13	9	46
Spring 2021*	0	5	22
Fall 2021	1	15	56
Total	48	61	183

Note: Small institutions have less than 5,000 students, while large institutions have more than 15,000 students.

115 institutions, in 32 different states and Canada. Tables one through five provide a summary of the final sample across semesters, including institution type, location and size, as well as course size.

The study sample was composed of a diverse sample of instructors, institutions, and disciplines. This enabled the Surveys to be tested with students representing different sociodemographic characteristics. Table six describes the sociodemographic characteristics of the study sample. The study sample was comprised of students who were; 53% White, 22% first in their families to go to college, 59% female, 29% not college ready (i.e., defined by SAT/ACT math and reading scores), 65% eligible for financial aid, and 69% had high a school GPA higher than 3.5

Study Methods

Prior to the start of the semester, participating instructors were given a short description of the Surveys, perceived benefits of usage, guidance on where to locate the Surveys in the Achieve program, and how to assign them to students. This occurred during a 45-minute overview of the Achieve program provided by a curriculum consultant. The consultant provided a recommended implementation path of assigning the Introductory Survey during the first couple weeks of their course, and then assigning Checkpoint surveys at natural intervals throughout the remainder of the semester. Although the consultant encouraged

Table 5. Number and Percent of Students by Discipline

Discipline	Total Number of Students	% of Sample
Chemistry	1127	15.60
Biochemistry	511	7.07
Biology	509	7.04
Precalc/Calculus	884	12.24
Psychology	2098	29.04
Economics	1301	18.01
English	795	11.00
Total	7225	100.00

Note: For 404 of the students the research team was unsure of the exact discipline.

Table 6. Sociodemographic Characteristics of Participants at Baseline

Characteristic	n	% of Respondents
Race		
White	3223	52.98
Non-White and Not Asian	2757	45.32
Other	103	1.69
First Generation College		
First Generation in College	1592	24.62
Not First Generation in College	4875	78.32
Gender		
Male	2196	41.21
Female	3133	58.79
College Ready		
College Ready	3578	70.87
Not College Ready	1471	29.13
Eligible for Financial Aid		
Eligible	3456	64.93
Not Eligible	1867	35.07
High School GPA		
GPA less than 3.5	2073	30.80
GPA greater or equal to 3.5	4657	69.20

Note: College ready students score above 480 SAT or 18 ACT in Reading and Writing, as well as also, scoring above 530 SAT or 22 ACT in Math.

instructors to try using the Surveys, use of the Surveys was not required, and implementation choices varied by instructor.

Throughout the semester, instructors made independent decisions about how many Surveys to assign, if any, and when to assign them to their students. In addition, instructors chose to assign the Surveys to students for credit or without credit. Ultimately, students chose to complete the Surveys or not. This meant that usage of the Surveys varied within the classrooms as well as across classrooms. The use and cadence of the Surveys was documented to better understand the potential impact of implementation variation.

Based on interviews with instructors, the main reasons the surveys were not assigned were:

1. Instructors did not plan their courses to include the surveys because they did not know enough about the surveys until later, or
2. They felt their own methods adequately supplied them the information needed for their purposes.

Student focus group feedback revealed that:

1. Many students will not seek out or attempt things that are not assigned as part of the course grade, and

2. A portion of the students already felt they knew what they needed to do, to be successful in the course, and did not need the surveys.

Students participating in the research study were asked to review an informed consent document at the beginning of the semester. Students who agreed to participate in the study gave permission for their instructors to share their course performance data and gave researchers permission to access their Survey usage data. Consenting students also completed two surveys (beginning and end of semester) to share sociodemographic information. During the fall 2021 semester, the student surveys also asked students to share their perceptions of the quality and utility of the Surveys.

Analysis

Complex statistical modeling was used to isolate the impact of the Surveys on student course performance. A general linear model was employed to statistically test group mean difference, and a consistent nested robust/empirical sandwich estimator was used to calculate standard errors for group means. A popular commercial statistical software suite was used to analyze the data.

In the model, several factors acted to control for differences between courses and students.

The factors were:

- course mean grade (i.e., akin to a random intercept for course),
- student college readiness (i.e., high school grade point average, SAT/ACT scores),
- student financial aid eligibility,
- student gender,
- student race/ethnicity,
- course enrollment total,
- number of course Achieve assignments assigned.
- and student number of course Achieve assignments completed.

It should be noted that the student demographic information (i.e., college readiness, gender, race/ethnicity, financial aid eligibility) are exogenous covariates. Exogenous covariates are not affected by the study treatment, in this case the Surveys. This methodology enables pre-existing differences between students to be made equal through a statistical model. Of particular note are the variables for college readiness and/or prior academic performance factors (i.e., high school grade point average, SAT/ACT scores). These variables are important because they, to the extent possible, equate students on their prior achievement and prowess as students. Essentially quelling the alternative hypothesis that better course grades seen in groups completing more surveys are due, at least in part, to 'better' students completing more surveys.

In addition, because grade percent is non-normal (i.e., bounded and negatively/lower tailed skewed with half the scores between 80% to 100%) and students' grades are nested in course, the researchers used robust asymptotically consistent standard errors (i.e., H3 sandwich estimator). The H3 formulation was chosen because it tends to be robust to the following:

- non-normal percent scores,
- liberal statistical tests due to nesting of students in courses,

- influential cases (outliers),
- unequal group variances (heteroscedasticity).

RESULTS

Figure one shows student course performance (in percent points earned) by the number of Surveys completed. Course performance was used as the outcome measure for two reasons, first it is important to both the instructor and student, and second, the surveys are expected to positively impact students' approach to the course as a whole. A total of 2,529 students were in a class that had at least one Survey assigned by their instructor during the semester.

The height of the bars in figure one indicates the increase in course performance relative to the students that did not complete any Surveys assigned to them (n = 326). The findings indicate that students who completed two or more Surveys tend to perform better in their courses compared to students in their courses who do not complete any Surveys, as well as students who complete only one Survey. This finding aligns with the Survey developer's theory during the development of the Surveys that students must not only set their goals (plan), but also monitor and evaluate their progress toward their goals in order for the Surveys to be successful. Students only completing one Survey - which tends to focus on goal-setting - are not achieving the same level of course performance compared to their peers who complete additional surveys to monitor and evaluate their progress toward their goals.

There is also a generally positive linear trend indicating that as the number of Surveys completed increases, so does course performance. The exception is for students who complete four Surveys - their course performance was lower than students who completed three Surveys, but still higher than students who did not complete any Surveys. While the researchers are unsure why there is a dip in performance for students completing four Surveys, the trend generally reinforces that students become more skilled in monitoring their progress toward their goals as they complete more Surveys and undertake the appropriate activities to meet their goals.

Further examination of the findings suggest that students achieve greater benefits when completing three or more Surveys. In terms of practical significance, a six percent increase in course performance represents slightly more than half a letter grade increase for the course. This finding also suggests an ideal implementation path is to assign three to five Surveys for instructors hoping to maximize student benefits.

Across the semesters, there were also 5,100 students in courses where instructors did not assign any of the Surveys. These students performed at a level between those students completing one or two Surveys, and 2.0 to 5.6 points lower than students completing three to five Surveys. Again, monitoring and evaluation of goals seems to be a key activity to help students achieve maximum benefits of using Surveys.

Table seven shows the sample sizes and standard errors for the comparisons in figure one. The small standard errors indicate that, practically speaking, any orthogonal set of comparisons between bars would be statistically significant. Given that, instructors can consider what number of Surveys are practical for their course and when the Surveys should be assigned.

Comparison Analysis From Natural Experiment

As mentioned earlier, the COVID 19 pandemic occurred during the spring 2020 semester and completely changed the modality of instruction for study participants. Table eight presents the modality of

Figure 1. Students' Comparative (0 Surveys) Course Performance (In Percent Points Earned) By the Number of Surveys Completed

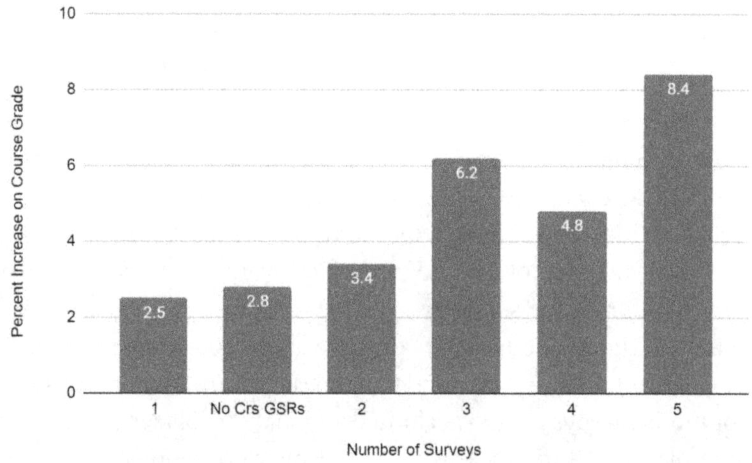

instruction by semester for student participants. During the height of the pandemic (spring 2020, fall 2020, and spring 2021), instruction became exclusively either fully virtual or a mixture of modalities (i.e., hybrid). Immediately prior to the pandemic (fall 2019 and beginning of spring 2020), instruction was almost exclusively face-to-face. As semesters have progressed further from the pandemic, the data is beginning to indicate that the change in modality of instruction may have a longer-term impact on how higher education courses are taught. Compared to the pre-pandemic environment of exclusively face-to-face instruction, the post-pandemic semesters (spring 2022 and fall 2022) have moved to around half of all students enrolled in a mix of fully virtual and hybrid modalities.

Implementation of Surveys

Implementation of the Surveys varied by semester. Table nine provides an overview of the number of surveys that were completed by semester. The Surveys were in beta phase during the fall 2019 and spring 2020 semesters. In fall 2019 the surveys were introduced to instructors through an Innovation

Table 7. Sample Sizes and Standard Errors for the Comparisons in Figure 1

Surveys	Number Courses Assigning	Number Students	Standard Error
5	11	458	0.5553
4	15	474	0.0999
3	17	502	0.1072
2	15	360	0.1065
1	18	409	0.1083
0	NA	326	NA
No Course Surveys	216	5,100	0.0468

Table 8. Instruction Modalities as a Percent of Study Instructors by Semester

Semester	Not Certain	Face-to-Face	Hybrid	Virtual
Fall 2019		86.67	0.00	13.33
Spring 2020	100	—	—	—
Fall 2020		0.00	34.48	65.52
Spring 2021		0.00	17.65	82.35
Fall 2021		53.19	31.91	14.89
Spring 2022	2.17	45.65	36.96	15.22
Fall 2022*	16.67	50.00	27.78	5.5

Note: Hybrid refers to a mixture of face-to-face and online course instruction.

*Outcome and usage data is not available for the fall 2022 semester yet but instructional modality data is included here to express the changing instructional environment.

area on the Achieve platform, but the instructors were not formally introduced or trained on how to use the Surveys during that semester. As a result, none of the instructors in the fall 2019 study discovered the Surveys on their own and used them.

At the beginning of the spring 2020 semester, the researchers chose to introduce the Surveys to the instructors during their training on the Achieve platform. The Surveys were still in beta phase, and still hosted in an Innovation section of the platform. Very few instructors chose to assign the Surveys, and when data was available during that semester, only 48 students completed a Survey.

Survey usage greatly increased beginning in the fall 2020 semester. At this time the Surveys were out of the beta phase and introduced as a regular resource in the Achieve platform. Students tended to complete either one or two Surveys when they were assigned by their instructors. During the spring 2021 semester, however, Survey usage increased with students beginning to complete more Surveys per semester. The average student now completed 3 - 5 Surveys instead of only one or two. This trend continued into the fall 2021 semester.

Results of Natural Experiment

The researchers treated a comparison of the fall 2020 and spring 2021 semester to the fall 2021 semester as a natural experiment. The fall 2020 and spring 2021 semesters constitute a cohort of survey users and non-users from fully virtual and hybrid courses. The fall 2021 semester is composed of a split of face-to-face and hybrid courses. Comparison of these two cohorts gives insight into how the surveys

Table 9. Number of Surveys Completed by Semester

Semester	No Course Use	1 Survey	2 Surveys	3-5 Surveys	No Surveys
Spring 2020	546	48	—	—	277
Fall 2020	1020	155	168	71	30
Spring 2021	193	56	43	415	13
Fall 2021	6	155	149	948	651

Note: Table does not include Fall 2019, with no survey use.

Figure 2. Students' Comparative (0 Surveys) Course Performance (In Percent Points Earned) By The Number of Surveys Completed By Semester

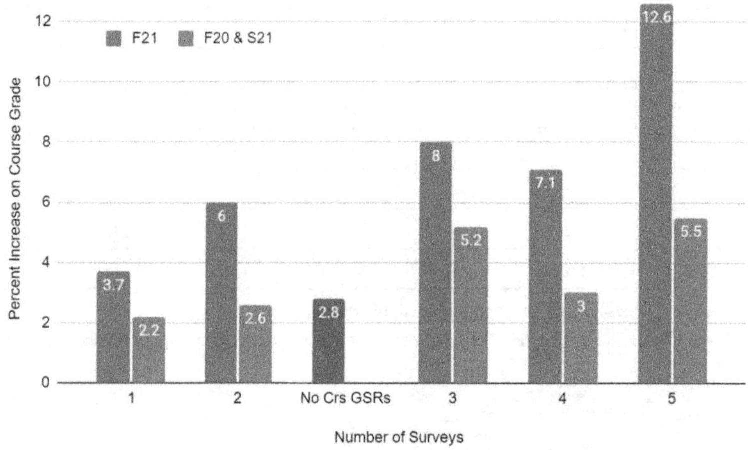

may benefit students under the two instruction modalities. Additionally, the fall 2019 and spring 2020 semesters serve as another natural comparison group composed of students in courses where instructors did not assign any of the Surveys, but also span pre-during-post pandemic time points.

Figure 2 shows the contrast in comparative student course performance by the number of Surveys completed. As with figure one, the height of the bars indicates the increase in course performance relative to the students that did not complete any Surveys assigned to them. Students enrolled in strictly online courses during the pandemic saw gains in course performance beyond non-users if they completed three or more Surveys. Students completing less than three Surveys performed comparably to their non-user peers. Students enrolled in a combination of face-to-face and hybrid courses tended to have greater gains in student performance regardless of the number of Surveys they completed. Students that completed just one Survey outperformed their peers who didn't complete any Surveys, and the gains increased as they completed more Surveys.

The results from the comparison analysis are preliminary and will benefit as additional semesters become available to understand if the trend in greater improvements when using Surveys in face-to-face and hybrid courses continues as more data is available for those cohorts. Another consideration is whether the instructional modality affects the performance associated with the Surveys, or if this is an isolated impact resulting from students just beginning to return to classrooms post-pandemic. It will be important to continue replicating the studies as students return to campuses to better understand if the instructional modality is the compelling factor, or if there is a combination of events associated with coming back from the pandemic.

Student Perceptions of Surveys

In addition to the relationship between Surveys completed and students' grades, results from the fall 2021 student surveys also indicated that students believed the Surveys helped them become better students. Fifty-eight percent of participating study students responded to the fall 2021 survey, with 780 students reporting they completed a Goal Setting and Reflection Survey. Table ten presents student responses to the

Table 10. Student Responses to Questions about Goal setting and Reflection Surveys

Survey Question	Agree or Strongly Agree	Neutral
I improved as a student this semester	75%	19%
Surveys valuable use of my time	62%	25%
Surveys helped me think about my goals/learning habits in/outside class	80%	15%
I learned something new about how I can manage my time, studying, or learning this semester.	79%	15%

Note: This table represents data from only the Fall 2021 semester.

survey questions. A majority of students felt the surveys were a valuable use of their time (62%), helped them establish goals and learning habits (80%), and taught them how to manage their time better (79%). Overall, the majority of students indicated they were satisfied with the quality and utility of the Surveys.

DISCUSSION

The shift to online learning has presented both advantages and disadvantages. One disadvantage is the decrease in instructor-to-student interaction. This limits the instructor's ability to identify strengths as well as gaps for their students in order to support and bolster knowledge and skills where needed. Self-regulated learning, including metacognitive skills, is pivotal to students' success. The ability to plan, monitor, and evaluate their learning and progress enables adaptive strategy use and help-seeking when needed. The current work was an attempt to bridge the gap between instructors and students in an online environment, while supporting and increasing students' self-regulated learning and metacognition skills. To this end, Macmillan Learning developed a series of surveys administered online to support the three phases of metacognition: planning (goal setting & strategic planning), monitoring (self-instruction, attention focusing, & help-seeking), and evaluating (self-evaluation & causal attribution).

Macmillan Learning funded a series of research studies, across five semesters (i.e., Fall 2019 thru Fall 2021), to examine the impact of using the Surveys on student course performance. Our theory, given previous research, was that usage of the Surveys would improve student course performance. The sample of students the research team was able to track and collect data on was large. It includes 136 unique instructors, teaching 292 courses, in eight subject areas (chemistry, biochemistry, biology, calculus, precalculus, psychology, economics, English), from 115 institutions, in 32 different states and Canada. Further, the students were diverse. The sample included students who were non-White or Asian (47%), first in their families to go to college (22%), not college ready (29%), eligible for financial aid (65%), and had a high school GPA lower than 3.5 (31%).

Overall, the findings from this study indicate that not only did students report they benefited from using the Surveys embedded within the Achieve digital platform, but they also showed a strong trend toward better course performance as they completed more of the Surveys. Furthermore, when examining students from courses that did not use the Surveys as a comparison group, students who completed the recommended three Surveys saw significant course performance benefits. The pandemic, starting during the study period, allowed for a large-scale natural experiment. The positive trend in students' grades increased both during the height of the pandemic and the semester immediately following. It will be interesting to see how the results hold for the semesters following the fall of 2021.

An additional benefit of the statistical model utilized was the inclusion of student demographic and college readiness information (particularly high school grade point average and SAT/ACT scores). Due to the inclusion of these variables and equating in the statistical models, the researchers believe the alternative hypothesis that better course grades seen in groups completing more surveys are due mainly to 'better' students completing more surveys, has been mitigated.

Students who completed the Surveys at regular intervals were given opportunities to reflect on their goals and strategies. This opportunity and exercise may have prompted students to engage in metacognitive monitoring and evaluation which led to a positive impact on their course performance. This replicates prior work implementing self-regulated learning, and metacognitive interventions aimed at directly instructing students on these skills/strategies (e.g., Bernacki et al., 2020), as well as having students reflect after learning (e.g., Stanton et al., 2015). The current work builds upon this prior work by including both opportunities for reflection and short, digestible direct instruction within the same resource. Furthermore, the current work not only examined how the intervention impacted student course performance, but also examined students' perceptions of the intervention.

Limitations

The current work used a convenience sample, and while the sample was large and diverse, included a comparison group, and variables were used as statistical controls for course differences and differences in students, it was not a true experiment with random assignment of the Surveys. Also, different instructors may value and emphasize self-regulated learning and metacognition in their instruction. This was not controlled for in the current work. Lastly, due to the pandemic, it is difficult to discern how much of the Surveys' impact on student performance is due to instructional modality and how much is an isolated impact resulting from students just beginning to return to classrooms post-pandemic. It will thus be important to continue replicating the studies into future semesters.

FUTURE RESEARCH DIRECTIONS

This area of study could certainly benefit from further research in several ways. Experimental studies, where possible, could test the impact of the Surveys and similar treatments by random assignment of students within the same course/instructor in order to rule out students' individual differences, as well as instructional differences. In combination with experimental studies, future research could benefit from complementary qualitative methods. Mixed methods studies would document instructional differences in promoting self-regulated learning and metacognition, then examine how these differences add or take away from the impact of the Surveys. As previously mentioned, the literature will also benefit from furthering the 'natural experiment' the pandemic allowed for by comparing results into future semesters as the post-pandemic world shapes instructional modalities and the instructional strategies around Self-regulated learning and metacognition.

Lastly, continued research into ideal online implementation of self-regulated learning and metacognition interventions would be beneficial. Interventions need to be accessible and perceived as useful to instructors and students. Interventions that are not accessible, or perceived as useful or relevant, even if impactful, will not be used and sadly have no impact.

ACKNOWLEDGMENT

This research was supported by Macmillan Learning.

REFERENCES

Alamri, H., Lowell, V., Watson, W., & Watson, S. L. (2020). Using personalized learning as an instructional approach to motivate learners in online higher education: Learner self-determination and intrinsic motivation. *Journal of Research on Technology in Education*, *52*(3), 322–352. doi:10.1080/15391523.2020.1728449

Aleven, V. A., & Koedinger, K. R. (2002). An effective metacognitive strategy: Learning by doing and explaining with a computer-based cognitive tutor. *Cognitive Science*, *26*(2), 147–179. doi:10.120715516709cog2602_1

Bernacki, M. L., Vosicka, L., & Utz, J. C. (2020). Can a brief, digital skill training intervention help undergraduates "learn to learn" and improve their STEM achievement? *Journal of Educational Psychology*, *112*(4), 765–781. doi:10.1037/edu0000405

Boekaerts, M., & Corno, L. (2005). Self-regulation in the classroom: A perspective on assessment and intervention. *Applied Psychology*, *54*(2), 199–231. doi:10.1111/j.1464-0597.2005.00205.x

Bombaerts, G., & Nickel, P. J. (2017, April). Feedback for relatedness and competence: Can feedback in blended learning contribute to optimal rigor, basic needs, and motivation? In *2017 IEEE global engineering education conference (EDUCON)* (pp. 1089-1092). doi:10.1109/EDUCON.2017.7942984

Broadbent, J., Panadero, E., Lodge, J. M., & Barba, P. D. (2020). Technologies to enhance self-regulated learning in online and computer-mediated learning environments. In M. J. Bishop, E. Boling, J. Elen, & V. Svihla (Eds.), *Handbook of research in educational communications and technology* (pp. 37–52). Springer. doi:10.1007/978-3-030-36119-8_3

Carpenter, J. P., Krutka, D. G., & Kimmons, R. (2020). # RemoteTeaching & #RemoteLearning: Educator tweeting during the COVID-19 pandemic. *Journal of Technology and Teacher Education*, *28*(2), 151–159. https://eric.ed.gov/?id=EJ1257425

Chiu, T. K. (2021). Digital support for student engagement in blended learning based on self-determination theory. *Computers in Human Behavior*, *124*, 1–10. doi:10.1016/j.chb.2021.106909

Cogliano, M., Bernacki, M. L., & Kardash, C. M. (2021). A metacognitive retrieval practice intervention to improve undergraduates' monitoring and control processes and use of performance feedback for classroom learning. *Journal of Educational Psychology*, *113*(7), 1421–1440. doi:10.1037/edu0000624

Colthorpe, K., Zimbardi, K., Ainscough, L., & Anderson, S. (2015). Know Thy Student! Combining Learning Analytics and Critical Reflections to Increase Understanding of Students' Self-Regulated Learning in an Authentic Setting. *Journal of Learning Analytics*, *2*(1), 134–155. doi:10.18608/jla.2015.21.7

Delaney, J. G., Johnson, A., Johnson, T. D., & Treslan, D. (2010). *Students' perceptions of effective teaching in higher education. Project Report.* Memorial University of Newfoundland. https://research.library.mun.ca/8370/

Dinsmore, D. L., Alexander, P. A., & Loughlin, S. M. (2008). Focusing the conceptual lens on metacognition, self-regulation, and self-regulated learning. *Educational Psychology Review*, *20*(4), 391–409. doi:10.100710648-008-9083-6

Donker, A. S., De Boer, H., Kostons, D., Van Ewijk, C. D., & van der Werf, M. P. (2014). Effectiveness of learning strategy instruction on academic performance: A meta-analysis. *Educational Research Review*, *11*, 1–26. doi:10.1016/j.edurev.2013.11.002

Dörrenbächer, L., & Perels, F. (2016). Self-regulated learning profiles in college students: Their relationship to achievement, personality, and the effectiveness of an intervention to foster self-regulated learning. *Learning and Individual Differences*, *51*, 229–241. doi:10.1016/j.lindif.2016.09.015

Ellis, J. (2014). *Preparing Future Professors: Highlighting the Importance of Graduate Student Professional Development Programs in Calculus Instruction.* North American Chapter of the International Group for the Psychology of Mathematics Education. https://files.eric.ed.gov/fulltext/ED599810.pdf

Garrison, D. R., & Kanuka, H. (2004). Blended learning: Uncovering its transformative potential in higher education. *The Internet and Higher Education*, *7*(2), 95–105. doi:10.1016/j.iheduc.2004.02.001

Hudesman, J., Crosby, S., Flugman, B., Issac, S., Everson, H., & Clay, D. B. (2013). Using formative assessment and metacognition to improve student achievement. *Journal of Developmental Education*, *37*(1), 2. doi:10.4324/9781315623856

Iyer, L. S., Bharadwaj, S., Shetty, S. H., Verma, V., & Devanathan, M. (2022). Advancing equity in digital classrooms: A personalized learning framework for higher education institutions. In *Socioeconomic Inclusion During an Era of Online Education* (pp. 225–245). IGI Global. doi:10.4018/978-1-6684-4364-4.ch011

Lambert, S. R. (2020). Do MOOCs contribute to student equity and social inclusion? A systematic review. *Computers & Education*, *145*, 103693. doi:10.1016/j.compedu.2019.103693

Meichenbaum, D. (1985). Metacognitive methods of instruction: Current status and future prospects. *Special Services in the Schools*, *3*(1-2), 23–32. doi:10.1300/J008v03n01_03

Nelson, T. O., & Narens, L. (1990). Metamemory: A theoretical framework and new findings. *Psychology of Learning and Motivation*, *26*, 125–173. doi:10.1016/S0079-7421(08)60053-5

Patterson, D. A., Waya, S. W., Ahuna, K. H., Tinnesz, C. G., & Vanzile-Tamsen, C. (2014). Using self-regulated learning methods to increase Native American college retention. *Journal of College Student Retention*, *16*(2), 219–237. doi:10.2190/CS.16.2.d

Rogers, G. (2004). History, learning technology and student achievement: Making the difference? *Active Learning in Higher Education*, *5*(3), 232–247. doi:10.1177/1469787404043811

Schraw, G. (2009). A conceptual analysis of five measures of metacognitive monitoring. *Metacognition and Learning*, *4*(1), 33–45. doi:10.100711409-008-9031-3

Schunk, D. H. (2008). Metacognition, self-regulation, and self-regulated learning: Research recommendations. *Educational Psychology Review*, *20*(4), 463–467. doi:10.100710648-008-9086-3

Schunk, D. H., & Ertmer, P. A. (2000). Self-regulation and academic learning: Self-efficacy enhancing interventions. In *Handbook of self-regulation* (pp. 631–649). Academic Press. doi:10.1016/B978-012109890-2/50048-2

Stanton, J. D., Neider, X. N., Gallegos, I. J., & Clark, N. C. (2015). Differences in metacognitive regulation in introductory biology students: When prompts are not enough. *CBE Life Sciences Education*, *14*(2), ar15. Advance online publication. doi:10.1187/cbe.14-08-0135 PMID:25976651

Tate, T., & Warschauer, M. (2022). Equity in online learning. *Educational Psychologist*, *57*(3), 192–206. doi:10.1080/00461520.2022.2062597

Theobald, M. (2021). Self-regulated learning training programs enhance university students' academic performance, self-regulated learning strategies, and motivation: A meta-analysis. *Contemporary Educational Psychology*, *66*, 101976. doi:10.1016/j.cedpsych.2021.101976

Valdez, A. (2013). Student metacognitive monitoring: Predicting test achievement from judgment accuracy. *International Journal of Higher Education*, *2*(2), 141–146. doi:10.5430/ijhe.v2n2p141

Wright, R. D. (Ed.). (2015). *Student-Teacher Interaction in Online Learning Environments*. IGI Global. doi:10.4018/978-1-4666-6461-6

Zepeda, C. D., Richey, J. E., Ronevich, P., & Nokes-Malach, T. J. (2015). Direct instruction of metacognition benefits adolescent science learning, transfer, and motivation: An in vivo study. *Journal of Educational Psychology*, *107*(4), 954–970. doi:10.1037/edu0000022

Zimmerman, B., & Campillo, M. (2003). Motivating Self-Regulated Problem Solvers. In J. Davidson & R. Sternberg (Eds.), *The Psychology of Problem Solving* (pp. 233–262). Cambridge University Press. doi:10.1017/CBO9780511615771.009

Zimmerman, B. J., & Schunk, D. H. (Eds.). (2001). *Self-regulated learning and academic achievement: Theoretical perspectives*. Routledge. https://www.routledge.com/Self-Regulated-Learning-and-Academic-Achievement-Theoretical-Perspectives/Zimmerman-Schunk/p/book/9780805835618

Zimmerman, B. J., & Schunk, D. H. (2018). *Handbook of self-regulation of learning and performance*. Routledge. doi:10.4324/978131569704

ADDITIONAL READING

Alamri, H., Lowell, V., Watson, W., & Watson, S. L. (2020). Using personalized learning as an instructional approach to motivate learners in online higher education: Learner self-determination and intrinsic motivation. *Journal of Research on Technology in Education*, *52*(3), 322–352. doi:10.1080/15391523.2020.1728449

Broadbent, J., Panadero, E., Lodge, J. M., & Barba, P. D. (2020). Technologies to enhance self-regulated learning in online and computer-mediated learning environments. In M. J. Bishop, E. Boling, J. Elen, & V. Svihla (Eds.), *Handbook of research in educational communications and technology* (pp. 37–52). Springer. doi:10.1007/978-3-030-36119-8_3

Carpenter, J. P., Krutka, D. G., & Kimmons, R. (2020). # RemoteTeaching & #RemoteLearning: Educator tweeting during the COVID-19 pandemic. *Journal of Technology and Teacher Education*, *28*(2), 151–159. https://eric.ed.gov/?id=EJ1257425

Chiu, T. K. (2021). Digital support for student engagement in blended learning based on self-determination theory. *Computers in Human Behavior*, *124*, 1–10. doi:10.1016/j.chb.2021.106909

Garrison, D. R., & Kanuka, H. (2004). Blended learning: Uncovering its transformative potential in higher education. *The Internet and Higher Education*, *7*(2), 95–105. doi:10.1016/j.iheduc.2004.02.001

Iyer, L. S., Bharadwaj, S., Shetty, S. H., Verma, V., & Devanathan, M. (2022). Advancing equity in digital classrooms: A personalized learning framework for higher education institutions. In *Socioeconomic Inclusion During an Era of Online Education* (pp. 225–245). IGI Global. doi:10.4018/978-1-6684-4364-4.ch011

Rogers, G. (2004). History, learning technology and student achievement: Making the difference? *Active Learning in Higher Education*, *5*(3), 232–247. doi:10.1177/1469787404043811

Tate, T., & Warschauer, M. (2022). Equity in online learning. *Educational Psychologist*, *57*(3), 192–206. doi:10.1080/00461520.2022.2062597

KEY TERMS AND DEFINITIONS

Cognitive Strategies: Mental processes that are implemented to achieve goals or solve problems.

Evaluating: Phase of metacognition. Evaluating occurs when the learner assesses their solutions and whether their goals have been satisfied, reviewing the strategies used and making adjustments as needed.

Metacognition: Our thinking about our own thinking. It is our knowledge and self-awareness of our own cognitive processes and behaviors.

Monitoring: Phase of metacognition. Monitoring occurs as the learner tracks their current state during the task, monitoring their progress towards their goals.

Planning: Phase of metacognition. Planning occurs when the learner sets goals for the task, identifies the task components and critical features, and plans strategies accordingly.

Self-Regulated Learning: Includes a set of interrelated cognitive and motivational skills that control learning.

SRL Interventions: Methods of supporting students' self-regulated learning.

Chapter 6
Supporting Student Self-Regulation:
Designing and Deploying Effective Microsurveys and Warning Systems to Help Learners Help Themselves

Jeff Bergin
General Assembly, USA

Kara McWilliams
ETS, USA

ABSTRACT

Microsurveys are a powerful tool to gather data to enable improved learner self-regulation, which can contribute to improved learner outcomes. However, for microsurveys to be effective, researchers may need to refactor their research, design, and evaluation processes to address microsurvey creation, deployment, and optimization. This chapter considers how researchers may develop microsurveys by formulating a research base, developing initial designs, and then conducting formative evaluation for ongoing improvement.

INTRODUCTION

Despite decades of research on student outcomes, students continue to withdraw, fail, and dropout of higher education (in particular at two-year and other broad access institutions) at an alarming rate. According to the National Student Clearinghouse Research Center, of those students who started college in the fall of 2016, 26% of students did not persist at any institution the following year, and 38% were not retained by their initial institution. At two-year institutions, only 48% were retained (NSC Research Center, 2018). Research has shown that when students feel less motivated to attend a class or do not see the relevance of that class to their degree goals, they visit the learning environment less frequently

DOI: 10.4018/978-1-6684-6500-4.ch006

(Simpson, 2013). Courses taken online have a 10-20% higher drop rate than face-to-face courses, with 40-80% of online students dropping depending upon the institution and course (Bawa, 2016). Therefore, online courses and degree programs need systems that help to identify students who are at risk of dropping in time for instructors, advisors, and administrators to attempt to intervene. Traditionally, the main source of this data was end-of-course surveys, which by their very nature were too late (Hu, Lo & Shih, 2014). Today, early warning systems provide the opportunity to identify students early enough to provide an intervention.

Some of the best early warning systems and their associated interventions are those that help learners to better self-regulate. Self-regulation involves planning, monitoring, and improving one's learning using a variety of strategies. Interventions that enable better self-regulation can not only help learners with the experience at hand, they can also help learners become better at learning in general. Self-regulation doesn't just apply to learning; for example, work has been done to support self-regulation in behavioral and health contexts, including one scale that was designed to capture self-regulation associated with health risk behaviors (Scherer et al., 2022). Self-regulation refers to the ability to enlist one's affective, behavioral, and cognitive resources to approach and achieve goals. The centrality of self-regulation to all goal-motivated behaviors, including learning, has prompted researchers to develop an ontology of self-regulation that can benefit microsurveys and associated interventions (Eisenberg et al., 2018).

According to the research, SRL strategies overwhelmingly improve learning performance (Dignath & Büttner 2008; Dignath et al., 2008; Hattie et al., 1996; Richardson et al., 2012; Sitzmann & Ely, 2011; Theobald, 2021). Researchers conducted a systematic review of 14 papers, qualified from an initial set of more than 239 studies, and determined that SRL strategies positively correlate with non-academic outcomes (Anthonysamy et al., 2020). However, SRL is most often associated with academic outcomes. For example, researchers found that students' learning outcomes were influenced by their self-control, SRL, and course participation. The impact of self-control on learning outcomes was mediated through SRL and course participation; specifically, self-control and SRL predicted final grades in the course (Zhu et al., 2016).

Early warning systems leverage student data to develop algorithms that can give instructors and administrators warnings about student behavior in time for intervention and remediation (Howard, Meehan & Parnell, 2018; National Forum on Education Statistics, 2018). Early warning systems can be used in any educational context including traditional face-to-face classes; hybrid, blended, or computer-enabled courses; or fully online courses. However, much interest has been directed to incorporating them into online courses, where student/instructor interaction may be more limited or where higher failure, drop, and withdrawal rates may exist (Bawa, 2016). Furthermore, online contexts typically provide more data, whether on student logins, time-on-task, behaviors, and performance, compared to other contexts. This data can be used to develop early warning systems by mining learner data, discovering trends that reveal at-risk students, and devising algorithms to prompt alerts. Many studies indicate that early warning systems can in fact enable successful interventions, if implemented with fidelity which, in turn, can drive learner outcomes in both blended and online courses (Jokhan, Sharma & Singh, 2018; National Forum on Education Statistics, 2018; Sneyers & De Witte, 2018). These interventions may include prompts for strategies that enable better and more effective self-regulation.

While early warning systems are an important mechanism for improving outcomes, many are based primarily on behavioral data (National Forum on Education Statistics, 2018). Surveys, however, can provide a meaningful compliment to the other datastreams typically used in early warning systems. Specifically, microsurveys—short surveys that are limited in both the number of survey items and the length of those items—a unique opportunity to gather real time data on students' affective states. This data can complement behavioral and cognitive data gleaned by traditional coursework or courseware platforms and, therefore, be a valuable data input into early warning systems. Microsurveys can also provide valuable metacognitive insights focused on learners' perceptions of their behavioral and cognitive performance. Such metacognitive insights are a critical component of self-regulation.

Creating, deploying, interpreting, and improving microsurveys comes with a series of considerations that are unique from their longer-form counterparts. This chapter provides a brief background on the relationship between microsurveys and early warning systems; describes how to devise a foundational research base to underpin the microsurveys; focuses on initial and iterative design issues, such as microsurvey creation and modification, microsurvey formats and usability, microsurvey deployment protocols (such as first occurrence, frequency, and deployment tiers) and microsurvey transparency; as well as delineating a formative evaluation plan (including the construction of student archetypes, progressive refinement, and theory building.

BACKGROUND

Effective early warning systems rely upon data from multiple domains—affective, behavioral, and cognitive—to develop predictive models that provide alerts when students hit specific risk thresholds (National Forum on Education Statistics, 2018). Then, when the model triggers an alert, students can receive an intervention to improve their likelihood of meeting a particular outcome (McMahon & Sembiante, 2019). Often, that outcome is to achieve an educational goal such as completing a course, persisting through their first year, and being retained through to the completion of a degree—three common outcomes that institutions measure. (Bawa, 2016; NCS Research Center, 2018; Rumberger, 2011). One precursor to completing a course is keeping students engaged in their courses; thus, measuring and improving student engagement has become a common undertaking at institutions and a focal point for both traditional course surveys and early warning systems.

The domains that inform early warning systems—those focused on student engagement—may include academic performance, behaviors, attitudes, and demographics (Rumberger, 2011). Increasingly, these domains may also include indicators of learner self-regulation, such as their time management, self-appraisal of performance, and plans for improvement. Blending indicators from different domains into a single "on-track" indicator both enhances its predictive power (Balfanz, Herzog & MacIver, 2007) and general usability (McMahon & Sembiante, 2019). This is because the causes of dropouts are often complex issues that cross domains. Typically, researchers gather datasets from institutional student information systems or large, national surveys. The former contains readily available data; however, it is predominantly behavioral (such as a student's time-on-task) and cognitive (such as a student's performance on assessment items). To inform the early warning systems with affective data, the system needs complementary inputs, often derived through self-reporting of students' subjective perceptions which help explain the "why" behind student disengagement, thereby strengthening early warning systems (McMahon & Sembiante, 2019).

Traditionally, self-reported data have been gathered at the end of a course, when there is little time to affect change for those students who may have failed, withdrawn, or dropped. Advancements in technologies, such as learning management systems, courseware, and mobile devices, enable the integration of microsurveys into students' daily activities. Microsurveys are both shorter in the number of items they present at one time and the length of those items and their associated responses than traditional end-of-term surveys that are traditionally delivered both in the number of items they present at one time and the length of those items and their associated responses. In fact, microsurveys can involve just a few clicks in under a few minutes.

Over the past few years, there has been increased interest in using microsurveys to understand self regulation. Researchers examining how students self-regulate online have relied on self-report surveys, sometimes combining this data with system or platform data (Cho & Yoo, 2017). One challenge of self-report data is insufficient effort responding; however, according to one study, while inattentive and attentive learners differ in some attributes, the inclusion of inattentive student data did not fundamentally change inferences or conclusions drawn (Iaconelli and Walters, 2020). Notably, self-report instruments that support the practice of self-assessment are a critical component of the SRL process. Self-assessment including self-reflection influences self-directed feedback seeking, which in turn was a strong positive predictor of academic achievement (Yan, 2020).

The benefits to properly developed and deployed microsurveys are many: they make data capture and collection easier and more efficient; they provide real time rather than retroactive data, which may be less likely to suffer from the effects of poor recall or social desirability; they enable researchers to compliment behavioral and cognitive data with metacognitive and affective data for more comprehensive and targeted archetypes and interventions; and, perhaps most importantly, they foster earlier intervention—early enough to improve an outcome (Fredricks & McColskey, 2012). Microsurveys can also help learning designers understand student reactions to specific pedagogical approaches and resources, such as self-regulation strategies, and optimize each accordingly. Microsurveys also inform researchers' understanding of learner engagement. Researchers have used microlevel data to collect subjective data, to complement other data sources, and to solicit students' reflections on their own engagement (Balasooriya et al., 2017). Timely microlevel data enriches traditional learning analytics to enable a more robust understanding of student learning as well as cognitive patterns, affective states, and success behaviors while enabling better instructor feedback and institutional responsiveness (Balasooriya et al., 2018). However, microsurveys also bring inherent challenges, many of which are related to the validity, reliability, and usability of the microsurvey instruments which threaten to reduce their ultimate impact on interventions and outcomes.

The next sections explore the special considerations that researchers and designers encounter when conceptualizing, designing, validating, and optimizing microsurveys, as summarized in Table 1. These are derived from a review of the literature on microsurvey design and development, as well as best practices in educational technology research, design and evaluation. In particular, the emphasis on anchoring the early warning system in foundational research and then conducting formative evaluation to demonstrate an impact on outcomes and contribute to theory building aligns this approach with the core tenets of design-based research (Barab & Squire, 2004). The following approach also aligns to the Plan, Implement, Use, Evaluate proposed in the Forum Guide to Early Warning Systems (National Forum on Education Statistics, 2018).

Table 1. Microsurvey design, development, deployment, and iteration considerations

Phase	Consideration	Purpose
Foundational Research	Underlying theory	Enables researchers and designers to understand the body of research pertaining to self-regulated learning and student outcomes.
	Outcome definition	Enables researchers and designers to set clear outcomes that the early warning systems and associated microsurveys will then support.
	Change for logic	Enables researchers and designers to establish all relationships among the outcomes and instructional and intervention schemes.
	Existing tools	Review tools that may already exist within the domain of self-regulated learning.
Initial and Iterative Design	Microsurvey design	Enables microsurvey items to be most effective in particular contexts.
	Microsurvey formats and usability	Enables microsurvey items to be readily usable by students.
	Deployment protocols	Enables microsurvey items to be deployed based on a strategy.
	Microsurvey transparency	Enables microsurvey items to support student self-regulation and data ethics.
Formative Evaluation	Learner archetypes	Enables microsurveys to provide valuable data that interventions can leverage to support specific subgroups of learners.
	Progressive refinement	Enables microsurveys to be optimized based on initial testing.
	Theory building	Enables microsurvey evaluation findings to validate (or invalidate) the broader theoretical framework and contribute to advancement within education.

DEVELOPING MICROSURVEYS

Foundational Research

Underlying Theory

Before beginning to design and develop microsurveys for early warning systems that embed SRL strategies and interventions, it's important to anchor the effort in a thorough understanding of SRL theories. Researchers and scientists have studied self-regulated learning (SRL) theories and strategies for more than three decades, as evidenced by at least three meta-analyses (Dignath & Büttner, 2008; Dignath et al., 2008; Sitzmann & Ely, 2011) and a critical review (Panadero, 2017). SRL involves using strategies to manage, monitor, and actively improve one's learning. There are at least six SRL models: Zimmerman, Boekaerts, Winne, Pintrich, Efklides and Hadwin, Järvelä, and Miller (Panadero, 2017). Zimmerman's Cyclical model—revised in 2009—is both widely referenced and accepted within the field and relatively easily applied. It is divided into three phases: the forethought phase, the performance phase, and the self reflection phase. According to Zimmerman, self regulated learning is "The degree to which students are metacognitively, motivationally, and behaviorally active participants in their own learning processes" (2013, p.137). It involves metacognition, or being aware of one's cognition and being able to regulate their memories and learning processes (Sperling, et al., 2004). Learners use their metacognitive skills when they make plans to begin learning; contemplate how they are learning; and reflect on what they have just learned.

Table 2. Zimmerman's Self Regulated Learning Categories

Categories of Strategies	Definitions
1. Self-evaluation	Statements indicating student-initiated evaluations of the quality or progress of their work, e.g., "I check over my work to make sure I did it correct."
2. Organizing and transforming	Statements indicating student initiated overt or covert rearrangement of instructional materials to improve learning, e.g., "I make an outline before I write my paper."
3. Goal-setting and planning	Statements indicating student initiated setting of educational goals or subgoals and planning for sequencing, timing, and completing activities related to those goals, e.g., "First I start studying 2 weeks before exams, and I pace myself."
4. Seeking information	Statements indicating student-initiated efforts to secure further task information from nonsocial sources when undertaking an assignment, e.g., "Before beginning to write the paper, I go to the library to get as much information as possible concerning the topic."
5. Keeping records and monitoring	Statements indicating student efforts to record events or results, e.g., "I took notes of the class discussion." "I kept a list of the words I got wrong."
6. Environmental structuring	Statements indicating student-initiated efforts to select or arrange the physical setting to make learning easier, e.g., "I isolate myself from anything that distracts me." "I turned off the radio so I can concentrate on what I am doing."
7. Self-consequences	Statements indicating student arrangement or imagination of rewards or punishment for success or failure, e.g., "If I do well on a test, I treat myself to a movie."
8. Rehearsing and memorizing	Statements indicating student-initiated efforts to memorize material by overt or covert practice, e.g., "In preparing for a math test, I keep writing the formula down until I remember it."
9 - 11. Seeking social assistance	Statements indicating student-initiated efforts to solicit help from peers (9), teachers (10), and adults (1 1), e.g., "If I have problems with math assignments, I ask a friend to help."
12 -14. Reviewing records	Statements indicating student-initiated efforts to reread tests (12), notes (13), or textbooks (14), to prepare for class or further testing, e.g., "When preparing for a test, I review my notes."
15. Other	Statements indicating learning behavior that is initiated by other persons such as teachers or parents, and all unclear verbal responses, e.g., "I just do what the teachers says."

Numerous researchers have offered classification schemes for self regulated learning strategies (see Hattie, Biggs and Purdie (1996), Ergen and Kanadli (2017), and Theobald (2021)). Zimmerman (2013) advanced fifteen categories (excerpted in Table 2). Aligning microsurvey items and interventions to these strategies can be helpful when developing early warning systems.

Outcome Definition

When developing an early warning system that includes a microsurvey, it is tempting for developers to devise common sense questions or to try to reuse a legacy survey by interspersing the existing questions throughout a course, with little modification. However, legacy surveys may not have been intended to drive a prevention or intervention scheme, nor were they likely crafted for the context in which the microsurveys will be deployed. Thus, researchers and designers should ground their microsurvey design in research on best practices. Floyd Fowler Jr. wrote *Survey Research Methods*, an excellent review of the guidelines for survey research. There are other seminal books and articles that provide a comprehensive outline for designing surveys that can be applied to microsurvey development (e.g. Rea & Parker, 1992). The guidelines and steps that follow in this section were derived from previous research on survey development, educational research on higher education outcomes, and the authors' personal experiences.

Microsurvey developers should first consider the outcomes that they are hoping to measure and improve for both their institutions and their students. These outcomes should drive the development of both the early warning system at large and the microsurvey component. When establishing outcomes microsurvey developers should be careful to ensure that they are meaningful and measurable. Similarly, that they are the outcomes of interest and not merely leading indicators of those outcomes.

Common outcomes of interest include course completion, persistence through the first year, retention through a program of study, and completion. Unfortunately, monitoring and measuring these broader outcomes, while important in terms of programmatic and institutional initiatives, may not enable early enough intervention to successfully improve an outcome. Rather, these broader outcomes are dependent upon students remaining engaged within courses throughout their academic programs.

Therefore, institutions, administrators, and educators should focus on leading indicators of engagement when developing microsurveys. Student engagement is typically considered to be a combination of three dimensions: affect, cognition, and behavior (although some researchers differentiate cognitive and meta-cognitive dimensions and yet others differentiate between academic and cognitive dimensions) (Appleton et al., 2006; Reschly & Christenson, 2006). When developing an early warning system, all domains that measure student engagement should be considered. By incorporating multiple domains, the early warning systems will be able to draw more holistic inferences into what causes a student to dropout and, therefore, pinpoint more effective interventions on the most malleable causes (McMahon & Sembiante, 2019).

Logic for Change

Once broad outcomes and leading indicators of student engagement in multiple learning environments have been drafted, researchers can begin to build the logic models or theories of change that will inform how the outcomes will be measured, monitored, and improved through instructional techniques or, in the case of early warning systems, intervention schemes.

Theories of change are critical to the development of an early warning system because they ground both the intended outcome and the steps that are planned to reach that outcome. They also support the identification of the data sources that will be needed to measure, directionally, whether a student is on track to meet the intended broader outcome. While there are a variety of methods that can be used to develop a logic model or theory of change, there is seminal research on the topic that can guide a developer's thinking. The development of a logic model or theory of change can be supported by basing it on a proven theoretical framework like Finn's Participation-Identification Theory (Finn, 1989) or Tinto's Interactionalist Theory (Tinto, 1987). Alternatively, it can be based on a theoretical model, such as the What Works? Model of Student Retention and Success (Thomas, 2012). Importantly, a logic model or theory of change can also be based on—or aligned to—a self-regulation framework. These theoretical frameworks and model each advance specific theories of why students may not achieve outcomes in either an online or brick-and-mortar classroom. However, these authors suggest that a logic model or theory of change is more critical in an online course because of the uniqueness of the learning environment and the learners who are participating in the course.

In addition to theoretical frameworks grounding a researcher's thinking about intended outcomes, they also help researchers and designers understand the previously researched and often empirically based factors that influence these outcomes. In doing so, previously conducted research can be appropriately factored into a theory of change or logic model. Moreover, situating an early warning system or the microsurveys it includes within a theoretical framework enables a more thoughtful and comprehensive understanding of the student experience. This, in turn, enables researchers who are developing early warning systems and associated microsurveys to more clearly identify the student perceptions, attributes, and behaviors that are related to student engagement and goal attainment—or student disengagement and withdrawal, failure, or dropout (McMahon & Sembiante, 2019). In short, theoretical frameworks help researchers and designers to develop hypotheses about how specific instructional and interventional approaches may drive outcomes, collect data on them using early warning systems (specifically microsurveys), and measure the validity of their hypotheses through impact research.

An outcome ladder, informed by a theoretical framework, can serve as a backbone for a logic model or theory of change. An outcome ladder is a graphical representation of intended outcomes on a continuum, identifying the most foundational outcome to the most substantial outcome. For example, an outcome ladder might begin with "a student is attending class" and progress through "a student is engaging in class," "a student is performing adequately in class," "a student has successfully completed class," and "a student has progressed on to the next phase of study in class." Theoretical frameworks and outcome ladders are two ways of ensuring that the intervention scheme driven by the early warning system will likely improve the intended outcomes. This foundational work will enable effective interventions rather than serving up interventions that do not actually facilitate meaningful change. Logic models and theories of change need not be elaborate to be effective; however, they should map the outcomes, leading indicators, and interventional schemes. Researchers and developers can then return to these logic models and theories of change to guide early warning system and microsurvey design decisions.

More specific logic models and theories of change may include key performance indicators and their associated datastreams and measurement schemes, if helpful for researchers and designers.

Datastreams related to student affect may require the development of microsurvey self-response items. When constructing those items, researchers and designers may benefit from adopting or adapting research-based, validated instruments, such as the National Survey of Student Engagement (Kuh, 2009) or Student Engagement Questionnaire (Coates, 2007). When considering adopting or adapting an instrument, it is important to evaluate whether it has made a demonstrable impact on student outcomes for a population of students that approximates those targeted by your early warning system and whether it has been used for prevention or intervention, or both, and under what circumstances. Perhaps most importantly, the instrument should include student (not just school) factors—ideally those that pertain to malleable student attributes that can most easily be modified through intervention and subsequent change (McMahon & Sembiante, 2019).

Existing Tools

Several instruments assess learner self regulation and may be adapted. These include the Academic SRL Scale (A-SRL-S), Motivated Strategies for Learning Questionnaire (MSQL) and Learning Attitudes and Study Strategies Inventory (LASSI) and the Learning Strategy Scale (LSS).

- *Academic SRL Scale (A-SRL-S)* This instrument was based on data from 1454 college students on eight protocols, which were based on six learning contexts. In total, 111 items were generated and organized according to 14 categories (Magno, 2010).
- *Motivated Strategies for Learning Questionnaire (MSQL)* This instrument was developed to assess college students' motivation and learning strategies and includes two sections: a motivation

section and a learning strategies section. The 1991 version contains 81 items, with 31 items that assess learners' goals, beliefs about their skill to succeed, and anxiety about tests; 31 items regarding learners' use of cognitive and metacognitive strategies; and 19 items concerning learner resource management (Pintrich et al., 1991).

- *Learning Attitudes and Study Strategies Inventory (LASSI)* This 10-scale, 60-item instrument assesses learners' understanding and use of learning strategies that can be optimized through specific interventions (Weinstein et al., 2016).
- *Learning Strategy Scale (LSS)* This five-factor scale based on the Learning Attitude and Study Strategies Inventory (LASSI), covers strategies such as elaboration, comprehension monitoring, and rehearsal (Guven, 2008).

Initial and Iterative Design

There are many options for researchers and developers of early warning systems and microsurveys. They might leverage a validated, research-based instrument, implement a trusted legacy instrument, or utilize some combination of both. Whatever path is chosen, some modification of those instruments will have to occur. While instruments might be validated, they will not hold the same psychometric properties when modified to be used as microsurveys, and they may not be appropriate for deployment as such. Further, it is critical that they are working in service of the early warning system intervention scheme. Finally, a survey developed and validated in traditional brick-and-mortar courses may not seamlessly translate to online environments. Modification typically involves developing or revising survey items or scales; pilot testing and measuring the psychometric soundness of the items and scales; devising microsurvey protocols; developing usable microsurvey formats; and considering issues pertaining to student transparency.

Microsurvey Design

Great care should be taken when constructing a microsurvey and the effort should be led by (or conducted in partnership with) an experienced psychometrician. Three areas should be paid close attention throughout the process: alignment of items or scales to the outcomes being measured; length of items and/or scales; and psychometric soundness of the resulting items or scales.

Aligning Items to Outcomes

When identifying or developing individual items for a microsurvey a psychometrician should evaluate the extent to which that item aligns to its associated outcome and ensure that it is representing the appropriate domain. When selecting validated scales, or developing new scales, the underlying construct that the scale is intended to measure should align with the intended outcome. To do this, first consult the literature to understand what previous research has been done on the construct of interest. Search for valid predictors of that construct. In this process existing scales to measure the construct of interest may be available. It is often more useful to identify existing scales that have been validated so that you know it is aligned to the outcome. When selecting validated scales, or developing new scales, the underlying construct that the scale is intended to measure should align with the intended outcome. Given the nature of microsurveys, lengthy scales may become intrusive or unusable and require revision, but the revised sets of items should still measure one construct and align to the outcome. If items need to be developed, they should be reviewed by a subject matter expert who can evaluate whether they are aligned to the outcome. Their perspective will support reliability.

Length of Items/Scales

Survey and item length, in general, should be carefully considered. Often, longer engagement instruments need to be substantially trimmed to fit the microsurvey context, focusing on retaining only the most critical items that correspond directly to relevant activities, resources, and interventions (Balasooriya, Mor & Rodríguez, 2017). Once those items have been selected, and any gaps identified, existing questions can be revised, new questions can be created, and nonessential items can be removed. It is critical to use simple, concise, and clear language. This means taking care to avoid asking double barrel questions (e.g., How much did you enjoy the reading *and* the activities?) and paying special attention to avoid readability issues, cultural colloquialisms, and biased language. The nature of a microsurvey is that it is an immediate collection of data in real time. If a great deal of cognitive load is required for a student to understand what the survey question is asking, they will become disengaged, resulting in a loss of data. Brief, concise questions will keep a student's attention while not over taxing them.

Psychometric Soundness of Items/Scales

As with all survey construction, microsurvey development should adhere to psychometric standards. That is, as noted by the American Psychological Association, sound measures must demonstrate content-validity, criterion-related validity, construct validity, and internal consistency. These requirements exist within microsurveys as well. Additionally, as with all self-report instruments, microsurvey items should be developed for accuracy and to remove inherent biases. In particular, the items may be compromised by the social desirability effect (whereby responders select the answer that they feel is most socially acceptable); acquiescence bias (whereby responders agree with an assertion); the recency effect (whereby responders select the most recent in a series of answer choices); and/or the order, contrast, or assimilation effects (whereby prior questions influences the responders answer). Therefore, it is critical to review each microsurvey question carefully and critically. Poorly functioning items can be identified during pilot testing and either modified or removed before finalizing the microsurvey. For a complete list of biases, see Choi and Pak (2005).

Pilot Testing

A host of research, and the first-hand experience of the authors has demonstrated that the following processes are best practice when pilot testing microsurveys. Before finalizing a microsurvey it should be pilot tested and revised if needed. The target population that will be using the microsurvey should be clearly defined (e.g. students at two- and four-year institutions that are public and private and range in their level of selectivity). A clear definition will help establish the sample of students that the microsurvey should be pilot tested with. Then a stratification can be developed (e.g. 70% students at two-year institutions, 30% students at four-year institutions) and students recruited to take the survey. A power analysis can help researchers know the size sample they require to measure the psychometric properties of the microsurvey.

To investigate reliability; stability and internal consistency of the microsurvey should be investigated. To measure stability students can be asked to complete the survey and a few days later asked to complete it again. Then, the intraclass correlation coefficient can be calculated to measure stability while taking into account measurement error. It is best practice to wait no longer than two weeks before retesting the survey. Internal consistency tells us the extent to which all of the items that are meant to measure a similar construct are in fact measuring that construct. For example, if nine items are meant to measure student's engagement, all of those items should clearly align to that construct. To calculate this in pilot testing, Cronbach's alpha coefficient—which demonstrates the covariance level between the items of a scale—can be used. Although there is no set parameter for a "good" Cronbach's alpha, generally values .70 and higher are considered sufficient. However, with microsurveys it is important to note that the small number of items may deflate a Cronbach's alpha, as the value is highly dependent on the number of items measuring the construct. Care should be taken when interpreting the alpha of a microsurvey and the addition of items to increase internal consistency weighted against the need to keep the microsurvey brief. It might be that a lower alpha (closer to .50) is still acceptable to reduce survey length. Note that if the microsurvey has items that are dichotomous, Kruder-Richardson will be more appropriate than Cronbach's alpha to measure internal consistency.

To measure the validity of a newly developed or adapted microsurvey, minimally construct, content, and criterion validity should be considered. If appropriate steps were taken to align items and/or scales to the constructs of interest, the survey has likely achieved content validity. Construct validity is gathered through a statistical test measuring whether a set of items that are intended to measure a construct are measuring that construct. Researchers typically use confirmatory factor analyses to measure construct validity. As above, to gather evidence of content validity once a microsurvey has been developed an expert should review the alignment between items and the construct of interest. Content validity evidence is qualitative but can still be rigorous is an appropriate expert is selected to review. Criterion validity, sometimes referred to as predictive validity measures the correlation between the microsurvey and the criterion. In the case of microsurveys, the relationship between student responses and student engagement may be investigated to measure criterion validity. To achieve this a separate measure that has been validated to measure engagement should also be completed by students and items on the microsurvey that are intended to measure engagement should be correlated with responses to the engagement survey. If there is a high correlation this provides evidence of criterion validity.

Microsurvey Formats and Usability

Design of microsurvey questions must be based on the context in which those questions will be deployed. That is, will they be deployed within a learning management system, by email, or by mobile or another handheld device? Will students be interacting via laptop, mobile phone, or other hardware? Will there be any kind of sensory prompt (such as a vibration or auditory signal) or any attempt to capture physiological data, such as heart rate, facial expressions, or eye movement? Identifying and prioritizing all possible deployment contexts is critical for establishing the best response formats, character constraints, and interaction patterns for the questions (Goetz, Bieg & Hall, 2016). When specifically targeting a population of students who are taking courses online other considerations must be taken into account: surveys can be somewhat longer form since students are used to typical asynchronous engagement, microsurveys should be positioned in announcements or somewhere else prevalent that students can easily see and access them, and the response formats have to be appropriate for online completion. The following guidelines are based on research on microsurvey development best-practice.

Response Formats

Questions may be closed-ended (selected response), open-ended (constructed response) or ordinal (such as a Likert scale). Each of these formats has its benefits and challenges. Closed-ended and ordinal items may be more efficient for students to submit and for researchers to code and correlate with domains but may yield less insightful responses from students. Closed-ended items that are lengthy may not be considered readily usable from a student perspective and may, therefore, encourage the recency effect or other aforementioned biases. Ordinal formats may be preferable from a usability perspective—in particular on mobile devices with limited screen real estate—and may be consistent with typical mobile behaviors (e.g., rating services or liking/disliking social media posts).

Question Set Constraints

Question set constraints pertain to the limits that researchers and designers impose on how many microsurvey items get released to students at one time and the degree to which those items are sequenced in a specific order or randomized. Some research indicates microsurveys question sets should consist of one to three total items per instance (Balasooriya et al., 2017; Gogol et al., 2014). Randomization of items (including the reversal of ordinal items) can help avoid the recency effect and other biases but may add complexity to both the microsurvey deployment and the early warning system algorithm that drives interventions.

Character Constraints

Mobile screens, in particular, may constrict characters and, therefore, dictate word choice, question formats, and interaction patterns to some degree. In addition, for open-ended (constructed response) questions, there may be character limits pertaining to what a student may enter, which may limit the effectiveness of these formats.

Interaction Patterns

Interaction patterns are exact steps that learners will go through when they receive and respond to a microsurvey question or series of questions. These include how the question is initially presented to them as well as how the actual question stem and responses are presented and the number of clicks or taps necessary to enter, select, or submit a response. These patterns also must include what happens if a student does not respond to a question; that is, can a question be bypassed, dismissed, or deferred—and, what are the associated implications?

Accessibility

Developing microsurveys may involve more usability considerations than their longer-form counterparts often did. Students may be visually impaired or have mobility issues that preclude them from being able to readily use their computers or mobile phones to respond to microsurvey items—especially if those items are particularly small, include any kind of color coding, or involve fine motor skills, such as radio-button selection, text entry, swiping, or tapping. Ensuring that all items and item functionality adheres with best practices in universal design and accessibility is an important way to ensure that all students can respond to survey items. In some cases, this may involve developing alternate delivery formats for items or working directly with those students who cannot access or complete the microsurvey items.

Testing the response formats, question set constraints, character constraints, interaction patterns, and accessibility is critical. Many of the design decisions involve substantial user testing to refine and when the target population is students in online courses, the testing should be conducted in this environment. Ultimately, the response formats, question set constraints, character constraints, and interaction patterns should all support a usable, learnable, and accessible student experience to both facilitate data gathering and to avoid further frustrating already at-risk students. As these undergo rounds of usability testing, it is important to consider how many clicks (or taps) are required of students to complete each instance of the survey and whether there should be a reward system to encourage or reinforce student responses. Finally, researchers and designers must consider whether the microsurvey design inadvertently privileges or disadvantages learners in its visual design, color choices, language, or overall usability.

Deployment Protocols

Another important design consideration is the microsurvey deployment protocol. The protocol delineates how early and how often microsurveys should be deployed within a particular learning context, as well as the relationship between the trigger for a survey question or question set and the associated interventions. There are several important considerations to defining the best protocol, including: the first occurrence, the frequency of subsequent occurrences, and the structure of deployment tiers based upon response or nonresponse.

First Occurrence

An effective early warning system captures indicators that a student may be at risk (of failing, withdrawing, or dropping from a course or course of study) early enough that an intervention or series of interventions may be successfully deployed (McMahon & Sembiante, 2019). Therefore, questions around student interest and motivation (precursors to engagement) may be initiated at the onset of a course and questions around the affective domain of student engagement may be initiated prior to the onset of any risk indicators (both to establish a baseline understanding of affective engagement and to begin to identify those resources or interactions that students experience as highly engaging). Indeed, research has indicated that when students lack interest or motivation, or cannot understand the relevance of a class to their degree or goals, they engage less frequently (Simpson, 2013).

Frequency

The frequency of deploying subsequent questions or question sets is dependent, in part, on whether the early warning system is intended to focus on prevention or intervention. Prevention systems may be intended to catalog student engagement for every instructional interaction and resource, requiring more frequent questions or question sets. Intervention systems may be intended to identify only those students needing additional support and, therefore, may include less frequent and more reactive questions (triggered by elevated risk indicators). In general, researchers need to determine if microsurvey question sets are deployed at certain intervals within a course or term; deployed based upon certain conditions being met or unmet; or deployed based upon specific instructional or assessment resources being accessed. For example, the experience sampling method (ESM) involves issuing a sampling protocol whereby assessments are issued at pre-designated time intervals, events, or signals and thus “disrupt” the learning experience to gather self-reports from learners (Goetz et al., 2016).

Deployment Tiers

Microsurvey deployment tiers are the conditional statements that prompt initial and subsequent questions or question sets. These need to account for conditions whereby students do not respond to a question or question set or respond in certain ways that may trigger additional questions. In addition, these rules need to consider whether unanswered items are followed by secondary or tertiary prompts, or if they are delayed and later redeployed (and if so, at what time interval or subsequent trigger).

Microsurvey Transparency

One of the issues researchers and designers must face when developing early warning systems at large and microsurveys is how transparent to be in sharing the purpose and implications of this data gathering. Ethically, researchers and designers need to consider to what degree students should be informed about the purposes, uses, and security of their data; whether students should be able to opt-in or opt-out of the microsurveys (and indeed the early warning system intervention schemes altogether); and whether students should have access to raw or interpreted views of their responses for their own edification or self-regulation. When gathering attitudinal, affective, and self-perception data for the purposes of understanding learner self-regulation, it is particularly critical that learners realize the value of providing accurate self-reports in the interest of helping themselves, and that this will not be used for assessment, grading, or any other commercial purposes.

Similarly, researchers and designers must consider the inadvertent effects of both the microsurvey questions and question sets as well as the subsequent interventions on student attitudes and behaviors. For instance, at what point will microsurveys become too intrusive or too familiar, resulting in student aggravation or premature dismissal? Could a microsurvey degrade the student experience by inadvertently fostering frustration or negative appraisals of a student's own learning or learning environments? Could frequent microsurvey questions spark the negativity bias and reduce students' self-efficacy?

Furthermore, few of these systems offer robust student interfaces that enable students to manage and monitor their own performance and risk and make informed modifications. (Balasooriya, Mor & Rodríguez, 2018). Does the student see their own results over time, potentially enabling important metacognitive or self-regulatory skills, or does this then turn the data collection process into an intervention of its own, inadvertently influencing student thinking and behavior (Goetz et al., 2016; Wheeler & Reis 1991)? If students are enabled to see their own results, how is the data visualized and how is student interaction with the data measured and analyzed?

Perhaps most importantly, researchers and designers must consider the safety of the students—both in terms of the influence of the microsurvey questions and the use to which these questions are put, how the responses are safeguarded, and the transparency with which they are delivered. From a data ethics perspective, it is important that students understand how and why their data is being collected and safeguarded, and their rights regarding how this data is or may be used. It is equally important for this data to be safeguarded from any other commercial uses, such as marketing or advertising.

Formative Evaluation

Developing early warning systems including microsurveys that measure the affective domain require ongoing formative evaluation efforts that subsequently inform both the operation of the system at large as well as the accuracy of the microsurvey questions, the ways in which they are formatted and designed, and how they are structured vis-a-vis their overarching protocols. Such ongoing formative evaluation should be conducted early in the design process and prior to the system and microsurveys being deployed in situ. There are three important considerations for formative evaluation efforts as they pertain to the microsurveys: developing student archetypes, progressive refinement, and theory building.

Learner Archetypes

Today, it is insufficient to just identify at-risk students; rather, early warning systems need to provide interventions that address specific and changeable student-level indicators (Gaertner & McClarty, 2015; MacIver & Messel, 2013; McMahon & Sembiante, 2019; Parr & Bonitz, 2015). Attendance, academic performance, and attitudes are considered changeable, whereas socio-economic status, for example, is not (McMahon & Sembiante, 2019). It is important for early warning systems to be able to cluster students into robust student archetypes and then pinpoint those students who exhibit multiple indicators, so that the system can then provide a more targeted and effective intervention (McMahon & Sembiante, 2019).

Unfortunately, archetype development requires actual student use to better enable researchers to identify those clusters of affective, behavioral, and cognitive elements that contribute to the particular archetypes—and, how members of these archetypes respond both to microsurvey questions and to specific interventions. Thus, it is important for researchers and designers to plan for a round of pilot testing to further refine the archetypes and adjust survey and intervention algorithms accordingly.

As researchers design, pilot, and test their microsurvey instruments it is critical to do so in tandem with the associated interventions. And this requires designers to carefully conceptualize exactly which archetypes receive which interventions, at what threshold the intervention or scaffolded interventions are triggered, who receives the trigger, and what type of explicit action the intervention takes to both minimize the risk and drive the outcome—and indeed if there is one or a series of cascading interventions based on risk severity.

Progressive Refinement

Microsurvey items need to be piloted with an appropriate sample of students, have poor items removed or replaced, and then be beta tested for impact in an actual class setting with proper IRB approval and disclosures. This beta testing will help researchers and designers to understand how effectively the microsurvey contributes to the larger early warning systems and how effectively it supports intervention, remediation, and outcome attainment. The plan for this multi-stage testing process should be articulated from the onset, with appropriate time to develop and refine the evaluation methodology. There should also be proper time, between piloting, beta testing, and broad deployment to iterate on the items and the overall microsurvey design—including potential changes to the broader early warning systems including its intervention scheme.

Theory Building

As stated earlier, one of the benefits of orienting an early warning system within a theoretical framework is that it enables researchers to establish hypotheses to validate or invalidate through evaluation. It is important that, as this work is done, it contributes to the larger body of scholarship that helps researchers to evolve both their understanding of these theories and contribute to the empirical research base upon which they are founded. By participating in this scholarship, researchers and designers who develop early warning systems and microsurveys are not just improving outcomes for the learners with whom they come in contact; they are sharing important results that may have a much broader impact. Such theory building may unlock enormous opportunities for understanding learner self-regulation strategies and best-practices.

FUTURE RESEARCH DIRECTIONS

Given that microsurvey use in early warning systems is in its infancy, little evidence exists on their impact. Early warning systems would benefit greatly from research comparing the use of systems with microsurveys soliciting affective data to those systems that are based predominantly or exclusively on behavioral and/or cognitive data. Early warning systems would also benefit from research indicating which metacognitive data can inform interventions, and which interventions can drive improved self-regulation. Specifically, there is substantial opportunity to evaluate the long-term benefits of SRL, the strategies that are most effective for specific learner populations, and the relationship between SRL and specific markers of academic achievement (Cetin, 2015; de Boer et al., 2018; Sitzmann & Ely, 2011). Furthermore, research on the ideal number length of surveys, length of survey questions, format of those questions, and deployment protocols would help developers optimize existing and future systems. There is also a dearth of research on empirically validated student archetypes—and, how those archetypes benefit from specific types of interventions and intervention schemes, including tiered or scaffolded interventions. Finally, there needs to be research on the validity and reliability of affective instruments and scales, and their relative effectiveness.

While very little research has been conducted on early warning systems and microsurveys in general, even less has been conducted on developing, deploying, validating, and using microsurveys and early warning systems specifically in online environments. It will be important that future research in this area focuses specifically on that educational context and that student population. Research-based instruments that have been piloted and validated in face-to-face environments should have their psychometric properties re-calculated when data are collected in online environments. Similarly, if surveys have been modified for use in online environments, they should be pilot tested with that population. Because deployment protocols will be specific in online environments, the same testing should be done to ensure that effective deployment in a face-to-face environment translates to an online environment. And, although student engagement can likely be measured in many of the same ways between face-to-face and online environments, there are likely additional metrics that can be captured in an online environment that can be considered.

CONCLUSION

After decades of research on the factors that influence student outcomes, institutions still struggle to improve student retention and graduation rates (NSC Research Center, 2018). Broad access institutions, such as two-year institutions, have particularly poor retention rates, and students in online courses are particularly likely to drop out (Bawa, 2016; NSC Research Center, 2018). Students in online courses and degree programs can benefit from systems that help support them at the first sign that they are at risk of dropping. Many institutions turn to such early warning systems to help them prevent student failure, withdrawal, or dropouts, or to intervene early enough to improve outcomes. They also use these systems to better understand the range of factors—including the perceived relevance of a course and a student's interest in it and motivation to succeed—to make more informed interventions.

However, early warning systems rely on data drawn from student information and learning platforms which often lack sufficient data on student emotions to prevent withdrawals, failures, and dropouts or to intervene early enough to improve outcomes. Therefore, researchers and designers are increasingly using microsurveys to understand the student experience as early as fully and as early as possible. Yet, microsurveys are in their infancy and little research has been conducted on their efficacy in driving learning outcomes, particularly those related to persistence, retention, and completion in online courses and programs. However, there are steps that researchers, designers, and evaluators can take to ensure that microsurveys are a strong complement to other early warning system elements. Indeed, they provide numerous opportunities for early warning systems to not only improve outcomes, but to do so by improving learner self-regulation—a skill that benefits learners beyond any one course or experience.

Successfully designing and deploying microsurveys requires researchers and designers to address considerations unique to microsurvey creation, deployment, and optimization, including formulating a foundational research base, developing initial designs, and then refining those through formative evaluation. These considerations include devising a foundational research base to underpin the microsurveys; focusing on early and progressive design issues, such as microsurvey creation and modification, formats and usability, deployment protocols, accessibility, and transparency; and developing a formative evaluation plan. These steps enable microsurveys to be a critical and effective component of any early warning system and to support those student and institutional outcomes that are so challenging to improve.

REFERENCES

Anthonysamy, L., Koo, A. C., & Hew, S. H. (2020). Self-regulated learning strategies and non-academic outcomes in higher education blended learning environments: A one decade review. *Education and Information Technologies*, *25*(5), 3677–3704. doi:10.100710639-020-10134-2

Appleton, J. J., Christenson, S. L., Kim, D., & Reschly, A. L. (2006). Measuring cognitive and psychological engagement: Validation of the student engagement instrument. *Journal of School Psychology*, *44*(5), 427–445. doi:10.1016/j.jsp.2006.04.002

Balasooriya, I., Mor, E., & Rodríguez, M. E. (2017). Design of a microlevel student engagement data capture system. In *Proceedings of the 12th International Conference on P2P, Parallel, Grid, Cloud and Internet Computing* (pp. 632-641). Springer International Publishing.

Balasooriya, I., Mor, E., & Rodríguez, M. E. (2018). Engagement Analytics: A Microlevel Approach to Measure and Visualize Student Engagement. In S. Caballé & J. Conesa (Eds.), *Software Data Engineering for Network eLearning Environments. Lecture Notes on Data Engineering and Communications Technologies, 11*. Springer. doi:10.1007/978-3-319-68318-8_3

Balasooriya, I., Mor, E., & Rodríguez, M. E. (2018). Understanding user engagement in digital education. In *Learning and Collaboration Technologies. Learning and Teaching Lecture Notes in Computer Science* (pp. 3–15). Springer International Publishing. doi:10.1007/978-3-319-91152-6_1

Balasooriya, I., Rodríguez, M. E., & Mor, E. (2017). Assessment of Engagement: Using Microlevel Student Engagement as a Form of Continuous Assessment. In E. Ras & A. Guerrero Roldán (Eds.), Technology Enhanced Assessment. TEA 2017. Communications in Computer and Information Science. Academic Press.

Balfanz, R., Herzog, L., & MacIver, D. (2007). Preventing student disengagement and keeping students on the graduation path in urban middle-grades schools: Early identification and effective interventions. *Educational Psychologist*, *42*(4), 223–235. doi:10.1080/00461520701621079

Barab, S., & Squire, K. (2004). Design-based research: Putting a stake in the ground. *Journal of the Learning Sciences*, *13*(1), 1–14. doi:10.120715327809jls1301_1

Bawa, P. (2016). Retention in online courses. *SAGE Open*, *6*(1). Advance online publication. doi:10.1177/2158244015621777

Cho, M., & Yoo, J. S. (2017). Exploring online students' self-regulated learning with self-reported surveys and log files: A data mining approach. *Interactive Learning Environments*, *25*(8), 970–982. doi:10.1080/10494820.2016.1232278

Choi, B. C., & Pak, A. W. (2005). A catalog of biases in questionnaires. *Preventing Chronic Disease*, *2*(1), A13. PMID:15670466

Coates, H. (2007). A model of online and general campus-based student engagement. *Assessment & Evaluation in Higher Education*, *32*(2), 121–141. doi:10.1080/02602930600801878

de Boer, H., Donker, A. S., Kostons, D. D. N. M., & van der Werf, G. P. C. (2018). Long-term effects of metacognitive strategy instruction on student academic performance: A meta-analysis. *Educational Research Review*, *24*, 98–115. doi:10.1016/j.edurev.2018.03.002

Eisenberg, I. W., Bissett, P. G., Canning, J. R., Zeynep Enkavi, A., Whitfield-Gabrieli, S., Gonzalez, O., Green, A. I., Greene, M., Kiernan, M., Jung Kim, S., Li, J., Lowe, M. R., Mazza, G. L., Metcalf, S. A., Onken, L., Parikh, S. S., Peters, E., Prochaska, J. J., Scherer, E. A., ... Poldrack, R. A. (2018). Applying novel technologies and methods to inform the ontology of self-regulation. *Behaviour Research and Therapy*, *101*, 46–57. doi:10.1016/j.brat.2017.09.014 PMID:29066077

Finn, J. D. (1989). Withdrawing from school. *Review of Educational Research*, *59*(2), 117–142. doi:10.3102/00346543059002117

Fredricks, J. A., & McColskey, W. (2012). The measurement of student engagement: A comparative analysis of various methods and student self-report instruments. In S. Christenson, A. Reschly, & C. Wylie (Eds.), *Handbook of Research on Student Engagement* (pp. 763–782). Springer Science & Business Media. doi:10.1007/978-1-4614-2018-7_37

Gaertner, M., & McClarty, K. (2015). Performance, perseverance, and the full picture of college readiness. *Educational Measurement: Issues and Practice*, *34*(2), 20–33. doi:10.1111/emip.12066

Goetz, T., Bieg, M., & Hall, N. C. (2016). Assessing academic emotions via the experience sampling method. In M. Zembylas & P. Schutz (Eds.), *Methodological Advances in Research on Emotion and Education* (pp. 245–258). Springer International Publishing. doi:10.1007/978-3-319-29049-2_19

Gogol, K., Brunner, M., Goetz, T., Martin, R., Ugen, S., Keller, U., Fischbach, A., & Preckel, F. (2014). "My Questionnaire is Too Long!" The assessments of motivational-affective constructs with three-item and single-item measures. *Contemporary Educational Psychology*, *39*(3), 188–205. doi:10.1016/j.cedpsych.2014.04.002

Howard, E., Meehan, M., & Parnell, A. (2018). Contrasting prediction methods for early warning systems at undergraduate level. *The Internet and Higher Education*, *37*, 66–75. doi:10.1016/j.iheduc.2018.02.001

Hu, Y., Lo, C., & Shih, S. (2014). Developing early warning systems to predict students' online learning performance. *Computers in Human Behavior*, *36*, 469–478. doi:10.1016/j.chb.2014.04.002

Iaconelli, R., & Wolters, C. A. (2020). Insufficient Effort Responding in Surveys Assessing Self-Regulated Learning: Nuisance or Fatal Flaw? *Frontline Learning Research*, *8*(3), 104–125. doi:10.14786/flr.v8i3.521

Jokhan, A., Sharma, B., & Singh, S. (2018). Early warning system as a predictor for student performance in higher education blended courses. *Studies in Higher Education*, *44*(11), 1900–1911. doi:10.1080/03075079.2018.1466872

Kuh, G. D. (2009). The national survey of student engagement: Conceptual and empirical foundations. *New Directions for Institutional Research*, *2009*(141), 5–20. doi:10.1002/ir.283

MacIver, M. A. M., & Messel, M. (2013). The ABCs of keeping on track to graduation: Research findings from Baltimore. *Journal of Education for Students Placed at Risk*, *18*(1), 50–67. doi:10.1080/10824669.2013.745207

McMahon, B. M., & Sembiante, S. F. (2019). Re-envisioning the purpose of early warning systems: Shifting the mindset from student identification to meaningful prediction and intervention. *Review of Education*, *8*(1), 266–301. doi:10.1002/rev3.3183

National Forum on Education Statistics. (2018). *Forum Guide to Early Warning Systems* (NFES2019035). U.S. Department of Education. Washington, DC: National Center for Education Statistics.

NSC Research Center. (2018). *Persistence & Retention – 2018*. Retrieved from https://nscresearchcenter.org/snapshotreport33-first-year-persistence-and-retention/

Parr, A. K., & Bonitz, V. S. (2015). Role of family background, student behaviors, and school-related beliefs in predicting high school dropout. *The Journal of Educational Research*, *108*(6), 504–514. doi:10.1080/00220671.2014.917256

Reschly, A. L., & Christenson, S. L. (2006). Prediction of dropout among students with mild disabilities: A case for inclusion of student engagement variables. *Remedial and Special Education*, *27*(5), 276–292. doi:10.1177/07419325060270050301

Rumberger, R. W. (2011). *Dropping out: why students drop out of high school and what can be done about it*. Harvard University Press. doi:10.4159/harvard.9780674063167

Scherer, E. A., Kim, S. J., Metcalf, S. A., Sweeney, M. A., Wu, J., Xie, H., Mazza, G. L., Valente, M. J., MacKinnon, D. P., & Marsch, L. A. (2022). Momentary Self-regulation: Scale Development and Preliminary Validation. *JMIR Mental Health, 9*(5), e35273. doi:10.2196/35273 PMID:35536605

Simpson, O. (2013). Student retention in distance education: Are we failing our students? *Open Learning: The Journal of Open, Distance, and eLearning, 28*(2), 105-119.

Sneyers, E., & De Witte, K. (2018). Interventions in higher education and their effect on student success: A meta-analysis. *Educational Review, 70*(2), 208–228. doi:10.1080/00131911.2017.1300874

Thomas, L. (2012). *Building student engagement and belonging at a time of change in higher education*. Paul Hamlyn Foundation.

Tinto, V. (1987). *Leaving college: Rethinking the causes and cures for student attrition*. University of Chicago Press.

Wheeler, L., & Reis, H. T. (1991). Self-recordings of everyday life events: Origins, types, and Uues. *Journal of Personality, 59*(3), 339–354. doi:10.1111/j.1467-6494.1991.tb00252.x

Yan, Z. (2020). Self-assessment in the process of self-regulated learning and its relationship with academic achievement. *Assessment & Evaluation in Higher Education, 45*(2), 224–238. doi:10.1080/02602938.2019.1629390

Zhu, Y., Au, W., & Yates, G. (2016). University students' self-control and self-regulated learning in a blended course. *The Internet and Higher Education, 30*, 54–62. doi:10.1016/j.iheduc.2016.04.001

ADDITIONAL READING

Fredricks, J. A., & McColskey, W. (2012). The measurement of student engagement: A comparative analysis of various methods and student self-report instruments. In S. Christenson, A. Reschly, & C. Wylie (Eds.), *Handbook of Research on Student Engagement* (pp. 763–782). Springer Science & Business Media. doi:10.1007/978-1-4614-2018-7_37

Gogol, K., Brunner, M., Goetz, T., Martin, R., Ugen, S., Keller, U., Fischbach, A., & Preckel, F. (2014). "My Questionnaire is Too Long!" The assessments of motivational-affective constructs with three-item and single-item measures. *Contemporary Educational Psychology, 39*(3), 188–205. doi:10.1016/j.cedpsych.2014.04.002

Howard, E., Meehan, M., & Parnell, A. (2018). Contrasting prediction methods for early warning systems at undergraduate level. *The Internet and Higher Education, 37*, 66–75. doi:10.1016/j.iheduc.2018.02.001

Hu, Y., Lo, C., & Shih, S. (2014). Developing early warning systems to predict students' online learning performance. *Computers in Human Behavior, 36*, 469–478. doi:10.1016/j.chb.2014.04.002

Jokhan, A., Sharma, B., & Singh, S. (2018). Early warning system as a predictor for student performance in higher education blended courses. *Studies in Higher Education, 44*(11), 1900–1911. doi:10.1080/03075079.2018.1466872

McMahon, B. M., & Sembiante, S. F. (2019). Re-envisioning the purpose of early warning systems: Shifting the mindset from student identification to meaningful prediction and intervention. *Review of Education*, *8*(1), 266–301. doi:10.1002/rev3.3183

National Forum on Education Statistics. (2018). *Forum Guide to Early Warning Systems* (NFES2019035). U.S. Department of Education. Washington, DC: National Center for Education Statistics.

Sneyers, E., & De Witte, K. (2018). Interventions in higher education and their effect on student success: A meta-analysis. *Educational Review*, *70*(2), 208–228. doi:10.1080/00131911.2017.1300874

KEY TERMS AND DEFINITIONS

Alerts: Signals, nudges, or warnings sent to students, instructors, and/or administrators that are triggered when data-driven student performance or behaviors indicate a drop below a specified threshold or match a specified pattern.

Archetype: A typology representing a group of people with shared or clustered attributes.

Domain: Specific spheres of activity or knowledge, pertaining to learning, that include affective, behavioral, cognitive, and metacognitive.

Engagement: The degree of attention and interest students demonstrate (through their emotional responses, behaviors, and cognition) while learning.

Logic Model: A visualization of the relationships between outcomes, interactions, and interventions that shows a self-evident and defensible logic.

Microsurvey: A short question or question set that help researchers gather data in open-ended, closed-ended, or ordinal formats at strategic points in time.

Outcome: Broadly agreed, measurable change used to monitor the impact of a particular approach or intervention.

Theory of Change: An illustration of how and why a change should happen in a specific context.

Usability: The degree to which something is readily able to be used by a person.

Chapter 7
Metacognitive Knowledge and Self-Regulation of In-Service Teachers in an Online Learning Environment

Shirley Miedijensky
Oranim Academic College of Education, Israel

ABSTRACT

The study aimed at exposing expressions of metacognitive knowledge and self-regulation among in-service teachers taking an online course, examining the changes they applied in the tasks they developed in the course and characterizing their perceptions regarding the online course design principles. Teachers' blogs were analyzed inductively, based on a metacognition and self-regulation rubric developed in this study, as well as on design principles for online learning environments. The findings indicate increased expressions of knowledge of the task, people, and strategies. However, obstacles regarding time management were mentioned. Teachers' perceptions analysis indicates that learning from and with peers, course organization, and making thinking visible were the most significant principles promoting their learning. It seems that the online course offered the teachers a constructive, supportive learning environment, enabling them to express their metacognition and self-regulation skills, as well as the insights they will consider when designing tasks in the future.

INTRODUCTION

Modern technologies and the internet's rapid development have generated various advantages in the delivery of higher education, enabling the recruitment of more students at lower costs (Castro & Tumibay, 2019; Chen & Carliner, 2020). In the last decade, higher education institutions have expanded the number of online courses, which requires lecturers to become familiar with the design principles on which these courses are based, or develop new design principles according to their course needs. Taking online courses, particularly asynchronous ones, requires students to be responsible and self-directed (Zhu

DOI: 10.4018/978-1-6684-6500-4.ch007

& Bonk, 2022). Hence, the course design is significant. Design principles can help lecturers organize course structure and content, express diverse pedagogies or ones adapted to the specific course and its goals, and encourage the promotion of student learning (Engeness, 2021; Kali et al., 2009). Online courses promoting peer learning and student engagement expose students to self-regulation as well as to social knowledge construction, which can enhance their socially-shared metacognitive regulation (Binali et al., 2021). If teachers wish to relate to the pragmatic aspect of metacognition development and enable its expression among their students, they need to be aware of their own metacognitive knowledge and processes, and have sound pedagogical knowledge in the context of teaching metacognition and high order thinking skills (Eldar & Miedijensky, 2015; Lin et al., 2017; Miedijensky et al., 2021; Zohar & Barzilai, 2013). Unfortunately, research indicates that metacognition is still a vague concept for most teachers (Zohar & Ben-Ari, 2022). This chapter focuses on metacognitive knowledge and self-regulation among in-service teachers taking an online course as part of their M.Ed. program at a College of Education. Its aim is to understand the way learning in an online course is perceived by the teachers, and how self-regulation and metacognitive knowledge are expressed in their task design process during the course. Thus, the research questions are:

1. How do teachers perceive the design principles of the online course?
2. How are metacognitive knowledge and self-regulation expressed by the teachers in the course?

BACKGROUND

Design Principles in the Online Learning Environment

In the last decade online learning environments have become popular in higher education, and universities face the challenge of developing such courses, using advanced pedagogical approaches and making efficient use of digital technologies (Morris et al., 2020), as well as promoting students' capacity of learning how to learn (Engeness, 2021). In addition, the methods and learning materials used in online learning environments should also include use of interactive and technological resources (Sezgin & Yüzer, 2022). The way in which online learning environments are designed might affect students' self-directed learning and outcomes (Engeness, 2021; Jaggars & Xu, 2016). One way to handle such complex learning environments is to use design principles that can help educators in implementing their pedagogical approaches (Kali, 2006). Design principles are perceived as an organizational unit for synthesizing design knowledge (Linn et al., 2004). Based on this approach, the Design Principles Database was developed to combine emerging design knowledge about the use of technologies for education and enable educators and researchers to share their design knowledge in the form of design principles (Kali et al., 2009). The following five design principles were implemented in this study. Four meta-design principles based on the Design Principles Database (Kali & Ronen-Fuhrman, 2011), and one based on Moore (2013):

1. *Learning from and with peers:* the teachers learn from their colleagues' ideas and interpret them, gaining new perspectives.
2. *Making thinking visible:* the teachers integrate new knowledge, reflect upon it and connect it to their own or others' ideas, distinguishing them from or reconciling them with others.

3. *Making content accessible:* the course included many different elements that were available to the teachers - simulations, media resources, academic materials, activities, blogs and discussions, which introduced the teachers to rich, varied learning environments and encouraged them to reconsider their existing ideas and connect them to new ones.
4. *Promoting autonomy:* establishing a rich, wide-ranging learning environment, encouraging the teachers to take responsibility for their own learning and develop into lifelong learners.
5. *Course organization:* a clear structure and instructions that explicitly guide the teachers to navigate the course successfully.

Teachers' Metacognition and Self-Regulation

Metacognition is known as: "one's knowledge concerning one's own cognitive processes…and the active monitoring and consequent regulation and orchestration of these processes" (Flavell, 1976, p.232). Scholars (e.g., Brown, 1987; Flavell, 1979; Schraw & Moshman, 1995) have noted that metacognition includes metacognitive skills (MS) or regulation of cognition, as well as metacognitive knowledge. MS focus on self-regulation processes, which include setting goals, planning, testing, revising and evaluating learning progress and strategies (Andrade, 2019; Brown, 1987; Brown & Harris, 2014). Metacognitive knowledge includes knowledge of strategies used for different tasks, the conditions under which they might be used and the extent to which they are effective, as well as knowledge regarding people (the self and others). Success in a learning task requires several abilities: the ability to choose and understand the rationale; the ability to set goals; the ability to choose appropriate strategies to achieve those goals; the ability to monitor progress in the learning process; and the ability to adjust the implementation of strategies as needed, that is, regulation (Zohar & Ben-Ari, 2022). Self-regulation is comprised of actions that enable students to select and use strategies, monitor their learning and behavior and regulate them (Zimmerman, 2008); for instance, planning one's time-management in order to carry out a task (Pintrich, 2004). Dinsmore and colleagues (2008) noted that "differences between metacognition, self-regulation, and self-regulated learning may lie in *what* is being monitored or controlled. In self-regulation and self-regulated learning, monitoring or control refer to behavior, or motivation, while metacognition likely emphasizes monitoring and control of cognition specifically" (p. 401). In the current study, we view self-regulation as part of metacognition (Dinsmore et al., 2008), particularly in relation to metacognitive knowledge, and the online course design principles as the platform enabling expressions of metacognitive knowledge and self-regulation skills (see Figure 1). We discuss metacognitive knowledge, focusing on three main components:

1. *Knowledge of the task*: How comprehension of the task is presented - what is the task about, its rationale, structure and components, its significance, and when to apply it or its components. Regarding self-regulation, we discuss monitoring and time management.
2. *Knowledge of people*: How one examines and monitors his/her thinking processes; how one studies others' thinking; how one interacts and collaborates with others, praising or providing constructive feedback.
3. *Knowledge of strategies*: How one employs strategies in an effort to improve performance.

Figure 1. Course principles as a platform for metacognitive knowledge and self-regulation expressions

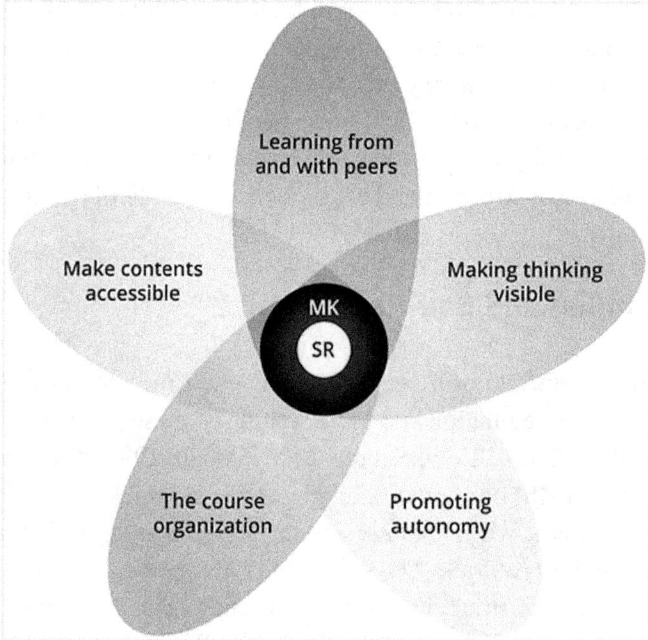

METHODOLOGY

Participants and Learning Environment

The participants included 146 in-service teachers attending an online course as part of their M.Ed. program at a College of Education. The online course, entitled Gifted Education, focused on gifted students, effective curriculum models for the gifted, and giftedness in science and mathematics. The course was asynchronous and included weekly learning units. Each unit included learning materials, media and various short activities in a specific subject in gifted education. In the course, the teachers were required to develop activities for gifted students, explore a variety of resources, and introduce their activities in the course online discussions, relating to their colleagues' questions and feedback. The goals of the course were to help teachers promote self-regulation skills and metacognition for learning. The teachers' activities encouraged expression of creativity and higher order thinking skills. In addition, each teacher had a personal blog on the course website. The course design is presented in Figure 2, which shows how the design principles are embedded in the course throughout the entire learning process.

Data Collection and Analysis

The data included teachers' blogs, the tasks they developed and the online discussions. In this chapter we discuss the teachers' blogs. The personal blog included a weekly post at the end of each learning unit, as well as a discussion of the final course assignment (developing a task for gifted students) entered at the end of the course.

Figure 2. Course design

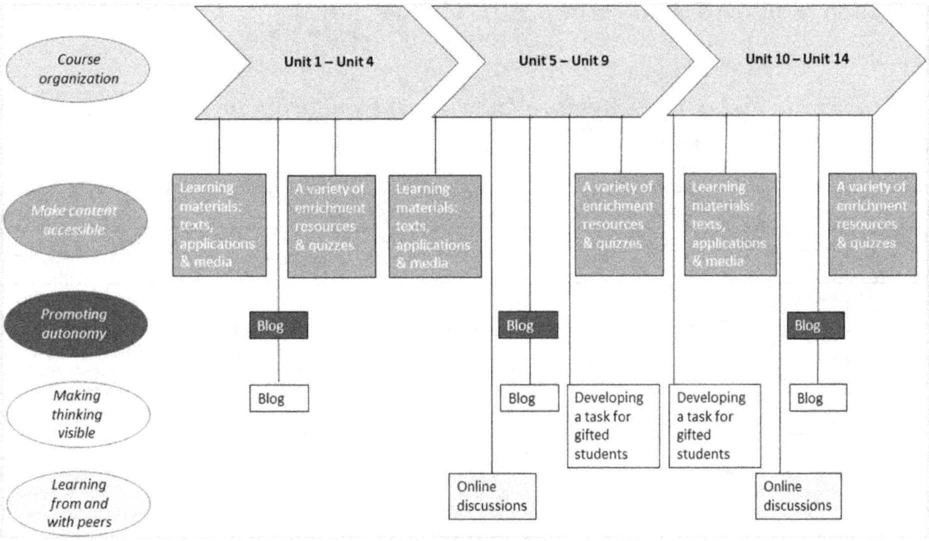

In their weekly posts, the teachers were asked to refer to the subjects they had studied, the articles they had read, the activities they had experienced, the media resources they had watched, and learning from and with their colleagues in the forum discussion. In addition, they were required to complete a short questionnaire/quiz, indicating whether they had acquired new knowledge and, if so, what, and whether they had acquired knowledge about themselves as learners and their thought processes. Did they feel responsible for their learning? What was significant and valuable to them and why, were there topics and/or activities that were valuable to them beyond the course itself, did it affect their way of thinking and if so, how? Did the course encourage them to come up with ideas for implementation at school or as students in the MEd program? In addition, the teachers were asked to indicate what their strengths were, and at which points in the course did they feel in control of what was taught. What were the difficulties they had experienced? Were there things they did not understand and/or that were unclear to them? The teachers were required to indicate in detail how they intended to deal with these difficulties. These questions were part of the course metacognitive scaffolding, aimed at developing teachers' metacognitive knowledge regarding their own learning processes.

In their reference to the task for the gifted they developed, teachers were required to describe its rationale and indicate how it adds/contributes to the gifted curriculum. In addition, they were asked to note which curriculum model for the gifted they had selected and adapted. They were required to describe the task, its components, the skills it develops (e.g., critical thinking, problem solving, judgment, creative thinking), strategies they used, strengths and/or weaknesses regarding task development, their colleagues' feedback, the teacher's role, other factors involved, what prior knowledge is required, and whether the students will work individually or in groups.

For the first research question, the data analysis was based on metacognitive knowledge components as defined in the current study, as well as on a rubric (see Table 1) developed by the author and another researcher, relating to metacognitive knowledge and aspects of monitoring and time management. This rubric was validated by four other researchers, three specializing in metacognition and one in self-regulation. The inter-rater reliability was 0.85 (Krippendorff, 2013). For the second research question, the teachers' perceptions were analyzed inductively, based on the five design principles described in the Background section (Kali & Ronen-Fuhrman, 2011; Moore, 2013).

Table 1. A rubric for assessing metacognitive knowledge, monitoring and time management levels in the tasks developed by the teachers

	Low Level	Intermediate Level	High Level
	At least one of the following characteristics exists	At least two of the following characteristics exist	All of the following characteristics exist
Knowledge of the task	The teacher doesn't present aims at all or presents aims irrelevant to the task; the teacher doesn't explain how the task structure & content suit its demands; there's no mention of the model the task is based on; the teacher mentions the model the task is based on but it doesn't suit the task.	There's partial comprehension of the task; the teacher describes the task aims & structure, but doesn't sufficiently connect the task aims, structure & content; the teacher relates to the model the task is based on but the explanation is partial and/or the model doesn't suit the presented task.	There's full comprehension of the task and its content; the teacher explains task aims fully; the teacher connects task aims, structure & content; a suitable model the task is based on is presented and a full, coherent explanation is provided.
Knowledge of strategies	The teacher doesn't present any strategies, or presents strategies irrelevant for the task; the teacher doesn't present insights regarding new strategies s/he wishes to use following peer feedback.	The teacher describes one or more strategies, but doesn't sufficiently connect them to the task components & content; the teacher presents one insight only regarding new strategies s/he wishes to use following peer feedback.	There is clear knowledge & comprehension regarding strategies related to the task & its content; the teacher presents strategies relevant to the task; the teacher presents two insights or more regarding new strategies s/he wishes to use following peer feedback about the task.
Knowledge of self	There is no expression of the teacher's strengths and/or weaknesses regarding task development; there is no expression of the teacher's thought characteristics and/or insights regarding task development.	One of the teacher's strengths and/or weaknesses regarding task development is mentioned; there is an expression of one of the teacher's thought characteristics and/or insights regarding task development.	Two or more of the teacher's strengths and/or weaknesses regarding task development are mentioned; there is an expression of two or more of the teacher's thought characteristics and/or insights regarding task development.
Knowledge of others	There is no expression of colleagues' thought processes and/or strengths and/or weaknesses; there is no expression of interactions or cooperation with colleagues.	There is expression of one colleague's thought processes and/or strengths and/or weaknesses; there is an undetailed expression of colleagues' thought processes; there is interaction and/or cooperation with one colleague.	There is expression of two or more colleagues' thought processes and/or strengths and/or weaknesses; there is a full, detailed discussion of colleagues' thought processes; there is expression of interactions and cooperation with more than two colleagues.
Monitoring	The teacher doesn't relate at all to his/her thinking process while carrying out the task; the teacher doesn't mention or explain whether or not his/her aim has been achieved and/or changes to the task should be made; there is no mention of new knowledge and/or skills acquired during task development; there is no expression of expectations for the next learning process.	The teacher relates to his/her thinking process while carrying out the task, but doesn't explain or provides a partial, undetailed explanation; the teacher mentions whether s/he has found the task reasonable, and/or s/he has achieved the aim, and/or s/he needs to make any changes, but the explanation is lacking or is not accompanied by examples; there is expression of expectations for the next learning process, including mention of at least one conclusion.	The learner relates to his/her thought processes while carrying out the task. S/he differentiates between former knowledge & skills s/he has implemented during the learning process and new knowledge and/or skills acquired during it; s/he examines his/her work vis-à-vis the plan, locates gaps if any and can explain them; s/he critically summarizes the learning process while engaging in expressions of expectations for the next learning process, relating to two or more positive/negative conclusions.
Time management	The teacher doesn't relate to time management while carrying out the task.	The teacher relates to time management while carrying out certain elements of the task, not relating to the entire task; there is mention of one advantage and/or one difficulty relating to time management.	The teacher relates to time management while carrying out the entire task; there is mention of more than two advantages and/or difficulties relating to time management.

RESULTS

Teachers' Perceptions of the Course Design Principles

Analysis of the teachers' perceptions indicates that learning from and with peers, course organization, and making thinking visible were the most significant design principles, promoting their learning in the course. The themes that emerged from the teachers' references to these principles included: Critical Thinking, Knowledge Expansion and Reflection.

Learning From and With Peers

This principle enabled the teachers to benefit from their colleagues' ideas, introduced new perspectives and motivated them to interpret these ideas. As described above, this course included online discussions which usually lasted one to two weeks. This time period enabled the teachers to think, raise questions and discuss relevant issues with their colleagues. Most of the teachers (89%) stated that the opportunity to learn from colleagues during the discussions helped them think critically, understand how to improve the task they had developed and expand their knowledge, as can be seen in the following quotes:

One of the significant things in the course was the opportunity to learn from the discussions we held throughout the semester. I was able to get feedback on the task and regarding the questions I needed an answer to, and I also wrote clarifying questions regarding other teachers' activities. Each discussion taught me more, I expanded my knowledge.

The discussions in the course enabled me to stop and think about my assignment, as well as my way of thinking in relation to the other teachers. It was like self-criticism, every time. The fact that the discussion lasted a week and I could relate to my colleagues when it suited me gave me time to think and process all the information I learned that week, and think about if and how I need to improve my assignment.

Course Organization

This principle relates to a clear structure and instructions explicitly guiding students in their navigation of the course. Most teachers (75%) referred to the directions on the course website, which included clear instructions, a division of content, a schedule, and a place to submit assignments and activities.

It was very easy to navigate the course website. The order in the course, its organization and the opening of activities according to schedule and providing the option of choosing to explore the content related to gifted education helped me deepen my knowledge regarding the gifted in science education.

When I take an online course, particularly an asynchronous one, it is important to me that things are clear from the beginning to the end of the course. In this course it is evident that a lot of thinking was put into its planning, so that it will be clear for us. We were given the best conditions. It was rare that I didn't understand something and had to write an email to the lecturer. It also helped me and others in the course to submit assignments on time, and I'm usually the type to postpone my submissions.

Making Thinking Visible

This principle allows the teachers to integrate knowledge, reflect upon new information and engage in differentiating or reconciling their own or their peers' ideas from or with each other. In the course, almost all the teachers (95%) experienced this on their own when they wrote their reflections regarding their activities, and collaboratively when they participated in online discussions, as can be seen in the following quote:

In almost every post on my blog I referred to the fact that I am going through a reflective process in the course, revealing my thinking to myself, to my colleagues and to those who will review this work. I worked individually on all assignments, that's what I decided to do. I enjoyed proving that I went from being able to write about things at a technical level only to a level where I related to details and was able to reasonably explain what my thought processes were throughout the course, and what went through my mind during the stage of planning the task and presenting it to my colleagues.

The following design principles, *Making Content Accessible,* and *Promoting Autonomy,* stood out less in the teachers' words.

Making Content Accessible

The course included a variety of components: academic articles, on-line quizzes, media resources and discussions. These components formed a rich and diverse learning environment that helped the teachers during the learning process and when designing their assignments. Exposure to this content and its various elements allowed the teachers to reflect on their learning, as well as their thinking processes. Nevertheless, 45% of the teachers' mentioned it explicitly. It seems that most teachers did not relate to this design principle as a stand-alone principle. It is possible that *Making Content Accessible* is seen as embedded in the other design principles, or that it serves as a basic platform for them.

The reading materials and the media components on the website helped me get ideas for developing the task. The short movie about the brain and sleep helped me understand the importance of chemical processes in our bodies. All these sources helped me answer the quizzes and give my colleagues feedback. Regarding my task, it consisted of several steps, I had to really gather information, research, check if what I teach at school can be adapted to a higher level for gifted students. I was not always able to do this, and in the end, I changed the subject of the task several times.

Promoting Autonomy

This principle involved the establishment of a rich learning environment, encouraging teachers to take responsibility for their own learning and develop as lifelong learners, as one of the teachers noted:

Throughout the course I studied alone, I have insights into how to study in an asynchronous course. This is entirely the learner's responsibility. We really had everything on the site. There are things that I have already implemented in other courses, and maybe when I return from my sabbatical, I will implement them at school as well.

The data analysis revealed that this design principle did not stand out for most of the teachers. Approximately a third of the teachers (34%) stated that they would have preferred less choice in the reading assignments and the short exercises in the course. Some indicated that it sometimes caused them

Table 2. Levels of metacognitive knowledge, monitoring and time management expressions (N=146)

	Low Level	Intermediate Level	High Level
Knowledge of the task	0%	23%	77%
Knowledge of strategies	5%	49%	46%
Knowledge of self	0%	4%	96%
Knowledge of others	0%	11%	89%
Monitoring	0%	25%	75%
Time management	0%	10%	90%

confusion. It was difficult for them to choose, make decisions and write responses to open questions in the peer discussions. They needed almost constant assistance from the lecturer.

Teachers' Expressions of Metacognitive Knowledge and Self-Regulation Aspects

In this section we present teachers' metacognitive knowledge and aspects of self-regulation as expressed by the teachers regarding the task they developed for the gifted as well as their learning process. Table 2 presents the percentage of teachers rated at each level regarding expressions of metacognitive knowledge, monitoring and time management according to the three levels of the rubric.

It seems that most of the teachers knew how to refer to metacognitive knowledge of the self and their knowledge of their colleagues, as well as how to relate to issues of task monitoring and time management. Nevertheless, it seems that they had some difficulties expressing their knowledge of strategies regarding the task. Below are examples of expressions of metacognitive knowledge, monitoring and time management at the high level, as emerging from the data analysis.

Knowledge of the Assignment

This task deals with the Mobius Strip and is based on the epistemological model and the process–product model. Students will also be exposed to the philosophical aspects of the topic and will discuss the concept of 'structure' in biology and other contexts. They will be required to develop models of new cell structures for organisms, explore why the new structure suits the function of the organism, and list its advantages and disadvantages as compared to the existing structure. The task relates to receptors and processes that occur both on the surface of the cell and within it. The objective of the task is to develop creative, interdisciplinary learning.

This task dealt with the effect of persuasion in language and in the media. Its objectives included transmitting knowledge and principles and acquiring skills in the areas of language and communication. The linguistic aspect focused on identifying an impersonal subject in a sentence, recognizing its functions in a dialogue, and understanding the circumstances and objectives of its use. The learning objectives in the area of communication focused on the effect of persuasion: familiarizing students with the two main types of persuasion in advertising and understanding the advantages and disadvantages of each. The area of skills focused on cognitive and social skills, analytic thinking abilities, critical thinking, teamwork and creativity. The task is particularly suitable for classes of gifted students, but it is also appropriate for gifted students in regular classrooms. The task can be adapted to gifted students from several aspects, including learning through discussions that encourage creativity and self-expression.

Knowledge of Strategies

After thoroughly assessing the feedback I received from my colleagues, I made several changes in order to make the task less structured. I changed the research to an open one, and the students had to propose new research questions and suggest additional research topics. They also had the option of choosing two out of four of the guidelines. Teachers must be flexible, particularly with gifted students. It is necessary to provide clear guidelines, while allowing the students a certain degree of freedom in their research.

Integrating cooperative learning into my task was an excellent idea that I got from the class forum. I read about it and realized that it is very suitable to my activities and can also contribute to social cohesion among gifted students. I included a matrix that explains the components of cooperative learning and its various levels. I allowed the students to choose which level suited them, while providing an explanation for their choice.

Knowledge of Self

My choice of the topic order and disorder stems from my extensive interest in chaos. I understood that I can think differently and allow room for imagination, creativity and critique. These things are expressed in nature and in other strange ideas. This led me to be more flexible and not adhere to the strict laws of physics. I now look at things differently and teach differently.

I have planned lessons all my life, but I have always based them on existing materials because I was afraid of making mistakes. The material in the course and my experience with the activities enabled me to open up, and I rediscovered myself. I have been a teacher for 16 years, but I now feel as if I were a new teacher and full of enthusiasm. I learned that I can take risks and grow. I have adopted this message for myself as well as for my students – particularly for the gifted child in my class.

Knowledge of Others

My colleagues' feedback in the course reflected their thinking processes to me: what their rationale for developing their activities was, how they thought about building them, how they dealt with challenges, and the difficulties they experienced. We presented questions that we wanted our colleagues to relate to. I debated whether to explain the concept of biomimicry to my students or let them understand it for themselves. I asked Tal and Kim (pseudonyms) on the forum, and they helped me understand how they dared to teach differently. They were not afraid to make mistakes, or even admit their mistakes to their students. I also understood that it is preferable not to reveal the topic to gifted students, because they will eventually discover it themselves.

Martin (pseudonym) wrote that he supported the task that I wanted. He asked me to answer questions that he wrote, and conveyed the message that he was critical, while at the same time helping me with the final development of my task. We talked after each meeting on the forum, and our telephone conversations strengthened me. He had wonderful ideas, and I understood how good it was to think together. He has extensive general knowledge and excellent analytical abilities.

Monitoring

I had to understand all the components of integrative learning while I was developing the assignment. I had to cope with my perception of multi-disciplinarity and inter-disciplinarity, because I hadn't previously been familiar with integrative learning. I noticed that this sometimes prevented me from making progress in building the assignment. I decided to cope and solve the problem myself. I composed a question about vectors that combined physics and mathematics. I understood that in order to develop activities in the future I would need to learn things comprehensively, make sure I understand them, practice, compose questions about the topic, and verify that I could answer them. It's also important to examine the target audience for whom the task is intended.

The assignment about the river that I developed has scientific, mathematical, social and cultural aspects. I had to relate to the cultural aspect in an extremely sensitive manner, because the students come from a variety of cultural backgrounds. I researched all their cultures in depth and made sure that there was at least one question pertaining to each culture. At first, I only noted facts about what is acceptable in each culture, but the questions I received from my colleagues made me realize that was not enough. I began to use concepts from each specific culture that we dealt with in the assignment. This was combined with illustrations, links to relevant podcasts and newspaper articles. I felt my thinking was also developing with each stage of the assignment.

Time Management

Time management was the most difficult part for me. I have a bit of dissonance and am aware of my problem, but I haven't succeeded in solving it. I know I was supposed to deal with each part of the assignment during a specific period of time. I planned to do so, but planning the assignment, writing the objectives and planning the skills took me more than a month. I found myself devoting far too much time to this, more than I had planned, because I am easily distracted. Halfway through the course I already had enough knowledge, and I saw that others were also dealing with problems of time management while building the assignment. One suggestion was to set an alarm and work on the assignment at a certain time each day. If we completed the daily objective without being distracted, we would have a Zoom meeting to have a cup of coffee together. This increased our motivation and helped us bond socially.

I divided the construction of the assignment and all the studying according to the days of the week. Each day I invested a half hour in the course and assignment construction. On weekends I designated an hour and a half to working on the course. I discovered that I was able to accomplish this, and I completed the assignment before the end of the semester. This made me feel that I was skilled in managing my time in my personal life as well. There were also difficulties, which frustrated me. I felt pressure towards the end of the semester because of other courses, and it interfered with my time with my family.

DISCUSSION

The findings indicate that teachers perceive 'course organization', 'learning from and with peers', and 'making thinking visible' as the most substantial design principles for their learning process and task design. The importance of a clear structure of online learning environments, instructions that help students navigate the course and ease of use were mentioned by several scholars (e.g., Crews & Wilkinson, 2015; Jaggars & Xu, 2016; Martin et al., 2019; Mo et al., 2021; Moore, 2013). Nevertheless, it is worth mentioning that although course organization is important, it does not automatically predict learner outcomes (Jaggars & Xu, 2016; Mubarak et al., 2022). It seems that the design principles, 'learning from and with peers' and 'making thinking visible', promoted the teachers' critical thinking and their ability to write coherent and constructive feedback to their colleagues. At the same time, these principles contributed to their self-reflection regarding the assignment they had developed. These design principles enabled the establishment of a community of inquiry for the teachers, perceived as significant for promoting their learning and reflection-in-action regarding the task they had developed (Fiock, 2020; Mumford & Dikilitas, 2020; Schön, 1983). Regarding the design principle of promoting autonomy, as mentioned in the Findings section, over a third of the teachers stated that they would have liked to have been given less choice regarding the course reading assignments and exercises, and some said that this confused them. This is understandable, since learners are required to cope with large amounts of information from multiple sources and are responsible for regulating their own learning process (Blau et al., 2020). This highlights the need for a rational design which considers design principles in course planning in general, and in asynchronous online courses specifically, particularly regarding self-regulation, since there are learners who find it difficult to bridge the gap between this type of learning and learning in face-to-face courses (Xu & Jaggars, 2014).

Regarding expressions of metacognition, the findings indicate that most of the teachers knew how to discuss metacognitive knowledge of the self and their peers, and most of them knew how to talk about issues of task monitoring and time management. Significantly, the fact that the teachers related to their time management skills did not indicate that they did not encounter difficulties relating to this self-regulation component. However, regarding the component of knowledge about strategies, it is evident that half of the teachers knew how to refer to this in a coherent, explicit manner, while the others had some difficulties in expressing this metacognitive knowledge component, referring to it at a medium to low level.

Our findings show that the design of the online course and the use of various digital tools promoted the teachers' metacognitive knowledge. As Dinsmore (2008) and Miedijensky and Tal (2016) noted, self-regulation and metacognition can be developed and expressed based on the person's interaction with a learning environment that stimulates a great deal of highly conscious reflection. It seems that the teachers constructed their metacognitive knowledge personally, while writing their own blogs and through interactions with their colleagues during online discussions and the development of their teaching activities. Receiving feedback from peers seems to have enhanced their ability to monitor and regulate their progress in the learning process (Efklides, 2019). This is supported by Engeness (2021), who noted that feedback provided to students in digital environments assists them in developing their conceptual understanding and enhancing their understanding of how to go about learning.

The current study indicates that the course design described in the study created a supportive learning environment and promoted teachers' understanding of the course learning materials, encouraging positive interactions among the learners. The present study offers both theoretical and practical contributions.

Theoretically, the study contributes to the bodies of knowledge dealing with educational technology, asynchronous online courses and design principles in teaching and learning, as well as metacognition and self-regulation. From a practical point of view, the findings may help lecturers in higher education in designing online courses, as well as developing workshops dealing with this topic.

FUTURE RESEARCH DIRECTIONS

In the current chapter findings were presented concerning metacognitive knowledge and two particular aspects of self-regulation (time management and monitoring). Findings concerning additional aspects of self-regulation are presented in an upcoming paper. It is recommended that future research examines metacognition and affect. Specifically, teachers' metacognitive feelings and emotions while learning in online courses designed to promote a community of inquiry. In addition, it is recommended that researchers study metacognitive expressions and self-regulation among students whose teachers participated in training programs focusing on metacognition and self-regulation. The author is currently working on expansion of the model (Figure 1) presented in this chapter, including cognitive neuroscience perspectives, psychology of learning, and additional dimensions of cognition regulation and design principles for online learning environments.

REFERENCES

Andrade, H. L. (2019). A critical review of research on student self-assessment. *Frontiers in Education*, *4*(87), 87. Advance online publication. doi:10.3389/feduc.2019.00087

Binali, T., Tsai, C. C., & Chang, H. Y. (2021). University students' profiles of online learning and their relation to online metacognitive regulation and internet-specific epistemic justification. *Computers & Education*, *175*, 104315. Advance online publication. doi:10.1016/j.compedu.2021.104315

Blau, I., Shamir-Inbal, T., & Avdiel, O. (2020). How does the pedagogical design of a technology-enhanced collaborative academic course promote digital literacies, self-regulation, and perceived learning of students? *The Internet and Higher Education*, *45*, 100722. Advance online publication. doi:10.1016/j.iheduc.2019.100722

Brown, A. (1987). Metacognition, executive control, self-regulation, and other more mysterious mechanisms. In F. E. Weinert & R. H. Kluwe (Eds.), *Metacognition, motivation and understanding* (pp. 65–116). Erlbaum.

Brown, G., & Harris, L. R. (2014). The future of self-assessment in classroom practice: Reframing self-assessment as a core competency. *Frontline Learning Research*, *2*(1), 22–30. doi:10.14786/flr.v2i1.24

Castro, M. D. B., & Tumibay, G. M. (2019). A literature review: Efficacy of online learning courses for higher education institution using meta-analysis. *Education and Information Technologies*, *26*(2), 1367–1385. doi:10.100710639-019-10027-z

Chen, Y., & Carliner, S. (2020). A special SME: An integrative literature review of the relationship between instructional designers and faculty in the design of online courses for higher education. *Performance Improvement Quarterly*, *33*(4), 471–495. doi:10.1002/piq.21339

Crews, T. B., & Wilkinson, K. (2015). Online quality course design vs. quality teaching: Aligning quality matters standards to principles for good teaching. *The Journal of Research in Business Education*, *57*(1), 47–63.

Dinsmore, D. L., Alexander, P. A., & Loughlin, S. M. (2008). Focusing the conceptual lens on metacognition, self-regulation, and self-regulated learning. *Educational Psychology Review*, *20*(4), 391–409. doi:10.100710648-008-9083-6

Efklides, A. (2019). Gifted students and self-regulated learning: The MASRL model and its implications for SRL. *High Ability Studies*, *30*(1-2), 79–102. doi:10.1080/13598139.2018.1556069

Eldar, O., & Miedijensky, S. (2015). Designing a metacognitive approach to the professional development of experienced science teachers. In A. Peña-Ayala (Ed.), *Metacognition: Fundaments, Applications, and Trends. A Profile of the Current State-Of-The-Art* (pp. 299–319). Springer. doi:10.1007/978-3-319-11062-2_12

Engeness, I. (2021). Developing teachers' digital identity: Towards the pedagogic deign principles of digital environments to enhance students' learning in the 21st century. *European Journal of Teacher Education*, *44*(1), 96–114. doi:10.1080/02619768.2020.1849129

Fiock, H. (2020). Designing a community of inquiry in online courses. *The International Review of Research in Open and Distributed Learning*, *21*(1), 135–153. doi:10.19173/irrodl.v20i5.3985

Flavell, J. H. (1976). Metacognitive aspects of problem-solving. In L. B. Resinck (Ed.), *The nature of intelligence* (pp. 231–236). Erlbaum.

Flavell, J. H. (1979). Metacognition and cognitive monitoring: A new area of cognitive-developmental inquiry. *The American Psychologist*, *34*(10), 906–911. doi:10.1037/0003-066X.34.10.906

Jaggars, S. S., & Xu, D. (2016). How online course design features influence student performance? *Computers & Education*, *95*, 270–284. doi:10.1016/j.compedu.2016.01.014

Kali, Y. (2006). Collaborative knowledge building using the Design Principles Database. *Computer Supported Learning*, *1*(2), 187–201. doi:10.100711412-006-8993-x

Kali, Y., Levin-Peled, R., & Dori, Y. J. (2009). The role of Design-Principles in designing courses that promotes collaborative learning in higher-education. *Computers in Human Behavior*, *25*(5), 1067–1078. doi:10.1016/j.chb.2009.01.006

Kali, Y., & Ronen-Fuhrmann, T. (2011). Teaching to design educational technologies. *International Journal of Learning Technology*, *6*(1), 4–23. doi:10.1504/IJLT.2011.040147

Krippendorff, K. (2013). *Content analysis: An introduction to its methodology* (3rd ed.). Sage.

Lin, Y.-R., Hung, C.-Y., & Hung, J.-F. (2017). Exploring teachers' meta-strategies knowledge of science argumentation teaching with the repertory grid technique. *International Journal of Science Education*, *39*(2), 105–134. doi:10.1080/09500693.2016.1270476

Linn, M. C., Bell, P., & Davis, E. A. (2004). Specific design principles: Elaborating the scaffolded knowledge integration framework. In Internet environments for science education. Lawrence Erlbaum Associates.

Martin, F., Ritzhaupt, A., Kymar, S., & Budhrani, K. (2019). Award-winning faculty online teaching practices: Course design, assessment and evaluation, and facilitation. *The Internet and Higher Education*, *42*, 34–43. doi:10.1016/j.iheduc.2019.04.001

Miedijensky, S., Sasson, I., & Yehuda, I. (2021). Teachers' learning communities for developing high order thinking skills—A case study of a school pedagogical change. *Interchange*, *52*(4), 577–598. doi:10.100710780-021-09423-7

Miedijensky, S., & Tal, T. (2016). Reflection and assessment for learning in science enrichment courses for the gifted. *Studies in Educational Evaluation*, *50*, 1–13. doi:10.1016/j.stueduc.2016.05.001

Mo, C. Y., Hsieh, T. H., Lin, C. L., Jin, Y. Q., & Su, Y. S. (2021). Exploring the critical factors, the online learning continuance usage during Covid-19 pandemic. *Sustainability*, *13*(10), 5471. doi:10.3390u13105471

Moore, M. G. (2013). The theory of transactional distance. In M. G. Moore (Ed.), *Handbook of Distance Education* (3rd ed.). Routledge. doi:10.4324/9780203803738.ch5

Morris, N. P., Ivancheva, M., Coop, T., Mogliacci, R., & Seinnerton, B. (2020). Negotiating growth of online education in higher education. *International Journal Educational Technology in Higher Education*, *17*(1), 48. doi:10.118641239-020-00227-w

Mubarak, A. A., Cao, H., & Zhang, W. (2022). Predication of students' early dropout based on their interaction logs in online learning environment. *Interactive Learning Environments*, *30*(8), 1414–1433. doi:10.1080/10494820.2020.1727529

Mumford, S., & Dikilitas, K. (2020). Pre-service language teachers reflection development through online interaction in a hybrid learning course. *Computers & Education*, *144*, 103706. Advance online publication. doi:10.1016/j.compedu.2019.103706

Pintrich, P. R. (2004). A conceptual framework for assessing motivation and self-regulation learning in college students. *Educational Psychology Review*, *16*(4), 385–407. doi:10.100710648-004-0006-x

Schön, D. A. (1983). *The reflective practitioner: How professionals think in action*. Basic Books.

Schraw, G., & Moshman, D. (1995). Metacognitive theories. *Educational Psychology Review*, *7*(4), 351–371. doi:10.1007/BF02212307

Sezgin, S., & Yüzer, T. V. (2022). Analyzing adaptive gamification design principles for online courses. *Behaviour & Information Technology*, *41*(3), 485–501. doi:10.1080/0144929X.2020.1817559

Xu, D., & Jaggars, S. S. (2014). Performance gaps between online and face-to-face courses: Differences between types of students and academic subject areas. *The Journal of Higher Education*, *85*(5), 633–659. doi:10.1353/jhe.2014.0028

Zhu, M., & Bonk, C. J. (2022). Guidelines and strategies for fostering and enhancing self-directed online learning. *Open Learning: The Journal of Open, Distance and eLearning*. doi:10.1080/02680513.2022.2141105

Zimmerman, B. J. (2008). Investigating self-regulation and motivation: Historical background, methodological developments, and future prospects. *American Educational Research Journal*, *45*(1), 166–183. doi:10.3102/0002831207312909

Zohar, A., & Barzilai, S. (2013). A review of research on metacognition in science education: Current and future directions. *Studies in Science Education*, *49*(2), 121–169. doi:10.1080/03057267.2013.847261

Zohar, A., & Ben-Ari, G. (2022). Teachers' knowledge and professional development for metacognitive instruction in the context of higher order thinking. *Metacognition and Learning*, *17*(3), 855–895. Advance online publication. doi:10.100711409-022-09310-1

ADDITIONAL READING

Azevedo, R. (2020). Reflection on the field of metacognition: Issues, challenges, and opportunities. *Metacognition and Learning*, *15*(2), 91–98. doi:10.100711409-020-09231-x

Brown, A. H., & Green, T. D. (2020). *The essentials of instructional design: Connecting fundamental principles with process and practice* (4th ed.). Routledge Taylor & Francos Group.

Carter, R. A. Jr, Rice, M., Yang, S., & Jackson, H. A. (2020). Self-regulated learning in online learning environments: Strategies for remote learning. *Information and Learning Sciences*, *121*(5/6), 321–329. doi:10.1108/ILS-04-2020-0114

Dori, Y. J., Mevarech, Z., & Baker, D. (Eds.). (2018). *Cognition, Metacognition and Culture in STEM Education: Learning, Teaching and assessment*. Springer. doi:10.1007/978-3-319-66659-4

Greenhow, C., Graham, C. R., & Koehler, M. J. (2022). Foundation of online learning: Challenges and opportunities. *Educational Psychologist*, *57*(3), 131–147. doi:10.1080/00461520.2022.2090364

Shea, P., Richardson, J., & Swan, K. (2022). Building bridges to advance the community of inquiry framework for online learning. *Educational Psychologist*, *57*(3), 148–161. doi:10.1080/00461520.2022.2089989

Tarricone, P. (2011). *The taxonomy of metacognition*. Psychology Press. doi:10.4324/9780203830529

Xu, X., Zhu, X., & Chan, F. M. (2020). System design of Pintrich's SRL in a supervised-PLE platform: A pilot test in higher education. *Interactive Learning Environments*, 1–18. Advance online publication. doi:10.1080/10494820.2020.1802296

Zhao, L., & Ye, C. (2020). Time and performance in online learning: Applying the theoretical perspective of metacognition. *Decision Sciences Journal of Innovative Education*, *18*(3), 435–455. doi:10.1111/dsji.12216

KEY TERMS AND DEFINITIONS

Community of Inquiry: A group of online learners who share knowledge, information, values, support, and a sense of commitment.

Design Principles: Elements in the learning environment that have a pedagogical rationale.

Metacognitive Knowledge: Knowledge that learners have about a certain task, about their selves and others, and about different strategies they can apply.

Metacognitive Skills: Processes of monitoring and regulating cognition that include planning, monitoring, and assessing processes and their outcomes.

Online Learning Environment: An environment of computer platforms and the Internet in which teaching and learning take place which include synchronous and asynchronous courses.

Reflection: Conscious thinking about actions, thoughts, experiences, performance, and emotions.

Self-Regulation: The ability to monitor and control one's thoughts, performance, emotions, and evaluation processes.

Section 3

Learning Technologies and Pedagogies for Promoting Self-Regulated Learning

Chapter 8
Intelligent Self-Regulation: Bridging AI and Learning Science to Support Student Success

Kara McWilliams
ETS, USA

ABSTRACT

Digital education tools have revolutionized how learning solutions can be personalized for the benefit of all learners. When advances in technology are paired with knowledge of how individuals learn most effectively, more efficacious learning solutions can be developed. In this chapter, the authors contend that not only should learning science principles drive the technologies learners engage with, but combining these principles with the algorithms that personalize a learner's experience will greatly impact learning outcomes at scale. They offer a brief discussion of automation and self-regulation in educational technology, then provide an example of a novel learning solution that pairs personalization—through automated intelligence—with learning science principles to impact outcomes. A practical discussion of how to design and develop learning solutions for maximum impact is shared, as well as best practices for conducting validity and efficacy research to measure the extent to which intelligent self-regulation features are supporting learning outcomes.

INTRODUCTION

Digital education has transformed how we can personalize learning at scale; and recent advances in machine learning and natural language processing have enhanced learning efficiencies, created flexibilities, and enabled dynamic and actionable insights. In some cases, however, the technology is out in front of, or developed in absence of the learning theory it is supposed to be representing–such as self-regulated learning (SRL). In this chapter, we contend that not only should learning science principles drive the technologies learners engage with but combining learning science principles with the algorithms that personalize a learner's experience will greatly impact learning outcomes at scale.

DOI: 10.4018/978-1-6684-6500-4.ch008

Understanding when, and in what context certain features will support individual student success can help target these kinds of interventions and create more impactful learning experiences. Particularly when including SRL features in a tool, personalization and targeted interventions are critical. Some SRL features, like goal setting, are likely to benefit all learners and should be a standard feature in that tool and made available to all learners. Other features, like those that encourage and support self-monitoring, should be personalized. Sensitive, complex algorithms can drive how often learners are asked to self-monitor, determine whether they have the agency to engage in monitoring, and the extent to which they can monitor their learning. Models that become increasingly intelligent as a learner engages with a tool have the potential to personalize both the learning content they interact with, and the SRL features themselves.

In this chapter, we discuss the importance of leveraging learning science principles in conjunction with developing sophisticated algorithms to create meaningful SRL features in personalized digital tools that target a learner's needs. Following brief discussions of both AI and SRL in EdTech, this chapter will be divided into three sections that relate to bringing AI and learning science together to enable automated self-regulation supports in digital solutions.

The first section of the chapter focuses on product. Using a novel learning solution that is currently under development as an example, we will provide recommendations for how learning- science-based AI can offer intelligent SRL. The product offers SRL-promoting features to learners when they are most in need of them while not overburdening learners who may not be benefiting from them. We will outline the specific features built into the example tool, share insight into the logic that personalizes the features of the tool, and discuss the impact that those features are expected to have on learning.

The example product is a classroom-based automated writing evaluation tool that is designed to be used in middle school classrooms. It helps learners plan their writing, connect that planning to their writing, and create multiple drafts based on automated evaluation and feedback. This tool was selected because engaging in, progressing through, and completing the writing process can be a very challenging task for learners. Research suggests that learners tend to become frustrated during the writing process and potentially disengage if they lack confidence or feel that they are not successful in the instructional strategy.

The second section of the chapter focuses on product development. We will discuss considerations for the research and development of SRL tools, focusing specifically on the importance of successful collaboration amongst the teams responsible for designing and building features into the products. We posit that a Scrum team that includes Learning Scientists, User Experience Researchers, Software Developers, and AI/NLP Engineers who are sprinting together will build the most effective tools. Our contention is that fully dedicated cross-functional teams making product development decisions together will ensure that meaningful, automated SRL features are prioritized. Continuing with the product examples shared in the first section of the chapter, we will discuss the successes and challenges of those teams and make practical recommendations for Scrum teams working cross-functionally.

The third section of the chapter focuses on product evaluation. We will discuss considerations for measuring the effectiveness of personalized and automated SRL features in EdTech. A specific focus will be placed on the release of AI-based SRL features at the beginning of the development process, and how to manage the "cold start" challenge. Then, we discuss how, as more data are collected, algorithms can be optimized, and features updated. We will offer recommendations for rapid cycle evaluations, data mining, and efficacy studies that can provide concrete evidence of the impact of automated SRL features. Following the example provided earlier in the chapter, we offer insight into how the product has been optimized based on product evaluation studies to help product development teams avoid pitfalls previously encountered.

The chapter will conclude with concise and specific implications for EdTech vendors and practical recommendations for the research and development of digital learning tools that leverage AI to support SRL.

BACKGROUND

There exists a large body of research that generally agrees on the fundamental learning benefits of SRL (Duncan et al., 2007; McClelland et al., 2000).When learners can manage their own learning process in a way that allows them to take ownership over how they are going to achieve their learning goals, determine what paths they are going to take to most efficiently achieve those goals, and how they will customize those paths as needed, they are more likely to be successful (Schunk, 2013; Zimmerman, 2000).

There is an emerging body of research around the application of SRL to digital solutions. The most seminal models of SRL—Zimmerman (2000), Pintrich (2000), and Winne and Hadwin (1998)—are each most appropriate for a certain modality of learning. The once scarce research on SRL features in digital solutions has grown in the past two decades, though there isn't clear evidence of application in the current literature (e.g. Bannert et al., 2014 and Sedrakya et al., 2016). However, we argue that components of the Zimmerman et al. (2000) theories can be applied to digital solutions.

The Zimmerman model suggests that self-regulation is not solely driven by the learner. Rather, it is influenced by personal, behavioral, and environmental processes. Each of these components are present in digital solutions. For example, learners may choose to engage in optional practice opportunities demonstrating that they are taking control over their mindset and personally aiming to improve their learning outcomes. Additionally, learners may choose to come into the system for shorter bursts of time to implement spaced practice if they are seeing their performance declining over long periods of time, demonstrating behavioral self-regulation. Learners may choose to "receive a hint" or "ask my teacher for support" through available buttons in the application, leveraging environmental self-regulation. Each of these things may happen multiple times, representing Zimmerman's triadic form of SRL and its cyclical nature (Zimmerman, 2000).

The social-cognitive model of SRL developed by Pintrich is applicable to digital solutions as well. Pintrich suggests that there are four phases of self-regulation: planning, goal-setting, controlling, and reflecting (Jakesova & Kalenda, 2014). The applications of Pintrick's model are largely represented in the discussion of Zimmerman's model. However, in the case of Pintrich's model, motivation is the primary driver whereas Zimmerman, and other models, emphasize cognitive and behavioral factors (Zimmerman & Schunk, 2001). A potential application to digital solutions could be the inclusion of a self-report tool that asks learners to indicate their level of motivation, adapted from the Motivational Strategies Learning Questionnaire (McKeachie et al, 1985). The insights gleaned from these survey data could be included in models that are used to personalize a solution based on how motivated a learner is based on their self-report.

Winne and Hadwin (1998) developed an SRL model that is based around "Conditions, Operations, Products, Evaluation, and Standards" (COPES). The COPES model is fluid, but unique processing occurs at each stage of the model. One of the primary differences between the Winne and Hadwin model as compared to Zimmerman or Pintrich, is that it focuses specifically on how a learner processes information that is presented to them through each of the conditions of the model (Azevedo et al., 2010). A potential application of this model in digital solutions is to progressively reveal insights while a learner is engaging with digital learning content. The learner may start their learning path based on concrete definitions, but as insights about how they are progressing on various components of the instructional content are revealed, they may process that information and refine how they are engaging with the task. This behavior demonstrates that the learner is receiving, processing, and implementing the information.

An analysis of the seminal, and largely agreed on SRL models in the literature suggests that there are some consistencies in how the application of SRL is defined. For the purposes of this chapter, and to frame the following sections, the authors offer the following conceptual understanding of SRL as it relates to digital solutions. Note that these definitions are largely based on the influential works previously discussed and simply offer a context by which to consider the applicability within digital learning tools. When applied in the context of digital solutions, self-regulation emerges to users through cognitive, metacognitive, and affective product features. Cognitive features are product components that help learners actively exercise the learning processes that will help them meet their goals (Winne, 2018). These take the form of things like scaffolding, feedback, and voluntary practice opportunities. Metacognitive features emerge to the learners through components of the product that promote the consideration of one's learning process (Azevedo et al., 2015). These take the form of things like goal-setting, choice of how to engage in the learning, monitoring one's progress toward their defined goals, and reflecting on progression through the learning process. Affective components of a product influence emotion and mindset, which are impacted by the product's components and features. Often features in digital learning tools like congratulatory indicators, positive nudges, and a focus on the learners' strengths can boost confidence and influence the learner's motivation to persist, even through challenging learning experiences.

While the authors postulate that efficacious digital solutions is designed and developed based on core learning science principles like SRL, we further argue that learning science principles can emerge to users in more meaningful ways if paired with advanced technology, like automation and machine learning. For example, automated intelligence (AI) algorithms can enable more efficient and nuanced scaffolding for learners or motivational prompts at times appropriate for the unique needs of a learner. Certainly, learning science-based AI is still in its infancy and, while shown to be effective in lower-level instructional strategies, like feedback, there is a great deal of work to do to support more complex instructional strategies like peer-to-peer interaction or authentic assessment of skills-based learning (Koedinger et al., 2012). Yet still, advances in AI methods like eye tracking, head posture, and emotion detection are being used to provide signals about things like confidence and motivation which may widely advance a developer's ability to provide intelligent SRL supports within digital learning tools (Blikstein, 2013).

To leverage advanced technologies and what the field knows about how learners meet their learning goals most effectively, learning science-based AI should be ethically and responsibly applied to digital solutions. However, more research and continued partnerships are needed to apply it to the best effect. This requires bringing together scientists, engineers, educators, learners, and user experience experts to co-design solutions that will meet the deep needs of educators and learners. The core thesis of this chapter is that when the appropriate co-design partnerships are developed and learning science-based AI is applied ethically to digital learning solutions, it can support learners' self-regulation of their learning and help them meet their learning goals more efficiently and effectively. The authors propose that "intelligent self-regulation," defined as algorithms that surface features to users to promote self-regulation at times that are most appropriate for the learner's unique needs, can promote learning outcomes.

To support this argument, the next section offers three overviews of digital learning solutions that are in development and specifically leverage learning-science-based AI to surface SRL features to learners. Following the overview of the three products, insight into how the products are being developed and evaluated during development are offered. The goal of the authors is to provide insights into best practices and common challenges when attempting to apply learning-science-based AI.

HOW INTELLIGENT SELF-REGULATION CAN BE SUPPORTED IN DIGITAL LEARNING SOLUTIONS

To prove a practical context for the theoretical definition of intelligent self-regulation, the next section of this chapter shares an example of a product that leverages learning science-based AI to surface features that promote self-regulation to meet learner's unique needs. The product presented here is currently under iterative development and the features discussed in this chapter reflect the features on the roadmap at the time of publication.

A Description of the Example Solution

One of the most often-communicated challenges of middle school English Language Arts teachers is supporting personalized writing progressions in their classroom. With so many students in the class and each student having individual needs, teachers lack the time needed to provide personalized feedback and offer one-on-one support. Teachers also often report that students find it difficult to begin the writing process, to organize their writing, and persist toward their writing goals. Lastly, teachers note that a student's lack of confidence in their writing ability can have negative impacts on the writing process. The solution is intended to meet the needs of students by helping plan their writing, so they are prepared to begin the process, supporting individualized writing progression, and building a learner's confidence in their writing ability.

The tool is a student-led, AI-based writing tool that supports students through the planning, drafting, reflection, and revision process. Students are taken through a series of activities that help them form main ideas and develop supporting details. They are then scaffolded in beginning the writing process and persisting through it. An automated writing capability scores their writing in sections and provides immediate feedback on mechanics as well as content alignment to the writing genre (e.g., persuasion or argumentation). Learning-science-based AI is built into the system at various points to support self-regulation.

A broad feature set makes up the end-to-end experience of the solution. We will provide a subset of those features focused specifically on those that promote intelligent self-regulation at various points throughout the writing process. Table 1 lists the features with a description, the applicable SRL principle, and a summary of the AI integration. This is followed by a brief discussion of each feature and a visual representation of how it surfaces to the user.

Pax

During the learner's onboarding session, they interact with "Pax," an automated writing guide who chats with the learner to promote self-regulation.

Table 1. Features in the solution that support intelligent self-regulated learning.

	Description	SRL Principle	AI-enablement
Pax	A personalized writing guide that learners have an initial discussion with to share their feelings about the writing process, their interests, and their learning goals.	Learners set goals for the instructional strategy. Learners prepare to engage in the instructional strategy.	Pax's responses to the learner in the chat are personalized based on the data inputs learners include in the conversation.
Prepare and pre-flect	Learners are presented with learning objectives and writing skills. Learners review the rubric that will be used to assess the essay and pre-flect on how they believe they will perform against each measure.	Learners meaningfully prepare for the instructional strategy. Learners understand what is expected of them in the instructional strategy.	The amount of detail that is presented to students is based on data inputs from students about their level of confidence and how well they expect to perform in the instructional strategy.
Prompt selection	Learners are provided three prompts and asked to select one that will guide their writing.	Learners react to stimuli that evoke a cognitive and/or emotional reaction. Learners take agency over the writing process by being offered choice. Learners are motivated by stimuli aligned to their personal interest.	Prompt choices are selected by the system based on data inputs learners have provided.
Plan	Learners are scaffolded through a planning process where they identify a main idea, select supporting details, and organize the structure of their essay.	Learners plan their instructional strategy. Learners engage in sense-making. Learners organize their approach to the instructional strategy. Learners execute several steps and try different approaches when first approach is not successful.	Scaffolding is automated based on learner needs. System redirects student based on level of success in initial attempts to form main ideas and develop supporting details.
Confidence in preparation check	Learners are asked to reflect on the planning process and the resulting organization of their essay outline. Where appropriate, they are provided a nudge to reach out to a teacher.	Learners leverage learning aids where appropriate. Learners reach out for support when it is needed.	Communication from the product to the learner is based on cognitive and metacognitive data inputs from the learner. Prompt to reach out to teacher is based on metacognitive data inputs from the learner.
Ongoing motivation	Learners receive motivational messages throughout the planning and writing process.	Learners gain confidence in their ability. Learners are motivated to continue the process.	Content in, and cadence of, motivational messages are based on the cognitive and metacognitive data inputs from the learner.
Personalized feedback	Throughout the writing process learners receive automated personalized feedback on their writing quality.	Learners develop self-awareness of their strengths and weaknesses. Learners reflect on the instructional strategy. Learners consider perspectives other than their own.	Natural language processing models provide signals about the grammar, usage, mechanics, and style of the learners writing. An interpretation layer helps learners understand the NLP signals and use them to meaningfully incorporate the feedback into their writing.
Reflection	Learners complete the same rubric they completed during pre-flection in reflection and compare the two rubrics. They are asked to leave a written reflection on the comparison.	Learners reflect on the instructional strategy. Learners consider their own change from pre-flection to reflection.	An algorithm compares the pre-flection to the reflection to learn more about a learner's progress and personalize future paths and communications.

Pax prompts the learner to identify and define their learning goals, and if the goals are not specific enough, support the learner in more clearly defining their goals. Goal setting is an important component of self-regulation and focused and specific goal setting will support learners as they return and reflect on their goals (Pintrich, 2000b). Pax also asks about the learner's level of confidence in their writing ability and then personalizes responses based on a learner's inputs. For example, if the learner lacks confidence, Pax offers encouragement to promote confidence and motivation. If the learner reports feeling confident at that time, Pax congratulates the learner. Nudges of encouragement are environmental supports that can promote motivation, if used appropriately. Pax also asks the learner about their interests so that the writing process can be personalized, supporting motivation and perseverance. If a learning strategy is aligned with a learner's interests it can promote engagement and persistence (McKeachie & Pintrich, 1985). At the end of the conversation Pax assures the learner that they will be with them along the writing journey and motivates the learner to progress.

Prepare

Learners are provided with a set of interactive screens that help them think about the learning objectives of the writing process. They are also provided an overview of the writing skills that they will be demonstrating and evaluated on during this assignment.

Preparing for an instructional strategy helps learners organize themselves cognitively and emotionally before beginning the process (Zimmerman, 2000). A learner's preparation is based on prior data collected in the system such that there is more detailed review of skills experience if they are less confident in their writing ability.

Pre-flection

As part of a student preparing for the instructional strategy, they are presented with a set of rubrics that clearly illustrate how they will be scored on their writing. Learners are asked to complete a pre-flection indicating how they believe they will perform on each of the traits evaluated.

Pre-flection helps learners think deeply about the learning process (Zimmerman, 2000). The data collected during the pre-flection will be used in an algorithm that will determine how much support the product should provide that student. By combining data on a learner's self-reported level of confidence and how they expect they will perform, an appropriate set of motivational features and nudges can be served up to the learner at the appropriate times in the learning process.

Personalized Prompts

Offering learners a stimuli helps them engage in the instructional strategy in a thoughtful way. The stimuli might spark a cognitive or emotional reaction in the learner and prompt them to think about how they will approach the instructional strategy. During preparation learners are presented with writing prompts as stimuli.

Giving learners choice gives them agency over the learning process (Winne, 2018). Providing them choice that is aligned to their personal interests helps them engage and stay motivated (Winne, 2018). As part of the preparation process learners are offered three prompts that are personalized based on the various interest areas they shared with Pax. In addition to providing choices aligned to a learner's interest, it is important to introduce learners to topic areas they may not be familiar with and could become interested in. The logic-based prompt presentation offers learners two topics directly aligned with their interest area and one topic adjacent to their interest area.

Plan

Learners are scaffolded through a set of steps to help them plan their writing. First, they are given three minutes to brainstorm as many ideas as possible. If they can't think of at least three ideas at the end of the three minutes, they attempt another process for brainstorming main ideas. Prompting a learner to execute several steps in a row, including trying different methods if their first attempt was not successful helps keep a learner motivated but also scaffolds them to try different paths to reach the intended outcome (Zimmerman, 2000).

Throughout scaffolded planning learners select and prioritize their main ideas, eventually choosing the idea that resonates most. They are then scaffolded through activities that help them add supporting details to the main ideas and eventually organizing their outline. Where the product determines that a learner is struggling to complete the intended activities, personalized nudges help them stay motivated.

After learners have completed the planning process they are asked to share their level of confidence in the writing process, based on their plan.

Where learners report that they are lacking confidence, a supportive message appears and learners are prompted to reach out to their teacher if they need additional support. These features both align with a learner's level of confidence to promote motivation and enable environmental factors that allow them to take control over the learning process by using learning aids (reaching out to the teacher) for support if they need it.

Ongoing Motivation

To support persistence and develop confidence in learners, motivational prompts are provided along the learner's writing journey. Importantly, the prompts, and the cadence at which they are presented to learners should be determined based on what the product knows about the learner – their level of confidence at that time, how they are progressing in the writing process, and whether they appreciate the personalized notes. Imagine seven presents an example motivational prompt and measure of confidence.

Learners may find ongoing motivational prompts distracting, particularly if they are not lacking confidence, they are performing well, and they are reaching their learning goals efficiently. Models that can identify which learners will and will not benefit from prompts mitigate any negative influence of ongoing motivational prompts.

Personalized Feedback

The writing process itself is scaffolded such that learners complete one section of their essay at a time. After each section is completed natural language processing (NLP) models provide learners personalized feedback on their mechanics and alignment to the selected genre. Personalized and targeted feedback allows learners to reflect on the instructional strategy, think about their work in a different way, and revise their output.

In addition to providing personalized feedback about what a learner may want to revise, the product offers in-draft feedback on areas where the learner may be interested in focusing attention during the revision process. Again, targeted in-draft feedback helps learners reflect and reconsider the instructional strategy.

Reflection

When learners complete their first draft, they are asked to reflect on the writing process by again completing the rubric that they completed in the preparation process. Learners are presented a comparison of their pre-flection and reflection and asked to comment on anything that is interesting about the comparison. By reviewing both rubrics learners can think about the writing process, reflect on their first draft, and be more prepared to revise their first draft. On the back end of the product, an algorithm is comparing the rubrics and determining the type of communication to provide to learners based on the analysis. Targeted communication going into subsequent drafts will motivate learners more than generic messages congratulating them and moving them on to the next draft. Reflection, revision, and personalized communication is iterative throughout the writing process until the learner submits their final draft.

This section provided an overview of the features within the tool that support intelligent self-regulation based on the learning science principles discussed earlier in this chapter. Note that the motivation for the inclusion of these features were to support student self-regulation, but also to meet the needs of the educators' supporting learners. These features, and the broader feature set in the solution, enable personalization of the writing process for learners in the class and provide actionable insights to the teacher so that the teacher knows when their intervention with a learner is needed.

PRODUCT DEVELOPMENT TO SUPPORT INTELLIGENT SELF-REGULATION

The process of designing and developing efficacious digital learning tools including features that promote and support self-regulation is complex. This section offers insight into best practices, calls out challenges, and provides implications for product development vendors. The section is divided into two parts. First, we discuss the importance of the design and development team make-up. Then, we provide an overview of user-centered design and its importance in developing these products.

Team makeup. One of the biggest challenges of building products that leverage learning-science-based AI is ensuring that the right people are on the design and development team at the appropriate stages of the product development lifecycle. The authors have found most success when building teams that are made up of individuals from diverse backgrounds and perspectives. The team structure is fully cross-functional, and the team is self-contained, such that they are 100% dedicated to only one product. The authors have further found that a cross-functional agile team is the most effective method for building a solution that meets user needs, has a high degree of usability, and has an impact on the intended outcome (Fowler et al., 2001 and Manifesto of agile software development, 2021).

Bringing together cross-functional teams with experts from diverse contexts enables rapid development and deployment, but more importantly ensures that the team is appropriately bringing learning science, engineering, and automation together in a way that will be easily understood by learners and help them meet their learning goals efficiently and effectively. For example, a learning scientist can work directly with a data scientist and an AI engineer to identify specific areas where automation can be applied to enhance a learning science principle, while a user experience designer can ensure the visual representation of that feature is captured in a way that doesn't negatively impact the learning experience and software engineers can be engaged in all of these areas to ensure that the development reflects the theory and intended user experience. Because of the importance of the composition of the development

Table 2. Roles and responsibilities of a cross-functional agile research and development team

Role	Responsibilities
AI/ML Engineer	AI/ML Engineers understand learning/assessment objectives, where AI/ML models can help achieve them, and then design and develop effective methods of AI/ML model testing during development, deployment, and recalibration.
Data Scientist	Data Scientists develop and build the user data footprint, conduct the preprocessing of structured and unstructured data, and lead on the research and development of statistical models and algorithms to glean meaningful insights.
Data Architect	Data Architects plan the implementation of solutions, identify the right technologies to meet user needs, and direct and oversee the development of data ingestion and data transformation infrastructure.
Product Owner	Product Owners ensure the voice of the user is represented in the team's backlog and serve as a liaison between the project team, the business, and the market to align needs and priorities.
Research/Learning Scientist	Research/Learning Scientists apply foundational research principles to the theory-driven solutions and apply learning science principles, learning design principles, and user-centered research to development processes.
Software Developer	Software Developers lead on the technical component of translating wireframes into engaging, interactive, and highly functioning solutions.
User Experience Designer	User Experience Designers lead on the UI/UX aspects of the user experience, building needs into sketches and lo- and hi-fidelity prototypes.
User Experience Researcher	User Experience Researchers engage with users in interviews, observations, focus groups and other data collection activities to understand their needs and translate them into features and capabilities that will be designed by a User Experience Designer.

team, we outline the recommended roles and responsibilities in Table 2 when designing and developing AI based solutions.

Each of the roles described in Table 2 represent a unique area of expertise, but only the cross-functional collaboration coordinated by the product owner will lead to combining all areas of expertise meaningfully and ensuring that automation offers efficiencies, flexibility, and insights. To that end, the team will be more successful, and the product will be more impactful if the team sprints together through all phases of the design and development process, from discovery through to optimization.

User-centered design. The research field largely agrees on the need for, and benefit from, applying a use-centered approach when building digital solutions (e.g., Hassenzahl, 2010; Interactive Design Foundation, 2021; Vrendenburg et al., 2002). The authors argue that it's even more critical when developing a complex product like a student-led automated writing evaluation tool. By leveraging a user-centered approach the team can form a deep understanding of the students and educators who will be using the product, understand needs from their perspectives and within their individual contexts, and build features that promote self-regulations in the ways that are most meaningful to the target population. Once the team has built empathy for the students and educators, the students can work in ideation and co-design sessions with the designers and developers, apply an evaluation-based design to the features, and continue to optimize features in partnership with students and educators.

A user-centered approach will not only support the development of a solution that meets user needs but will inform how learning science-based AI is leveraged to best help students regulate their learning. To follow the example of the current solution, the development team collaborated with a representative sample of learners in 5th through 8th grade and educators teaching 5th through 8th grade English Language

Arts. The following sections describe the design and development components of the product development lifecycle that are relevant to building solutions that include learning-science-based AI.

Discovery is one of the initial stages of the product development lifecycle where teams are working toward the identification and validation of the problem the solution will solve based on the needs the team has hypothesized exist in the market. Throughout discovery a series of user experience research methods are employed to empathize with users and gain an understanding of their values, beliefs, and experiences. Building empathy helps development teams identify user pain points, which leads to a prioritized list of problems to be solved. To provide a concrete example of this phase, the product development team initiated their discovery efforts by examining user journeys that had been defined during the development of a different product targeting the same user group. Leveraging that research, they then began talking with users of existing automated writing evaluation tools to understand what was working and what was less helpful in the tool. While only the User Experience Researcher conducted the interviews, all members of the Scrum team either attended the virtual interviews on mute with their cameras off, or they reviewed the interview recordings after the interview. It is important that the entire team build empathy for the users because each expert contribution will impact the efficacy and user acceptance of the product. The information the team gathered offered important insight into what impacts learners' confidence, motivation, and willingness to engage, as well as what contributes to them persisting in the product or ultimately disengaging.

Insights from discovery were used to begin initial feature design during the co-design session. A very high-level, end-to-end flow of the user journey was mapped out and, together with learners and educators, points on that journey were identified where learners might need a confidence check, some additional scaffolding, feedback, or a chance to reflect. Learners were asked to describe what they thought they would be feeling at that point in the journey and what they would need to succeed. Prompts were used to spark discussion. For example, "Would you prefer an automated guide or to reach out to your teacher here?" and, "Would you like a feature that lets you ask for a hint here or would you like to try it on your own one more time?" as well as, "If you run out of time would you like to try again or would you like to engage in a different experience to see if you can achieve the same goal?" Conversations among learners, between learners and educators, among the development team, and with the development team and educators and learners brings creative solutioning to the product that is likely to meet a broader group of learner's needs.

Other important discussions with learners and educators included how they would want AI to be used to offer flexibility, efficiencies, and insights and whether it would concern them that AI is being leveraged. In the conversations around the solution under development learners were open about being nervous about AI scoring their essays, so we included features that require "teacher review before finalizing grades." Learners also said they were more likely to tell the tool that they lacked confidence rather than tell the teacher directly and appreciated that AI was leveraged to personalize the solution based on how they were feeling and how they were performing.

Following co-design sessions, the team further fleshes out feature sets and begins to create visual representations, called wireframes, of what the features would look like and how they would emerge to learners. The designs are validated with educators and learners. Using the same solution example, Pax was originally designed to be a video conference with "Pax" and the team quickly learned that might be too intimidating and some learners might be demotivated and feel less confident if they had to go on camera. So, the feature was modified to represent a chat that 6th grade students would feel comfortable with. Additionally, students initially felt overwhelmed with the amount of automated feedback they were receiving on their drafts, so designs were optimized to offer progressive feedback in small pieces that learners could implement over time.

Once wireframes are validated, usability testing can further refine features that are meant to support self-regulation. The product team conducted moderated usability testing where they would have users click through the wires and User Experience Researchers would ask them to think aloud while they were going through the flow and ask questions on specific screens such as, "What would you be feeling now?" In some cases, learners responded with excitement that they received confetti and congratulations and thought it seemed like they were doing a great job. In other cases, learners were confused by how the system knew something or why things were recommended, prompting designers to include supporting information about why some things were personalized. Moderated usability testing with learners thinking aloud and reflecting on questions and prompts is a great way to refine the product before beginning to build it.

User-centered design extends to how automation can support a learner's ability through promoting self-regulation. That is, a system can facilitate support based on how it learns that a user might benefit from SRL tools. However, those features should be co-designed with learners. That is, how often and when the learner wants a system to make decisions for them or whether full autonomy is preferred.

User-centered design does not end once a digital product begins to be built. Rather, it is an iterative process throughout the product development lifecycle and continues well into a product being used at scale in the market. The next section of this chapter discusses how to evaluate the effectiveness and efficacy of self-regulation features built on learning-science-based AI. The approach to research and evaluation described in this chapter also includes a user-centered design approach.

EVALUATING THE EFFICACY OF INTELLIGENT SELF-REGULATION FEATURES IN DIGITAL SOLUTIONS

There are many efficacy frameworks used to measure the effectiveness of digital learning tools (e.g., McWilliams et al., 2017; Mattern, 2019; Pearson, 2020) and existing frameworks to support validity and effectiveness of assessments, interventions, and learning tools (e.g., Arieli-Attali et al., 2019; Kane, 2006; Mislevy et al., 2003). Although some of these frameworks are customized for their institution to meet their unique mission, there are some common elements across frameworks that are relevant for the purposes of this chapter. That is, most published efficacy frameworks call out the importance of measuring the incremental efficacy of features within a product. Many research studies look at the overall relationship between use of a product and a learning outcome of interest, but it is also important to study individual features and how they contribute to the overall efficacy. In doing so, product development teams can make important decisions about feature optimization or inclusion. This principle is even more critical when evaluating features that leverage learning-science-based AI to support learner self-regulation. If specific features are not contributing to the overall efficacy of a product, designers should remove the feature to increase learning efficiency or optimize the feature so that it adds incremental value over the existing relationship.

The authors recommend a particular adaptation of many of the published efficacy frameworks. The proposed framework emphasizes user obsession, continuous evaluation, and equity throughout. To generate meaningful evidence that support claims for effectiveness and efficacy of the features included in products, it is important to set the foundation by identifying problems and defining outcomes, and then work backwards to identify viable solution pathways. This foundation creates the opportunity to identify broad claims that we want to make about a solution and helps to shape and prioritize research goals for continuously evaluating and gathering evidence for effectiveness, efficacy, and equity.

When measuring the efficacy of features within products it is important to establish a clear problem statement which will support narrowing of the defined outcomes (i.e., measurable changes that address a problem) for the targeted user group by understanding their specific metrics and criteria needed to reach those outcomes (e.g., identifying the criteria to define success). Outcomes can be affective (i.e. how a learner feels about the learning strategy), behavioral (i.e. how the learner is engaging with the learning solution), or cognitive (i.e. learners progressing toward or achieving their learning goals). In some cases learning outcomes can be two, or even three of those constructs.

Following the example of the solution we have been discussing, one of the defined outcomes was that learners would meaningfully reflect on the writing process and revise their draft essay. While this outcome is behavioral, it is also cognitive as the expectation is that the learner will improve their writing. Another outcome was that learners would progress through the writing process without disengaging. This outcome is behavioral, because they would progress but also affective because they would be motivated to continue.

As measurable outcomes are being defined, teams also need to think about the desired high-level product claims or assertions that are associated with those outcomes and measurable changes. These high-level claims are related to the long-term outcomes we want to define to generate a real-world impact for the solution. Impact refers to the degree to which a solution solves a real-world problem. For example, the example solution seeks to develop the writing ability in young learners and also increase their confidence in their writing so that they are more likely to write in the future. Working backwards from high-level outcomes will help the team determine the most effective path, product features to develop, and the types of evidence needed to collect and justify the high-level claims.

In addition to broader learning, educational, and societal outcomes, we must also define specific outcomes as they relate to the features included in the product and how those feature outcomes moderate the longer-term outcomes. For example, Pax is intended to support learners clearly and specifically in defining their goals and provide confidence as they embark on their writing journey. The theory is that if learners have defined their goals and feel confident, they will more effectively progress through the learning process and improve as writers. A product development team should go through each of the features in their product that define specific outcomes of the features and how they are meant to influence the longer term, more high-level outcomes.

The authors propose that feature and product efficacy measurement should begin during the design and discovery process. Table 3 presents an overview of the Efficacy and Equity framework that these authors use in all products that they develop and is being used for measuring the efficacy of the features in the product.

By measuring the effectiveness and efficacy of a product, including features, during the design and development process it not only enables product teams to make road mapping and optimization decisions, but it allows the development of a portfolio of evidence. Developing a portfolio of evidence gives learners and educators the input they need to make adoption and implementation decisions. It also provides educators with insights around learner self-regulation and the efficacy of specific features. In that way, educators know that engagement with the tool is supporting their needs of personalization at scale.

Table 3. Overview of an Efficacy and Equity Framework

Phase	Study Type	Methods	Questions Answered	Use of Results
Discovery	User Experience Research	Large scale survey data User interviews Focus groups	· Have subgroups within the target population been articulated? · Are user journeys understood? · Have user's pain points been identified and validated? · Has a problem statement been articulated and validated?	Needs validation
Ideation	User Experience Design and Research	Large scale survey data User interviews Focus groups	· Has foundational research been leveraged? · Has consultation with subject matter experts occurred? · Have scientists reconciled the literature with meeting user needs?	Concept validation
Prototyping	Alpha and Beta	·Mixed Methods, largely descriptive	· Have a representative sample of users co-designed the solution? · Have moderated and unmoderated studies of usability occurred? · Have out-of-context and in-context evaluations measuring acceptance, sentiment, and perception of effectiveness occurred?	Pre-market solution optimization
In market	Effectiveness	·Mixed Methods, descriptive, and correlational	· Have relationships been established between user needs and outcomes? · Have data been disaggregated by subgroup to examine trends? · Have platform data been explored to identify engagement, persistence, and progression trends within and between subgroups? · Have feature and component evaluations within and between subgroups occurred?	Adoption and implementation evidence and solution optimization
Optimization	Efficacy	Mixed Methods, descriptive, correlational, and causal	· Do research study designs lend themselves to valid causal statements of impact on need? · Were a representative sample of users included in the studies? · Has differential efficacy been examined?	Adoption and implementation evidence, solution optimization, advancing the field

FUTURE RESEARCH

As we noted in our introduction there is still a great deal of work to be done to understand theories and frameworks for how learning-science-based AI can be leveraged in digital technology to best effect. Two of the key areas of interest for these authors is understanding whether features that are meant to support self-regulation demonstrate differential efficacy (that they support all subgroups of learners in the same way), and that when they are used at scale the same trends emerge that are being seen in testing. Both research studies will be conducted when the product goes to market and is being implemented in context, rather than as part of a discrete study. This section briefly describes the two planned research studies to answer the described research questions.

To measure the differential efficacy of the features in the example product, a background questionnaire will be included in the beginning of the user journey that captures information on the learner's background and demographics. Behavioral data of the features promoting self-regulation in the product will be disaggregated by learner subgroup and individual analyses of use of the features and subsequent motivation, engagement, confidence, persistence, and performance will be conducted. Data scientists will analyze whether there are any statistically significant differences between the relationships among subgroups. If differences are found, additional user research with specific subgroups will be planned to understand why the features promoting self-regulation are impacting some learners differently than others.

To measure whether the same behavioral and performance trends are observed at scale as are observed in testing, data scientists on the product team have worked closely with a Data Innovation team to develop dashboards that demonstrate real time implementation patterns and present key performance metrics that are coded into the dashboard. The insights gathered from alpha and best testing will be posted on the dashboard as the product goes to scale, and as more users engage in the product, we will compare the trends. If data scientists observe that there are substantially different implementation patterns, an implementation study will be conducted among subsets of users to understand whether there are more efficacious implementation patterns that users should be guided toward.

Two things are critical when planning future research around features that promote self-regulation in digital learning tools, and specifically in the example tool here. First, it is imperative that design and development teams work together to build an intentional user data footprint in the backend of the digital learning solution. Learning and data scientists should leverage both learning and measurement theory-driven and user research-focused approaches when constructing the learner data footprint. They will also work closely with user experience researchers and designers as well as developers to ensure data architecture can translate appropriately to the user's experience in the system.

It is equally important that design and development teams adhere to strict data privacy and security guidelines when leveraging learner and educator data to conduct these analyses. Terms and conditions should be clear to the learners, and all personally identifiable data should be removed before analyses are conducted. Finally, learner data should be destroyed as soon as analyses have been conducted and insights derived.

CONCLUSION

The benefits of learners regulating their learning process are largely agreed. However, with technology developing so quickly it is critically important that technology developers and the learners and educators who use their tools understand when, and in what context, certain features will support individual student success. By closely examining the needs of the users, designing solutions with users, and measuring the incremental value of tools that support intelligent SRL, development teams can help target such interventions and create more impactful learning experiences.

As we discussed throughout this chapter there are some SRL features that are likely to support the broadest set of learners, like goal setting. However, it is still the case that personalization can help scaffold the goal setting process in a way that makes it more impactful for individual learners. Other features are likely support some learners, but not others. For example, motivational prompts and nudges might be beneficial to some and a distraction to others. Algorithms that are built on usage, perception, and performance data can drive how often learners receive motivational nudges and what form they come in.

To develop learning-science-based AI features to best effect it is critical that a development team leverage user-centered design. In this way the learning science, technology, and needs and perspectives of users can come together in ways that are most useful for learners. And ongoing evaluation and efficacy studies should be continuously collecting data on how users are engaging with the features, what their perceptions of the features are, and whether the subsequent behaviors that users demonstrate are those intended during feature development.

In this chapter we discussed the importance of leveraging learning science principles in conjunction with the development of sophisticated algorithms to create meaningful SRL features in digital tools that are personalized and targeted to a learner's needs. We offered a brief discussion of both AI and SRL in EdTech, and then divided the chapter into three sections. First, we discussed product and provided an example of a novel automated writing evaluation tool and shared examples of the features that are based on learning science principles and driven by automation. Then, we discussed best practices and implications for developing learning-science-based AI features to support SRL. Next, the importance of evaluating features meant to support SRL and how insights from those evaluations can be used, was discussed. We ended with planned future research and implications.

Our expectation was that this chapter would offer some insight into challenges and best practices when combining learning science and AI to deliver features within digital solutions that support learner self-regulation. These insights are expected to support additional work in this area.

ACKNOWLEDGMENT

The authors would like to acknowledge the product design and development team that is working, together with the authors, to bring the solution that we have been using an example to educators and learners. We appreciate the team allowing us to showcase this important work.

REFERENCES

Arieli-Attali, M., Ward, S., Thomas, J., Deonovic, B., & von Davier, A. A. (2019). The expanded evidence centered design (e-ECD) for learning and assessment systems: A framework for incorporating learning goals and processes within assessment design. *Frontiers in Psychology*, *10*, 853. doi:10.3389/fpsyg.2019.00853 PMID:31105616

Azevedo, R., Moos, D., Johnson, A., & Chauncey, A. (2010). Measuring Cognitive and Metacognitive Regulatory Processes During Hypermedia Learning: Issues and Challenges. *Educational Psychologist*, *45*(4), 210–223. doi:10.1080/00461520.2010.515934

Bannert, M., Reimann, P., & Sonnenberg, C. (2014). Process mining techniques for analysing patterns and strategies in students' self-regulated learning. *Metacognition and Learning*, *9*(2), 161–185. doi:10.100711409-013-9107-6

Blikstein, P. (2013). Multimodal learning analytics. In *Proceedings of the third international conference on learning analytics and knowledge* (pp. 102-106). ACM. 10.1145/2460296.2460316

Duncan, G. J., Dowsett, C. J., Claessens, A., Magnuson, K., Huston, A. C., Klebanov, P., Pagani, L. S., Feinstein, L., Engel, M., Brooks-Gunn, J., Sexton, H., Duckworth, K., & Japel, C. (2007). School readiness and later achievement. *Developmental Psychology*, *43*(6), 1428–1446. doi:10.1037/0012-1649.43.6.1428 PMID:18020822

Jakešováa, J., & Kalendab, J. (2015). Self-regulated learning: Critical-realistic conceptualization. *Social and Behavioral Sciences, 171,* 178–189. https://linkinghub.elsevier.com/retrieve/pii/S1877042815001354

Kane, M. (2006). Validation. In R. Brennan (Ed.), *Educational measurement* (4th ed., pp. 17–64). American Council on Education/Praeger.

Koedinger, K. R., Corbett, A. T., & Perfetti, C. (2012). The Knowledge-Learning-Instruction framework: Bridging the science-practice chasm to enhance robust student learning. *Cognitive Science*, *36*(5), 757–798. doi:10.1111/j.1551-6709.2012.01245.x PMID:22486653

Mattern, K. (2019). *ACT's efficacy framework: Combining learning, measurement, and navigation to improve learner outcomes.* ACT.

McClelland, M., Morrison, F. J., & Holmes, D. L. (2000). Children at risk for early academic problems: The role of learning-related social skills. *Early Childhood Research Quarterly*, *15*(3), 307–329. doi:10.1016/S0885-2006(00)00069-7

McKeachie, W. J., Pintrich, P. R., & Lin, Y. (1985). Teaching learning strategies. *Educational Psychologist*, *20*(3), 153–160. doi:10.120715326985ep2003_5

McWilliams, K., Black, A., Bergin, J., & Warnakulasooryia, R. (2017). *Unpacking the black box of efficacy: A framework for evaluating the effectiveness and researching the impact of digital learning tools*. Macmillan Learning.

Mislevy, R. J., Almond, R. G., & Lukas, J. F. (2003). *A brief introduction to evidence-centered design* (ETS Research Report RR-03-16). Educational Testing Service.

Pearson. (2020). *Efficacy reporting framework.* https://www.pearson.com/content/dam/one-dot-com/one-dot-com/global/Files/efficacy-and-research/reports/audited/Pearson_EfficacyFramework_2020.pdf

Pintrich, P. R. (2000a). The role of goal orientation in self-regulated learning. In M. Boekaerts, P. R. Pintrich, & M. Zeidner (Eds.), *Handbook of self-regulation* (pp. 451–502). Academic Press. doi:10.1016/B978-012109890-2/50043-3

Pintrich, P. R. (2000b). Multiple goals, multiple pathways: The role of goal orientation in learning and achievement. *Journal of Educational Psychology*, *92*(3), 544–555. doi:10.1037/0022-0663.92.3.544

Schunk, D. (2005). Self-Regulated Learning: The Educational Legacy of Paul R. Pintrich. *Educational Psychologist*, *40*(2), 85–94. doi:10.120715326985ep4002_3

Sedrakyan, G., De Weerdt, J., & Snoeck, M. (2016). Process Mining enabled feedback: "Tell me what I did wrong" vs. "tell me how to do it right. *Computers in Human Behavior*, *57*, 352–376. doi:10.1016/j.chb.2015.12.040

Winne, P. (2018). Theorising and researching levels of processing in self-regulated learning. *The British Journal of Educational Psychology*, *88*(1), 9–20. doi:10.1111/bjep.12173 PMID:28791689

Winne, P. H., & Hadwin, A. F. (1998). Studying as self-regulated learning. In D. J. Hacker, J. Dunlosky, & A. Graesser (Eds.), *Metacognition in educational theory and practice* (pp. 277–304). Routledge.

Zimmerman, B. J. (2000). Attaining self-regulation, a socio-cognitive perspective. Handbook of self-regulation, 13-39.

Zimmerman, B. J., & Schunk, D. H. (Eds.). (2001). *Self-regulated learning and academic achievement: Theoretical perspectives* (2nd ed.). Lawrence Erlbaum Associates, Inc.

ADDITIONAL READING

Afzaal, M., Nouri, J., Papapetrou, P., Forse, U., Wu, Y., Li, X., & Weegar, R. (2021). Explainable AI for Data-Driven Feedback and Intelligent Action Recommendations to Support Student Self-Regulation. *Frontiers in Artificial Intelligence, 4*. https://www.frontiersin.org/articles/10.3389/frai.2021.723447/full

Araka, E., Maina, E., Gitongo, R., & Oboko, R. (2020). Research trends in measurement and intervention tools for self-regulated learning for e-learning environments – systematic review (2008-2018). *Research and Practice in Technology Enhanced Learning*, *15*(1), 6. doi:10.118641039-020-00129-5

Bjork, R. A., Dunlosky, J., & Kornell, N. (2013). Self-regulated learning: Beliefs, techniques, and illusions. *Annual Review of Psychology*, *64*(1), 417–444. doi:10.1146/annurev-psych-113011-143823 PMID:23020639

English, M., & Kitsantas, A. (2013). Supporting student self-regulated learning in problem- and project-based learning. *The Interdisciplinary Journal of Problem-Based Learning*, *7*(2), 128–150. doi:10.7771/1541-5015.1339

Fyfe, E. R., & Rittle-Johnson, B. (2016). Feedback both helps and hinders learning: The causal role of prior knowledge. *Journal of Educational Psychology*, *108*(1), 82–97. doi:10.1037/edu0000053

Herodotou, C., Naydenova, G., Boroowa, A., Gilmour, A., & Rienties, B. (2020). How can predictive learning analyrics and motivational interventions increase student retention and enhance administrative support in distance education? *Journal of Learning Analytics*, *7*(2), 72–83. doi:10.18608/jla.2020.72.4

Lodge, J., Panadero, E., Broadbent, J., & de Barba, P. (2018). Supporting self-regulated learning with learning analytics. In Learning Analytics in the Classroom. Routledge. doi:10.4324/9781351113038-4

Sawyer, K. (Ed.). (2014). *The Cambridge handbook of the learning sciences* (2nd ed.). Cambridge University Press. doi:10.1017/CBO9781139519526

KEY TERMS AND DEFINITIONS

Automated Writing Evaluation: The use of natural language processing to automate the scoring and feedback of written text.

Intelligent Self-Regulation: Surfacing features to a learner within a digital solution that support their ability to control their own learning process.

Learner Confidence: A learner believing that they can successfully engage in and complete an instructional strategy.

Learner Insights: Applying an interpretation to signals provided by scoring to help learners contextualize the scores they are provided and action the insights.

Learner Motivation: A learner feeling encouraged to engage in and persist through an instructional strategy.

Natural Language Processing and Scoring: The use of textual or spoken language to model learner performance and provide signals about that performance.

Student-Led Product: A digital learning tool that students are meant to be able to successfully engage with and complete without direction from the teacher.

Chapter 9
Re-Imagining Health and Medicine Education:
Implementing a Mobile-Based Gamification App for Improved Affective Learner Engagement

Nicolene Lottering
Bond University, Australia

Iris Lim
https://orcid.org/0000-0001-5866-8968
Bond University, Australia

Suzanne Gough
https://orcid.org/0000-0002-1320-3558
Bond University, Australia

ABSTRACT

Gamification is an active-learning approach commonly used in education to promote learner engagement. This chapter provides an overview of how gamified approaches can be applied to enable university students comprising of Generation Z and Y learners, to access authentic learning resources to self-regulate their learning in preparation for assessment. Methods and flexible strategies that can be incorporated into undergraduate and postgraduate education programs worldwide are provided. Three case studies illustrate the use of technology-enhanced weekly quizzes to optimise student engagement, knowledge retention, and academic performance. Key educational theories and practices that underpinned the case studies include social constructivism, disuse theory, and complexity theory alongside the use of scaffolding, chunking, flipped classroom, deliberate practice, and periodic revisitation. The chapter concludes with 12 pearls of wisdom to optimize leaner engagement using a gamified approach to enhance the students' ability to self-regulate their learning and achieve their learning goals.

DOI: 10.4018/978-1-6684-6500-4.ch009

INTRODUCTION

As higher education curricula continue to be condensed through accelerated degree programs, which feature integrated teaching and learning activities on-campus, remotely and at clinical sites, efficient learning strategies in university is increasingly critical. In degree programs such as Medicine and Physiotherapy, discipline knowledge and innovation in practice continues to compound at an accelerating pace. The pre-requisite for long-term and rapid knowledge retention of information obtained in early years of their studies will contribute to competence and future professional practice. As generation Z learners (born 1997-2010) return to University campuses (or digital classrooms), it is clear that the pervasive influence of digital exposure has impacted their learning preferences, needs and attitudes (Shorey et al., 2021). Academic faculty members and learning designers are astutely aware that the majority of healthcare students belong to the generation Z (undergraduate enrollments) and generation Y (postgraduate) cohorts, who are immersed in a predominantly digital world through social activities, work, and study (García-Viola et al., 2019). The effective use of technology in blended learning initiatives, including gamification, is well documented in the feat to address student retention and declining levels of student engagement, attributed to this generation now entering college/university education. The rapid advancement of technology has significantly changed society and the way of human learning across the educational sector and social culture. This places a new demand for adaptation to this growing confluence between the digital and education worlds by reforming and re-imagining traditional pedagogical methods and approaches with technology implementation. Shorey and colleagues (2021) provide some insights to healthcare educators of generation Z students on how to create a vibrant learning community using creative approaches that combine technology, social media, active-learning, online modules, and social interactions to develop critical thinking skills and foster affective engagement. It appears that generation Z have questioned the value-add of higher education in the United States, with the National Student Clearinghouse Research Center (2022) reporting a 4.1% decline in undergraduate degree-program enrollments between spring 2021 and 2022, and total decline of 7.4% or 1.3 million students since 2020. If Universities are unable to reflect on current challenges in light of post-COVID patterns and generation changes in students, issues pertaining to retention, engagement and, consequently the acquisition of skills required by the labour market are foreseen. For school leavers that opt to embark upon tertiary education, the expectations of "value-add" will be at the forefront, as first-year retention is brought into the limelight, as higher education competes against global online learning platforms such as Coursera (https://about.coursera.org/).

Van der Meer and colleagues (2018) present a holistic framework of student engagement, subdivided into two core pillars of academic engagement and campus and community engagement; contributing influences including psycho-social variables, and ultimate intended outcomes during and beyond a student's tertiary studies. The authors define four areas of academic engagement in undergraduate students: (i) cognitive, (ii) emotional, (iii) behavioural, and (iv) relational engagement. Cognitive engagement relates to the way a student processes information; emotional or affective engagement includes variables including self-efficacy beliefs, self-regulation, and intrinsic motivation, which demonstrate a relationship with academic attainment (Beatson et al., 2020); while behavioural engagement focuses on the voluntary actions of the learner which may include attendance or opting into downloading educational apps. Beatson et al. (2020) explain that involuntary activities, such as opting in and access patterns within an optional mobile-based gamification app, are a measure of behavioral engagement. In a large undergraduate accounting subject, their results using the mobile-based gamification app utilized in this study support the underlying principle of gamification, in which earning badges, points, and leaderboard position can drive behaviour and influence desired performance changes. In this chapter, through data analytics pertaining to app access patterns, cumulative point aggregates, and question/module completion, student engagement is discussed through the lens of the emotional and behavioural components of the aforementioned framework.

While serious games, game-based learning and gamification are usually considered as a whole and not separately, there are notable differences between these terms and the way they are used and implemented. The focus of this chapter is the latter. Gamification is the use of game elements (points, leader boards, badges, levels, progress bars, completion tracking, and instant feedback), game mechanics, and game principles (competition and collaboration) in non-game environments, such as in the educational context (Aparicio et al., 2019). Gamification is a widespread and relevant approach to increase motivation and student participation in learning activities. Some of the characteristics that gamification offers include collaboration, engagement, motivation, task commitment, enjoyment and acquirement of critical thinking and personal learning skills (Mora et al., 2017). These characteristics have been shown to activate and significantly shape desired intrinsic behaviours within learners. Additionally, most games also provide extrinsic motivators in the form of prizes or rewards for achievement as a strategic addition to solicit engagement with the game. If utilised carefully, these extrinsic motivators can also further increase engagement and lead to autonomous motivation (Kusurkar et al., 2011). To achieve these positive outcomes of gamification, the process of design of learning tasks and immersion in activities to build and foster behavioural engagement requires a great deal of effort and thought. Different approaches have shown varying rates of success (Mora et al., 2017).

Flow theory elucidates the notion of why and how users or learners spend significant energy, effort, and time on specific activities. The flow experience is coined as the simultaneous experience of concentration, interest, and enjoyment (Guo et al., 2016). The theory argues that there are three channels for learning (Sharek & Wiebe, 2011): (i) Flow *channel*: As a learner completes and proceeds through a task, this state is likely to be preserved, provided the difficulty of the following task increases to match developing skills. (ii) *Boredom channel*: This results from a challenge that lacks skill and ability development, interest, or engagement; and (iii) *Frustration channel*: When the skill or ability level of the individual is not comparable to the difficulty of the task. The relationship between engagement and flow is supported by Beatson and colleagues' (2020) results, where the development of a rhythm of play through consistent engagement throughout the duration of undergraduate accounting and management units, correlated well with superior academic outcomes. In this study, the authors report that 'active status' of a gamification app, and the total points acquired in the app, were powerful indicators to predict higher final grades.

The main purpose of gamifying education is to make learning a more positive and fun experience, while stimulating learning in a no-stakes, informal manner. Therefore, well-designed gamification approaches which encourage learner movements toward an attainable and objective goal support the flow channel. Gamification also provides learners with a sense of autonomy and control over their own learning process. It has been shown that activities with a higher sense of self-initiation increase and maintain the interest and engagement of learners (Guo et al., 2016). Gamification, as an active learning approach, is becoming widely utilised in healthcare education to promote student engagement and participation in learning activities associated with complex content (Tavares, 2022; van Gaalen et al., 2021). Previous studies have reported an increase in perceived engagement, motivation and challenge in a gamified curriculum compared to traditional, non-gamified, lecture-based didactic methods within medical education (Gue et al., 2022).

Self-regulated learning (SRL) is an essential part of the development of healthcare professionals, and an indicator for emotional or affective engagement of the learner. Broadly speaking, the work of Zimmerman (1986) dominates the early SRL literature, first defining SRL as the degree to which students are metacognitively, motivationally and behaviorally active participants in the learning process. There has been a myriad of literature on the importance of SRL in healthcare education, and the benefits associated, including greater self-efficacy and academic achievement, enhanced intrinsic motivation and obtainment of a lifelong learning attitude (de Bruin et al., 2017; Lucieer et al., 2016; Sandars & Cleary, 2011; Spooner et al., 2021). Within educational institutions, both students and educators share the responsibility to develop self-regulated learning to ensure the learners are capable of reflecting on their own performance and modifying their approach and strategies for future attempts. The utility of gamification advancements have enabled educators to consider how trace measures of SRL can assess changes in self-regulation and self-motivation during learning, which ultimately influence overall academic performance. The use of gamification elements is aligned with Boekaert's (2011) Dual Processing model, emphasizing the role that positive and negative emotions play in adaptative learning, where learner appraisals are crucial to "goal pathway" activation. The authors summarize that the purpose of self-regulation during the learning journey is to (i) expand knowledge and skills, (ii) protect the student's commitment to the learning activity and (iii) prevent harm to the self. Gamification elements such as badge awards, point acquisition, highly visual and interactive user-interfaces, provide a non-threatening online learning environment. where learners can employ emotional self-regulation strategies in pursuit of their goal pathway.

Spooner et al. (2021) proposed that the self-regulated learner should be proactively engaged in planning their learning journey, which includes participating in activities, continuously drawing on internal and external assessment to monitor their own progress. This can be achieved with the use of learner analytics or trace measures to capture progress, achievement of learning objectives and allow students to set their own goals. Constant feedback from gamification methods allows students to re-evaluate and amend strategies and behaviours aims to optimise their learning gains, through which self-observation and self-reflection, subprocesses of Zimmerman's (2000) cyclical phases model, feeds self-regulatory behaviour. It is well known that feedback is considered to effect transformational change in learners (Black & William, 1998; Hattie & Timperley, 2007; Chou & Zou, 2020). While many methods of enhancing self-regulation can be practically implemented in learning and teaching, gamification of educational systems has become increasingly popular (Bouchrika et al., 2019; Huang et al., 2019). To 'gamify' learning through formative assessment e.g., quizzes, provides learners the autonomy for goal setting and strategic planning (forethought self-regulatory phase; Zimmerman, 2000), obtain achievements and instant gratification, relate, and socialize with their peers and demonstrate their competence with the progression and completion of the game (performance self-regulatory phase).

The phenomena of new knowledge acquisition and forgetting, which forms the basis of the Ebbinghaus Forgetting Curve indicates that an exponential relationship exists between memory retention and time (Ebbinghaus, 1885). A replication of the Ebbinghaus experiment by Murre and Dros (2015) demonstrates that between 32% and 44% of information is retained an hour after the initial learning event, in contrast to 27 to 33% retention after 24 hours, without deliberate practice. Evidence-based learning strategies that facilitate durable learning and long-term retention include (i) elaboration, (ii) interleaving, (iii) retrieval practice and (iv) distributed practice. Retrieval practice refers to a strategy in which recalling information from memory through testing, rather than listening or rereading, subsequently enhances and boosts learning. The retrieval effort hypothesis (Gardiner et al., 1973) maintains that the effort involved in retrieval, through testing that require the production of an answer, provides greater benefits for long-term retention. The user-interface of gamification software which employ notification features, content scheduling and question time-limits, are designed with the aforementioned models and hypotheses. This is not only to engage modern learners, but to maximize learning potential and the development of self-regulation skills. Bjork and Bjork (1992) propose the theory of disuse, which posits that memory has two components: storage strength and retrieval strength. Consistent with this theory, retrieval events not only improve overall memory, but improve storage strength, with the effects most pronounced at the point of forgetting e.g., 24 hours post-instruction. Distributed practice or spaced repetition learning, which employs a schedule of practice that incorporates intervals between multiple study activities over a set duration, is well established to be superior to massed practice or 'cramming'. User-interface design of modern gamification apps such as the one implemented in this study, exploit distributed practice through the ability to carefully schedule and 'drip feed' content and provides opportunities for retrieval practice, if used as a post-class testing opportunity. Our approaches to using gamified learning and weekly formative assessment quizzes provide conscious opportunities to retain knowledge through periodic revisitation, under the post-class component of a flipped classroom framework that features in many subjects within our Faculty (Figure 1). Additionally, this constant feedback offers the students continual immediate feedback, promoting self-monitoring by tracking performance (Zimmerman, 2008). Within this framework, behavioural engagement using the extensive learner analytics recorded in the mobile app gaming environment including a learner's active status, growth points, duration, accuracy, completion, date/time of access and number of attempts, offer suitable data for educators to 'keep our finger on the pulse' to identify at-risk users and provide early support interventions. Student in-app analytics regarding progress, performance, badges earned and peer-comparison via the leaderboard feature continually enable the students to self-regulate their own learning.

In this chapter, the authors share their collective experiences of implementing a mobile-based gamification app through three case studies within an Australian Health Science and Medicine Faculty and provide examples of the gamification app has been introduced within an intensive subject, a standard semester-long subject, and a full year of the medical program, to enhance self-regulation of learning and improve student engagement.

CASE STUDY 1: DOCTOR OF PHYSIOTHERAPY PROGRAM (INTENSIVE SUBJECT)

Educational Context

The first case study provides an example of the use of the gamified mobile app as a form of continual feedback opportunities across an intensive subject, delivered across two semesters a year apart. The Doctor of Physiotherapy (DPHTY) program at an Australian private university is an intensive, six semester programs. The program design features an innovative problem- and case-based learning model of physiotherapy education to prepare entry-level physiotherapists for their roles and responsibilities as first-contact practitioners. The curriculum features clinical, pathological, and related basic sciences content with the physiotherapy knowledge, skills and professional behaviors and attitudes required to

Figure 1. Inquiry-based learning model that informs the curriculum structure within undergraduate and postgraduate degree programs within the Faculty of Health Science and Medicine.
Note. The flipped classroom approach is utilized by many educators, and the three components of this framework are represented as 'pre-class', 'in-class' and 'post-class' learning opportunities. Using Examples of software and platforms frequently used for testing opportunities within the in-class component are represented in black text boxes. Formative assessment opportunities within Year 2 of the Medical Program and the format of summative assessment are represented in the black text boxes for the post-class component. Opportunities for the integration of the gamification app (red boxes) into the existing structure are illustrated.

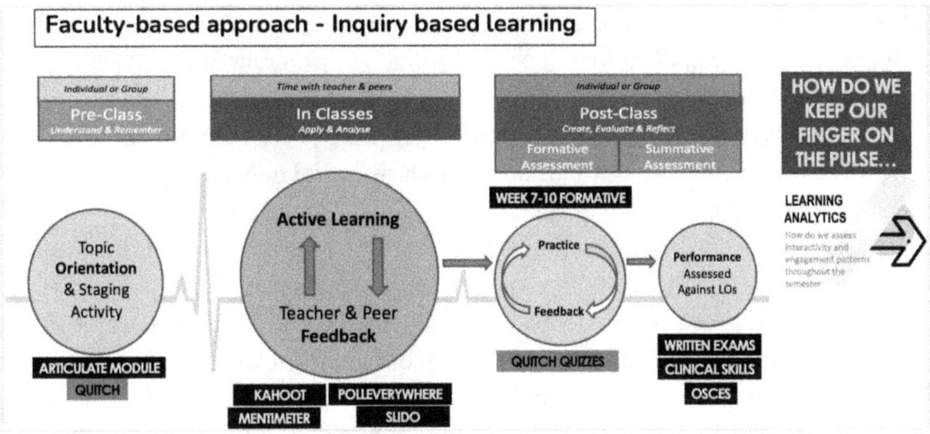

examine, diagnose, and treat physiotherapy clients (Bond University, 2022). The curriculum is informed by social constructivism theory and key educational practices include scaffolding, chunking (Thalmann et al., 2019), use of the flipped classroom (Roehl et al., 2013), deliberate practice (Ericsson et al., 1993) of key skills, and spaced repetition learning (Fields, 2005) to prepare students for clinical practice placements and transition to the workforce.

The recent global COVID-19 pandemic created the need to rapidly redesign the delivery of both coursework and clinical placements subjects within healthcare education (Cleland et al., 2020; Gordon et al., 2020; Keegan et al., 2020; Torda et al., 2020; World Physiotherapy 2020a). To enable healthcare programs to continue to recruit domestic and international students, allied health and medical programs responded by re-sequencing academic and placement subjects to ensure compliance with accreditation requirements (AHPRA 2020; CSP 2020; GMC 2020; Gough et al., 2021; MacDougall et al., 2020; Torda et al., 2020; World Physiotherapy 2020a,b,c). The resultant change for the subject in this case study was the division of theoretical content delivered as a three-week intensive subject in the first semester, coupled with a practical three-week intensive period in semester three of six, as illustrated in Figure 2. To optimize learning across the four semesters, the original six-week subject content was carefully deconstructed and re-scaffolded to allow theoretical content to be delivered and summatively assessed in week 3 via an examination and written report.

During the global pandemic, the closure of state and international borders in Australia, restricted the ability for students to attend on-campus face-to-face classes. Sub-cohort divisions arose, with approximately, 40% of the cohort studying overseas, 20% interstate, and 40% in the physical classroom (Gough et al., 2021).

Implementation

To enrich the engagement of students with the intensive content, interaction points were incorporated to both service as edutainment, and as a knowledge check for the academic. Edutainment is the blending of education and entertainment, to facilitate the student to acquire knowledge in an interesting, exciting, engaging, and entertaining format (Anikina & Yakimenko 2015). The subject conveners applied the conceptual framework of game-informed principles for health professional education, as outlined by Ellaway (2016). The learning activities were supplemented with a variety of gamified approaches and quiz questions with a range of software applications such as Kahoot! (https://kahoot.it/) Blackboard Collaborate (https://www.anthology.com/en-apac) polls and Poll Everywhere (https://www.polleverywhere.com/).

One of the drawbacks of polling software applications in the lack of learner analytics, which allows academics to track student progress over time and particularly track knowledge accuracy and engagement with supplementary learning activities. The incorporation of the mobile app within this subject was used to provide 24-7 revisitation opportunities of content. Any quiz/polls used within the learning activities were replicated on the mobile app and related at the end of the session. This allowed the academics to access the learner analytics for each student via the educator portal. The purpose of this duplication was to optimize the chances of embedding the subject theoretical knowledge in the students' long-term memory. Figure 2 illustrates key points during the intensive delivery where students' engagement in the classroom was supplemented with questions on the mobile app. As the summative assessment was delivered on Blackboard iLearn, students were also provided with formative assessment opportunities to familiarize themselves with the assessment application (Figure 2). Questions in the polls/quizzes/iLearn formative assessments and the mobile app all mirrored the style of questioning on the summative exam.

To help overcome potential memory decline, the app was made available for the entire duration of the two-year program. This aims to allow the students to periodically revisit the content and re-check their knowledge recall and application with purposefully scaffolded case studies. The question sets posted in the mobile app focus on the theoretical and practical application of the knowledge required within the objective structured clinical examinations (OSCEs) during the second intensive delivery period in semester 4 and later whilst on clinical placements (semesters 4-6). One key consideration was the number and frequency of questions released over an intensive period. Questions were released in batches of 5 or 10's, which was purposely chosen, to minimize cognitive overload (Dong et al., 2015; Miller 1956; Sweller, 1988, 1999), which is well known to have detrimental impacts on learning (Dong et al., 2015).

Design for SRL

The integration of the mobile app within the subject aimed to allow the physiotherapy students to self-regulate their own learning (Zimmerman, 2008) and progress over the three weeks of the intensive subject. One of the key processes of SRL is goal setting. Through engagement with the application, students were able to set short-term goals linked to the attainment of their knowledge, prior to the summative assessment. Immediate feedback and access to their learner (analytic) profile enabled students to refine their study through the process of self-monitoring against session content and overall achievement of the subject learning outcomes. The ability to review their own process on a daily level allowed the students to self-evaluation against the subject outcomes and seek help from the academics to accomplish their own SRL goals. Engagement in these self-regulatory processes aimed to enhance the students' own motivational beliefs, achievement of learning and performance (Zimmerman, 2008). Access to question

Figure 2. (A) Cardiorespiratory Physiotherapy subject roadmap illustrating the content delivered across two intensive three-week teaching blocks in different semesters and respective assessment items. (B) Graph extracted from educator dashboard in the mobile app, showing the typical trend of learner activity in number of questions answered throughout a semester within the Cardiorespiratory Physiotherapy subject. Timeline of graded assessment due dates are also shown.

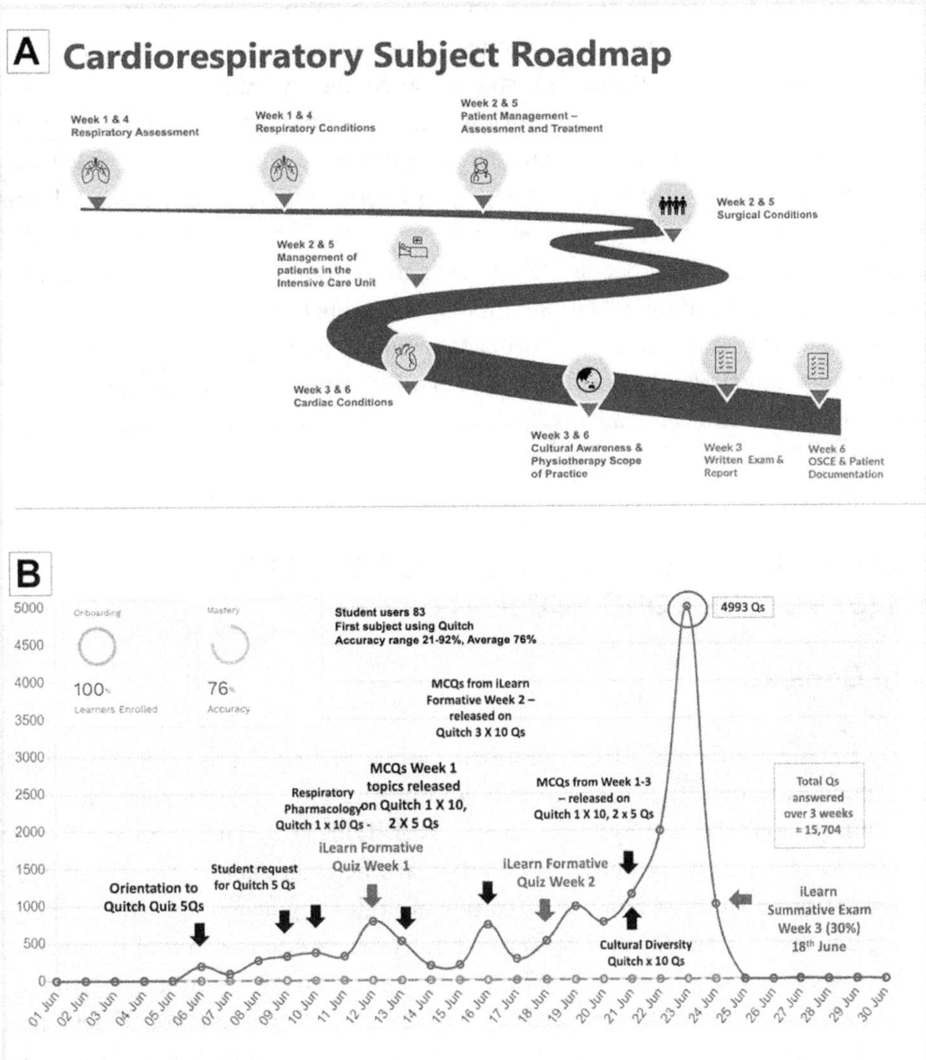

sets from this subject three semesters later and during subsequent clinical placement, affords students the opportunity to review knowledge, reset short and long-term goals to strive to optimize their performance.

Outcomes

All 83 students enrolled in the subjects accessed the mobile application, which was made available at no monetary cost to the students. Activity varied across the three-week subject leading up to the summative assessment in week 3 (Figure 2), with peak activities at the end of each week and the day before the summative exam. Similar trends have been observed over two cohorts (2021 and 2022). Students utilized the learner analytics (incorrect responses and lower accuracy areas within the questions sets) to structure specific questions to academics during subsequent resource sessions. Students utilized adaptive help-seeking behaviors (Zimmerman, 2008); to identify knowledge gaps, deepen their understanding and seek guidance on relevant resources to close the knowledge gaps. Whilst the students were predominantly focused on their recall and cramming for their summative assessment, this was expected owing to an intensive three-week learning period and high-stakes subject theory exam.

Academics utilized the educator portal to track learner enrollment, progress (completion of question sets released), and masters (accuracy). The traffic light system (red, amber, and green) assists the visual identification of potential 'at risk' students who have low completion and low mastery levels. Ongoing access to the application and subject question sets affords students the ability to re-test their knowledge and re-engage in the cyclical SRL processes (Zimmerman, 2008) as they complete the clinical aspect of the subject three semesters later and when on clinical placements prior to the end of their degree. The mobile app learner analytics can also help inform academics to identify those students who do not self-initiate SRL/do not use adaptive help-seeking behaviors. Referrals for academic and/or university-level support may be appropriate to allow students to identify SRL progresses to optimize learning throughout their degree.

CASE STUDY 2: BIOMEDICAL AND HEALTH SCIENCES PROGRAM (SEMESTER-LONG SUBJECT)

Educational Context

This case study focuses on the use of the gamified mobile platform in a subject generally taken by undergraduate students in their first year of study within Bachelor of Biomedical Sciences or Health Sciences program, (Human Control Systems subject: BMED11-112). The majority of students within these programs aim to pursue a postgraduate degree (e.g., medicine, higher degree research, occupational therapy, physiotherapy, nutrition and dietetics and others) following the completion of their current undergraduate degree. This Human Control Systems subject focuses on the structure and function of the nervous and hormonal control systems of the body and their interaction with the internal and external environments. Students undertake an integrated study of the anatomy and function of the musculoskeletal system of the axial and appendicular skeleton, the major structural components of the central nervous system and the neurohormonal axis. The subject materials presented also explains how sensations are recorded and interpreted, movements are controlled and the way the body regulates and integrates body function via the nervous and endocrine systems. There is also some coverage of the clinical aspects of disorders associated with control systems.

While this subject has traditionally been taught only in face-to-face mode, following the COVID-19 pandemic, the subject was transformed for multi-modal delivery. For the duration of this case study, the students who participated were either studying physically on-campus and/or remotely. Regardless of the delivery mode, the subject typically runs for a total of 12 teaching weeks across the semester, followed by a study week and a final assessment period. Each week, a specific topic is covered, and in-class sessions usually include a two-hour interactive lecture followed by an hour student-focused tutorial session. The interactive lecture incorporates flipped learning and content chunking, where small blocks of content are spaced with the use of Poll Everywhere polling questions as knowledge check-in points. Additionally, there are also four 3-hour practical sessions throughout the semester, three of which are anatomy sessions while the fourth being a physiology laboratory exercise. Assessment items that contribute towards students' final grades in the subject include the writing of a laboratory report, an anatomy quiz, a mid-semester test and a final exam.

While the use of polling questions in the lectures for this subject promoted in-class learner engagement, the lead educator sought an integrated platform that students could engage with outside the classroom. Students from past cohorts also requested a bank of practice questions that they could utilize for revision prior to examinations. This case study provides an example of how this mobile application was embedded to support semester-long retention and recall.

Implementation

In this context, the mobile app was offered as an optional revision tool for students to utilize. The lead educator of the subject posted 2 weekly quizzes on the platform across the 12 teaching weeks, related to the weekly topics that were covered. The first quiz generally consisted of 8-10 questions that tested the student's recall of knowledge from the weekly content of the subject. This was released immediately following the lecture of the week. The second quiz was comprised of 6 questions that required application and problem-solving using the concepts learnt within the topic. This quiz was released at the end of every teaching week. Additionally, three additional quizzes that contained purely anatomy questions were also released following practical sessions. All quizzes included multiple-choice and true or false questions.

Following the completion of a semester, application learner activity data and final grades of students were obtained from the educator portal and the university learning management system, respectively. The data collected were imported into GraphPad Prism software for the generation of graphs. A one-way ANOVA with Tukey's multiple comparisons of learner activity within the mobile app between final grade groups was performed, to explore possible co-relation of app engagement with students' academic performance in the subject.

Design for SRL

The mobile app was implemented consistently in this subject with a bi-weekly quiz release on the same days throughout the semester to promote self-regulated learning. The implementation design in this subject embeds a cyclical process that encourages the students to plan, monitor and reflect. With a recurrent and consistent quiz release schedule, students to plan and organize when and where they would undertake the quizzes in the week. This could be immediately when the quizzes are released, or after the teaching week is completed. This is followed by the ability to monitor their understanding based on their performance, as measured in the app using leaderboard scores and accuracy of their responses. This leads to a reflection by both the student (individually) and the educator (for the cohort) on performance in the quizzes. The reflection is supported by the straightforward traffic light system implemented by the mobile app, that clearly shows which questions had high or low accuracy rates. The educator can then decide to emphasize revision on content that students appear to have weakness in understanding and students will also be able to direct their time and effort on topics that they individually struggle with.

Outcomes

A total of 143 out of 155 (92%) students across 3 semesters used the application with varying levels of completion of available question sets. As can be seen in Figure 3A, peak levels of activity in the app occurred prior to the mid-semester test, anatomy quiz, and final examination. This is not surprising, as students are likely to revise content and practice questions immediately before these types of assessments. However, this observation did not align with the intended SRL design of a weekly cyclical process of plan, monitor, and reflect. While a minority did choose to use the mobile app in this manner, the majority of students instead chose the period (for most, the day) immediately prior to the assessment as a revision tool. The process of plan, monitor, and reflect might have still occurred, albeit in a short amount of time. This meant that the educator did not have enough time to reflect on the content that the cohort had weakness in understanding on and therefore, could not provide revision specific to this as intended.

The overall leaderboard score obtained from the mobile app at the end of the semester, immediately prior to the final assessment, is indicative of learner activity in the mobile application. This score considers the number of questions completed, the accuracy of answers, the number of attempts, and the time taken to answer for each user. The overall mobile app scores of students who obtained a High Distinction (85% and above) in the subject were significantly higher than the scores of those in other grade groups (Figure 3B). The app leaderboard scores in every other grade group (except credits vs pass and pass vs fails) were also significantly different from one another; with declining scores, there was a decline in the final grade obtained in the subject (HD vs D: $p = 0.0012$, HS vs P, C, and F: $p<0.0001$, D vs C: $p=0.0039$, D vs P and F: $p<0.0001$, C vs P: $p=0.0015$, C vs F: $p=0.1267$, P vs F: $p=0.9940$). While it is likely that this is due to the low number of students who failed the subject, it is interesting to note that there was no significant difference in leaderboard scores between the pass and fail groups. Based on these observations, it is apparent that using the mobile app to support students' learning experience in a semester-long course is effective in improving their overall academic performance.

CASE STUDY 3: PRE-CLINICA, BYEARS OF A MEDICAL PROGRAM (CURRICULUM INTEGRATION)

Educational Context

The final case-study focusses on the pilot of the mobile application within the second year of study in the Doctor of Medicine Program. This explores the complexities and considerations of the introduction of a new learning tool into an undergraduate program with multiple student entry cohorts, delivered by 36 to 41 unique academic and clinical educators, and the co-existence of multiple discipline streams in each week of teaching and learning activities. Although an undergraduate program of study, the variation in learner pre-entry context for science studies and in self-regulation skills poses a unique challenge, since the cohort comprises an amalgam of high school leavers, health science lateral entry students and a proportion of mature-age, postgraduate students.

The medicine curriculum team decided upon the second year of pre-clinical studies for the pilot, as it is notoriously dense given the proportion of foundational science content (e.g., Anatomy, Physiology, Pathology) represented and the expected learning and mastery of new clinical skills, such as systemic history-taking and physical examination within Clinical Practice. As represented in Figure 4, this year-

Figure 3. (A) Graph extracted from educator dashboard in the mobile app, showing the typical trend of learner activity in number of questions answered throughout a semester within the subject Human Control Systems (BMED11-112). Timeline of graded assessment due dates are also shown. (B) Box and whiskers plot showing students final leader board score prior to the final examination of the subject.
Note. Summative final grades represented as HD, High Distinction; D, Distinction; C; Credit, P; Pass, F; Fail. A one-way ANOVA was performed between final grade groups (p<0.05 vs HD, ^ p<0.05 vs D, # p<0.05 vs C).*

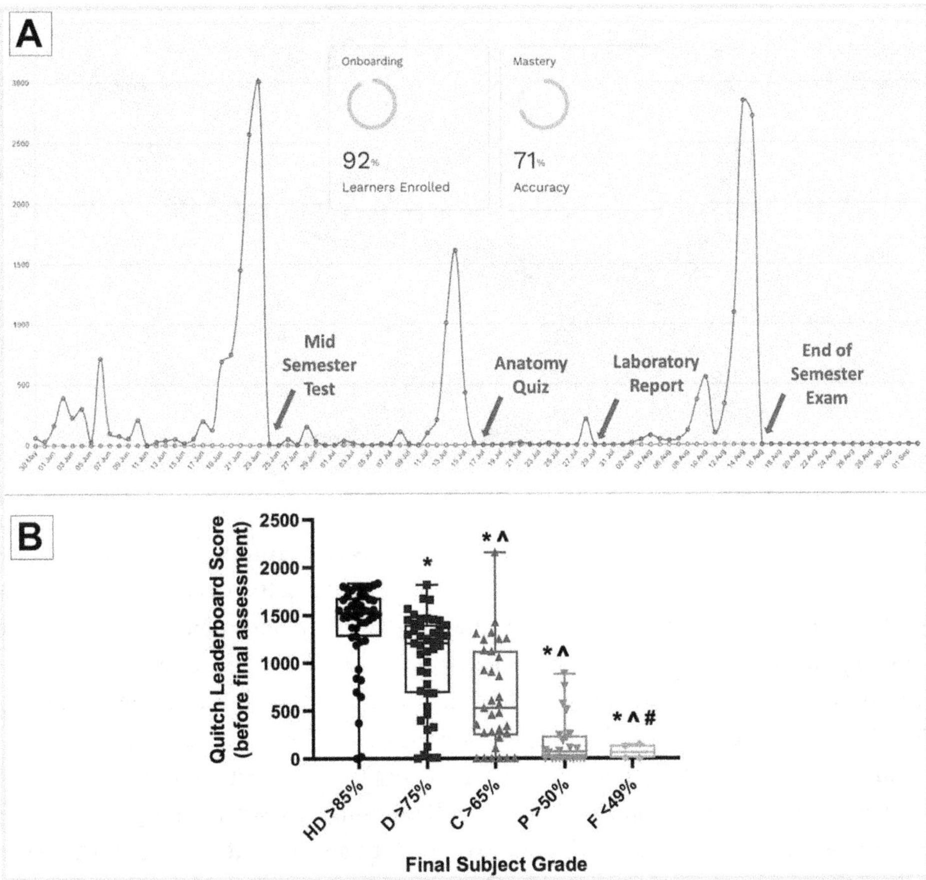

long subject is comprised of three trimesters, each featuring 12 teaching weeks; each trimester is then segregated into human body system blocks, which feature common clinical scenarios that inform integrated learning activities across four Domain areas (Science and Scholarship, Clinical Practice, Health and Society, Professionalism and Leadership). The complexity of this year level is compounded by two additional entry points of study: (i) approximately 18 lateral entry students with prior credit from another Health degrees (e.g., Biomedical Sciences, Doctor of Physiotherapy) commencing MEDI12-201 (subject 1) in January; and (ii) Year 1 September-entry students commencing MEDI12-202 (subject 2) in the May semester. Summative assessment opportunities feature at the end of each semester in the form of a clinical skills performance portfolio and written examination, combined with competency assessment in small-group learning and procedural skills, as well as an in-semester Health and Society assignment. Two formative assessment opportunities for performance control and self-reflection (Zimmerman, 2000), are provided between weeks 7 and 10 in preparation for the end-of-semester summative assessments.

Figure 4. Curriculum overview of Year 2 of the Medical Program illustrating the organisational and content breakdown over the course of the academic year.

Note. This year within the pre-clinical phase contains three (3) subjects/units that run over 12 weeks, containing three body systems and associated clinical cases. The complexity of each subject based on the discipline breakdown, number of unique educators, points of entry from Year 1 or lateral entry options are represented. Additionally, the timing of key formative assessment opportunities for clinical skills (CSF) and a Science and Scholarship written formative exam (WF) in each semester are represented in yellow.

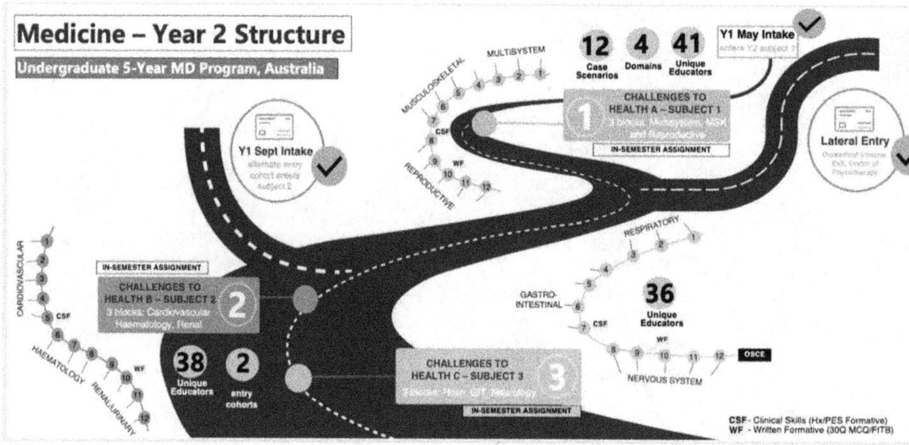

The learning tool was used as a way to motivate students to regularly engage in difficult learning activities across semesters, by providing them with opportunities to repeatedly engage in frequent, no-stakes weekly quizzes. Rich literature on the testing effect in undergraduate education supports the positive effects on memory and long-term knowledge retention (Karpicke & Blunt, 2011; Roediger & Karpicke, 2006), including the importance of feedback provision on information retention (Butler & Roediger, 2008). Bjork and Bjork's (1992) theory of disuse posits that retrieval practice improves storage strength, which is particularly important for medical students who are required to retain foundational science knowledge, for effective clinical reasoning in their clinical years of study and practice.

Educators are currently challenged with a lack of learner engagement, low visibility on learner performance in real-time and delayed data and insights into content performance. Two factors contribute to these challenges in our program. Firstly, the large number of educators that contribute to each unit mandates regulation of access and edit privileges in the nominated learning management system (LMS) to ensure the integrity of content and resources. As a result, the creation of weekly quizzes using the University LMS is not a viable option, which has resulted in a heavy reliance on student-generated, non-Faculty-endorsed Anki flashcards (https://apps.ankiweb.net/) within the student population. Under the 'in-class' component of the inquiry-based framework (Figure 1), an assortment of audience response tools such as Kahoot!, Poll Everywhere, Mentimeter (https://www.mentimeter.com/) and Slido (https://www.slido.com/) are frequently used in lectures or workshops, but only provide superficial learning analytics. The mobile app addresses this challenge by providing comprehensive, real-time data on learner performance to both parties, which allows for early intervention and opportunities for student support.

Table 1. Summary of content build data for contributing disciplines, topic, and question breakdown for each of the three semesters of the phase 1 pilot in 2021.

	MEDI12-202	MEDI12-203	MEDI12-201
No. of Contributing Disciplines	2 - Anatomy & Clinical Practice (Hx & PES)	4 - Anatomy, Clinical Practice, Pharmacology (EOB), Physiology (EOB)	5 - Anatomy, Clinical Practice (Hx & PES), Procedural Skills, Pharmacology, HS
No. of Topics	17	36	45
Questions created	126	205	229
App Enrolment	93.5% (n=175)	97% (n=183)	99% (n=212)
Inactive Users	8	7	2
Total questions	35, 692	81, 644	100, 984
Average no. of questions/day	375.71	951.81	1030.45
Average no. questions per student/day	2.15	5.43	4.77

Note. Student enrollment data and question engagement (total, average number of questions attempted each day and per student) are provided to illustrate exponential growth in uptake across the 12-month period. EOB – End of Block; PES – Physical Examination; HS – Health and Society Domain.

Implementation

A two-phase implementation strategy of the mobile application learning tool was conceived by the Year 2 Assessment and Clinical Practice leads in 2021, to tackle key challenges pertaining to post-COVID student engagement changes, encourage positive out-of-class learning tendencies and to provide consolidation of knowledge opportunities. Phase 1 aimed to conduct an initial 12-month pilot for 210 Year 2 students, in the form of weekly formative quizzes (ranging from 5 to 10 questions each) in the discipline areas of anatomy and clinical practice, commencing May 2021. In the mobile app, students were also directed to program generated and/or endorsed resources such as lightboard videos, VOPPS and infographics, to ensure horizontal and vertical spiraling of curriculum. As demonstrated in Table 1, for each subsequent semester from implementation, the discipline reach and adoptability by educators increased. In the first semester of roll-out (MEDI12-202) a total of 17 quizzes were created: increasing to 36 quizzes in MEDI12-203 and 45 quizzes in the final pilot semester (MEDI12-201). Following the 12-month pilot subphase, the focus shifted to transferability of the content-build approach to all other discipline and Domain areas, and support from key educators would be critical in 2022 to ensure adequate sampling and representation of content across the broader curriculum. Phase 2 will focus on a vertical roll-out strategy into all other subjects within the pre-clinical phase, starting in 2022.

Design for SRL

The mobile app was implemented across the three subjects in Medicine as an 'optional' formative assessment tool, to provide consistency in the quality of question provision and mitigate the reliance on external, non-peer reviewed resources. Centered around the week's case-based learning sessions, between two to five quizzes (n=5 MCQ per quiz) were released to students, featuring a sampler of content across the four-domain areas, each week. Each quiz was scheduled at least 24 hours post-delivery, to address the Ebbinghaus forgetting curve. An in-app notification is automatically pushed to the students' mobile devices as a reminder that new content is available – serving as a gentle prompt in assisting the learner with self-efficacy and control of learning. While the student is provided with the opportunity for immediate retrieval practice of core content via the platform, it should be noted that self-regulation of resource management, includes managing time and study environment, pace of content review, and effort management, will vary based on each student's individual learning strategies and metacognitive skills. The core issue we wanted to investigate using trace measures in the online platform, was whether modern learners display personal initiative, perseverance, and adaptive skill. Via the educator portal, learner activity data for each quiz including growth points, accuracy, completion, and attempt lapse since release were extracted from the educator portal within the mobile app. This data is useful to assess SRL as a metacognitive construct, where educators can access performance data prior to a teaching-sessions, to help learners to address knowledge gaps and content errors through encouraging rehearsal, elaboration, and critical thinking. This also provides immediate feedback opportunities for students to target their retrieval practice, re-evaluate study techniques, reflect on inefficiencies in their learning environments/ approaches or be more proactive in help seeking or peer learning.

To investigate SRL as a behavioral construct, specifically whether the learner engages with distributed versus massed practice, a new ordinal engagement tool was developed. Learning behaviors were classified into ordinal stages of "high", "moderate", "just-in-time" or "minimal/none", to allow cluster analysis and inter-group comparison measures of the end-of-semester summative grades, in consideration of the number of weeks lapsed since release of each quiz. Pilot data were imported into GraphPad Prism for exploratory analysis and one-way ANOVA with Tukey's multiple comparisons between final grade groups (combined score for end-of-semester written and clinical practice summative assessment) as well as engagement groups, to explore the relationship between engagement and academic attainment. It is anticipated that these rudimentary statistical comparisons will provide an insight into the proactive qualities of learners and their motivations to using the app, in consideration of intrinsic-extrinsic goal orientation. Student testimonials captured in routine subject student satisfaction surveys (eTEVAL) and quality assurance initiatives including focus groups, were also extracted to in an attempt to gain qualitative insights of learner motivation for the mobile app usage (e.g., valuing, expectation and affect measures).

Outcomes

Demonstrated in Table 1, student initiative to enroll in the optional mobile app learning module across the three consecutive semesters of the pilot phase increased from 93.5% (n=175), to 97% (n=183) and 99% (n=212); while enrolment rates reduced from 4.4% to 0.9%. This coincides with exponential growth in content built with each semester, with respect to the number of topics, questions, and unique educators, as student satisfaction and positive feedback in subject evaluation data became apparent. Conception in the first semester was limited to two select but co-dependent disciplines – Anatomical sciences and Clinical Skills (Physical Examination and History Taking), to iron out software teaching issues and monitor student behaviors and tenancies. By the third semester of utility (MEDI12-201), contributions had extended to five discipline areas and 16 educators. Usage trends across a semester indicate spikes in learner activity prior to in-semester clinical assessment (CSS), applied clinical skills workshops, and at the end of each content block (weeks 7 and week 12) (Figure 5). Not surprisingly, the number of questions completed in the period immediately prior to the written examination in Week 14 significantly increased to an average of 2,100/day in week 13 and 12, 551 questions the day prior to the module closing. The massed practice observed in week 13, while not a surprising observation for undergraduate University students, does not align with the intended SRL implementation of the mobile app. 2.1% of the cohort only downloaded the app for the first time the week prior to the examination, which may provide an insight of this group's interpretations of the purpose of the learning tasks featured on the app and/or learner intention with respect to self-concept of ability.

Exploratory analysis of engagement data or trace measures from the Educator portal appears to correlate with student academic performance. Similar to case-study two, growth points which include accuracy, completion, number of attempts and time measures for each question attempted by the student, were significantly higher for students who obtained greater than 85% on the end-of-semester assessment, than the scores of those in other grade groups (Figure 5B). Students with grades >85% completed approximately 94.3% of available questions in MEDI12-201. A general decline in points is noted across the groups, while a significant difference in leaderboard scores between the pass (>50%) group with those who obtained a credit (>65%) or distinction (>75%) was reported. Similarly, declining trends in completion patterns of available content is seen across grade groups, with significant differences in completion between students with grades below 49% (37.5% average) and those who scored a pass ($p < 0.05$; mean completion - 64%), credit ($p < 0.001$; mean completion – 76.3%) and distinction ($p < 0.001$; mean completion – 81%). These observations may reflect the two different goal paths described by Boekaerts and Niemivirta (2000); as students with low completion rates and points may perceive the learning tasks to be threatening to their well-being/ego or associated with negative cognitions and emotions, in turn activating the 'wellbeing' pathway rather than the mastery/growth pathway for self-regulation of learning. Further research on learner intention in the pursuit of task goals using the app is required.

Results of the newly developed engagement tool, which assesses the correlation between distributed practice and academic performance, demonstrates that students classified as 'highly engaged', who completed most topics within 2 weeks of release, scored significantly higher ($p < 0.05$; Δ 10.6%) than students who completed the quizzes in week 13/SWOTVAC for the first time (Figure 5C). Students with negligible or no regular engagement with the mobile app (n=27) obtained significantly lower scores than all other student groups (just-in-time - $p < 0.001$; Δ 8.9%, moderate - $p < 0.001$; Δ 15.6%, high engagement - $p < 0.001$; Δ 18.64%). DiBenedetto and Zimmerman (2010) suggest that "higher achievers" show more use of the subprocesses from Zimmerman's model (2000), which may explain the correlation between performance and engagement observed in our undergraduate students. The new trace measure of 'time lapse' (between first attempt and date of scheduled release), may provide a snapshot of the role of self-monitoring in SRL, where a 'highly engaged' student demonstrates stronger skills in the forethought phase and performance phase (including self-instruction, monitoring of progress of self-control strategies to be cognitively engaged). The impact of weekly formative quizzes, and provision of instant feedback in the platform has generally demonstrated positive benefits to the learning culture within Year 2 of the Medical Program and aims to support student commitment to long-term knowledge retention, resulting in improved mastery of end-of-semester assessment items.

Qualitative unsolicited student testimonials support the cyclic phases and subprocesses of self-regulation, with the positive benefits noted in relation to self-reflection, evaluation/monitoring and refinement of study and encoding techniques, based on retrieval practice. Gamification elements such as the traffic-light system to identify accuracy and leaderboard also appear to stimulate emotional engagement, based on informal unsolicited student feedback through "*I ensured each question had a 'green dot' at minimum, which signified an 80% success rate for that individual quiz. I found that this sustained repetition, paired with the competitiveness of seeing my rank climb in the leaderboard, allowed me to have better depth*

Figure 5. (A) Learner activity graph extracted from the Quitch Educator portal, demonstrating the number of questions completed each day, throughout the duration of a 12-week trimester within Year 2 of the Medical Program (MEDI12-201). (B) Box and whiskers plot showing students Quitch growth points (that inform the leaderboard position) based on summative assessment scores (not including competency and in-semester assignments). (C) Box and whiskers plot showing end-of-semester (EOS) summative assessment scores for each engagement group, using ordinal ratings of 1: high engagement, 2: moderate engagement, 3: just-in-time (SWOTVAC) and 4: minimal or no engagement with the app.
*Note. In graph A, the average number of questions completed each day in a given week are represented. Select activity spikes correspond to pretesting opportunities prior to the Applied Clinical Skills Workshops (ACSW), while clinical skills in-semester summative assessment timepoints (CSS) are also delineated on the graph. In graph B, group allocation is based on the generic University grade classification (HD, High Distinction; D, Distinction; C; Credit, P; Pass, F; Fail), and is not representative of medical program convention for individual assessment pieces. Results for the one-way ANOVA with Tukey's multiple comparison tests between grade groups are represented: #p<0.05 vs HD, ^ p<0.05 vs D, *p<0.05 vs C. For graph C, mean scores for each group are shown in yellow, while one-way ANOVA with Tukey's multiple comparison test results between engagement groups are represented: #p<0.05 vs just in time, ^ p<0.05 vs moderate, *p<0.05 vs high engagement.*

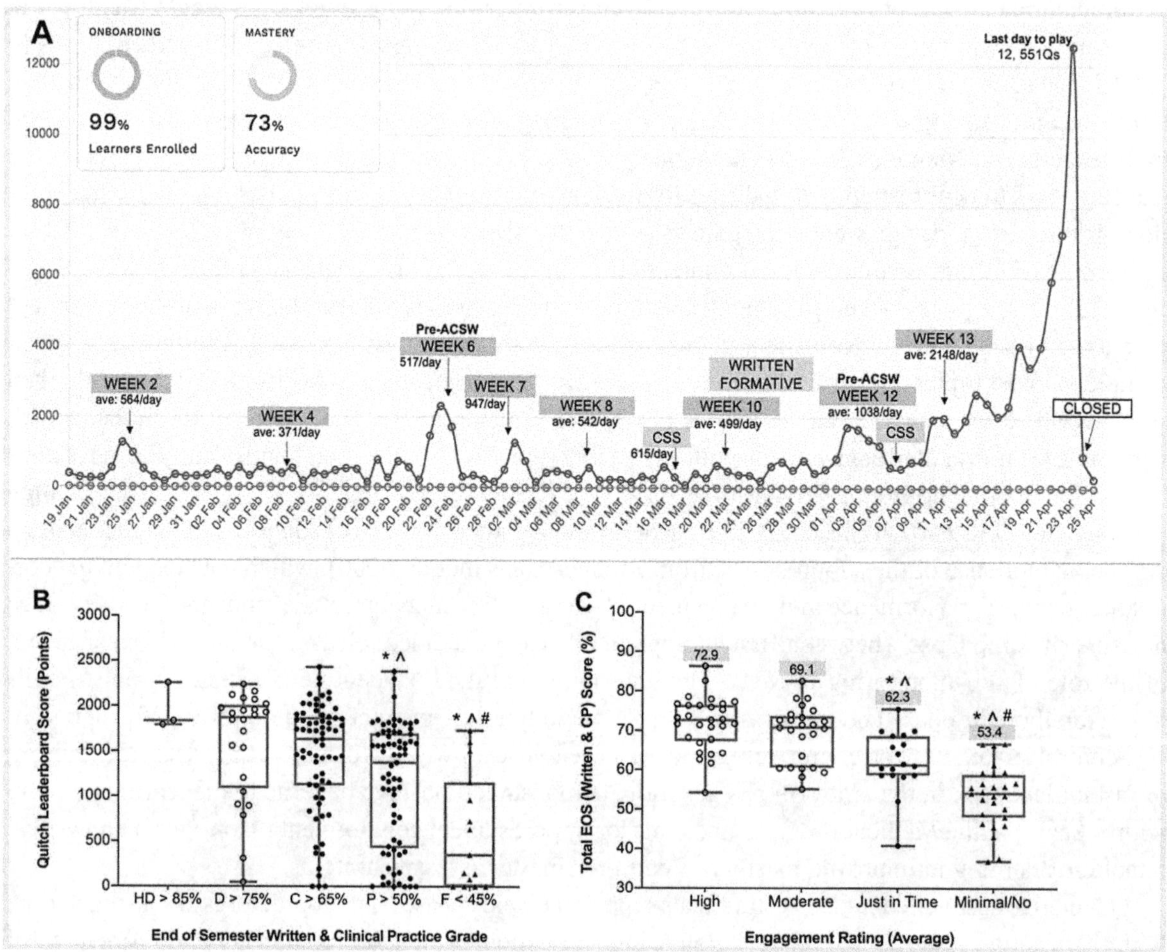

of knowledge than if I had just crammed in the days before the exam" (Year 2 MD Student, 2022 email correspondence). Critical at this stage in their pre-clinical studies, consistent retrieval practice has provided medical students with an opportunity to employ self-regulatory subprocesses to strategically plan, evaluate and refine their study and encoding strategies which results in positive habit-building in their learning approaches (Wlodarczyk et al., 2021). In addition, the fun, gamification elements and customized curriculum content build, provides modern learners with an easily accessible (mobile-based) tool to expand their knowledge and skills in a non-threatening digital environment, which aims to trigger positive emotions and cognitions.

DISCUSSION

Prior to the COVID-19 pandemic in March 2020, most University education programs favored on-campus delivery, with the exception of the Open University. In November 2020, Maguire and colleagues outlined expectations of a 10-year shift towards a greater blended learning approach, likely to comprise online lectures, online and in-person tutorials, and seminars, to give rise to priority to in-person workshops, skills, and simulation-based and laboratory-based practical work. Whilst there remains an importance of the learning environment as a physical space, it is essential that in this post-pandemic era, educators and learning designers recreate this same experience for learners who are receiving a blended learning delivery mode. New innovative and dynamic technologies offer opportunities and solutions to re-imagine blended learning environments through technology-driven educational approaches, but unless they are founded upon sound pedagogy, the outcomes may disappoint. Digital technology should be implemented and embedded in education intentionally to ensure that it is inclusive of all learners, including those with learning impairments (Maguire et al., 2020).

Beatson and colleagues (2020) advocate that the user-interface of gamification apps like the one implemented in this study, enable active engagement in course content over the duration of the semester due to its ease of access and integration with pre-existing generation Z mobile-phone access behaviors e.g., scrolling through social media, due to its modern and attractive, visually aesthetic design in comparison to a 'standard' LMS. The novelty effect and its impact on long-term engagement should be considered by educators and may be overcome by employing diversity in question format and embarking on content refresh initiatives every two years. Educators and coordinators are encouraged to carefully pre-plan the scheduling of question release in consideration of existing teaching activities in a given week or semester, to reduce cognitive load. This assists students to maintain the 'flow' in constant, repeated engagement to maintain concentration, interest and build self-efficacy; in contrast to larger assessment pieces which feature at the end-of-the semester in traditional assessment design. The app was predominantly used for the post-class component (e.g., 24 hours after the lecture) of the flipped classroom model to encourage retrieval opportunities and address the Ebbinghaus forgetting curve. Interestingly, clinical practice educators in Medicine opted to utilize learning tool for pre-testing opportunities for an integrated Applied Clinical Skills workshop held at the end of system block, accounting for the learner activity spikes in Figure 5A. Bjork and colleagues (1992) discuss the effectiveness of 'pretesting' as a primer for learning, to alert them to key concepts and learning outcomes to focus on during their instruction in the face-to-face session, or areas of their study where further elaboration is required. The rich analytics and traffic-light indicators for each question, available from the content landing page in the educator portal, allow academics to quickly gauge problematic areas and knowledge gaps, as well as which students have not prepared adequately, to plan face-to-face instruction accordingly.

Figure 6 provides a visual representation of the features of the mobile-based app. The in-app learner dashboard features student progress, overview of badges earned and performance relative to the class

(Figure 6A), which facilitates self-monitoring, self-evaluation, and self-management of learning. This feature allows learners to take personal initiative and self-diagnose their positions in comparison to their peers. For learners who are driven by competition, the external motivators of leaderboard placement and badge attainment may promote their drive to answer more questions on the app and/or spend more time and effort on understanding content The traffic light system of question competency is represented in each topic/quiz and provides a measure to monitor knowledge gaps. This; a gamification feature that promotes the student's learning to be goal-oriented and facilitates self-instruction of revision areas. From the educator perspective, this competency data can be readily reviewed prior to or within a teaching session, to help learners address knowledge gaps and correct content errors/misconceptions, through tailoring activities which encourage elaboration and critical thinking. Students can view educator generated or recommended 'resources' for guided revision more about difficult concepts (Figure 6B). This feature facilitates micro-learning where the learner can self-evaluate their understanding and knowledge on content that is specific to their course/subject/program. This targeted direction/linking toward credible resources assists students with digital literacy and source discrimination; imperative for a generation of learners exposed to more inaccurate and unverified online information than ever before. The number of attempts and example of instant feedback for each correct question is shown in Figure 6E. Examples of MCQ single and multiple response options with attached embedded images to appeal to Gen Z learners are illustrated in screenshots 6D and 6F.

Table 2 provides 12 pearls of wisdom for re-imagining and enhancing learner engagement using the learning tool within university education. Whilst the authors draw on their collective experiences, the pearls can be applied across other undergraduate and postgraduate program. The pearls similarly can be applied to single subjects or entire programs. Challenges overcome throughout the implementation of the three case studies have been highlighted across key stages of curriculum integration: onboarding of students to the application via the educator portal, question design, question release and student support. Additionally, ways in which these facilitates the SRL process are also outlined.

There has been an exponential growth of the availability of high-quality engaging online content through an emergence of a plethora of new subscription-based platforms. For example, common platforms used by medical students include Osmosis, AMBOSS, Boards and Beyond, which range from AU$179.99 to $498.00 per year, per platform. The recent emergence of such platforms (that include high-quality video and animated content, question banks and flashcards, as a health science and medicine faculty), poses a new challenge pertaining to learner equity, affordability, inclusivity, and the impact that external subscriptions have on the overall learning culture. A rationale for the mobileapp implementation included creating a level playing field for all students by the provision of baseline formative questions, competitive to the standard of the commercial medical education entities, which is designed by academics to mirror their curriculum. In light of this new market of online content provision and broader changes in the higher education sector, Maguire (2020) cautions that if universities fail to adapt to generation Z learners and reimagine learning and teaching, their organizations may fall behind the rest of the educational sector.

LIMITATIONS

A few of the limitations of the mobile app implementation for educators and/or administrators to consider concerns the fact that the app is currently not integrated with traditional learning management systems (LMS), and therefore combined learner analytic reports and grade-center integration is not possible.

Figure 6. A visual representation of the user-interface and unique features of the mobile-based app (student view)

Different output formats and variables of the LMS, Quitch educator portal or other software consulted in a program, may be a source of frustration for data management and analyses.

The preference for multiple-choice-type questions for the initial content build, allowed for minimal administrative burden on the institution and educators, as pre-existing questions created in other platforms such as Kahoot! or archival question banks, could be easily migrated and replicated. While the mobile app user-interface supports short-answer type questions (SAQ), the burden on educators of large student cohorts is heavy due to the manual marking and feedback required for each question. The strength of testing effect is generally dependent on how cognitively demanding the retrieval process is during practice opportunities, with short-answer practice questions generally resulting in increased score performance on the final exam, in comparison to MCQ only quizzes (Kang et al., 2007). Given the marking limitations of the SAQ format in the mobile app, the 'select all that apply' MCQ format was frequently utilized by disciplines such as clinical practice and physiotherapy, which require higher levels of critical thinking and reasoning, to improve the strength of the testing effects. While this condition is not identical to the

Table 2. Twelve pearls of wisdom for integrating the learning tool into university education.*

	Example Challenges	Pearls of Wisdom	Facilitating SRL Process
Onboarding			
1	Managing, recording, and licensing requirements of unique student and staff users.	• Accuracy of record keeping is essential with large cohort sizes, to ensure tracking of licenses allocated. • Co-ordination of license keys with a university Information Technology Service Team is advisable to aid cyber security and track licenses as users graduate, avoiding un-necessary costs.	
2	Staff proficiency and ability to answer queries	• Staff training is essential to ensure proficiency of use, optimal question design and familiarity of the learner analytics.	
3	Familiarity with mobile application	• Release a non-content related trivia (e.g., pop culture, general knowledge) as the first quiz to give learners the opportunity to familiarize with the app design and layout.	
Question design			
4	Appropriately constructing and formatting questions	• Construction of questions is essential, given the independent nature of the app. If question design is weak, this may detrimentally impact learner engagement. • Diversity in question types to strengthen retrieval skills and elaboration opportunities. For example, in case-study three, a combination for MCQ single correct, MCQ multiple-correct, true/false. • Question wording and type should mirror those of the summative assessments/exam (e.g., Multiple choice, true/false, fill in the blank, free text) to ensure familiarity. • Multiple choice questions can also aid recall of short answer free text questions as the learners are exposed to a range of correct/incorrect answers.	• The app provides the ability for academics to include feedback for each answer, to aid knowledge confirmation/correction of inaccuracies. Thus, micro-learning opportunities are provided to the users • Enabling multiple-retakes of question sets (e.g., 'number of lives' feature), facilitates self-monitoring (of accuracy/attainment progress), self-evaluation and self-management (through reflection). • Regular exposure to assessment quality questions, coupled with instant feedback, impacts learners motivational feelings and beliefs relating to sustained changes in their self- regulation of learning, resulting in higher self-efficacy beliefs and reduced performance anxiety in exams.
5	Creating question hints	• Question hints can be added within the question edit field. This can assist learners who are struggling to differentiate answers. Hyperlinks or prompts can also be added here. • When using the "select all" question type, student feedback recommends specifying the number of correct combinations e.g. Which three of the following are correct?	• Hints and answer explanations provide additional micro-learning opportunities to simply provide prompts, reaffirm knowledge or correct inaccuracies. Additionally, users have the freedom to click the 'hint' button or not, which promotes self-monitoring. • Explanation answers also facilitate students to evaluate their responses to questions, and can help maintain focus on accuracy, breadth, and depth. • Explanations can also include hyperlinks and/or refer to in-app 'resources' to provide targeted direction for those that have incorrect answers. • Frequent checks on knowledge and understanding provide internal feedback opportunities for the students. This coupled with external feedback from formative/summative progress contributes to the development of strategic learning.
6	Generating answer explanations	• Explanation of the answers can be added within the question edit field. This helps the learner to understand the incorrect/correct answers. It can be used to re-enforce key concepts.	
7	Text-based questions are more difficult for generation Z to process and are considered unappealing	• Accompanying questions with images used within a learning event/pre-requisite study task can aid memory recall (Rothman, 2016). • Public domain and Open Access websites provide a wide range of multi-media items (images, clip art, icons, videos, animations, and sounds) that can be added to the questions. open-source images. • Image use can help digital learners who prefer to process visuals (images and video), sounds and colour before processing text (Medina, 2008). • Ensure that you appropriately acknowledge the source of the digital media. This can be added within the answer explanation section when building the question. Ensure that copyright registration is not breached.	
8	Question similarity but not identical to the summative assessment item	• In some circumstances, academics may choose to avoid replicating identical summative questions within this formative platform, owing to the ability for unlimited attempts. • Alternatively, unlimited repetition and spaced-and-paced learning have been shown to improve recall and knowledge retention (Fields, 2005). Therefore, academics may choose to consider including a subset of modified questions into the summative assessment. Positive rewards may also facilitate consistent in-semester engagement.	• Questions written in the same format/style as the summative assessments helps students to contextualize their learning and can aid recall and retention, boost self-efficacy and address performance anxiety.
Question release			
9	Staff co-ordination & scheduling release of question sets	• Other polling platforms may be used within classroom-based learning activities, and questions can be duplicated in the mobile app, to enable anytime and inclusive learning. This allows access to learner analytics of content irrespective of initial question release. • Considerations include whether learners are undertaking other subjects which may also be using mobile apps or releasing flipped classroom activities for completion. • Co-ordinating release of learning activities across the week helps to reduced cognitive load. • Withholding the mobile app prior to an assessment/exam may increase learner stress and anxiety during revision. However, adult learners should be able to determine their own study habits. • Sequential release of question sets throughout a subject can help to encourage a distributed study habit and help to avoid cramming, which may lead to increased stress and potential burnout over time.	• Scheduling is important to allow students the time to self- monitor and utilise adaptive help-seeking behaviours (Zimmerman, 2008); to identify knowledge gaps, deepen their understanding and seek guidance on relevant resources to close the knowledge gaps. • Signpost to students various opportunities to seek goal-directed help from resources, peers, academics (Karabenick & Berger, 2013).
10	Inadequate preparation by students at face-to-face classes	• Question sets can be released as pre-requisite study to inform the academic of the knowledge base prior to delivery of the content in a particular session/activity. Learner analytics within the educator dashboard include a leader board, individual learner performance and question summary data. These are useful indicators for educators to quantify student preparedness and to identify problem areas to address within the instructional session.	• Staged release of questions as pre-requisite learning can also assist students to develop and exercise 'executive help seeking skills' whereby the students ask for explanations or hints rather than direct help to answer the questions/ resolve knowledge gaps. In turn executive help-seeking skills decrease the need for help and thus subsequent dependency on peers/academics (Karabenick & Berger, 2013).
Student support			
11	Supporting learners through remediation	• Learner analytics are powerful for those students' requiring remediation, after a subject has completed. • Question sets may also be used to capitalize on spaced-and-paced learning to aid long-term memory recall for placements or scaffolded content in later subjects within a program of study.	• The availability of questions sets post-assessment can facilitate continual self-regulation of their own performance. Initially reflecting and self-evaluating their performance (e.g., goal achievement/assessment success) and identifying primary factors causing them to struggle/succeed (Sandars & Cleary, 2011). • Weiner (1986) suggests that identification of causal attributions for success/ struggles is highly predictive of students' subsequent behaviours and ultimate motivations for successful and or sustained learning. • Teaching the cyclical process of self-regulation may contribute to successful remediation.
12	Reminders via in-app announcement functionality	• Given the external nature of the app, which is not integrated with the official learning management system yet, students often forget that new content will be released or ignore (or even turn off) the notifications. • The announcements functionality, which can target 'at risk' (<50% of content completion) or 'non-participation' students, offers an opportunity to remind students via notifications to their devices.	• Research has shown SRL to be a distinguishing characteristic of low/high academic achieving students (Sandars & Cleary, 2011). High-achievers typically setting higher strategic goals, self-monitoring their own progress and sing self-evaluations on test/exam performance. Thus, in-app reminders may help energize learners, guide their actions, and facilitate proactive choices about engagement with learning strategies/resources. Conversely, low achievers can be monitored and specifically targeted to seek engagement and offer support rather than wait for those students to seek help (Sandars & Cleary, 2011).

Note. *In the table, reference to 'learner', includes any user e.g., staff or student, as the platform can be used for any learning purpose.

question type featured in the written examination, it is anticipated that the higher cognitive processing required to deduce the correct combination of answers positively influence retrieval strength, storage strength and subsequently long-term retention. The choice of question format should be informed by the context, learning outcomes and learner challenges. For example, educators may want to consider diversity using recall, MCQ, fill-in-the-blank and true/false questions for first year units where the focus is on engagement with the content and promoting positive study habits; in year of the medical program, the focus shifts to integrating discipline content using clinical vignette style MCQ questions, to prepare them for the format and language associated with the end-of-semester written examination.

Engagement is a theoretical concept, and its complexity informed by a multitude of indicators, variables, and influences, that are not limited to the online environment. Preliminary pilot data provided in this chapter illustrates the potential of the mobile app to explore behavioral engagement measures but is by no means exhaustive in consideration of the multiple variables that inform the complexity of engagement models. The inferred relationship between behavioral engagement in the form of mobile app growth points and student performance (Figures 3 and 5) is consistent with existing literature (Beatson et al., 2020). However, multivariable modelling approaches may prove more informative. Factors that account for intrinsic motivation and broader engagement tendencies inclusive of face-to-face attendance data, extra-curricular involvement, and completion/performance of broader formative assessment tasks within the traditional curriculum structure need to be accounted for in a prediction model. The aforementioned indicators are congruent with characteristics for a 'highly engaged' student, and perhaps it is these students who are better at self-regulating their learning and display higher levels of self-motivation, thereby being likely to embrace any new app or platform introduced (Trowler, 2015). Unanswered questions to consider include, 'whether mobile app usage *results* in increased academic attainment', or 'are students with high measures of academic performance and cognitive engagement more engaged' with various aspects of curriculum which align with higher learner activity in the mobile app? Undergraduate nursing study who regularly engaged with 'weekly participation tasks' that included MCQ quizzes, were also more likely to engage with and attend face-to-face tutorials (Hughes et al., 2020). The app user interface, digital features and mobile-based accessibility may also provide a modern, technologically relevant, and comfortable learning environment that seamlessly allows for the development, application of and maintenance of self-resulted learning phases and subprocesses.

CONCLUSION

As many universities worldwide transition back to campus learning post-pandemic, the sector grapples with student disaffection or change of regarding face-to-face delivery which has been so pronounced that educator's resort to circulate photos of giving lectures and seminars to empty rooms, on prominent social media platforms. In discussing the psychology underpinning low on-campus attendance, Penn (2022) challenges that institutions cannot afford to assume that returning to pre-pandemic models of operation will be effective, however convenient that may be. Educationalists are at a watershed, where the sector must urgently seek empirical evidence to establish how to adapt to meet the needs of students and be able to articulate what added value on-campus delivery will provide (Maguire et al., 2020).

This chapter has provided an overview of the implementation strategy of a mobile-based gamification app within an intensive six-week subject, a standard 12-week semester and at a specific year level, within the Faculty of Health Sciences and Medicine. All three case-studies illustrate that data is a gift;

the analytical data output beneficial to the educator to monitor behavioral and affective engagement, and to the learner to encourage retrieval opportunities and improve storage strength for long-term knowledge retention and academic attainment. Twelve pearls of wisdom and how these facilitate SRL, skill development and self-motivation have been proposed to educators looking at the feasibility of integrating the mobile app into their subject(s) or program. These pearls may address post-COVID challenges and responding to the changing learning behaviors of generation Z students.

ACKNOWLEDGMENT

The authors would like to acknowledge the non-monetary support of the development team from Quitch, and Dr Grainne Oates, who assisted in the training of academic staff across the faculty in the user interface of the app. The authors would like to acknowledge Dr. Sacha Kennedy for her role developing Quitch content for the Medicine program Clinical Practice Domain. The authors would like to also acknowledge all academic staff who embraced the app and assisted in the delivery of subject content and questions across the programs featured in the case studies. Kylie Flack and Sian Daniel from Executive and Business Services are acknowledged for their assistance with license acquisition and management.

This research received no specific grant from any funding agency in the public, commercial, or not-for-profit sectors. The authors have no conflicts of interest to declare pertaining to this project. This research is approved by the institutional Ethics Committee (Project ID: IL00030).

REFERENCES

Anikina, O. V., & Yakimenko, E. V. (2015). Edutainment as a modern technology of education. *Procedia: Social and Behavioral Sciences*, *166*, 475–479. doi:10.1016/j.sbspro.2014.12.558

Aparicio, M., Oliveira, T., Bacao, F., & Painho, M. (2019). Gamification: A key determinant of massive open online course (MOOC) success. *Information & Management*, *56*(1), 39–54. doi:10.1016/j.im.2018.06.003

Australian Health Practitioner Regulation Agency (AHPRA). (2020). *National principles for clinical education during COVID-19.* https://www.ahpra.gov.au/News/COVID-19/National-principles-for-clinical-education-during-COVID-19.aspx

Beatson, N. J., Berg, D. A. G., & Smith, J. K. (2019). The influence of self-efficacy beliefs and prior learning on performance. *Accounting and Finance*, *60*(2), 1271–1294. doi:10.1111/acfi.12440

Bjork, R. A., & Bjork, E. L. (1992). A new theory of disuse and an old theory of stimulus fluctuation. In A. Healy, S. Kosslyn, & R. Shiffrin (Eds.), *From Learning Processes to Cognitive Processes: Essays in Honor of William K. Estes* (p. 35067). Erlbaum.

Black, P., & William, D. (1998). Assessment and classroom learning. *Assessment in Education: Principles, Policy & Practice*, *5*(1), 7–74. doi:10.1080/0969595980050102

Boekaerts, M., & Niemivirta, M. (2000). Self-regulated learning: finding a balance between learning goals and ego-protective goals. In M. Boekaerts, P. R. Pintrich, & M. Zeidner (Eds.), *Handbook of Self-Regulation* (pp. 417–451). Academic Press. doi:10.1016/B978-012109890-2/50042-1

Bond University. (2022). *Doctor of physiotherapy program.* https://bond.edu.au/program/doctor-physiotherapy#about

Bouchrika, I., Harrati, N., Wanick, V., & Wills, G. (2019). Exploring the impact of gamification on student engagement and involvement with e-learning systems. *Interactive Learning Environments*, 1–14. doi:10.1080/10494820.2019.1623267

Butler, A. C., & Roediger, H. L. I. I. I. (2008). Feedback enhances the positive effects and reduces the negative effects of multiple-choice testing. *Memory & Cognition, 36*(3), 604–616. doi:10.3758/MC.36.3.604 PMID:18491500

Chartered Society of Physiotherapy (CSP). (2020). *COVID-19 guidance for higher education institutions (updated October 2020).* Chartered Society of Physiotherapy. https://www.csp.org.uk/system/files/documents/2020-10/COVID_19%20Guidance%20Oct%202020_0.pdf

Chou, C. Y., & Zou, N. B. (2020). An analysis of internal and external feedback in self-regulated learning activities mediated by self-regulated learning tools and open learner models. *Int J Educ Technol High Educ, 17*(55), 1–17. doi:10.118641239-020-00233-y

Cleland, J., McKimm, J., Fuller, R., Taylor, D., Janczukowicz, J., & Gibbs, T. (2020). Adapting to the impact of COVID-19: Sharing stories, sharing practice. *Medical Teacher, 42*(7), 1–4. doi:10.1080/0142159X.2020.1757635 PMID:32401079

de Bruin, A. B. H., Dunlosky, J., & Cavalcanti, R. B. (2017, June). Monitoring and regulation of learning in medical education: The need for predictive cues. *Medical Education, 51*(6), 575–584. doi:10.1111/medu.13267 PMID:28332224

Deterding, S., Khaled, R., Nacke, L. E., & Dixon, D. (2011). *Gamification: Toward a Definition.* CHI 2011 Gamification Workshop Proceedings, Vancouver, Canada.

DiBenedetto, M. K., & Zimmerman, B. J. (2010). Differences in self-regulatory processes among students studying science: A microanalytic investigation. *The International Journal of Educational and Psychological Assessment, 5*, 2–24.

Dong, C., & Goh, P. S. (2015). Twelve tips for the effective use of videos in medical education. *Medical Teacher, 37*(2), 140–145. doi:10.3109/0142159X.2014.943709 PMID:25110154

Ebbinghaus, H. (1885). *Urmanuskript "Ueber das Gedächtniß".* Passavia Universitätsverlag.

Ellaway, R. H. A. (2016). Conceptual framework of game-informed principles for health professions education. *Advances in Simulation (London, England), 1*(28), 1–9. doi:10.118641077-016-0030-1 PMID:29449997

Ericsson, K. A., Krampe, R. T., & Tesch-Römer, C. (1993). The role of deliberate practice in the acquisition of expert performance. *Psychological Review, 100*(3), 363–406. doi:10.1037/0033-295X.100.3.363

Fields, R. D. (2005). Making Memories Stick. *Scientific American*, 58–63. PMID:15715394

García-Viola, A., Garrido-Molina, J. M., Márquez-Hernández, V. V., Granados-Gámez, G., Aguilera-Manrique, G., & Gutiérrez-Puertas, L. (2019). The influence of gamification on decision making in nursing students. *The Journal of Nursing Education*, *58*(12), 718–722. doi:10.3928/01484834-20191120-07 PMID:31794039

Gordon, M., Patricio, M., Horne, L., Muston, A., Alston, S. R., Pammi, M., Thammasitboon, S., Park, S., Pawlikowska, T., Rees, E. L., Doyle, A. J., & Daniel, M. (2020). Developments in medical education in response to the COVID-19 pandemic: A rapid BEME systematic review: BEME guide no. 63. *Medical Teacher*, *42*(11), 1202–1215. doi:10.1080/0142159X.2020.1807484 PMID:32847456

Gough, S., Orr, R., Stirling, A., Raikos, A., Schram, B., & Hing, W. (2021). Health Sciences and Medicine Education in Lockdown: Lessons Learned During the COVID-19 Global Pandemic. In D. Nestel, G. Reedy, L. McKenna, & S. Gough (Eds.), *Clinical Education for the Health Professions*. Springer. doi:10.1007/978-981-13-6106-7_141-1

Gue, S., Ray, J., & Ganti, L. (2022). 2022/08/30). Gamification of graduate medical education in an emergency medicine residency program. *International Journal of Emergency Medicine*, *15*(1), 41. doi:10.118612245-022-00445-1 PMID:36042403

Guo, Z., Xiao, L., Van Toorn, C., Lai, Y., & Seo, C. (2016). 2016/03/01/). Promoting online learners' continuance intention: An integrated flow framework. *Information & Management*, *53*(2), 279–295. doi:10.1016/j.im.2015.10.010

Hattie, J., & Timperley, H. (2007). The power of feedback. *Review of Educational Research*, *77*(1), 81–112. doi:10.3102/003465430298487

Huang, B., Hew, K. F., & Lo, C. K. (2019). Investigating the effects of gamification-enhanced flipped learning on undergraduate students' behavioral and cognitive engagement. *Interactive Learning Environments*, *27*(8), 1106–1126. doi:10.1080/10494820.2018.1495653

Kang, S. H. K., McDermott, K. B., & Roediger, H. L. III. (2007). Test format and corrective feedback modify the effect of testing on long–term retention. *The European Journal of Cognitive Psychology*, *19*(4-5), 528–558. doi:10.1080/09541440601056620

Karabenick, S. A., & Berger, J.-L. (2013). Help seeking as a self-regulated learning strategy. In H. Bembenutty, T. Cleary, & A. Kitsantas (Eds.), *Applications of self-regulated learning across diverse disciplines: A tribute to Barry J. Zimmerman* (pp. 237–261). IAP Press.

Karpicke, J. D., & Blunt, J. R. (2011). Retrieval practice produces more learning than elaborative studying with concept mapping. *Science*, *331*(6018), 772–775. doi:10.1126cience.1199327 PMID:21252317

Keegan, D. A., Chan, M., & Chan, T. (2020). Helping medical educators worldwide pivot their curricula online: PivotMedEd.com. *Medical Education*, *54*(8), 766–767. doi:10.1111/medu.14220 PMID:32392352

Kusurkar, R. A., Ten Cate, T. J., van Asperen, M., & Croiset, G. (2011). Motivation as an independent and a dependent variable in medical education: A review of the literature. *Medical Teacher*, *33*(5), e242–e262. doi:10.3109/0142159X.2011.558539 PMID:21517676

Lucieer, S. M., Jonker, L., Visscher, C., Rikers, R. M. J. P., & Themmen, A. P. N. (2016). Self-regulated learning and academic performance in medical education. *Medical Teacher, 38*(6), 585–593. doi:10.3109/0142159X.2015.1073240 PMID:26313552

MacDougall, C., Dangerfield, P., Katz, D., & Strain, W. (2020). The impact of COVID-19 on medical education and medical students. How and when can they return to placements? *MedEdPublish, 9*(1), 159. doi:10.15694/mep.2020.000159.1

Maguire, D., Dales, L., & Pauli, M. (2020). *Learning and teaching reimagined. A new dawn for higher education?* JISC. https://repository.jisc.ac.uk/id/eprint/8150

Mayer, R. E., & Moreno, R. (2003). Nine ways to reduce cognitive load in multimedia learning. *Educ Psychol, 38*(1), 43–52. doi:10.1207/S15326985EP3801_6

Miller, G. A. (1956). The magical number seven, plus or minus two: Some limits on our capacity for processing information. *Psychological Review, 63*(2), 81–97. doi:10.1037/h0043158 PMID:13310704

Mora, A., Riera, D., González, C., & Arnedo-Moreno, J. (2017). Gamification: A systematic review of design frameworks. *Journal of Computing in Higher Education, 29*(3), 516–548. doi:10.100712528-017-9150-4

Murre, J. M. J., & Dros, J. (2015). Replication and analysis of Ebbinghaus' forgetting curve. *PLoS One, 10*(3), e0120644. doi:10.1371/journal.pone.0120644 PMID:26148023

National Student Clearinghouse Research Centre. (2022). *Overview: Spring 2022 Enrollment Estimates.* https://nscresearchcenter.org/wp-content/uploads/CTEE_Report_Spring_2022.pdf

Penn, P. (2022) *Psychology explains why students aren't flocking back to campus.* https://www.timeshighereducation.com/blog/psychology-explains-why-students-arent-flocking-back-campus

Physiotherapy, W. (2020). *Worldphysiotherapy response to COVID-19 briefing paper 1: immediate impact on the higher education sector and response to delivering physiotherapist entry level education.* World Physiotherapy. https://world.physio/sites/default/files/2020-07/Education-Briefing-paper-1-HEI.pdf

Roediger, H. L. I. I. I. III, & Karpicke, J. D. (2006). The power of testing memory: Basic research and implications for educational practice. *Perspectives on Psychological Science, 1*(3), 181–210. doi:10.1111/j.1745-6916.2006.00012.x PMID:26151629

Roehl, A., Reddy, S. L., & Jett, G. (2013). The Flipped Classroom: An Opportunity to Engage Millennial Students through Active Learning Strategies. *Journal of Family and Consumer Sciences, 105*(2), 44–49. doi:10.14307/JFCS105.2.12

Rutledge, C., Walsh, C. M., Swinger, N., Auerbach, M., Castro, D., Dewan, M., Khattab, M., Rake, A., Harwayne-Gidansky, I., Raymond, T. T., Maa, T., & Chang, T. P. (2018). Gamification in Action: Theoretical and Practical Considerations for Medical Educators. *Academic Medicine, 93*(7), 1014–1020. doi:10.1097/ACM.0000000000002183 PMID:29465450

Sandars, J., & Cleary, T. J. (2011). Self-regulation theory: Applications to medical education: AMEE Guide No. 58. *Medical Teacher, 33*(11), 875–886. doi:10.3109/0142159X.2011.595434 PMID:22022899

Sharek, D., & Wiebe, E. (2011). Using Flow Theory to Design Video Games as Experimental Stimuli. *Proceedings of the Human Factors and Ergonomics Society Annual Meeting*, *55*(1), 1520–1524. doi:10.1177/1071181311551316

Shorey, S., Chan, V., Rajendran, P., & Ang, E. (2021). Learning styles, preferences and needs of generation Z healthcare students: Scoping review. *Nurse Education in Practice*, *57*, 103247. doi:10.1016/j.nepr.2021.103247 PMID:34768214

Spooner, M., Duane, C., Uygur, J., Smyth, E., Marron, B., Murphy, P. J., & Pawlikowska, T. (2022). Self-regulatory learning theory as a lens on how undergraduate and postgraduate learners respond to feedback: A BEME scoping review: BEME Guide No. 66. *Medical Teacher*, *44*(1), 3–18. doi:10.1080/0142159X.2021.1970732 PMID:34666584

Sweller, J. (1988). Cognitive load during problem solving: Effects on learning. *Cognitive Science*, *12*(2), 257–285. doi:10.120715516709cog1202_4

Sweller, J. (1999). *Instructional design in technical areas (Australian Education Review)*. Australian Council for Education.

Tavares, N. (2022). The use and impact of game-based learning on the learning experience and knowledge retention of nursing undergraduate students: A systematic literature review. *Nurse Education Today*, *1117*, 105484. doi:10.1016/j.nedt.2022.105484 PMID:35917707

Thalmann, M., Souza, A. S., & Oberauer, K. (2019). How does chunking help working memory? *Journal of Experimental Psychology. Learning, Memory, and Cognition*, *45*(1), 37–55. doi:10.1037/xlm0000578 PMID:29698045

Torda, A. J., Velan, G., & Perovic, V. (2020). The impact of the COVID-19 pandemic on medical education. *MJA, 23*(4), 1187–8.

Trowler, V. (2015). Negotiating Contestations and 'Chaotic Conceptions': Engaging 'Non-Traditional' Students in Higher education. *Higher Education Quarterly*, *69*(3), 295–310. doi:10.1111/hequ.12071

van der Meer, J., Scott, D., & Pratt, K. (2018). First semester academic performance: The importance of early indicators of non-engagement. *Student Success*, *9*(4), 1–12. doi:10.5204sj.v9i4.652

van Gaalen, A., Brouwer, J., Schönrock-Adema, J., Bouwkamp-Timmer, T., Jaarsma, A., & Georgiadis, J. R. (2021). Gamification of health professions education: A systematic review. *Advances in Health Sciences Education: Theory and Practice*, *26*(2), 683–711. doi:10.100710459-020-10000-3 PMID:33128662

Weiner, B. (1986). *An attributional theory of motivation and emotion*. Springer-Verlag. doi:10.1007/978-1-4612-4948-1

Xu, Y., Lau, Y., Cheng, L. J., & Lau, S. T. (2021). Learning experiences of game-based educational intervention in nursing students: A systematic mixed-studies review. *Nurse Education Today*, *107*, 105139. doi:10.1016/j.nedt.2021.105139 PMID:34563963

Zimmerman, B. J. (2000). Attaining self-regulation: a social cognitive perspective. In M. Boekaerts, P. R. Pintrich, & M. Zeidner (Eds.), *Handbook of Self-Regulation* (pp. 13–40). Academic Press. doi:10.1016/B978-012109890-2/50031-7

Zimmerman, B. J. (2008). Investigating Self-Regulation and Motivation: Historical Background, Methodological Developments and Future Prospects. *American Educational Research Journal Manth*, *45*(1), 166–183. doi:10.3102/0002831207312909

ADDITIONAL READING

Denden, M., Tlili, A., Chen, N.-S., Abed, M., Jemni, M., & Essalmi, F. (2022). The role of learners' characteristics in educational gamification systems: A systematic meta-review of the literature. *Interactive Learning Environments*, 1–23. Advance online publication. doi:10.1080/10494820.2022.2098777

Könings, K. D., Mordang, S., Smeenk, F., Stassen, L., & Ramani, S. (2021). Learner involvement in the co-creation of teaching and learning: AMEE Guide No. 138. *Medical Teacher*, *43*(8), 924–936. doi:10.1080/0142159X.2020.1838464 PMID:33153367

Maguire, D., Dales, L., & Pauli, M. (2020). *Learning and teaching reimagined. A new dawn for higher education?* JISC. https://repository.jisc.ac.uk/id/eprint/8150

Ozdemir, E. K., & Dinc, L. (2022). Game-based learning in undergraduate nursing education: A systematic review of mixed-method studies. *Nurse Education in Practice*, *62*, 103375. doi:10.1016/j.nepr.2022.103375 PMID:35749962

Pierce, C., Corral, J., Aagaard, E., Harnke, B., Irby, D. M., & Stickrath, C. (2020). A BEME realist synthesis review of the effectiveness of teaching strategies used in the clinical setting on the development of clinical skills among health professionals: BEME Guide No. 61. *Medical Teacher*, *42*(6), 604–615. doi:10.1080/0142159X.2019.1708294 PMID:31961206

Pylman, S., & Ward, A. (2020). 12 tips for effective questioning in medical education. *Medical Teacher*, *42*(12), 1330–1336. doi:10.1080/0142159X.2020.1749583 PMID:32297833

Seemiller, C., & Grace, M. (2017). Generation Z: Educating and Engaging the Next Generation of Students. *About Campus: Enriching the Student Learning Experience*, *22*(3), 21–26. doi:10.1002/abc.21293

Wlodarczyk, S., Muller-Juge, V., Hauer, K. E., Tong, M. S., Ransohoff, A., & Boscardin, C. (2021). Assessment to Optimize Learning Strategies: A Qualitative Study of Student and Faculty Perceptions. *Teaching and Learning in Medicine*, *33*(3), 245–257. doi:10.1080/10401334.2020.1852940 PMID:33439035

KEY TERMS AND DEFINITIONS

Active Learning: Learning activity where learner participates and interacts with the process.
Edutainment: The use of entertainment for educational purposes.

Game-Based Learning: Is a pedagogical approach that aims to motivate students/learners to regulate their own learning.

Gamification: Implementation of game design elements into traditionally non-game contexts.

Generation Y: Refers to learners born approximately between 1981 – 1995, or commonly referred to as Millennials.

Generation Z: Refers to learners born approximately between 1995 – 2015.

Retrieval Practice: This focuses bringing key information to the forefront of a learner's mind instead of cramming.

Spaced and Paced Learning: Refers to learning activities featuring highly condensed learning content being repeated several times interspersed with short breaks with distractor activities.

Student Engagement: The extent of attention, interest, and passion that learners show during the learning and teaching process.

Chapter 10
AI Chatbot to Assist Students Applying APA (7th Edition) Style in Their Academic Writing in a Polytechnic in Singapore

Linda Fang
Temasek Polytechnic, Singapore

Huiyu Zhang
Temasek Polytechnic, Singapore

Jang Yuan Chao
Temasek Polytechnic, Singapore

Ester Goh
Temasek Polytechnic, Singapore

ABSTRACT

This chapter focuses on a pilot project that utilized an artificial intelligence chatbot named the APABot to help 24 students from the Diploma in Psychology Studies apply APA (7th edition) style in their 400- to 500-word essay. This writing task was a requirement for Communication and Information Literacy, a fundamental subject for all first-year students in Temasek Polytechnic, Singapore. The four research questions were as follows: 1) How did the students respond to the APABot? 2) What strategies did the students use to learn from the APABot? 3) How did the APABot assist students to comply with the APA (7th edition) conventions in their writing? and 4) What were the characteristics of successful self-regulators using the APABot? Data from user logs, the number and types of errors, and a survey provided insights to the above questions.

DOI: 10.4018/978-1-6684-6500-4.ch010

INTRODUCTION

Temasek Polytechnic (TP) is an institute of higher learning (IHL) in Singapore that offers 43 diploma courses to post-secondary students. Those who have passed their GCE "O" levels or obtained a certificate from the Institute of Technical Education (ITE) can apply for a place in the polytechnic. Those with "N" levels are required to complete a one-year bridging programme before joining the polytechnic. Pre-Employment Training (PET) courses are offered to full-time students who would have recently completed their secondary or ITE education, while Continuing Education Training (CET) courses are for part-time students who are working adults.

Technology has been increasingly used for teaching and training since early 2000. Staff have been trained to use e-Learning in a blended mode for their face-to-face classes. Business Continuity Plans (BCP) stipulated by the Ministry of Education (MOE) after the SARS outbreak in 2003 required polytechnics to set aside an e-Learning week every year, where lessons are conducted fully online, off campus. These plans had to be fully deployed when the Corona Virus (CV) 19 pandemic required classes to be moved online from the April 2020 semester.

TP academic staff have been encouraged to explore the use of new technologies to enhance teaching, training and learning from the late 1990s. Since 2000, funding has been made available for staff to explore the use of specific technologies for teaching and learning, and conduct research on their effectiveness. For example, external funding could come from the National Research Foundation, the MOE Tertiary Research Fund, the Institute of Adult Learning Workforce Development Applied Research Fund, while internal funding would come from the TP Technology Enhanced Fund and Research Fund.

TP academic staff started exploring the use of educational chatbots from 2019. In June 2020, the School of Informatics and IT (IIT) received a SGD50k grant from the TP Research Fund to develop AI chatbots for two collaborator schools, namely the School of Applied Science (AS) and School of Humanities and Social Sciences (HSS). While existing administrative TP chatbots provided students with simple answers to their queries regarding their assignments, these AI chatbots would be used to help students learn content, offering functions that would surpass the capability of the TP administrative chatbots. AI chatbots have been used for subjects such as Airline Management, Microservices, Social Media Analytics, Programming Game Engines, Network Technology, Data Analytics and Visualisation, Electronic Devices and Circuits, and even for the optional independent learning of Microsoft Excel (2016 version).

Students in academic institutions are expected to conduct research, and then cite and reference their research correctly in their writing. In TP, two citation styles are used: APA is used by students in the Humanities and Social Science, Design, and Business diploma courses, and IEEE is used by students in the Engineering, IIT and Applied Science diploma courses. Despite stipulating the use of the respective citation style for assignments, students have difficulty applying it correctly. They either make gross errors when applying the format or avoid applying it altogether. To rectify this, all first-year students were required to use the assigned citation style in their assignments for their core subject "Communication and Information Literacy" (ICOMM).

Offered by the then Centre for Communication Skills in HSS, ICOMM was initially designed for face-to-face delivery. It was quickly adapted for online learning for the April 2020 semester because the circuit breaker period of the Covid 19 pandemic meant no one was allowed on campus. Teaching materials were placed on the LMS (Blackboard) while online synchronous classes were conducted via MS teams. This arrangement continued for the next four semesters.

In early 2021, an AI Chatbot was initiated by the HSS subject leader and co-developed with an IIT development team. Named the APABot, it was designed to help students learn the APA (7th edition) style and apply it in an assigned essay. Designed for independent, self-regulated learning (SRL), it was hoped that it would mitigate the challenges of fully online learning while greatly reducing the number of online queries for the tutor. It was trialled with first-year students from the Diploma in Psychology Studies, HSS during the April 2021 semester.

This chapter attempts to look at how the introduction of an AI chatbot could impact the application of APA (7th edition) style in a short essay. Using the APABot required specific learning skills, namely self-regulation. Hence, the research questions were as follows:

How did the students respond to the APABot?
What strategies did the students use to learn from the APABot?
How did the APABot assist students to comply with the APA (7th edition) conventions in their writing?
What were the characteristics of successful self-regulators using the APABot?

Teaching faculty, learning designers, curriculum developers and evaluators will benefit from this research as it seeks to explore how AI chatbots can support self-regulated online learners and the impact on their learning.

BACKGROUND

Chatbots

Chatbots are conversational interfaces that have been infused with artificial intelligence that allow them to interact with users in a human-like way (DeeAnn, 2012). They can converse in the form of text messages similar to how we have been interacting with our contacts in instant messaging applications (Smutny & Schreiberova, 2020). Some, including Alexa, Siri, and Google Assistant, can also process human speech in audio form and respond in the same manner (Garcia Brustenga et al., 2018). They aim to provide the experience for the user similar to interacting with a human agent, be it asking for information, making a reservation, or recommending services and products.

There are basically two types of chatbots: rule-based and artificial intelligence (AI). Rule-based ones use a series of pre-defined rules to drive the user conversation (Adamopoulou & Moussiades, 2020). These guide the user at each step with the 'if-then' logic by posing the user a question, and decide what would be the follow-up questions based on the user response and eventually lead to the correct resolution typically with call-to-action buttons (Srivastava, n.d.). These chatbots cannot understand or answer any questions outside of the defined rules. AI chatbots are more complex programmed chatbots based on machine learning (ML) algorithms such as the Natural Language Processing (NLP) techniques. The people behind the chatbots train them to understand a user's intents and context in their free text conversations and also identify the entities- subjects of the conversations, to correctly provide the response. The AI chatbot can become more intelligent with more ML training and be more accurate in providing resolution to the users whereas rule-based chatbots are not designed to learn and become smarter over time (Swivl, n.d.). Hence, for a computer program to be defined as a chatbot, it must possess the following elements: user interface (UI) and platform, user experience (UX), conversational AI and conversational flow.

Educational Chatbots for Teaching and Learning

Educational chatbots are one of the most recent tools for technology-mediated learning today. AI chatbots have been involved in the several functions in educational setting: teaching and learning, administration, assessment, advising, as well as research and development (Okonkwo & Ade-Ibijola, 2021). In this literature review, the focus would be on AI chatbots for teaching and learning, in particular, their uses, impact and methods of evaluation for language classes.

Educational chatbots have been applied in many domains. Hwang and Chang (2021) noticed that studies of educational chatbots between 1999 and 2020 were in these areas: languages, engineering or computers, Science, Health, Medical or Nursing, Social Science / Social Studies, Business and Management, Arts or Design, and Mathematics. Educational chatbots can be used for on-campus and off-campus learning. Hannan and Liu (2021) highlighted the key role of the AI Chatbot could play as teaching assistants, especially when there is a disconnect between students and their education. Indeed, many recent papers mention the use of AI chatbots for online education during the Corona Virus (CV)19 pandemic.

AI chatbots have been used to generate knowledge similar to a tutor in formal as well as non-formal educational settings. Learning is promoted through the interaction with conversational bots (Pérez et al., 2020). AI bots are able to teach as well as human teaching assistants. For instance, in 2016, *Jill Watson,* the virtual teaching assistant chatbot, proved it was able to effectively teach students in the Georgia Tech's Online Master of Science in Computer Science Program (College of Computing, 2020) because of its AI and adaptive learning functions. *Jill Watson* is currently pairing up with *VERA,* a virtual research assistant, to act as a virtual teaching assistant for science experiments (Georgia Tech, n.d.).

AI chatbots have been widely used for language learning. Since using a chatbot requires communicative exchange, chatbots are useful for enhancing dialogue-based learning (Garcia Brustenga et al., 2018). Fryer and Carpenter (2006) identified a myriad of possibilities for foreign language learning, from free speaking in the classroom, review, self-analysis, listening, with the opportunity for teachers to keep track of student conversations. The technology is so advanced that *CLIVE*, an AI chatbot that provides a beginner conversational practice in a foreign language, is able to converse in English and understand a response in another language e.g. Greek (Zakos & Capper, 2008).

AI Chatbots have been used in writing programs. Pengel et al. (2021) designed a chatbot that supported students in reading texts by offering writing assignments and providing automated feedback on these, as well as implementing a design for self-study activities. Schmitt and Buschek (2021) explored the use of *CharacterChat*, a chatbot that helps writers shape fictional character through conversation, which they describe as Progressive Manifestation. Lin and Chang (2020) designed a chatbot to provide instructions to help post-secondary writers refine their thesis statements based on peer feedback. However, there have not been chatbots used to help students learn and apply APA style in their writing.

Self-Regulated Learning (SRL)

Zimmerman (1990) defined self-regulated learners as students who are able to approach educational tasks with confidence, diligence and resourcefulness. They should also be aware of whether or not they know a fact or possess a skill. They proactively find ways to succeed in their tasks even when they encounter obstacles. According to Weinstein et al. (2011), strategic learning requires both skill and will. Self-regulation is described as "both the glue and the engine that help students manage their strategic learning on both a global and real time levels" (p. 47). The latter includes the use of metacognition for monitoring learning success, as well as the monitoring and regulating the use of effective and efficient learning strategies and focusing attention. Self-regulated learning is linked to performance. According to Zimmerman and Schunk (2011), "Self-regulated learning and performance refers to the process whereby learners personally activate and sustain cognitions, affects, and behaviours that are systematically oriented towards the attainment of personal goals" (p.1).

SRL for Chatbots

Intelligent tutoring system (ITS) is defined as "a computer learning environment that helps students master knowledge and skills by implementing intelligent algorithms that adapt to students at a fine-grained level and that instantiate complex principles of learning" (Graesser et al., 2018, p. 246). There are mainly two approaches to SRL in ITS: design an ITS which have built-in SRL mechanism, and add the SRL mechanism to an existing ITS. One such system using the former approach is the *MetaTutor*- a hypermedia-based ITS designed to scaffold college students' SRL while they learn about the human circulatory system (Azevedo et al., 2004; Greene & Azevedo, 2009; Moos, 2011). It contains four respective pedagogical agents to foster students' SRL skills in terms of providing adaptive prompts and feedback to students: the first, specialising in providing an information guide for student navigation; the second, assisting the setting up of learning goals and making plans; the third, monitoring student actions to guarantee that they will attain the goals; and the fourth, directing students to diverse learning support tools to adopt the learning strategies they want. Over their years of studies, the team behind *MetaTutor* found that students who are able to perform self regulation in learning with ITS are more likely to acquire a conceptual understanding of complex topics as compared to those who cannot. They also found that students need to be taught how to discover the microlevel SRL processes that are effective for them and to utilize them frequently to be engaged in the macrolevel of SRL processes of planning, strategy use, and monitoring (Greene et al., 2011). In terms of adding on pedagogical agents to improve students' SRL within an existing ITS system, the *Help Tutor* (Aleven et al., 2006) teaches students to be better help-seekers by offering advice through learning-by-doing, i.e. let students practice help-seeking skills and then giving appropriate feedback, and topping up with another Self-Assessment Tutor (Roll et al., 2011) to help students evaluate their learning progress. Eventhough the AI chabot by definition falls into the category of ITS, research or studies on SRL in AI chatbots are far and few between.

Evaluating Chatbots

Researchers focus on a range of aspects to understand the impact of AI bots for teaching and learning. Neo (2022) looked at the acceptance of an AI bot used in a multimedia course. Her students found the chatbot to be helpful in their learning process and it had improved their understanding of the course material. Lee et al. (2022) wanted to learn about the effectiveness of an AI bot for an after-class revision for a public health unit. They found that the AI bot helped improve the students' academic performance, self-efficacy, learning attitude, and motivation; overall, it helped students become more active in their learning process. Lin and Chang (2020), who studied an AI bot that guided students in a writing program, found a significant improvement in the writing of the experimental group compared to the control group. Most students enjoyed using the chatbot. They felt that it helped them identify new issues, improve how they gave effective feedback, become better reviewers and enhanced their skills in evaluating a thesis statement.

In their meta-analysis of 80 chatbots, Pérez et al. (2020) found that chatbots as teaching tools varied in their purposes, for instance, to promote learning or teach content. There could be different ways to obtaining data: through self-assessment and self-reflection, questionnaire, or the results of students. Chatbots as learning tools could be evaluated by comparing the self-perceived learning of control versus experimental groups. Hwang and Chang (2021) noted that chatbots tend to be evaluated most using quantitative methods, followed by mixed methods, and then qualitative methods. Most frequently used tools for analysis were ANCOVA/MANCOVA followed by interview, descriptive statistics, ANOVA/MANOVA, t-test, correlation, GLLAM), CFA and chi-square.

While the experimental design was frequently used, the mixed method approach provided more insights when comparing the experimental and control groups. Lee et al. (2022), who evaluated the use of AI bots for after-class revision for an infectious disease unit in a public health course, collected data using pre-and post-tests as well as pre-and post-questionnaires. Lin and Chang (2020), who evaluated the use of an AI bot to guide students in a writing program, collected quantitative data in the form of student grades for their outlines and ratings in their questionnaire, while qualitative data was collected from the open-ended questions of the questionnaire. Neo (2022), who studied the acceptance of an AI chatbot in their learning process, collected quantitative data using a 5-point Likert scale questionnaire, while qualitative data was collected from the open-ended questions in the survey. Essel et al. (2022), who compared the pre- and post-test scores of their control and experimental groups, also looked at user behaviour of the two groups i.e. number of students using the What's app chats during the course, number of chats per hour and the number of daily queries by students; they also conducted focus group interviews. Data collected by the AI bots have much potential in providing insights of the learners. However, studies that look at learner logs to reveal their learning patterns are lacking.

It is important to look at the intentionality of AI chatbots. If they are for exercise and practice, they lend themselves to behaviourist and cognitivist approaches; if they are teaching agents that act as learning companions, providing dialogue, collaboration and reflection, they lend themselves to socio-constructivist teaching and learning (Garcia Brustenga et al., 2018). Evaluations should also highlight how students are aligning to the pre-determined teaching approaches. As SRL becomes an important way to manage independent online learning, this should be the focus of research too.

As this was the first time the APAbot was used in TP, there was a need to understand the impact of the use of AI chatbots. Hence, this exploratory pilot study focused on how learners were using the APABot. With this area of research is still in its infant stage, the team had to decide on how to collect data that would uncover much of the unknowns. Adopting a grounded theory (Glaser & Strauss, 1967) approach might help make sense of the way users interact with AI chatbots to learn from them. This chapter aims to provide insights on how students are using an AI chatbot specially designed for self-regulated learning, and its impact on their application of APA (7th edition) style in academic writing.

METHODOLOGY

ADDIE Process

The duration of the funded project was from November 2020 to August 2021. The following sections describe how the ADDIE Instructional Design process was applied.

Analyse Stage (November - December 2020)

Home-based learning (HBL) was the "new normal" during the COVID-19 pandemic. Although it was convenient and safe to learn from home, HBL has its disadvantages over face-to-face learning for the following reasons:

a lack of immediate responses from tutors
a sense of isolation from fellow classmates and tutors
a lack of engagement and motivation because of remote learning.

In order to overcome the above challenges, as well as help students with the application of APA (7th edition) style, the SL proposed exploring the use of a personalized chatbot with AI technology to act like a teaching assistant. The customized AI learning pathways could help students get specific answers they needed. These were guided by the constant type errors made by previous cohorts. It had to be engaging enough to sustain interest while being available online 24/7. No administrative information was to be provided.

Design Stage (January- February 2021)

Decisions had to be made regarding the following:

Type of chatbot development platform to be adopted
Features required to improve the intelligence of the chatbot through analysis of user interaction and other relevant data
Dashboard to generate types of learning analytics
Conversational flow to start, sustain and end the interaction between student and chatbot
User interface of the chatbot
Features required to support self-regulated learning (SRL).

The learning experience design was based on Zimmerman's (1998) three cyclic phases of SRL, namely forethought, performance and self-reflection. The forethought phase refers to the processes to set the stage for learning, including goal-setting, strategic planning, self-efficacy beliefs, goal orientation and intrinsic interest. The performance stage refers to processes that occur during the learning that will affect concentration and performance, including self-instruction and self-monitoring. At the last phase of self-reflection, processes that occur after learning, including self-evaluation, attributions to success or failure, self-reactions that ultimately leads to being more adaptive. These self-reflection processes in turn influence subsequent forethought, and the cyclic process continues. The team interpreted the most important SRL processes as critical phases in the design of the APABot. These were goal-setting, action, monitoring, awareness and refinement respectively. See Figure 1 for the conceptual SRL model used to develop the APABot.

The three phases were then matched with the desired SRL behaviors to the features of the chatbot. See Table 1 for more details.

Figure 1. Conceptual Learning Model

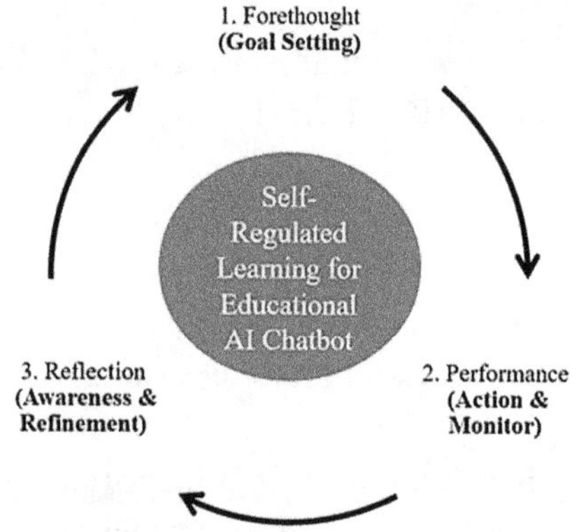

Table 1. Features to support SRL

Stage	Desired SRL behaviours	AI Chatbot features
Forethought (Goal Setting)	Students to set SMART goals: Specific: Use chat to improve application of APA (7th edition) style in an essay Measurable: Tie outcome to reducing number of errors Achievable: Learn from bite-sized lessons Relevant: Look at curated learning menu Time-bound: Complete within allocated time.	Provide curated menu in different APA categories: Reference List, In-text Citations, Elements of an APA Paper and Writing style and Grammar. Provide enlarged chatbot window as there can be quite a long list of items to guide students. Make available 24/7
Performance (Action and Monitoring)	Students to explore how to use the curated menu or free text utterances to obtain guidance on how to use the APA (7th edition) style. Students to monitor what aspects they were lacking in terms of APA (7th edition) style in their submission. Students to get personalised recommendation menu based on errors made: Students to learn from specific items listed in the menu Students to use free text to ask the chatbot specific questions.	Provide curated menu in different APA categories: Reference List, In-text Citations, Elements of an APA Paper and Writing style and Grammar. Show breakdown of errors made and a recommended menu to focus and work on (Areas for Improvement). Keep responses short and clear Provide responses in the form of clickable links to navigate the students to the APA website for more details. Provide related intents e.g. 'You may also like ....' for the users to continue exploring related citation elements.
Reflection (Awareness and Refinement)	Students to be aware of remaining learning gaps to bridge and know when task is adequately performed.	Provide the original curated learning menu and the personalized recommended menu based the performance of the last task.

For this project, the activity stops at Reflection (Awareness and Refinement). When the learner undertakes the next task using another AI chatbot, (s)he returns to the Forethought (Goal-setting Stage) hopefully with more experience and strategies to navigate the next two sections better.

The choice of the chatbot development platform was highly influenced by functionalities it could provide. Examples were webhook services to use the data extracted to generate dynamic responses, or trigger actions; conversation history to evaluate and improve the performance of the chatbot for cases such as unmatched intents. For an AI chatbot to become more intelligent with more ML training, it had to be designed with an "up vote" or "down vote" chatbot response. Data would be made available to the tutor/subject leader to adopt an iterative design approach to make continuous improvements to the training dataset for the chatbot.

For the dashboard to generate learning analytics, built-in graphs had to be considered. These were time series charts to show seasonality of the usage, cards showing metrics such as average time spent per visit and total unique users, bar charts displaying most frequently asked topics, with drill down functions available at the class level. These learning analytics were selected to provide behavioural insights to students' motivation or self-regulation level and allow tutors to, for example, nudge the students as part of the interventions to get a task completed on time.

Develop Stage (February- April 2021)

As this was a funded project, it was possible to hire a technical specialist to develop the chatbot. She was adept in cloud platforms, had sound knowledge and rich experience in AI algorithms, computer programming languages such as HTML, CSS, JavaScript, MySQL, and Python, and data visualisation/ dashboarding with commercial tools such as Tableau and Power BI. The SL curated the intents and responses that the chatbot should be trained for in a comma separated value (csv) file. This file was used to implement the menu that the chatbot would present to the students. Interns supported the work of both the technical specialist and the tutor who was also the SL.

Implement Stage (May - June 2021)

The technical specialist was also involved in this stage. The chatbot was implemented within the Google Cloud Platform (GCP) using Dialogflow and Firebase to enable the features to support students in SRL. The APABot was deployed in the form of a web application, whereby the instructor embedded the URL into the LMS (Blackboard) and was therefore available 24/7. Alpha and Beta tests were conducted in May 2021 to ensure that the APABot was functioning as planned. The final version was released to students on 25 June 2021. Instructions were provided via email, as well as on the webpage where the APABot was hosted, with the aim to assist students to access it. Students were hence introduced to the APABot and could learn how best to use its features for their learning. See Appendix 1 for details on how the APABot could be accessed.

Evaluate Stage (June - Aug 2021)

Data collected between June and July 2021 were analyzed in August 2021. Most of the time was spent reviewing the data derived from the APABot.

Figure 2.TP LibGuide APA citation webpage

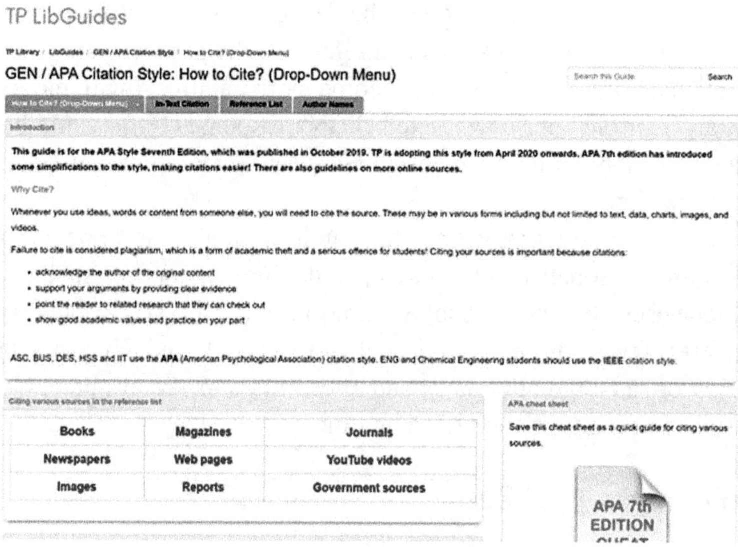

The Subject

ICOMM is a two-credit, 30-hour module offered by HSS to all first-year full-time students in Temasek Polytechnic. The aim was to develop competent, digital and information literate, communicative and collaborative students (School of Humanities and Social Science, 2018). This fundamental subject was designed with the following objectives:

To equip students with the skills to effectively search for relevant information from a variety of sources e.g., print, the Internet, online databases

To teach students to evaluate information, cite sources and communicate information coherently and appropriately in written and oral form.

Originally designed for face-to-face teaching, it had to be adapted for fully online learning. The existing materials on the LMS (Blackboard) continued to be used, but synchronous online classes were conducted using MS teams for the April 2020 semester. It remained the same for the April 2021 semester.

The Writing Task

As a non-examination subject, assessments were based on course work. To develop their skills in citation of sources, students had to write a 400-to-500-word essay demonstrating the correct use of APA (7th Edition) style. Students were first assigned a broad topic. They then worked with their tutor to find a focus for their essay. Following that, they had to conduct relevant research on their own. That researched information had to be clearly evident in their essay and indicated through in-text citations. They were required to have a minimum of three references from at least two different types of sources in the reference list. Four hours were allocated to tutor facilitation, and two hours for independent research work,

Table 2. Marking criteria

Elements of APA paper	In-text citation	Reference list
Cover Page Abstract Body Page and Headers Format for Reference List General Format	Author Basics Format In-Text Citation Type	Author Date Title Source Abbreviation Format Punctuation Reference Type Missing Element

which included learning how to use the APA (7th edition) style from the TP library webpage. Figure 2 provides examples of information on citation on the TP Library webpage (Temasek Polytechnic, 2022).

Students first submitted a draft essay whereby they applied the APA (7th edition) style. The tutor then marked the draft based on the criteria she designed. See Table 2 for the marking criteria.

Each student received feedback from the tutor via the LMS in terms of the number and types of errors made in the three above sections: Elements of APA paper, in-text citation and reference list. They then had to revise their essay and submit their final version. For the April 2021 Semester, instead of asking students to refer to the online library resources again to revise their writing, the APABot was introduced on 25 June 2021. It provided each student with personalised feedback on the number and types of errors they made under elements of the paper, in-text citations and references, and a recommended menu. See Appendix 1 for more details. Students then referred to it to correct errors for their final version. Refer to Table 3 for a summary of the sequence of events.

Table 3. Sequence of events

Wk (s)	Sequence	Date
1	Students were introduced to their subject and library resources.	Week starting 19 April 2021
2 to 3	Students were introduced to their writing task, assigned broad themes, and discussed online in groups with their tutor to finalise their individual topics.	Weeks starting 26 April and 3 May 2021
3 to 5	Students conducted online research and referred to APA (7th edition) guidelines on the library webpage.	Weeks starting 3, 10 and 17 May 2021
6	Students submitted their draft essay.	Submission deadline 28 May 2021
10	Students received individual feedback on their drafts via the LMS. Students revised their essay writing using the APABot.	Feedback received 25 June 2021
12	Students submitted their final essay.	Submission deadline 7 Jul 2021
13	Final draft marked, students receive feedback regarding their numbers and types of errors via the LMS.	Feedback received on 16 July 2021

While this study aimed to find out the impact of the APABot in their revisions using APA (7th edition) style, it also allowed the team to investigate how the students were reacting to it and using it. The research questions were as follows:

How did the students respond to the APABot?
What strategies did the students use to learn from the APABot?
How did the APABot assist students to comply with the APA (7th edition) conventions in their writing?
What were the characteristics of successful self-regulators using the APABot?

Research Context

The study involved 24 first-year, first semester students from the Diploma in Psychological Studies. As they were new to polytechnic education, they were unfamiliar with academic writing and the APA (7th edition) style. There were 23 females and one male, all Singaporeans between 16 to 17 years of age. Data was collected in the following ways:

Grading: The difference between the errors in initial draft and final essay would be one way to show its effectiveness of the APABot.

Survey: A survey, conducted after students used the APABot, captured their learning experience and reaction to the APABot. See Appendix 2 for the online survey questions and response options.

Analytics: The data collected by the APABot provided insights on its use: frequency, duration, types of inquiry, and types of responses; in short, how students were monitoring and regulating their learning. This is because the APABot, implemented within the Google Cloud Platform (GCP) using Dialogflow and Firebase, enabled the log features to reveal self-regulated learning.

See Table 4 for more details.

Table 4. Data collection

Sources of data	Critical dates	Types of data	Purpose
Draft Essay	23 June 2021	Tutor provided feedback on marked drafts by number and types of errors	To compare the quality of draft and final essays in terms of number and types of errors
Final Essay	16 Jul 2021	Tutor provided feedback on marked drafts by number and types of errors and overall marks	
Survey	8 - 13 Jul 2021	Student feedback on the use of the APABot	To capture user experience: accessibility, system, learning and user experience
Analytics from APABot	June - Jul 2021	Duration and frequency of use; topics accessed, the way they were accessed	To examine the approach to using APABot and intents in using APABot

Triangulating these sets of data would provide insights into the characteristics of successful self-regulated learners.

FINDINGS

Reaction

This section reflects how the students reacted to the APABot. From the survey conducted between 8 and 13 July 2021, participants were generally positive about the chatbot.

Accessibility: Participants accessed the APABot using the following devices: Laptop, 21 (87.5%), Desktop, one (4.2%), Tablet, one (4.2%), and Mobile phone, one (4.2%).

Ease of Use: Participants generally found it easy to use the APABot, as 17 participants (70.8%) strongly agreed or agreed that they only needed a few clicks to get their doubts clarified as opposed to four (16.7%) who were neutral and three (12.5%) who disagreed.

System Intelligence: In fact, nine participants (37.5%) strongly agreed or agreed that the APABot understood their questions as opposed to 11 (45.8%) who were neutral or four (16.7%) who disagreed or strongly disagreed. The APABot was able to answer most or all of the queries of 21 participants (87.5%) who strongly agreed or agreed versus three (12.5%) who were neutral. In addition, 21 participants (87.5%) strongly agreed or agreed that they found the responses clear and easy to follow as opposed to three (12.5%) who were neutral. APABot was perceived to have recommended useful resources automatically even though users did not particularly search for them for 21 participants (87.5%) who strongly agreed or agreed versus two (8.3%) who were neutral and one (4.2%) who disagreed.

Learning: The majority of the participants felt that the APABot was useful for several reasons. In fact, seven (29.2%) used the upvote button to indicate that the recommendations displayed by Spambot were useful. The following examples show the format of Topic, specific recommended response and number of up-votes:

APA Format
Body of paper (one participant or 4.2%)
Pages (two participants or 8.3%)
Plagiarism (one participant or 4.2%)
Reference List - Basics (3 participants or 12.5%)

There were 16 participants (66.7%) who felt that they could plan their learning with the help of the APABot as opposed to eight (33.3%) who were neutral. In addition, 19 participants (79.2%) strongly agreed or agreed that they used the APABot to find out more before approaching tutor for further clarifications versus four (16.7%) who were neutral and one (4.2%) who disagreed. While 16 participants (66.7%) strongly agreed or agreed about feeling confident of their ability in APA (7th edition) style after using the APABot, eight (33.3%) were neutral in their response. However, only four (16.7%) felt that the APABot was necessary to help enhance their APA skills.

Motivation: The APABot was seen as being able to provide the motivation to learn more about the subject by 12 participants (50%) who strongly agreed or agreed versus 10 (41.7%) who were neutral and two (8.3%) who disagreed. In fact, 16 participants (66.7%) strongly agreed or agreed that they felt encouraged and motivated to search for solutions and answers via the APABot versus seven (29.2%) who remained neutral and one (4.2%) who disagreed.

Figure 3. APABot usage (June – Jul 2022)

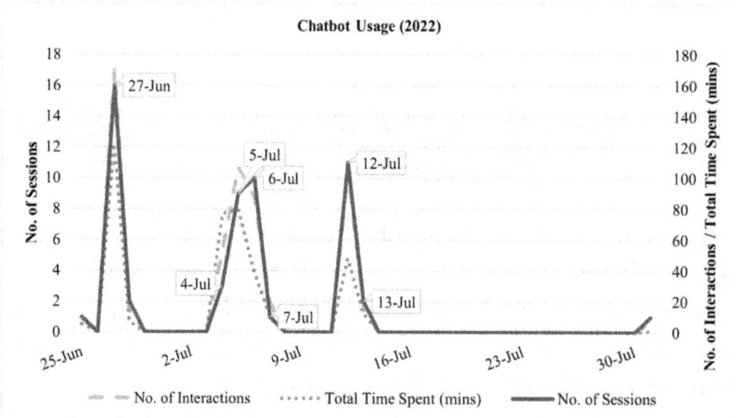

Overall experience: The ratings ranged from 8 (33.3%) for 'Excellent' to 16 (66.7%) for 'Fair'. In fact, 14 participants (58.3%) felt that the APABot was easy to use, and that it provided clear answers and information related to their questions or doubts. While only one participant (4.2%) appreciated the recommended menu, five (20.8%) said it helped them understand the APA formatting.

Added features

Six participants (25%) wanted the menu and responses to be shorter.

Two participants (8.3%) wanted the APABot to provide more examples for the covered formats.

Six participants (25%) wanted more topics in APA Style Formatting.

One participant (4.2%) wanted a chatbot to help edit the entire essay.

One participant (4.2%) wanted the development team to ensure all clickable links to external websites were working.

Continued use: In fact, 20 participants (83.3%) were ready to recommend the APABot to their friends (having rated 6 to 10 out of 11 points). They were open to using a chatbot for other subjects for the following reasons:

10 (41.7%) felt that a chatbot would be helpful in providing quick and clear information, serving as a one single resource to get most or all of the required information.

Four (16.7%) liked its 24/7 availability and hence the ability to seek some clarifications from it before approaching a tutor.

One (4.2%) would continue to use such a chatbot as it points her to what she had done wrong so that she can make improvements.

Three participants (12.5%) would not like to continue to use a chatbot for learning as they preferred to ask help directly from their tutor. The reasons they quoted that they were not tech savvy enough to use the chatbot.

Their reactions could also be reflected in terms of their usage patterns. Data in terms of interactions also reveal the participants' interest in using the APABot. Figure 3 shows the number of interactions between 25 June 2021 and 31 July 2021. Usage peaked when it was first released on 25 June 2021 and when it was closer to the submission deadline of the final essay which was 7 July 2021. It was interesting that the usage continued, albeit sporadically beyond the deadline, implying that the APABot might have been referred to for other pieces of work.

Strategies

This section explored the strategies participants used when learning from the APABot. The data showed three distinct groups determined by the number of sessions, the number of interactions and time spent. The team described them as Explorers, Focused Learners and Window Shoppers.

Explorers: There were 11 participants (45.8%) in this group. They used the APABot multiple times and each time, interacted with more than ten intents. They looked at different sections and then decided what they wanted to view. They had an open agenda.

Focused Learners: There were nine participants (37.5%) in this group. They used the APABot specifically and zoomed into specific intents to view specific content.

Window Shoppers: There were four participants (16.7%) in this group. They only logged in to the system once to view the curated learning menu. They were looking at it at the surface level and did not venture further into the content.

See Table 5 for details of usage in terms of sessions, interactions and time spent.

Table 5. Usage patterns

Types of Users	No. of Users	No. of Sessions		No. of Interactions		Time Spent (mins)	
		Total	Average	Total	Average	Total	Average
Explorer	11	36	3.3	396	36	336	30.5
Focused Learner	9	9	1	136	15.1	74	8.2
Window Shopper	4	5*	1.3	24	6	7	1.8
Total	24	50	2.1	556	23.2	417	17.4

One Winder Shopper clicked the menu twice but only looked at it once.

All participants viewed the recommended menu to see what the personalized areas were highlighted, based on their performance. However, usage varied. Only the Explorers and Focused Learners drilled down further into specific intents branched from either the full menu or the recommended one. It was observed that five Explorers (20.8%) and one Focused Learner (4.2%) used the APABot learning function, which was to ask a free text question rather than just interacting with the curated full menu which was the teaching function. Window shoppers only used the APABot to view one response which showed their number of errors made in the different sections.

It is interesting to note how the Explorers used the APABot. The first time was to view the personalized recommended menu to find out what were the sections they were making mistakes in. The period of usage was typically within five minutes. For subsequent use of the APABot, they spent longer time to revisit the recommended menu, drilling down one by one, specifically, the recommended intents that provided the APA style formatting guide in the areas they were weaker in. In each session, they could spend around five minutes on each of these intents, which was another indication that they were working on their writing task in these specific areas while using the APABot. Some of these Explorers needed more sessions with the APABot on the same specific intents as they were aware that the writing task was not adequately done performed and continued to bridge the gaps. But this was not the case of the other two types of users. The examples of logs of one session of three users provide evidence of how the different types of users interacted with the APABot.

```
Key:  A: Login or Welcome Intent
   1: Menu item
   D: Specific intent
Log of an Explorer (Participant 9):
A - Default Welcome Intent
1 - Menu - Result Log In
A - welcome.name
1 - Menu - RECOMMENDED - ITC
1 - Menu - RECOMMENDED - ITC - Author
D1 - In-Text Citation Basics- Authors 1
D1 - In-Text Citation Basics- Authors 2
D1 - In-Text Citation Basics- Authors 3
D1 - In-Text Citation Basics- Authors 6
D1 - In-Text Citation Basics- Authors 4
D1 - In-Text Citation Basics- Authors 5
1 - Menu - RECOMMENDED
1 - Menu - RECOMMENDED - RL
1 - Menu - RECOMMENDED - RL - Format
D5 - Information Sources 8
D5 - Information Sources 9
D5 - Reference List Basics 7
1 - Menu - RECOMMENDED - RL
1 - Menu - RECOMMENDED - RL - Reference Type
D5 - Information Sources 2
Log of a Focused Learner (Participant 8):
A - Default Welcome Intent
0 - Menu - LEARN - ITC
0 - Menu - LEARN - ITC - Format
D1 - In-Text Citation Basics- Format 3
0 - Menu - LEARN - ITC - Type
D1 - In-Text Citation Basics - Info Sources 1
D1 - In-Text Citation Basics- Info Sources 2
0 - Menu - LEARN - ITC - Basics
D1 - Plagiarism2
A - User Feedback (Helpful)
A - Default Welcome Intent
1 - Menu - Result Log In
```

```
A - welcome.name
1 - Menu - RECOMMENDED - ITC
1 - Menu - RECOMMENDED - RL
1 - Menu - RECOMMENDED - RL - Author
1 - Menu - RECOMMENDED
Log of a Window Shopper (Participant 20):
A - Default Welcome Intent
1 - Menu - Result Log In
A - welcome.name
1 - Menu - RECOMMENDED - RL
A - Default Welcome Intent
1 - Menu - Result Log In
A - welcome.name
1 - Menu - RECOMMENDED - RL
1 - Menu - RECOMMENDED - ELE
1 - Menu - RECOMMENDED - ITC
```

Improvement

This section examines the extent the APABot was able to assist participants to improve their writing to comply with the APA (7th edition) style. By comparing the errors identified in the draft and final essays the following categories was defined as follows:

Improved: Those who successfully reduced their errors
No Change: Those who showed no reduction in their errors
Worse: Those who ended with more errors.

Overall, 22 participants (91.7%) were able to correct and reduce between 6 to 34 errors, while one participant (4.2%) had more errors in the final draft. The remaining one participant (4.2%), who supposedly had no change in the number of errors, had actually corrected an error under Elements of APA but made an error under in-text citation. Table 6 shows the number of errors for their draft essay (D), their final essay (F), and the difference between them (F minus D) would be considered as improvement (I).

While Participants 1 to 21 were able to reduce their errors, it was worrying that there were errors made in the revisions of participants 22 to 24. Figure 4 shows the distribution of the different types of users by total number of errors reduced.

By categorizing error reduction by three groups, namely higher range (20 and above errors reduced), middle range (10 to 19 errors reduced), and lower range (9 and fewer errors reduced), the following clusters emerged. See Table 7 for more details.

Successful Self-regulators

Overall, the Explorers seemed to have managed to reduce the most errors, followed by the Focused Learners and Window Shoppers (see Tables 8 and 9). While one Window Shopper (Participant 24, the only male) certainly did not benefit at all from using the APABot, having made more errors, the outlier Window Shopper (Participant 1) seemed to be able to reduce errors in all three areas despite logging in only once. That is the reason for the higher-than-expected number of errors reduced. Without her, the average number of errors reduced would be 5.7 instead of 12.8 in Table 8.

Table 6. Errors corrected by specific areas

Partici-pant	Elements of APA Paper			In-Text Citations			Reference List			Total Errors Reduced	User Type
	D	F	I	D	F	I	D	F	I		
1	12	6	6	12	2	10	21	3	18	34	Window Shopper
2	7	2	5	12	1	11	15	2	13	29	Explorer
3	10	5	5	12	4	8	16	2	14	27	Explorer
4	10	3	7	9	0	9	10	3	7	23	Explorer
5	12	2	10	10	4	6	10	4	6	22	Focused Learner
6	8	3	5	8	3	5	16	5	11	21	Focused Learner
7	8	0	8	5	1	4	6	1	5	17	Window Shopper
8	4	0	4	8	3	5	13	5	8	17	Focused Learner
9	6	1	5	6	0	6	7	2	5	16	Explorer
10	4	1	3	6	1	5	8	1	7	15	Explorer
11	9	1	8	8	2	6	0	0	0	14	Explorer
12	12	5	7	8	2	6	3	2	1	14	Focused Learner
13	6	0	6	4	1	3	3	0	3	12	Focused Learner
14	8	8	0	8	7	1	18	7	11	12	Focused Learner
15	8	3	5	5	2	3	9	6	3	11	Explorer
16	4	0	4	3	1	2	4	1	3	9	Focused Learner
17	2	0	2	5	0	5	4	2	2	9	Explorer
18	3	1	2	3	0	3	5	1	4	9	Focused Learner
19	2	1	1	3	0	3	4	0	4	8	Explorer
20	2	2	0	4	1	3	4	1	3	6	Window Shopper
21	4	0	4	2	1	1	1	0	1	6	Explorer
22	8	5	3	4	0	4	0	1	-1	6	Explorer
23	2	1	1	1	2	-1	2	2	0	0	Focused Learner
24	6	8	-2	6	8	-2	6	8	-2	-6	Window Shopper

Figure 4. Number of errors reduced by types of users

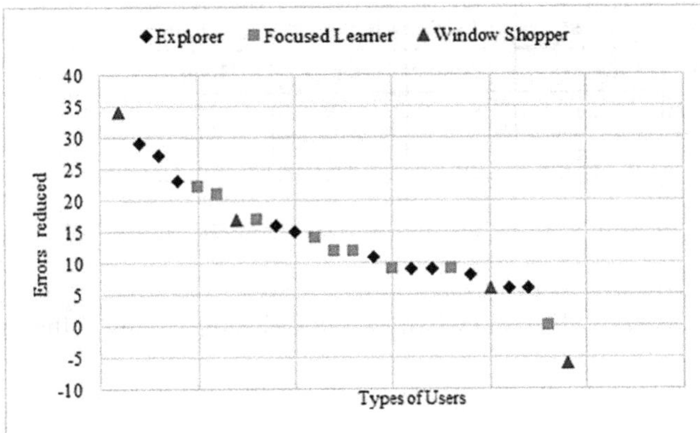

Table 7. Clusters of errors reduced

Users	Higher range	Middle range	Lower range
Explorer	Three participants (12.5%) between 23 and 29 errors reduced	Four participants (16.7%) between 11 and 16 errors reduced	Four participants (16.7%) between 6 and 9 errors reduced
Focused Learner	Two participants (8.3 %) between 21 and 22 errors reduced	Four participants (16.7%) between 12 and 17 errors reduced	Three participants (12.5%) between 0 and 9 errors reduced
Window Shopper	One participant (4.2%) with 34 errors reduced	One participant (4.2%) with 17 errors reduced	Two participants (8.3 %) between 6 and - 6 errors reduced

Table 8. Overall errors

Type of Usage Pattern	Participants		Number of Reduced Errors			No change in number of errors	Number of Increased Errors
	No.	%	Range	Total	Average		
Explorer	11	45.8%	6 to 29	164	14.9	0	0
Focused Learner	9	37.5%	0 to 22	116	12.9	1	0
Window Shopper	4	16.7%	-6 to 34	51	12.8	0	6
Total	24	100%	-	331	0	1	6

DISCUSSION

Reaction

The APABot was sufficiently interesting for the participants to use it at least once, especially to view the number of errors that they made. However, the Explorers used it most in terms of the number of

Table 9. Average errors reduced by sections

Usage	Elements of APA Style		In- Text Citations		Reference List		Overall	
	Total	Average	Total	Average	Total	Average	Total	Average
Explorer	48	4.4	61	5.5	55	5	164	14.9
Focused Learner	39	4.3	30	3.3	47	5.2	116	12.9
Window Shopper	12	3	15	3.8	24	6	51	12.8

log-ins and time spent. Similar to Lin and Chang's study (2020), many of the participants perceived it to be useful and enjoyable.

Strategies

The analytics from the APABot provided insights into how participants used it. The Explorers and Focused Learners were seen to be regulating their learning by the way they sent out their intents and how they viewed the menu. The majority of participants showed interest in improving their work by using the menu function more than asking questions to delve deeper. It was observed that the Window Shoppers missed out on the SRL experience and were not able to perform the tasks adequately (apart from Participant 1). Spending less than 2 mins in their only log-in could stem from the lack of interest in setting goals for reducing the errors in the use of APA (7th edition) style. This could also be because of the lack of skill and will (Weinstein et al., 2011).

The Explorers clearly displayed SRL traits (Zimmerman, 1998) when they used the APABot repeatedly:

Forethought: Viewing personalized recommended menu was in sync with the first phase of setting SMART goals. They needed to know and plan how to use the APABot to improve in the final essay. The subsequent time(s) they visited the APABot again, it would be according to the 'T' of their SMART goal- when to use and when to complete.

Performance: Subsequent visits to the recommended menu were longer for their intents. This was the phase of performance. When they proceeded to click on the prompts provided by the APABot to continue exploring related citation elements, they were monitoring what other aspects they could be lacking in. They needed more sessions to improve their work.

Reflection: Explorers who needed more sessions with the APABot on the same specific intents were probably aware that their writing task was not adequately done and continued to bridge the gaps. This is an indication of being aware and apply refinement to their work.

However, Explorer (Participant 22), Focused Learner (Participant 23) and Window Shopper (Participant 24) actually made more mistakes when editing their work, showing weakness in their performance and reflection.

Impact

The participants were able to use the APABot to help themselves apply APA (7th edition) style for their essay writing. Improvements could be attributed to the use of the APABot as it helped reduce and address errors for all except for three participants. Not only did the participants appreciate the ease of its use, it helped identify their gaps and served as a single reliable resource to learn the APA (7th edition) style. One limitation of the study was the lack of comparison with the previous cohorts. With the vastly different teaching environment e.g., face-to-face (pre-Covid) versus fully online (during CV19) and with no AI bot in 2020 versus CV19 with APABot in 2021, no provision was made to systematically compare cohorts. Another limitation was the absence of an interview after the participants had used the APABot. That would have provided the opportunity to find out why the Window Shopper (Participant 1) was able to make the corrections without much use of the APA Bot.

Successful self-regulated learners

Although the APABot was designed for SRL, not every user applied SRL skills when using it. This was evident with the Window Shoppers. While the Explorers and Focused Learners displayed the tendency to probe further by interacting with the APABot, a few who supposedly displayed SRL behaviors were not yet fully skilled. This implies that there is a need to train users in SRL to fully benefit from the APABot. Perhaps, the tutor needed to allocate time to demonstrate its use, and check on the usage dashboard during the semester to help those who are struggling with its use, by suggesting SRL strategies.

FUTURE RESEARCH DIRECTIONS

For a repeat run of the subject using the APABot, it would be beneficial to include interviews to uncover more insights linked to the survey data, especially the motivation to use the chatbot, user experience and strategies for the different types of users. A survey at the beginning of the semester on the familiarity with chatbots, learner's attitudes towards using chatbots, and their SRL skills could provide more relevant insights to their pre-usage patterns. Students lacking in the necessary SRL skills could be briefed on strategies before they use the APABot and observed if they applied the SRL strategies in the current and subsequent semesters. Coaching could be enhanced with weekly learning analytics reports from the dashboard. There could be a study on the effectiveness of supporting learners this way. Studies could also focus on students from other diplomas to see if the APABot appeals to them as well as special needs students.

CONCLUSION

The pioneering work in the research on the use of AI chatbots in education generated an SRL design model for AI chatbots for learning at the polytechnic level. This study allowed researchers, designers and developers, implementers to gain insights into the use of the APABot to help learners grasp what the APA (7th edition) style entails and apply it correctly in a writing task. It also identified different kinds of strategies used, and the extent they reflected SRL.

ACKNOWLEDGMENT

This project was supported by the 2020 Temasek Polytechnic Research Fund [Q1B]

REFERENCES

Adamopoulou, E., & Moussiades, L. (2020). Chatbots: History, technology, and applications. *Machine Learning with Applications*, *2*(100006), 1–18. doi:10.1016/j.mlwa.2020.100006

Aleven, V., Mclaren, B., Roll, I., & Koedinger, K. (2006). Toward meta-cognitive tutoring: A model of help seeking with a cognitive tutor. *International Journal of Artificial Intelligence in Education*, *16*(2), 101–128.

Allison, D. A. (2012). Chatbots in the Library: Is it Time? *Library Hi Tech*, *30*(1), 95–107. doi:10.1108/07378831211213238

College of Computing. (2020, Jan 24). *Jill Watson, a pioneer in AI education, turns 4*. Retrieved Dec 2022, from Georgia Tech. https://www.ic.gatech.edu/news/631545/jill-watson-ai-pioneer-education-turns-4

Essel, H. B., Vlachopoulos, D., Tachie-Menson, A., Johnson, E. E., & Baah, P. K. (2022). The impact of a virtual teaching assistant (chatbot) on students' learning in Ghanaian higher education. *International Journal of Educational Technology in Higher Education*, *19*(1), 1–19. doi:10.118641239-022-00362-6 PMID:35013716

Fryer, L. K., & Carpenter, R. (2006). Bots as Language Learning Tools. *Language Learning & Technology*, *10*, 8–14.

Garcia Brustenga, G., Fuertes-Alpiste, M., & Molas-Castells, N. (2018). *Briefing paper: chatbots in education*. eLearn Center. Universitat Obertade Catalunya. doi:10.7238/elc.chatbots.2018

Georgia Tech. (n.d.). *Georgia Tech is developing artificially intelligent agents that are unleashing the potential of lifetime learning*. Retrieved from Georgia Tech. https://emprize.gatech.edu/

Glaser, B., & Strauss, A. (1967). *The discovery of grounded theory: Strategies for qualitative research*. Aldine.

Graesser, A., Hu, X., & Sottilare, R. (2018). Intelligent tutoring systems. International Handbook of the Learning Sciences, 246-255. doi:10.4324/9781315617572

Greene, J., Moos, D., & Azevedo, R. (2011). Self-regulation of learning with computer-based learning environments. *New Directions for Teaching and Learning*, *126*(126), 107–115. doi:10.1002/tl.449

Greene, J. A., & Azevedo, R. (2009). A macro-level analysis of SRL processes and their relations to the acquisition of a sophisticated mental model of a complex system. *Contemporary Educational Psychology*, *34*(1), 18–29. doi:10.1016/j.cedpsych.2008.05.006

Hannan, E., & Liu, S. (2021). AI: New source of competitiveness in higher education. *Competitiveness Review*. Advance online publication. doi:10.1108/CR-03-2021-0045

Hwang, G. J., & Chang, C. Y. (2021). A review of opportunities and challenges of chatbots in education. *Interactive Learning Environments*, 1–14. Advance online publication. doi:10.1080/10494820.2021.1952615

Lee, Y. F., Hwang, G. J., & Chen, P. Y. (2022). Impacts of an AI-based chatbot on college students' after-class review, academic performance, self-efficacy, learning attitude, and motivation. *Educational Technology Research and Development*, *70*(5), 1843–1865. doi:10.100711423-022-10142-8

Lin, M. P. C., & Chang, D. (2020). Enhancing Post-secondary Writers' Writing Skills with a Chatbot: A Mixed-Method Classroom Study. *Journal of Educational Technology & Society*, *23*(1), 78–92.

Moos, D. C. (2011). Self-regulated learning and externally generate feedback with hypermedia. *Journal of Educational Computing Research*, *44*(3), 265–297. doi:10.2190/EC.44.3.b

Neo, M. (2022). The Merlin Project: Malaysian Students' Acceptance of an AI Chatbot in Their Learning Process. *Turkish Online Journal of Distance Education*, *23*(3), 31–48. https://doi-org.tp-library.idm.oclc.org/10.17718/tojde.1137122

Okonkwo, C. W., & Ade-Ibijola, A. (2021). Chatbots applications in education: A systematic review. *Computers and Education: Artificial Intelligence*, *2*, 1–10. doi:10.1016/j.caeai.2021.100033

Pengel, N., Martin, A., Meissner, R., Arndt, T., Neumann, A. T., de Lange, P., & Wollersheim, H. W. (2021). *TecCoBot: Technology-aided support for self-regulated learning*. doi:10.48550/arXiv.2111.11881

Pérez, J. Q., Daradoumis, T., & Puig, J. M. M. (2020). Rediscovering the use of chatbots in education: A systematic literature review. *Computer Applications in Engineering Education*, *28*(6), 1549–1565. doi:10.1002/cae.22326

Roll, I., Aleven, V., McLaren, B. M., & Koedinger, K. R. (2011). Metacognitive practice makes perfect: Improving students' self-assessment skills with an intelligent tutoring system. *Artificial Intelligence in Education*, *6738*, 288–295. doi:10.1007/978-3-642-21869-9_38

Schmitt, O., & Buschek, D. (2021). *CharacterChat: Supporting the Creation of Fictional Characters through Conversation and Progressive Manifestation with a Chatbot*. doi:10.1145/3450741.3465253

School of Humanities and Social Sciences. (2018). *Subject syllabus document: Communication & Information Literacy*. Temasek Polytechnic.

Smutny, P., & Schreiberova, P. (2020). Chatbots for learning: A review of educational chatbots for the Facebook Messenger. *Computers & Education*, *151*(103862), 1–11. doi:10.1016/j.compedu.2020.103862

Srivastava, E. (n.d.). *Decision Tree Vs Natural Language Processing: What Chatbot Type Is Better?* HappyFox Inc.

Swivl. (n.d.). Which is a better option: Ai-power or rule-based chatbots? *Swivl Blog*. Retrieved August 20, 2022, from https://tryswivl.com/blog/ai-powered-chatbot/which-is-the-best-option-ai-powered-or-a-rule-based-chatbot/

Temasek Polytechnic. (2022). *TP LibGuides*. Retrieved from TP Library: https://tp.libguides.com/apa

Weinstein, C. E., Acee, T. W., & Jung, J. H. (2011). Self-regulation and learning strategies. *New Directions for Teaching and Learning*, *2011*(126), 45–53. doi:10.1002/tl.443

Zakos, J., & Capper, L. (2008). CLIVE – An Artificially Intelligent Chat Robot for Conversational Language Practice. In J. Darzentas, G. A. Vouros, S. Vosinakis, & A. Arnellos (Eds.), Lecture Notes in Computer Science: Vol. 5138. *Artificial Intelligence: Theories, Models and Applications. SETN 2008*. Springer. doi:10.1007/978-3-540-87881-0_46

Zimmerman, B. J. (1990). Self-regulated learning and academic achievement: An overview. *Educational Psychologist*, *25*(1), 3–17. doi:10.120715326985ep2501_2

Zimmerman, B. J. (1998). Developing self-fulfilling cycles of academic regulation. In Self-regulated learning: From teaching to self-reflective practice. Guilford Publications.

Zimmerman, B. J., & Schunk, D. H. (2011) Self-regulated learning and Performance. In Handbook of Self-regulation of learning and performance. Routledge.

ADDITIONAL READING

Burden, D., & Savin-Baden, M. (2019). *Virtual humans: Today and tomorrow*. CRC Press LLC. doi:10.1201/9781315151199

Chassignol, M., Khoroshavin, A., Klimova, A., & Bilyatdinova, A. (2018). Artificial Intelligence trends in education: A narrative overview. *Procedia Computer Science*, *136*, 16–24. doi:10.1016/j.procs.2018.08.233

de Leon, D., Levas, E., & Li, Y. (2021, March 3). *A smart class chatbot for improving student learning and engagement* [Conference session]. 2021 Computer Science Conference for CSU Undergraduates, Virtual. https://cscsu-conference.github.io/index.html

Holmes, W., Bialik, M., & Fadel, C. (2019). *Artificial intelligence in education: promises and implications for teaching and learning*. The Center for Curriculum Redesign.

Meyer von Wolff, R., Nörtemann, J., Hobert, S., & Schumann, M. (2020). Chatbots for the Information Acquisition at Universities – A Student's View on the Application Area. In *Chatbot Research and Design: CONVERSATIONS 2019* (pp. 231–244). Springer. doi:10.1007/978-3-030-39540-7_16

Saks, K., & Leijen, A. (2014). Distinguishing Self-Directed and Self-Regulated Learning and Measuring them in the E-learning Context. *Procedia: Social and Behavioral Sciences*, *112*, 190–198. doi:10.1016/j.sbspro.2014.01.1155

Zawacki-Richter, O., Marín, V. I., Bond, M., & Gouverneur, F. (2019). Systematic review of research on artificial intelligence applications in higher education – where are the educators? *International Journal of Educational Technology in Higher Education, 16*(1), 1–27. doi:10.118641239-019-0171-0

Zhang, H., Fang, L., Miao, H., & Goh, E. (2022). *AI Chatbot to teach Microsoft Excel*. Singapore Institute of Technology. Poster. doi:10.25447it.19210686.v1

KEY TERMS AND DEFINITIONS

AI Chatbot: A program within a website or an application that leverages on machine learning and natural language processing techniques to understand the intent behind queries and answer them in a human-like way.

Analytics: The process of analyzing data to discover, interpret and communicate significant patterns or insights to eventually drive or influence decision-making. Learning Analytics is the measurement, collection, analysis and reporting of data for purposes of understanding and optimizing learning and the environments in which it occurs.

Chatbot Development Platform: An application used for developing a chatbot. It typically comes with a framework with ready-made cloud-based tools and technology.

Conversational Flow: The design logic behind how to start, sustain or end a conversation with the user is determined by the purpose of the chatbot. It could be implemented as a tree-like flow that guides the user with follow-up questions to eventually achieve the learning purpose.

Entity: The subject that the user refers to, e.g., when the user asks 'How do you do that'; What does 'that' refer to?

Intent: This refers to the chatbot user's intention, namely, what does (s)he wants from the conversation.

Menu: A listing of what the chatbot can respond to in the form of buttons and chips. In the case of APABot, this refers to the curated APA style sections which students will need to be aware of in their APA formatted writing.

Response: The reply by the chatbot in response to a detected user's intent.

User Experience (UX): The experience provided to the user that allows a natural, intelligent and logical conversation to be conducted.

User Interface (UI) and Platform: This is where the user can see or hear the conversational exchange. The chatbot needs to be hosted or integrated into either a website or mobile application including mobile instant messaging applications such as Facebook, Telegram.

APPENDIX 1: ACCESSING THE APABOT

The APABot could be used in two ways, namely, by accessing a menu, and by asking questions.

Method 1: Using the Menu

Figure 5 shows what the user sees when (s)he logs in.

Figure 5. Log–in page

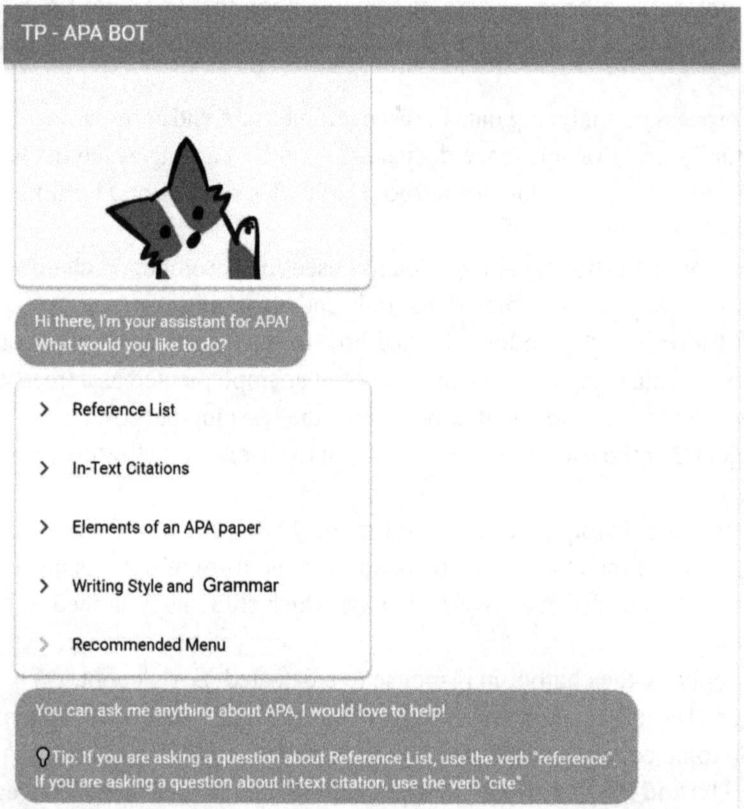

If the user proceeds to click on the Recommended Menu, the number and types of errors will be displayed, along with the recommended intents to focus on (see Figure 6).

If user clicks on the two highlighted areas of focus respectively, the following sub-menu will be displayed (see figure 7):

Figure 6. Recommended menu page

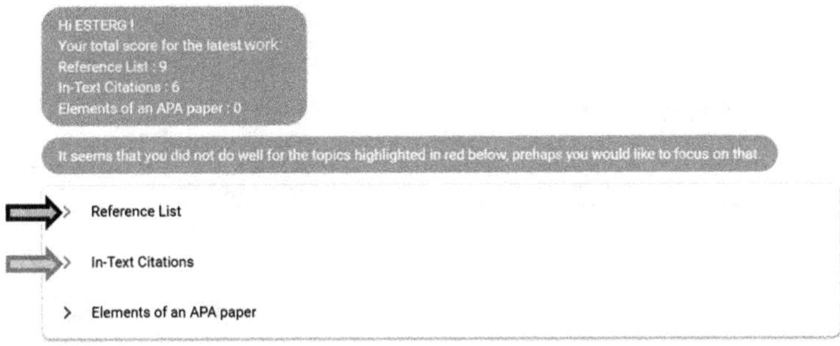

Figure 7. Recommended sub-menu page

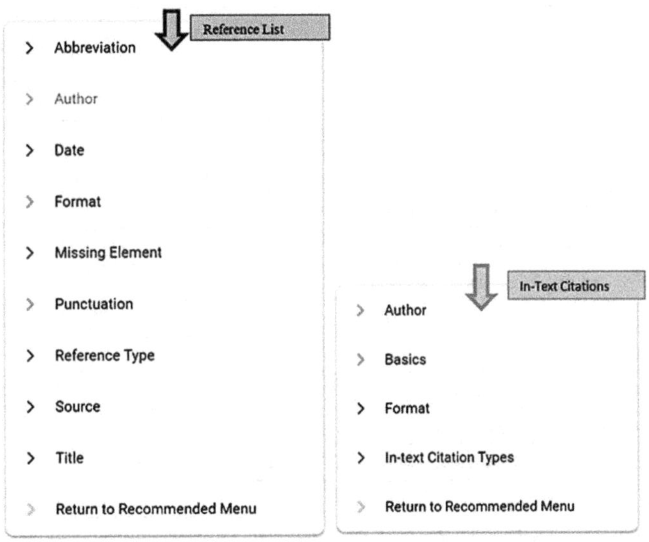

Method 2: Asking the APABOT Questions

The user can type in free text to ask questions related to APA (see Figure 8).

Figure 8. Free text input

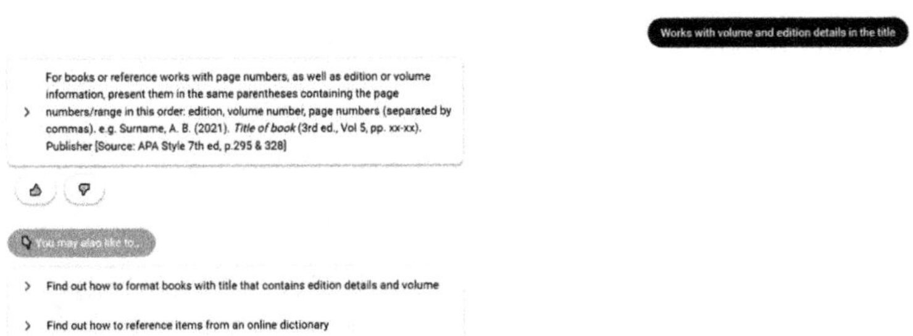

APPENDIX 2: SURVEY

Table 10. Survey questions and response types

Questions	Response Types
1. On average, how many times did you use the APABot?	Options: • Almost every day • About every other day • Less than three times • Only one time
2. On average, how much time did you spend on the APABot?	Options: • More than 60 mins • Around 30 to 60 mins • Around 15 to 30 mins • Around 5 to 15 mins • Less than 5 mins
3. What did you use to access APABot?	Options: • Desktop • Laptop • Tablet • Mobile phone
4. I am able to use the APABot to answer most, if not all, of my queries or doubts.	For Q4 - Q14 Five-point Likert Scale ranging from Strongly Agree to Strongly Disagree
5. The APABot recommends me some useful resources (through the Menu function) even though I did not particularly search for it.	
6. I feel encouraged and motivated to search for solutions and answers via the APABot.	
7. The responses provided by the APABot are clear and easy to follow.	
8. I feel confident of my ability in APA Style after using the APABot.	
9. I have sufficient knowledge of APA Style after using the APABot	
10. I can plan for my learning with the help of the APABot.	
11. Having the APABot as a learning companion, motivates me to learn more about ICOMM.	
12. I use the APABot to seek answers or solutions before turning to tutor/ instructor for help.	
13. I am able to enhance my knowledge and skills in APA Style Referencing even without the chatbot.	
14. I often find that the APABot is not able to understand my questions	
15. What is something you hope the APABot can do to help you in your learning, but not achieved by this current one?	Free Text
16. Overall, how was your experience with the APABot?	Options: • Excellent • Fair • Poor • Very Poor
17. Share with us the reason(s) why you rated your experience in such as way?	Free Text
18. How likely are you to recommend the APABot to a friend?	Options: Eleven-point scale from 0 (not likely at all) to 10 (extremely likely)
19. Would you like to use a chatbot for the learning of other subjects or skills?	Options: Yes / No
20. Share with us the reason(s) why you prefer/ not prefer using a chatbot to learn another subject or skill?	Free text

Section 4

Self-Regulated Learning Across Contexts

Chapter 11
Self-Regulation, Motivation, Emotion, and Skill Mastery of Online Learning:
New Evidence From a Survey During COVID-19

Jiao Guo
Institute of Higher Education, East China Normal University, China

Qinnan Ding
National Institutes of Educational Policy Research, East China Normal University, China

ABSTRACT

Self-regulation is a core concept associated with the metacognitive, motivational, and emotional aspects of learning. The COVID-19 pandemic provides a large-scale setting to collect new empirical evidence to test this conceptual framework in an authentic online learning environment. By reference to 64,949 participants enrolled at 39 universities in China, the authors developed the Undergraduate Online Self-Regulated Learning Questionnaire and estimated the associations among self-regulation, motivation, emotion, and skill mastery with regard to online learning across different subgroups of a diverse student body. The results demonstrated that males, rural students, lower-division undergraduates, first-generation college students, SEAM majors, and students at elite universities reported significantly lower UOSL scores. After controlling for motivation and emotion, these gaps decreased substantially and become statistically nonsignificant. The findings highlight the critical role played by targeted interventions in the creation of a supportive online environment for disadvantaged subgroups.

INTRODUCTION

Self-regulation is a core concept associated with the nature of learning that emphasizes the self-driven learning motivation exhibited by learners. During the past three decades, the notion of self-regulated

DOI: 10.4018/978-1-6684-6500-4.ch011

learning (SRL) has developed into a sophisticated conceptual framework used by high-impact scholars and featuring theoretical models, empirical evidence, and established instruments (Panadero, 2017). The multidimensional construct of SRL reflects the perplexing aspects of learning by mapping observable behaviors (e.g., setting goals, monitoring progress, reflection) onto metacognition, motivation, emotion, culture, and other hidden drives internalized by learners. This mapping work enables education researchers and practitioners to unpack some myths associated with overachievers from disadvantaged backgrounds (e.g., the upward mobility of first-generation college students) or underachievers who waste their potential (e.g., the downward mobility of students who exhibit lower educational attainment than their parents) (Zimmerman & Risemberg, 1997). SRL has been proven to play a critical role not only in academic performance (e.g., course grades) but also in nonacademic outcomes (e.g., student engagement) (Anthonysamy et al., 2020), which matter more with regard to long-term knowledge retention and transferrable skills. Our chapter contributes to this line of investigation with regard to SRL by focusing on the associations among learners' background, their learning behaviors, the latent mechanisms that drive their behaviors, and self-reported skill mastery in terms of nonacademic outcomes.

Early SRL theory studies were usually conducted in a strictly controlled psychological laboratory. However, one obvious trend is recent research on learning behavior has been to focus on real educational situations. The outbreak of COVID-19 led to dramatic changes in school teaching methods worldwide. These changes also provided a large-scale setting for collecting new empirical evidence to test this conceptual framework in an authentic online learning environment. For example, students might exhibit different modes or methods of learning in different disciplines, which feature different course designs and are based on different self-regulated learning models (Struyven et al., 2006; Nijhuis et al., 2008). These difference could even be found with regard to different groups in a single class because their learning strategies are diverse (e.g., deep learning vs. surface learning) (Winne & Hadwin, 1998).

BACKGROUND

The positive association between SRL and learning outcomes has been supported by evidence across various learning environments, but the estimated effect sizes of SRL have varied substantially. This situation challenges researchers to identify which SRL mechanism is most effective where and when in further detail. The role of SRL is expected to be more important in an online learning environment, which features more autonomy and less guidance than traditional face-to-face classrooms (Barnard et al., 2009). A meta-analysis of 12 studies on academic outcomes (i.e., GPA), however, found that the effect of SRL in the online setting is weaker than its effect in offline classrooms (Broadbent & Poon, 2015). The outbreak of COVID-19, despite its disruption of normal schooling, triggered a large-scale learning environment switch from offline to online. This unexpected and massive switch provided a retrospective opportunity for learners to compare the two different learning settings, i.e., the online learning that took place during COVID-19 and the offline learning just before the switch. Our chapter aims to use a multi-institutional survey conducted during the pandemic to investigate whether a substantial gap in learning outcomes associated with SRL exists between the online and offline learning contexts. This investigation has practical implications with regard to concerns pertaining to the long-term effects of this massive offline-to-online switch during the pandemic on learners' learning behaviors, metacognition, psychological mechanisms, and skill mastery.

To reduce the complexity of the survey design and implementation, the participants in our survey were undergraduates at 39 four-year universities located in a metropolitan city of China during the pandemic. As a result of the large sample size (N=64,949) and the diversity of the student body (e.g., 18.3% of participants were from rural families, and 48.6% were first-generation college students; see Table 1 for more details regarding the sample distribution), we were able to use the survey data to compare subgroups and subsequently to highlight heterogeneous effects (if any). The literature on online SRL has shown that demographic information (e.g., age, gender, country of origin), personal background (e.g., educational attainment, social economic status), motivation (e.g., intention to take a job-related online course), and other individual-level differences (e.g., prior online learning experience) are linked with SRL behaviors and learning outcomes (Guo & Reinecke, 2014; Hansen & Reich, 2015; Kizilcec et al., 2017); however, most of these findings have been limited to massive open online courses (MOOCs), whose target population and outcome measures (e.g., watching course lectures) differ from those of formal schooling. To address this gap in our current understanding of online SRL, our investigation aims to provide insights into a formal higher education system that serves a heterogeneous student population and to produce empirical findings that can inform future smart interventions that are tailored to the special needs of different subgroups, for example, a supportive online learning environment design that targets students from low income, rural families or other disadvantaged backgrounds with the aim of inspiring their internal drives or enabling them to cope with negative feelings experienced during online learning.

METHODOLOGY

Participants

The data were collected using a multi-institutional survey during the outbreak of the COVID-19 pandemic in the summer of 2020. An invitation to participate in the online survey was sent to students at 39 four-year universities located in a metropolitan city in China. A total of 84,720 undergraduates responded and completed the survey. After deleting the responses of participants who completed their surveys in too short (i.e., less than 5 minutes) or too long (i.e., more than an hour) a period of time, the final valid sample for our survey included 64,949 undergraduates. Given that the focus of our investigation was to compare different subgroups and identify the heterogeneous effects (if any) of online SRL on skill mastery, the task of ensuring the sample diversity in terms of demographic information and educational backgrounds was a major concern during the data-collection process. See Table 1 for the distribution of the sample with regard to selected variables.

Measures

The outcome variable used to measure online learning achievement in our survey was the participant's self-rated skill mastery. A total of eight skills were rated, including three subject-specific skills (basic knowledge, frontier research, and practical skills) and five transferrable skills (effective communication, information processing, critical thinking, problem solving, and planning). Each of these eight skills was rated by participants on a Likert scale ranging from one to five. During the online data-collection process, the survey platform reminded participants to report their skill mastery after comparing their online learning during COVID-19 against their offline learning prior to the pandemic.

Table 1. Sample distribution with regard to selected variables (N=64,949)

Selected Variables	Categories	Sample Distribution (%)
Gender	Female	61.2
	Male	38.8
Household residency	Rural	18.3
	Urban	81.7
Family socioeconomic status[1]	First-generation college student	48.6
	Second-generation college student	51.4
	Freshman	41.0
	Sophomore	32.1
Year	Junior	25.3
	Senior	1.6[2]
Subject field	Humanities and social sciences Science, engineering, agriculture, and medicine	60.4 39.6
University type	Elite university[3] Other university	24.2 75.8

[1]Family socioeconomic status was measured in terms of the educational attainment of parents. In our chapter, first-generation college students refer to undergraduates whose parents never attended college.

[2]The response rate was low for seniors (i.e., the class of 2020) because the survey was conducted in the summer of 2020, when most seniors had already graduated; accordingly, few seniors took online courses during COVID-19.

[3]In our research design, elite universities refer to 42 universities selected by China's Ministry of Education for World-Class University Construction and 95 other universities selected for World-Class Discipline Construction in 2017. Both constructions are known in China as the Double World-Class Construction (DWC) project in the context of higher education.

The question variable in our chapter was measured using the Undergraduate Online Self-Regulated Learning Scale (UOSL). Built on previously developed instruments (Barnard et al., 2009) used to measure online SRL, the UOSL scores consisted of six items that aimed to address this latent construct in terms of three dimensions: planning, execution, and reflection. The Cronbach's alpha value is 0.942, which indicated the internal consistency of the scale. The construct validity of the UOSL scores was measured by conducting an exploratory factor analysis. Both orthogonal rotation and oblique rotation demonstrated essentially the same results. See Table 2 for the results of the orthogonal rotation. All standardized factor loadings of the six items included in UOSL scores ranged from 0.606 to 0.874.

In addition to online SRL, motivation and emotion are two other hidden mechanisms that drive the hypothesized online learning behaviors of undergraduates. Motivation was measured in our survey using five items, including three items measuring internal drive resulting from (1) pure interest to satisfy participants' academic curiosity, (2) problem solving with regard to striving to overcome learning challenges, and (3) reading habits with respect to enjoying subject-related books or materials; in addition, two items measured external drive resulting from (4) course performance due to the desire to obtain good grades and (5) career goals with regard to finding a subject-related job. Emotion was measured in our survey using four items that asked participants to report whether they (1) struggled to keep up with the pace of the course, (2) were bored while they continued to engage in online learning, (3) felt nervous participating in online learning activities, and (4) became exhausted by thinking about upcoming online courses.

Table 2. Construct validity of the UOSL scores based on the factor analysis (N=64,949)

UOSL Items	Factor 1 Planning	Factor 2 Execution	Factor 3 Reflection
1. I plan for short-term and long-term goals more frequently.	0.874		
2. I am more capable of completing weekly assignments.		0.642	
3. I am more capable of adjusting my reading methods to suit difficult materials.		0.710	
4. I am more capable of adjusting my learning methods to cope with the pace of the course.		0.718	
5. I am better at summarizing what I have learned.			0.606
6. I ask myself whether I understand the new content more frequently.			0.719

Hypothesized Associations

Our investigation aimed to test our four hypotheses based on the following equation:

$$\text{Skill}=\beta_0+\beta_1\,\text{UOSL}+\beta_2\,\text{Motivation}+\beta_3\,\text{Emotion}+\sum_{j=4}^{n}\beta_j\,X_j \tag{1}$$

where β_0 is the constant term.

1. SRL is positively associated with skill mastery with regard to online learning. The hypothesized association can be proven by a positive and statistically significant coefficient, β_1, of participants' self-rated UOSL scores.
2. Motivation is also positively associated with online learning outcomes, which can be proven by the hypothesized positive and statistically significant coefficient, β_2, of participants' motivation, such as academic curiosity, problem solving, reading habits, course grades, or career goals.
3. Emotions such as feelings of struggling or being bored, nervous or tired during the online learning process are negatively associated with the online learning effect. The corresponding coefficient, β_3, is hypothesized to be negative and statistically significant.

H0: Emotions such as feelings of struggling or being bored, nervous or tired during the online learning process are not associated with the online learning effect. The corresponding coefficient, β_3, is hypothesized to be statistically nonsignificant.

4. The background variables, X_j, in the hypothesized regression model include gender, household residency, the educational attainment of the participant's parents, subject field and institutional type (i.e., elite universities versus other four-year universities). Males, rural residents, first-generation college students, SEAM (science, engineering, agriculture, or medical) majors, and undergraduates at nonelite universities are hypothesized to represent disadvantaged subgroups who face more challenges with regard to online learning than do other subgroups. The corresponding set of coefficients, β_j, are hypothesized to be negative and statistically significant.

Table 3. Descriptive statistics of the self-rated UOSL scores (N=64,949)

UOSL Items	Mean	SD
1. I plan for short-term and long-term goals more frequently.	3.197	0.803
2. I am more capable of completing weekly assignments[1].	3.335	0.835
3. I am more capable of adjusting my reading methods to suit difficult materials.	3.251	0.801
4. I am more capable of adjusting my learning methods to cope with the pace of the course.	3.347	0.801
5. I am better at summarizing what I have learned.	3.245	0.791
6. I ask myself whether I understand the new content more frequently.	3.267	0.790
TOTAL	19.64	4.246

H0: The background variables, X_j, in the hypothesized regression model are not associated with the online learning effect. The corresponding set of coefficients, β_j, are hypothesized to be statistically nonsignificant.

RESULTS

Descriptive Statistics

We began with descriptive statistics of the survey data before conducting further analysis. With regard to the sum of all six items of the UOSL scores, participants reported an average value of 19.64 (Median=18, SD=4.246) with a minimum value of 6 and a maximum value of 30. Due to the large sample size (N=64,949), the self-rated UOSL scores approximate a normal distribution. Specifically (see Table 3), the highest SRL item rated by participants was adjustment for course pace (Mean=3.347), thus supporting the expected high autonomy of online learning; the lowest SRL item pertained to goal setting in both the short-term and the long-term (Mean=3.197).

This item-specific pattern was consistent across different subgroups; for example, both first-generation college students and second-generation college students reported the highest mean score for pace adjustment and the lowest mean score for goal setting. Our focus of comparison and interpretation, therefore, was the sum of UOSL scores rather than each of the six items individually. Based on the *t test* used to compare the mean scores across different subgroups, we found that males, rural students, first-generation college students, SEAM majors and undergraduates at elite universities reported lower average UOSL scores in the context of online learning than did other subgroups, and all the self-reported gaps among subgroups were statistically significant (see Table 4). All the results (except those pertaining to elite universities) supported the hypothesis that disadvantaged subgroups face larger challenges in online SRL. The *t* test comparison across subgroups indicated a similar pattern with respect to skill mastery with regard to online learning. The measure of this outcome was the total sum of participants' self-rated mastery with regard to eight skills (Mean=25.73, Median=24, SD=5.475). Subgroups that reported lower levels of online SRL also reported a lower average sum of skill mastery (see Table 5). To address the multiple testing issue in this preliminary analysis, the hypothesized regression models were tested, and their results are interpreted later in this chapter.

Table 4. t test used to compare mean total UOSL scores across different subgroups (N=64,949)

Undergraduate Subgroups	UOSL Scores (subgroup=0)	UOSL Scores (subgroup=1)	t Value
Males	19.867	19.285	16.477***
Rural residents	19.748	19.164	14.136***
First-generation college students	19.396	19.873	14.386***
SEAM majors	19.801	19.398	14.136***
Students at nonelite universities	19.544	19.673	3.352***

***p<0.001

Table 5. t test used to compare the mean total skill improvement across different subgroups (N=64,949)

Undergraduate Subgroups	Skill Improvement (subgroup=0)	Skill Improvement (subgroup=1)	t Value
Males	25.971	25.356	13.496***
Rural residents	25.869	25.122	13.922***
First-generation college students	26.078	25.368	16.602***
SEAM majors	26.046	25.254	18.035***
Students at nonelite universities	25.609	25.772	3.355***

***p<0.001

Correlation Analysis

We conducted a correlation analysis to confirm the associations among learners' background, online self-regulation, and skill mastery (see the corresponding columns in Table 6). The patterns remained essentially the same. We identified negative correlations between online SRL and four background variables (i.e., males, rural residency, first-generation college students, and SEAM majors) as predicted by Hypothesis 4 (see Section 2.3.). Only the correlation between online SRL and nonelite universities was positive in opposition to the hypothesis. All the correlation coefficients were statistically significant but weak, ranging from 0.013 to 0.071. This finding reminded us of the importance of exploring other internal drives besides SRL that mediate the relationship between learners background and skill mastery.

We extended the investigation by adding two other latent mechanisms, i.e., motivation and emotion, to the correlation analysis focused on skill mastery with regard to online learning. Motivation was measured as the total sum of five participant-rated items regarding their internal drives (e.g., pure curiosity) and external drives (e.g., career goals). The mean of motivation was 17.22 (Median=17, SD=3.092). Emotion was measured as the total sum of four self-rated items pertaining to negative feelings (e.g., feelings of struggling) during the online learning process. The mean of emotion was 11.73 (Median=12, SD=3.331). The correlation analysis between the two mechanisms and learners' backgrounds exhibited a similar pattern featuring the same disadvantaged subgroups as identified above. All the correlation coefficients (with the exception of the correlation between gender and emotion) are statistically significant but weak (ranging from 0.005 to 0.081). The correlations between participants' self-rated skill mastery and the

Table 6. Correlations between learners' background, self-regulation, motivation, emotion, and skill mastery with regard to online learning (N=64,949)

	Self-regulation (UOSL scores)	Motivation	Emotion	Skill mastery With regard to Online Learning
Males	-0.067***	-0.067***	0.005	-0.055***
Rural residents	-0.053***	-0.050***	0.079***	-0.053***
First-generation college students	-0.056***	-0.067***	0.081***	-0.065***
SEAM majors	-0.045***	-0.048***	0.056***	-0.071***
Students at nonelite universities	0.016***	0.040***	-0.025***	0.013***
Self-regulation		0.504***	-0.169***	0.641***
Motivation			-0.325***	0.594***
Emotion				-0.373***

***$p<0.001$

three mechanisms (self-regulation, motivation, and emotion) were all positive, statistically significant, and moderate to strong (ranging from 0.373 to 0.641). This finding provides insights into the critical role played by the three latent mechanisms in the online learning environment.

Regression Analysis

Hypothesis 5

The baseline regression model included a set of variables pertaining to learners' demographic information and educational backgrounds due to the associations between these factors and online learning outcomes. All regression coefficients were statistically significant and in the same direction as predicted by Hypothesis 4 (see *2.3. Hypotheses*, bullet 4), with the exception of the coefficient of nonelite universities. See the detailed results of the baseline model in Table 7. The findings relevant to demographics were consistent. Males, rural residents, and first-generation college students face more challenges in online learning. Their self-reported skill mastery with regard to online learning was lower than that of the other subgroups, and all these gaps were statistically significant ($p<0.001$). The findings pertaining to educational background were mixed. Lower-division undergraduates (e.g., freshmen or sophomores) and SEAM majors reported lower skill mastery with regard to online learning than did other subgroups. The regression coefficient of nonelite universities, however, was positive, in opposition to the hypothesis. This perplexing pattern is interpreted further in the discussion section.

Self-Regulation and Skill Mastery Regarding Online Learning (Hypothesis 1)

After adding the question predictor, i.e., self-regulation, to the regression model (see Model 2 in Table 7), the variation in self-rated skill mastery explained by the model increased substantially. The adjusted R^2 value rose from 0.011 in the baseline model to 0.413 in Model 2 with UOSL scores. The standardized regression coefficient of UOSL scores, β_1, was positive and statistically significant, and the effect size

Table 7. Regression analysis of learners' background, self-regulation, motivation, emotion and skill mastery with regard to online learning (N=64,949)

Undergrad Subgroups	Variables	Model 1 Baseline	Model 2 + Self-regulation	Model 3 + Motivation	Model 4 + Emotion
B Information	Male	0.041***	-0.004	0.004	0.001
	Rural Residency	-0.029***	-0.008*	-0.005	0.003
	First Generation	-0.050***	-0.024***	-0.013	-0.005
Educational Background	Year	0.031***	0.017***	0.021***	0.008***
	SEAM Majot	-0.044***	-0.028***	-0.016***	-0.008***
	Nonelite U	0.012**	0.004	0.021***	0.017***
	Self-regulation		0.637***	0.456***	0.399***
	Motivation			0.363***	0.362***
	Emotion				-0.180***
	df	64942	64941	64940	64939
	Adjusted R	0.011	0.413	0.510	0.539
	F value	119	6521	8457	8432

*$p<0.05$, **$p<0.01$, ***$p<0.001$, the standardized regression coefficients are reported.

was 0.637, thus supporting our hypothesis regarding the association between online SRL and learning outcomes. Furthermore, after controlling for individual-level differences in self-regulation, the gaps in skill mastery across different demographical subgroups decreased substantially. Specifically, the self-reported gaps in skill mastery related to rural residency and first-generation college students decreased by 72%, i.e., (0.008-0.029)/0.029, and 52%, respectively. The gender gap in skill mastery decreased by 90% and became statistically nonsignificant. A similar pattern was illustrated with regard to educational background. The gap in skill mastery associated with a linear variable of the student's year decreased by 45%, and the gap associated with the dummy variable for SEAM majors decreased by 36% in terms of effect size. The predicted advantage associated with nonelite universities in the online learning effect became statistically nonsignificant.

Motivation and Skill Mastery Regarding Online Learning (Hypothesis 2)

Another potential mechanism included in our investigation was motivation. After controlling for learners' motivation, the adjusted R^2 increased to 0.510, indicating that all the predictors in the regression model explained more than half of the variation in the outcome variable. See Model 3 in Table 7 for detailed results. As predicted (see *2.3.*, bullet 2), the regression coefficient of motivation, β_2, was positive and statistically significant, and the effect size was 0.363. The effect size of self-regulation decreased slightly to 0.456, but its positive and statistically significant association with learning outcome remained the same. Moreover, the gaps pertaining to learners' demographics decreased in terms of effect size and became statistically nonsignificant. This pattern indicates that the two latent constructs, i.e., both self-regulation and motivation, are key elements that must be integrated into the online learning environment design. The pattern found with regard to educational background was mixed. The gap related to SEAM majors decreased in terms of effect size by 43% but remained statistically significant. The gaps associated with the student's year and the university type (i.e., nonelite universities) even increased in terms of effect size after adding the measure of learners' motivation.

Emotion and Learning Outcomes (Hypothesis 3)

The regression results (see Model 4 in Table 7) remained essentially the same after adding one more latent construct, i.e., emotion. The adjusted R^2 increased further to 0.539. The regression coefficient of emotion, β_3, was negative and statistically significant, and the effect size was 0.180, as the predicted (see *2.3.*, bullet 3). The estimates of the other two constructs, i.e., self-regulation and motivation, were consistent, positive, and statistically significant. The gaps pertaining to learners' demographic background decreased in terms of effect size and became statistically nonsignificant. The perplexing pattern associated with educational background remained; however, the effect size associated with the student's year and SEAM majors decreased substantially. These empirical results offer inspiration for further investigation. In-depth interviews with some participants after they submitted the survey revealed that one reason that lower-division undergraduates, SEAM majors, and students in elite universities felt as if they struggled more or were more exhausted in the face of online learning is because they have more credit hours to complete or tougher course requirements to satisfy.

Subgroup Analysis With the Aim of Identifying Specific Challenges for Each Subgroup

To analyze the differences among subgroups, each of the eight skills (instead of their sum) were taken as outcome measures of the regression model (see Table 8). The coefficients of the three latent constructs, i.e., self-regulation, motivation, and emotion, were consistent across the eight model specifications. For example, all the coefficients of self-regulation were positive and statistically significant, with effect sizes ranging from 0.296 to 0.399. Similar patterns could be observed for motivation and emotion. These results confirm the important role played by these three constructs in the online learning context for all eight skills in general as well as for some transferable skills (e.g., communication and planning) in particular.

Another purpose of the subgroup analysis in Table 8 was to identify the specific challenges faced by each subgroup, which is key to designing and delivering future smart interventions that are tailored to the special needs of these subgroups. With regard to demographic information, the gender gap of online learning identified in Table 8 includes three skills for females (i.e., frontier research, practical skills, and critical thinking) and four skills for males (i.e., communication, IT competency, problem solving, and planning). These gaps in skill mastery must be interpreted with caution for the following three reasons. First, skill mastery was self-rated by undergraduates themselves, so these results focus on perceived gaps rather than actual gaps. Second, undergraduates' skill mastery in online learning settings during COVID-19 was compared with their retrospective memory of their offline learning experience before the pandemic. Third, some disadvantaged subgroups perceived more mastery in at least one skill in online learning settings, representing the silver lining for every cloud. For example, undergraduates from rural families self-reported more mastery in frontier research, practical skills, and planning than undergraduates from urban families in the online learning setting during COVID-19. See Table 8 for a complete list of advantages and disadvantages in self-rated skill mastery with regard to online learning for all the subgroups included in our survey.

Table 8. Regression analysis of eight skills self-rated by undergraduate subgroups on self-regulation, motivation, and emotion in the context of online learning (N=64,949)

Undergraduate Subgroups	Variables	Basic Knowledge	Frontier Research	Practical Skills	Communication	Critical Thinking	IT Competency	Problem-Solving	Planning
Demographic background	Male Rural First-generation	0.002 0.000 -0.008*	0.022*** 0.008* -0.007*	0.017*** 0.007* -0.001	-0.016*** -0.011** -0.009**	0.011*** 0.005 -0.005	-0.010*** -0.002 -0.001	-0.030*** 0.000 -0.004	-0.007* 0.014*** 0.003
Educational background	Year SEAM major Nonelite university	0.016*** -0.004 0.005	0.013*** -0.008* 0.026***	0.007* -0.063** 0.057***	-0.005 -0.008** 0.010**	0.001 0.004 0.010**	0.012*** 0.015** -0.010***	0.011*** 0.014*** -0.004	0.004 0.005 0.021***
	Self-regulation	0.356***	0.342***	0.296***	0.399***	0.359***	0.343***	0.359***	0.363***
	Motivation	0.327***	0.290***	0.237***	0.362***	0.335***	0.358***	0.351***	0.321***
	Emotion	-0.200***	-0.180***	-0.150***	-0.180***	-0.140***	-0.147***	-0.137***	-0.143***
	Df	64939	64939	64939	64939	64939	64939	64939	64939
	Adjusted R	0.462	0.392	0.289	0.539	0.430	0.442	0.449	0.421
	F value	6207	4645	2928	8432	5435	5726	5892	5249

*$p<0.05$, **$p<0.01$, ***$p<0.001$, the standardized regression coefficients are reported.

DISCUSSION

We conducted a multi-institutional survey during the pandemic to understand the metacognitive, motivational, and emotional aspects of online learning. The outbreak of COVID-19 provided a large-scale setting to test the conceptual framework of SRL in an authentic online learning environment. By reference to 64,949 participants at 39 universities located in a metropolitan city in China, we developed the Undergraduate Online Self-Regulated Learning Questionnaire (UOSL) and subsequently constructed regression models to estimate the associations among online SRL, motivation, emotion, and skill mastery in the online learning setting across different subgroups in the context of a heterogeneous student population.

Theoretical Contribution

Our chapter made two contributions to the literature on SRL. First, we developed the Undergraduate Online Self-Regulated Learning Questionnaire (UOSL). UOSL is based on part of an established instrument (i.e., OSLQ) used to measure online SRL (Barnard et al., 2009). Both the reliability and construct validity of the UOSL were proven by reference to our survey data. Due to the fact that it includes only six items, UOSL is easy to apply to a combination of measurements in a large-scale survey. This combination enables researchers to use one survey to simultaneously collect data from other measurements, such as the motivational and emotional scales that the literature on SRL has lacked (Roth et al., 2015) and ultimately to highlight the multidimensional nature of this complex construct. Second, our results highlight the critical role played by psychological factors in the online learning setting. This finding links our chapter to the rich literature on higher education from the psychological perspective that has focused on motivation, self-efficacy, and student engagement. For example, we identified the positive association between learners' motivation and skill mastery. This pattern confirmed the conclusions of a previous multi-institutional study conducted in China that connected self-regulation and motivation with adaptive engagement in the traditional face-to-face learning setting (Yin, 2018).

Practical Implications

The large sample size and the diverse student body of survey participants included in this study enabled us to provide insights into the associations among self-regulation, motivation, emotion, and skill mastery in the context of a heterogeneous population. The regression results identified special needs for different subgroups in the online learning environment that can be used to inform targeted interventions. The particular challenges identified for each subgroup could be a target for future smart interventions, such as effective online communication workshops tailored to males, rural residents, first-generation college students, and SEAM majors.

Previous work on this topic has summarized the design principles that can be used to promote online SRL, e.g., scaffolding activities in MOOCs. One such design principle was that online learning platforms should send reminders to learners with lower levels of SRL to encourage them to set goals, allocate time, reduce distractions, seek help, and visualize their progress (Lee et al., 2019). Our findings built on those principles to highlight the critical role played by the hidden mechanisms of motivation and emotion in driving learners' self-regulation behaviors. We encourage future smart intervention design not only to send alerts about learning tips but also to boost learners' internal drives (e.g., by encouraging them to write down their intentions and commit time to online learning) (Kizilcec et al., 2020).

Limitations

Two limitations of our research design should be noted. One such limitation pertains to the external validity of our sample. Participants in our survey were undergraduates at 39 four-year universities located in a metropolitan city in China during COVID-19. Due to the disruption of formal schooling by the pandemic, disadvantaged subgroups (e.g., rural, first-generation college students) in the diverse student population were required to study at home. Our survey data demonstrated that these subgroups faced online learning challenges (e.g., poor bandwidth coverage in rural villages, distractions from other family members) that were similar to those faced by other learners in developing countries. This cultural context is likely to be intertwined with motivations, emotions, and other hidden mechanisms associated with self-rated skill mastery with regard to online learning, which requires further investigation based on additional empirical evidence collected from other countries.

The other limitation pertains to the internal validity of our instrument. The measurements of online SRL, motivation, emotion, and skill mastery were self-rated by the participants included in our survey sample. Although learning behaviors can be observed and recorded in an authentic online learning environment (Kizilcec et al., 2020), we argue that metacognitive, psychological, or other hidden mechanisms should nevertheless be measured in part by established instruments (Roth et al., 2015) that are tailored to the population of interest and the cultural context in question. A combination of multiple sources consisting of observed behaviors, self-reported perceptions, platform logs, and experimental results can be discussed further, thus providing a direction for future investigations.

FUTURE RESEARCH DIRECTIONS

Our chapter yielded some inspiring findings for future research. One perplexing pattern in the results of our study is the associations among university type, online SRL, and self-rated mastery of skills.

After controlling for learners' background, motivation, and emotions in the context of online learning, undergraduates at elite universities reported lower levels of online SRL and lower-rated skill mastery. This pattern contradicts our hypothesis but illustrates the essentially context-dependent nature of SRL. SRL is highly context dependent, a term which refers to the critical role played by learning environment design in promoting SRL strategies, shaping learners' behaviors, and internalizing these behaviors into habits. Due to the disruption of formal schooling during the pandemic, participants at elite universities were separated from labs, libraries, study rooms and other offline spaces designed to facilitate advanced learning and scientific inquiry. They were also separated from college dorms, cafeterias, gyms, and other offline social spaces that previously allowed them to interact with other students. Our survey demonstrated that formal or informal interactions (e.g., feedback regarding hands-on lab skills during face-to-face instruction, playing games or simply hanging out with peers on a basketball court or soccer field) were the activities that participants reported they missed the most with respect to their online learning experience during the pandemic. A focus on these interactions or the adoption of a social or collaborative perspective represents a direction for future research aimed at extending our current understanding of online SRL (Hadwin et al.).

Another direction for future investigation is the improvement of research designs regarding SRL and other metacognitive or psychological mechanisms in the online learning environment. Specifically, we suggest three future research directions in terms of measures and methods. First, in addition to questionnaires, other self-report instruments (such as in-depth interviews, think-aloud techniques, and learning diaries) (Roth et al., 2015) should be incorporated into the research design to take advantage of both quantitative and qualitative methods. Second, using MOOCs and other online learning platforms, the current development of learning analytics enables a shift in the investigation of SRL from the traditional personal level to the finer-grained level of learning tasks (Efklides, 2011; Kizilcec et al., 2020). Platform logs provide an opportunity to automatically record the traces left by each learner in an authentic online learning environment. Trace-based learning process mining and other log analytic instruments have been used to understand the associations among SRL, motivation, and emotion (Winne & Baker, 2013) and to predict the mastery of writing skills (Cascallar et al., 2006). Third, to address skeptical concerns regarding interventions that consist of prompts offering learning tips (e.g., an alert tool to remind the user of time allocation or a distraction tool intended to block irrelevant websites) (Patterson, 2018), we encourage future intervention designs to address learners' internal drives such as metacognition, motivation and emotion deeply. For example, asking the learner to write down his or her personal intention to take an online course was proven to be an effective intervention for MOOC learners from developing countries (Kizilcec et al., 2020). Randomized control experiments have been conducted to support causal inferences regarding the unbiased effect of those interventions across different learning environments (Alpert et al., 2016; Bowen et al., 2013). Hispanic students, males, and low achievers have been found to face larger challenges in online learning (Figlio et al., 2013). Most of these experiments, however, have been conducted in the context of a single course (e.g., an introductive microeconomics course) at a single university. More rigorous empirical evidence combining mixed methods, learning analytics, and experimental design must be collected on a large scale to inform future smart interventions aimed at promoting the SRL of online learners from disadvantaged backgrounds.

CONCLUSION

Our analysis demonstrated that three hidden mechanisms, i.e., self-regulation, motivation, and emotion, have statistically significant and moderate to strong associations with participants' self-rated skill mastery in the online learning environment. We found that males, rural students, lower-division undergraduates, SEAM majors, and first-generation college students report lower average UOSL scores and skill mastery than do other subgroups. The patterns are consistent across descriptive statistics, correlation analysis, and regression analysis. After controlling for these three mechanisms, the gaps among subgroups in terms of self-rated skill mastery decreased substantially and became statistically nonsignificant. This finding provides insights into the critical role played by metacognitive, motivational, and emotional factors in the conceptual framework of online SRL in the context of a heterogeneous learner population that can inform future smart interventions that are intended to target the special needs of different subgroups in general and to be tailored to disadvantaged subgroups in particular.

ACKNOWLEDGMENT

This research was funded by the Peak Project of the Faculty of Education at East China Normal University; the Humanities and Social Science Research Planning Fund at China's Ministry of Education Project "Undergraduate Online Learning Behavior Analysis Based on Trace-SRL" [grant number 21YJA880014]; and the National Social Science Foundation of China Ministry of Education Youth Project "Research on the trends, influencing factors and policy implications of college graduates in the Yangtze river delta from the perspective of regional integration development" [grant number EIA220521].

REFERENCES

Alpert, W. T., Couch, K. A., & Harmon, O. R. (2016). A randomized assessment of online learning. *The American Economic Review*, *106*(5), 378–382. doi:10.1257/aer.p20161057

Anthonysamy, L., Koo, A.-C., & Hew, S.-H. (2020). Self-regulated learning strategies and non-academic outcomes in Higher Education Blended Learning Environments: A one decade review. *Education and Information Technologies*, *25*(5), 3677–3704. doi:10.100710639-020-10134-2

Barnard, L., Lan, W. Y., To, Y. M., Paton, V. O., & Lai, S.-L. (2009). Measuring self-regulation in online and blended learning environments. *The Internet and Higher Education*, *12*(1), 1–6. doi:10.1016/j.iheduc.2008.10.005

Bowen, W. G., Chingos, M. M., Lack, K. A., & Nygren, T. I. (2013). Interactive learning online at public universities: Evidence from a six-campus randomized trial. *Journal of Policy Analysis and Management*, *33*(1), 94–111. doi:10.1002/pam.21728

Broadbent, J., & Poon, W. L. (2015). Self-Regulated Learning Strategies & Academic Achievement in Online Higher Education Learning Environments: A systematic review. *The Internet and Higher Education*, *27*, 1–13. doi:10.1016/j.iheduc.2015.04.007

Cascallar, E., Boekaerts, M., & Costigan, T. (2006). Assessment in the evaluation of self regulation as a process. *Educational Psychology Review*, *18*(3), 297–306. doi:10.100710648-006-9023-2

Efklides, A. (2011). Interactions of metacognition with motivation and affect in self-regulated learning: The MASRL model. *Educational Psychologist*, *46*(1), 6–25. doi:10.1080/00461520.2011.538645

Figlio, D., Rush, M., & Yin, L. (2013). Is it live or is it internet? experimental estimates of the effects of online instruction on student learning. *Journal of Labor Economics*, *31*(4), 763–784. doi:10.1086/669930

Guo, P. J., & Reinecke, K. (2014). Demographic differences in how students navigate through moocs. In *Proceedings of the first ACM conference on learning@ scale conference (L@S 2014)*. ACM. 10.1145/2556325.2566247

Hadwin, A. F., Järvelä, S., & Miller, M. (n.d.). Self-regulated, co-regulated, and socially shared regulation of learning. Handbook of Self-Regulation of Learning and Performance. doi:10.4324/9780203839010.ch5

Hansen, J. D., & Reich, J. (2015). Democratizing education? examining access and usage patterns in massive open online courses. *Science*, *350*(6265), 1245–1248. doi:10.1126cience.aab3782 PMID:26785488

Kizilcec, R. F., Pérez-Sanagustín, M., & Maldonado, J. J. (2017). Self-regulated learning strategies predict learner behavior and goal attainment in massive open online courses. *Computers & Education*, *104*, 18–33. doi:10.1016/j.compedu.2016.10.001

Kizilcec, R. F., Reich, J., Yeomans, M., Dann, C., Brunskill, E., Lopez, G., Turkay, S., Williams, J. J., & Tingley, D. (2020). Scaling up behavioral science interventions in online education. *Proceedings of the National Academy of Sciences of the United States of America*, *117*(26), 14900–14905. doi:10.1073/pnas.1921417117 PMID:32541050

Lee, D., Watson, S. L., & Watson, W. R. (2019). Systematic literature review on self-regulated learning in Massive open online courses. *Australasian Journal of Educational Technology*, *35*(1). Advance online publication. doi:10.14742/ajet.3749

Nijhuis, J., Segers, M., & Gijselaers, W. (2008). The extent of variability in learning strategies and students' perceptions of the learning environment. *Learning and Instruction*, *18*(2), 121–134. doi:10.1016/j.learninstruc.2007.01.009

Panadero, E. (2017). A review of self-regulated learning: Six models and four directions for Research. *Frontiers in Psychology*, *8*, 422. Advance online publication. doi:10.3389/fpsyg.2017.00422 PMID:28503157

Patterson, R. W. (2018). Can behavioral tools improve online student outcomes? Experimental evidence from a massive open online course. *Journal of Economic Behavior & Organization*, *153*, 293–321. doi:10.1016/j.jebo.2018.06.017

Roth, A., Ogrin, S., & Schmitz, B. (2015). Assessing self-regulated learning in higher education: A systematic literature review of self-report instruments. *Educational Assessment, Evaluation and Accountability*, *28*(3), 225–250. doi:10.100711092-015-9229-2

WinneP. H.BakerR. S. J. (2013). The potentials of educational data mining for researching metacognition, motivation and self-regulated learning. Zenodo.

Winne, P. H., & Hadwin, A. F. (1998). Studying as self-regulated learning. In D. J. Hacker, J. Dunlosky, & A. C. Graesser (Eds.), Metacognition in educational theory and practice (pp. 277-304). Lawrence Erlbaum Associates Publishers.

Yin, H. (2018). What motivates Chinese undergraduates to engage in learning? insights from a psychological approach to student engagement research. *Higher Education*, *76*(5), 827–847. doi:10.100710734-018-0239-0

Zhu, Y., Au, W., & Yates, G. (2016). University students' self-control and self-regulated learning in a blended course. *The Internet and Higher Education*, *30*, 54–62. doi:10.1016/j.iheduc.2016.04.001

Zimmerman, B. J., & Risemberg, R. (1997). Self-regulatory dimensions of academic learning and motivation. Handbook of Academic Learning, 105–125. doi:10.1016/b978 012554255-5/50005-3

ADDITIONAL READING

Barnard, L., Lan, W. Y., To, Y. M., Paton, V. O., & Lai, S.-L. (2009). Measuring self-regulation in online and blended learning environments. *The Internet and Higher Education*, *12*(1), 1–6. doi:10.1016/j.iheduc.2008.10.005

Panadero, E. (2017). A review of self-regulated learning: Six models and four directions for Research. *Frontiers in Psychology*, *8*, 422. Advance online publication. doi:10.3389/fpsyg.2017.00422 PMID:28503157

Roth, A., Ogrin, S., & Schmitz, B. (2015). Assessing self-regulated learning in higher education: A systematic literature review of self-report instruments. *Educational Assessment, Evaluation and Accountability*, *28*(3), 225–250. doi:10.100711092-015-9229-2

Saint, J., Whitelock-Wainwright, A., Gasevic, D., & Pardo, A. (2020). Trace-SRL: A Framework for Analysis of Micro-level Processes of Self Regulated Learning from Trace Data. *IEEE Transactions on Learning Technologies*, *13*(4), 861–877. Advance online publication. doi:10.1109/TLT.2020.3027496

Schunk, D. H., & Greene, J. A. (2018). *Handbook of Self-Regulation of Learning and Performance* (2nd ed.). Routledge.

Winne, P. H., & Hadwin, A. F. (1998). Studying as self-regulated learning. In D. J. Hacker, J. Dunlosky, & A. C. Graesser (Eds.), *Metacognition in Educational Theory and Practice* (pp. 277–304). Lawrence Erlbaum Associates Publishers.

Zimmerman, B. J. (1990). Self-Regulated Learning and Academic Achievement: An Overview. *Educational Psychologist*, *25*(1), 3–17. doi:10.120715326985ep2501_2

Zimmerman, B. J., & Schunk, D. H. (2011). *Handbook of Self-Regulation of Learning and Performance. Routledge.*

KEY TERMS AND DEFINITIONS

Elite Universities: One hundred thirty-seven universities identified by China's Ministry of Education in 2017 as elite higher-ed institutions.

First-Generation College Students: Undergraduates whose parents never attended college.

Motivation: Internal or external factors that drive individuals to change their behaviors.

Motives: Unverbalized intentions and values of individual agents.

SEAM Majors: Science, engineering, agriculture, and medical majors.

Self-Regulation Strategies: Actions and processes aimed at the acquisition of information or skills that involve agency, purpose, and instrumentality perceptions on the part of learners.

Skill Mastery: Undergraduates' self-rated improvement in subject-specific skills (e.g., basic knowledge) and transferrable skills (e.g., problem solving).

Chapter 12
Development, Sustainment, and Scaling of Self-Regulated Learning Analytics:
Prediction Modeling and Digital Student Success Initiatives in University Contexts

Matthew L. Bernacki
University of North Carolina at Chapel Hill, USA

ABSTRACT

Undergraduates who engage in high structure, high enrollment, active learning courses tend to perform best when they self-regulate their learning. Student self-regulated learning is encouraged by active learning designs that provide resources used to enact strategies and engage in planning, monitoring, and evaluation of one's learning processes. Some learners may need to "learn to learn" before these resources can be leveraged effectively. This chapter documents a scalable co-design and learning analytics project led by learning scientists and science, technology, engineering, and math (STEM) instructors who enhanced digital resources of large-lecture courses' learning management systems (LMSs). Students' course engagement produced data about self-regulated learning processes, affording feature engineering, prediction modeling and provision of timely support to students predicted to struggle. The authors report initial results through the lens of self-regulated learning theory and elaborate cases demonstrating institutionalization and replicability to research and regional institutions.

INTRODUCTION

In response to issues with student performance, retention, progression, and completion (Arroway et al., 2016), many universities and their educational software providers are embracing *learning analytics* (Lang et al., 2017, 2022) to understand the student learning experience through the *learning event* data that undergraduates produce while they learn in their courses (Bernacki, 2018). Those data can be used to

DOI: 10.4018/978-1-6684-6500-4.ch012

improve instructional practices, support for student learning, and institutional resources that encourage students' retention, progression, and completion. The rise of interest among university administrators and information technology leaders is well documented in trade publications such as the Campus Computing Project's annual report (Green, 2019), and industry trend reports such as EDUCAUSE's Horizon Report for Higher Education (Pelletier et al., 2022). However, fervor about the promise of learning analytics for revolutionizing higher education that was forecast in earlier editions (e.g., Adams Becker et al., 2017) has been tempered in more recent years. In 2022, Pelletier et al. (2022, p. 9) describe "learning analytics and big data" with more reservation:

The promise of harnessing big data to improve student outcomes and increase automation of services such as the LMS has been enticing to many institutional leaders over the past five years. However, the implementation of big-data systems has not resulted in much change for campuses. Large amounts of data are collected but rarely harnessed to effect meaningful change in outcomes or even systems. Mature, institution-wide data mining strategies are needed to see progress on learning analytics and big data. Some barriers to success include student privacy and equity concerns, lack of buy-in from faculty, and investment in staff and resources for data reporting. A path forward needs to rely heavily on collaboration with all the key stakeholders at the table, including faculty, and starts with a clear vision of what big questions need to be answered.

In this paper, we address this tempered enthusiasm and document an initiative that aligns to their "path forward" by reflecting on an illustrative course-specific learning analytics initiative that was intended to enable university instructors and administrators to (1) identify which of their students are most in need of learning support, (2) leverage low-cost digital learning supports, and (3) promote timely enrollment of students into the university's existing student success programs to leverage existing resources, increase return on this investment, and improve student success. We closely document the heavy collaboration of faculty and educational psychologists, share the clear vision that guided an initiative ground to learning theory and analytics, and detail the roles and sensibilities of the key stakeholders who were indeed essential to the initiative's success. We briefly overview those empirical successes, and transition to documentation of the multiple paths forward that have been forged since the initiative began. The first is a model for sustainability and scaling within the university where the initiative was conducted. The second is a demonstration of the replicability of the course-specific learning analytics approach in a second research university context with a different student population, key performance indicators that guided the work, and distinct teaching, learning and technology infrastructures including learning management systems and instructor approaches. The third case is a contrast to the second and demonstrates a second instance of replication in a regional college context where faculty, administrative, and technology support were limited, but the initiative could be replicated in a minimally viable fashion and sustain the ability to collect and interpret learning analytics data, use it to predict achievement, and deliver timely learning support to students predicted to benefit from it. Throughout, we apply *self-regulated learning* frameworks (SRL; Pintrich, 2000; Winne & Hadwin, 1998; Zimmerman, 2000) as a theoretical lens that informs the interpretation of students' engagement with resources in the LMS and how such framing produces *learning events* (Bernacki, 2018) that can be engineered to reflect learning processes, interpret prediction models, and guide the design of digital resources to support learning.

BACKGROUND

Institution-Level Learning Analytics: "Early Warning" Products

One of the most prominent learning analytics methods is the use of tabular and event data about learner characteristics and behaviors to predict a learning outcome (Brooks & Thompson, 2017). Prediction modeling is a pragmatic method that can allow researchers with access to such data to observe how learners' characteristics and behavior patterns associate with levels of achievement, and models can be developed to identify those students whose behaviors are predictive of undesirable outcomes (Gardner & Brooks, 2018). To the degree that prediction models rely only on the earliest of events within a learning task, these models can be tuned to provide accurate predictions about student outcomes with sufficient notice that instructors could use model results to identify and support students who appear to struggle. These kinds of "early warning systems" are well represented in the learning analytics literature (e.g., Arnold & Pistilli, 2012; Bernacki, 2018, 2020a; Dawson, Jovanovic, Gašević, & Pardo, 2017; Ferguson, Clow, Macfadyen, Essa, Dawson, & Alexander, 2014; Sønderlund, Hughes, & Smith, 2018) and have become incorporated into the analytics package of many products sold as supplements to digital learning platforms sold to universities.

All early warning systems involve the development of a data model that collects information about the characteristics of the learner from educational technology platforms. These data frequently include tabular data describing learner characteristics commonly managed by to admissions departments (i.e., prior achievement in high school, demographic information, financial aid information) and university registrars (i.e., transcript data on recent prior achievement in university coursework). Many models also comprise data from university- or cloud-hosted logs of student engagement with software platforms designed to support learning. Most often, these logs capture students' use of the system in the form of logins, and accesses to learning objects that are coarsely categorized by tool type or other hard-coded meta data: download of a digital object, post to a forum, check of a gradebook, completion of a quiz, and at times, performance on lower stakes assignments. These data are often sufficient to produce reasonably accurate predictions about an eventual student learning outcome. However, two key opportunities exist to improve their impact on student success. Both reflect an insufficient consideration of the context in which learning occurs.

Potential Area for Improvement #1: A Paucity of Theory Application and the Potential Value of Aligning to a Self-Regulated Learning Framework

The first limitation in the typical approach to prediction modeling of student success is that event data are seldom considered through the lens of learning theory. Without considering the content of a learning object, the learning activity it affords, and the kinds of learning behaviors the instructor designed it to support, it is difficult to discern why such events are predictive of achievement. Models are of course predictive and not casual, but educational psychologists and faculty designers can appraise models as they reflect student use – and potential misuse – of thoughtfully designed learning objects. When student behaviors reflect deviation from the intended use of objects, interventions can guide students to learn in ways that align to instructors' intentions, which themselves align to techniques known to enhance learning and performance. Course-specific appraisal of models thus reveals clearer associations between behaviors and achievement.

A potential solution is to apply a flexible learning framework that can describe students based on their learning characteristics and how their engagement with digital resources might reflect their motivations, affective responses, or cognitive and metacognitive processes during learning (Azevedo et al., 2018). Theoretical frameworks that describe *self-regulated learning* are particularly well-suited to this approach, so long as they involve learning analytics tools managed by researchers who collaborate closely with courses designers to understand how digital events might be interpreted to reflect self-regulated *learning events* (Bernacki, 2018).

A Brief Self-Regulated Learning Primer

Theoretical models of SRL include several similar frameworks that describe the ways that students actively engage in learning tasks by regulating the motivational, cognitive, metacognitive, and affective processes that occur during learning (Panadero, 2017; Pintrich, 2000; Winne & Hadwin, 1998, Zimmerman, 2000). Many scholars have developed research methodologies to examine these SRL processes, including those who obtain traces of the activity by users of learning technology. These are logged unobtrusively while individuals engage with the content and tools on the platform (e.g., Aleven et al., 2010; Bernacki, 2018; Greene & Azevedo, 2010). More recently, researchers have begun to collect *multimodal* traces of SRL events including two channels of information, such as aligning log event data with verbal event data collected and coded through think-aloud protocols (Greene & Azevedo, 2009), to corroborate the verbalized traces of students' SRL processes to understand the SRL involved in concurrent digital traces of learning (e.g., Bernacki et al., 2022; Fan et al., 2022). These processes enable learning analytics researchers to observe the loosely sequenced, cyclical phases of the SRL model (Salehian Kia et al., 2022), including the planning, strategy enactment, monitoring, and adaptation behaviors that comprise the SRL cycle in theoretical frameworks (e.g., Winne & Hadwin, 1998).

Potential Area for Improvement #2: A Paucity of Responsive Intervention, and the Potential Value of Explainable Artificial Intelligence Methods to Develop SRL-Aligned Interventions

A second limitation to be overcome within prediction modeling research in learning analytics and educational data mining is that much effort is spent on the development of accurate prediction models, but little effort is spent deploying interventions based on them and evaluating their success. The literature is replete with impressively precise confusion matrices reflecting models with tremendous potential to identify learners in time to intervene. However, few papers describe thoughtfully designed intervention approaches that are sensitive to theory about what learning techniques are highly effective, and which of these are well-suited to a course's specific learning objectives and the content an instructor provides to help students master them (e.g., Bernacki et al., 2020a, 2020b, 2021; Cogliano et al., 2022). To optimize their effectiveness, interventions must be designed so they address the learning activities that are germane to the instructional design of the course, can be deployed in a timely fashion, and without requiring undue effort from students who can little afford to take time away from their study of course content.

Close alignment to learning theories like frameworks for self-regulated learning can afford a solution to this problem as well. When digitally traced events are understood to reflect learning processes, models that associate specific events with a measure of success or failure and with a mapping to specific learning processes can produce an *explainable artificial intelligence* solution (Khosravi et al., 2022;

Turek, 2018) informed by a learning theory like self-regulated learning. Predictive models are not causal models but can be cautiously interpreted as reflecting theory-based, potentially causal processes one might infer from learning events. These can then be treated as potentially explanatory events that inform the design of interventions that can be experimentally tested to gauge their effectiveness in supporting future learners who exhibit the behaviors that predicted poor outcomes in the training data, and that can be observed when the model is applied to current students' data.

Aims

This paper describes a multidisciplinary effort across universities to develop contextualized learning analytics solutions in large lecture STEM courses found to be critical bottlenecks in the local STEM workforce pipeline. Educational psychologists teamed with course instructors to revise the design of these courses to enhance the digital learning objects available to students to provide learning opportunities, and the LMS event data that students generate when learning with them. This collaborative instructional design allowed the team to classify learners' events in the LMS as they reflect theory-aligned learning events which were found to be predictive of achievement in the specific STEM course. Interventions were then crafted in light of learning techniques known to be effective for the objectives of the course, and that past successful students in the course confirmed were critical to their success. Details about the design and testing of models and interventions are provided, as are the organizational elements that are key to development and sustainment of the approach. Thereafter, case studies illustrate the investments that are necessary to scale such a solution within a single institution (Case 1) and across like (Case 2) and distinct institution types (Case 3) to accommodate variance in instructors, course design features, learning platforms, achievement criteria, student populations, and resources available to support student success. We close by presenting a set of regression models that predicted a measure of student success at each institution, note how self-regulated learning theory was used to build a schema for classifying these learning events as traces of the planning, monitoring, or strategy enactments described in frameworks of SRL, and how a SRL-aligned consideration of models informs future efforts to observe and support future students' learning.

METHODOLOGY

The original project, *Learning Theory and Analytics as Guides to Improve STEM Education* was supported by an external research award wherein the research team employed students' own course-specific event data in a learning management system (LMS) to predict course performance and to intervene to improve learning and achievement.

Learning Management System Events as Traces of Learning Processes

Undergraduate students utilize a learning management system (LMS) for multiple functions, and the kinds of learning processes that can be observed are dictated by course objectives and the kinds of digital learning resources instructors provide for student learning. For example, in a biology course requiring mastery of declarative knowledge about anatomical features and conceptual and procedural knowledge of physiological system functioning, students can use digital resources provided by the instructor to

Table 1. Empirically Supported Cognitive and Metacognitive Self-Regulated Learning Processes and Digital Content That Support Their Enactment

Self-regulated Learning Processes	Digital Resources in the LMS Course Site to Support Enactment
Cognitive	
[Spaced] Retrieval Practice	Chapter quizzes with item pools designed for repeated use (ungraded; provides correctness feedback, textbook reference)
Self-Explanation	Self-assessment opportunities providing prompts to self-explain & evaluate answers
Worked Examples	Annotated, diagrammatic presentation of biological systems in graphic or video form
Metacognitive	
Planning	Exam Blueprints with weighting topic & depth of knowledge
Monitoring Learning	Detailed Feedback with correctness and pointers to content areas for restudy after self-assessment completion (above)
Monitoring Progress towards Mastery	Self-assessment of Learning Goal Mastery (Editable Worksheet of Learning Goals per Chapter, Unit & level of mastery to date)
Monitoring Performance	Digital Gradebook

engage in cognitive strategies (i.e., enactment phase of the Winne & Hadwin, 1998 framework) and metacognitively monitor the standards for their learning in the learning objectives, their learning using feedback provided on interactive assignments, and on the products of their learning using gradebooks, (i.e., the COPES model, as described by Winne & Hadwin, 1998; see Table 1). Clicks on these resources produce requests to servers and events in the server logs, and these can be mined, reorganized, and tagged with these SRL event tags to produces records of learning events (Bernacki, 2018).

In addition to using SRL frameworks to classify learning events as they reflect cognitive and metacognitive SRL processes, learning scientists who engineer log data into learning events must consider how resources are hosted in technology platforms and how this influences that students' behavior that they can(not) represent with event logs. For example, it is more appropriate to model the use of downloadable files like exam blueprints as a dichotomous event that should impact learning if it occurs once (indicating that a student has obtained the file) compared to zero times (indicating the student has not). In contrast, resources designed for repeated use online, such as practice quizzes, are best captured as count data (Bernacki, 2018; Greene, Costa & Dellinger, 2011).

Data Modeling and Development of Algorithms to Predict Student Success

A key phase of the original project was to test different algorithms that could balance prediction accuracy obtained by the model, and coherence of model implementation where university data systems could record learning events in ways that could be programmed back into a model that provided the real time predictions of a student's likelihood of success that informed timely interventions. We examined implications of different representations of LMS resource use on the accuracy of prediction models, examine whether the most accuracy model predicts performance in subsequent samples, and whether the model can provide a basis for alerting students about their potential for poor achievement (Bernacki et al., 2020a).

For the biology course described above, prediction modeling involved data extracted from server logs of users' learning events in the LMS from the first four weeks of the course (i.e., prior to any exam). Early warnings could then be generated and sent in time for learners to adjust tactics or seek help a full week prior to their first unit exam (i.e., in Week 5). Events were aggregated and enriched using Splunk, a platform for search and modeling of machine data, and tables of metadata about content items. Classification of items into resource types was handled by human research programmers. Models were built and evaluated in RapidMiner. We compared models that involved different levels of aggregation of learning events (i.e., count, dichotomous representations per content items and classes of resources) and tested different temporal aggregations (i.e., the day or week of the semester). These combinations of feature classes were submitted to algorithms including forward selection logistic regressions, decision trees (J-48, J-Rip), Naïve Bayes, and K-Star. Models were cross validated using k-fold methods (usually with 10 folds). With data from an initial semester of learners (roughly 325) and with a focus on the recall metric within confusion matrices, we settled on the use of a forward selection logistic regression that could identify 4 of 5 (^{3} 80%) students likely to fail to obtain the B average needed to move forward to the next course in the biology sequence for health science majors (i.e., the goal of most students enrolled).

Sustainability and Generalizability of the Prediction Model

Sustainability of Model Accuracy Over Multiple Semesters

We monitored drift in the course over the subsequent semesters of biology students and refit the model once when adjustments to course materials warranted. Examination of model accuracy for students in our control group (i.e., those predicted as eligible for intervention but who were only tracked and did not receive an intervention) indicated that were able to sustain a lower bound of 75% accurate recall over the three years when the prediction model was applied in the course, as evidenced by confusion matrix reports. The modeling approach was later extended to a Calculus and an Engineering course. A similar level of prediction accuracy was achieved with the same feature engineering approach, despite changes in the number of weeks available to collect learning events and sparser digital content in some course sites. These models also demonstrated that, when instructional design features, including digital course content and assessment practices, were held constant across multiple course sections and taught by different instructors of record (i.e., a master LMS course site is developed, and instructors adopt identical course pacing, exam timings, items, and scoring), prediction models can maintain their accuracy (Bernacki et al., 2020a).

Intervention to Support Students Predicted to Struggle

Students whose LMS data informed the prediction model were classified a week before their first exams via logistic regression as likely to obtain a B or Better in the course or likely to obtain a C or worse and need to re-enroll again next semester. Because such models are diagnostic but not causal, intervention efforts were not tailored to model features. Rather, students were encouraged to consider adopting (or developing) learning strategies known to promote achievement on tasks aligned with course learning objectives. Students with prediction values indicating a grade of C or Worse was likely (i.e., > 0) were randomized into a Control group that received a message from the instructor (Figure 1; first and last lines only) that reminded them about the upcoming exam, or to an Intervention group whose message also

Figure 1. Resource Sheet for LMS System

A Check-in on your learning !

Hi [Name]!

Our first course exam is coming up in a week or so.

[I'm a little concerned that you might not score so well because of the way you've been using the resources provided on WebCampus so far this semester.]

I want to check-in to make sure each student is on top of our content, learning in appropriate ways, and able to perform well. So, I'd like to direct you to two resources that can help you with learning the material in our course:

1. The first is a one-page summary of advice from students who have completed the course in the past.
   These students each passed the course with an excellent grade, and they have shared some of the strategies that helped them perform well in the course.
2. A set of learning modules called "The Science of Learning to Learn."
   These modules describe learning strategies you can use with our course materials. Each has been shown to help college students learn in the past, and students who completed this training scored about 4 points better on their exams afterwards.

Both resources can be found on the [LMS] course site under the **STEM Learning Resources** link in the left panel (and provided in this announcement, below).

I hope you find that these resources help you to learn and perform well!

Dr. [NAME]

recommended an advice page (entirety of Figure 1 and link to Figure 2 content; Bernacki et al., 2020a). Students could also access a training program called the *Science of Learning to Learn* (Bernacki et al., 2020b, Figure 3) that provides roughly two-hours of independent, digital training to develop students' cognitive learning strategies and ability to self-regulate their learning by considering their course, developing a plan, enacting the strategies they identified as likely to help them reach a learning goal, and monitoring and adapting this process over the course of the semester (Winne & Hadwin, 1998). Those who received the intervention message and accessed the advice resources (56%) significantly outperformed Control students on subsequent exams in Biology (*ds* = .2 to .4; Bernacki et al., 2020a) and Mathematics (*ds* [3] .6 Hong & Bernacki 2018). These findings were sufficiently encouraging that efforts were made to scale the prediction modeling efforts to additional learning contexts at new institutions, and to use the insights drawn from prediction processes to consider causal relations between behaviors and outcomes that could inform intervention designs.

In the years that followed, the initiative leaders pursued both internal supports to sustain the initiative and broaden its impact on the academic success of the local undergraduate population, as well as to expand their research into methods of improving their methods for collaboratively designing courses with discipline-based educational researchers who also teach and wish to study their own large lecture courses. Having summarized an exemplar case that validates the prognosis in the 2022 Horizon Report (Pelletier et al., 2022), we next elaborate three cases that introduce the way forward for learning analytics to sustain and scale after an initial stakeholder community develops an initiative (Case 1), and how stakeholder communities that span multiple higher education solutions can adapt the practices of demonstration cases to suit the aspirations and resources of their research (Case 2) and regional (Case 3) higher education institutions.

Figure 2. Students Were Asked to Reflect on Their Experience Learning in Their Anatomy and Physiology Lecture Courses

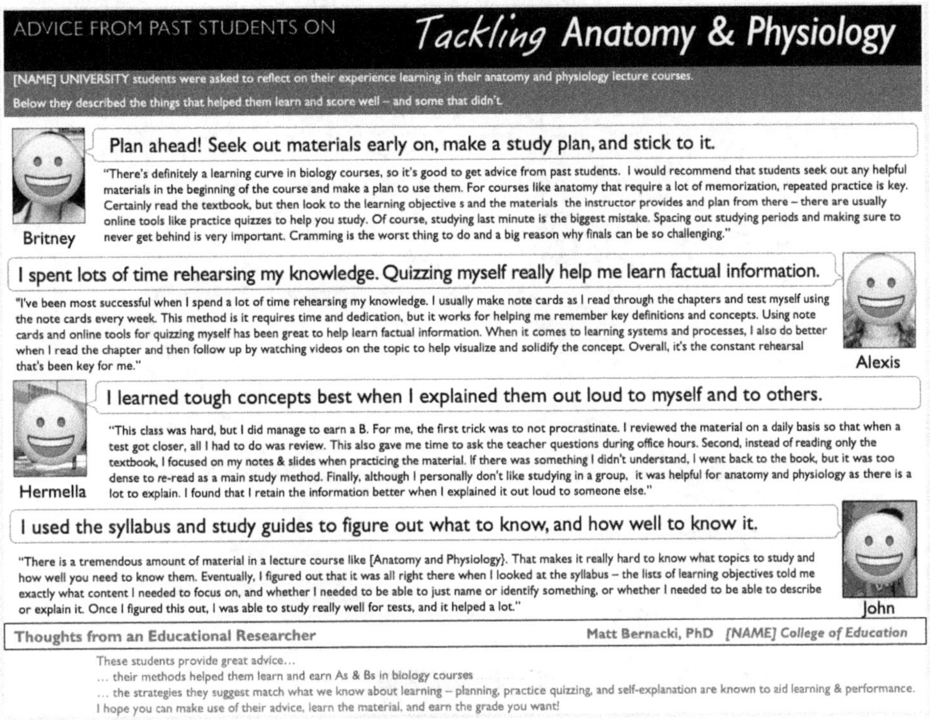

SCALABILITY CASE #1: GENERALIZING A LEARNING ANALYTICS RESEARCH SOLUTION TO A UNIVERSITY LEARNING ANALYTICS INITIATIVE

The University Context

At the large public university where the learning analytics research solution was developed, the student body is largely comprised of first-generation college students who graduated from low-resource high schools (i.e., receiving supplemental federal funding via U.S. Title 1 grants) and who hail from ethnic groups that are historically under-represented in higher education and STEM fields. Issues with academic achievement and retention, progression, and completion of degree programs are pronounced challenges, and university leadership sought to leverage local learning analytics research to address a university's need. Campus stakeholders were gathered by the provost and the research team, and a partnership spanning course instructors, Information Technology, and Online Education offices were assembled to scale the research solution to serve students in ten courses.

Figure 3. Modules for Optimized Learning

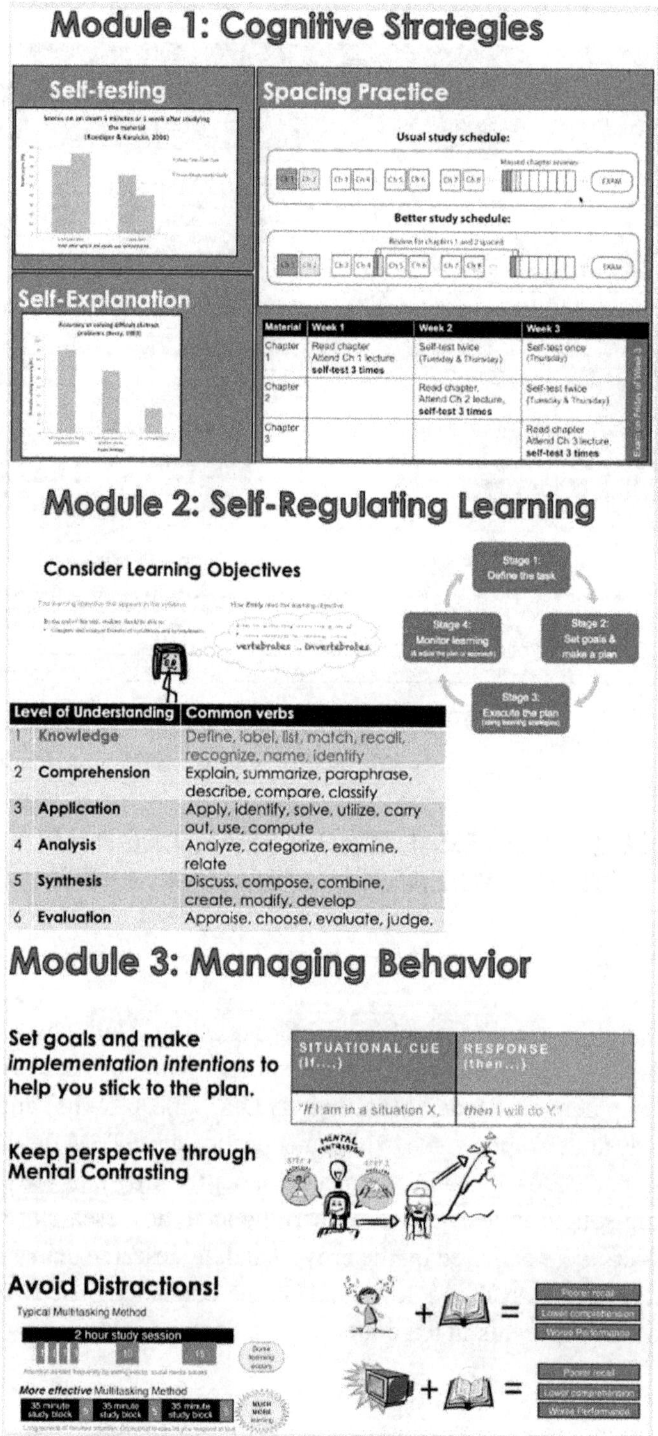

Scaling Components to Convert Research Effort to a University-Wide Initiative

Staffing the Initiative

A staff of three individuals composed the Learning Analytics Initiative team (LAI; noted by * in Table 2). This group worked with campus stakeholders in existing units to replicate and extend a scope of work that involved instructional design efforts in each course, a common data infrastructure serving all courses, and a feature engineering, data mining, and prediction modeling process per course. Interventions specific to courses followed.

Course Selection

Candidate courses were first selected from those with the largest impact on university retention progression and completion metrics. The Provost's Office provided a list of courses with high enrollment and high rates of grades awarded that delayed students' progress toward the major. An exemplar subset appears in Table 3. The top 20 courses were then cross-examined for their current potential to provide features predictive of achievement, using digital content items already on LMS course sites. Content items reflect current development efforts and could be supplemented with instructional design support to digitize existing print materials, link textbook content, or design new learning objects. Thereafter, assessment format and consistency (i.e., alignment to objectives, common exam item pool across instructors and course sections) were confirmed to ensure a robust and sustainable course design so the learning analytics implementation could be achieved.

Instructional Design to Sustain Features Predicting a Fixed Criterion Variable

When instructor groups responsible for course delivery agreed to partner with the LAI to support their students, they agreed to a collaborative evaluation of their assessment process, involving the alignment of exam format and items to instructional objectives listed in the course, and the design or acquisition of digital and print materials that addressed these objectives. This is a common instructional design process but was new and intriguing for many in disciplines where formal instructional design training was not a requirement during preparation for a faculty role. The lead course instructor and LAI instructional designer effectively produced a master course that provided a standardized digital offering across all sections of the face-to-face, large-lecture course. This master course was to be used and unchanged for the two years of the initiative, after which course revision could be undertaken and prediction models could be refit as needed. This afforded protection of instructors' academic freedom – they could teach however they wished within the course schedule during course meetings – and simply adhered to the course schedule and design established by their department and required to ensure the durability of the learning analytics infrastructure (i.e., the digital component of the course – the LMS course site).

Planning to Adapt to Change: Iterative Redesign, Partnership, and Redundancy

Universities are dynamic instructional contexts. Student enrollments fluctuate, degree program requirements and course policies shift, and the instructional goals of courses must adapt to accommodate new demands of students and programs, as well as new opportunities provided by learning technologies (e.g.,

Table 2. Organizational Chart for the Learning Analytics Initiative

Position	Scope of Work	Affiliation	Effort
Learning Science Team			
Faculty Director*	Advise on digital course enrichment, feature engineering, prediction modeling; lead grant writing, academic presentations & publications	College of Education	Course release or equivalent
Learning Scientist*	Liaison with faculty and units providing learning support. Oversee initial development of prediction models and coordination of learning supports. Lead evaluation of effectiveness of learning supports (i.e., on course grade & completion; RPC metrics).	College of Education	100% FTE; postdoctoral scholar with learning sciences background
Instructional Team			
Course instructor	(Previously) develop digital course materials; maintain a master course over multiple semesters so that prediction can be conducted; message students predicted to perform poorly	Home Academic Department	None
Instructional Design Graduate Assistant*	Support Learning Scientist; Conduct individual consultations with faculty partners; lead build, maintenance and inventory of digital contents enriched for target courses	College of Education (EPHE Dept)	12-month Graduate Assistantship
System Management Team			
Data Modeler	develop and maintain data ingestion infrastructure; build, validate, and maintain a data model per course; assist in prediction modeling; lead build of infrastructure to calculate student success projections to inform learning support.	IT Operations	25% FTE; IT Specialist, Operations or Institutional research
IT Support	Support Data Scientist; conduct ongoing integrity checking of existing models; assist in building of new data models, troubleshooting, and data management.	IT Operations	Hourly, work study or wage worker

new content, or features provided by a publisher) or developments in the field (e.g., new content that must be covered to provide a relevant, contemporary course). The course redesign and learning analytics refitting process accommodated most of these design challenges, but additional plans needed to be made to accommodate changes in staffing within the LAI, instructional group delivering supported courses,

Table 3. Courses with Highest Total Enrollment and DFW Rate with Digital Content Count

Course	Title	Enrollment	Digital Content Items
English	Composition I	2049	95
Math	College Algebra	1442	33
Philosophy	Critical Thinking & Reasoning	1301	0
Political Science	Introduction to American Politics	1100	50
Sociology	Principles of Sociology	967	131
Psychology	General Psychology	962	75
Communications	Oral Communication	853	135
Developmental Math 1	Elementary, Algebra	1143	20
Developmental Math 2	Intermediate Algebra	1195	15
Biology	Fundamentals of Life Science	725	105

and campus units providing data services and student support. To ensure activities could continue uninterrupted in the event that a member of the Initiative left to assume a new role, redundancies were built into each Initiative team (Table 2). In addition, a master documentation infrastructure was maintained using the campus' collaboration platform. This required specific tasking of lead individuals per team to maintain documentation and the preservation of a version history to ensure redundancy of these materials to offset periodic file loss, as is common in collaborative work.

Funding the Initiative and Partnering to Scale Student Support

Whereas research solutions rely on external support to address research questions that align to the agenda of a program, the LAI was funded entirely with existing University resources. The provost redirected existing funds generated by course technology fees to employ a postdoctoral Learning Scientist who could manage the project under the Director, who received releases from teaching to support the other instructor-partners who subscribed to LAI services. Graduate students pursuing relevant degrees were hired to assistantships to support instructional design. These components of the initiative are critical to the SRL-theory-aligned components of the course, and the effort required to administer learning analytics solutions needs to be scaled for each additional course enrolled in the initiative. Thereafter, a substantial infrastructure is already in place in this institution and many others, which make the adoption and scaling of such initiatives plausible, once a funding model is achieved for the Learning Science component of the staffing plan described above and atop Table 2.

Because offices of Information Technology already possess infrastructure to observe LMS event logs, they could provide data, trouble shooting, and reporting services within their core business offerings to campus; current employees' time managing these existing data was allotted accordingly. The efforts of the Intervention Team are again comprised of pre-existing campus units that offer learning support to students (e.g., Academic Success Centers who offer coaching and tutoring, and units that offer course specific supplemental instruction. Fully digital interventions could be maintained by the Office of Online Education and administered at close to zero cost by simply enrolling future learners into LMS courses that housed intervention materials like the learning skill training program described in Figure 3.

Evaluating the Initiative, and Return on the Provost's Investment

The Learning Analytics Initiative was initially funded for a two-year period, which afforded the opportunity to develop digital content and assessments, initial data collection and prediction modeling, then semesters of master course delivery during which prediction models could be applied and interventions provided. In these semesters, course achievement metrics from periods following interventions (i.e., subsequent exam performance, course performance, re-enrollment data) are monitored to examine the effectiveness of the interventions and inform decisions about returns on nearly costless (i.e., digital, scalable interventions, Figure 1 and 2) versus resource-intensive interventions. Summatively, the collective impact of the Learning Analytics Initiative can be observed by plotting achievement and retention metrics across semesters and examining the overall impact as well as the impact for target populations (e.g., first-generation college students). These data can inform whether the Initiative should receive continued or expanded university support.

CASE 1: PRODUCTS AND RESULTS

Two ingredients are essential for a prediction algorithm to provide accurate predictions across multiple sections of a university course: (1) a consistent set of digital learning objects that inform the predictive model that are deployed in the course from one semester to the next, and (2) a uniform assessment approach that retains a criterion variable to be predicted. In addition to ensuring the quality of prediction modeling in courses, these elements serve as process measures for evaluation that indicate courses are achieving the richness of instructional opportunities targeted in recent prominent instructional design position papers (i.e., President's Council report on undergraduate STEM education; Olsen & Riordan, 2012) and position papers that argue for consistency and rigor in higher education assessment practices (Campbell, Dortch & Burt, 2018).

In order to ensure that the prediction model we develop in our initial course partnerships can retain its predictive accuracy in future semesters, we partnered with the instructional faculty who teach a target course to co-design a mastery set of digital resources. Instructors developed a common set of instructional objectives that were essential for students to master and established a consistent set of topics to be covered within an exam period. The timing of coverage varied slightly based on the lecture schedule (e.g., days of week, number and length of sessions). Instructors adopted a common set of digital resources students could access to plan their study (e.g., unit study guides), monitor their progress towards mastery (e.g., learning objectives checklists, self-assessment quizzes populated with publisher content), and consume resources that align to lecture topics. Slide decks that aligned to the lecture were consistent in their number to preserve their scope of contribution to the digital learning resources. Importantly, instructors decided that the ability to exercise one's intellectual freedom was critical to obtaining initial buy-in. No one was interested in teaching directly from someone else's uneditable materials, and the group proposed that affording future instructors full ownership of the lecture sessions was critical to ensuring that others would be willing to instruct within the bounds of a course designated for prediction modeling and student success interventions.

In addition to aligning the curriculum and the learning resources meant to support student learning and achievement, instructors also collaborated to align their assessment instruments. With the help of learning analysts, instructors designed tables of specifications that identified critical learning objectives to be assessed, the number of items needed to assess them, and the level of understanding each would assess. Once consensus was reached, pools of candidate items were obtained from publisher test banks and archived exams, and instructors generated additional items to fill gaps in the bank where extant items did not address learning objectives. Instructors were able to generate multiple forms for each section to diminish the potential for academic dishonesty when exams were scheduled with time for students in earlier sessions to debrief with their peers in later ones.

Psychometric analyses of initial assessments confirmed that exams were highly internally reliable (Cronbach's alphas > .8), and when instructors designed and adhered to tables of specifications that determined the coverage of exams by topic and level of understanding described by the learning objectives assessed on exams, exam means, and distributions were consistent across sections of the course taught by instructor groups (Bernacki et al., 2020b). These assessment features, when considered alongside the consistent set of digital resources available to students across sections, demonstrate a consistent and high-quality of the educational experience for students. This ensures equity in the instruction delivered to students enrolled across multiple sections of the partner course and provides future instructors greater confidence that grades based on aligned exams can be relied upon to reflect whether their incoming students have had a known level of exposure to and mastery of prerequisite knowledge they will need to rely on when teaching more advanced topics in later courses. While not the focus of a learning analytics initiative, these essential ingredients improve the quality of instruction, and help partner courses align with the university's educational mission.

SCALABILITY CASES 2 AND 3

Generalizing a Learning Analytics Research Solution Across Multiple University and Technology Contexts

The focus of this multi-university generalizability project was described to the funder as aiming to support, retain, and increase the achievement of undergraduates who traditionally do not persist in STEM majors (e.g., underrepresented minority groups, first-generation college students) by (1) applying an existing data-driven solution to identify struggling STEM learners before they begin to fail, (2) developing targeted, effective achievement and retention interventions combining the expertise of two universities who are leading sources of empirically supported approaches for STEM success, and (3) demonstrating the applicability of these solutions to a variety of higher education contexts.

The primary benefits to this generalizability effort are to provide higher education institutions with a proof of concept that learning analytics solutions developed at one institution can be adapted and employed at another, and to provide exemplar cases such that leadership of any future institution can select an exemplar that most closely mirrors their own institutional features and design their learning analytics solutions accordingly. This model further allows each institution to conduct a self-study of the resources available for collecting data on student learning (i.e., their LMS and other technologies for student support), their access to these data (Table 4), and their existing intervention resources that can be efficiently directed to support their students' success when prediction models identify students whose learning event data suggest a need for learning support.

The primary challenges to scaling such a learning analytics solution are three-fold. The first is to establish an appropriate collaborative stakeholder group similar to the one needed to scale the research solution in Case 1. The latter challenge is to map the data collection and prediction modeling solution to new learning management systems and data infrastructures that capture and can afford the prediction of achievement using students' learning events. Whereas the first challenge is covered sufficiently in Case 1, Cases 2 and 3 require a description of the variability in campus infrastructure for data collection and modeling, and the various software contracts that dictate which LMSs university instructors can use. Further, different institutions serve different student populations and are staffed by instructors with different levels of commitment to the university (i.e., tenure-track and teaching-track faculty, adjunct instructors, etc.). Attention must thus be paid to partnerships with instructional units, so that they can design, sustain, and thoughtfully iterate through an established instructional design plan that guides course objectives, content, and assessment required to initiate and continue employing a learning analytics solution. A final challenge is to revisit the self-regulated learning frameworks that guided the development of learning analytics solutions and use these and the algorithms they generate to inform the kinds of interventions that instructors might adopt or design to meet the needs of struggling students.

Profiles of Project Partner Institutions

Three institutions came together to propose and ultimately undertake this scope of work: Institution 1 is the same research university where the initial efforts took place, and the second wave of learning analytics research and implementation were embedded within the scope described in Case 1.

Case 2 is a second research university that serves as a flagship campus for a university system. Admission is selective, and students tend to enter the university having achieved high GPAs in high school, and many have completed advanced placement and similar college-oriented courses prior to enrollment. This second research university has a decorated teaching faculty whose efforts to deliver high structure, active learning course experiences predated the grant and were readily adaptable to the co-design and prediction modeling phases of the project. The information technology capacity of the second research university exceeds the first, and the IT team were able to staff the data modeler and IT support roles (Table 4) as part of their core business offerings to campus partners, at zero cost to the project. This cost savings afforded opportunities to grow the learning sciences team and engage in additional feature engineering to produce digital traces of learning that more precisely describe self-regulated learning processes, and that produced more accurate prediction models than could be achieved in the original initiative, as we document in the results section.

Case 3 is a contrasting case of a regional institution that serves a similar student body to Case 1, and many students who attend one often take classes at the other institution. The regional university is a member institution of the state system of higher education and serves a large enrollment of students who pursue two and four year degrees, often while working full time and attending to familial responsibilities including primary caregivers. Students here are predominantly first-generation college students, and the institution enrolls many adult learners. The faculty at this institution are primarily full-time and the balance of their effort is primarily on teaching, with minimal levels of research or service. Given the higher teaching load, they have less ability to act as committed stakeholders to research and development initiatives as described in the Horizon Report's (Pelletier et al., 2002) characterization of learning analytics projects. As a result, this case required a leaner approach that could be achieved with limited faculty involvement outside the semester, a smaller, cheaper data infrastructure, and staffing by an educational technology team that had less capacity to treat the project as a core business service.

In the following section and Table 4, we summarize the key features of the learning analytics initiative as instantiated at each institution. In Table 5, we further document the data infrastructure the teams were able to develop, and the prediction models that differ in their content but rely on analogous biology-course-specific raw data collected from students who use resources on the course learning management system site to predict a key achievement outcome that influences their progression through their chosen degree plan.

Considering Campus Infrastructure for Data Collection and Modeling

Across the three universities that serve as research sites for this generalizability project, learning management systems varied, and included LMS-A, LMS-C, and LMS-B. Further, the capacity of each institution's infrastructure, personnel, expertise, and budget for information technology platforms and personnel within operations management units varied considerably. These institutional uniquenesses led to variations in project staffing, as well as to the design of data collection and modeling platforms, even when two institutions supported the same LMS. To illustrate how these differences impacted the generalizability

Table 4. Institutional, Team and Design Features of Learning Analytics Initiatives across Three Partner Sites

Feature	Case 1: Research University	Case 2: Research University	Case 3: Regional College
Institution			
Enrollment	>31,000	>30,000	>44,000
Study Body Served	State institution, designated Minority-Serving Institution (MSIs), Hispanic-Serving Institution (HSI), and Asian American and Native American Pacific Islander-Serving Institution (AANAPISI), predominantly first-generation college students who pursue 4-year degrees; acceptance rate = 81%	State institution, Predominantly White enrollment (60%), 18% first generation college students; acceptance rate = 25%,	State institution, A designated Minority-Serving Institution (MSIs), Hispanic-Serving Institution (HSI) and Asian American and Native American Pacific Islander-Serving Institution (AANAPISI); predominantly first-generation college students who pursue 2- and 4-year degrees; open admission
Team			
Instructional Team	Full-time teaching faculty member as lead, with team of 4-6 teaching faculty instructors who maintain and deliver a master course design that holds pace, topic, activity and assessment constant	Full-time teaching faculty member as lead, with team of 4 full-time instructors who maintain and deliver a master course design that holds pace, topic, activity and assessment design constant	Full-time teaching faculty member as lead; additional instructors allowed students to participate through the laboratory, but did not co-design
Learning Sciences Team	Learning Sciences faculty member as lead, additional faculty members in education and quantitative psychology, postdoctoral researcher and graduate research assistants (2)	Learning Sciences faculty member as lead, additional faculty member in education, postdoctoral researcher and graduate research assistant (1)	Learning Sciences Faculty from Case 2 institution as site lead; periodic support from graduate student from institution at Case 2
System Management Team	Data Modeler, as lead; LMS consultant, IT support from a core IT data group	Data Modeler as lead; LMS consultant, IT support from a core IT data group	e-learning designer as lead; ad-hoc customer support from data modeling tool provider, outsourced central IT
Design			
Course	Introductory Biology	Introductory Biology	Anatomy and Physiology
Outcome to be Predicted	A or B vs. C or worse; Final Exam	A or B vs. C or worse; Course Grade	A or B or C vs. D or worse; Exam 1
Raw data available to predict	LMS-B course events + digital textbook companion activity	LMS-C course events	LMS-C course events

of the project, the parallel methods of tracing the same learning events are summarized in Table 5. The first column illustrates the nature of an event obtained from logs of servers hosting the LMS-A utilized in the original learning analytics solution. The methods required to collect the same events on LMS-B appear in the second column. The third and fourth columns demonstrate data collection methods for gathering the same learning events from cloud-hosted instances of LMS-C but accessed through different methods. The LMS-C Data API was chosen by the 4-year institution where the LMS-A model was first built. This university changed LMS providers after the project and required a new data collection

Table 5. Learning Events Obtained from LMS-A, LMS-B, and LMS-C-Data and LMS-C-Events Data Infrastructures

Key Values	SRL Process	Where found in LMS-A (From Server Logs)	LMS-B (log)	LMS-C-Events (log)	LMS-C-Data (API Tables)
Timestamp	temporally ordered event	in each event in log (date, HH:MM:SS)	Same	Same	available in request table
Student identifier	student-initiated event	LMS specific "duid"; can be matched via lookup to student ID	Same	user_id in Body of JSON formatted events	available in request table
Course, Section identifier	context-specific event	available in each server event as a registrar-provided value (lookup table)	Same	Same	available in request table
Navigation (links, folders)	context-specific event	GET request for specific "content_id" (metadata human coded)	Same	Same	available in request table
Downloading syllabus	planning course engagement	GET request, content_id	syllabus.read event in log	appears as asset. accessed	available in request table
Download of study guide	planning future study	GET request, content_id	webcontent. Read event	appears as asset. accessed	available in request table
Use of Ungraded Self-assessment quizzes	rehearsal, monitoring learning	GET request "assessment_id" value; Note: this is a limitation of the server log approach, as assessment_id events collapse attempts at items and review of feedback on items into a single type of logged event.	Assessment. Event Metadata: assessment table (score)	appears as asset. accessed event with dedicated identifier for course	event in request table; metadata in Quiz_ submission_fact
Checking gradebook	monitoring performance	Identify GET request with specific, hard-coded tool_id for Gradebook (i.e., same identifier is applied in all courses, making this event simpler to capture than course-specific content)	gradebook. StudentView event	asset.accessed event	event in request table; metadata in grading_ period_score_ fact

solution to sustain two additional research projects and to scale the original learning analytics solution into a service to meet university demand for data-driven student support (i.e., Case 1). The final partner on the generalizability project also utilized a cloud-hosted instance of LMS-C but had a pre-existing need to capture learning event data via a different data modeling tool – LMS-C Events – that informed software for accessibility and learner accommodations. Unlike LMS-C Data, the LMS-C Events API infrastructure captures only a subset of user activity.

CASE 2 AND 3: ADDITIONAL PRODUCTS AND RESULTS

Scaling the Initiative Across Research Universities and to a Regional College

Four years into our efforts to scale the original learning analytics solution, these challenges have largely been overcome, and an initiative is in place at each institution that includes one or more courses that have been co-designed by an instructor and learning sciences team, a data model that logs students' learning events and enriches them with labels that reflect students' self-regulated learning processes, and a prediction model is in place that can be applied incoming semesters for students who consent to share their data, and who may wish to receive learning support. Table 6 demonstrates the features of each algorithm that accurately classify students into groups of those achieving or failing to achieve the targeted performance on the key outcome variable selected by faculty. Across institutions, the models consistently achieve the sensitivity necessary to identify the majority of students who would benefit from learning support and do so in advance of the first exam administered in the course (see *sensitivity* which reflects the percent of the students who ultimately achieved the undesirable outcome that were identified by the prediction model, Table 6 row 4; *Model Performance*). This sensitivity, achieved within a prediction window this brief and early, provides enough time to identify learners who might benefit from support, deliver advice, learning skill training, or referrals to existing campus services like general academic coaching or course-specific supplemental instruction.

Abstracting Common SRL Themes From Cases and Their Potential for Scalability

In each institution described in these cases, the characteristics of their student enrollment, course subjects, and instructional design features varied. So too did the LMS platform where such materials were hosted, and the data logging infrastructure that recorded learners' use of the tools and content that instructors provided. Despite these differences, the metadata that are produced when log data are reconsidered through the lens of SRL theory to treat them as SRL events provides an opportunity to observe the commonality in the SRL-aligned variables that predict success in early, large enrollment STEM courses. The first common predictor was a test of students' prior knowledge which, when administered predicted a substantial amount of variance in students' outcomes. This knowledge reflects an *affordance* that learners bring with them to the task environment and is considered a learner characteristic in SRL models like the COPES model (Winne & Hadwin, 1998). Thereafter, *task affordances* include the resources provided by instructors that afford opportunities to engage in metacognitive planning or monitoring or to enact cognitive strategies using the resources. Across courses, learners could access materials that provided novel information they needed to acquire to master the declarative and conceptual knowledge indicated by learning objectives, and they could rehearse that knowledge using quizzes that afforded retrieval practice opportunities. When quizzes were ungraded and hosted in ways that autoscored students' answers, those same resources could afford formative assessment opportunities, and the feedback they provide could inform learners' metacognitive monitoring judgements about their own learning (i.e., interactive quizzes in Cases 1, 2, and 3 in Table 6). Students who use interactive quizzes may produce *evaluations* about the *products* of their *cognitions* and *operations* during learning, given *standards* established for content mastery, illustrating the SRL processes described in the COPES model (Winne & Hadwin, 1998). Those judgments could inform adaptation in learning processes over time, where students adapt their strategy selection, or choose to seek help within the course, or from services on campus (e.g., attend biology tutoring or access coaching services at a Learning Center; Case 2 in Table 6).

Table 6. Prediction Model Features by Case

	Case 1	Case 2	Case 3
Classification	A or B vs. C or Worse (Final Grade)	A or B vs. C or Worse (Final Exam)	A or B or C vs. Worse (Exam 1)
Observation window	2 weeks (Exam 1 in Week 3 or 4)	3weeks (Exam 1 in Week 4 or 5)	1 week (Exam 1 in Week 3)
Prediction algorithm	Logistic Regression	LASSO Regression	Logistic Regression
Model performance	73% accuracy, 79% sensitivity (base rate =51%) K =.37	73% accuracy, 71% sensitivity (base rate =51%) K =.37	67% accuracy, 79% sensitivity (base rate =69%)
Predictors in model	Prior knowledge (score on a pretest) Module view (week before course; contain information, links, resources) Announcement view (Week 1; views of announcements) Assignment view (Week 1; views of detailed descriptions of course assignments) External tool view (Week 1; use of links to access external resources, e.g., e-text) Files view (Week 1; number of file attachments opened to view in browser) Grades view (Week 1; visit to the grade book that displays assignments, scores) All behaviors (Week 1; total number of events in LMS site) Discussion topic view (Week 2; views of posts in discussion forum)	Prior knowledge (score on a pretest) Download of Lesson 0 lecture slides (which described key course features) Forum Question event (indicating students asking or answering questions) Download of Lesson 3 lecture slides Saved submission of Guided Reading Questions #1 Download Guided Reading Question set 7 Attend review session provided by Peer Mentors View assignment instructions for Guided Reading Question set 1 Attend 1:1 writing coaching at the Learning Center Download of Lesson 0 group assignment (for in-class discussions) Submission of Guided Reading Questions 4 Attend one-on-one peer mentoring session with Biology tutor Revision of Guided Reading Question Set 4 submission Revision of Guided Reading Question Set 1 submission Access course calendar on Learning Management System course site Download of package of all Course Outlines	*No prior knowledge given* Views of Chapter 1 Learning Outcomes Attempted Chapter 1 Practice Quiz Total views of Chapter 4 Outline Views of Helpful Chapter 1 Videos Distinct Count Views/ Attempts: Chapter Learning Objective Sets Chapter Outlines Practice Quizzes
Self-regulated learning processes afforded by resources included in algorithm	Measures of learner characteristics; Enactment/Behavioral Engagement (information acquisition); Metacognitive Monitoring	Measures of learner characteristics; Planning (using advanced organizers, calendars); Enactment/Behavioral Engagement Strategies (information acquisition; self-testing; help-seeking)	Planning (using Learning Objectives, Outcomes, Outlines); Enactment/Behavioral Engagement Strategies (information acquisition; self-testing) Metacognitive Monitoring

FUTURE RESEARCH DIRECTIONS

Scaling Up Learning Analytics Within an Institution

These cases overview scalability considerations in one institutional context and the way variants in infrastructure across contexts pose challenges to the generalizability of a single solution. Hundreds of learning analytics solutions are in place in higher education, but few are evaluated for their effectiveness

(Sønderlund, Hughes, & Smith, 2018). More exemplar cases need to be evaluated to identify principles that can inform design, and so that learning analytics solutions are worth scaling. From our development process and early efforts to scale and replicate a solution, we share some specific lessons we learned that can serve others aiming to adopt and scale similar learning analytics solutions in additional learning contexts, customize their solution, and maintain their fidelity once established (Table 5).

Scaling Up Across Multiple Institutions

Each institution's local context will pose challenges to the development and sustainment of a learning analytics initiative. Scaling such an initiative to one or more new contexts poses additional challenges as features of additional campuses differ in ways that will force changes in the composition of the stakeholder group that runs the project, the institutional needs and priorities the project addresses, and the campus systems that compose the learning analytics infrastructure. Some of these adaptations can be achieved systematically such as bridging to new data systems that afford similar resources to observe learning events via different data fields (i.e., Table 5). Others are more nuanced, and require that learning analytics leaders develop policy, and management skills more often possessed by university administrators rather than researchers. Table 7 and 8 highlight some of the challenges to be navigated when scaling an existing learning analytics solution to a novel university context.

Table 7. Lessons Learned from Prediction Modeling, Intervention, and Replication Studies: Initial Site

Lesson	Insights and Implications
Start with instructional design and work closely with instructors.	Learning about instructors' goals and designing content and assessments accordingly increases course quality and prediction accuracy. Well-designed master courses can be easily replicated to ensure consistency, minimizing variability that undermines predictions. Maintaining an active partnership limits drift in course design and implementation.
Satisfice when choosing a prediction algorithm.	A model needs to produce accurate predictions and to also be programmable in order to produce them in real time. Simpler algorithms ease implementation in data models and enable timely action.
During model selection, select criteria for judging accuracy pragmatically.	The purpose of the prediction model dictates how accuracy should be appraised. For example, identifying those likely to fail was critical and our intervention was not so costly that overapplication is a problem. Choosing a model with high recall was important to identify those needing support, and the risk was small: lower precision meant only that we suggested learning resources to some who did not need them.

CONCLUSION

Administrators at higher education institutions are under increasing pressure to embrace learning analytics to address institutional challenges. This provides opportunities for teams of learning scientists, instructors and information technology stakeholders to develop initiatives that (1) produce new scholarship on teaching and learning that can refine learning theories as they are observed in authentic settings, and at scale (2) contribute to the university's educational mission. This project provides evidence that, within the university, a systematic approach to partnership with faculty members that begins with collaborative instructional design and assessment yields data that can inform learning analytics models. When those models are further interpreted through an SRL framework, insights can be derived that make models

Table 8. Lessons learned when scaling a learning analytics project to additional institutions

Lesson	Insights and Implications
Institutional policies will dictate implementation, Analytics policies must emerge	Policies around data governance (i.e., ownership of data systems, their contents), and use (i.e., interpretation of FERPA guidelines, IRB decisions about risk, data sharing) differ by institution, and learning analytics projects need to adapt to abide the data climate on campus. Emerging learning analytics policy resources such as the SHEILA Framework (Tsai, et al., 2018a, 2018b) and a manual for use by policy makers (Gašević & Tsai, 2019) can serve as tools for planning and self-study by the learning analytics group, and institutional leaders.
Determine what is "core business" and what is not, and budget accordingly	The organizational theory that governs information technology differs by campus, and the implications for learning analytics are immense. IT can be centralized, distributed, or both. Core services can be provided to the whole campus at no additional cost or itemized. Some can be subcontracted and thus not adjustable in their delivery. Learning how to work within the structure of campus IT and culturing a collaborative relationship is a critical first piece of a stakeholder community. This will require ample time to learn the system and the people in charge of it, and some of the things you will request of them may require funding to reach an agreement. Ask.
Educating stakeholders is essential and requires an adaptive approach.	Learning analytics is an emerging concept that is on the minds of higher education administrators, but their understanding of what it comprises, and how it could look on campus is often hazy. The team must educate stakeholders to obtain their buy-in, and this typically involves identifying the data resources the campus possesses and how they can be leveraged. Collaborators' campus responsibilities and prior knowledge about data should dictate the approach. Data savvy administrators charged with improving retention and achievement are quick studies and can be compelled by an aspirational case study. Overworked IT administrators often require detailed funding and feasibility plans; some are enticed by the chance to directly contribute to university mission. Faculty partners are the most variable of all; even the earliest of adopters can require thorough orientation and ongoing education and support.
Stakeholder relationships are the lifeblood of a learning analytics project.	Whereas much of the work of growing and maintaining a learning analytics project involves management of resources like course sites, databases, data models, and sets of analyses, the management of relationships with stakeholders is equally critical to ensuring project success. Each stakeholder has unique responsibilities outside of the learning analytics project that can threaten their ability to contribute consistently. Frequent reporting on progress to the whole leadership group maintains awareness and buy-in. Periodic meetings to take the temperature and appraise new and upcoming challenges can inform the adjustments that will need to be made to a project in order to adapt to changes at the university (e.g., leadership, policy, or technology changes) that can derail project activities.

explainable and inform ways to support learners. The cases presented serve as models from which features can be abstracted, and lessons can be learned. Learning analytics is a powerful emergent approach that is maturing in terms of research methodologies (Lang et. al, 2017, 2022), alignment to learning theories (Gašević, et al., 2015; Wise & Shaffer, 2015) and especially self-regulated learning (Bernacki, 2018; Winne, 2017, 2022) and through policy tools (Gašević & Tsai, 2019) that can yield tremendous benefits to higher education when institutions partner thoughtfully to leverage the human and data resources on campus and address academic challenges that are critical for their institution to overcome.

REFERENCES

Adams Becker, S., Cummins, M., Davis, A., Freeman, A., Hall Giesinger, C., & Ananthanarayanan, V. (2017). *NMC Horizon Report: 2017 Higher Education Edition*. The New Media Consortium.

Aleven, V., Roll, I., McLaren, B. M., & Koedinger, K. R. (2010). Automated, unobtrusive, action-by-action assessment of self-regulation during learning with an intelligent tutoring system. *Educational Psychologist*, *45*(4), 224–233. doi:10.1080/00461520.2010.517740

Arnold, K. E., & Pistilli, M. D. (2012, April). Course signals at Purdue: Using learning analytics to increase student success. In *Proceedings of the 2nd international conference on learning analytics and knowledge* (pp. 267-270). ACM. 10.1145/2330601.2330666

Arroway, P., Morgan, G., O'Keefe, M., & Yanosky, R. (2016). *Learning Analytics in Higher Education. Research report.* ECAR.

Azevedo, R., Taub, M., & Mudrick, N. V. (2018). Understanding and reasoning about real-time cognitive, affective, and metacognitive processes to foster self-regulation with advanced learning technologies. In *Handbook of self-regulation of learning and performance* (pp. 254–270). Routledge.

Bernacki, M. L. (2018). Examining the cyclical, loosely sequenced, and contingent features of self-regulated learning: Trace data and their analysis. In D. H. Schunk & J. A. Greene (Eds.), *Handbook of Self-Regulated Learning and Performance* (pp. 370–387). Routledge.

Bernacki, M. L., Chavez, M. M., & Uesbeck, P. M. (2020a). Predicting STEM achievement with learning management system data: Prediction modeling and a test of an early warning system. *Computers & Education, 158*. Advance online publication. doi:10.1016/j.compedu.2020

Bernacki, M. L., Greene, J. A., Plumley, R. D., Yu, L., Duke, R. F., Freed, R., Hollander, C., & Hogan, K. (2022, April 21-26). *Code What I Say, Not Just What I Do! Multimethod Investigations into Digitally Traced Behaviors* [Paper Presentation]. Annual Meeting of the American Education Research Association, San Diego, CA, United States.

Bernacki, M. L., Vosicka, L., & Utz, J. C. (2020b). Can brief, web-delivered training help STEM undergraduates "learn to learn"? *Journal of Educational Psychology, 112*(4), 765–781. doi:10.1037/edu0000405

Bernacki, M. L., Vosicka, L., Utz, J. C., & Warren, C. (2021). Effects of digital learning skill training on the academic performance of undergraduates in science and mathematics. *Journal of Educational Psychology, 113*(6), 1107–1125. doi:10.1037/edu0000485

Brooks, C., & Thompson, C. (2017) Predictive Modelling in Teaching and Learning. In C. Lang, G. Siemens, A. Wise, & D. Gašević (Eds.), Handbook of Learning Analytics (pp. 61-68). SoLAR. doi:10.18608/hla17.005

Campbell, C. M., Dortch, D., & Burt, B. A. (2018). Reframing rigor: A modern look at challenge and support in higher education. *New Directions for Higher Education, 2018*(181), 11–23. doi:10.1002/he.20267

Cogliano, M. C., Bernacki, M. L., Hilpert, J. C., & Strong, C. L. (2022). A self-regulated learning analytics prediction-and-intervention design: Detecting and supporting struggling biology students. *Journal of Educational Psychology, 114*(8), 1801–1816. doi:10.1037/edu0000745

Dawson, S., Jovanovic, J., Gašević, D., & Pardo, A. (2017). From prediction to impact: Evaluation of a learning analytics retention program. In *Proceedings of the Seventh International Learning Analytics & Knowledge Conference* (pp. 474-478). ACM. 10.1145/3027385.3027405

Fan, Y., Lim, L., van der Graaf, J., Kilgour, J., Raković, M., Moore, J., Molenaar, I., Bannert, M., & Gašević, D. (2022). Improving the measurement of self-regulated learning using multi-channel data. *Metacognition and Learning*, *17*(3), 1–31. doi:10.100711409-022-09304-z

Ferguson, R., Clow, D., Macfadyen, L., Essa, A., Dawson, S., & Alexander, S. (2014, March). Setting learning analytics in context: overcoming the barriers to large-scale adoption. In *Proceedings of the Fourth International Conference on Learning Analytics and Knowledge* (pp. 251-253). ACM. 10.1145/2567574.2567592

Gardner, J., & Brooks, G. (2018). Evaluating Predictive Models of Student Success: Closing the Methodological Gap. *Journal of Learning Analytics*, *5*(2), 105–125. doi:10.18608/jla.2018.52.7

Gašević, D., Dawson, S., & Siemens, G. (2015). Let's not forget: Learning analytics are about learning. *TechTrends*, *59*(1), 64–71. doi:10.100711528-014-0822-x

Gašević, D., & Tsai, Y. S. (2019). *The Sheila Project*. https://sheilaproject.eu/

Green, K. C. (2019). *Campus Computing 2019: The 30th National Survey of Computing and Information Technology in American Higher Education*. Campus Computing.

Greene, J. A., & Azevedo, R. (2009). A macro-level analysis of SRL processes and their relations to the acquisition of a sophisticated mental model of a complex system. *Contemporary Educational Psychology*, *34*(1), 18–29. doi:10.1016/j.cedpsych.2008.05.006

Greene, J. A., & Azevedo, R. (2010). The measurement of learners' self-regulated cognitive and metacognitive processes while using computer-based learning environments. *Educational Psychologist*, *45*(4), 203–209. doi:10.1080/00461520.2010.515935

Hong, W., & Bernacki, M. L. (2018, April) *Data-Driven Digital Alerts and Learning Support: Effects on Achievement and Moderation by Unintended Course Events* [Poster Presentation]. Annual Meeting of the American Educational Research Association, New York, NY, United States.

Khosravi, H., Shum, S. B., Chen, G., Conati, C., Tsai, Y. S., Kay, J., ... Gašević, D. (2022). Explainable artificial intelligence in education. *Computers and Education: Artificial Intelligence*, *3*, 100074.

Lang, C., Siemens, G., Wise, A. F., & Gašević, D. (2017). *Handbook of Learning Analytics*. SoLAR. doi:10.18608/hla17

Lang, C., Siemens, G., Wise, A. F., Gašević, D., & Merceron, A. (Eds.). (2022). Handbook of Learning Analytics (2nd. ed.). SoLAR. DOI: doi:10.18608/hla22

Olson, S., & Riordan, D. G. (2012). *Engage to Excel: Producing One Million Additional College Graduates with Degrees in Science, Technology, Engineering, and Mathematics*. Report to the President. Executive Office of the President. https://files.eric.ed.gov/fulltext/ED541511.pdf

Pelletier, K., McCormack, M., Reeves, J., Robert, J., & Arbino, N. (2022). *EDUCAUSE Horizon Report, Teaching and Learning Edition*. EDUCAUSE.

Pintrich, P. R. (2000). The role of goal orientation in self-regulated learning. In M. Boekaerts, P. R. Pintrich, & M. Zeidner (Eds.), *Handbook of self-regulation* (pp. 451–502). Academic Press. doi:10.1016/B978-012109890-2/50043-3

Salehian Kia, F., Hatala, M., Baker, R. S., & Teasley, S. D. (2021, April). Measuring students' self-regulatory phases in LMS with behavior and real-time self-report. In *LAK21: 11th International Learning Analytics and Knowledge Conference* (pp. 259-268). 10.1145/3448139.3448164

Sønderlund, A. L., Hughes, E., & Smith, J. (2018). The efficacy of learning analytics interventions in higher education: A systematic review. *British Journal of Educational Technology*. Advance online publication. doi:10.1111/bjet.127208

Tsai, Y.-S., Gašević, D., Whitelock-Wainwright, A., Muñoz-Merino, P. J., Moreno-Marcos, P. M., Fernández, A. R., Kloos, C. D., Scheffel, M., Jivet, I., Drachsler, H., Tammets, K., Calleja, A. R., & Kollom, K. (2018). *SHEILA: Supporting Higher Education to Intergrade Learning Analytics Research Report*. https://sheilaproject.eu/results/

Tsai, Y. S., Moreno-Marcos, P. M., Jivet, I., Scheffel, M., Tammets, K., Kollom, K., & Gaševic, D. (2018). The SHEILA Framework: Informing Institutional Strategies and Policy Processes of Learning Analytics. *Journal of Learning Analytics*, *5*(3), 5–20. doi:10.18608/jla.2018.53.2

Turek, M. (2018). *Explainable artificial intelligence (XAI)*. Defense Advanced Research Projects Agency. https://www darpa. mil/program/explainable-artificial-intelligence

Winne, P. H. (2017). Learning Analytics for self-regulated learning. In Handbook of learning analytics. SOLAR. doi:10.18608/hla17.021

Winne, P. H. (2022). Learning analytics for Self-Regulated Learning. In Handbook of Learning Analytics (2nd. ed., pp. 78-85). SoLAR. DOI: doi:10.18608/hla22

Winne, P. H., & Hadwin, A. F. (1998). Studying as self-regulated learning. In D. J. Hacker, J. Dunlosky, & A. C. Graesser (Eds.), *Metacognition in educational theory and practice* (pp. 227–304). Erlbaum.

Wise, A. F., & Shaffer, D. W. (2015). Why theory matters more than ever in the age of big data. *Journal of Learning Analytics*, *2*(2), 5–13. doi:10.18608/jla.2015.22.2

Zimmerman, B. J. (2000). Attaining self-regulation: A social cognitive perspective. In M. Boekaerts, P. R. Pintrich, & M. Zeidner (Eds.), *Handbook of Self-Regulation* (pp. 13–39). Academic Press. doi:10.1016/B978-012109890-2/50031-7

ADDITIONAL READING

Gardner, J., & Brooks, G. (2018). Evaluating Predictive Models of Student Success: Closing the Methodological Gap. *Journal of Learning Analytics*, *5*(2), 105–125. doi:10.18608/jla.2018.52.7

Gašević, D., Dawson, S., & Siemens, G. (2015). Let's not forget: Learning analytics are about learning. *TechTrends*, *59*(1), 64–71. doi:10.100711528-014-0822-x

Gašević, D., & Tsai, Y. S. (2019). *The Sheila Project*. Retrieved from https://sheilaproject.eu/

Green, K. C. (2019). *Campus Computing 2019: The 30th National Survey of Computing and Information Technology in American Higher Education*. Campus Computing.

Greene, J. A., & Azevedo, R. (2009). A macro-level analysis of SRL processes and their relations to the acquisition of a sophisticated mental model of a complex system. *Contemporary Educational Psychology*, *34*(1), 18–29. doi:10.1016/j.cedpsych.2008.05.006

Matcha, W., Gasevic, D., Uzir, N. A. A., Jovanovic, J., Pardo, A., Lim, L., ... Tsai, Y. S. (2020). Analytics of Learning Strategies: Role of Course Design and Delivery Modality. *Journal of Learning Analytics*, *7*(2), 45–71. doi:10.18608/jla.2020.72.3

Rodriguez, F., Yu, R., Park, J., Rivas, M. J., Warschauer, M., & Sato, B. K. (2019, March). Utilizing learning analytics to map students' self-reported study strategies to click behaviors in STEM courses. In *Proceedings of the 9th international conference on learning analytics & knowledge* (pp. 456-460). 10.1145/3303772.3303841

Winne, P. H. (2020). Construct and consequential validity for learning analytics based on trace data. *Computers in Human Behavior*, *112*, 106457. doi:10.1016/j.chb.2020.106457

KEY TERMS AND DEFINITIONS

Feature Engineering: Any actions taken to create a new trace from raw event data captured in a logfile. Learning analytics practitioners will engage in feature engineering as they label and organize learning events of interest to educators who aim to make decisions or inferences about learners in a learning environment.

Learning Environment: Addressed in this chapter and further described by Matcha and colleagues in recommended additional readings, a learning environment includes the digital technology platform on which a learner engages in a task and the instructional design of the task. The learning goal set out by the designer, instructor, or learner and the assessment practices used to evaluate performance will determine the types of learning resources provided to the learner, and these will vary across the course sites on a learning management system. Tracing learning events is thus context-dependent, and definitions will vary from one environment to the next.

Learning Event: Elaborated in recommended readings (Bernacki, 2018), a learning event is a timestamped event captured as a trace from process data in a learning environment that can reliably be interpreted to reflect a theoretically-grounded learning process. This requires validation of the event using corroborating data from the learner, and a theory that describes the learning process the data reflect.

Learning Resource: Elaborated in recommended readings (Bernacki, 2018), a learning resource is a digital or physical piece of educational media provided to a learner within a learning environment. Educators can consider the resource and how it aligns to the learning objectives and assessments and consider learning theories to determine how access and use of a learning resource might produce traces that reflect a learning event.

Log (or Logfile): Any record of timestamped events recorded by a software that can be used to observe traces of learner actions, which can be interpreted through theory to reflect learning events.

Log(file) Analysis: Any variety of descriptive, inferential or machine learning analysis of data derived. From a logfile and inferred to trace learning events.

Trace: A recorded observation of an event that occurs during a session. The observation may be captured from the logfile produced by a learning technology or may be captured from audio or video recording. This isolated trace then needs to be considered through the lens of a learning theory to determine whether it reflects a specific learning event.

Chapter 13
Using Written Responses to Reflection Questions to Improve Online Student Retention:
A Text Analysis Approach

Danny Glick
University of California, Irvine, USA

Anat Cohen
https://orcid.org/0000-0002-8373-3511
Tel Aviv University, Israel

Hagit Gabbay
https://orcid.org/0000-0002-2012-1964
Tel Aviv University, Israel

ABSTRACT

Online learning has been recognized as a promising approach to improve learning outcomes in developing countries where high-quality learning resources are limited. Concomitant with the boom in online learning, there are escalating concerns about academic accountability, specifically student outcomes as measured by persistence and success. This chapter examines whether evidence of reflection found in student written responses to a set of skill-building videos predicts success in online courses. Using a text analysis approach, this study analyzes 1,871 student responses to four reflection questions at a large online university in Panama. A Kruskal-Wallis test found median final course grade differences between students who showed no evidence of significant learning in their written responses and those using 1-13 words associated with significant learning. These results suggest that persistence and performance in online courses can be predicted by evidence of reflection found in student written responses to reflection questions.

DOI: 10.4018/978-1-6684-6500-4.ch013

INTRODUCTION

Online learning has been growing in both popularity and practice over the past thirty years, with a drastic acceleration since the onset of the COVID-19 pandemic (Ginder, Kelly-Reid, & Mann, 2019; National Student Clearinghouse Research Center, 2022; Seaman, Allen, & Seaman, 2018; Xu & Xu, 2019).While online education has traditionally been viewed as an alternative pathway for nontraditional students seeking higher education opportunities, the emergence of the COVID-19 pandemic has forced students and educators across all levels of education to rapidly adapt to online learning. The pandemic has created the largest disruption of education systems in history, affecting nearly 1.6 billion learners in more than 190 countries, forcing K-20 education to shift to online learning (United Nations, 2020). Today, learners engage in online or blended learning in primary, secondary, post-secondary, workforce training, and workplace learning like never before in modern history.

Concomitant with the boom in online learning are escalating concerns about academic accountability, specifically with respect to student outcomes as measured by persistence and success. These concerns emerge from research indicating that dropout rates in online courses are significantly higher than in traditional brick-and-mortar learning environments (Soffer & Cohen, 2019). A 2019 report by Xu and Xu found that online students are up to 15 percent more likely to drop out than are students in face-to-face classes at community colleges in North America (Xu & Xu, 2019). This finding is very problematic, as lower retention rates among online students have been connected to overall lack of academic success in higher education (Xu & Jaggars, 2011). Xu and Jaggars' study points to the importance of online course success, particularly in view of evidence suggesting that failing online college courses early in one's college career may impede progression towards graduation (Xu & Jaggars, 2011).

While online learning is growing in popularity, many students struggle in such settings, especially students lacking certain personal attributes - such as being goal-oriented and self-disciplined - that are essential for online success. Learners need to be able to navigate, engage, and persist in such environments with more autonomy and self-directedness than was otherwise needed in traditional brick-and-mortar learning environments. This, in turn, requires learners to adopt, practice, and internalize self-regulated learning strategies. Students who self-regulate are more likely to improve their academic performance, find value in their learning process, and continue to be effective lifelong learners (Zimmerman, 2002). However, online students often struggle to self-regulate, which may contribute to lower academic performance. It is important, therefore, to be able to identify early in the course students who lack self-regulation skills in order to improve retention and graduation.

A growing body of research is seeking to respond to this challenge by employing learning analytics techniques to analyze student online learning behavior, log files, and clickstream data (Cohen et al., 2019). However, research examining other types of analytics (e.g., text data mining, text analysis, etc.) is scarce. Therefore, the purpose of this study is to employ text analysis techniques to analyze student reflective responses to a set of skill-building videos incorporated into online courses. Specifically, this study aims to examine whether persistence and performance of online Latin American students may be predicted by evidence of significant learning found in student written responses to post-video reflection questions.

This study contributes to the literature on persistence in online learning in several important ways. First, this study performs what appears to be the first attempt to use text analysis techniques to examine whether persistence is affected by evidence of significant learning found in student written responses. By answering this question, university leaders and online course administrators will be able to identify at-risk students using a more holistic approach, which integrates learning analytics with text analysis techniques, thus improving graduation by targeting individual students in meaningful ways. Second, course administrators often use midterm scores to predict success in online courses (Glick et al., 2019). Although midterm scores prove to be a strong predictor of students' final grades, they are collected at a point when students have already finished a significant amount of the coursework. Therefore, more research is needed to explore factors such as text analysis techniques, which may prove effective in identifying at-risk students by analyzing reflective responses submitted early in the course. Finally, while a growing number of institutions across Latin America are transitioning from brick-and-mortar to online teaching (Glick et al., 2019; Xu et al., 2019), many Latin American students struggle in such settings. Therefore, to improve persistence and performance in online courses implemented in developing countries, it is important to examine whether Latin American students who are at-risk of dropping out can be identified using text analysis techniques – a previously understudied but critically important approach.

BACKGROUND

Online Learning in Developing Countries

Despite steady investment in public education made by developing countries over the past few decades, national efforts to improve student learning outcomes in developing countries often remain ineffective (Glick et al., 2019). Typical challenges include a shortage of qualified teachers, lack of teacher certification or training, limited access to high-quality learning resources, large class sizes, and poorly designed curricula (Ministerio de Educación, Perú, 2016; OECD, 2015). In view of these challenges, online learning has increasingly been viewed as a possible way to remove the barriers associated with traditional teaching by providing low-cost, quality education (Glick et al., 2019; Seaman et al., 2018; Sife, Lwoga, & Sanga, 2007; Soffer & Cohen, 2019; Xu et al., 2019). Recent studies suggest that technology-based instruction implemented in developing countries has a significant, positive impact on student course grades and course completion rates compared to traditional face-to-face instruction (Bai, Mo, Zhang, Boswell, & Rozelle, 2016; Banditvilai, 2016; Glick et al., 2016; Xu et al., 2019). This, however, has not been free of challenges. The most pressing issues include: student attitude towards e-learning, lack of student motivation, inadequate teacher training, and low level of technological readiness (Ngampornchai & Adams, 2016; Sigama & Kalema, 2018; Tarus, Gichoya, & Muumbo, 2015).

While online learning is a promising approach to deliver more desirable learning outcomes, many students struggle in such settings (Allen et al., 2016; Cohen, 2017), especially Latin American students with poor self-regulation skills. Online learning, by its very nature, gives greater autonomy to students as it offers flexibility of time, place and pace (Jansen et al., 2017). However, unlike traditional learning environments where the teacher guides and supports students, students in online courses are responsible for their own learning (Littlejohn, Hood, Milligan, & Mustain, 2016), which often leads to higher dropout rates. Online learning environments require certain self-regulation skills, which students with little or no familiarity with online learning, may lack. Therefore, to improve persistence and performance in online courses, it is important to be able to identify at-risk students early in the course, especially in online learning environments, where the absence of face-to-face accountability may cause students to disengage with the course much more than they would in traditional classrooms (Park et al., 2018).

Self-Regulated Learning, Reflection and Performance in Online Courses

Self-Regulated Learning (SRL) refers to *proactive* processes employed by the student in order to achieve a set of learning objectives. Such processes may include goal setting, effort regulation and time management. Through monitoring and self-reflection, these processes are monitored and modified to enhance one's progression towards goal achievement (Broadbent, 2017). Self-regulated learners are motivated, persistent, manage their time effectively, and seek help when needed (Pintrich, Smith, Garcia, & McKeachie, 1993). Several types of self-regulated learning models can be found in the literature (e.g., Pintrich et al., 1993; Zimmerman, 2008), yet they all share two common characteristics: first, SRL is a cyclical process which includes cognitive, metacognitive, behavioral, motivational, and emotional/affective aspects of learning; second, self- regulated learning skills can be developed and enhanced (Panadero & Alonso-Tapia, 2014).

Research has shown that developing student self-reflection is essential for student success (Cui, Wise, & Kenneth, 2019; Van den Boom, Paas, Van Merrienboer, & Van Gog, 2004; Zimmerman, 2000, 2008). For example, Saito and Miwa (2007) examined the effects of self-reflection questions on student learning outcomes in an online course. They found that students who demonstrated skills of reflection and self-awareness significantly outperformed those who did not. Similarly, Lew & Schmidt (2011) found that reflective journals used in undergraduate courses led to improved learning outcomes.

Self-regulation plays a particularly important role in online learning environments where students are required to take greater responsibility to control and regulate their own learning (Appana, 2008; Duffy & Kirkley, 2003). Research suggests that self-regulated learners are engaged in more effective learning processes, which leads to improved learning outcomes (Bernacki, Aguilar, & Byrnes, 2011). A growing body of research (e.g., Broadbent & Poon, 2015; Wong et al., 2019) has found a significant positive relationship between SRL strategies and improved learning outcomes in online courses, suggesting that developing students' self-regulated learning strategies through reflection may lead to improved learning outcomes. We, therefore, hypothesize that evidence of self-reflection found in student written responses to reflection questions may prove effective in predicting student persistence and performance in online courses.

Text Analysis and Academic Performance

Text analysis, sometimes referred to as content analysis or text data mining, is the action of obtaining patterns or insights from text-based resources)Kovanović et al., 2018). Through automated text analysis, it is now possible to find patterns to determine and extract useful information from a written text. Exploiting the capabilities of automated text analysis techniques can provide educators with the ability to analyze students' answers and make better judgement on their performance (Cunningham-Nelson, Mukherjee, Goncher, & Boles, 2018). Abd-Elrahman, Andreu, and Abbott (2010) used automated text data mining techniques to analyze student answers to a set of course evaluation questions in order to identify unrevealed aspects that may affect the teaching process. The answers from the student course evaluations were scored manually and automatically. The manually, and automatically, scored evaluation values were then compared. The researchers found a strong correlation between the values of the manually interpreted and automatically-mined techniques, suggesting that text mining of student answers can provide efficient alternative measure to identify unrevealed aspects affecting the teaching process (Abd-Elrahman et al., 2010). Research has shown that text analysis is an effective methodology to spot clues of SRL events within students' written messages. Dettori and Persico (2008) used content analysis to analyze the messages exchanged by a group of students in online learning communities. They found that content analysis could help understand the practice and development of SLR in Virtual Learning Communities. Similarly, Lew and Schmidt (2011) used an automated coding procedure to examine whether reflective journal writing was effective in promoting self-reflection and learning. Outcomes of the textual context analysis suggest that student self-reflection may prove effective in improving academic performance (Dettori & Persico, 2008).

Predicting Persistence in Online Courses

A growing number of institutions seek to reduce dropout rates by targeting students who are most likely to drop out, so that targeted interventions and support can be provided when needed (Hachey et al., 2014; Liu, Gomez, Khan, & Yen, 2007). Responding to this demand, educational researchers have examined the effects of early warning models using learning analytics techniques. These predictive models utilize student behavioral data and online learning behavior collected during the course (Moreno-Marcos et al., 2020). For example, Macfadyen and Dawson (2010) found that the final grade in an online academic course can be predicted by analyzing the number of discussion messages posted by students, the number of completed assignments and the number of sent messages. Zacharis (2015) built a predictive model utilizing 29 behavioral variables collected during the course. Similarly, Xind and Du (2019) and Strang (2017) analyzed different sets of event-based variables to predict success in online courses. However, research suggests that predictive models based entirely on analysis of student log files, especially when collected after students have already finished significant amount of the coursework, may have limited value (Moreno-Marcos et al., 2020; Pardo, Ellis, & Calvo, 2015). Such predictive models may fail to predict at-risk students who drop out as early as week one (Moreno-Marcos et al., 2020).

The current study aims to fill a gap in the literature, investigating whether analysis of written responses to a set of reflection questions can predict student persistence. In what appears to be a first attempt to predict success by analyzing written responses, this study utilizes text analysis techniques to analyze 1,871 Latin American students' responses to a set of four reflection questions. The purpose of this study, therefore, is to examine whether learning outcomes can be predicted by evidence of significant learning found in Latin American student written responses to reflection questions. Specifically, this study seeks to answer the following research questions: Q1 Is student *persistence* in online courses affected by evidence of significant learning found in student written responses to post-video reflection questions? Q2 Is student *performance* in online courses affected by evidence of significant learning found in student written responses to post-video reflection questions?

METHODOLOGY

Research Context

This study was conducted at a large private university in Panama. The university enrolls roughly 9,000 students annually in 17-degree programs, all of which are delivered online. Participants were 511 Spanish-speaking undergraduate students enrolled in online courses from winter 2019 to summer 2019. About 54% of the student body was female, and 73% 24 years old or older. Over two-thirds of the enrollees

Table 1. Skill-building Videos Skill Focus and Reflection Questions

Video	Skill Focus	Reflection Questions
1	Effective Online Learning Behavior	Do you agree with the following statement: *Spreading out the study time throughout the course will produce more long-lasting learning.*
2	Effective Time Management	What are the advantages of spreading out the study time throughout the course, over studying for an intense period of time close to the exam?
3	Socialization in Online Learning	How can social media help spur socialization among online students?
4	Effective Test-taking Strategies	Which test-taking strategy did you find most useful, and why?

came from low or middle socioeconomic backgrounds, and about 40% of them had little or no prior online experience. The courses were moderated by certified Panamanian teachers, who receive training in online teaching methodologies. The student-to-teacher ratio was approximately 35 online students per teacher. The online courses were developed locally by groups of subject matter experts (SME), instructional designers and media production specialists. Courses were completed over a period of five weeks and combined interactive computer lessons completed in self-access with weekly sync lessons. The final grade was based on students' score on the final test, online quizzes, written assignments, and a student research project. The final grade was assigned on a 100-point scale.

Skill-building Videos and Reflection Questions

To help students develop the skills needed to be successful online learners, the university - guided by e-learning specialists and educational researchers from the University of California, Irvine's Digital Learning Lab, and Tel-Aviv University's Educational Technology Department - produced a set of four skill-building videos. The videos were scripted, and featured 2nd- and 3rd-year Spanish-speaking students sharing effective online learning practices with first-time online learners. Each video lasted about 4 minutes and provided online students with useful study tips on how to become more successful self-regulated learners by utilizing effective time management, goal setting, and self-assessment strategies. To provide opportunities for meaningful application-oriented learning, which goes beyond an understand-and-remember type of learning, students were asked to respond to open-ended reflection and application questions after watching each of the four skill-building videos. The study tips and the reflection questions are summarized in Table 1.

Text Analysis Process

To examine whether student written responses to the reflection questions show evidence of significant learning, automated text analysis techniques were applied. A dataset of 1,871 reflective responses collected from 511 students enrolled in 17 different online courses were analyzed. The text analysis process consisted of eight phases. First, a list of words associated with significant learning was developed. This word list was adapted from Fink's taxonomy (2003), which provides the language for interpreting and evaluating multiple kinds of student learning. Specifically, Fink's taxonomy encompasses and integrates a wide range of literature and published statements on desirable kinds of learning, and provides a list of 36 verbs, associated with significant learning (e.g., *analyze*, *assess*, *identify*, *relate*, etc.). To deal with

Table 2. Examples of Nouns and Verbs Derived from Fink's Verbs for Significant Learning

Kinds of Learning	Fink's Verbs for Significant Learning	Extended Taxonomy
Foundational Knowledge	Remember, Understand, Identify	Identified, Identifying
Application	Use, Critique, Manage, Solve, Assess, Judge, Do, Imagine, Analyze, Calculate, Create, Coordinate, Make decisions	Analyzed, Analyzing, Analysis, Analyses
Integration	Connect, Relate, Compare, Integrate, Identify similarities, Identify interaction	Compared, Comparing, Comparison(s)
Human Dimension	Understand others, Decide to become, Interact with others regarding, Come to see themselves	Decided to become, Deciding to become
Caring	Get excited about, Be ready to, Be more interested in, Value	Valued, Valuing
Learning How to Learn	Read and study, Set a learning agenda, Identify source of information, Be able to construct knowledge, Frame useful questions, Create a learning plan	Created a learning plan, Creating a learning plan

morphological changes in the structure of words from the same morphological family (e.g., *assess, assessed, assessing*, etc.), an extended taxonomy, which includes nouns, adjectives and adverbs derived from Fink's verb list, was developed by the researchers for the purpose of this study. Examples of nouns and verbs derived from Fink's taxonomy are shown in Table 2. Appendix 1 provides a full list of nouns, verbs, adjectives and adverbs derived from Finks's taxonomy.

Next, the extended taxonomy was translated into Spanish by a certified English-Spanish translator. To prepare for text analysis, all special characters and accent marks, called *Tildes* in Spanish, which appear above the letter (e.g., *ñ, ú,* etc.), were removed. To automate the text analysis process, all the written responses were exported to SQL, which has a word count query that allowed us to search for the words from the extended taxonomy across all students' written responses. It then provided a frequency distribution of words appearing in each of the student individual written responses. Next, all the written responses were exported to Excel as a matrix with the 1,871 student written responses as the rows, and the distribution of words from the extended taxonomy found in each written response as the columns. We then used the AutoSum function to sum the word frequency distribution across all written responses for each individual student. Lastly, the sum of word frequency of each individual student was coded as 0, 1 or 2 (*None, Low* or *High* respectively). Students who showed no evidence of significant learning in their written responses (i.e., SQL found no words from the extended taxonomy in their written responses) were coded as 0; one or two words were coded as 1; and three to 13 words were coded as 2. We named this new categorical variable WordSum. The text analysis process is summarized in Table 3.

Data Analysis

Based on 1,871 written responses to a set of four post-video reflection questions, the aim of this study was to employ text analysis techniques to examine whether performance and persistence in online courses were affected by the independent variable WordSum, which is the sum of the frequency of words of significant learning found across all reflective responses of each individual student. This study utilizes data collected from three different sources: 1,871 reflective responses coded as 0, 1 or 2; LMS course

Table 3. Summary of the Text Analysis Process

Phase	Description
1	A list of 36 verbs, associated with significant learning, was identified in the literature.
2	An extended taxonomy, which includes nouns, adjectives and adverbs derived from Fink's verbs for significant learning, was developed by the researchers for the purpose of this study.
3	The extended taxonomy was translated into Spanish by a certified English-Spanish translator.
4	All special characters and accent marks were removed.
5	All written responses were exported to SQL to search for words from the extended taxonomy across all student written responses.
6	All written responses were exported to Excel. AutoSum function was used to sum the word frequency distribution across all written responses for each individual student.
7	The sum of word frequency of each individual student was coded as 0, 1 or 2 (*None*, *Low* or *High* respectively).
8	A new categorical variable, named WordSum, was created.

data containing the winter 2019 to summer 2019 course reports data for all 511 students; and a pre-course student demographic survey (see Appendix 2). Data were analyzed using descriptive and inferential statistics, using IBM SPSS statistics version 25.

We used logistic regression to explore Research Question 1 – whether student *persistence* in online courses was affected by evidence of significant learning found in student written responses. Student *Completer/Dropout* status was used as the outcome variable, which was dummy coded to 0 (*Dropouts*) or 1 (*Completers*). Students who took the end-of-course exam and completed the course were coded as 1 (*Completers*); students who dropped after census, withdrew from the course, or missed the end-of-course exam were coded as 0 (*Dropouts*). WordSum (coded as 0, 1 or 2), and the demographic variables *gender* and *age*, were used as independent variables.

Analysis for Research Question 2 – whether student *performance* in online courses was affected by evidence of significant learning found in student written responses – was conducted in three phases. The first phase checked Normality assumptions and obtained a sense of the data using boxplots and the Shapiro-Wilk test, which many researchers recommend as the best choice for testing the normality of data (Thode, 2002). The second phase included the Kruskal-Wallis test, which compares several populations on the basis of independent random samples from each population. The Kruskal-Wallis test can replace the ANOVA F test if the Normality assumption is violated (Pallant, 2013). Finally, pairwise comparisons with adjusted p-values were carried out for the three groups. A significance level of alpha $<.05$ was chosen to denote statistical significance.

RESULTS

Descriptive Statistics

Descriptive data of the most frequent terms and their relative frequency (see Table 4) show that the most frequently used word was *use* (22%) and its morphologically-related family members (*used*, *using*, *usage*). The second most frequently used word was *solve* (11.4%), and its morphologically-related family members (*solved*, *solving*, *solution*). The relative frequency of the words *understand, manage, create,* and *analyze* – and their morphologically-related family members – ranged from 6.1% to 7.9%. Counter-intuitively, the least frequent words were *compare* (0.6%), *identify* (0.6%) and *make decisions* (0.5%). Appendix 3 provides descriptive data of frequency counts of each term and its relative frequency. Examples of reflective responses of students who show evidence of significant learning in their writing can be found in Appendix 4.

Table 4. Summary of the Most Frequent Terms

Word	Frequency	Relative Frequency
Use, Used, Using, Usage	146	22%
Solve, Solved, Solving, Solution	76	11.4%
Understand, Understood, Understanding	53	7.9%
Manage, Managed, Managing	44	6.6%
Create, Created, Creating, Creation	42	6.3%
Analyze, Analyzed, Analyzing, Analysis	41	6.1%
Remember, Remembered, Remembering	36	5.4%
Relate, Related, Relating	34	5.1%

Inferential Statistics

Research Question 1

Is student *persistence* in online courses affected by evidence of significant learning found in student written responses to post-video reflection questions?

The logistic regression analysis was carried out in a hierarchical, block-wise fashion. First, we ran the analysis specifying WordSum as the main effect (Model 1). Then we added the demographic variables *gender* (Model 2) and *age* (Model 3). Finally, we specified an interaction effect, which is the combined effect of WordSum and *age* (Model 4). The overall model summary statistics for each of the four models is shown in Table 5. Model 1 yielded a chi-square of 35.125, which was highly significant ($p < .001$). Adding *gender* ($\chi^2 = 0.557, p = .456$) and *age* ($\chi^2 = 0.148, p = .701$) had virtually no effect on the fit of the model. Finally, we added the WordSum and gender interaction term to the model. As before, the change in chi-square was very non-significant ($\chi^2 = 0.882, p = .633$), indicating that adding the interaction term to the model had no effect. Additionally, the R^2 value, which tells approximately how much variation in the outcome variable is explained by the model, indicates that adding *gender* and *age* to the model had no effect on R^2 change. Finally, the predicted group membership probabilities in Model 1 indicates that the model is correctly classifying the outcome of 73.3% of the cases. Adding the other explanatory variables to the model (*gender*, *age*, and the interaction term) had no effect on the classification accuracy. We, therefore, proceeded with Model 1, which demonstrated an improvement over the intercept-only baseline model.

Table 5. Model Summary

	Model 1		Model 2		Model 3		Model 4	
Model chi-square	35.125		35.682		35.830		36.712	
Improvement over Previous model		$p <$ .001	.557	$p = .456$	.148	$p = .701$	.882	$p = .663$
Nagelkerke R^2	.101		.102		.103		.104	
Classification Accuracy	73.3%		73.3%		73.3%		73.3%	

The results of the logistic regression show that Model 1, which includes WordSum as the main effect, was statistically significant ($\chi^2 = 35.125, p < .001$), indicating that words from the extended taxonomy found in student written responses significantly predicted the outcome variable *persistence*. The logistic regression results summarized in Table 6 show the estimate, Wald tests, odds ratios, and confidence intervals for WordSum. The odds ratio value of 3.484 indicates that, holding all other variables constant, for a one unit change in WordSum (e.g., change from *Low* to *High*), the odds of earning a passing grade increase by 3.484.

Table 6. Coefficients of the Model Predicting Student Persistence by WordSum and Student Demographics

	B	Wald	Sig.	Odds	Lower	Upper
Constant	0.26	2.658	.103			
WordSum	1.25	16.834	.000	3.48	1.92	6.32

Note. $R^2 = .07$ (Cox & Snell) .1 (Nagelkerke). Model $\chi^2(1) = 35.125, p < .01$

Research Question 2

Is student *performance* in online courses affected by evidence of significant learning found in student written responses to post-video reflection questions?

A boxplot was used to compare the median and spread of the final course grade by WordSum, the new categorical variable. The boxplot (see Figure 1) suggests that written responses that fall into WordSum Category 0 (*None*) have a lower median, and the bottom 50% of the values are more spread out compared to the other groups. Specifically, the boxplot tells us that the final course grade values of WordSum Category 0 are concentrated on the lower end of the scale. This could indicate skewness and a violation of the normal distribution requirements for analysis with ANOVA (Weinberg & Abramowitz, 2008).

To assess Normality, we used the Shapiro-Wilk test (see Table 7). As shown in the final column of the Shapiro-Wilk normality test, the final course grade values are not normally distributed, as the *p*-value is less than .05. Levene's test also shows that the assumption of homogeneity of variance has been violated, $F(2, 360) = 29.51, p < .001$, because the *p*-value in the table in less than .05. As such, these data are not normally distributed, and the groups have heterogeneous variance.

We, therefore, used the Kruskal–Wallis test to examine median differences across the three groups. The null hypothesis is that all three populations have the same median final course grade. The alternative hypothesis is that not all three median final course grades are equal. The results show median final

Figure 1. Boxplot of Final Course Median Score by WordSum

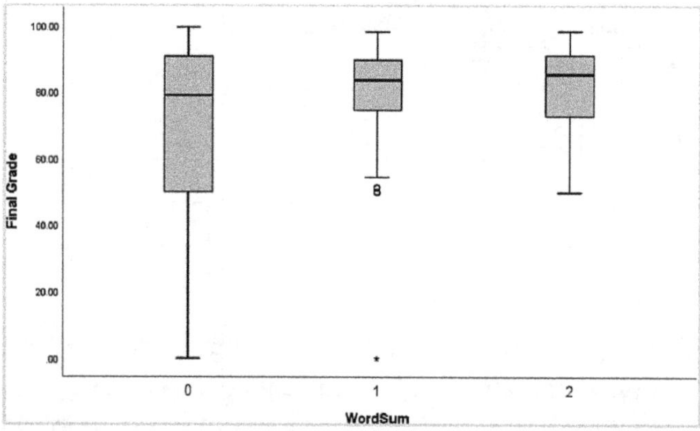

course grade differences across different subgroups $H(2) = 8.82, p < .05$. Thus, the null hypothesis was rejected. Pairwise comparisons with adjusted p-values were carried out for the three groups. Overall, significant differences were found ($p = .024$) between groups 0 (*None*) and 2 (*High*). The median final course grade for WordSum Category 2 students was 85.55 compared to 79.16 in Category 0. Similarly, WordSum Category 1 students (*Low*) showed higher median final course grade of 83.83 compared to Category 0 students ($p = .039$). No significant differences were found between Categories 1 and 2.

DISCUSSION

Online learning has been recognized as a promising approach to improve learning outcomes in developing countries where high-quality learning resources are limited (Bai et al., 2016; Glick et al., 2016). There are, however, escalating concerns about the high dropout rates associated with online learning (Hachey et al., 2013; Jaggars & Xu, 2016), especially in low-income countries. Therefore, identifying factors that predict student performance in online courses can inform institutions and instructors of interventions to improve learning experiences and success in online courses (Ai & Laffey, 2007; Cohen, 2017; Romero & Ventura, 2007). Research has shown that SRL may prove effective in predicting student performance in online courses (Eom & Ashill, 2018; Glick et al., 2019). The authors, therefore, produced a set of four skill-building videos, which provide online students with study tips on how to become successful self-regulated learners. We used text analysis techniques to examine whether student learning outcomes – as

Table 7. Shapiro-Wilk Test of Normality and Levene Test of Homogeneity of Variances

Category	Shapiro-Wilk			Levene			
	Statistic	df	Sig.	*F*	df1	df2	Sig.
0	.864	113	.000				
1	.849	168	.000				
2	.896	82	.000				
				29.51	2	360	.000

measured by persistence and performance – are affected by evidence of significant learning found in student written responses to reflection questions. Based on analysis of 1,871 student responses to four post-video reflection questions, this study identifies several important predictors of Latin American student success in online courses.

We first used a binary logistic regression to examine whether student performance in online courses was affected by evidence of significant learning found in student reflective responses. The results show that words from the extended taxonomy found in student written responses significantly predict student persistence in online courses. Specifically, we found that for a one-point increase in WordSum (e.g., change from *None* to *Low*), the odds of earning a passing grade increase by 3.484. In exploring the relationship between student performance and evidence of words of significant learning found in student written responses, we found median final course grade differences across the three groups (None, Low, and High). Specifically, we found median final course grade differences between students who showed no evidence of significant learning in their written responses, and those using 1-2 or 3-13 words associated with significant learning (79.16, 83.83, and 85.55 respectively). These results strongly suggest that persistence and performance in online courses are affected by evidence of reflection found in student written responses to a set of reflection questions. These results are consistent with a number of other studies (e.g., Broadbent & Poon, 2015; Moreno-Marcos et al., 2020; Wong et al., 2019) that found a significant positive relationship between SRL-related strategies and success in online courses. Our results thus support using student reflection as a promising strategy to improve learning outcomes in online courses.

These results have several theoretical and practical implications. First, prior studies on student reflection mainly focused on online courses in developed countries. Our study fills a gap in the literature by extending this line of research on student reflection to online courses implemented in developing countries, which differ substantially from developed countries in terms of student and teacher characteristics. Our results suggest that use of words from the extended taxonomy may prove effective in identifying at-risk students in developing countries – a previously understudied context. Overall, these results provide guidance on how to identify at-risk students in developing countries by analyzing student reflective responses, using automated text analysis techniques.

Second, research has shown that the course midterm score proves to be a strong success predictor in online courses (Glick et al., 2019). However, course midterm tests are usually administered when students have finished a significant amount of the coursework, by which time at-risk students may have already dropped out. Hence, a set of reflection tasks assigned early in the course may prove effective in identifying at-risk students early on. Once identified, targeted interventions and individualized student support can be provided to get struggling students back on track. Alternatively, students who make extensive use of words from the extended taxonomy – whose odds of earning a passing grade increase significantly – should be advised to enroll in for-credit courses if they have to decide between two course or program choices. Unlike free or audit courses which do not award a certificate, paid, for-credit online courses award students a certificate upon successful completion of the course.

Finally, we found that use of specific words from the extended taxonomy (e.g., use, solve, understand, create, analyze, etc.) was a significant predictor of student success. Based on this word list, institutions can now identify at-risk students by analyzing - automatically or manually – student responses to a set of reflection questions. Students who show no evidence of significant learning in their reflective responses may be classified as being at-risk. The moment at-risk students are identified, instructors can provide timely pedagogical interventions to get them back on track (Jaggars & Xu, 2016). Such support could take the form of a diagnostic intervention, in which course administrators assess the students through video interviews to identify specific areas for support, and then provide the individualized counseling and guidance needed (Hachey et al., 2014).

CONCLUSION

While self-regulation strategies - and the models that underpin them - have been the subject of considerable research and publication, their direct application to online and blended learning remains nascent but quickly evolving. To put it plainly, while both self- regulated learning and online learning have been the focus of increased research, far less research has brought these two concepts together, critical and complimentary as they are. This chapter addresses a number of important considerations related to learner self-regulation in online environments. The literature indicates that self-regulation is indeed an effective practice for enhancing student success, engagement and retention among students. While it is closely tied to motivation, emotion, and skill mastery, the nature of these relationships remains elusive. Indeed, the very notion of self-regulation is often surrounded by misconceptions, myths, and biases that impede the adoption or implementation of successful practices.

Technology is opening up the concept of self-regulated learning in exciting and innovative ways. Increasingly, learning technologists are able to invoke self-regulated learning strategies in their platform, feature, and AI designs. For example, AI can be leveraged to develop algorithms that can automate and personalize self-regulation at scale and can enable technologies, such as chatbots, that can help learners to self-regulate in a variety of courses. Active learning designs can foster self-regulated learning and inform the development of technologies that enable it at scale, including learning platform features, predictive modeling, and targeted support. Gamification can both be informed by self-regulated learning and promote self-regulated learning in ways that are based on a host of learning science and pedagogical principles. And self-regulated learning methods provide an opportunity to address the dropout rates and boost student success in self-paced Massive Open Online Courses (MOOCs) through risk detection and improved design.

Increased awareness of self-regulated learning is enabling learning designers and instructors to adopt simple processes to begin to implement self-regulated learning strategies in their programs, courses, and pedagogies. Common learning technologies, such as LMSs and course authoring systems, enable instructors to more readily develop and facilitate online courses in ways that are aligned with self-regulated learning. Simple tools that can foster self-regulation, especially with students at a distance from their instructors, need to be deployed to help learners plan, monitor, and evaluate their own progress. Yet, adherents would do well to consider philosophical issues such as the degree to which self-regulation is a skill that learners can and should acquire or the result of being in a community of practice that fosters their own motivation, agency, self-direction, and curiosity.

Most importantly, learners themselves need encouragement and opportunities in their earliest online courses to practice, embrace, and benefit from self-regulated learning strategies and resources. This includes practice with metacognitive monitoring – based in part on learner perceptions and the feedback that informs those perceptions – which is a critical component of both learner expectations and choices. Being able to successfully think about one's thinking, learning, and performance is of course foundational to the very concept of self-regulation.

FUTURE RESEARCH DIRECTIONS

The current study examined student persistence and performance using text analysis techniques at a university in Panama. While the results are promising, further studies in more diverse settings are required to confirm these results. Nevertheless, this study provides evidence that student persistence and performance are affected by evidence of significant learning found in student written responses to a set of reflection questions in a higher education context of a developing country.

REFERENCES

Abd-Elrahman, A., Andreu, M., & Abbott, T. (2010). Using text data mining techniques for understanding free-style question answers in course evaluation forms. *Research in Higher Education*, *9*, 1.

Ai, J., & Laffey, J. (2007). Web mining as a tool for understanding online learning. *Journal of Online Learning and Teaching*, *3*(2), 160–169.

Allen, I. E., Seaman, J., Poulin, R., & Straut, T. T. (2016). *Online report card: tracking online education in the United States*. Babson Survey Research Group and Quahog Research Group.

Appana, S. (2008). A review of benefits and limitations of online learning in the context of the student, the instructor and the tenured faculty. *International Journal on E-Learning*, *7*(1), 5–22.

Bai, Y., Mo, D., Zhang, L., Boswell, M., & Rozelle, S. (2016). The impact of integrating ICT with teaching: Evidence from a randomized controlled trial in rural schools in China. *Computers & Education*, *96*, 1–14. doi:10.1016/j.compedu.2016.02.005

Banditvilai, C. (2016). Enhancing student's language skills through blended learning. *The Electronic Journal of E-Learning, 14*(3), 220-229. Available from www.ejel.org

Bernacki, M. L., Aguilar, A. C., & Byrnes, J. P. (2011). Self-regulated learning and technology enhanced learning environments: An opportunity-propensity analysis. *Fostering Self-Regulated Learning through ICT*, 1-26.

Broadbent, J. (2017). Comparing online and blended learner's self-regulated learning strategies and academic performance. *The Internet and Higher Education*, *33*, 24–32. doi:10.1016/j.iheduc.2017.01.004

Broadbent, J., & Poon, W. L. (2015). Self-regulated learning strategies & academic achievement in online higher education learning environments: A systematic review. *The Internet and Higher Education*, *27*, 1–13. doi:10.1016/j.iheduc.2015.04.007

Cohen, A. (2017). Analysis of student activity in web-supported courses as a tool for predicting dropout. *Educational Technology Research and Development*, *65*(5), 1285–1304. doi:10.100711423-017-9524-3

Cohen, A., Shimony, U., Nachmias, R., & Soffer, T. (2019). Active learners' characterization in MOOC forums and their generated knowledge. *British Journal of Educational Technology*, *50*(1), 177–198. doi:10.1111/bjet.12670

Cui, Y., Wise, A. F., & Allen, K. L. (2019). Developing reflection analytics for health professions education: A multi-dimensional framework to align critical concepts with data features. *Computers in Human Behavior*.

Cunningham-Nelson, S., Mukherjee, M., Goncher, A., & Boles, W. (2018). Text analysis in education: A review of selected software packages with an application for analysing students' conceptual understanding. *Australasian Journal of Engineering Education*, *23*(1), 25–39.

Dettori, G., & Persico, D. (2008). Detecting self-regulated learning in online communities by means of interaction analysis. *IEEE Transactions on Learning Technologies*, *1*(1), 11–19. doi:10.1109/TLT.2008.7

Duffy, T. M., & Kirkley, J. R. (2003). *Learner-centered theory and practice in distance education: Cases from higher education*. Routledge. doi:10.4324/9781410609489

Eom, S. B., & Ashill, N. J. (2018). A System's View of E-Learning Success Model. *Decision Sciences Journal of Innovative Education*, *16*(1), 42–76. doi:10.1111/dsji.12144

Fink, L. D. (2003). *Creating significant learning experiences: An integrated approach to designing college courses*. Jossey-Bass.

Ginder, S. A., Kelly-Reid, J. E., & Mann, F. B. (2019). *Enrollment and employees in postsecondary institutions, fall 2017; and financial statistics and academic libraries, fall 2017*. U.S. Department of Education, National Center for Education Statistics. https://nces.ed.gov/pubs2019/2019021REV.pdf

Glick, D., Cohen, A., Festinger, E., Xu, D., & Warschauer, M. (2019). Predicting success, preventing failure: Using learning analytics to predict at-risk students and improve retention in online English language courses. In D. Ifenthaler, D. K. Mah, & J. Y. K. Yau (Eds.), *Utilizing Learning Analytics to Support Study Success* (pp. 249–273). Springer. doi:10.1007/978-3-319-64792-0_14

Glick, D., Xu, D., Warschauer, M., Rodriguez, F., Li, Q., & Cung, B. (2016, August). *Maximizing learning outcomes through blended learning: What research shows*. Paper presented at the 2016 Association of Bilingual Centers of Latin America Conference, Houston, TX.

Hachey, A., Conway, K., & Wladis, C. (2013). Community colleges and underappreciated assets: Using institutional data to promote success in online learning. *Online Journal of Distance Learning Administration*, *16*(1), 1–18.

Hachey, A. C., Wladis, C. W., & Conway, K. M. (2014). Do prior online course outcomes provide more information than GPA alone in predicting subsequent online course grades and retention? An observational study at an urban community college. *Computers & Education*, *72*, 59–67. doi:10.1016/j.compedu.2013.10.012

Jaggars, S. S., & Xu, D. (2016). How do online course design features influence student performance? *Computers & Education*, *95*, 270–284. doi:10.1016/j.compedu.2016.01.014

Jansen, R. S., Van Leeuwen, A., Janssen, J., Kester, L., & Kalz, M. (2017). Validation of the self-regulated online learning questionnaire. *Journal of Computing in Higher Education*, *29*(1), 6–27. doi:10.100712528-016-9125-x

Kovanović, V., Joksimović, S., Mirriahi, N., Blaine, E., Gašević, D., Siemens, G., & Dawson, S. (2018). Understand students' self-reflections through learning analytics. *Proceedings of the 8th International Conference on Learning Analytics and Knowledge*, 389-398. 10.1145/3170358.3170374

Lew, D. N. M., & Schmidt, H. G. (2011). Writing to learn: Can reflection journals be used to promote self-reflection and learning? *Higher Education Research & Development*, *30*(4), 519–532. doi:10.1080/07294360.2010.512627

Littlejohn, A., Hood, N., Milligan, C., & Mustain, P. (2016). *Learning in MOOCs: Motivations and self-regulated learning in MOOCs*. doi:10.1016/j.iheduc.2015.12.003

Liu, S., Gomez, J., Khan, B., & Yen, C. J. (2007). Toward a learner-oriented community college online course dropout framework. *International Journal on E-Learning*, *6*(4), 519–542.

Macfadyen, L. P., & Dawson, S. (2010). Mining LMS data to develop an "early warning system" for educators: A proof of concept. *Computers & Education*, *54*(2), 588–599. doi:10.1016/j.compedu.2009.09.008

Ministerio de Educación. Perú. (2016). *Currículo nacional de la educación básica*. Retrieved from http://www.minedu.gob.pe/curriculo/pdf/curriculo-nacional-2016-2.pdf

Moreno-Marcos, P. M., Muñoz-Merino, P. J., Maldonado-Mahauad, J., Pérez-Sanagustín, M., Alario-Hoyos, C., & Delgado Kloos, C. (2020). *Temporal analysis for dropout prediction using self-regulated learning strategies in self-paced MOOCs*. doi:10.1016/j.compedu.2019.103728

National Student Clearinghouse Research Center. (2022). *Overview: Spring 2022 enrollment estimates*. https://nscresearchcenter.org/stay-informed/

Ngampornchai, A., & Adams, J. (2016). Students' acceptance and readiness for E-learning in Northeastern Thailand. *International Journal of Educational Technology in Higher Education*, *13*(1), 34. doi:10.118641239-016-0034-x

OECD. (2015). *Education at a glance 2015: OECD indicators*. OECD Publishing. doi:10.1787/eag-2015-

Pallant, J. (2013). *SPSS survival manual: A step by step guide to data analysis using IBM SPSS* (5th ed.). Allen & Unwin.

Panadero, E., & Alonso-Tapia, J. (2014). How do students self-regulate?: Review of Zimmerman's cyclical model of self-regulated learning. *Anales De Psicologia*.

Pardo, A., Ellis, R. A., & Calvo, R. A. (2015). Combining observational and experiential data to inform the redesign of learning activities. *Proceedings of the Fifth International Conference on Learning Analytics and Knowledge*, 305-309.

Park, J., Yu, R., Rodriguez, F., Baker, R., Smyth, P., & Warschauer, M. (2018). Understanding student procrastination via mixture models. *Proceedings of the 11th International Conference on Educational Data Mining*.

Pintrich, P. R., Smith, D. A., Garcia, T., & McKeachie, W. J. (1993). Reliability and predictive validity of the motivated strategies for learning questionnaire (MSLQ). *Educational and Psychological Measurement, 53*(3), 801–813. doi:10.1177/0013164493053003024

Romero, C., & Ventura, S. (2007). Educational data mining: A survey from 1995 to 2005. *Expert Systems with Applications, 33*(1), 135–146. doi:10.1016/j.eswa.2006.04.005

Saito, H., & Miwa, K. (2007). Construction of a learning environment supporting learners' reflection: A case of information seeking on the web. *Computers & Education, 49*(2), 214–229. doi:10.1016/j.compedu.2005.07.001

Seaman, J. E., Allen, I. E., & Seaman, J. (2018). *Grade Increase: Tracking Distance Education in the United States.* Babson Survey Research Group.

Sife, A., Lwoga, E., & Sanga, C. (2007). New technologies for teaching and learning: Challenges for higher learning institutions in developing countries. *International Journal of Education and Development Using ICT, 3*(2).

Sigama, K., & Kalema, B. M. (2018, November). Conceptualizing moocs implementation for higher education in developing countries. In *2018 IEEE 6th International Conference on MOOCs, Innovation and Technology in Education (MITE)* (pp. 14-18). IEEE. 10.1109/MITE.2018.8747114

Soffer, T., & Cohen, A. (2019). Students' engagement characteristics predict success and completion of online courses. *Journal of Computer Assisted Learning, 35*(3), 378-389. doi:10.1111/jcal.12340

Strang, K. D. (2017). Beyond engagement analytics: Which online mixed-data factors predict student learning outcomes? *Education and Information Technologies, 22*(3), 917–937. doi:10.100710639-016-9464-2

Tarus, J. K., Gichoya, D., & Muumbo, A. (2015). Challenges of implementing e-learning in Kenya: A case of Kenyan public universities. *International Review of Research in Open and Distributed Learning, 16*(1), 120-141.

Thode, H. C. (2002). *Testing for normality* (Vol. 164). CRC Press. doi:10.1201/9780203910894

Ullmann, T. D. (2011). *An architecture for the automated detection of textual indicators of reflection.* Academic Press.

United Nations. (2020). *Policy Brief: Education during COVID-19 and beyond.* https://unsdg.un.org/resources/policy-brief-education-during-covid-19-and-beyond

Van den Boom, G., Paas, F., Van Merrienboer, J. J., & Van Gog, T. (2004). Reflection prompts and tutor feedback in a web-based learning environment: Effects on students' self-regulated learning competence. *Computers in Human Behavior, 20*(4), 551–567. doi:10.1016/j.chb.2003.10.001

Weinberg, S. L., & Abramowitz, S. K. (2008). *Statistics using SPSS: An integrative approach.* Cambridge University Press.

Wong, J., Baars, M., Davis, D., Van, D. Z., Houben, G., & Paas, F. (2019). Supporting self-regulated learning in online learning environments and MOOCs: A systematic review. *International Journal of Human-Computer Interaction*, *35*(4-5), 356–373. doi:10.1080/10447318.2018.1543084

Xing, W., & Du, D. (2019). Dropout prediction in MOOCs: Using deep learning for personalized intervention. *Journal of Educational Computing Research*, *57*(3), 547–570. doi:10.1177/0735633118757015

Xu, D., Glick, D., Rodriguez, F., Cung, B., Qiujie, L., & Warschauer, M. (2019). Does blended instruction enhance English language learning in developing countries? Evidence from Mexico. *British Journal of Educational Technology*.

Xu, D., & Jaggars, S. S. (2011). *Online and hybrid course enrollment and performance in Washington state community and technical colleges.* CCRC working paper no. 31. Community College Research Center, Columbia University.

Xu, D., & Xu, Y. (2019). *The promises and limits of online higher education: Understanding how distance education affects access, cost, and quality*. American Enterprise Institute. https://www.aei.org/research-products/report/the-promises-and-limits-of-online-higher-education

Zacharis, N. Z. (2015). A multivariate approach to predicting student outcomes in web-enabled blended learning courses. *The Internet and Higher Education*, *27*, 44–53. doi:10.1016/j.iheduc.2015.05.002

Zimmerman, B. J. (1990). Self-regulated learning and academic achievement: An overview. *Educational Psychologist*, *25*(1), 3–17. doi:10.120715326985ep2501_2

Zimmerman, B. J. (2000). *Attaining self-regulation: A social cognitive perspective. In Handbook of self-regulation*. Elsevier. doi:10.1016/B978-012109890-2/50031-7

Zimmerman, B. J. (2002). Becoming a self-regulated learner: An overview. *Theory into Practice*, *41*(2), 64–72. doi:10.120715430421tip4102_2

Zimmerman, B. J. (2008). Investigating self-regulation and motivation: Historical background, methodological developments, and future prospects. *American Educational Research Journal*, *45*(1), 166–183. doi:10.3102/0002831207312909

ADDITIONAL READING

Butler, D. L., & Winne, P. H. (1995). Feedback and Self-Regulated Learning: A Theoretical Synthesis. *Review of Educational Research*, *65*(3), 245–281. doi:10.3102/00346543065003245

Clark, I. (2012). Formative Assessment: Assessment Is for Self-regulated Learning. *Educational Psychology Review*, *24*(2), 205–249. doi:10.100710648-011-9191-6

Gašević, D., Dawson, S., Rogers, T., & Gasevic, D. (2016). Learning analytics should not promote one size fits all: The effects of instructional conditions in predicting academic success. *The Internet and Higher Education*, *28*, 68–84. doi:10.1016/j.iheduc.2015.10.002

Kostons, D., Van Gog, T., & Paas, F. (2012). Training self-assessment and task-selection skills: A cognitive approach to improving self-regulated learning. *Learning and Instruction*, *22*(2), 121–132. doi:10.1016/j.learninstruc.2011.08.004

Lai, C. (2013). A framework for developing self-directed technology use for language learning. *Language Learning & Technology*, *17*(2), 100–122.

Papamitsiou, Z., & Economides, A. A. (2014). Learning Analytics and Educational Data Mining in Practice: A Systematic Literature Review of Empirical Evidence. *Journal of Educational Technology & Society*, *17*(4), 49–64. doi:10.2307/jeductechsoci.17.4.49

Roll, I., & Winne, P. H. (2015). Understanding, evaluating, and supporting self-regulated learning using learning analytics. *Journal of Learning Analytics*, *2*(1), 7–12. doi:10.18608/jla.2015.21.2

Sun, S. Y. (2014). Learner perspectives on fully online language learning. *Distance Education*, *35*(1), 18–42. doi:10.1080/01587919.2014.891428

Ullmann, T. D. (2017). Reflective writing analytics - Empirically determined keywords of written reflection. *ACM International Conference Proceeding Series*, 163–167. 10.1145/3027385.3027394

KEY TERMS AND DEFINITIONS

At-Risk Students: Students who are low performing or come from low socioeconomic backgrounds.

Developing Country: A country with a less developed industrial base and a low Human Development Index relative to other countries.

Early Warning System: A pedagogical-technological system that uses machine learning to identify at-risk students early in the course.

Reflection: A process which involves constructing meaning by linking current experience to previous learning, and by applying what one has learned to contexts beyond the original situation.

Retention: The continuous enrollment of students from one fall semester to the following fall semester.

Self-Regulated Learning: A cyclical process wherein the student plans for a task, monitors their performance, and then reflects on the outcome.

Text Analysis: The action of obtaining patterns or insights from text-based resources.

APPENDIX 1

Table 8.

Kinds of Learning	Fink's Verbs for Significant Learning	Extended Taxonomy
Foundational Knowledge	Remember, Understand, Identify	Remembered, Remembering, Understood, Understanding, Identified, Identifying
Application	Use, Critique, Manage, Solve, Assess, Judge, Do, Imagine, Analyze, Calculate, Create, Coordinate, Make decisions	Used, Using, Usage, Criticized, Criticizing, Managed, Managing, Solved, Solving, Solution, Assessed, Assessing, Assessment, Judged, Judging, Did, Doing, Imagined, Imagining, Analyzed, Analyzing, Analysis, Analyses, Calculated, Calculating, Created, Creating, Creation, Coordinated, Coordinating, Coordination, Made decision, Making decision
Integration	Connect, Relate, Compare, Integrate, Identify similarities, Identify interaction	Connected, Connecting, Connection, Related, Relating, Compared, Comparing, Comparison(s), Integrated, Integrating, Integration(s), Identified similarities, Identifying similarities, Identified interaction, Identifying interaction
Human Dimension	Understand others, Decide to become, Interact with others regarding, Come to see themselves	Understood others, Understanding others, Decided to become, Deciding to become, Interacting with others regarding, Coming to see themselves
Caring	Get excited about, Be ready to, Be more interested in, Value	Got excited about, Getting excited about, Was/am/is/are ready to, Has/have been ready to, Will be ready to, Valued, Valuing
Learning How to Learn	Read and study, Set a learning agenda, Identify source of information, Be able to construct knowledge, Frame useful questions, Create a learning plan	Reading and studying, Setting a learning agenda, Identified a source of information, Identifying a source of information, Was/am/is/are able to construct knowledge, Will be ready to construct knowledge, Framed useful questions, Framing useful questions, Created a learning plan, Creating a learning plan

APPENDIX 2

Thank you for taking time to complete this questionnaire. Please answer each question to the best of your knowledge. Your thoughtfulness and candid responses will be greatly appreciated. Your individual name or identification number will not at any time be associated with your responses. Your responses will be kept completely confidential.

1. What is your gender?
   a. Female
   b. Male
2. What is your age? Numeric characters only:
3. What is your major?
4. How many for-credit online courses have you taken prior to this term?

a. 0
b. 1
c. 2
d. 3
e. 4
f. 5
g. 6 or more

5. What was your high school GPA?

APPENDIX 3

Table 9.

Word	Frequency	Relative Frequency
Use, Used, Using, Usage	146	22%
Solve, Solved, Solving, Solution	76	11.4%
Understand, Understood, Understanding	53	7.9%
Manage, Managed, Managing	44	6.6%
Create, Created, Creating, Creation	42	6.3%
Analyze, Analyzed, Analyzing, Analysis	41	6.1%
Remember, Remembered, Remembering	36	5.4%
Relate, Related, Relating	34	5.1%
Read and Study, Reading and Studying	33	4.9%
Construct/Constructed/Constructing Knowledge	30	4.5%
Do, Did, Doing	27	4%
Assess, Assessed, Assessing	19	2.8%
Interact, Interacting	17	2.6%
Be able to	12	1.8%
Be ready to	9	1.4%
Connect, Connected, Connecting, Connection	9	1.4%
Integrate, Integrated, Integrating, Integration(s)	7	1.2%
Imagine, Imagined, Imagining	6	1%
Judge, Judged, Judging	6	1%
Coordinate, Coordinated, Coordinating, Coordination	5	0.9%
Identify, Identified, Identifying	4	0.6%
Compare, Compare, Comparing, Comparison(s)	4	0.6%
Make/Made/Making decisions	3	0.5%
Total	663	100%

APPENDIX 4

Provided below are two examples of reflective responses of students who show evidence of significant learning in their writing. Words associated with significant learning appear in bold, followed by the English translation.

Example 1:

Em mi opinion extender el tiempo a lo largo del curso es favorable ya que nos permite poder desarrollar una mejor forma de lograr la captura de la informacion que necesitamos **aprendar (Study), en comparacion (Comaparison)** *a realizarlo cercano al examen ya que saturamos nuestro cerebro de informacion mezclada y que quizas no* **entendamos (Understand)** *para realizar el examen.*

Example 2:

las ventajas que tienen en mi opinión, primero que si organizamos bien nuestro tiempo todos los días para que los temas se puedan **leer (Read)**, **entenderemos (Undersatn***d) mejor los conceptos, tenemos tiempo para aclarar dudas, hacer consultas si es necesario y elaboramos mejor los trabajos y* **aprender (Study)** *más. Una* **comparación (Comparison)** *de alguien que deja todo hasta el último momento saturado de trabajo no hará bien las lecturas de los temas o los trabajos y lo más importante, no* **aprenderán (Study).**

Chapter 14
Developing Students' Self-Regulation Skills Within and Outside Academic Modules

Peng Cheng Wang
Singapore Institute of Technology, Singapore

Eric C. P. Chua
Singapore Institute of Technology, Singapore

Karin Avnit
https://orcid.org/0000-0001-8126-0768
Singapore Institute of Technology, Singapore

Sok Mui Lim
Singapore Institute of Technology, Singapore

ABSTRACT

COVID-19 has accelerated the adoption of online learning, and the authors' university (like many others) is settling into a blended learning approach. In this chapter, the authors share their experiences in improving students' self-regulation of online learning. The first learning experience for most students at the Singapore Institute of Technology is in online, self-paced courses in Mathematics, Physics, and Chemistry. Beyond content, these courses provide students opportunities to embrace the 'norm' of self-paced, self-directed online learning and to expose and encourage them to develop self-regulation skills. Students are required to self-assess and refer to different learning resources independently, based on their identified needs. The authors have also developed another intervention based on Zimmerman's self-regulated learning model, guiding students to plan, monitor, and adjust their learning plans and develop self-efficacy through this process. For students to transfer these skills into their actual studies, the authors provide individual coaching sessions to facilitate students' implementation.

DOI: 10.4018/978-1-6684-6500-4.ch014

INTRODUCTION

COVID-19 has accelerated the adoption of online learning (García-Morales et al., 2021), and our university, like many others, is settling into a blended learning approach for the new endemic norm. Online learning therefore plays a larger role in our students' learning compared to before.

In this context we take online learning to be the use of synchronous and asynchronous interaction and communication within a virtual environment, which contrasts with traditional learning where student – teacher interaction and communication occur face-to-face in a classroom (Broadbent & Poon, 2015). Effective online learning requires effort from both the instructor and the student. While instructors gain expertise in effective online teaching (Lim, 2020; Fung et al., 2020), it is necessary for students to also enhance their skills for effective online learning.

Online learning can be more challenging for students than face-to-face instruction, as it requires them to be much more independent and self-directed (Broadbent & Poon, 2015). Success in an online learning environment also relies heavily on a student's ability to engage in the learning process autonomously and actively (Broadbent & Poon, 2015; Wang et al., 2013). Furthermore, research has shown that students who struggle in face-to-face classes are likely to struggle even more with online learning (Loeb, 2020). For example, in an institutional study on online learning early in the COVID-19 pandemic, we found that many of our students struggled to self-regulate. We also found that weaker students tended to struggle more, reporting low or declining motivation, with additional challenges in time management.

Given the increased importance of online learning and its associated challenges for our students, our university has been finding ways to support our students and help them build capacity for online learning. We are guided by evidence that helping students increase their ability for self-regulation improves their learning. For example, via a systematic review, self-regulated learning strategies of metacognitive self-regulation, time management, effort regulation and critical thinking was found to positively associate with academic success in an online environment (Broadbent & Poon, 2015). We therefore identified that our students may benefit from self-regulated learning training to increase their self-efficacy for online learning.

At the university's teaching and learning unit, the authors are involved in two initiatives for enhancing self-regulated learning in our students. The first is a large-scale online bridging program for newly matriculated students to brush up on foundational STEM subjects including mathematics, physics, and chemistry. The second is a small-group, non-credit-bearing module that helps students apply self-regulation skills to improve their learning. In this chapter, our main purpose is to share our experience with these two initiatives.

Before discussing the two initiatives, we would like to share our university's context, to aid readers in understanding the context of the work, and in evaluating its applicability to other contexts. Our university is a large technological university that has several campuses across Singapore. It is a relatively young university established in 2014 to pioneer an applied learning pathway. It offers undergraduate degree programs across a wide range of disciplines including engineering, infocomm technology, health sciences, business, and design. The university enrols roughly 9,000 students. It is one of six publicly funded universities in Singapore, which together provides subsidised university places for 40% of each cohort (Ministry of Education of Singapore, 2022). In Singapore, students typically enter university after completing either 'A' levels or a polytechnic diploma. In our case, most students come from the diploma route.

Self-Regulated Learning Models

There are several self-regulated learning (SRL) models in the literature. In a recent review Panadero suggested six models, namely those of Zimmerman, Boekaerts, Winne and Hadwin, Pintrich, Efklides and Hadwin, Järvelä and Miller (Panadero, 2017).

In Zimmerman's Cyclical Phases Model, self-regulated learning is taken as the conceptual framework of learners in charge of their learning, monitoring and cyclically adjusting their plan according to the outcomes of learning and developing self-efficacy through this process (Zimmerman, 2000). The 'forethought' phase involves proper goal setting and deciding on a learning strategy. The 'performance' requires student self-discipline to carry out the plan as well as self-monitoring how well the plan is working. The 'self-reflection' phase examines one's performance with regards to the goals set and determines what to improve going forward.

In Boekaerts' Dual Processing Model, emotions are critical in determining 'goal pathways' one chooses for a task. If the task is aligned with one's personal goals, positive emotions will be triggered, leading one to activate a 'mastery/growth pathway' and adopt top-down strategies. On the other hand, if the task is perceived to be threatening to one's well-being, negative emotions will be triggered, leading one to activate a 'well-being pathway' and adopt bottom-up strategies. The third scenario is a transition between the 'well-being pathway' and the 'mastery/growth pathway'.

In Winne and Hadwin's model, SRL occurs in 4 connected phases in a feedback loop. These phases are (a) 'task definition', where one understands the task; (b) 'goal setting and planning', where one sets goals and develops a plan to attain the goals; (c) 'enacting tactics and strategies', where one carries out the actions required to accomplish the goals; and (d) 'metacognitively adapting', where one makes changes in to his or her motivations, beliefs, and strategies for the future.

In Pintrich's SRL model, SRL occurs in four phases: (a) forethought, planning and activation, (b) monitoring, (c) control and (d) reaction and reflection. In each of the 4 phases, there are four different areas for regulation, namely cognition, motivation/affect, behaviour and context. For each phase and area, several SRL processes were articulated, for example target goal setting for cognition regulation during the first (forethought, planning and activation) phase.

In Efklides's Metacognitive and Affective Model of Self-Regulated Learning (MARSH), there are 2 levels - the Person level, and the Task x Person level. The Person level represents one's personal characteristics, and consists of cognition, motivation, self-concept, affect, volition, metacognitive knowledge and skills. The Task x Person level is where the task interacts with one's personal characteristics, where task execution occupies one's attention and actions are data-driven and bottom–up.

Hadwin, Järvelä and Miller's Shared Regulation of Learning Model (SSRL) addresses SRL in a collaborative setting. In the model, shared regulation happens in 4 loops. In the first loop, groups develop shared task perceptions. In the second loop, groups set shared task goals and develop shared plans. In the third loop, groups coordinate their collaboration, monitor their progress and modify their task perceptions, goals, plans, or strategies. In the fourth loop, groups review and regulate for future tasks.

The interventions our institution adopted are based on Zimmerman's model (Zimmerman, 2000). This model was chosen because it is one of the more common models (Panadero, 2017), and was deemed easy to understand and apply. In addition, it was felt it was a comprehensive approach considering different aspects of learning and the importance placed on the continuous adjustments of personal (cognitive and affective states), behavioural (performance) and environmental (learning conditions and outcomes) determinants. Furthermore, we believe that our students become better learners through interactions with their instructors and peers, in line with the social cognitive theory that underpins Zimmerman's model.

Interventions for Developing Self-Regulated Learning

There is a considerable body of literature on interventions for developing self-regulated learning in various settings, and corresponding systematic reviews. For example, Hattie et al. (1996) reviewed 51 interventions on improving study skills and found that they were most effective when situated in-context and fostered student activity and metacognitive awareness. Dignath et al. (2008) reviewed 48 self-regulation training programs for primary school students and found that effective interventions are based on social-cognitive theories, train cognitive, metacognitive, and motivational strategies, and provide knowledge about strategy use and about its benefit. Jansen et al. reviewed self-regulated learning interventions in higher education (Jansen et al., 2019). Among other findings, the review found that intervention characteristics of inclusion of cognitive strategies, format, timing, tailoring to the learning context, and SRL activity supported, did not significantly moderate the positive effect of SRL interventions on achievement. The authors noted that this may suggest there is no 'wrong' interventions in the context of higher education. Wong et al. recently reviewed 35 studies on supporting SRL in massive open online courses (MOOC), and found that while prompts, feedback, and an integrated support system can be effective, it is necessary to consider human factors (Wong et al., 2018).

Response to Intervention Model

In creating interventions to help our students build SRL capacity, our institution has adopted the Response to Intervention (RtI) model (Berkeley et al., 2009). In brief, RtI is a tiered approach for supporting students' learning and behaviour. The general principle is to begin by ensuring high-quality and universal intervention for the target student population. Students who are struggling and require additional support are then identified and provided with further interventions at increasing levels of intensity. RtI is generally considered to have three tiers. Tier 1 is preventive with universal screening and broad intervention. When Tier 1 intervention is insufficient, Tier 2 features targeted, small-group interventions and close progress monitoring. Tier 3 involves high-intensity, longer duration individualised interventions, and frequent progress monitoring.

For Tier 1, our institution has created our bridging program for STEM disciplines in an online, self-paced, and adaptive manner (Wang et al., 2020). This is the first learning experience for most students, covering foundational knowledge in Mathematics, Physics and Chemistry. This set of self-paced adaptive courses is designed to address the challenge of a heterogenous profile of students with varying competencies in these subjects at the point of entering the institution. The profile is heterogenous because while most of our students come from the diploma route, some have diplomas from similar disciplines while others are from non-related diplomas. Furthermore, they would have had different exposures to Mathematics, Physics and Chemistry depending on their subject choices before entering polytechnic (during their secondary school education).

Beyond technical content, this adaptive learning environment also provides students with the opportunity to build SRL capacity by embracing the 'norm' of self-paced, self-directed online learning, and to encourage them to develop learning traits that are essential in this digital space. Self-regulated learning has been much discussed and reviewed towards academic outcomes, and the literature clearly suggests that more can be done to drive towards non-academic outcomes, especially in the digital environment (Anthonysamy et al., 2020). Recent literature also observed that students with good self-regulatory learning skills behave differently from other learners who are not as strong, and they are more likely to revisit previously learnt materials (Jivet et al., 2020). Students today have also started to become more independent in their learning, whether driven by the pandemic or otherwise (Anthonysamy, 2021), often desiring, or wanting to take charge of their own learning (Freire & Santos, 2021). These skills are therefore useful and relevant, not only for the immediate term to complete their undergraduate studies (Tadesse et al., 2022), but also on the longer term for adult learning (Morris, 2019; Silamut & Sovajassatakul, 2021).

Following RtI principles (Berkeley et al., 2009), for Tier 2, we developed a program that provides targeted, small-group intervention for students who needed more help at improving their self-regulated learning for online learning, with close and personalised progress monitoring by instructors. For this intervention, we focused on metacognitive self-regulation, time and study environment management, and effort regulation strategies. This was guided by an internal study conducted to understand students' learning strategies. 132 second-year students completed the Motivated Strategies for Learning Questionnaire (MSLQ) (Pintrich & de Groot, 1990). On average, compared to students from the traditional route ('A' levels), students from the diploma route scored lower on average in the following learning strategies – metacognitive self-regulation, time and study environment management, and effort regulation (all $p < 0.03$). On the motivational scales, on average they reported lower self-efficacy and higher test anxiety (all $p < 0.03$). In addition, we found that students' self-efficacy was positively associated with metacognitive self-regulation, time and study environment management and effort regulation, after controlling for academic background (all $p < 0.001$). Given that our students are predominantly from the diploma route and they appeared to be less equipped than their peers from a more traditional route in terms of metacognitive self-regulation, time and study environment management, and effort regulation, and that these variables are associated with students' self-efficacy, we decided to focus on these areas.

Design of the Adaptive Learning System

Online learning often requires good use of the learner's time, with good concentration and attention for the learning to be effective (Pearl & Arunfred, 2019; Szpunar et al., 2013). The digital space provides many external links and temptations for one to digress from the original intention of learning a particular content/subject, causing distraction (Pearl & Arunfred, 2019). What is critical therefore, is for that short span of 'undivided attention' time to be used to the fullest potential, and this adaptive learning system endeavours to achieve this.

The focus of the courses within the adaptive learning system is on active learning, rather than on teaching. Students are required to self-assess, assume a bigger responsibility in their learning and refer to different learning resources independently, based on their identified needs. This is a paradigm shift moving away from purely focusing on the subject matter, into developing good learning practices and processes (Tadesse et al., 2022). When faced with different challenges, the courses react to errors made by the learner and provide references to different online resources to strengthen the understanding of relevant concepts. This includes providing prompts (van Alten et al., 2020) and hints, such as reminding them of a certain critical concept, or potential pitfalls, nudging students to re-watch video tutorials (van Alten et al., 2020) and directing them to other online resources that are aimed at the specific mistakes/struggles encountered by the student. These video tutorials or online resources could be either developed in-house by our faculty members, or from public domain resources. Similar exercises, additional work examples and practice problems are then offered to ensure mastery of skills before moving on to a different topic. This inherently helps students to focus their attention on what they are not yet competent in, and in the process makes better use of their learning time. Through this, students learn to self-regulate their learning, pace themselves, and more critically pick up the all-important skill of 'learning to learn' independently online. Thus, the three phases discussed by Jivet et al. (2020) (forethought, performance, and reflection) can be met, amongst others found in the literature (Anthonysamy et al., 2021). Through this, students learn to put in more thought to their learning (Tadesse et al., 2022), to set their own goals (of what they would like to learn or address) and to plan and manage their time focusing on what may require immediate attention. The online system allows students to track and evaluate their own performance – if they do well, they can move on to more advanced topics, and if not, to dwell or look deeper into concepts to improve the competencies. After this self-evaluation, they learn to reflect and thus seek necessary and relevant help (from the system, their peers, and the faculty members).

Design of Learning to Learn Better

One important goal we had was for our students to transfer the skills learnt and improve their actual studies. Learning from the evidence discussed earlier, we identified that the intervention should be situated, be based on experiential learning approaches, and be closely contextualised to students' actual coursework. Following these principles, the intervention targeted online learning instead of learning in general. Taking reference from the intervention characteristics described by Jensen et al. (2019), our intervention is aimed at both metacognitive and resource management activities, includes cognitive strategy instruction tailored to the learning context, and includes instruction, application and prompts. In addition, its pedagogy is experiential learning-based, including a weekly reflective log component covering coursework in question, strategies used and why, compliance, challenges encountered, and actions taken or plan to take to overcome the challenges. It is also supported by short, facilitated sessions focussing on group sharing and discussion of experiences.

The intervention is run as a non-credit bearing module called Learning to Learn Better. The module runs over an entire academic term and spans 15 weeks. The intended learning outcomes are (a) identify personal learning goals and create a learning plan, (b) organise and carry out the planned learning activities, (c) assess and revise the learning plan, (d) identify concrete solutions to manage learning challenges. There are no assessments per se; instead, there are tasks spread across the module to help students apply the learning onto their own situation and to track their progress. These tasks are: 1) creating SMART goals, 2) creating a learning plan, 3) completing the (partial) Motivated Strategies for Learning Questionnaire (once each at the beginning and the end of the module), 4) completing the Self-Regulated Learning Interview Schedule (SRLIS). For the MSLQ, only the following sub-scales were used – self-efficacy, test anxiety, metacognitive self-regulation, time and study environment, and effort regulation. These are selected as our institutional data indicated these as weak areas for our students. The learning activities were made up of 6 classes spread across the term, and two 1:1 coaching sessions to review progress (once in the middle and once towards the end of the module). The class schedule, including the learning activities and tasks, is shown in Table 1.

To evaluate the Learning to Learn Better intervention, a mixed-method, quasi-experimental design is used. The study consisted of two arms – an intervention arm where students were enrolled in Learning to Learn Better, and a control arm made up of students not taking Learning to Learn Better. This study

Table 1. Schedule for Learning to Learn Better.

Week	Learning Activities	Tasks
3	Metacognitive cycle • Planning and organising learning schedule • Monitoring and identifying challenges for learning • Evaluating learning • Improving and managing learning	SMART goals for current term MSLQ
4	Managing time effectively for learning • Realising and acknowledging procrastination factors Support and resources needed	Learning plan for current term
5	Staying motivated for learning • Acknowledging successes and reinforcing sources of motivation Recovering from challenging learning situations and moving forward positively	SRLIS Actigraphy
6 – 7	Coaching session 1 • Review goals and progress (metacognitive cycle)	
8	Learning with others effectively online • Group contract • Establishing trust and workable partnership • Learning Pyramid Communicating effectively online	
9 – 10	Coaching session 2 • Review goals and progress (metacognitive cycle)	
11	Sleep and Learning Managing assessments • Online assessments • Stress and anxiety • Wellbeing	MSLQ Reflection
15	Reviewing past term (Metacognitive cycle)	SMART goals (for next term) SRLIS Module feedback

started in January 2021 and is expected to complete in June 2023, and the study is on-going at the time of writing.

For the treatment arm, participants were recruited from students enrolled in Learning to Learn Better, with a target of 60 research participants over 4 runs of the module. Consent was sought from students and anonymised coursework data was extracted for research purposes. The anonymised data collected consisted of demographics, submissions for smart goals, learning plans, and self-reflections, written notes taken by the coaches during the coaching sessions, MSLQ responses, SRLIS responses, actigraphy data, and module feedback responses. For the control arm, participants were recruited from students not taking Learning to Learn Better, with a target of 60 research participants. To provide comparison data, participants were asked to provide demographic data, complete the MSLQ and SRLIS, and to provide actigraphy data. These study procedures were carried out at the same junctures of the academic term as the intervention arm participants, and the data collected were de-identified.

Evaluation of the Adaptive Learning System

As we emphasised the need to embrace and practice 'forethought, performance and reflection' (Jivet et al., 2020), one aspect that is equally crucial in this system is to evaluate the learning process and

Figure 1. Self-reported confidence level before and after learning through Quest, Academic Years 2021-2022

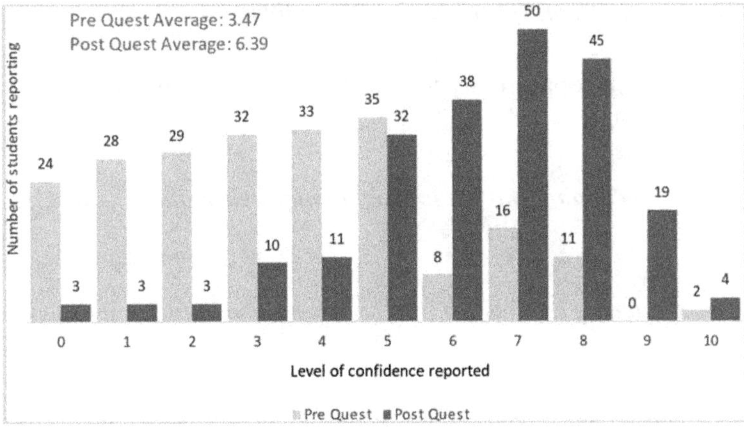

experience of the students. Here, two things are looked at. First, the students are asked to 'forethought' and evaluate their own confidence in the subject prior to starting the online learning system. This is an essential first-step self-reflection for the students to be self-critical, and to assess their own confidence, and inherently, their competency. As seen from Figure 1 below, most students who reflected are trending towards 5 and below. This data is consistent to what was observed in the last 5 to 6 years since the online system was set up. Once the students finished the online learning system, the same question was asked again. Now, the students get to practice the 'performance and reflection'. It can be observed from Figure 1 that there is a shift in students' self-perception of their own confidence in attempting the questions in the online learning system. The results are encouraging and show that students grew in confidence as they journeyed through this online learning system on their own.

Secondly, students were also asked on their motivation to do independent learning. The results indicate that 65% of the students surveyed agreed that through adaptive Math courses, they were more motivated and encouraged to embrace independent learning. This resonates with our earlier hypothesis and justifications that our well-designed online learning system will help our students to focus on what is necessary for them (be it to gain confidence, or mastery) and to make better use of their learning time. The ability to self-regulate their learning and to pace themselves to be independent learners is therefore developed throughout this learning process.

Evaluation of Learning to Learn Better

As this project is on-going, here we present some preliminary data from the initial runs of Learning to Learn Better. From initial analysis of student demographics and reasons for joining the program, we observed that students who enrolled in Learning to Learn Better tend to be average- to above-average students (in terms of their GPA) who expressed a desire to further improve themselves through this program.

Based on preliminary analysis of qualitative feedback after students completed Learning to Learn Better students, students shared that the module helped them manage their time better, encouraged active reflection and helped them explore learning strategies to develop themselves.

"The metacognitive cycle helps find out my strengths and weaknesses"

"I implemented breaks in between my learning and felt motivated".

Students also appreciated the opportunity to connect with like-minded peers and the peer learning that results.

"Gives an opportunity to meet others who are looking to improving study methods, to discuss and share ideas".

"Discussing each other's learning experiences, helps you realise things you never realised was a problem (before)."

DISCUSSION

Adaptive Learning System

As mentioned earlier, our institution welcomes students of diverse backgrounds every year. Coupled with the lack of immediate response from the instructors (comparing to face-to-face class), personalised learning and adaptive learning to the learner's needs becomes even more important (Peng et al., 2019). We want to achieve a personalised learning pathway to create a learner-centric environment (King & South, 2017), and to be adaptive for a better learning experience (Apoki et al., 2022). For students who are already strong in their concepts, they perhaps do not need to go through as many resources or links compared to those who are struggling. Instead, time can be spent on more challenging activities that can stretch their potential, or simply put, to be spent on other subjects that require their attention. This is extremely helpful to this group of students who have prior knowledge and could further harness the impact of self-regulated learning (such as self-reflection, better monitoring behaviour) during this process (Yang et al., 2018). For students who are struggling with a certain subject, it makes sense for their attention to be focused on that area. Here, maximising the use of the students' time is critically important – to ensure that each student is stimulated cognitively to want to learn and achieve the desired competency. This requires careful management, both digitally via the system, and with timely human intervention, which will be described later. What the digital systems aims to develop is beyond just learning how to answer a question correctly, but to develop the students' ability to learn actively, and eventually able to independently pick up and discern relevant learning resources that can help them in their learning. There is therefore no point to repeatedly ask a student to 're-attempt' the questions he/she is struggling with. Instead, relevant resources, or subtle guides/hints can show the student that with the right information, knowledge and skills can be picked up.

Research shows that discipline and dedication from both the faculty (in terms of providing support) and students are required for students to stay engaged in the learning process. This adjustment to active learning needs time, and thus the additional support and nudging is required to help the students in this journey. For students who need the extra motivation to join and participate actively in the system, an automated intelligent system will nudge them with friendly reminders to go onto the system. For students who are already in the system, the system is also able to pick up students who are having difficulties in attempting the questions. They will first be referred to an online community (which will be described in detail later), where peer teaching is offered, and a live forum is available for doubts to be clarified. If this help is insufficient, students will be further referred to subject matter experts (SMEs) who will then be able to offer a more focused help. The above three steps are all made possible through a dedicated tracking system, both online and offline, and managed by the adaptive learning system product team.

A learning community can promote engagement with the learnt content as well as with instructors and peers. This promotes active learning practices and inherently support student learning (Kuh, 2009; Sengsouliya et al., 2020). An online community is thus set up to encourage peer-to-peer learning, monitored by the academic staff, to complement the adaptive system. For the last two years, at least 600 students enrolled into the learning community. This creates an ecosystem where students can confidently share their queries and have the assurance that they will be addressed and answered. The benefits are observed to be two-fold. One, students who were able to support the peers not only demonstrated their understanding in the topic, but by sharing the knowledge, they found themselves knowing the topic better. Two, at the receiving end, the students not only got their queries/doubts answered, but they were also able to learn from their peers how the challenges could be addressed. Such online engagement, sharing of information and having intentional discussion on the topics can help develop students cognitively – this in turn will continue to encourage students to engage in positive and productive discussions (Freire & Santos, 2021). Academic staff are also on hand to provide timely guidance, and at the same time, provide current learning resources at various checkpoints to motivate students in their learning. Beyond this, academic staff were also able to sieve out critical points of learning struggles that can be addressed. This creates a feedback loop for both current students and future cohorts. This ranges from the online content (whether it is relevant, current, or has any errors), to the mode of delivery (such as length of video, accessibility of videos) to topics that the majority struggles with (whether more intervention or deliberate re-design of content) that needs to be re-examined. This combination of monitoring, interaction in this online community (or discussion forum), and the use of learning data analytics is usually critical and essential to make this work (Freire & Santos, 2021). This also brings up another equally important point that the adaptive learning system product team hopes to achieve – which is to ensure that good interactivity between the students and the content within learning environment needs to be achieved (Le et al., 2022).

This high-tech (adaptive learning system) – high touch (instructions and community support) (Avnit et al., n.d.) targeted learning is essential for our students to pick up the necessary skills to prepare them for the subsequent modules. It is not so straightforward, as students take time to change their learning behaviours, or are not aware of good cognitive learning practices, hence not optimising their learning strategies (van Alten et al., 2020), or they are simply not equipped with the skills (Anthonysamy, 2021). It is certainly not easy too, from the educator's point of view, as discussed earlier on the need for a sound and robust curriculum design and good technological tools to support this initiative (Mirata et al., 2020). What is promising though, is that over the last few years, improvement in the confidence and competencies of the students was observed (Tan et al., 2019; Wang et al., 2020), as shown in Figure 1. More importantly, the confidence level of the students in attempting these topics have also increased, and an increase in motivation for students to be more independent in their learning was also observed. This points us to similar findings found in the literature, where there is a positive correlation of self-regulated learning to intrinsic/extrinsic motivation, self-efficacy (Anthonysamy et al., 2020), and finally to academic achievements (El-Adl & Alkharusi, 2020).

The adaptive learning system described earlier fits within a larger program in our university. This program helps students build capacity for learning using a tiered approach based on the Response to

Intervention (RtI) model (Berkeley et al., 2009). The system sits in Tier 1, which is characterised by first-line early interventions made available to all freshmen. Other than this adaptive learning system, our institution has also implemented under Tier 1 a first-line early intervention for freshmen at risk of poor academic performance. This intervention is known as AdventureLEARN. It focuses on enhancing learning approaches and well-being (Lim et al., 2021) and is delivered via an online gamified micro-learning platform. Freshmen identified with a history of poor well-being, ineffective learning approaches, and/or poor pre-university academic performance receive personalised resource recommendations, on-demand micro-lessons, and progress tracking over their freshman year.

Learning to Learn Better

Although the project and its evaluation are still on-going, there are several learning points to-date from our experience, as described below.

Audience

While the intervention is open to all students, the faculty wanted to reach especially the academically weaker students, and to provide this group of students the additional support based on the evidence that weaker students struggle even more with online learning (Loeb, 2020). To do that, the team partnered with faculty members serving as program leaders or academic advisors to identify and encourage this group of students to attend. Perhaps not surprisingly, it was challenging to reach this group of students at-scale, and we had only limited success. What we noticed was that students who completed the Learning to Learn Better intervention were students with a GPA of 3 or 4 on a 5-point scale, who wanted to improve their GPA. This seems to suggest that sufficient motivation to do better academically may be necessary for students to take up such an intervention, particularly when it is non-credit bearing.

Peer Learning

In delivering the classes, the faculty had planned for group discussions and sharing to stimulate active learning. What the faculty had not planned for was a more intentional use of peer learning as a method to achieve the learning outcomes. This turned out to be a point of improvement and opportunity as anecdotally, students shared that what they enjoyed was to have made new friends who share similar goals and challenges, and to have learnt strategies from them that, on reflection, they can adapt or adopt for themselves.

Collaboration

The Learning to Learn Better intervention was implemented using a collaborative translational approach between our institution and the National University of Singapore (NUS). NUS has been running their version of Learning to Learn Better as an elective credit-bearing module for its undergraduate population since 2017. Our version of Learning to Learn Better as described earlier in this chapter was adapted from this NUS module to suit our different student profile, and to highlight the online learning aspect. Within the local Singaporean context, this project is a good example of inter-varsity translational collaboration, where universities collaborate in common goals and share knowledge and material.

Model

The current model to reach students across the university is to offer a small-group, one-term non-credit bearing module. While this is aligned to the overall Response to Intervention model and is a practical first step for our university, the reach is inherently small with such a model. There are many students who could have benefited that we are unable to reach. To extend the reach, one possible approach is to equip faculty members serving as academic advisors with the knowledge and skills in Learning to Learn Better. In our institution, this is facilitated by a parallel effort to equip all faculty members with coaching skills. In this way, academic advisors can then have coaching conversations with advisees, guiding them on setting goals, developing plans, and monitoring and adjusting their plans. As a further extension, these faculty members may also be able to include these elements into the design and delivery of the modules they teach, thereby reaching yet another group of students.

CONCLUSION

Given the increased importance of online learning and its associated challenges for our students, our university has been finding ways to help our students build SRL capacity. In this process, we are guided by evidence that helping students increase their ability for self-regulation improves their learning (Broadbent & Poon, 2015). We therefore identified that our students may benefit from self-regulated learning training to increase their self-efficacy for online learning. Following the tiered Response to Intervention model (Berkeley et al., 2009), we developed two interventions based on Zimmerman's self-regulated learning model (Zimmerman, 2000). In this chapter, our main purpose is to share our experience to-date with these interventions. The first is via the mass online, self-paced and adaptive learning system to socialise incoming freshmen to online learning, and the second is via the one-term, small-group Learning to Learn Better module to coach students on applying self-regulation to their coursework. While we have been able to achieve these aims, there are challenges of reach, particularly the weaker students who are the main target. One possible approach to extending reach may be to increase the awareness among educators on the importance of developing self-regulation, and to equip them with the skills to promote it in their daily work, such as via curriculum design of the modules they teach, and via the conversations they have with students as academic advisors or faculty members. This may be facilitated through leveraging faculty development programs where most faculty members attend. Peer learning was an important learning point and an exciting area of opportunity. Further efforts to more intentionally use peer learning to help develop self-regulation may yield better models for doing so. In addition, while our focus was on implementation, we could have evaluated our interventions more rigorously in the research sense. Finally, developing self-regulation for online learning is a common goal for many in higher education. Efforts to share models, material, and resources towards achieving that common goal should be highly encouraged.

REFERENCES

Anthonysamy, L. (2021). The use of metacognitive strategies for undisrupted online learning: Preparing university students in the age of pandemic. *Education and Information Technologies, 26*(6), 6881–6899. doi:10.100710639-021-10518-y PMID:33897268

Anthonysamy, L., Ah Choo, K., & Soon Hin, H. (2021). Investigating Self-Regulated Learning Strategies for Digital Learning Relevancy. *Malaysian Journal of Learning and Instruction, 18*(1), 29–64. doi:10.32890/mjli2021.18.1.2

Anthonysamy, L., Koo, A.-C., & Hew, S.-H. (2020). Self-regulated learning strategies and non-academic outcomes in higher education blended learning environments: A one decade review. *Education and Information Technologies, 25*(5), 3677–3704. doi:10.100710639-020-10134-2

Apoki, U. C., Hussein, A. M. A., Al-Chalabi, H. K. M., Badica, C., & Mocanu, M. L. (2022). The Role of Pedagogical Agents in Personalised Adaptive Learning: A Review. *Sustainability, 14*(11), 6442. doi:10.3390u14116442

Avnit, K., Wang, P. C., & Iyer, P. (n.d.). *High tech and high touch: designing a bridging system to help students prepare for STEM studies.* https://www.timeshighereducation.com/campus/high-tech-and-high-touch-designing-bridging-system-help-students-prepare-stem-studies

Berkeley, S., Bender, W. N., Gregg Peaster, L., & Saunders, L. (2009). Implementation of response to intervention: A snapshot of progress. *Journal of Learning Disabilities, 42*(1), 85–95. doi:10.1177/0022219408326214 PMID:19103800

Broadbent, J., & Poon, W. L. (2015). Self-regulated learning strategies & academic achievement in online higher education learning environments: A systematic review. *Internet High. Educ., 27*, 1–13. doi:10.1016/j.iheduc.2015.04.007

Dignath, C., Buettner, G., & Langfeldt, H. P. (2008). How can primary school students learn self-regulated learning strategies most effectively? A meta-analysis on self-regulation training programmes. *Educational Research Review, 3*(2), 101–129. doi:10.1016/j.edurev.2008.02.003

El-Adl, A., & Alkharusi, H. (2020). Relationships between self-regulated learning strategies, learning motivation and mathematics achievement. *Cypriot Journal of Educational Sciences, 15*(1), 104–111. doi:10.18844/cjes.v15i1.4461

Freire, M., & Santos, A. (2021). *How Cognitive Engagement Strategies' can improve Learning Outcomes in Higher Education.* Position Paper.

Fung, M. F., Magdeline, T. N., & Kamei, K. R. (2020, June 10). *How to create engaging online learning amid COVID-19 pandemic: Lessons from Singapore.* The Conversation. https://theconversation.com/how-to-create-engaging-online-learning-amid-covid-19-pandemic-lessons-from-singapore-138979

García-Morales, V. J., Garrido-Moreno, A., & Martín-Rojas, R. (2021). The Transformation of Higher Education After the COVID Disruption: Emerging Challenges in an Online Learning Scenario. *Frontiers in Psychology*, *12*, 196. doi:10.3389/fpsyg.2021.616059 PMID:33643144

Hattie, J., Biggs, J., & Purdie, N. (1996). Effects of learning skills interventions on student learning: A meta-analysis. *Review of Educational Research*, *66*(2), 99–136. doi:10.3102/00346543066002099

Jansen, R. S., van Leeuwen, A., Janssen, J., Jak, S., & Kester, L. (2019). Self-regulated learning partially mediates the effect of self-regulated learning interventions on achievement in higher education: A meta-analysis. *Educational Research Review*, *28*, 100292. Advance online publication. doi:10.1016/j.edurev.2019.100292

Jivet, I., Scheffel, M., Schmitz, M., Robbers, S., Specht, M., & Drachsler, H. (2020). From students with love: An empirical study on learner goals, self-regulated learning and sense-making of learning analytics in higher education. *The Internet and Higher Education*, *47*, 100758. doi:10.1016/j.iheduc.2020.100758

King, J., & South, J. (2017). *Reimagining the role of technology in higher education: A supplement to the national education technology plan*. US Department of Education, Office of Educational Technology.

Kuh, G. D. (2009). The national survey of student engagement: Conceptual and empirical foundations. *New Directions for Institutional Research*, *141*(141), 5–20. doi:10.1002/ir.283

Le, B., Lawrie, G. A., & Wang, J. T. H. (2022). Student Self-perception on Digital Literacy in STEM Blended Learning Environments. *Journal of Science Education and Technology*, *31*(3), 303–321. doi:10.100710956-022-09956-1 PMID:35132301

Lim, M. (2020, March 20). *Educating despite the Covid-19 outbreak: Lessons from Singapore*. Times Higher Education. https://www.timeshighereducation.com/blog/educating-despite-covid-19-outbreak-lessons-singapore

Lim, S. M., Devilly, O., Jasin, J., Kok, K. X.-F., Tan, C. T., & Foo, Y. L. (2021). Effectiveness of AdventureLEARN, an Online Gamified Platform for Improving Approaches to Learning. *Asian Journal of the Scholarship of Teaching and Learning*, *11*(2), 76–92.

Loeb, S. (2020). How effective is online learning? What the research does and doesn't tells us. *Education Week*. https://www.edweek.org/ew/articles/2020/03/23/how-effective-is-online-learning-what-the.html

Ministry of Education of Singapore. (2022, March 7). *Expanding pathways & opportunities across a life course: investing in our learners for life*. https://www.moe.gov.sg/news/press-releases/20220307-expanding-pathways-and-opportunities-across-a-life-course-investing-in-our-learners-for-life

Mirata, V., Hirt, F., Bergamin, P., & van der Westhuizen, C. (2020). Challenges and contexts in establishing adaptive learning in higher education: Findings from a Delphi study. *International Journal of Educational Technology in Higher Education*, *17*(1), 1–25. doi:10.118641239-020-00209-y

Morris, T. H. (2019). Self-directed learning: A fundamental competence in a rapidly changing world. *International Review of Education*, *65*(4), 633–653. doi:10.100711159-019-09793-2

Panadero, E. (2017). A Review of Self-regulated Learning: Six Models and Four Directions for Research. *Frontiers in Psychology*, *8*(APR), 422. Advance online publication. doi:10.3389/fpsyg.2017.00422 PMID:28503157

Pearl, J. B., & Arunfred, N. (2019). A Comparative Study on the Concentration Skill between E-Learning Methods and Traditional Learning Methods among Higher Education Students. *Asia Pacific Journal of Multidisciplinary Research*, *7*(4), 67–73.

Peng, H., Ma, S., & Spector, J. M. (2019). Personalized adaptive learning: An emerging pedagogical approach enabled by a smart learning environment. *Smart Learning Environments*, *6*(1), 9. doi:10.118640561-019-0089-y

Pintrich, P. R., & de Groot, E. (1990). Motivational and Self-Regulated Learning Components of Classroom Academic Performance. *Journal of Educational Psychology*, *82*(1), 33–40. doi:10.1037/0022-0663.82.1.33

Sengsouliya, S., Soukhavong, S., Silavong, N., Sengsouliya, S., & Littlepage, F. (2020). An investigation on predictors of student academic engagement. *European Journal of Education Studies*.

Silamut, A., & Sovajassatakul, T. (2021). Self-directed learning with knowledge management model on academic achievement and digital literacy abilities for employees of a Thai energy organization. *Education and Information Technologies*, *26*(5), 5149–5163. doi:10.100710639-021-10484-5

Singapore Institute of Technology. (2014, March 28). *SIT is officially Singapore's new autonomous university*. https://www.singaporetech.edu.sg/digitalnewsroom/sit-is-officially-singapores-new-autonomous-university/

Szpunar, K. K., Moulton, S. T., & Schacter, D. L. (2013). Mind wandering and education: From the classroom to online learning. *Frontiers in Psychology*, *4*, 495. doi:10.3389/fpsyg.2013.00495 PMID:23914183

Tadesse, T., Asmamaw, A., Getachew, K., Ferede, B., Melese, W., Siebeck, M., & Fischer, M. (2022). Self-Regulated Learning Strategies as Predictors of Perceived Learning Gains among Undergraduate Students in Ethiopian Universities. *Education Sciences*, *12*(7), 468. doi:10.3390/educsci12070468

Tan, R. Z., Wang, P. C., Lim, W. H., Ong, S. H. C., & Avnit, K. (2019). Early Prediction of Students' Mathematics Performance. *Proceedings of 2018 IEEE International Conference on Teaching, Assessment, and Learning for Engineering, TALE 2018*. 10.1109/TALE.2018.8615289

The World Bank. (2020, July 15). *Remote learning, EdTech and COVID-19*. https://www.worldbank.org/en/topic/edutech/brief/edtech-covid-19

van Alten, D. C. D., Phielix, C., Janssen, J., & Kester, L. (2020). Self-regulated learning support in flipped learning videos enhances learning outcomes. *Computers & Education*, *158*, 104000. doi:10.1016/j.compedu.2020.104000

Wang, C. H., Shannon, D. M., & Ross, M. E. (2013). Students' characteristics, self-regulated learning, technology self-efficacy, and course outcomes in online learning. *Distance Education*, *34*(3), 302–323. doi:10.1080/01587919.2013.835779

Wang, P. C., Avnit, K., Tan, R. Z., Ng, T. H., & Lim, W. H. (2020). Learning Mathematics through Technology-enhanced Pedagogy. In *Applied Learning in Higher Education*. Perspective, Pedagogy, and Practice.

Wong, J., Baars, M., Davis, D., van der Zee, T., Houben, G. J., & Paas, F. (2018). Supporting Self-Regulated Learning in Online Learning Environments and MOOCs: A Systematic Review. *International Journal of Human-Computer Interaction, 35*(4–5), 356–373. doi:10.1080/10447318.2018.1543084

Yang, T.-C., Chen, M. C., & Chen, S. Y. (2018). The influences of self-regulated learning support and prior knowledge on improving learning performance. *Computers & Education, 126*, 37–52. doi:10.1016/j.compedu.2018.06.025

Zimmerman, B. J. (2000). Attaining self-regulation. In M. Boekaerts, P. Pintrich, & M. Zeidner (Eds.), *Handbook of Self-Regulation* (pp. 13–39). Academic Press. doi:10.1016/B978-012109890-2/50031-7

ADDITIONAL READING

Berkeley, S., Bender, W. N., Gregg Peaster, L., & Saunders, L. (2009). Implementation of response to intervention: A snapshot of progress. *Journal of Learning Disabilities, 42*(1), 85–95. doi:10.1177/0022219408326214 PMID:19103800

Broadbent, J., & Poon, W. L. (2015c). Self-regulated learning strategies & academic achievement in online higher education learning environments: A systematic review. *The Internet and Higher Education, 27*, 1–13. doi:10.1016/j.iheduc.2015.04.007

Dignath, C., Buettner, G., & Langfeldt, H. P. (2008). How can primary school students learn self-regulated learning strategies most effectively? A meta-analysis on self-regulation training programmes. *Educational Research Review, 3*(2), 101–129. doi:10.1016/j.edurev.2008.02.003

Hattie, J., Biggs, J., & Purdie, N. (1996). Effects of learning skills interventions on student learning: A meta-analysis. *Review of Educational Research, 66*(2), 99–136. doi:10.3102/00346543066002099

Jansen, R. S., van Leeuwen, A., Janssen, J., Jak, S., & Kester, L. (2019). Self-regulated learning partially mediates the effect of self-regulated learning interventions on achievement in higher education: A meta-analysis. *Educational Research Review, 28*, 100292. Advance online publication. doi:10.1016/j.edurev.2019.100292

Panadero, E. (2017). A Review of Self-regulated Learning: Six Models and Four Directions for Research. *Frontiers in Psychology, 8*(APR), 422. Advance online publication. doi:10.3389/fpsyg.2017.00422 PMID:28503157

Wong, J., Baars, M., Davis, D., van der Zee, T., Houben, G. J., & Paas, F. (2018). Supporting Self-Regulated Learning in Online Learning Environments and MOOCs: A Systematic Review. *International Journal of Human-Computer Interaction, 35*(4–5), 356–373. doi:10.1080/10447318.2018.1543084

Zimmerman, B. J. (2000). Attaining Self-Regulation: A Social Cognitive Perspective. Handbook of Self-Regulation, 13–39. doi:10.1016/B978-012109890-2/50031-7

KEY TERMS AND DEFINITIONS

Blended Learning: An approach to education that combines online educational materials and opportunities for interaction online with physical place-based classroom methods.

Higher Education: Tertiary education leading to award of an academic degree.

Learning Strategies: An individual's way of organising and using a particular set of skills in order to learn content or accomplish other tasks more effectively and efficiently in school as well as in non-academic settings.

Online Learning: Use of synchronous and asynchronous interaction and communication within a virtual environment.

Response to Intervention: A system of supports that schools put in place to provide high-quality education to students with disabilities.

Self-Efficacy: An individual's belief in his or her capacity to execute behaviours necessary to produce specific performance attainments.

Self-Regulated Learning: One's ability to understand and control one's learning environment.

Chapter 15
Teaching Students to Be Students:
Facilitating Self-Regulated Learning in Transitional Studies

Michael Gooch
DeVry University, USA

ABSTRACT

Previous studies of self-regulated learning have focused primarily on K-12 learners in a co-present environment. This study focuses on the benefits of self-regulated learning techniques for adult learners taking transitional studies courses in the online modality. Advances in educational technology, including learning management systems and numerous interactive learning tools, have made it easier for subject matter experts, or SMEs, to design courses in which students learn key topics with minimal instructor intervention. This does not eliminate the instructor's role, but instead provides tools to allow the instructor to facilitate learning more effectively.

INTRODUCTION

The term *transitional studies* is often used to refer to foundational courses in reading, writing, or mathematics offered to incoming college students who do not meet the admissions requirements to be placed in standard courses. Generally, these courses are required to move forward in the plan of study but may not count directly for degree credit. Very often, these courses have titles that include words like "introduction," "foundations," or "basic."

Students may be enrolled in these courses because they scored below the required level on an admissions test, or they are returning to school after many years and are unable to provide the necessary documentation in order to gain admission to standard courses. In either case, students may come into these courses with a sense of anxiety or disappointment. Previous experience has convinced them that they are not prepared for college-level work, or the nature of higher education has changed so much over

DOI: 10.4018/978-1-6684-6500-4.ch015

their time away from school that they fear they will be unable to successfully adapt. In addition, some students feel that they should have been placed in standard courses and that the transitional courses add to their expenses without a legitimate academic need.

While the primary focus of a transitional studies course is the subject matter of the course itself, such as reading, writing, or mathematics, there is another underlying objective: to teach students the skills and behaviors associated with academic success at the college level. These skills include time management, persistence, and professionalism. In other words, the goal of these courses is not just to make students better readers, writers, or mathematicians so that they can succeed in subsequent courses, but to assist in developing the necessary skills to be an accountable, self-regulated learner who can reach their educational goals with increasing autonomy.

While some students attend college simply for the love of learning, most are hoping to learn new skills and earn credentials that will help them to succeed in their careers. One of the most important skills an employee can possess, aside from position-specific knowledge, is the ability to complete tasks with minimal oversight from supervisors. In other words, employers prize reliable, self-regulated employees. As such, colleges serve their students best when they foster self-regulated behaviors in their students.

Fortunately, advances in educational technology have made it easier for colleges to design transitional studies courses to encourage students to learn important skills in a self-regulated fashion. This chapter provides an analysis of educational technology tools that can be instrumental, in the author's anecdotal experience, in helping students to become more effective, successful, and independent learners.

BACKGROUND

While the literature of self-regulated learning is extensive, the application of self-regulated learning strategies in college-level online courses is still developing. Much of the literature devoted to self-regulated learning predates contemporary approaches to online education, with studies focused on K-12 students in a traditional physical classroom. Self-regulated learning strategies are arguably even more important for students learning online because the instructor is not physically present to help students to plan, monitor, and evaluate their learning. Such strategies are crucial in transitional studies courses in reading and writing, as students in such courses are considered at risk. An at risk-student is anyone who falls into a category of individuals who either fail courses at a higher rate than average, or who drop out of college at a higher rate than is usual for that institution. A simple example of an at-risk student at the course level is any student who is retaking the course due to failing or withdrawing from it previously.

Fortunately, there are many educational technology tools that can help to foster self-regulated learning in online reading and writing courses. One common denominator of these tools is that they provide students with immediate and actionable automated feedback. Unlike feedback from instructors, which is limited by time and workload, these educational technology tools almost never need a break, other than occasional pauses for maintenance and upgrades. This quick feedback helps to build self-efficacy in students, which in turn can contribute to student success.

One of the most important benefits of self-regulated learning strategies is the fostering of self-efficacy. Bandura (1977) defines self-efficacy as a personal belief in one's ability to face challenges and overcome obstacles. Self-efficacy is especially important in an online learning environment, and even more so for at-risk students, like those placed in foundational learning courses in reading and writing. Students placed in these courses are there because their reading and writing skills have been evaluated to be insufficient to succeed at the college level without remediation. This student population tends to have a weak sense of self-efficacy based on their prior levels of performance. In addition, such students are often new to the online learning environment and may struggle to navigate a complex internet-based learning management system (LMS).

Very often, students in traditional learning environments fail to build self-regulated learning skills. Instead, they rely on external regulation, in the form of repeated guidance and verbal reminders from instructors. Studies have shown that when students rely upon external regulation, they do not build self-regulated learning skills such as metacognition, planning, monitoring, and evaluating (Weinert et al., 1989). To function in an online learning environment, in which the instructor is not physically present, students must practice self-regulated learning strategies. There is a clear obstacle, however: students accustomed to relying on external regulation typically encounter difficulty when those external supports are removed (Kurtz & Weinert, 1989). One method used to counteract that difficulty is known as *fading* (Collins et al., 1991), which refers to the gradual removal of external supports; however, this process of fading is often difficult to carry out successfully once students have become used to receiving a certain level of assistance.

More recent studies have focused on the concept of metacognition as it relates to self-regulated learning. Simply put, metacognition in self-regulated learning refers to the benefits of learners gaining an awareness of not only what they are learning, but how and why they are learning. Nelson (1996) was among the first researchers to study the effects of metacognition and to posit the notion that this building of self-awareness might have a beneficial impact on learning, while Veenman (2017) extended Nelson's work by looking specifically at how students might go about gaining this self-awareness. However, according to a recent review of literature on the topic (Dignath & Veenman, 2021), most studies on self-regulated learning show that self-regulation is most often taught indirectly, with little attention paid to the importance of metacognition. College students are primed to comprehend and benefit from a metacognitive approach, thus this is an area of opportunity for researchers to explore further. Specifically, there is an opportunity to incorporate metacognition into online learning tools in a more direct and intentional fashion.

As this chapter will show, there are numerous educational technology tools available to help online learners build a sense of self-efficacy and help them to succeed, including those aimed at enabling retrieval practice, providing guided practice, offering automated writing feedback, and making videos more interactive, each of which have demonstrated success in supporting learning (see Agarwal et al., 2021; Garcia, 2018; Wilson and Roscoe, 2020; and Zhang et al, 2006). Unlike studies of self-regulated learning, which are typically found in the pages of peer-reviewed scholarly publications, studies of educational technology tools are often organized by the creators of the tools themselves and focused more broadly on general academic performance than specific self-regulated learning strategies or theories.

In addition to these studies conducted by the creators of the educational technology tools, there are a small, but growing number of published studies on these tools as well. Studies on the use of originality verification or academic integrity technology, one type of automated writing evaluation, are among the most numerous (Balbay & Killis, 2019; Kaktins, 2019; Pavelich, 2019), with fewer on guided learning tools which enable guided practice (Zumalt & Williamson, 2016) and interactive video quiz tools (Su & Chiu, 2021). Studies of academic integrity tools, a use for automated writing evaluation, often critique their effectiveness at preventing plagiarism (Balbay & Killis, 2019; Katkins, 2019) or question their impact on improving student writing (Pavelich, 2019), but they do not discuss impact on self-efficacy. Existing studies of guided learning tools (Zumalt & Williamson, 2016) and interactive video quiz tools

(Su & Chiu, 2021) focus on how they might help create a more enjoyable learning process, but neither specifically addresses issues of self-efficacy or self-regulated learning.

Some might argue that educational technology tools constitute a form of external support, but there is a key difference between the educational technology tools that will be discussed in depth and the external supports provided by instructors. In the case of external supports provided by instructors, it is the instructor who is providing the support, regardless of whether the student has asked for it. In contrast, the student who takes advantage of a technological tool does so by choice and must make some effort to make use of it. One may think of it as being somewhat analogous to the difference between having a math tutor and using a calculator.

What all these tools have in common is the ability to provide quick, actionable feedback to students, allowing them to create their own strategies for success without necessary intervention from the instructor. The specific tools, to be discussed ahead, focus on retrieval practice, guided practice, automated writing evaluation, and interactive video quizzes.

ANALYSIS METHODOLOGY

This chapter will provide a broad overview of the educational technology tools noted previously, all of which the author has used in transitional studies courses, and describe the degree to which they can be leveraged to promote self-regulated learning skills in students, often with promising results. While this chapter is based on the author's anecdotal experience, it provides a powerful commentary on how such tools—often created for other purposes—can help learners to become better at the task of self-regulated learning. Lastly, this chapter will provide researchers with suggestions for opportunities for empirical research that might further validate the use cases advanced here. Individually, each of these tools can support specific self-regulation strategies; together, their effect can be even more impactful.

LEARNING TOOLS COMMONLY USED IN TRANSITIONAL STUDIES COURSES

Retrieval Practice Tools

A common lament among instructors of transitional studies courses is that students either do not read the assigned textbook at all, or do not understand or remember the concepts presented well. Given that the concepts discussed in the textbook often form the basis of course assignments—such as essays, quizzes, and exams—students who fail to read, understand, or recall the textbook material are likely to have poor outcomes. In on-site based courses, a traditional and still often used solution to the problem of students not reading the textbook might be for the instructor to create a quiz based on each chapter and use class time for students to complete it. This approach has a few shortcomings—first, it takes time to create these quizzes, even if the educational technology company provides a test bank or similar resource to accompany the textbook. Second, it takes time out of the class period to administer the quiz. Third, it takes time to grade the quiz and record the results. Fourth, such quizzes may be impractical in an online, asynchronous learning environment.

A solution to many of the problems associated with typical reading quizzes can be found through educational technology quizzing features. These are products used in or with a wide variety of textbooks.

Some such products guide students through an assigned chapter of the textbook and ask them a series of questions based on the material covered in each section. These products enable retrieval practice, also known as the testing effect, whereby learning is enhanced by deliberately recalling information (Agarwal et al, 2021).

The number of questions asked, as well as the topics covered within the chapter, can be selected by either the individual instructor, the subject-matter expert (SME), or the development team in charge of creating the course. Those portions of the chapter deemed most important are highlighted, allowing students to focus their attention on the sections the questions will be drawn from.

These retrieval practice products often provide course developers with an estimated time it will take the typical student to complete the assigned chapter based on the number of topics selected and allow the developers to determine how many points an assignment is worth. Course developers can then adjust the number of topics covered, as well as the points assigned, so that the activity has its intended purpose of helping students to better understand the assigned reading, while at the same time not making the requirements so stringent that students are overwhelmed by the activities and have little time left to focus on other course requirements.

There are numerous advantages to retrieval practice products over the traditional reading quiz. First, they are often automatically graded, and the scores generally transfer into the LMS. Second, they are often mastery based, meaning that if a question is missed, additional questions will be assigned until the student demonstrates mastery. Third, they are designed for use in an asynchronous learning environment, allowing students to complete these tasks at a time that is convenient for them.

Since students in transitional studies courses are generally new to college or may have been away from school for many years, it is important that any technological tool be easy to use, and these retrieval practice products are generally intuitive and user-friendly. To access an assigned chapter, students click on a link in the LMS, which brings them to the assignment. Students can often choose to either begin with questions, if they feel they are familiar with the material already, or to start by reading – this choice is central to the concept of self-regulated learning.

After reading a section of text, students are typically prompted to answer a question or question set. Most questions are multiple choice, including some that ask students to check all that apply. If a student is not sure of an answer, the student may choose to return to the text and will be brought back to the specific section the question is based on. An additional feature of these retrieval practice products is that students may be asked to not only answer the question, but to indicate how sure they feel about the answer they are selecting. This feature encourages self-regulation by asking students to reflect, if only briefly, on the perceived difficulty of the question or their confidence in their own response. In addition, this feature may be said to incorporate an element of metacognition, in the sense that it makes the students more self-aware of the learning process they are engaged in.

To help students plan their schedule, these products often include an estimations of learner time. Students are shown some indicator of their progress as they go through the assignment, and they can save their progress and pick up where they left off as needed. These features allow students to work on assignments whenever it is convenient for them, and to fit study time around other responsibilities such as work and family, and in so doing ultimately complete their work on time.

Typically, these products are based on a variety of learning principles as well as formative or evaluative research conducted indicating successful implementations with users. In this author's experience as both an instructor of courses that use these products as well as a SME, it has been anecdotally observed that their use has a modestly positive impact on grades and overall success rates for courses they've been used in to date. Because students who complete the retrieval practice activities earn full credit, those who complete all the activities are likely to raise their grade, and certainly will not lower it. At the same time, there is a strong correlation between students completing the retrieval practice activities and successful submission of the other course assignments, such as essays, so it doesn't appear that students are failing to submit assignments due to spending excessive time on the retrieval practice tasks. However, it should be noted that the author is not authorized to share data on grades and pass rates at the institutional level, and such data at the individual level would not be statistically meaningful.

Retrieval practice products can also help instructors understand where learners are struggling and offer the best individual and cohort interventions, including those based on self-regulated learning. Similarly, these products can also help safeguard against academic dishonesty. For example, instructors can often see how long it takes students to complete the retrieval practice activities. A telltale sign of academic dishonesty would be a large proportion of students completing these assignments much more quickly than the estimated time provided. For example, if the estimated time to complete a certain assignment was thirty minutes, but many students were completing the assignment in less than five minutes while others were still taking thirty minutes or more, this would likely indicate academic dishonesty. Instead, the author has observed that students most often spend significantly *more* than the estimated time on these assignments rather than less. As a SME who takes part in the design of numerous courses at a large institution with multiple sections of each course, this author has not yet observed widespread cases of academic dishonesty. Nevertheless, it is recommended that SMEs who are considering retrieval practice products for their own institutions periodically review and revise the retrieval practice activities by switching up concept coverage or the chapters assigned to encourage academic integrity.

Through the use of retrieval practice products, instructors can also be enabled to help learners better manage their time—a hallmark of good planning and self-monitoring. As a best practice, it is recommended that course developers not rely on estimated times when determining the number of items to assign in a chapter. Instead, it is better to tentatively select a certain number of items, and then complete the assignment and record the actual amount of time it took to finish it successfully. It often takes a student two to three times longer to complete an assignment successfully than it takes an instructor. If possible, it is best to pilot the use of retrieval practice assignments in a single course section, or a few sections, to see how well students do and to figure out how long it takes students to complete them. The assignments can then be modified as needed before using them in all sections of the course.

The third opportunity for self-regulation that these products represent is to help learners manage their own online attendance. In some colleges, attendance is taken in online courses via a system that tracks activity in the LMS. For example, if a student participates in a graded online discussion, submits a writing assignment, or completes a quiz or exam hosted in the LMS, this may—depending upon an institution's policies—contribute to some portion of an engagement, interaction or even attendance grade. In this way, learners can begin to regulate their own behavior by engaging in activities that may contribute to additional learning goals. However, it is incumbent upon developers to make the determination if these products are integrated into their learning management systems in such a way that captures and records engagement into their course gradebook.

When adopting these products, it is recommended that an institution move deliberately, by piloting products in a few course sections and monitoring the results prior to use in all courses. The author has found that the assignments nearly always take longer for students to complete than the estimated time given. As such, the author has, after discussion with colleagues, reduced the length of retrieval practice assignments in several courses recently, often by as much as 50%.

Guided Practice Tools

Another well-known type of educational technology is guided practice tools that are worthy of serious consideration by colleges offering transitional studies courses. This type of tool provides a wide variety of learning activities, enabling a SME to build an entire course around guided practice activities, reducing or even eliminating the need for instructors or course developers to come up with their own assignments. Guided practice, whereby learners receive direct guidance through materials or instruction, can be an effective instructional strategy that shows promise for introductory online and blended learning courses (Garcia).

Unlike retrieval practice tools, in which students are taken straight to the textbook and directed to read before or after answering questions, guided practice activities feature a variety of other learning assessments based on the material covered by the textbook. In other words, while students would benefit from reading the assigned textbook chapter prior to taking an assessment, this product is not designed in such a way as to require students to do so. The benefit of a guided practice tool is that it more directly encourages students to read the text, and in so doing students may be more likely to read. At the same time, if the goal is for students to become more self-sufficient and independent learners, allowing them greater latitude in choosing how to complete their assigned work, as guided practice activities do, may be preferable.

The author recently concluded development work on a transitional studies course in business communication. The premise behind the course is that students who wish to study business, but need a transitional studies course in writing and reading, may benefit from a course with a focus on business communication principles rather than a broader focus on reading and writing in general. The author taught this course twice, using a guided practice product for most assignments. The textbook chosen for this course focused on basic written business communication skills, such as learning the parts of speech, avoiding run-on sentences, and mastering the rules of capitalization, with examples drawn from the business world, such as emails, memos, and reports. The guided practice activities are designed to assess students understanding of these concepts. For each chapter, students take a pretest, a posttest, and complete an editing exercise.

Just as it sounds, the pretest is intended to determine how much students already know about a concept. For example, in one pretest, students are given a sentence and asked to determine the part of speech of a word through a multiple-choice question. In the default assignment settings, students may take the pretest an unlimited number of times, based on the premise that students will learn about the concept simply by the process of completing the assignment. Similarly, the posttest is meant to see what students have learned, both from reading the assigned text and from taking the pretest.

In between the pretest and the posttest, students are given an editing exercise for each chapter. Each exercise features a typical business document, such as a workplace email, memo, or report. Throughout the document, certain sections and are left blank. Students must click on that blank space to reveal a dropdown menu with several possible choices to correctly fill in the blank. Unlike the pretest and posttest, students are given a maximum number of attempts at these exercises.

From prior experience in using a similar guided practice tool in a college readiness course, this author can attest that this product has many of the same positive attributes as the retrieval practice tools previously mentioned. In each case, the activities are graded automatically, and the scores are transferred to the LMS quickly and easily. An interesting feature related to self-regulation is the ability of students to check the correctness of a response prior to finalizing it. This allows students the possibility of a second chance on a question and encourages students to spend more time thinking through a question rather than rushing through to completion.

When a student clicks on a link to a guided practice activity from the LMS, they are taken to the edtech company's environment, which is regarded as an external tool by the attendance-taking system and therefore not tracked. This is a potentially serious issue for this particular product. These guided practice activities may constitute either all or most of the assignments in courses that use it. Therefore, there may be very few opportunities in a guided-learning-based online course for students to otherwise consider and demonstrate engagement, interaction, or attendance. By contrast, retrieval practice activities are typically just one of many assignments given in courses using this tool. It is highly recommended, therefore, that in online courses in which attendance is taken through the recording of academic events in the LMS, specific weekly assignments, such as graded online discussions, are included as well to avoid limiting student opportunities to achieve these self-regulated learning opportunities or institutional requirements.

As with a retrieval practice product, the possibility of academic dishonesty can be managed and minimized. To combat academic dishonesty, it may be worthwhile to assign only certain chapters in the textbook for guided practice assignments, or certain assignments in a chapter, and to periodically change some chapters. Retrieval practice activities and guided practice assignments can both help to facilitate self-regulated learning, albeit in different ways. Retrieval practice tools appear to follow more of a behavioral approach, such as that favored by Sunstein and Thaler (2009), who advocate for behavioral nudges. A nudge is an encouragement to take an action that is in that person's best interest, but that still allows the individual to make a choice. Retrieval practice products "nudge" students to do something that is in their own best interests: reading the textbook. In contrast, the guided practice product allows students the freedom to learn through a process of trial and error, based on the understanding that in the long run students need to be able to decide for themselves what is in their own best interests. Each approach can work, so the decision of whether to adopt a textbook that focuses on retrieval practice, or one that favors guided practice will likely come down to how well aligned the textbook is with the goals of the course.

According to studies cited on some guided practice activity web sites, claims may be made for improved grades and course success rates as well as links to case studies of instructors and specific courses highlighting better grades and course success rates.

In the business communication course mentioned previously, the author experienced a significantly higher student success rate as compared to the traditional introductory composition course that he frequently teaches. These results should be kept in context, however, due to the small sample size and limited amount of time the course has been offered, as well as the author's personal role in teaching the course. As the course continues to be offered and is taught by a wide range of instructors, its effectiveness will be judged more accurately.

While the anecdotal evidence is promising, there is still considerable room for further independent verification of claims of success, both by individual instructors as well as institutions who have adopted guided practice on a large scale. Ideally, such studies would compare the results of similar courses in which this product was used in some sections but not others. Alternatively, a before and after approach could also be illuminating, though less definitive.

Automated Writing Evaluation Tools

Many educators are becoming increasingly familiar with automated writing evaluation tools, including originality verification tools, that help students ensure that their work is their own. In the minds of many, these tools are associated with either catching students who may, intentionally or accidentally, plagiarize written work. However, they can be valuable tools to help learners understand what constitutes plagiarism and how easy it is to accidentally plagiarize work. They can also help learners understand the value of reflection and revision as they improve their own self-regulated learning strategies.

Depending on whether a school has an LMS integrated with these products, students either submit their essays directly to a web site, or via the LMS as they upload their assignments for grading. When an essay is submitted, the product detects "matching" from a wide array of print and online sources and is assigned an originality score based on the percentage of matching that is detected. Instructors may adjust settings, such as excluding bibliographic information, direct quotations, or small matches, meaning that the same essay submitted to two different instructors might have different originality scores.

While some of these products may be largely used to detect and deter plagiarism, there is another way of thinking about these products that relates directly to the topic of self-regulated learning. Educational technology tools can help facilitate self-regulated learning among college students in transitional studies courses. Just as the previous products mentioned help students to learn with minimal instructor oversight, originality verification products can similarly help students to improve their research and writing skills independently.

The key to maximizing effectiveness in this regard is for course developers, or individual instructors, to be thoughtful about the product settings, and clear in their expectations of students. For example, as mentioned previously, automated writing evaluation allows for the exclusion of small matches, direct quotations, and bibliographic material. If these are all excluded, then the acceptable match rate for a typical essay should be very low, ideally less than 5%. If quotations are not excluded, the instructor might be doing so in order to encourage students to use a certain amount of quoting, such as between 0 to 5%. In this instance, the product allows students to see if they have quoted too little or too much. A final suggestion for course developers is to include this product as a default setting in the LMS rather than requiring individual instructors to enable the feature for each course section, enhancing ease-of-use.

The best way to use automated writing evaluation to facilitate self-regulated learning is to allow students to submit their drafts to it prior to submission of the final essay. By allowing students to submit their work early, as well as providing clear guidelines on how to interpret the feedback score, students can analyze their own work and make necessary improvements prior to the assignment deadline. This helps put students in charge of their own learning, a key element of self-regulation.

It has been this author's experience that the use of automated writing evaluation products both helps to deter plagiarism and increases the quality of student work. In the author's experience, students sometimes submit drafts of research-based writing with relatively high match rates of 20% or more. However, by submitting such drafts prior to their due date, the students ensure that they have provided proper credit for source use and are able to revise their work accordingly.

Interactive Video Quizzes

The final tool analyzed in this chapter that can help students to become better self-regulated learners is interactive video quizzes. Indeed, learners who used interactive video have been shown to achieve higher performance and higher satisfaction than video used in other contexts (Zhang et al, 2006). These tools often allow instructors to create video quizzes based either on their own videos or videos from external sources, such as YouTube or TED. Prior to using someone else's videos, instructors should always be sure to obtain permission from the copyright holder.

Much like retrieval practice tools help support students to learn from a text, this quiz creation tool helps students to better understand a video. Just as retrieval practice tools embed questions related to the assigned reading, video quiz creation tools allow instructors to place quiz questions into the video at any point. The instructor or course developer can choose whether to allow students to retake a quiz, as well as allowing students to fast forward or rewind.

As with products previously mentioned, this product can be integrated with an LMS so that the grades of a quiz can be transferred to the gradebook. In addition, instructors can choose to make a quiz ungraded, providing it simply to help students to learn an important concept. Using ungraded quizzes can be particularly useful for lesson pages in the LMS to make them more engaging.

Unlike previously referenced types of products, in which the assignments may be created by the educational technology providers, this product requires instructors or developers to create their own quizzes. For that reason, creating a video quiz may be a more time-consuming process. For this author, that process is as follows:

1. Begin by creating a short slide deck on the topic being taught, such as how to summarize a source.
2. Make a screen recording of the slide deck.
3. Open the product, retrieve the screen recording, and create the quiz.
4. Create an assignment in the LMS and upload the quiz.

As this brief recounting of the process shows, an instructor or developer needs to have a good basic understanding of technological teaching tools to create a video quiz successfully. For that reason, this author advises those interested in creating video quizzes to allow adequate time for completion. Once completed, video quizzes can be a welcome addition to a transitional studies course. Most of this author's students enjoy videos, and these quizzes provide a change of pace from the usual weekly assignments. It is recommended that the settings be adjusted to allow students to retake the quiz, as well as to be able to fast forward or rewind as needed. This puts students in charge of their own learning, thus fostering more self-regulation. It has been this author's experience that these quizzes are an additional engaging feature in most classes.

DISCUSSION

This analysis has argued that educational technology tools can help online college students in transitional studies courses to be more self-regulated learners who benefit from self-directed intervention. Some of the most popular and effective of these educational technology tools focus on retrieval practice, guided practice, automated writing evaluation, and interactive video quizzes. While each of these educational technology tools has a specific use, what they all have in common is the ability to help students learn without significant direct instruction or intervention from an instructor. Unlike instructors, whose availability is often limited to class time and office hours, these educational technology tools are available all day, every day. In addition, since today's students are technologically adept, students are used to working with technology and may enjoy using these tools just as much or more than they enjoy learning in traditional ways, such as through lecture and discussion.

As noted earlier, a major goal of self-regulated learning is the fostering of feelings of self-efficacy in students. While some college students simply wish to learn for the sake of learning, or to gain a sense of personal fulfillment, for the vast majority the goal is to earn a credential, most often in the form of a completed degree or certificate, that will enable the student to be able to compete for employment in a field of his or her choice. Likewise, a common belief about higher education is that it should prepare students for the "real world." In other words, students should learn concepts in college that help them to be successful in their careers. Increasingly, jobs that offer competitive salaries and benefits packages are those that require employees to be able to master the organization's ever-expanding and changing array of educational technology tools, including software, databases, videoconferencing tools, and so on.

The more educational technology tools students gain a mastery over during their studies, the easier it will be to adapt to new forms of technology on the job. As such, these educational technology tools serve a double benefit. They not only help students to learn the skills related to the goals of the class they are taking, but they also help students to gain a sense of self-efficacy in using technology more broadly. Students who learn how to use educational technology tools in college will feel comfortable and confident to learn about new tools while on the job, thus enhancing students' chances of long-term career success.

FUTURE RESEARCH DIRECTIONS

Going forward, research around the efficacy of these tools at acquiring self-regulated learning strategies and improved learning performance is warranted. While many of these tools have been the foci of other types of research studies and publications, examining their impact on specific self-regulated learning strategies and other moderating variables would shed greater light on how such tools can most effectively advance learner autonomy, agency, and motivation. Furthermore, empirical studies of the effectiveness of these educational technology tools vis-à-vis self-regulated learning would underscore their value to students, as well as to instructors and institutions, so that students could more effectively select and use tools that provide the most learning value.

CONCLUSION

In summary, this author's experience suggests that the use of a variety of educational technology tools in online transitional studies courses can help students to become better self-regulated learners with healthy levels of self-efficacy. Each of the tools analyzed in this chapter appears to be a promising way to help support students to learn material more effectively while at the same time reducing the need for heavy supervision by the course instructor. In addition, these tools reduce the need for instructor administration. Time saved using these educational technology tools allows instructors to spend their time in more effective ways, such as in online discussions, live lessons, and providing detailed feedback on essays or presentations.

REFERENCES

Balbay, S., & Kilis, S. (2019). Perceived effectiveness of Turnitin in detecting plagiarism in presentation slides. *Contemporary Educational Technology, 10*(1), 25–36. doi:10.30935/cet.512522

Bandura, A. (1977). Self-efficacy: Toward a unifying theory of behavioral change. *Psychological Review, 84*(2), 191–215. doi:10.1037/0033-295X.84.2.191 PMID:847061

Collins, A., Brown, J. S., & Holmes, A. (1991). Cognitive apprenticeship: Making thinking visible. *American Educator, 15*, 6–11.

Dignath, C., & Veenman, M. V. J. (2021). The role of direct strategy instruction and indirect activation of self-regulated learning—Evidence from classroom observation studies. *Educational Psychology Review, 33*(2), 489–533. doi:10.100710648-020-09534-0

Kaktiņš, L. (2019). Does Turnitin support the development of international students' academic integrity? *Ethics and Education, 14*(4), 430–448. doi:10.1080/17449642.2019.1660946

Kurtz, B. E., & Weinert, F. E. (1989). Metamemory, metaperformance, and causal attributions in gifted and average children. *Journal of Experimental Child Psychology, 48*(1), 45–61. doi:10.1016/0022-0965(89)90040-4 PMID:2754388

Nelson, T. O. (1996). Consciousness and metacognition. *The American Psychologist, 51*(2), 102–116. doi:10.1037/0003-066X.51.2.102

Su, C. Y., & Chiu, C. H. (2021). Perceived enjoyment and attractiveness influence Taiwanese elementary cchool students' intention to use interactive video learning. *International Journal of Human-Computer Interaction, 37*(6), 574–583. doi:10.1080/10447318.2020.1841423

Thaler, R., & Sunstein, C. (2009). *Nudge: Improving decisions about health, wealth, and happiness.* Penguin.

Veenman, M. V. J. (2017). Learning to self-monitor and to self-regulate. In R. E. Mayer & P. A. Alexander (Eds.), Handbook of research on learning and instruction (2nd ed., pp. 233–257). Routledge.

Weinert, F. E., Schrader, F. W., & Helmke, A. (1989). Quality of instruction and achievement outcomes. *International Journal of Educational Psychology, 13*(8), 895}912.

Zumalt, C., & Williamson, V. (2016). Does the arrangement of embedded text versus linked text in homework systems make a difference in students' impressions, attitudes, and perceived learning? *Journal of Science Education and Technology, 25*(5), 704–714. doi:10.100710956-016-9625-5

ADDITIONAL READING

Agarwal, P. K., Nunes, L. D., & Blunt, J. R. (2021). Retrieval practice consistently benefits student learning: A systematic review of applied research in schools and classrooms. *Educational Psychology Review, 33*(4), 1409–1453. doi:10.100710648-021-09595-9

Dignath, C., & Veenman, M. V. J. (2020). The role of direct strategy instruction and indirect activation of self-regulated Learning—Evidence from classroom observation studies. *Educational Psychology Review, 33*(2), 489–533. doi:10.100710648-020-09534-0

Garcia, S. (2018). Improving Classroom Preparedness Using Guided Practice. *SIGCSE: Proceedings of the 49th ACM Technical Symposium on Computer Science Education*, 326-331. 10.1145/3159450.3159571

Ma, Y., Yang, X. M., Hong, L., & Tang, R. J. (2022). The influence of stress perception on academic procrastination in postgraduate students: The role of self-efficacy for self-regulated learning and self-control. *International Journal of Digital Multimedia Broadcasting, 2022*, 1–11. doi:10.1155/2022/6722805

Nückles, M., Roelle, J., Glogger-Frey, I., Waldeyer, J., & Renkl, A. (2020). The self-regulation-view in writing-to-learn: Using journal writing to optimize cognitive load in self-regulated learning. *Educational Psychology Review, 32*(4), 1089–1126. doi:10.100710648-020-09541-1

Palalas, A., & Wark, N. (2020). The relationship between mobile learning and self-regulated learning: A systematic review. *Australasian Journal of Educational Technology, 36*(4), 151–172. doi:10.14742/ajet.5650

Papamitsiou, Z., & Economides, A. A. (2019). Exploring autonomous learning capacity from a self-regulated learning perspective using learning analytics. *British Journal of Educational Technology, 50*(6), 3138–3155. doi:10.1111/bjet.12747

van Gog, T., Hoogerheide, V., & van Harsel, M. (2020). The role of mental effort in fostering self-regulated learning with problem-solving tasks. *Educational Psychology Review, 32*(4), 1055–1072. doi:10.100710648-020-09544-y

Wang, C., Shannon, D. M., & Ross, M. E. (2013). Students' characteristics, self-regulated learning, technology self-efficacy, and course outcomes in online learning. *Distance Education, 34*(3), 302–323. doi:10.1080/01587919.2013.835779

Wilson, J., & Roscoe, R. D. (2020). Automated Writing Evaluation and Feedback: Multiple Metrics of Efficacy. *Journal of Educational Computing Research, 58*(1), 87–125. doi:10.1177/0735633119830764

Wirth, J., Stebner, F., Trypke, M., Schuster, C., & Leutner, D. (2020). An interactive layers model of self-regulated learning and cognitive load. *Educational Psychology Review, 32*(4), 1127–1149. doi:10.100710648-020-09568-4

Wolters, C. A., & Brady, A. C. (2021). College students' time management: A self-regulated learning perspective. *Educational Psychology Review, 33*(4), 1319–1351. doi:10.100710648-020-09519-z

Zhang, D., Zhou, L., Briggs, R. O., & Nunamaker, J. Jr. (2006). Instructional video in e-learning: Assessing the impact of interactive video on learning effectiveness. *Information & Management, 43*(1), 15–27. doi:10.1016/j.im.2005.01.004

KEY TERMS AND DEFINITIONS

At-Risk Students: An at-risk student is one who is thought to possess the characteristics of an individual who is at higher-than-average possibility of either failing a course or dropping out of college altogether.

Automated Writing Evaluation: Tool providing students and instructors with a detailed report on source use in an assignment in order to improve the quality of writing, including discouraging plagiarism and encouraging ethical research.

Contract Cheating: Hiring someone else to complete an academic assignment, especially a written assignment.

Guided Practice: Describes a variety of learning activities in which students are guided through important concepts. These activities are usually automatically graded.

Interactive Video Quiz: Product that provides instructors and course developers with the ability to embed graded or ungraded quizzes into videos.

Learning-Management System: A comprehensive electronic tool that facilitates teaching and learning in online courses. It is commonly abbreviated as LMS.

Retrieval Practice Tool: A product that encourages students to read assigned textbooks by asking questions based on the concepts discussed in the text.

Self-Efficacy: The sense of belief in one's ability to overcome obstacles and achieve success in life. It is closely associated with the work of Alfred Bandura.

Self-Regulated Learning: The ability to learn independently of external supports, especially those provided by instructors, advisers, and tutors.

Subject-Matter-Expert: An individual with thorough knowledge of a certain academic field who uses that knowledge to develop curriculum for one or more institutions. It is commonly abbreviated as SME.

Transitional Studies: Courses offered in college, most often in reading, writing, or mathematics, for incoming students who do not meet the requirements for placement into a standard, credit-bearing course.

Compilation of References

Abd-Elrahman, A., Andreu, M., & Abbott, T. (2010). Using text data mining techniques for understanding free-style question answers in course evaluation forms. *Research in Higher Education*, *9*, 1.

Abushanab, B., & Bishara, A. J. (2013). Memory and metacognition for piano melodies: Illusory advantages of fixed- over random-order practice. *Memory & Cognition*, *41*(6), 928–937. doi:10.375813421-013-0311-z PMID:23508339

Adamopoulou, E., & Moussiades, L. (2020). Chatbots: History, technology, and applications. *Machine Learning with Applications*, *2*(100006), 1–18. doi:10.1016/j.mlwa.2020.100006

Adams Becker, S., Cummins, M., Davis, A., Freeman, A., Hall Giesinger, C., & Ananthanarayanan, V. (2017). *NMC Horizon Report: 2017 Higher Education Edition*. The New Media Consortium.

Adesope, O. O., Trevisan, D. A., & Sundararajan, N. (2017). Rethinking the use of tests: A meta-analysis of practice testing. *Review of Educational Research*, *87*(3), 659–701. doi:10.3102/0034654316689306

Agarwal, P. K., Bain, P. M., & Chamberlain, R. W. (2012). The value of applied research: Retrieval practice improves classroom learning and recommendations from a teacher, a principal, and a scientist. *Educational Psychology Review*, *24*(3), 437–448. doi:10.100710648-012-9210-2

Agarwal, P. K., D'Antonio, L., Roediger, H. L. III, McDermott, K. B., & McDaniel, M. A. (2014). Classroom-based programs of retrieval practice reduce middle school and high school students' test anxiety. *Journal of Applied Research in Memory and Cognition*, *3*(3), 131–139. doi:10.1016/j.jarmac.2014.07.002

Agarwal, P. K., Nunes, L. D., & Blunt, J. R. (2021). Retrieval practice consistently benefits student learning: A systematic review of applied research in schools and classrooms. *Educational Psychology Review*, *33*(4), 1409–1453. doi:10.100710648-021-09595-9

Ai, J., & Laffey, J. (2007). Web mining as a tool for understanding online learning. *Journal of Online Learning and Teaching*, *3*(2), 160–169.

Alamri, A., & Higham, P. A. (2022). The dark side of corrective feedback: Controlled and automatic influences of retrieval practice. *Journal of Experimental Psychology. Learning, Memory, and Cognition*, *48*(5), 752–768. doi:10.1037/xlm0001138 PMID:35389700

Alamri, H., Lowell, V., Watson, W., & Watson, S. L. (2020). Using personalized learning as an instructional approach to motivate learners in online higher education: Learner self-determination and intrinsic motivation. *Journal of Research on Technology in Education*, *52*(3), 322–352. doi:10.1080/15391523.2020.1728449

Aleven, V. A., & Koedinger, K. R. (2002). An effective metacognitive strategy: Learning by doing and explaining with a computer-based cognitive tutor. *Cognitive Science*, *26*(2), 147–179. doi:10.120715516709cog2602_1

Aleven, V., Mclaren, B., Roll, I., & Koedinger, K. (2006). Toward meta-cognitive tutoring: A model of help seeking with a cognitive tutor. *International Journal of Artificial Intelligence in Education, 16*(2), 101–128.

Aleven, V., Roll, I., McLaren, B. M., & Koedinger, K. R. (2010). Automated, unobtrusive, action-by-action assessment of self-regulation during learning with an intelligent tutoring system. *Educational Psychologist, 45*(4), 224–233. doi:10.1080/00461520.2010.517740

Allen, I. E., Seaman, J., Poulin, R., & Straut, T. T. (2016). *Online report card: tracking online education in the United States*. Babson Survey Research Group and Quahog Research Group.

Allison, D. A. (2012). Chatbots in the Library: Is it Time? *Library Hi Tech, 30*(1), 95–107. doi:10.1108/07378831211213238

Alpert, W. T., Couch, K. A., & Harmon, O. R. (2016). A randomized assessment of online learning. *The American Economic Review, 106*(5), 378–382. doi:10.1257/aer.p20161057

Andrade, H. L. (2019). A critical review of research on student self-assessment. *Frontiers in Education, 4*(87), 87. Advance online publication. doi:10.3389/feduc.2019.00087

Anikina, O. V., & Yakimenko, E. V. (2015). Edutainment as a modern technology of education. *Procedia: Social and Behavioral Sciences, 166*, 475–479. doi:10.1016/j.sbspro.2014.12.558

Anthonysamy, L. (2021). The use of metacognitive strategies for undisrupted online learning: Preparing university students in the age of pandemic. *Education and Information Technologies, 26*(6), 6881–6899. doi:10.100710639-021-10518-y PMID:33897268

Anthonysamy, L., Ah Choo, K., & Soon Hin, H. (2021). Investigating Self-Regulated Learning Strategies for Digital Learning Relevancy. *Malaysian Journal of Learning and Instruction, 18*(1), 29–64. doi:10.32890/mjli2021.18.1.2

Anthonysamy, L., Koo, A. C., & Hew, S. H. (2020). Self-regulated learning strategies and non-academic outcomes in higher education blended learning environments: A one decade review. *Education and Information Technologies, 25*(5), 3677–3704. doi:10.100710639-020-10134-2

Aparicio, M., Oliveira, T., Bacao, F., & Painho, M. (2019). Gamification: A key determinant of massive open online course (MOOC) success. *Information & Management, 56*(1), 39–54. doi:10.1016/j.im.2018.06.003

Apoki, U. C., Hussein, A. M. A., Al-Chalabi, H. K. M., Badica, C., & Mocanu, M. L. (2022). The Role of Pedagogical Agents in Personalised Adaptive Learning: A Review. *Sustainability, 14*(11), 6442. doi:10.3390u14116442

Appana, S. (2008). A review of benefits and limitations of online learning in the context of the student, the instructor and the tenured faculty. *International Journal on E-Learning, 7*(1), 5–22.

Appleton, J. J., Christenson, S. L., Kim, D., & Reschly, A. L. (2006). Measuring cognitive and psychological engagement: Validation of the student engagement instrument. *Journal of School Psychology, 44*(5), 427–445. doi:10.1016/j.jsp.2006.04.002

Arieli-Attali, M., Ward, S., Thomas, J., Deonovic, B., & von Davier, A. A. (2019). The expanded evidence centered design (e-ECD) for learning and assessment systems: A framework for incorporating learning goals and processes within assessment design. *Frontiers in Psychology, 10*, 853. doi:10.3389/fpsyg.2019.00853 PMID:31105616

Arnold, K. E., & Pistilli, M. D. (2012, April). Course signals at Purdue: Using learning analytics to increase student success. In *Proceedings of the 2nd international conference on learning analytics and knowledge* (pp. 267-270). ACM. 10.1145/2330601.2330666

Arroway, P., Morgan, G., O'Keefe, M., & Yanosky, R. (2016). *Learning Analytics in Higher Education. Research report.* ECAR.

Australian Health Practitioner Regulation Agency (AHPRA). (2020). *National principles for clinical education during COVID-19.* https://www.ahpra.gov.au/News/COVID-19/National-principles-for-clinical-education-during-COVID-19.aspx

Avnit, K., Wang, P. C., & Iyer, P. (n.d.). *High tech and high touch: designing a bridging system to help students prepare for STEM studies.* https://www.timeshighereducation.com/campus/high-tech-and-high-touch-designing-bridging-system-help-students-prepare-ste
m-studies

Azevedo, R., Moos, D., Johnson, A., & Chauncey, A. (2010). Measuring Cognitive and Metacognitive Regulatory Processes During Hypermedia Learning: Issues and Challenges. *Educational Psychologist, 45*(4), 210–223. doi:10.1080/00461520.2010.515934

Azevedo, R., Taub, M., & Mudrick, N. V. (2018). Understanding and reasoning about real-time cognitive, affective, and metacognitive processes to foster self-regulation with advanced learning technologies. In *Handbook of self-regulation of learning and performance* (pp. 254–270). Routledge.

Baddeley, A. D., & Longman, D. J. A. (1978). The influence of length and frequency of training session on the rate of learning to type. *Ergonomics, 21*(8), 627–635. doi:10.1080/00140137808931764

Bai, Y., Mo, D., Zhang, L., Boswell, M., & Rozelle, S. (2016). The impact of integrating ICT with teaching: Evidence from a randomized controlled trial in rural schools in China. *Computers & Education, 96*, 1–14. doi:10.1016/j.compedu.2016.02.005

Balasooriya, I., Mor, E., & Rodríguez, M. E. (2017). Design of a microlevel student engagement data capture system. In *Proceedings of the 12th International Conference on P2P, Parallel, Grid, Cloud and Internet Computing* (pp. 632-641). Springer International Publishing.

Balasooriya, I., Rodríguez, M. E., & Mor, E. (2017). Assessment of Engagement: Using Microlevel Student Engagement as a Form of Continuous Assessment. In E. Ras & A. Guerrero Roldán (Eds.), Technology Enhanced Assessment. TEA 2017. Communications in Computer and Information Science. Academic Press.

Balasooriya, I., Mor, E., & Rodríguez, M. E. (2018). Engagement Analytics: A Microlevel Approach to Measure and Visualize Student Engagement. In S. Caballé & J. Conesa (Eds.), *Software Data Engineering for Network eLearning Environments. Lecture Notes on Data Engineering and Communications Technologies, 11.* Springer. doi:10.1007/978-3-319-68318-8_3

Balasooriya, I., Mor, E., & Rodríguez, M. E. (2018). Understanding user engagement in digital education. In *Learning and Collaboration Technologies. Learning and Teaching Lecture Notes in Computer Science* (pp. 3–15). Springer International Publishing. doi:10.1007/978-3-319-91152-6_1

Balbay, S., & Kilis, S. (2019). Perceived effectiveness of Turnitin in detecting plagiarism in presentation slides. *Contemporary Educational Technology, 10*(1), 25–36. doi:10.30935/cet.512522

Balfanz, R., Herzog, L., & MacIver, D. (2007). Preventing student disengagement and keeping students on the graduation path in urban middle-grades schools: Early identification and effective interventions. *Educational Psychologist, 42*(4), 223–235. doi:10.1080/00461520701621079

Balota, D. A., Duchek, J. M., & Paullin, R. (1989). Age-related differences in the impact of spacing, lag, and retention interval. *Psychology and Aging, 4*(1), 3–9. doi:10.1037/0882-7974.4.1.3 PMID:2803609

Banditvilai, C. (2016). Enhancing student's language skills through blended learning. *The Electronic Journal of E-Learning, 14*(3), 220-229. Available from www.ejel.org

Bandura, A. (1977). Self-efficacy: Toward a unifying theory of behavioral change. *Psychological Review, 84*(2), 191–215. doi:10.1037/0033-295X.84.2.191 PMID:847061

Bandura, A. (1986). *Social foundations of thought and action: A social cognitive theory*. Prentice-Hall.

Bangert-Drowns, R. L., Kulik, C. L. C., Kulik, J. A., & Morgan, M. (1991). The instructional effect of feedback in test-like events. *Review of Educational Research, 61*(2), 213–238. doi:10.3102/00346543061002213

Bannert, M., Reimann, P., & Sonnenberg, C. (2014). Process mining techniques for analysing patterns and strategies in students' self-regulated learning. *Metacognition and Learning, 9*(2), 161–185. doi:10.100711409-013-9107-6

Barab, S., & Squire, K. (2004). Design-based research: Putting a stake in the ground. *Journal of the Learning Sciences, 13*(1), 1–14. doi:10.120715327809jls1301_1

Barber, S. J. (2020). The applied implications of age-based stereotype threat for older adults. *Journal of Applied Research in Memory and Cognition, 9*(3), 274–285. doi:10.1016/j.jarmac.2020.05.002 PMID:36032188

Barnard, L., Lan, W. Y., To, Y. M., Paton, V. O., & Lai, S.-L. (2009). Measuring self-regulation in online and blended learning environments. *The Internet and Higher Education, 12*(1), 1–6. doi:10.1016/j.iheduc.2008.10.005

Baticulon, R., Sy, J., Alberto, N., Baron, M., Mabulay, R., Rizada, L., Tiu, C., Clarion, C., & Reyes, J. (2021). Barriers to online learning in the time of COVID-19: A national survey of medical students in the Philippines. *Medical Science Educator, 31*(2), 615–628. doi:10.100740670-021-01231-z PMID:33649712

Bawa, P. (2016). Retention in online courses. *SAGE Open, 6*(1). Advance online publication. doi:10.1177/2158244015621777

Beatson, N. J., Berg, D. A. G., & Smith, J. K. (2019). The influence of self-efficacy beliefs and prior learning on performance. *Accounting and Finance, 60*(2), 1271–1294. doi:10.1111/acfi.12440

Bednall, T. C., & Kehoe, E. J. (2011). Effects of self-regulatory instructional aids on self-directed study. *Instructional Science, 39*(2), 205–226. doi:10.100711251-009-9125-6

Bentler, P. M. (1990). Comparative fit indexes in structural models. *Psychological Bulletin, 107*(2), 238–246. doi:10.1037/0033-2909.107.2.238 PMID:2320703

Berkeley, S., Bender, W. N., Gregg Peaster, L., & Saunders, L. (2009). Implementation of response to intervention: A snapshot of progress. *Journal of Learning Disabilities, 42*(1), 85–95. doi:10.1177/0022219408326214 PMID:19103800

Bernacki, M. L., Aguilar, A. C., & Byrnes, J. P. (2011). Self-regulated learning and technology enhanced learning environments: An opportunity-propensity analysis. *Fostering Self-Regulated Learning through ICT*, 1-26.

Bernacki, M. L., Greene, J. A., Plumley, R. D., Yu, L., Duke, R. F., Freed, R., Hollander, C., & Hogan, K. (2022, April 21-26). *Code What I Say, Not Just What I Do! Multimethod Investigations into Digitally Traced Behaviors* [Paper Presentation]. Annual Meeting of the American Education Research Association, San Diego, CA, United States.

Bernacki, M. L. (2017). Examining the cyclical, loosely sequenced, and contingent features of self-regulated learning: Trace data and their analysis. In *Handbook of Self-Regulation of Learning and Performance* (2nd ed.). Routledge. doi:10.4324/9781315697048-24

Bernacki, M. L. (2018). Examining the cyclical, loosely sequenced, and contingent features of self-regulated learning: Trace data and their analysis. In D. H. Schunk & J. A. Greene (Eds.), *Handbook of Self-Regulated Learning and Performance* (pp. 370–387). Routledge.

Bernacki, M. L., Chavez, M. M., & Uesbeck, P. M. (2020a). Predicting STEM achievement with learning management system data: Prediction modeling and a test of an early warning system. *Computers & Education, 158*. Advance online publication. doi:10.1016/j.compedu.2020

Bernacki, M. L., Nokes-Malach, T. J., & Aleven, V. (2015). Examining self-efficacy during learning: Variability and relations to behavior, performance, and learning. *Metacognition and Learning, 10*(1), 99–117. doi:10.100711409-014-9127-x

Bernacki, M. L., Vosicka, L., & Utz, J. C. (2020). Can a brief, digital skill training intervention help undergraduates "learn to learn" and improve their STEM achievement? *Journal of Educational Psychology, 112*(4), 765–781. doi:10.1037/edu0000405

Bernacki, M. L., Vosicka, L., Utz, J. C., & Warren, C. (2021). Effects of digital learning skill training on the academic performance of undergraduates in science and mathematics. *Journal of Educational Psychology, 113*(6), 1107–1125. doi:10.1037/edu0000485

Bills, D. B. (2019). The problem of meritocracy: The belief in achievement, credentials and justice. *Research Handbook on the Sociology of Education*, 88–105.

Binali, T., Tsai, C. C., & Chang, H. Y. (2021). University students' profiles of online learning and their relation to online metacognitive regulation and internet-specific epistemic justification. *Computers & Education, 175*, 104315. Advance online publication. doi:10.1016/j.compedu.2021.104315

Biswas, G., Baker, R. S., & Paquette, L. (2017). Data mining methods for assessing self-regulated learning. In *Handbook of Self-Regulation of Learning and Performance* (2nd ed.). Routledge. doi:10.4324/9781315697048-25

Biwer, F., de Bruin, A. B., Schreurs, S., & oude Egbrink, M. G. A. (2020). Future steps in teaching desirably difficult learning strategies: Reflections from the Study Smart program. *Journal of Applied Research in Memory and Cognition, 9*(4), 439–446. doi:10.1016/j.jarmac.2020.07.006

Bjork, E. L., & Bjork, R. A. (2011). Making things hard on yourself, but in a good way: Creating desirable difficulties to enhance learning. *Psychology and the real world: Essays illustrating fundamental contributions to society, 2*, 59-68.

Bjork, R. A. (1975). Retrieval as a memory modifier: An interpretation of negative recency and related phenomena. In R.L. Solso (Ed.), *Information Processing and Cognition: The Loyola Symposium* (pp. 123–144). Hillsdale, NJ: Erlbaum.

Bjork, R. A. (1994). Memory and metamemory considerations in the training of human beings. In J. Metcalfe & A. Shimamura (Eds.), *Metacognition: Knowing about knowing* (pp. 185–205). MIT Press.

Bjork, R. A., & Bjork, E. L. (1992). A new theory of disuse and an old theory of stimulus fluctuation. In A. Healy, S. Kosslyn, & R. Shiffrin (Eds.), *From Learning Processes to Cognitive Processes: Essays in Honor of William K. Estes* (p. 35067). Erlbaum.

Bjork, R. A., Dunlosky, J., & Kornell, N. (2013). Self-regulated learning: Beliefs, techniques, and illusions. *Annual Review of Psychology, 64*(1), 417–444. doi:10.1146/annurev-psych-113011-143823 PMID:23020639

Black, P., & William, D. (1998). Assessment and classroom learning. *Assessment in Education: Principles, Policy & Practice, 5*(1), 7–74. doi:10.1080/0969595980050102

Blasiman, R. N., Dunlosky, J., & Rawson, K. A. (2017). The what, how much, and when of study strategies: Comparing intended versus actual study behaviour. *Memory (Hove, England), 25*(6), 784–792. doi:10.1080/09658211.2016.1221974 PMID:27561889

Blau, I., Shamir-Inbal, T., & Avdiel, O. (2020). How does the pedagogical design of a technology-enhanced collaborative academic course promote digital literacies, self-regulation, and perceived learning of students? *The Internet and Higher Education, 45*, 100722. Advance online publication. doi:10.1016/j.iheduc.2019.100722

Blikstein, P. (2013). Multimodal learning analytics. In *Proceedings of the third international conference on learning analytics and knowledge* (pp. 102-106). ACM. 10.1145/2460296.2460316

Bloom, K. C., & Shuell, T. J. (1981). Effects of massed and distributed practice on the learning and retention of second-language vocabulary. *The Journal of Educational Research, 74*(4), 245–248. doi:10.1080/00220671.1981.10885317

Blunt, J. R., & Karpicke, J. D. (2014). Learning with retrieval-based concept mapping. *Journal of Educational Psychology, 106*(3), 849–858. doi:10.1037/a0035934

Boekaerts, M., & Corno, L. (2005). Self-regulation in the classroom: A perspective on assessment and intervention. *Applied Psychology, 54*(2), 199–231. doi:10.1111/j.1464-0597.2005.00205.x

Boekaerts, M., & Niemivirta, M. (2000). Self-regulated learning: finding a balance between learning goals and ego-protective goals. In M. Boekaerts, P. R. Pintrich, & M. Zeidner (Eds.), *Handbook of Self-Regulation* (pp. 417–451). Academic Press. doi:10.1016/B978-012109890-2/50042-1

Bombaerts, G., & Nickel, P. J. (2017, April). Feedback for relatedness and competence: Can feedback in blended learning contribute to optimal rigor, basic needs, and motivation? In *2017 IEEE global engineering education conference (EDUCON)* (pp. 1089-1092). doi:10.1109/EDUCON.2017.7942984

Bond University. (2022). *Doctor of physiotherapy program.* https://bond.edu.au/program/doctor-physiotherapy#about

Bouchrika, I., Harrati, N., Wanick, V., & Wills, G. (2019). Exploring the impact of gamification on student engagement and involvement with e-learning systems. *Interactive Learning Environments*, 1–14. doi:10.1080/10494820.2019.1623267

Bowen, W. G., Chingos, M. M., Lack, K. A., & Nygren, T. I. (2013). Interactive learning online at public universities: Evidence from a six-campus randomized trial. *Journal of Policy Analysis and Management, 33*(1), 94–111. doi:10.1002/pam.21728

Bransford, J. D., & Schwartz, D. L. (1999). Rethinking Transfer: A Simple Proposal with Multiple Implications. *Review of Research in Education, 24*, 61. doi:10.2307/1167267

Broadbent, J. (2017). Comparing online and blended learner's self-regulated learning strategies and academic performance. *The Internet and Higher Education, 33*, 24–32. doi:10.1016/j.iheduc.2017.01.004

Broadbent, J., Panadero, E., Lodge, J. M., & Barba, P. D. (2020). Technologies to enhance self-regulated learning in online and computer-mediated learning environments. In M. J. Bishop, E. Boling, J. Elen, & V. Svihla (Eds.), *Handbook of research in educational communications and technology* (pp. 37–52). Springer. doi:10.1007/978-3-030-36119-8_3

Broadbent, J., & Poon, W. L. (2015). Self-Regulated Learning Strategies & Academic Achievement in Online Higher Education Learning Environments: A systematic review. *The Internet and Higher Education, 27*, 1–13. doi:10.1016/j.iheduc.2015.04.007

Brooks, C., & Thompson, C. (2017) Predictive Modelling in Teaching and Learning. In C. Lang, G. Siemens, A. Wise, & D. Gašević (Eds.), Handbook of Learning Analytics (pp. 61-68). SoLAR. doi:10.18608/hla17.005

Brown, A. (1987). Metacognition, executive control, self-regulation, and other more mysterious mechanisms. In F. E. Weinert & R. H. Kluwe (Eds.), *Metacognition, motivation and understanding* (pp. 65–116). Erlbaum.

Brown, B. A. (2011). Isn't That Just Good Teaching? Disaggregate Instruction and the Language Identity Dilemma. *Journal of Science Teacher Education*, *22*(8), 679–704. doi:10.100710972-011-9256-x

Browne, M. W., & Cudeck, R. (1993). Alternative ways of assessing model fit. In K. A. Bollen & J. S. Long (Eds.), *Testing structural equation models* (pp. 111–135). Sage.

Brown, G., & Harris, L. R. (2014). The future of self-assessment in classroom practice: Reframing self-assessment as a core competency. *Frontline Learning Research*, *2*(1), 22–30. doi:10.14786/flr.v2i1.24

Bruso, J., Stefaniak, J., & Bol, L. (2020). An examination of personality traits as a predictor of the use of self-regulated learning strategies and considerations for online instruction. *Educational Technology Research and Development*, *68*(5), 2659–2683. doi:10.100711423-020-09797-y

Burgers, C., Eden, A., van Engelenburg, M. D., & Buningh, S. (2015). How feedback boosts motivation and play in a brain-training game. *Computers in Human Behavior*, *48*, 94–103. doi:10.1016/j.chb.2015.01.038

Butler, A. C. (2010). Repeated testing produces superior transfer of learning relative to repeated studying. *Journal of Experimental Psychology. Learning, Memory, and Cognition*, *36*(5), 1118–1133. doi:10.1037/a0019902 PMID:20804289

Butler, A. C., Karpicke, J. D., & Roediger, H. L. III. (2008). Correcting a metacognitive error: Feedback increases retention of low-confidence correct responses. *Journal of Experimental Psychology. Learning, Memory, and Cognition*, *34*(4), 918–928. doi:10.1037/0278-7393.34.4.918 PMID:18605878

Butler, A. C., Marsh, E. J., Slavinsky, J. P., & Baraniuk, R. G. (2014). Integrating cognitive science and technology improves learning in a STEM classroom. *Educational Psychology Review*, *26*(2), 331–340. doi:10.100710648-014-9256-4

Butler, A. C., & Roediger, H. L. I. I. I. (2008). Feedback enhances the positive effects and reduces the negative effects of multiple-choice testing. *Memory & Cognition*, *36*(3), 604–616. doi:10.3758/MC.36.3.604 PMID:18491500

Butler, A. C., & Roediger, H. L. III. (2007). Testing improves long-term retention in a simulated classroom setting. *The European Journal of Cognitive Psychology*, *19*(4-5), 514–527. doi:10.1080/09541440701326097

Butler, D. L., & Cartier, S. C. (2017). Advancing Research and Practice about Self-Regulated Learning: The Promise of In-Depth Case Study Methodologies. In *Handbook of Self-Regulation of Learning and Performance* (2nd ed.). Routledge. doi:10.4324/9781315697048-23

Butler, R. (1987). Task-involving and ego-involving properties of evaluation: Effects of different feedback conditions on motivational perceptions, interest, and performance. *Journal of Educational Psychology*, *79*(4), 474–482. doi:10.1037/0022-0663.79.4.474

Campbell, C. M., Dortch, D., & Burt, B. A. (2018). Reframing rigor: A modern look at challenge and support in higher education. *New Directions for Higher Education*, *2018*(181), 11–23. doi:10.1002/he.20267

Carlson, R. A., & Yaure, R. G. (1990). Practice schedules and the use of component skills in problem solving. *Journal of Experimental Psychology. Learning, Memory, and Cognition*, *15*(3), 484–496. doi:10.1037/0278-7393.16.3.484

Carpenter, J. P., Krutka, D. G., & Kimmons, R. (2020). #RemoteTeaching & #RemoteLearning: Educator tweeting during the COVID-19 pandemic. *Journal of Technology and Teacher Education*, *28*(2), 151–159. https://eric.ed.gov/?id=EJ1257425

Carpenter, S. K. (2009). Cue strength as a moderator of the testing effect: The benefits of elaborative retrieval. *Journal of Experimental Psychology. Learning, Memory, and Cognition*, *35*(6), 1563–1569. doi:10.1037/a0017021 PMID:19857026

Carpenter, S. K. (2011). Semantic information activated during retrieval contributes to later retention: Support for the mediator effectiveness hypothesis of the testing effect. *Journal of Experimental Psychology. Learning, Memory, and Cognition, 37*(6), 1547–1552. doi:10.1037/a0024140 PMID:21707217

Carpenter, S. K., Wilford, M. M., Kornell, N., & Mullaney, K. M. (2013). Appearances can be deceiving: Instructor fluency increases perceptions of learning without increasing actual learning. *Psychonomic Bulletin & Review, 20*(6), 1350–1356. doi:10.375813423-013-0442-z PMID:23645413

Carrier, L. M. (2003). College students' choices of study strategies. *Perceptual and Motor Skills, 96*(1), 54–56. doi:10.2466/pms.2003.96.1.54 PMID:12705510

Carrier, M., & Pashler, H. (1992). The influence of retrieval on retention. *Memory & Cognition, 20*(6), 633–642. doi:10.3758/BF03202713 PMID:1435266

Cascallar, E., Boekaerts, M., & Costigan, T. (2006). Assessment in the evaluation of self regulation as a process. *Educational Psychology Review, 18*(3), 297–306. doi:10.100710648-006-9023-2

Castel, A. D., McCabe, D. P., & Roediger, H. L. (2007). Illusions of competence and overestimation of associative memory for identical items: Evidence from judgments of learning. *Psychonomic Bulletin & Review, 14*(1), 107–111. doi:10.3758/BF03194036 PMID:17546739

Castro, M. D. B., & Tumibay, G. M. (2019). A literature review: Efficacy of online learning courses for higher education institution using meta-analysis. *Education and Information Technologies, 26*(2), 1367–1385. doi:10.100710639-019-10027-z

Caviglia-Harris, J., & Maier, K. (2020). It's not all in their heads: The differing role of cognitive factors and non-cognitive traits in undergraduate success. *Education Economics, 28*(3), 245–262. doi:10.1080/09645292.2020.1729702

Cepeda, N. J., Pashler, H., Vul, E., Wixted, J. T., & Rohrer, D. (2006). Distributed practice in verbal recall tasks: A review and quantitative synthesis. *Psychological Bulletin, 132*(3), 354–380. doi:10.1037/0033-2909.132.3.354 PMID:16719566

Cerasoli, C. P., Nicklin, J. M., & Ford, M. T. (2014). Intrinsic motivation and extrinsic incentives jointly predict performance: A 40-year meta-analysis. *Psychological Bulletin, 140*(4), 98. doi:10.1037/a0035661 PMID:24491020

Cetin, B. (2015). Academic motivation and self-regulated learning in predicting academic achievement in college. *Journal of International Education Research, 11*(2), 95-106.

Chartered Society of Physiotherapy (CSP). (2020). *COVID-19 guidance for higher education institutions (updated October 2020).* Chartered Society of Physiotherapy. https://www.csp.org.uk/system/files/documents/2020-10/COVID_19%20Guidance%20Oct%202020_0.pdf

Chen, Y., & Carliner, S. (2020). A special SME: An integrative literature review of the relationship between instructional designers and faculty in the design of online courses for higher education. *Performance Improvement Quarterly, 33*(4), 471–495. doi:10.1002/piq.21339

Cheryan, S., Plaut, V. C., Davies, P. G., & Steele, C. M. (2009). Ambient belonging: How stereotypical cues impact gender participation in computer science. *Journal of Personality and Social Psychology, 97*(6), 1045–1060. doi:10.1037/a0016239 PMID:19968418

Chetty, R., Jackson, M. O., Kuchler, T., Stroebel, J., Hendren, N., Fluegge, R. B., Gong, S., Gonzalez, F., Grondin, A., Jacob, M., Johnston, D., Koenen, M., Laguna-Muggenburg, E., Mudekereza, F., Rutter, T., Thor, N., Townsend, W., Zhang, R., Bailey, M., ... Wernerfelt, N. (2022). Social capital II: Determinants of economic connectedness. *Nature, 608*(7921), 7921. Advance online publication. doi:10.103841586-022-04997-3 PMID:35915343

Chi, M., & Wylie, R. (2014). The ICAP Framework: linking cognitive engagement to active learning outcomes. *Educational Psychologist*, *49*(4), 219-243.

Chiu, T. K. (2021). Digital support for student engagement in blended learning based on self-determination theory. *Computers in Human Behavior*, *124*, 1–10. doi:10.1016/j.chb.2021.106909

Choi, B. C., & Pak, A. W. (2005). A catalog of biases in questionnaires. *Preventing Chronic Disease*, *2*(1), A13. PMID:15670466

Cho, M., & Yoo, J. S. (2017). Exploring online students' self-regulated learning with self-reported surveys and log files: A data mining approach. *Interactive Learning Environments*, *25*(8), 970–982. doi:10.1080/10494820.2016.1232278

Chou, C. Y., & Zou, N. B. (2020). An analysis of internal and external feedback in self-regulated learning activities mediated by self-regulated learning tools and open learner models. *Int J Educ Technol High Educ*, *17*(55), 1–17. doi:10.118641239-020-00233-y

Clark, R., & Saxberg, B. (2018). Engineering Motivation Using the Belief-Expectancy-Control Framework. *Interdisciplinary Education and Psychology*, *2*. Advance online publication. doi:10.31532/InterdiscipEducPsychol.2.1.004

Cleary, T. J., & Callan, G. L. (2017). Assessing Self-Regulated Learning Using Microanalytic Methods. In *Handbook of Self-Regulation of Learning and Performance* (2nd ed.). Routledge. doi:10.4324/9781315697048-22

Cleland, J., McKimm, J., Fuller, R., Taylor, D., Janczukowicz, J., & Gibbs, T. (2020). Adapting to the impact of COVID-19: Sharing stories, sharing practice. *Medical Teacher*, *42*(7), 1–4. doi:10.1080/0142159X.2020.1757635 PMID:32401079

Coates, H. (2007). A model of online and general campus-based student engagement. *Assessment & Evaluation in Higher Education*, *32*(2), 121–141. doi:10.1080/02602930600801878

Cogliano, M. C., Bernacki, M. L., Hilpert, J. C., & Strong, C. L. (2022). A self-regulated learning analytics prediction-and-intervention design: Detecting and supporting struggling biology students. *Journal of Educational Psychology*, *114*(8), 1801–1816. doi:10.1037/edu0000745

Cogliano, M., Bernacki, M. L., & Kardash, C. M. (2021). A metacognitive retrieval practice intervention to improve undergraduates' monitoring and control processes and use of performance feedback for classroom learning. *Journal of Educational Psychology*, *113*(7), 1421–1440. doi:10.1037/edu0000624

Cohen, A. (2017). Analysis of student activity in web-supported courses as a tool for predicting dropout. *Educational Technology Research and Development*, *65*(5), 1285–1304. doi:10.100711423-017-9524-3

Cohen, A., Shimony, U., Nachmias, R., & Soffer, T. (2019). Active learners' characterization in MOOC forums and their generated knowledge. *British Journal of Educational Technology*, *50*(1), 177–198. doi:10.1111/bjet.12670

College of Computing. (2020, Jan 24). *Jill Watson, a pioneer in AI education, turns 4*. Retrieved Dec 2022, from Georgia Tech. https://www.ic.gatech.edu/news/631545/jill-watson-ai-pioneer-education-turns-4

Collins, A., Brown, J. S., & Holmes, A. (1991). Cognitive apprenticeship: Making thinking visible. *American Educator*, *15*, 6–11.

Colthorpe, K., Zimbardi, K., Ainscough, L., & Anderson, S. (2015). Know Thy Student! Combining Learning Analytics and Critical Reflections to Increase Understanding of Students' Self-Regulated Learning in an Authentic Setting. *Journal of Learning Analytics*, *2*(1), 134–155. doi:10.18608/jla.2015.21.7

Congleton, A., & Rajaram, S. (2012). The origin of the interaction between learning method and delay in the testing effect: The roles of processing and conceptual retrieval organization. *Memory & Cognition*, *40*(4), 528–539. doi:10.375813421-011-0168-y PMID:22160872

Corman, C., Tiru, L., Mesesan-Schmitz, L., Stanciu, C., & Bularca, M. (2020). Online teaching and learning in higher education during the Coronavirus pandemic: Students' perspective. *Sustainability*, *20*, 24.

Corno, L. (2011). *Studying self-regulation habits. Handbook of self-regulation of learning and performance*. Routledge.

Credé, M., Tynan, M. C., & Harms, P. D. (2017). Much ado about grit: A meta-analytic synthesis of the grit literature. *Journal of Personality and Social Psychology*, *113*(3), 492–511. doi:10.1037/pspp0000102 PMID:27845531

Crews, T. B., & Wilkinson, K. (2015). Online quality course design vs. quality teaching: Aligning quality matters standards to principles for good teaching. *The Journal of Research in Business Education*, *57*(1), 47–63.

Cui, Y., Wise, A. F., & Allen, K. L. (2019). Developing reflection analytics for health professions education: A multidimensional framework to align critical concepts with data features. *Computers in Human Behavior*.

Cunningham-Nelson, S., Mukherjee, M., Goncher, A., & Boles, W. (2018). Text analysis in education: A review of selected software packages with an application for analysing students' conceptual understanding. *Australasian Journal of Engineering Education*, *23*(1), 25–39.

Dawson, S., Jovanovic, J., Gašević, D., & Pardo, A. (2017). From prediction to impact: Evaluation of a learning analytics retention program. In *Proceedings of the Seventh International Learning Analytics & Knowledge Conference* (pp. 474-478). ACM. 10.1145/3027385.3027405

De Beni, R., & Moè, A. (2003). Presentation modality effects in studying passages. Are mental images always effective? *Applied Cognitive Psychology*, *17*(3), 309–324. doi:10.1002/acp.867

de Boer, H., Donker, A. S., Kostons, D. D. N. M., & van der Werf, G. P. C. (2018). Long-term effects of metacognitive strategy instruction on student academic performance: A meta-analysis. *Educational Research Review*, *24*, 98–115. doi:10.1016/j.edurev.2018.03.002

de Bruin, A. B. H., Dunlosky, J., & Cavalcanti, R. B. (2017, June). Monitoring and regulation of learning in medical education: The need for predictive cues. *Medical Education*, *51*(6), 575–584. doi:10.1111/medu.13267 PMID:28332224

Deci, E. L., Koestner, R., & Ryan, R. M. (2001). Extrinsic rewards and intrinsic motivation in education: Reconsidered once again. *Review of Educational Research*, *71*(1), 1–27. doi:10.3102/00346543071001001

Deci, E. L., & Ryan, R. M. (1985). *Intrinsic Motivation and Self Determination in Human Behaviour*. Plenum Press. doi:10.1007/978-1-4899-2271-7

Delaney, J. G., Johnson, A., Johnson, T. D., & Treslan, D. (2010). *Students' perceptions of effective teaching in higher education. Project Report*. Memorial University of Newfoundland. https://research.library.mun.ca/8370/

Dempster, F. N. (1988). The spacing effect: A case study in the failure to apply the results of psychological research. *The American Psychologist*, *43*(8), 627–634. doi:10.1037/0003-066X.43.8.627

Dent, A. L., & Koenka, A. C. (2016). The relation between self-regulated learning and academic achievement across childhood and adolescence: A meta-analysis. *Educational Psychology Review*, *28*(3), 425–474. doi:10.100710648-015-9320-8

Deterding, S., Khaled, R., Nacke, L. E., & Dixon, D. (2011). *Gamification: Toward a Definition*. CHI 2011 Gamification Workshop Proceedings, Vancouver, Canada.

Dettori, G., & Persico, D. (2008). Detecting self-regulated learning in online communities by means of interaction analysis. *IEEE Transactions on Learning Technologies*, *1*(1), 11–19. doi:10.1109/TLT.2008.7

DiBenedetto, M. K., & Zimmerman, B. J. (2010). Differences in self-regulatory processes among students studying science: A microanalytic investigation. *The International Journal of Educational and Psychological Assessment*, *5*, 2–24.

Dickinson, L. (1995). Autonomy and motivation a literature review. *System*, *23*(2), 165–174. doi:10.1016/0346-251X(95)00005-5

Dignath, C., & Büttner, G. (2008). Components of fostering self-regulated learning among students. a meta-analysis on intervention studies at primary and secondary school level. *Metacognition and Learning*, *3*(3), 231–264. doi:10.100711409-008-9029-x

Dignath, C., Büttner, G., & Langfeldt, H. (2008). How can primary school students learn self-regulated learning strategies most effectively? A meta-analysis on self-regulation training programmes. *Educational Research Review*, *3*(2), 101–129. doi:10.1016/j.edurev.2008.02.003

Dignath, C., & Veenman, M. V. J. (2021). The role of direct strategy instruction and indirect activation of self-regulated learning—Evidence from classroom observation studies. *Educational Psychology Review*, *33*(2), 489–533. doi:10.100710648-020-09534-0

Dinsmore, D. L., Alexander, P. A., & Loughlin, S. M. (2008). Focusing the conceptual lens on metacognition, self-regulation, and self-regulated learning. *Educational Psychology Review*, *20*(4), 391–409. doi:10.100710648-008-9083-6

Dong, C., & Goh, P. S. (2015). Twelve tips for the effective use of videos in medical education. *Medical Teacher*, *37*(2), 140–145. doi:10.3109/0142159X.2014.943709 PMID:25110154

Donker, A. S., De Boer, H., Kostons, D., Van Ewijk, C. D., & van der Werf, M. P. (2014). Effectiveness of learning strategy instruction on academic performance: A meta-analysis. *Educational Research Review*, *11*, 1–26. doi:10.1016/j.edurev.2013.11.002

Donoghue, G. M., & Hattie, J. A. (2021). A meta-analysis of ten learning techniques. In *Frontiers in Education* (p. 48). Frontiers.

Dörrenbächer, L., & Perels, F. (2016). Self-regulated learning profiles in college students: Their relationship to achievement, personality, and the effectiveness of an intervention to foster self-regulated learning. *Learning and Individual Differences*, *51*, 229–241. doi:10.1016/j.lindif.2016.09.015

Duffy, T. M., & Kirkley, J. R. (2003). *Learner-centered theory and practice in distance education: Cases from higher education*. Routledge. doi:10.4324/9781410609489

Duncan, G. J., Dowsett, C. J., Claessens, A., Magnuson, K., Huston, A. C., Klebanov, P., Pagani, L. S., Feinstein, L., Engel, M., Brooks-Gunn, J., Sexton, H., Duckworth, K., & Japel, C. (2007). School readiness and later achievement. *Developmental Psychology*, *43*(6), 1428–1446. doi:10.1037/0012-1649.43.6.1428 PMID:18020822

Dunlosky, J. (2013). Strengthening the student toolbox: Study strategies to boost learning. *American Educator*, *37*(3), 12–21.

Dunlosky, J., Rawson, K. A., Marsh, E. J., Nathan, M. J., & Willingham, D. T. (2013). Improving students' learning with effective learning techniques: Promising directions from cognitive and educational psychology. *Psychological Science in the Public Interest*, *14*(1), 4–58. doi:10.1177/1529100612453266 PMID:26173288

Dweck, C. S. (1986). Motivational processes affecting learning. *The American Psychologist*, *41*(10), 1040–1048. doi:10.1037/0003-066X.41.10.1040

Ebbinghaus, H. (1885). *Urmanuskript "Ueber das Gedächtniß"*. Passavia Universitätsverlag.

Ebbinghaus, H. (1995). *Memory: A contribution to experimental psychology* (H. A. Ruger & C. E. Bussenius, Trans.). Dover. (Original work published 1964)

Eccles, J. S., & Wigfield, A. (2020). From expectancy-value theory to situated expectancy-value theory: A developmental, social cognitive, and sociocultural perspective on motivation. *Contemporary Educational Psychology*, *61*, 101859. doi:10.1016/j.cedpsych.2020.101859

Eccles-Parsons, J. S. (1983). Expectancies, values, and academic behaviors. In J. T. Spence (Ed.), *Achievement and Achievement Motivations* (pp. 75–121). W. H. Freeman & Co.

Efklides, A. (2011). Interactions of metacognition with motivation and affect in self-regulated learning: The MASRL model. *Educational Psychology*, *46*(1), 6–25. doi:10.1080/00461520.2011.538645

Efklides, A. (2019). Gifted students and self-regulated learning: The MASRL model and its implications for SRL. *High Ability Studies*, *30*(1-2), 79–102. doi:10.1080/13598139.2018.1556069

Eisenberg, I. W., Bissett, P. G., Canning, J. R., Zeynep Enkavi, A., Whitfield-Gabrieli, S., Gonzalez, O., Green, A. I., Greene, M., Kiernan, M., Jung Kim, S., Li, J., Lowe, M. R., Mazza, G. L., Metcalf, S. A., Onken, L., Parikh, S. S., Peters, E., Prochaska, J. J., Scherer, E. A., ... Poldrack, R. A. (2018). Applying novel technologies and methods to inform the ontology of self-regulation. *Behaviour Research and Therapy*, *101*, 46–57. doi:10.1016/j.brat.2017.09.014 PMID:29066077

Ekuni, R., de Souza, B. M. N., Agarwal, P. K., & Pompeia, S. (2022). A conceptual replication of survey research on study strategies in a diverse, non-WEIRD student population. *Scholarship of Teaching and Learning in Psychology*, *8*(1), 1–14. doi:10.1037tl0000191

El-Adl, A., & Alkharusi, H. (2020). Relationships between self-regulated learning strategies, learning motivation and mathematics achievement. *Cypriot Journal of Educational Sciences*, *15*(1), 104–111. doi:10.18844/cjes.v15i1.4461

Eldar, O., & Miedijensky, S. (2015). Designing a metacognitive approach to the professional development of experienced science teachers. In A. Peña-Ayala (Ed.), *Metacognition: Fundaments, Applications, and Trends. A Profile of the Current State-Of-The-Art* (pp. 299–319). Springer. doi:10.1007/978-3-319-11062-2_12

Ellaway, R. H. A. (2016). Conceptual framework of game-informed principles for health professions education. *Advances in Simulation (London, England)*, *1*(28), 1–9. doi:10.118641077-016-0030-1 PMID:29449997

Ellis, J. (2014). *Preparing Future Professors: Highlighting the Importance of Graduate Student Professional Development Programs in Calculus Instruction.* North American Chapter of the International Group for the Psychology of Mathematics Education. https://files.eric.ed.gov/fulltext/ED599810.pdf

Engeness, I. (2021). Developing teachers' digital identity: Towards the pedagogic deign principles of digital environments to enhance students' learning in the 21st century. *European Journal of Teacher Education*, *44*(1), 96–114. doi:10.1080/02619768.2020.1849129

Engeström, Y. (1999). Activity theory and individual and social transformation. In R. Miettinen & R. L. Punamäki-Gitai (Eds.), *Perspectives on activity theory.* Cambridge University Press. doi:10.1017/CBO9780511812774.003

Engeström, Y. (2009). The Future of Activity Theory: A Rough Draft. In A. Sannino, H. Daniels, & K. D. Gutierrez (Eds.), *Learning and Expanding with Activity Theory* (pp. 303–328). Cambridge University Press. doi:10.1017/CBO9780511809989.020

Engeström, Y. (2011). From design experiments to formative interventions. *Theory & Psychology*, *21*(5), 598–628. doi:10.1177/0959354311419252

Eom, S. B., & Ashill, N. J. (2018). A System's View of E-Learning Success Model. *Decision Sciences Journal of Innovative Education*, *16*(1), 42–76. doi:10.1111/dsji.12144

Ergen, B., & Sedat, K. (2017). The effect of self-regulated learning strategies on academic achievement: A meta-analysis study. *Eurasian Journal of Educational Research*, *69*(69), 55–74. doi:10.14689/ejer.2017.69.4

Ericsson, K. A., Krampe, R. T., & Tesch-Römer, C. (1993). The role of deliberate practice in the acquisition of expert performance. *Psychological Review*, *100*(3), 363–406. doi:10.1037/0033-295X.100.3.363

Essel, H. B., Vlachopoulos, D., Tachie-Menson, A., Johnson, E. E., & Baah, P. K. (2022). The impact of a virtual teaching assistant (chatbot) on students' learning in Ghanaian higher education. *International Journal of Educational Technology in Higher Education*, *19*(1), 1–19. doi:10.118641239-022-00362-6 PMID:35013716

Fan, Y., Lim, L., van der Graaf, J., Kilgour, J., Raković, M., Moore, J., Molenaar, I., Bannert, M., & Gašević, D. (2022). Improving the measurement of self-regulated learning using multi-channel data. *Metacognition and Learning*, *17*(3), 1–31. doi:10.100711409-022-09304-z

Fazio, L. K., Huelser, B. J., Johnson, A., & Marsh, E. J. (2010). Receiving right/wrong feedback: Consequences for learning. *Memory (Hove, England)*, *18*(3), 335–35. doi:10.1080/09658211003652491 PMID:20408043

Ferguson, C., Van den Broek, E. L., & Van Oostendorp, H. (2020). On the role of interaction mode and story structure in virtual reality serious games. *Computers & Education*, *143*, 103671. doi:10.1016/j.compedu.2019.103671

Ferguson, R., Clow, D., Macfadyen, L., Essa, A., Dawson, S., & Alexander, S. (2014, March). Setting learning analytics in context: overcoming the barriers to large-scale adoption. In *Proceedings of the Fourth International Conference on Learning Analytics and Knowledge* (pp. 251-253). ACM. 10.1145/2567574.2567592

Fields, R. D. (2005). Making Memories Stick. *Scientific American*, 58–63. PMID:15715394

Figlio, D., Rush, M., & Yin, L. (2013). Is it live or is it internet? experimental estimates of the effects of online instruction on student learning. *Journal of Labor Economics*, *31*(4), 763–784. doi:10.1086/669930

Fink, L. D. (2003). *Creating significant learning experiences: An integrated approach to designing college courses.* Jossey-Bass.

Finn, B. (2015). Measuring motivation in low stakes assessment. Educational Testing Service, ETS RR-15-19. doi:10.1002/ets2.12067

Finn, B., & Tauber, S. K. (2015). When confidence is not a signal of knowing: How students' experiences and beliefs about Processing Fluency Can Lead to Miscalibrated Confidence. *Educational Psychology Review*, *27*(4), 567–586. doi:10.100710648-015-9313-7

Finn, J. D. (1989). Withdrawing from school. *Review of Educational Research*, *59*(2), 117–142. doi:10.3102/00346543059002117

Fiock, H. (2020). Designing a community of inquiry in online courses. *The International Review of Research in Open and Distributed Learning*, *21*(1), 135–153. doi:10.19173/irrodl.v20i5.3985

Firth, J. (2018). Teachers' beliefs about memory: What are the implications for in-service teacher education? *Psychology of Education Review*, *42*(2), 15–22. doi:10.53841/bpsper.2018.42.2.15

Fischhoff, B. (1982). Debiasing. In D. Kahneman, P. Slovic, & A. Tversky (Eds.), *Judgment under uncertainty: heuristics and biases* (pp. 422–444). Cambridge University Press. doi:10.1017/CBO9780511809477.032

Flavell, J. H. (1976). Metacognitive aspects of problem-solving. In L. B. Resinck (Ed.), *The nature of intelligence* (pp. 231–236). Erlbaum.

Flavell, J. H. (1979). Metacognition and cognitive monitoring: A new area of cognitive-developmental inquiry. *The American Psychologist, 34*(10), 906–911. doi:10.1037/0003-066X.34.10.906

Foerst, N., Klug, J., Jostl, G., Spiel, C., & Schober, B. (2017). Knowledge vs. action: Discrepancies in university students' knowledge about and self-reported use of self-regulated learning strategies. *Frontiers in Psychology, 8*, 27. doi:10.3389/fpsyg.2017.01288 PMID:28798713

Fong, C. J., Patall, E. A., Vasquez, A. C., & Stautberg, S. (2019). A meta-analysis of negative feedback on intrinsic motivation. *Educational Psychology Review, 31*(1), 121–162. doi:10.100710648-018-9446-6

Fredricks, J. A., & McColskey, W. (2012). The measurement of student engagement: A comparative analysis of various methods and student self-report instruments. In S. Christenson, A. Reschly, & C. Wylie (Eds.), *Handbook of Research on Student Engagement* (pp. 763–782). Springer Science & Business Media. doi:10.1007/978-1-4614-2018-7_37

Freire, M., & Santos, A. (2021). *How Cognitive Engagement Strategies' can improve Learning Outcomes in Higher Education*. Position Paper.

Fritz, C. O., Morris, P. E., Acton, M., Voelkel, A. R., & Etkind, R. (2007). Comparing and combining retrieval practice and the key-word mnemonic for foreign vocabulary learning. *Applied Cognitive Psychology, 21*(4), 499–526. doi:10.1002/acp.1287

Fryer, L. K., & Carpenter, R. (2006). Bots as Language Learning Tools. *Language Learning & Technology, 10*, 8–14.

Fung, M. F., Magdeline, T. N., & Kamei, K. R. (2020, June 10). *How to create engaging online learning amid COVID-19 pandemic: Lessons from Singapore*. The Conversation. https://theconversation.com/how-to-create-engaging-online-learning-amid-covid-19-pandemic-lessons-from-singapore-138979

Gaertner, M., & McClarty, K. (2015). Performance, perseverance, and the full picture of college readiness. *Educational Measurement: Issues and Practice, 34*(2), 20–33. doi:10.1111/emip.12066

Garcia Brustenga, G., Fuertes-Alpiste, M., & Molas-Castells, N. (2018). *Briefing paper: chatbots in education*. eLearn Center. Universitat Obertade Catalunya. doi:10.7238/elc.chatbots.2018

García-Morales, V. J., Garrido-Moreno, A., & Martín-Rojas, R. (2021). The Transformation of Higher Education After the COVID Disruption: Emerging Challenges in an Online Learning Scenario. *Frontiers in Psychology, 12*, 196. doi:10.3389/fpsyg.2021.616059 PMID:33643144

García-Viola, A., Garrido-Molina, J. M., Márquez-Hernández, V. V., Granados-Gámez, G., Aguilera-Manrique, G., & Gutiérrez-Puertas, L. (2019). The influence of gamification on decision making in nursing students. *The Journal of Nursing Education, 58*(12), 718–722. doi:10.3928/01484834-20191120-07 PMID:31794039

Gardner, J., & Brooks, G. (2018). Evaluating Predictive Models of Student Success: Closing the Methodological Gap. *Journal of Learning Analytics, 5*(2), 105–125. doi:10.18608/jla.2018.52.7

Garrison, D. R., & Kanuka, H. (2004). Blended learning: Uncovering its transformative potential in higher education. *The Internet and Higher Education, 7*(2), 95–105. doi:10.1016/j.iheduc.2004.02.001

Gašević, D., & Tsai, Y. S. (2019). *The Sheila Project*. https://sheilaproject.eu/

Gašević, D., Dawson, S., & Siemens, G. (2015). Let's not forget: Learning analytics are about learning. *TechTrends, 59*(1), 64–71. doi:10.100711528-014-0822-x

Gates, A. I. (1917). Recitation as a factor in memorizing. *Archives de Psychologie, 6*, 1–104.

Gee, J. P. (2003). What video games have to teach us about learning and literacy. *Computers in Entertainment, 1*(1), 20–22. doi:10.1145/950566.950595

General Assembly. (2020). *Student Outcomes Report: GA's Full-Time Program Data: Jan. 1, 2019-Dec. 31, 2019.* https://generalassemb.ly/sites/default/files/2021-08/GA_OutcomesReport_19_8.5.21.pdf

Georgia Tech. (n.d.). *Georgia Tech is developing artificially intelligent agents that are unleashing the potential of lifetime learning.* Retrieved from Georgia Tech. https://emprize.gatech.edu/

Gigerenzer, G., & Gaissmaier, W. (2011). Heuristic decision making. *Annual Review of Psychology, 62*(1), 451–482. doi:10.1146/annurev-psych-120709-145346 PMID:21126183

Gigerenzer, G., & Todd, P. M. ABC Research Group. (1999). *Simple heuristics that make us smart.* Oxford University Press.

Gilbert, T. F. (1957). Overlearning and the retention of meaningful prose. *The Journal of General Psychology, 56*(2), 281–289. doi:10.1080/00221309.1957.9920339 PMID:13429005

Ginder, S. A., Kelly-Reid, J. E., & Mann, F. B. (2019). *Enrollment and employees in postsecondary institutions, fall 2017; and financial statistics and academic libraries, fall 2017.* U.S. Department of Education, National Center for Education Statistics. https://nces.ed.gov/pubs2019/2019021REV.pdf

Glaser, B., & Strauss, A. (1967). *The discovery of grounded theory: Strategies for qualitative research.* Aldine.

Glenberg, A. M. (1979). Component-levels theory of the effects of spacing of repetitions on recall and recognition. *Memory & Cognition, 7*(2), 95–112. doi:10.3758/BF03197590 PMID:459836

Glick, D., Xu, D., Warschauer, M., Rodriguez, F., Li, Q., & Cung, B. (2016, August). *Maximizing learning outcomes through blended learning: What research shows.* Paper presented at the 2016 Association of Bilingual Centers of Latin America Conference, Houston, TX.

Glick, D., Cohen, A., Festinger, E., Xu, D., & Warschauer, M. (2019). Predicting success, preventing failure: Using learning analytics to predict at-risk students and improve retention in online English language courses. In D. Ifenthaler, D. K. Mah, & J. Y. K. Yau (Eds.), *Utilizing Learning Analytics to Support Study Success* (pp. 249–273). Springer. doi:10.1007/978-3-319-64792-0_14

Goetz, T., Bieg, M., & Hall, N. C. (2016). Assessing academic emotions via the experience sampling method. In M. Zembylas & P. Schutz (Eds.), *Methodological Advances in Research on Emotion and Education* (pp. 245–258). Springer International Publishing. doi:10.1007/978-3-319-29049-2_19

Gogol, K., Brunner, M., Goetz, T., Martin, R., Ugen, S., Keller, U., Fischbach, A., & Preckel, F. (2014). "My Questionnaire is Too Long!" The assessments of motivational-affective constructs with three-item and single-item measures. *Contemporary Educational Psychology, 39*(3), 188–205. doi:10.1016/j.cedpsych.2014.04.002

Gordon, M., Patricio, M., Horne, L., Muston, A., Alston, S. R., Pammi, M., Thammasitboon, S., Park, S., Pawlikowska, T., Rees, E. L., Doyle, A. J., & Daniel, M. (2020). Developments in medical education in response to the COVID-19 pandemic: A rapid BEME systematic review: BEME guide no. 63. *Medical Teacher, 42*(11), 1202–1215. doi:10.1080/0142159X.2020.1807484 PMID:32847456

Gough, S., Orr, R., Stirling, A., Raikos, A., Schram, B., & Hing, W. (2021). Health Sciences and Medicine Education in Lockdown: Lessons Learned During the COVID-19 Global Pandemic. In D. Nestel, G. Reedy, L. McKenna, & S. Gough (Eds.), *Clinical Education for the Health Professions.* Springer. doi:10.1007/978-981-13-6106-7_141-1

Graesser, A., Hu, X., & Sottilare, R. (2018). Intelligent tutoring systems. International Handbook of the Learning Sciences, 246-255. doi:10.4324/9781315617572

Green, D. P., Whitehead, J., & Sugden, D. A. (1995). Practice variability and transfer of a racket skill. *Perceptual and Motor Skills*, *81*(3, suppl), 1275–1281. doi:10.2466/pms.1995.81.3f.1275 PMID:8684925

Greene, J. A., & Azevedo, R. (2009). A macro-level analysis of SRL processes and their relations to the acquisition of a sophisticated mental model of a complex system. *Contemporary Educational Psychology*, *34*(1), 18–29. doi:10.1016/j.cedpsych.2008.05.006

Greene, J. A., & Azevedo, R. (2010). The measurement of learners' self-regulated cognitive and metacognitive processes while using computer-based learning environments. *Educational Psychologist*, *45*(4), 203–209. doi:10.1080/00461520.2010.515935

Greene, J. A., Deekens, V. M., Copeland, D. Z., & Yu, S. (2017). Capturing and Modeling Self-Regulated Learning Using Think-Aloud Protocols. In *Handbook of Self-Regulation of Learning and Performance* (2nd ed.). Routledge. doi:10.4324/9781315697048-21

Greene, J., Moos, D., & Azevedo, R. (2011). Self-regulation of learning with computer-based learning environments. *New Directions for Teaching and Learning*, *126*(126), 107–115. doi:10.1002/tl.449

Green, K. C. (2019). *Campus Computing 2019: The 30th National Survey of Computing and Information Technology in American Higher Education*. Campus Computing.

Grolnick, W. S., & Ryan, R. M. (1987). Autonomy in children's learning: An experimental and individual difference investigation. *Journal of Personality and Social Psychology*, *52*(5), 89. doi:10.1037/0022-3514.52.5.890 PMID:3585701

Gue, S., Ray, J., & Ganti, L. (2022). 2022/08/30). Gamification of graduate medical education in an emergency medicine residency program. *International Journal of Emergency Medicine*, *15*(1), 41. doi:10.118612245-022-00445-1 PMID:36042403

Gunesekera, A., Bao, Y., & Kibelloh, M. (2019). The role of usability on e-learning user interactions and satisfaction: A literature review. *Journal of Systems and Information Technology*, *21*(3), 368–394. doi:10.1108/JSIT-02-2019-0024

Guo, L. (2022). The effects of self-monitoring on strategy use and academic performance: A meta-analysis. *International Journal of Educational Research*, *112*, 112. doi:10.1016/j.ijer.2022.101939

Guo, P. J., & Reinecke, K. (2014). Demographic differences in how students navigate through moocs. In *Proceedings of the first ACM conference on learning@ scale conference (L@S 2014)*. ACM. 10.1145/2556325.2566247

Guo, Z., Xiao, L., Van Toorn, C., Lai, Y., & Seo, C. (2016). 2016/03/01/). Promoting online learners' continuance intention: An integrated flow framework. *Information & Management*, *53*(2), 279–295. doi:10.1016/j.im.2015.10.010

Gurung, R., & Chick, N. (Eds.). (2009). *Exploring Signature Pedagogies: Approaches to Teaching Disciplinary Habits of Mind*. Stylus Publishing.

Guven, M. (2008). Development of learning strategy scale: Study of validation and reliability. *World Applied Sciences Journal*, *4*(1), 31–36.

Hachey, A. C., Wladis, C. W., & Conway, K. M. (2014). Do prior online course outcomes provide more information than GPA alone in predicting subsequent online course grades and retention? An observational study at an urban community college. *Computers & Education*, *72*, 59–67. doi:10.1016/j.compedu.2013.10.012

Hachey, A., Conway, K., & Wladis, C. (2013). Community colleges and underappreciated assets: Using institutional data to promote success in online learning. *Online Journal of Distance Learning Administration, 16*(1), 1–18.

Hadwin, A. F., Järvelä, S., & Miller, M. (n.d.). Self-regulated, co-regulated, and socially shared regulation of learning. Handbook of Self-Regulation of Learning and Performance. doi:10.4324/9780203839010.ch5

Hadwin, A., Järvelä, S., & Miller, M. (2018). Self-regulation, co-regulation, and shared regulation in collaborative learning environments. In Handbook of self-regulation of learning and performance, 2nd ed (pp. 83–106). Routledge/Taylor & Francis Group.

Hadwin, A., Järvelä, S., & Miller, M. (2011). Self-regulated, co-regulated, and socially shared regulation of learning. In B. J. Zimmerman & D. H. Schunk (Eds.), *Handbook of Self-Regulation of Learning and Performance* (pp. 65–84). Routledge.

Hall, K. G., Domingues, D. A., & Cavazos, R. (1994). Contextual interference effects with skilled baseball players. *Perceptual and Motor Skills, 78*(3), 835–841. doi:10.1177/003151259407800331 PMID:8084699

Hannan, E., & Liu, S. (2021). AI: New source of competitiveness in higher education. *Competitiveness Review*. Advance online publication. doi:10.1108/CR-03-2021-0045

Hansen, J. D., & Reich, J. (2015). Democratizing education? examining access and usage patterns in massive open online courses. *Science, 350*(6265), 1245–1248. doi:10.1126cience.aab3782 PMID:26785488

Hartwig, M. K., & Dunlosky, J. (2012). Study strategies of college students: Are self-testing and scheduling related to achievement? *Psychonomic Bulletin & Review, 19*(1), 126–134. doi:10.375813423-011-0181-y PMID:22083626

Hattie, J. (2012). *Visible learning for teachers: Maximizing impact on learning*. Routledge. doi:10.4324/9780203181522

Hattie, J., Biggs, J., & Purdie, N. (1996). Effects of learning skills interventions on student learning: A meta-analysis. *Review of Educational Research, 66*(2), 99–136. doi:10.3102/00346543066002099

Hattie, J., & Timperley, H. (2007). The power of feedback. *Review of Educational Research, 77*(1), 81–112. doi:10.3102/003465430298487

Higham, P. A., Zengel, B., Bartlett, L. K., & Hadwin, J. A. (2022). The benefits of successive relearning on multiple learning outcomes. *Journal of Educational Psychology, 114*(5), 928–944. doi:10.1037/edu0000693

Hofstätter, F. (2021, November 16). *How learning reward functions can go wrong*. Medium. https://towardsdatascience.com/how-learning-reward-functions-can-go-wrong-6e794e42f4fc

Hong, W., & Bernacki, M. L. (2018, April) *Data-Driven Digital Alerts and Learning Support: Effects on Achievement and Moderation by Unintended Course Events* [Poster Presentation]. Annual Meeting of the American Educational Research Association, New York, NY, United States.

Howard, E., Meehan, M., & Parnell, A. (2018). Contrasting prediction methods for early warning systems at undergraduate level. *The Internet and Higher Education, 37*, 66–75. doi:10.1016/j.iheduc.2018.02.001

Huang, B., Hew, K. F., & Lo, C. K. (2019). Investigating the effects of gamification-enhanced flipped learning on undergraduate students' behavioral and cognitive engagement. *Interactive Learning Environments, 27*(8), 1106–1126. doi:10.1080/10494820.2018.1495653

Hudesman, J., Crosby, S., Flugman, B., Issac, S., Everson, H., & Clay, D. B. (2013). Using formative assessment and metacognition to improve student achievement. *Journal of Developmental Education, 37*(1), 2. doi:10.4324/9781315623856

Hu, L. T., & Bentler, P. M. (1998). Fit indices in covariance structure modeling: Sensitivity to underparameterized model misspecification. *Psychological Methods*, *3*(4), 424–453. doi:10.1037/1082-989X.3.4.424

Hutchins, E. (2006). Cognition in the wild. MIT Press.

Hu, Y., Lo, C., & Shih, S. (2014). Developing early warning systems to predict students' online learning performance. *Computers in Human Behavior*, *36*, 469–478. doi:10.1016/j.chb.2014.04.002

Hwang, G. J., & Chang, C. Y. (2021). A review of opportunities and challenges of chatbots in education. *Interactive Learning Environments*, 1–14. Advance online publication. doi:10.1080/10494820.2021.1952615

Iaconelli, R., & Wolters, C. A. (2020). Insufficient Effort Responding in Surveys Assessing Self-Regulated Learning: Nuisance or Fatal Flaw? *Frontline Learning Research*, *8*(3), 104–125. doi:10.14786/flr.v8i3.521

Iyer, L. S., Bharadwaj, S., Shetty, S. H., Verma, V., & Devanathan, M. (2022). Advancing equity in digital classrooms: A personalized learning framework for higher education institutions. In *Socioeconomic Inclusion During an Era of Online Education* (pp. 225–245). IGI Global. doi:10.4018/978-1-6684-4364-4.ch011

Jacoby, L. L., Kelley, C. M., & Dywan, J. (1989). Memory attributions. Varieties of memory and consciousness. *Essays in Honour of Endel Tulving*, *391*, 422.

Jaggars, S. S., & Xu, D. (2016). How online course design features influence student performance? *Computers & Education*, *95*, 270–284. doi:10.1016/j.compedu.2016.01.014

Jakešováa, J., & Kalendab, J. (2015). Self-regulated learning: Critical-realistic conceptualization. *Social and Behavioral Sciences, 171,* 178–189. https://linkinghub.elsevier.com/retrieve/pii/S1877042815001354

Janes, J. L., Dunlosky, J., Rawson, K. A., & Jasnow, A. (2020). Successive relearning improves performance on a high-stakes exam in a difficult biopsychology course. *Applied Cognitive Psychology*, *34*(5), 1118–1132. doi:10.1002/acp.3699

Jansen, R. S., Van Leeuwen, A., Janssen, J., Jak, S., & Kester, L. (2019). Self-regulated learning partially mediates the effect of self-regulated learning interventions on achievement in higher education: A meta-analysis. *Educational Research Review*, *28*, 100292. doi:10.1016/j.edurev.2019.100292

Jansen, R. S., Van Leeuwen, A., Janssen, J., Kester, L., & Kalz, M. (2017). Validation of the self-regulated online learning questionnaire. *Journal of Computing in Higher Education*, *29*(1), 6–27. doi:10.100712528-016-9125-x

Jivet, I., Scheffel, M., Schmitz, M., Robbers, S., Specht, M., & Drachsler, H. (2020). From students with love: An empirical study on learner goals, self-regulated learning and sense-making of learning analytics in higher education. *The Internet and Higher Education*, *47*, 100758. doi:10.1016/j.iheduc.2020.100758

Jokhan, A., Sharma, B., & Singh, S. (2018). Early warning system as a predictor for student performance in higher education blended courses. *Studies in Higher Education*, *44*(11), 1900–1911. doi:10.1080/03075079.2018.1466872

Kahneman, D. (2011). *Thinking, fast and slow*. Macmillan.

Kahneman, D., & Frederick, S. (2002). Representativeness revisited: Attribute substitution in intuitive judgment. In T. Gilovich, D. Griffin, & D. Kahneman (Eds.), *Heuristics and biases: The psychology of intuitive judgment* (pp. 49–81). Cambridge University Press. doi:10.1017/CBO9780511808098.004

Kahneman, D., & Tversky, A. (1979). Prospect theory: An analysis of decision under risk. *Econometrica*, *47*(2), 263. doi:10.2307/1914185

Kaktiņš, L. (2019). Does Turnitin support the development of international students' academic integrity? *Ethics and Education*, *14*(4), 430–448. doi:10.1080/17449642.2019.1660946

Kali, Y. (2006). Collaborative knowledge building using the Design Principles Database. *Computer Supported Learning*, *1*(2), 187–201. doi:10.100711412-006-8993-x

Kali, Y., Levin-Peled, R., & Dori, Y. J. (2009). The role of Design-Principles in designing courses that promotes collaborative learning in higher-education. *Computers in Human Behavior*, *25*(5), 1067–1078. doi:10.1016/j.chb.2009.01.006

Kali, Y., & Ronen-Fuhrmann, T. (2011). Teaching to design educational technologies. *International Journal of Learning Technology*, *6*(1), 4–23. doi:10.1504/IJLT.2011.040147

Kane, M. (2006). Validation. In R. Brennan (Ed.), *Educational measurement* (4th ed., pp. 17–64). American Council on Education/Praeger.

Kang, S. H. K., McDermott, K. B., & Roediger, H. L. III. (2007). Test format and corrective feedback modify the effect of testing on long-term retention. *The European Journal of Cognitive Psychology*, *19*(4-5), 528–558. doi:10.1080/09541440601056620

Kang, S. H. K., & Pashler, H. (2012). Learning painting styles: Spacing is advantageous when it promotes discriminative contrast. *Applied Cognitive Psychology*, *26*(1), 97–103. doi:10.1002/acp.1801

Kapp, K. M. (2012). *The gamification of learning and instruction: game-based methods and strategies for training and education*. John Wiley & Sons.

Karabenick, S. A., & Berger, J.-L. (2013). Help seeking as a self-regulated learning strategy. In H. Bembenutty, T. Cleary, & A. Kitsantas (Eds.), *Applications of self-regulated learning across diverse disciplines: A tribute to Barry J. Zimmerman* (pp. 237–261). IAP Press.

Karpicke, J. D. (2012). Retrieval-based learning: Active retrieval promotes meaningful learning. *Current Directions in Psychological Science*, *21*(3), 157–163. doi:10.1177/0963721412443552

Karpicke, J. D., & Blunt, J. R. (2011). Retrieval practice produces more learning than elaborative studying with concept mapping. *Science*, *331*(February), 772–775. doi:10.1126cience.1199327 PMID:21252317

Karpicke, J. D., Butler, A. C., & Roediger, H. L. III. (2009). Metacognitive strategies in student learning: Do students practice retrieval when they study on their own? *Memory (Hove, England)*, *17*(4), 471–479. doi:10.1080/09658210802647009 PMID:19358016

Karpicke, J. D., & Zaromb, F. M. (2010). Retrieval mode distinguishes the testing effect from the generation effect. *Journal of Memory and Language*, *62*(3), 227–239. doi:10.1016/j.jml.2009.11.010

Keegan, D. A., Chan, M., & Chan, T. (2020). Helping medical educators worldwide pivot their curricula online: PivotMedEd.com. *Medical Education*, *54*(8), 766–767. doi:10.1111/medu.14220 PMID:32392352

Kelley, C. M., & Jacoby, L. L. (1996). Adult egocentrism: Subjective experience versus analytic bases for judgment. *Journal of Memory and Language*, *35*(2), 157–175. doi:10.1006/jmla.1996.0009

Kerr, R., & Booth, B. (1978). Specific and varied practice of motor skill. *Perceptual and Motor Skills*, *46*(2), 395–401. doi:10.1177/003151257804600201 PMID:662537

Khosravi, H., Shum, S. B., Chen, G., Conati, C., Tsai, Y. S., Kay, J., ... Gašević, D. (2022). Explainable artificial intelligence in education. *Computers and Education: Artificial Intelligence*, *3*, 100074.

King, J., & South, J. (2017). *Reimagining the role of technology in higher education: A supplement to the national education technology plan*. US Department of Education, Office of Educational Technology.

Kinzer, C., Hoffman, D., Turkay, S., Gunbas, N., Chantes, P., Dvorkin, T., & Chaiwinij, A. (2012). The impact of choice and feedback on learning, motivation, and performance in an educational video game. In *Proceedings of the games, learning, and society conference* (Vol. 2, pp. 175-181). ETC.

Kirwan, J. R., Lounsbury, J. W., & Gibson, L. W. (2014). An Examination of Learner Self-Direction in Relation to the Big Five and Narrow Personality Traits. *SAGE Open*, *4*(2), 2158244014534857. doi:10.1177/2158244014534857

Kistner, S., Rakoczy, K., Otto, B., & Dignath, C. (2010). Promotion of self-regulated learning in classrooms: Investigating frequency, quality, and consequences for student performance. *Metacognition and Learning*, *5*(2), 157–171. doi:10.100711409-010-9055-3

Kizilcec, R. F., Pérez-Sanagustín, M., & Maldonado, J. J. (2017). Self-regulated learning strategies predict learner behavior and goal attainment in massive open online courses. *Computers & Education*, *104*, 18–33. doi:10.1016/j.compedu.2016.10.001

Kizilcec, R. F., Reich, J., Yeomans, M., Dann, C., Brunskill, E., Lopez, G., Turkay, S., Williams, J. J., & Tingley, D. (2020). Scaling up behavioral science interventions in online education. *Proceedings of the National Academy of Sciences of the United States of America*, *117*(26), 14900–14905. doi:10.1073/pnas.1921417117 PMID:32541050

Kluger, A. N., & DeNisi, A. (1996). The effects of feedback interventions on performance: A historical review, a meta-analysis, and a preliminary feedback intervention theory. *Psychological Bulletin*, *119*(2), 254–284. doi:10.1037/0033-2909.119.2.254

Kluger, A. N., & DeNisi, A. (1998). Feedback interventions: Toward the understanding of a double-edged sword. *Current Directions in Psychological Science*, *7*(3), 67–72. doi:10.1111/1467-8721.ep10772989

Knowles, M. S. (1975). *Self-Directed Learning: A Guide for Learners and Teachers*. Academic Press.

Knowles, M. S. (1975). Self-directed learning: A guide for learners and teachers (Vol. 2). Association Press.

Koedinger, K. R., Corbett, A. T., & Perfetti, C. (2012). The Knowledge-Learning-Instruction framework: Bridging the science-practice chasm to enhance robust student learning. *Cognitive Science*, *36*(5), 757–798. doi:10.1111/j.1551-6709.2012.01245.x PMID:22486653

Koenka, A. C., & Anderman, E. M. (2019). Personalized feedback as a strategy for improving motivation and performance among middle school students. *Middle School Journal*, *50*(5), 15–22. doi:10.1080/00940771.2019.1674768

Koenka, A. C., Linnenbrink-Garcia, L., Moshontz, H., Atkinson, K. M., Sanchez, C. E., & Cooper, H. (2021). A meta-analysis on the impact of grades and comments on academic motivation and achievement: A case for written feedback. *Educational Psychology*, *41*(7), 922–947. doi:10.1080/01443410.2019.1659939

Koriat, A. (1997). Monitoring one's own knowledge during study: A cue-utilization approach to judgments of learning. *Journal of Experimental Psychology. General*, *126*(4), 349–370. doi:10.1037/0096-3445.126.4.349

Koriat, A., Bjork, R. A., Sheffer, L., & Bar, S. K. (2004). Predicting one's own forgetting: The role of experience-based and theory-based processes. *Journal of Experimental Psychology. General*, *133*(4), 643–656. doi:10.1037/0096-3445.133.4.643 PMID:15584811

Koriat, A., Lichtenstein, S., & Fischhoff, B. (1980). Reasons for confidence. *Journal of Experimental Psychology. Human Learning and Memory*, *6*(2), 107–118. doi:10.1037/0278-7393.6.2.107

Kornell, N. (2009). Optimising learning using flashcards: Spacing is more effective than cramming. *Applied Cognitive Psychology*, *23*(9), 1297–1317. doi:10.1002/acp.1537

Kornell, N. (2012). A stability bias in human memory. In N. M. Seel (Ed.), *Encyclopedia of the sciences of learning* (pp. 4–7). Springer. doi:10.1007/978-1-4419-1428-6_1683

Kornell, N., & Bjork, R. A. (2007). The promise and perils of self-regulated study. *Psychonomic Bulletin & Review*, *14*(2), 219–224. doi:10.3758/BF03194055 PMID:17694904

Kornell, N., & Bjork, R. A. (2008). Optimizing self-regulated study: The benefits-and costs-of dropping flashcards. *Memory (Hove, England)*, *16*(2), 125–136. doi:10.1080/09658210701763899 PMID:18286417

Kornell, N., Castel, A. D., Eich, T. S., & Bjork, R. A. (2010). Spacing as the friend of both memory and induction in young and older adults. *Psychology and Aging*, *25*(2), 498–503. doi:10.1037/a0017807 PMID:20545435

Kornell, N., Rhodes, M. G., Castel, A. D., & Tauber, S. K. (2011). The ease-of-processing heuristic and the stability bias: Dissociating memory, memory beliefs, and memory judgments. *Psychological Science*, *22*(6), 787–794. doi:10.1177/0956797611407929 PMID:21551341

Kornell, N., & Son, L. K. (2009). Learners' choices and beliefs about self-testing. *Memory (Hove, England)*, *17*(5), 493–501. doi:10.1080/09658210902832915 PMID:19468957

Kovanović, V., Joksimović, S., Mirriahi, N., Blaine, E., Gašević, D., Siemens, G., & Dawson, S. (2018). Understand students' self-reflections through learning analytics. *Proceedings of the 8th International Conference on Learning Analytics and Knowledge*, 389-398. 10.1145/3170358.3170374

Krenn, B., Würth, S., & Hergovich, A. (2013). The impact of feedback on goal setting and task performance. *Swiss Journal of Psychology*, *2*(2), 79–89. doi:10.1024/1421-0185/a000101

Krippendorff, K. (2013). *Content analysis: An introduction to its methodology* (3rd ed.). Sage.

Krueger, W. C. F. (1929). The effect of overlearning on retention. *Journal of Experimental Psychology*, *12*(1), 71–78. doi:10.1037/h0072036

Kuh, G. D. (2009). The national survey of student engagement: Conceptual and empirical foundations. *New Directions for Institutional Research*, *2009*(141), 5–20. doi:10.1002/ir.283

Kühn, A. (1914). Über einprägung durch lesen und durch rezitieren. *Zeitschrift für Psychologie mit Zeitschrift für Angewandte Psychologie*, *68*, 396–481.

Kuhn, T. S. (1962). *The structure of scientific revolutions*. University Of Chicago Press.

Kuklick, L., & Lindner, M. A. (2021). Computer-based knowledge of results feedback in different delivery modes: Effects on performance, motivation, and achievement emotions. *Contemporary Educational Psychology*, *67*, 102001. doi:10.1016/j.cedpsych.2021.102001

Kulhavy, R. W., White, M. T., Topp, B. W., Chan, A. L., & Adams, J. (1985). Feedback complexity and corrective efficiency. *Contemporary Educational Psychology*, *10*(3), 285–291. doi:10.1016/0361-476X(85)90025-6

Kurtz, B. E., & Weinert, F. E. (1989). Metamemory, metaperformance, and causal attributions in gifted and average children. *Journal of Experimental Child Psychology*, *48*(1), 45–61. doi:10.1016/0022-0965(89)90040-4 PMID:2754388

Kusurkar, R. A., Ten Cate, T. J., van Asperen, M., & Croiset, G. (2011). Motivation as an independent and a dependent variable in medical education: A review of the literature. *Medical Teacher*, *33*(5), e242–e262. doi:10.3109/0142159X.2011.558539 PMID:21517676

Lambert, S. R. (2020). Do MOOCs contribute to student equity and social inclusion? A systematic review. *Computers & Education, 145*, 103693. doi:10.1016/j.compedu.2019.103693

Landin, D. K., Hebert, E. P., & Fairweather, M. (1993). The effects of variable practice on the performance of a basketball skill. *Research Quarterly for Exercise and Sport, 64*(2), 232–237. doi:10.1080/02701367.1993.10608803 PMID:8341849

Lang, C., Siemens, G., Wise, A. F., Gašević, D., & Merceron, A. (Eds.). (2022). Handbook of Learning Analytics (2nd. ed.). SoLAR. Doi:10.18608/hla22

Lang, C., Siemens, G., Wise, A. F., & Gašević, D. (2017). *Handbook of Learning Analytics.* SoLAR. doi:10.18608/hla17

Larrick, R. P. (2004). Debiasing. In D. J. Koehler & N. Harvey (Eds.), *Blackwell handbook of judgment and decision making* (pp. 316–337). Blackwell Publishing. doi:10.1002/9780470752937.ch16

Larsen, D. P., Butler, A. C., Lawson, A. L., & Roediger, H. L. III. (2013). The importance of seeing the patient: Test-enhanced learning with standardized patients and written tests improves clinical application of knowledge. *Advances in Health Sciences Education: Theory and Practice, 18*(3), 409–425. doi:10.100710459-012-9379-7 PMID:22618856

Lave, J., & Wenger, E. (1991). *Situated learning*. Cambridge University Press. doi:10.1017/CBO9780511815355

Le, B., Lawrie, G. A., & Wang, J. T. H. (2022). Student Self-perception on Digital Literacy in STEM Blended Learning Environments. *Journal of Science Education and Technology, 31*(3), 303–321. doi:10.100710956-022-09956-1 PMID:35132301

Lee, D., Watson, S. L., & Watson, W. R. (2019). Systematic literature review on self-regulated learning in Massive open online courses. *Australasian Journal of Educational Technology, 35*(1). Advance online publication. doi:10.14742/ajet.3749

Lee, Y. F., Hwang, G. J., & Chen, P. Y. (2022). Impacts of an AI-based chatbot on college students' after-class review, academic performance, self-efficacy, learning attitude, and motivation. *Educational Technology Research and Development, 70*(5), 1843–1865. doi:10.100711423-022-10142-8

Leont'ev, A. N. (2009). *The Development of Mind: Selected works of Aleksei Nikolaevich Leontyev*. Academic Press.

Lew, D. N. M., & Schmidt, H. G. (2011). Writing to learn: Can reflection journals be used to promote self-reflection and learning? *Higher Education Research & Development, 30*(4), 519–532. doi:10.1080/07294360.2010.512627

Lewis, K. L., Stout, J. G., Pollock, S. J., Finkelstein, N. D., & Ito, T. A. (2016). Fitting in or opting out: A review of key social-psychological factors influencing a sense of belonging for women in physics. *Physical Review. Physics Education Research, 12*(2), 020110. doi:10.1103/PhysRevPhysEducRes.12.020110

Lim, M. (2020, March 20). *Educating despite the Covid-19 outbreak: Lessons from Singapore*. Times Higher Education. https://www.timeshighereducation.com/blog/educating-despite-covid-19-outbreak-lessons-singapore

Lim, S. M., Devilly, O., Jasin, J., Kok, K. X.-F., Tan, C. T., & Foo, Y. L. (2021). Effectiveness of AdventureLEARN, an Online Gamified Platform for Improving Approaches to Learning. *Asian Journal of the Scholarship of Teaching and Learning, 11*(2), 76–92.

Linkous, H. M. (2021). Self-Directed Learning and Self-Regulated Learning: What's the Difference? A Literature Analysis. *American Association for Adult and Continuing Education 2020 Conference.*

Lin, M. P. C., & Chang, D. (2020). Enhancing Post-secondary Writers' Writing Skills with a Chatbot: A Mixed-Method Classroom Study. *Journal of Educational Technology & Society, 23*(1), 78–92.

Linn, M. C., Bell, P., & Davis, E. A. (2004). Specific design principles: Elaborating the scaffolded knowledge integration framework. In Internet environments for science education. Lawrence Erlbaum Associates.

Linnenbrink-Garcia, L., Durik, A. M., Conley, A. M., Barron, K. E., Tauer, J. M., Karabenick, S. A., & Harackiewicz, J. M. (2010). Measuring situational interest in academic domains. *Educational and Psychological Measurement*, *70*(4), 647–671. doi:10.1177/0013164409355699

Lin, Y.-R., Hung, C.-Y., & Hung, J.-F. (2017). Exploring teachers' meta-strategies knowledge of science argumentation teaching with the repertory grid technique. *International Journal of Science Education*, *39*(2), 105–134. doi:10.1080/09500693.2016.1270476

Lipkus, I. M., & Klein, W. M. (2006). Effects of communicating social comparison information on risk perceptions for colorectal cancer. *Journal of Health Communication*, *11*(4), 391–407. doi:10.1080/10810730600671870 PMID:16720537

Littlejohn, A., Hood, N., Milligan, C., & Mustain, P. (2016). *Learning in MOOCs: Motivations and self-regulated learning in MOOCs*. doi:10.1016/j.iheduc.2015.12.003

Liu, S., Gomez, J., Khan, B., & Yen, C. J. (2007). Toward a learner-oriented community college online course dropout framework. *International Journal on E-Learning*, *6*(4), 519–542.

Loeb, S. (2020). How effective is online learning? What the research does and doesn't tells us. *Education Week*. https://www.edweek.org/ew/articles/2020/03/23/how-effective-is-online-learning-what-the.html

Lucieer, S. M., Jonker, L., Visscher, C., Rikers, R. M. J. P., & Themmen, A. P. N. (2016). Self-regulated learning and academic performance in medical education. *Medical Teacher*, *38*(6), 585–593. doi:10.3109/0142159X.2015.1073240 PMID:26313552

MacDougall, C., Dangerfield, P., Katz, D., & Strain, W. (2020). The impact of COVID-19 on medical education and medical students. How and when can they return to placements? *MedEdPublish*, *9*(1), 159. doi:10.15694/mep.2020.000159.1

Macfadyen, L. P., & Dawson, S. (2010). Mining LMS data to develop an "early warning system" for educators: A proof of concept. *Computers & Education*, *54*(2), 588–599. doi:10.1016/j.compedu.2009.09.008

MacIver, M. A. M., & Messel, M. (2013). The ABCs of keeping on track to graduation: Research findings from Baltimore. *Journal of Education for Students Placed at Risk*, *18*(1), 50–67. doi:10.1080/10824669.2013.745207

Magno, C. (2010). Assessing academic self-regulated learning among Filipino college students: The factor structure and item fit. *The International Journal of Educational and Psychological Assessment*, *5*, 61–76.

Maguire, D., Dales, L., & Pauli, M. (2020). *Learning and teaching reimagined. A new dawn for higher education?* JISC. https://repository.jisc.ac.uk/id/eprint/8150

Martin, F., Ritzhaupt, A., Kymar, S., & Budhrani, K. (2019). Award-winning faculty online teaching practices: Course design, assessment and evaluation, and facilitation. *The Internet and Higher Education*, *42*, 34–43. doi:10.1016/j.iheduc.2019.04.001

Mattern, K. (2019). *ACT's efficacy framework: Combining learning, measurement, and navigation to improve learner outcomes*. ACT.

Mayer, R. E., & Moreno, R. (2003). Nine ways to reduce cognitive load in multimedia learning. *Educ Psychol*, *38*(1), 43–52. doi:10.1207/S15326985EP3801_6

Mayfield, K. H., & Chase, P. N. (2002). The effects of cumulative practice on mathematics problem solving. *Journal of Applied Behavior Analysis*, *35*(2), 105–123. doi:10.1901/jaba.2002.35-105 PMID:12102132

McCabe, J. (2011). Metacognitive awareness of learning strategies in undergraduates. *Memory & Cognition*, *39*(3), 462–476. doi:10.375813421-010-0035-2 PMID:21264604

McClelland, M., Morrison, F. J., & Holmes, D. L. (2000). Children at risk for early academic problems: The role of learning-related social skills. *Early Childhood Research Quarterly*, *15*(3), 307–329. doi:10.1016/S0885-2006(00)00069-7

McDaniel, M. A., & Masson, M. E. (1985). Altering memory representations through retrieval. *Journal of Experimental Psychology. Learning, Memory, and Cognition*, *11*(2), 371–385. doi:10.1037/0278-7393.11.2.371

McDermott, K. B., Agarwal, P. K., D'Antonio, L., Roediger, H. L., & McDaniel, M. A. (2014). Both multiple-choice and short-answer quizzes enhance later exam performance in middle and high school classes. *Journal of Experimental Psychology. Applied*, *20*(1), 3–21. doi:10.1037/xap0000004 PMID:24274234

McElrath, K. (2020). *Nearly 93% of households with school age children report some form of distance learning during Covid 19. In Schooling During the Covid-19 Pandemic*. U.S. Census Bureau.

McKeachie, W. J., Pintrich, P. R., & Lin, Y. (1985). Teaching learning strategies. *Educational Psychologist*, *20*(3), 153–160. doi:10.120715326985ep2003_5

McMahon, B. M., & Sembiante, S. F. (2019). Re-envisioning the purpose of early warning systems: Shifting the mindset from student identification to meaningful prediction and intervention. *Review of Education*, *8*(1), 266–301. doi:10.1002/rev3.3183

McNamara, D. S., Jackson, G. T., & Graesser, A. (2010). Intelligent tutoring and games (ITaG). In *Gaming for classroom-based learning: Digital role playing as a motivator of study* (pp. 44–65). IGI Global. doi:10.4018/978-1-61520-713-8.ch003

McWilliams, K., Black, A., Bergin, J., & Warnakulasooryia, R. (2017). *Unpacking the black box of efficacy: A framework for evaluating the effectiveness and researching the impact of digital learning tools*. Macmillan Learning.

Means, B., Toyama, Y., Murphy, R., & Baki, M. (2013). The effectiveness of online and blended learning: A meta-analysis of the empirical literature. *Teachers College Record*, *115*(3), 1–47. doi:10.1177/016146811311500307

Meehl, P. E. (1954). *Clinical versus statistical prediction: A theoretical analysis and a review of the evidence*. University of Minnesota. doi:10.1037/11281-000

Mehta, J., & Fine, S. (2019). *In Search of Deeper Learning—Jal Mehta, Sarah Fine*. Harvard University Press. https://www.hup.harvard.edu/catalog.php?isbn=9780674988392

Meichenbaum, D. (1985). Metacognitive methods of instruction: Current status and future prospects. *Special Services in the Schools*, *3*(1-2), 23–32. doi:10.1300/J008v03n01_03

Mertens, U., Finn, B., & Lindner, M. (2022, November). Effects of computer-based feedback on lower and higher order learning outcomes: A network meta-analysis. *Journal of Educational Psychology*, *114*(8), 1743–1772. doi:10.1037/edu0000764

Metcalfe, J., & Finn, B. (2008). Evidence that judgments of learning are causally related to study choice. *Psychonomic Bulletin & Review*, *15*(1), 174–179. doi:10.3758/PBR.15.1.174 PMID:18605499

Miedijensky, S., Sasson, I., & Yehuda, I. (2021). Teachers' learning communities for developing high order thinking skills—A case study of a school pedagogical change. *Interchange*, *52*(4), 577–598. doi:10.100710780-021-09423-7

Miedijensky, S., & Tal, T. (2016). Reflection and assessment for learning in science enrichment courses for the gifted. *Studies in Educational Evaluation*, *50*, 1–13. doi:10.1016/j.stueduc.2016.05.001

Miller, G. A. (1956). The magical number seven, plus or minus two: Some limits on our capacity for processing information. *Psychological Review*, *63*(2), 81–97. doi:10.1037/h0043158 PMID:13310704

Ministerio de Educación. Perú. (2016). *Currículo nacional de la educación básica*. Retrieved from http://www.minedu.gob.pe/curriculo/pdf/curriculo-nacional-2016-2.pdf

Ministry of Education of Singapore. (2022, March 7). *Expanding pathways & opportunities across a life course: investing in our learners for life*. https://www.moe.gov.sg/news/press-releases/20220307-expanding-pathways-and-opportunities-across-a-life-course-investing-in-our-learners-for-life

Mirata, V., Hirt, F., Bergamin, P., & van der Westhuizen, C. (2020). Challenges and contexts in establishing adaptive learning in higher education: Findings from a Delphi study. *International Journal of Educational Technology in Higher Education*, *17*(1), 1–25. doi:10.118641239-020-00209-y

Mironenko, I. (2013). Concerning Interpretations of Activity Theory. *Integrative Psychological & Behavioral Science*, *47*(3), 376–393. Advance online publication. doi:10.100712124-013-9231-5 PMID:23512520

Mislevy, R. J., Almond, R. G., & Lukas, J. F. (2003). *A brief introduction to evidence-centered design* (ETS Research Report RR-03-16). Educational Testing Service.

Mo, C. Y., Hsieh, T. H., Lin, C. L., Jin, Y. Q., & Su, Y. S. (2021). Exploring the critical factors, the online learning continuance usage during Covid-19 pandemic. *Sustainability*, *13*(10), 5471. doi:10.3390u13105471

Moore, M. G. (2013). The theory of transactional distance. In M. G. Moore (Ed.), *Handbook of Distance Education* (3rd ed.). Routledge. doi:10.4324/9780203803738.ch5

Moos, D. C. (2011). Self-regulated learning and externally generate feedback with hypermedia. *Journal of Educational Computing Research*, *44*(3), 265–297. doi:10.2190/EC.44.3.b

Mora, A., Riera, D., González, C., & Arnedo-Moreno, J. (2017). Gamification: A systematic review of design frameworks. *Journal of Computing in Higher Education*, *29*(3), 516–548. doi:10.100712528-017-9150-4

Morehead, K., Rhodes, M. G., & DeLozier, S. (2016). Instructor and student knowledge of study strategies. *Memory (Hove, England)*, *24*(2), 257–271. doi:10.1080/09658211.2014.1001992 PMID:25625188

Moreno-Marcos, P. M., Muñoz-Merino, P. J., Maldonado-Mahauad, J., Pérez-Sanagustín, M., Alario-Hoyos, C., & Delgado Kloos, C. (2020). *Temporal analysis for dropout prediction using self-regulated learning strategies in self-paced MOOCs*. doi:10.1016/j.compedu.2019.103728

Morris, N. P., Ivancheva, M., Coop, T., Mogliacci, R., & Seinnerton, B. (2020). Negotiating growth of online education in higher education. *International Journal Educational Technology in Higher Education*, *17*(1), 48. doi:10.118641239-020-00227-w

Morris, T. H. (2019). Self-directed learning: A fundamental competence in a rapidly changing world. *International Review of Education*, *65*(4), 633–653. doi:10.100711159-019-09793-2

Mory, E. H. (2013). Feedback research revisited. In *Handbook of research on educational communications and technology* (pp. 738–776). Routledge.

Mubarak, A. A., Cao, H., & Zhang, W. (2022). Predication of students' early dropout based on their interaction logs in online learning environment. *Interactive Learning Environments*, *30*(8), 1414–1433. doi:10.1080/10494820.2020.1727529

Mumford, S., & Dikilitas, K. (2020). Pre-service language teachers reflection development through online interaction in a hybrid learning course. *Computers & Education*, *144*, 103706. Advance online publication. doi:10.1016/j.compedu.2019.103706

Murphy, D. H., Huckins, S. C., Rhodes, M. G., & Castel, A. D. (2022). The effect of perceptual processing fluency and value on metacognition and remembering. *Psychonomic Bulletin & Review*, *29*(3), 910–921. doi:10.375813423-021-02030-8 PMID:34846689

Murre, J. M. J., & Dros, J. (2015). Replication and analysis of Ebbinghaus' forgetting curve. *PLoS One*, *10*(3), e0120644. doi:10.1371/journal.pone.0120644 PMID:26148023

Nathan, M. J., Koedinger, K. R., & Alibali, M. W. (2001). *Expert blind spot: When content knowledge eclipses pedagogical content knowledge.* Paper presented at the Annual Meeting of the American Educational Research Association.

National Forum on Education Statistics. (2018). *Forum Guide to Early Warning Systems* (NFES2019035). U.S. Department of Education. Washington, DC: National Center for Education Statistics.

National Student Clearinghouse Research Center. (2022). *Overview: Spring 2022 enrollment estimates.* https://nscresearchcenter.org/stay-informed/

National Student Clearinghouse Research Centre. (2022). *Overview: Spring 2022 Enrollment Estimates.* https://nscresearchcenter.org/wp-content/uploads/CTEE_Report_Spring_2022.pdf

Neelen, M., & Kirschner, P. A. (2020). *Evidence-Informed Learning Design.* Kogan Page. https://www.koganpage.com/product/evidence-informed-learning-design-9781789661415

Nelson, T. O. (1996). Consciousness and metacognition. *The American Psychologist*, *51*(2), 102–116. doi:10.1037/0003-066X.51.2.102

Nelson, T. O., & Narens, L. (1990). Metamemory: A theoretical frame-work and new findings. *Psychology of Learning and Motivation*, *26*, 125–141. doi:10.1016/S0079-7421(08)60053-5

Neo, M. (2022). The Merlin Project: Malaysian Students' Acceptance of an AI Chatbot in Their Learning Process. *Turkish Online Journal of Distance Education, 23*(3), 31–48. https://doi-org.tp-library.idm.oclc.org/10.17718/tojde.1137122

Ngampornchai, A., & Adams, J. (2016). Students' acceptance and readiness for E-learning in Northeastern Thailand. *International Journal of Educational Technology in Higher Education*, *13*(1), 34. doi:10.118641239-016-0034-x

Nijhuis, J., Segers, M., & Gijselaers, W. (2008). The extent of variability in learning strategies and students' perceptions of the learning environment. *Learning and Instruction*, *18*(2), 121–134. doi:10.1016/j.learninstruc.2007.01.009

Nisbett, R. E., & Wilson, T. D. (1977). Telling more than we can know: Verbal reports on mental processes. *Psychological Review*, *84*(3), 231–259. doi:10.1037/0033-295X.84.3.231

Nist, S. L., & Hogrebe, M. C. (1987). The role of underlining and annotating in remembering textual information. *Reading Research and Instruction*, *27*(1), 12–25. doi:10.1080/19388078709557922

NSC Research Center. (2018). *Persistence & Retention – 2018*. Retrieved from https://nscresearchcenter.org/snapshotreport33-first-year-persistence-and-retention/

OECD. (2015). *Education at a glance 2015: OECD indicators*. OECD Publishing. doi:10.1787/eag-2015-

Okonkwo, C. W., & Ade-Ibijola, A. (2021). Chatbots applications in education: A systematic review. *Computers and Education: Artificial Intelligence*, *2*, 1–10. doi:10.1016/j.caeai.2021.100033

Okonofua, J. A., & Eberhardt, J. L. (2015). Two strikes: Race and the disciplining of young students. *Psychological Science*, *26*(5), 617–624. doi:10.1177/0956797615570365 PMID:25854276

Olson, S., & Riordan, D. G. (2012). *Engage to Excel: Producing One Million Additional College Graduates with Degrees in Science, Technology, Engineering, and Mathematics*. Report to the President. Executive Office of the President. https://files.eric.ed.gov/fulltext/ED541511.pdf

Paivio, A., Walsh, M., & Bons, T. (1994). Concreteness effects on memory: When and why? *Journal of Experimental Psychology. Learning, Memory, and Cognition*, *20*(5), 1196–1204. doi:10.1037/0278-7393.20.5.1196

Pajares, F. (2006). Self-efficacy during childhood and adolescence: Implications for Teachers and Parents. In *Adolescence and education: Self-efficacy beliefs of adolescents* (Vol. 5, pp. 339–367). Information Age Publishing.

Pallant, J. (2013). *SPSS survival manual: A step by step guide to data analysis using IBM SPSS* (5th ed.). Allen & Unwin.

Panadero, E. (2017). A review of self-regulated learning: Six models and four directions for research. *Frontiers in Psychology*, *8*, 28. doi:10.3389/fpsyg.2017.00422 PMID:28503157

Panadero, E., & Alonso-Tapia, J. (2014). How do students self-regulate? Review of Zimmerman's cyclical model of self-regulated learning. *Anales de Psicología*, *30*, 450–462.

Panadero, E., & Alonso-Tapia, J. (2014). How do students self-regulate?: Review of Zimmerman's cyclical model of self-regulated learning. *Anales De Psicologia*.

Paolacci, G., & Chandler, J. (2014). Inside the Turk: Understanding Mechanical Turk as a participant pool. *Current Directions in Psychological Science*, *23*(3), 184–188. doi:10.1177/0963721414531598

Papies, E., & Aarts, H. (2016). Automatic self-regulation: from habit to goal pursuit. In K. D. Vohs & R. F. Baumeister (Eds.), *Handbook of Self-Regulation: Research, Theory, and Applications*. Guilford Press.

Pardo, A., Ellis, R. A., & Calvo, R. A. (2015). Combining observational and experiential data to inform the redesign of learning activities. *Proceedings of the Fifth International Conference on Learning Analytics and Knowledge*, 305-309.

Park, J., Yu, R., Rodriguez, F., Baker, R., Smyth, P., & Warschauer, M. (2018). Understanding student procrastination via mixture models. *Proceedings of the 11th International Conference on Educational Data Mining*.

Parr, A. K., & Bonitz, V. S. (2015). Role of family background, student behaviors, and school-related beliefs in predicting high school dropout. *The Journal of Educational Research*, *108*(6), 504–514. doi:10.1080/00220671.2014.917256

Pashler, H., Cepeda, N. J., Wixted, J. T., & Rohrer, D. (2005). When does feedback facilitate learning of words? *Journal of Experimental Psychology. Learning, Memory, and Cognition*, *31*(1), 3–8. doi:10.1037/0278-7393.31.1.3 PMID:15641900

Pastötter, B., & Bäuml, K. H. T. (2014). Retrieval practice enhances new learning: The forward effect of testing. *Frontiers in Psychology*, 286. PMID:24772101

Patterson, D. A., Waya, S. W., Ahuna, K. H., Tinnesz, C. G., & Vanzile-Tamsen, C. (2014). Using self-regulated learning methods to increase Native American college retention. *Journal of College Student Retention*, *16*(2), 219–237. doi:10.2190/CS.16.2.d

Patterson, R. W. (2018). Can behavioral tools improve online student outcomes? Experimental evidence from a massive open online course. *Journal of Economic Behavior & Organization*, *153*, 293–321. doi:10.1016/j.jebo.2018.06.017

Pearl, J. B., & Arunfred, N. (2019). A Comparative Study on the Concentration Skill between E-Learning Methods and Traditional Learning Methods among Higher Education Students. *Asia Pacific Journal of Multidisciplinary Research*, *7*(4), 67–73.

Pearson. (2020). *Efficacy reporting framework*. https://www.pearson.com/content/dam/one-dot-com/one-dot-com/global/Files/efficacy-and-research/reports/audited/Pearson_E fficacyFramework_2020.pdf

Pelletier, K., McCormack, M., Reeves, J., Robert, J., & Arbino, N. (2022). *EDUCAUSE Horizon Report, Teaching and Learning Edition*. EDUCAUSE.

Pengel, N., Martin, A., Meissner, R., Arndt, T., Neumann, A. T., de Lange, P., & Wollersheim, H. W. (2021). *TecCoBot: Technology-aided support for self-regulated learning*. doi:10.48550/arXiv.2111.11881

Peng, H., Ma, S., & Spector, J. M. (2019). Personalized adaptive learning: An emerging pedagogical approach enabled by a smart learning environment. *Smart Learning Environments*, *6*(1), 9. doi:10.118640561-019-0089-y

Penn, P. (2022) *Psychology explains why students aren't flocking back to campus*. https://www.timeshighereducation.com/blog/psychology-explain s-why-students-arent-flocking-back-campus

Pérez, J. Q., Daradoumis, T., & Puig, J. M. M. (2020). Rediscovering the use of chatbots in education: A systematic literature review. *Computer Applications in Engineering Education*, *28*(6), 1549–1565. doi:10.1002/cae.22326

Perkins, D. N. (2009). *Making learning whole: How seven principles of teaching can transform education* (1st ed.). Jossey-Bass.

Perry, S. & Martin, R. (2016) Authentic reflection for experiential learning at international schools. *International Journal of Research on Service-Learning and Community Engagement, 4*(1), 53-68.

Peterson, D. J., & Mulligan, N. W. (2013). The negative testing effect and multifactor account. *Journal of Experimental Psychology. Learning, Memory, and Cognition*, *39*(4), 1287–1293. doi:10.1037/a0031337 PMID:23421505

Peterson, S. E. (1992). The cognitive functions of underlining as a study technique. *Reading Research and Instruction*, *31*(2), 49–56. doi:10.1080/19388079209558078

Physiotherapy, W. (2020). *World physiotherapy response to COVID-19 briefing paper 1: immediate impact on the higher education sector and response to delivering physiotherapist entry level education.* World Physiotherapy. https://world.physio/sites/default/files/2020-07/Education-Briefing-paper-1-HEI.pdf

Pintrich, P. R., & Others, A. (1991). *A Manual for the Use of the Motivated Strategies for Learning Questionnaire (MSLQ)*. https://eric.ed.gov/?id=ED338122

Pintrich, P., Smith, D., Garcia, T., & McKeachie, W. (1991). *A manual for the use of the motivated strategies for learning questionnaire (MSQL).* National Center for research to Improve Post-secondary Teaching and Learning. Ann Arbor: MI: The Regents of the University of Michigan. Technical Report No. NCRIPTAL-91-B-004.

Pintrich, P. (2000). The role of goal orientation in self-regulated learning. In M. Boekaerts, P. R. Pintrich, & M. Zeidner (Eds.), *s), Handbook of Self-Regulation* (pp. 452–502). Academic Press. doi:10.1016/B978-012109890-2/50043-3

Pintrich, P. R. (2000b). Multiple goals, multiple pathways: The role of goal orientation in learning and achievement. *Journal of Educational Psychology*, *92*(3), 544–555. doi:10.1037/0022-0663.92.3.544

Pintrich, P. R. (2004). A conceptual framework for assessing motivation and self-regulation learning in college students. *Educational Psychology Review*, *16*(4), 385–407. doi:10.100710648-004-0006-x

Pintrich, P. R., & de Groot, E. (1990). Motivational and Self-Regulated Learning Components of Classroom Academic Performance. *Journal of Educational Psychology*, *82*(1), 33–40. doi:10.1037/0022-0663.82.1.33

Pintrich, P. R., Smith, D. A., Garcia, T., & McKeachie, W. J. (1993). Reliability and predictive validity of the motivated strategies for learning questionnaire (MSLQ). *Educational and Psychological Measurement*, *53*(3), 801–813. doi:10.1177/0013164493053003024

Postman, L. (1962). Retention as a function of degree of overlearning. *Science*, *135*(3504), 666–667. doi:10.1126cience.135.3504.666 PMID:14037399

Prensky, M. (2001). Digital natives, digital immigrants, part 1. *On the Horizon*, *9*(5), 1–6. doi:10.1108/10748120110424816

Pyc, M. A., & Rawson, K. A. (2010). Why testing improves memory: Mediator effectiveness hypothesis. *Science*, *330*(6002), 335–335. doi:10.1126cience.1191465 PMID:20947756

Pyc, M. A., & Rawson, K. A. (2012). Why is test–restudy practice beneficial for memory? An evaluation of the mediator shift hypothesis. *Journal of Experimental Psychology. Learning, Memory, and Cognition*, *38*(3), 737–746. doi:10.1037/a0026166 PMID:22060276

Rawson, K. A., & Dunlosky, J. (2022). Successive relearning: An underexplored but potent technique for obtaining and maintaining knowledge. *Current Directions in Psychological Science*, *31*(4), 362–368. doi:10.1177/09637214221100484

Rawson, K. A., Dunlosky, J., & Sciartelli, S. M. (2013). The power of successive relearning: Improving performance on course exams and long-term retention. *Educational Psychology Review*, *25*(4), 523–548. doi:10.100710648-013-9240-4

Reich, J., & Ruipérez-Valiente, J. A. (2019). The MOOC pivot. *Science*, *363*(6423), 130–131. doi:10.1126cience.aav7958 PMID:30630920

Reinecke, L., Tamborini, R., Grizzard, M., Lewis, R., Eden, A., & Bowman, D. N. (2012). Characterizing mood management as need satisfaction: The effects of intrinsic needs on selective exposure and mood repair. *Journal of Communication*, *62*(3), 437–453. doi:10.1111/j.1460-2466.2012.01649.x

Reschly, A. L., & Christenson, S. L. (2006). Prediction of dropout among students with mild disabilities: A case for inclusion of student engagement variables. *Remedial and Special Education*, *27*(5), 276–292. doi:10.1177/074193250 60270050301

Rhodes, M. G., & Castel, A. D. (2008). Memory predictions are influenced by perceptual information: Evidence for metacognitive illusions. *Journal of Experimental Psychology. General*, *137*(4), 615–625. doi:10.1037/a0013684 PMID:18999356

Rhodes, M. G., & Castel, A. D. (2009). Metacognitive illusions for auditory information: Effects on monitoring and control. *Psychonomic Bulletin & Review*, *16*(3), 550–554. doi:10.3758/PBR.16.3.550 PMID:19451383

Richardson, M., Abraham, C., & Bond, R. (2012). Psychological correlates of university students' academic performance: A systematic review and meta-analysis. *Psychological Bulletin*, *138*(2), 353–387. doi:10.1037/a0026838 PMID:22352812

Roberts, R. D., Martin, J. E., & Olaru, G. (2015). *A Rosetta stone for noncognitive skills: Understanding, assessing, and enhancing noncognitive skills in primary and secondary education*. Academic Press.

Roediger, H. L. III, & Karpicke, J. D. (2006). The power of testing memory: Basic research and implications for educational practice. *Perspectives on Psychological Science*, *1*(3), 181–210. doi:10.1111/j.1745-6916.2006.00012.x PMID:26151629

Roediger, H. L., & Pyc, M. A. (2012). Inexpensive techniques to improve education: Applying cognitive psychology to enhance educational practice. *Journal of Applied Research in Memory and Cognition*, *1*(4), 242–248. doi:10.1016/j.jarmac.2012.09.002

Roehl, A., Reddy, S. L., & Jett, G. (2013). The Flipped Classroom: An Opportunity to Engage Millennial Students through Active Learning Strategies. *Journal of Family and Consumer Sciences*, *105*(2), 44–49. doi:10.14307/JFCS105.2.12

Rogers, G. (2004). History, learning technology and student achievement: Making the difference? *Active Learning in Higher Education*, *5*(3), 232–247. doi:10.1177/1469787404043811

Rohrer, D., Dedrick, R. F., & Burgess, K. (2014). The benefit of interleaved mathematics practice is not limited to superficially similar kinds of problems. *Psychonomic Bulletin & Review*, *21*(5), 1323–1330. doi:10.375813423-014-0588-3 PMID:24578089

Rohrer, D., & Pashler, H. (2010). Recent research on human learning challenges conventional instructional strategies. *Educational Researcher*, *39*(5), 406–412. doi:10.3102/0013189X10374770

Rohrer, D., & Taylor, K. (2007). The shuffling of mathematics problems improves learning. *Instructional Science*, *35*(6), 481–498. doi:10.100711251-007-9015-8

Roll, I., Aleven, V., McLaren, B. M., & Koedinger, K. R. (2011). Metacognitive practice makes perfect: Improving students' self-assessment skills with an intelligent tutoring system. *Artificial Intelligence in Education*, *6738*, 288–295. doi:10.1007/978-3-642-21869-9_38

Romero, C., & Ventura, S. (2007). Educational data mining: A survey from 1995 to 2005. *Expert Systems with Applications*, *33*(1), 135–146. doi:10.1016/j.eswa.2006.04.005

Roth, A., Ogrin, S., & Schmitz, B. (2015). Assessing self-regulated learning in higher education: A systematic literature review of self-report instruments. *Educational Assessment, Evaluation and Accountability*, *28*(3), 225–250. doi:10.100711092-015-9229-2

Rowland, C. A. (2014). The effect of testing versus re-study on retention: A meta-analytic review of the testing effect. *Psychological Bulletin*, *140*(6), 1–32. doi:10.1037/a0037559 PMID:25150680

Rumberger, R. W. (2011). *Dropping out: why students drop out of high school and what can be done about it*. Harvard University Press. doi:10.4159/harvard.9780674063167

Rutledge, C., Walsh, C. M., Swinger, N., Auerbach, M., Castro, D., Dewan, M., Khattab, M., Rake, A., Harwayne-Gidansky, I., Raymond, T. T., Maa, T., & Chang, T. P. (2018). Gamification in Action: Theoretical and Practical Considerations for Medical Educators. *Academic Medicine*, *93*(7), 1014–1020. doi:10.1097/ACM.0000000000002183 PMID:29465450

Ryan, R. M., & Deci, E. L. (2000). Self-determination theory and the facilitation of intrinsic motivation, social development, and well-being. *The American Psychologist*, *55*(1), 68–78. doi:10.1037/0003-066X.55.1.68 PMID:11392867

Saito, H., & Miwa, K. (2007). Construction of a learning environment supporting learners' reflection: A case of information seeking on the web. *Computers & Education*, *49*(2), 214–229. doi:10.1016/j.compedu.2005.07.001

Salehian Kia, F., Hatala, M., Baker, R. S., & Teasley, S. D. (2021, April). Measuring students' self-regulatory phases in LMS with behavior and real-time self-report. In *LAK21: 11th International Learning Analytics and Knowledge Conference* (pp. 259-268). 10.1145/3448139.3448164

Sandars, J., & Cleary, T. J. (2011). Self-regulation theory: Applications to medical education: AMEE Guide No. 58. *Medical Teacher*, *33*(11), 875–886. doi:10.3109/0142159X.2011.595434 PMID:22022899

Scherer, E. A., Kim, S. J., Metcalf, S. A., Sweeney, M. A., Wu, J., Xie, H., Mazza, G. L., Valente, M. J., MacKinnon, D. P., & Marsch, L. A. (2022). Momentary Self-regulation: Scale Development and Preliminary Validation. *JMIR Mental Health*, *9*(5), e35273. doi:10.2196/35273 PMID:35536605

Schmader, T., & Johns, M. (2003). Converging evidence that stereotype threat reduces working memory capacity. *Journal of Personality and Social Psychology*, *85*(3), 440–452. doi:10.1037/0022-3514.85.3.440 PMID:14498781

Schmitt, O., & Buschek, D. (2021). *CharacterChat: Supporting the Creation of Fictional Characters through Conversation and Progressive Manifestation with a Chatbot*. doi:10.1145/3450741.3465253

Schön, D. A. (1983). *The reflective practitioner: How professionals think in action*. Basic Books.

School of Humanities and Social Sciences. (2018). *Subject syllabus document: Communication & Information Literacy*. Temasek Polytechnic.

Schraw, G. (2009). A conceptual analysis of five measures of metacognitive monitoring. *Metacognition and Learning*, *4*(1), 33–45. doi:10.100711409-008-9031-3

Schraw, G., & Moshman, D. (1995). Metacognitive theories. *Educational Psychology Review*, *7*(4), 351–371. doi:10.1007/BF02212307

Schunk, D. H., & Greene, J. A. (2018b). Historical, contemporary, and future perspectives on self-regulated learning and performance. In Handbook of self-regulation of learning and performance (2nd ed., pp. 1–15). Routledge/Taylor & Francis Group.

Schunk, D. (2005). Self-Regulated Learning: The Educational Legacy of Paul R. Pintrich. *Educational Psychologist*, *40*(2), 85–94. doi:10.120715326985ep4002_3

Schunk, D. H. (2008). Metacognition, self-regulation, and self-regulated learning: Research recommendations. *Educational Psychology Review*, *20*(4), 463–467. doi:10.100710648-008-9086-3

Schunk, D. H., & Ertmer, P. A. (2000). Self-regulation and academic learning: Self-efficacy enhancing interventions. In *Handbook of self-regulation* (pp. 631–649). Academic Press. doi:10.1016/B978-012109890-2/50048-2

Schunk, D. H., & Greene, J. A. (Eds.). (2018a). *Handbook of Self-Regulation of Learning and Performance* (2nd ed.). Routledge. https://www.routledge.com/Handbook-of-Self-Regulation-of-Learning-and-Performance/Schunk-Greene/p/book/9781138903197

Schunk, D. H., & Zimmerman, B. J. (1997). Social origins of self-regulatory competence. *Educational Psychologist*, *32*(4), 195–208. doi:10.120715326985ep3204_1

Schwinger, M., Wirthwein, L., Lemmer, G., & Steinmayr, R. (2014). Academic self-handicapping and achievement: A meta-analysis. *Journal of Educational Psychology*, *106*(3), 744–761. doi:10.1037/a0035832

Seaman, J. E., Allen, I. E., & Seaman, J. (2018). *Grade Increase: Tracking Distance Education in the United States*. Babson Survey Research Group.

Sedrakyan, G., De Weerdt, J., & Snoeck, M. (2016). Process Mining enabled feedback: "Tell me what I did wrong" vs. "tell me how to do it right. *Computers in Human Behavior*, *57*, 352–376. doi:10.1016/j.chb.2015.12.040

Sengsouliya, S., Soukhavong, S., Silavong, N., Sengsouliya, S., & Littlepage, F. (2020). An investigation on predictors of student academic engagement. *European Journal of Education Studies*.

Seufert, T. (2018). The interplay between self-regulation in learning and cognitive load. *Educational Research Review*, *24*, 116–129. doi:10.1016/j.edurev.2018.03.004

Sezgin, S., & Yüzer, T. V. (2022). Analyzing adaptive gamification design principles for online courses. *Behaviour & Information Technology*, *41*(3), 485–501. doi:10.1080/0144929X.2020.1817559

Shah, A. K., & Oppenheimer, D. M. (2008). Heuristics made easy: An effort-reduction framework. *Psychological Bulletin*, *134*(2), 207–222. doi:10.1037/0033-2909.134.2.207 PMID:18298269

Shah, A. K., & Oppenheimer, D. M. (2009). The path of least resistance: Using easy-to-access information. *Current Directions in Psychological Science*, *18*(4), 232–236. doi:10.1111/j.1467-8721.2009.01642.x

Sharek, D., & Wiebe, E. (2011). Using Flow Theory to Design Video Games as Experimental Stimuli. *Proceedings of the Human Factors and Ergonomics Society Annual Meeting*, *55*(1), 1520–1524. doi:10.1177/1071181311551316

Shea, J. B., & Morgan, R. L. (1979). Contextual interference effects on the acquisition, retention, and transfer of a motor skill. *Journal of Experimental Psychology. Human Learning and Memory*, *5*(2), 179–187. doi:10.1037/0278-7393.5.2.179

Shorey, S., Chan, V., Rajendran, P., & Ang, E. (2021). Learning styles, preferences and needs of generation Z healthcare students: Scoping review. *Nurse Education in Practice*, *57*, 103247. doi:10.1016/j.nepr.2021.103247 PMID:34768214

Shortt, M., Tilak, S., Kuznetcova, I., Martens, B., & Akinkuolie, B. (2021). Gamification in mobile-assisted language learning: A systematic review of Duolingo literature from public release of 2012 to early 2020. *Computer Assisted Language Learning*, 1–38. Advance online publication. doi:10.1080/09588221.2021.1933540

Shute, V. J. (2008). Focus on formative feedback. *Review of Educational Research*, *78*(1), 153–189. doi:10.3102/0034654307313795

Shute, V. J., & Ke, F. (2012). Games, learning, and assessment. In *Assessment in game-based learning* (pp. 43–58). Springer. doi:10.1007/978-1-4614-3546-4_4

Sife, A., Lwoga, E., & Sanga, C. (2007). New technologies for teaching and learning: Challenges for higher learning institutions in developing countries. *International Journal of Education and Development Using ICT, 3*(2).

Sigama, K., & Kalema, B. M. (2018, November). Conceptualizing moocs implementation for higher education in developing countries. In *2018 IEEE 6th International Conference on MOOCs, Innovation and Technology in Education (MITE)* (pp. 14-18). IEEE. 10.1109/MITE.2018.8747114

Silamut, A., & Sovajassatakul, T. (2021). Self-directed learning with knowledge management model on academic achievement and digital literacy abilities for employees of a Thai energy organization. *Education and Information Technologies*, *26*(5), 5149–5163. doi:10.100710639-021-10484-5

Simon, H. A. (1957). *Models of man: Social and rational.* Wiley.

Simons, D. J., & Chabris, C. F. (2011). What people believe about how memory works: A representative survey of the US population. *PLoS One*, *6*(8), e22757. doi:10.1371/journal.pone.0022757 PMID:21826204

Simons, D. J., & Chabris, C. F. (2012). Common (mis) beliefs about memory: A replication and comparison of telephone and Mechanical Turk survey methods. *PLoS One*, *7*(12), e51876. doi:10.1371/journal.pone.0051876 PMID:23272183

Simpson, O. (2013). Student retention in distance education: Are we failing our students? *Open Learning: The Journal of Open, Distance, and eLearning, 28*(2), 105-119.

Singapore Institute of Technology. (2014, March 28). *SIT is officially Singapore's new autonomous university*. https://www.singaporetech.edu.sg/digitalnewsroom/sit-is-officially-singapores-new-autonomous-university/

Sitzmann, T., & Ely, K. (2011). A meta-analysis of self-regulated learning in work-related training and educational attainment: What we know and where we need to go. *Psychological Bulletin, 137*(3), 421–442. doi:10.1037/a0022777 PMID:21401218

Sloman, S. A. (2002). Two systems of reasoning. In T. Gilovich, D. Griffin, & D. Kahneman (Eds.), *Heuristics and biases: The psychology of intuitive judgment* (pp. 379–396). Cambridge University Press. doi:10.1017/CBO9780511808098.024

Smith, S. M. (1982). Enhancement of recall using multiple environmental contexts during learning. *Memory & Cognition, 10*(5), 405–412. doi:10.3758/BF03197642 PMID:7176900

Smith, S. M., Glenberg, A., & Bjork, R. A. (1978). Environmental context and human memory. *Memory & Cognition, 6*(4), 342–353. doi:10.3758/BF03197465

Smith, S. M., & Rothkopf, E. Z. (1984). Contextual enrichment and distribution of practice in the classroom. *Cognition and Instruction, 1*(3), 341–358. doi:10.12071532690xci0103_4

Smutny, P., & Schreiberova, P. (2020). Chatbots for learning: A review of educational chatbots for the Facebook Messenger. *Computers & Education, 151*(103862), 1–11. doi:10.1016/j.compedu.2020.103862

Sneyers, E., & De Witte, K. (2018). Interventions in higher education and their effect on student success: A meta-analysis. *Educational Review, 70*(2), 208–228. doi:10.1080/00131911.2017.1300874

Snowman, J. (1986). Learning tactics and strategies. In G. D. Phye & T. Andre (Eds.), *Cognitive classroom learning: Understanding, thinking, and problem solving* (pp. 243–275). Academic Press.

Soderstrom, N. C., & Bjork, R. A. (2015). Learning versus performance: An integrative review. *Perspectives on Psychological Science, 10*(2), 176–199. doi:10.1177/1745691615569000 PMID:25910388

Soegaard, M., & Dam, R. F. (2012). *The encyclopedia of human-computer interaction*. Academic Press.

Soffer, T., & Cohen, A. (2019). Students' engagement characteristics predict success and completion of online courses. *Journal of Computer Assisted Learning, 35*(3), 378-389. doi:10.1111/jcal.12340

Sønderlund, A. L., Hughes, E., & Smith, J. (2018). The efficacy of learning analytics interventions in higher education: A systematic review. *British Journal of Educational Technology*. Advance online publication. doi:10.1111/bjet.127208

Sperling, R., Howard, B., Staley, R., & DuBois, N. (2004). Metacognition and self-regulated learning Constructs. *Educational Research and Evaluation, 10*(2), 117–139. doi:10.1076/edre.10.2.117.27905

Spitzer, H. F. (1939). Studies in retention. *Journal of Educational Psychology, 30*(9), 641–656. doi:10.1037/h0063404

Spooner, M., Duane, C., Uygur, J., Smyth, E., Marron, B., Murphy, P. J., & Pawlikowska, T. (2022). Self-regulatory learning theory as a lens on how undergraduate and postgraduate learners respond to feedback: A BEME scoping review: BEME Guide No. 66. *Medical Teacher, 44*(1), 3–18. doi:10.1080/0142159X.2021.1970732 PMID:34666584

Srivastava, E. (n.d.). *Decision Tree Vs Natural Language Processing: What Chatbot Type Is Better?* HappyFox Inc.

St. Evans, J. S. B. (2003). In two minds: Dual-process accounts of reasoning. *Trends in Cognitive Sciences*, *7*(10), 454–459. doi:10.1016/j.tics.2003.08.012 PMID:14550493

Stafford-Brizard, K. B. (2016). *Building blocks for learning: A framework for comprehensive student development.* Turnaround for Children. https://turnaroundusa.org/wp-content/uploads/2016/03/Turnaround-for-Children-Building-Blocks-for-Learningx-2.pdf

Stanovich, K. E., & West, R. F. (2000). Individual differences in reasoning: Implications for the rationality debate? *Behavioral and Brain Sciences*, *23*(5), 645–665. doi:10.1017/S0140525X00003435 PMID:11301544

Stanton, J. D., Neider, X. N., Gallegos, I. J., & Clark, N. C. (2015). Differences in metacognitive regulation in introductory biology students: When prompts are not enough. *CBE Life Sciences Education*, *14*(2), ar15. Advance online publication. doi:10.1187/cbe.14-08-0135 PMID:25976651

Sternberg, R. J., & Williams, W. M. (2010). *Educational psychology* (2nd ed.). Pearson.

Strang, K. D. (2017). Beyond engagement analytics: Which online mixed-data factors predict student learning outcomes? *Education and Information Technologies*, *22*(3), 917–937. doi:10.100710639-016-9464-2

Study International. (2017). Edtech and online learning are making higher education more accessible. *Online (Bergheim).*

Su, C. Y., & Chiu, C. H. (2021). Perceived enjoyment and attractiveness influence Taiwanese elementary cchool students' intention to use interactive video learning. *International Journal of Human-Computer Interaction*, *37*(6), 574–583. doi:10.1080/10447318.2020.1841423

Sweller, J. (1988). Cognitive load during problem solving: Effects on learning. *Cognitive Science*, *12*(2), 257–285. doi:10.120715516709cog1202_4

Sweller, J. (1999). *Instructional design in technical areas (Australian Education Review).* Australian Council for Education.

Sweller, J. (2010). Element interactivity and intrinsic, extraneous, and germane cognitive load. *Educational Psychology Review*, *22*(2), 123–138. doi:10.100710648-010-9128-5

Swivl. (n.d.). Which is a better option: Ai-power or rule-based chatbots? *Swivl Blog*. Retrieved August 20, 2022, from https://tryswivl.com/blog/ai-powered-chatbot/which-is-the-best-option-ai-powered-or-a-rule-based-chatbot/

Szpunar, K. K., Moulton, S. T., & Schacter, D. L. (2013). Mind wandering and education: From the classroom to online learning. *Frontiers in Psychology*, *4*, 495. doi:10.3389/fpsyg.2013.00495 PMID:23914183

Tadesse, T., Asmamaw, A., Getachew, K., Ferede, B., Melese, W., Siebeck, M., & Fischer, M. (2022). Self-Regulated Learning Strategies as Predictors of Perceived Learning Gains among Undergraduate Students in Ethiopian Universities. *Education Sciences*, *12*(7), 468. doi:10.3390/educsci12070468

Tan, R. Z., Wang, P. C., Lim, W. H., Ong, S. H. C., & Avnit, K. (2019). Early Prediction of Students' Mathematics Performance. *Proceedings of 2018 IEEE International Conference on Teaching, Assessment, and Learning for Engineering, TALE 2018.* 10.1109/TALE.2018.8615289

Tarus, J. K., Gichoya, D., & Muumbo, A. (2015). Challenges of implementing e-learning in Kenya: A case of Kenyan public universities. *International Review of Research in Open and Distributed Learning, 16*(1), 120-141.

Tate, T., & Warschauer, M. (2022). Equity in online learning. *Educational Psychologist*, *57*(3), 192–206. doi:10.1080/00461520.2022.2062597

Tavares, N. (2022). The use and impact of game-based learning on the learning experience and knowledge retention of nursing undergraduate students: A systematic literature review. *Nurse Education Today, 1117*, 105484. doi:10.1016/j.nedt.2022.105484 PMID:35917707

Taylor, K., & Rohrer, D. (2010). The effects of interleaved practice. *Applied Cognitive Psychology, 24*(6), 837–848. doi:10.1002/acp.1598

Temasek Polytechnic. (2022). *TP LibGuides*. Retrieved from TP Library: https://tp.libguides.com/apa

Thaler, R. H., & Sunstein, C. R. (2009). *Nudge: Improving decisions about health, wealth, and happiness*. Penguin.

Thalmann, M., Souza, A. S., & Oberauer, K. (2019). How does chunking help working memory? *Journal of Experimental Psychology. Learning, Memory, and Cognition, 45*(1), 37–55. doi:10.1037/xlm0000578 PMID:29698045

The World Bank. (2020, July 15). *Remote learning, EdTech and COVID-19*. https://www.worldbank.org/en/topic/edutech/brief/edtech-covid-19

Theobald, M. (2021). Self-regulated learning training programs enhance university students' academic performance, self-regulated learning strategies, and motivation: A meta-analysis. *Contemporary Educational Psychology, 66*, 1. doi:10.1016/j.cedpsych.2021.101976

Thode, H. C. (2002). *Testing for normality* (Vol. 164). CRC Press. doi:10.1201/9780203910894

Thomas, L. (2012). *Building student engagement and belonging at a time of change in higher education*. Paul Hamlyn Foundation.

Tinto, V. (1987). *Leaving college: Rethinking the causes and cures for student attrition*. University of Chicago Press.

Torda, A. J., Velan, G., & Perovic, V. (2020). The impact of the COVID-19 pandemic on medical education. *MJA, 23*(4), 1187–8.

Trowler, V. (2015). Negotiating Contestations and 'Chaotic Conceptions': Engaging 'Non-Traditional' Students in Higher education. *Higher Education Quarterly, 69*(3), 295–310. doi:10.1111/hequ.12071

Tsai, Y.-S., Gašević, D., Whitelock-Wainwright, A., Muñoz-Merino, P. J., Moreno-Marcos, P. M., Fernández, A. R., Kloos, C. D., Scheffel, M., Jivet, I., Drachsler, H., Tammets, K., Calleja, A. R., & Kollom, K. (2018). *SHEILA: Supporting Higher Education to Intergrade Learning Analytics Research Report*. https://sheilaproject.eu/results/

Tsai, Y. S., Moreno-Marcos, P. M., Jivet, I., Scheffel, M., Tammets, K., Kollom, K., & Gaševic, D. (2018). The SHEILA Framework: Informing Institutional Strategies and Policy Processes of Learning Analytics. *Journal of Learning Analytics, 5*(3), 5–20. doi:10.18608/jla.2018.53.2

Tucker, L. R., & Lewis, C. (1973). A reliability coefficient for maximum likelihood factor analysis. *Psychometrika, 38*(1), 1–1. doi:10.1007/BF02291170

Turek, M. (2018). *Explainable artificial intelligence (XAI)*. Defense Advanced Research Projects Agency. https://www darpa. mil/program/explainable-artificial-intelligence

Tversky, A., & Kahneman, D. (1974). Judgment under uncertainty: Heuristics and biases (Biases in judgments reveal some heuristics of thinking under uncertainty). *Science, 185*(4157), 1124–1131. doi:10.1126cience.185.4157.1124 PMID:17835457

Ullmann, T. D. (2011). *An architecture for the automated detection of textual indicators of reflection*. Academic Press.

United Nations. (2020). *Policy Brief: Education during COVID-19 and beyond*. https://unsdg.un.org/resources/policy-brief-education-during-covid-19-and-beyond

Valdez, A. (2013). Student metacognitive monitoring: Predicting test achievement from judgment accuracy. *International Journal of Higher Education*, *2*(2), 141–146. doi:10.5430/ijhe.v2n2p141

Vallerand, R. J., & Reid, G. (1988). On the relative effects of positive and negative verbal feedback on males' and females' intrinsic motivation. *Canadian Journal of Behavioural Science/Revue Canadienne des Sciences du Comportement, 20*(3), 239.

van Alten, D. C. D., Phielix, C., Janssen, J., & Kester, L. (2020). Self-regulated learning support in flipped learning videos enhances learning outcomes. *Computers & Education*, *158*, 104000. doi:10.1016/j.compedu.2020.104000

Van den Boom, G., Paas, F., Van Merrienboer, J. J., & Van Gog, T. (2004). Reflection prompts and tutor feedback in a web-based learning environment: Effects on students' self-regulated learning competence. *Computers in Human Behavior*, *20*(4), 551–567. doi:10.1016/j.chb.2003.10.001

Van der Kleij, F. M., Feskens, R. C., & Eggen, T. J. (2015). Effects of feedback in a computer-based learning environment on students' learning outcomes: A meta-analysis. *Review of Educational Research*, *85*(4), 475–511. doi:10.3102/0034654314564881

van der Meer, J., Scott, D., & Pratt, K. (2018). First semester academic performance: The importance of early indicators of non-engagement. *Student Success*, *9*(4), 1–12. doi:10.5204sj.v9i4.652

van Gaalen, A., Brouwer, J., Schönrock-Adema, J., Bouwkamp-Timmer, T., Jaarsma, A., & Georgiadis, J. R. (2021). Gamification of health professions education: A systematic review. *Advances in Health Sciences Education: Theory and Practice*, *26*(2), 683–711. doi:10.100710459-020-10000-3 PMID:33128662

van Merrienboer, J. J. G. (1997). *Training complex cognitive skills: A four-component instructional design model for technical training*. Educational Technology Publications. https://research.utwente.nl/en/publications/training-complex-cognitive-skills-a-four-component-instructional-

Van Merriënboer, J. J., Clark, R. E., & De Croock, M. B. (2002). Blueprints for complex learning: The 4C/ID-model. *Educational Technology Research and Development*, *50*(2), 39–61. doi:10.1007/BF02504993

Veenman, M. V. J. (2017). Learning to self-monitor and to self-regulate. In R. E. Mayer & P. A. Alexander (Eds.), Handbook of research on learning and instruction (2nd ed., pp. 233–257). Routledge.

Walton, G. M., Cohen, G. L., Cwir, D., & Spencer, S. J. (2012). Mere belonging: The power of social connections. *Journal of Personality and Social Psychology*, *102*(3), 513–532. doi:10.1037/a0025731 PMID:22023711

Wang, C. H., Shannon, D. M., & Ross, M. E. (2013). Students' characteristics, self-regulated learning, technology self-efficacy, and course outcomes in online learning. *Distance Education*, *34*(3), 302–323. doi:10.1080/01587919.2013.835779

Wang, P. C., Avnit, K., Tan, R. Z., Ng, T. H., & Lim, W. H. (2020). Learning Mathematics through Technology-enhanced Pedagogy. In *Applied Learning in Higher Education*. Perspective, Pedagogy, and Practice.

Weinberg, S. L., & Abramowitz, S. K. (2008). *Statistics using SPSS: An integrative approach*. Cambridge University Press.

Weiner, B. (1986). *An attributional theory of motivation and emotion*. Springer-Verlag. doi:10.1007/978-1-4612-4948-1

Weinert, F. E., Schrader, F. W., & Helmke, A. (1989). Quality of instruction and achievement outcomes. *International Journal of Educational Psychology, 13*(8), 895}912.

Weinstein, C. E., Palmer, D. R., & Acee, T. W. (2016). LASSI user's manual: Learning and study strategies. H&H.

Weinstein, C. E., Acee, T. W., & Jung, J. H. (2011). Self-regulation and learning strategies. *New Directions for Teaching and Learning*, *2011*(126), 45–53. doi:10.1002/tl.443

Weinstein, C., Palmer, D., & Acee, T. (2016). *LASSI user's manual: learning and study strategies inventory* (3rd ed.). H&H Publishing Company.

Weiss, M. (2020). *Long Life Learning: Preparing for Jobs that Don't Even Exist Yet*. Wiley.

Wheeler, L., & Reis, H. T. (1991). Self-recordings of everyday life events: Origins, types, and Uues. *Journal of Personality*, *59*(3), 339–354. doi:10.1111/j.1467-6494.1991.tb00252.x

Wigfield, A., & Eccles, J. S. (2000). Expectancy–value theory of achievement motivation. *Contemporary Educational Psychology*, *25*(1), 68–81. doi:10.1006/ceps.1999.1015 PMID:10620382

Winne, P. H. (2017). Learning Analytics for self-regulated learning. In Handbook of learning analytics. SOLAR. doi:10.18608/hla17.021

Winne, P. H., & Hadwin, A. F. (1998). Studying as self-regulated learning. In D. J. Hacker, J. Dunlosky, & A. C. Graesser (Eds.), Metacognition in educational theory and practice (pp. 277-304). Lawrence Erlbaum Associates Publishers.

Winne, P. (2018). Theorising and researching levels of processing in self-regulated learning. *The British Journal of Educational Psychology*, *88*(1), 9–20. doi:10.1111/bjep.12173 PMID:28791689

Winne, P. H. (1996). A metacognitive view of individual differences in self-regulated learning. *Learning and Individual Differences*, *8*(4), 327–353. doi:10.1016/S1041-6080(96)90022-9

WinneP. H.BakerR. S. J. (2013). The potentials of educational data mining for researching metacognition, motivation and self-regulated learning. Zenodo.

Winne, P. H., & Hadwin, A. F. (1998). Studying as self-regulated learning. In D. J. Hacker, J. Dunlosky, & A. Graesser (Eds.), *Metacognition in educational theory and practice* (pp. 277–304). Routledge.

Wirth, J., Stebner, F., Trypke, M., Schuster, C., & Leutner, D. (2020). An interactive layers model of self-regulated learning and cognitive load. *Educational Psychology Review*, *32*(4), 1127–1149. doi:10.100710648-020-09568-4

Wise, A. F., & Shaffer, D. W. (2015). Why theory matters more than ever in the age of big data. *Journal of Learning Analytics*, *2*(2), 5–13. doi:10.18608/jla.2015.22.2

Wissman, K. T., Rawson, K. A., & Pyc, M. A. (2012). How and when do students use flashcards. *Memory (Hove, England)*, *20*(6), 568–579. doi:10.1080/09658211.2012.687052 PMID:22671698

Wolters, C. A., & Won, S. (2017). Validity and the Use of Self-Report Questionnaires to Assess Self-Regulated Learning. In *Handbook of Self-Regulation of Learning and Performance* (2nd ed.). Routledge. doi:10.4324/9781315697048-20

Wong, J., Baars, M., Davis, D., Van, D. Z., Houben, G., & Paas, F. (2019). Supporting self-regulated learning in online learning environments and MOOCs: A systematic review. *International Journal of Human-Computer Interaction*, *35*(4-5), 356–373. doi:10.1080/10447318.2018.1543084

World Bank. (2003). *Lifelong Learning in the Global Knowledge Economy: Challenges for Developing Countries*. Author.

Wright, R. D. (Ed.). (2015). *Student-Teacher Interaction in Online Learning Environments*. IGI Global. doi:10.4018/978-1-4666-6461-6

Xing, W., & Du, D. (2019). Dropout prediction in MOOCs: Using deep learning for personalized intervention. *Journal of Educational Computing Research*, *57*(3), 547–570. doi:10.1177/0735633118757015

Xu, D., & Jaggars, S. S. (2011). *Online and hybrid course enrollment and performance in Washington state community and technical colleges.* CCRC working paper no. 31. Community College Research Center, Columbia University.

Xu, D., & Xu, Y. (2019). *The promises and limits of online higher education: Understanding how distance education affects access, cost, and quality.* American Enterprise Institute. https://www.aei.org/research-products/report/the-promises-an d-limits-of-online-higher-education

Xu, D., Glick, D., Rodriguez, F., Cung, B., Qiujie, L., & Warschauer, M. (2019). Does blended instruction enhance English language learning in developing countries? Evidence from Mexico. *British Journal of Educational Technology*.

Xu, D., & Jaggars, S. S. (2014). Performance gaps between online and face-to-face courses: Differences between types of students and academic subject areas. *The Journal of Higher Education*, *85*(5), 633–659. doi:10.1353/jhe.2014.0028

Xu, Y., Lau, Y., Cheng, L. J., & Lau, S. T. (2021). Learning experiences of game-based educational intervention in nursing students: A systematic mixed-studies review. *Nurse Education Today*, *107*, 105139. doi:10.1016/j.nedt.2021.105139 PMID:34563963

Yang, T., Chen, M. C., & Chen, S. (2018). The influences of self-regulated learning support and prior knowledge on improving learning performance. *Computers & Education*, *126*, 37–52. doi:10.1016/j.compedu.2018.06.025

Yan, V., Thai, K., & Bjork, R. (2014). Habits and beliefs that guide self-regulated learning: Do they vary with mindset? *Journal of Applied Research in Memory and Cognition*, *3*(3), 123. doi:10.1037/h0101799

Yan, Z. (2020). Self-assessment in the process of self-regulated learning and its relationship with academic achievement. *Assessment & Evaluation in Higher Education*, *45*(2), 224–238. doi:10.1080/02602938.2019.1629390

Yin, H. (2018). What motivates Chinese undergraduates to engage in learning? insights from a psychological approach to student engagement research. *Higher Education*, *76*(5), 827–847. doi:10.100710734-018-0239-0

Zacharis, N. Z. (2015). A multivariate approach to predicting student outcomes in web-enabled blended learning courses. *The Internet and Higher Education*, *27*, 44–53. doi:10.1016/j.iheduc.2015.05.002

Zakos, J., & Capper, L. (2008). CLIVE – An Artificially Intelligent Chat Robot for Conversational Language Practice. In J. Darzentas, G. A. Vouros, S. Vosinakis, & A. Arnellos (Eds.), Lecture Notes in Computer Science: Vol. 5138. *Artificial Intelligence: Theories, Models and Applications. SETN 2008.* Springer. doi:10.1007/978-3-540-87881-0_46

Zaromb, F. M., & Roediger, H. L. (2010). The testing effect in free recall is associated with enhanced organizational processes. *Memory & Cognition*, *38*(8), 995–1008. doi:10.3758/MC.38.8.995 PMID:21156864

Zepeda, C. D., Martin, R. S., & Butler, A. C. (2020). Motivational strategies to engage learners in desirable difficulties. *Journal of Applied Research in Memory and Cognition*, *9*(4), 468–474. doi:10.1016/j.jarmac.2020.08.007

Zepeda, C. D., Richey, J. E., Ronevich, P., & Nokes-Malach, T. J. (2015). Direct instruction of metacognition benefits adolescent science learning, transfer, and motivation: An in vivo study. *Journal of Educational Psychology*, *107*(4), 954–970. doi:10.1037/edu0000022

Zhu, M., & Bonk, C. J. (2022). Guidelines and strategies for fostering and enhancing self-directed online learning. *Open Learning: The Journal of Open, Distance and eLearning*. doi:10.1080/02680513.2022.2141105

Zhu, Y., Au, W., & Yates, G. (2016). University students' self-control and self-regulated learning in a blended course. *The Internet and Higher Education*, *30*, 54–62. doi:10.1016/j.iheduc.2016.04.001

Zimmerman, B. J. (1998). Developing self-fulfilling cycles of academic regulation. In Self-regulated learning: From teaching to self-reflective practice. Guilford Publications.

Zimmerman, B. J. (2000). Attaining self-regulation, a socio-cognitive perspective. Handbook of self- regulation, 13-39.

Zimmerman, B. J., & Risemberg, R. (1997). Self-regulatory dimensions of academic learning and motivation. Handbook of Academic Learning, 105–125. doi:10.1016/b978 012554255-5/50005-3

Zimmerman, B. J., & Schunk, D. H. (2011) Self-regulated learning and Performance. In Handbook of Self-regulation of learning and performance. Routledge.

Zimmerman, B. (2000). Attaining self-regulation: a social cognitive perspective. In M. Boekaerts, P. R. Pintrich, & M. Zeidner (Eds.), *s), Handbook of Self-Regulation* (pp. 13–40). Academic Press. doi:10.1016/B978-012109890-2/50031-7

Zimmerman, B. (2013). From cognitive modeling to self-regulation: A social cognitive career path. *Educational Psychologist*, *48*(3), 135–147. doi:10.1080/00461520.2013.794676

Zimmerman, B. J. (1990). Self-regulated learning and academic achievement: An overview. *Educational Psychologist*, *25*(1), 3–17. doi:10.120715326985ep2501_2

Zimmerman, B. J. (2002). Becoming a self-regulated learner: An overview. *Theory into Practice*, *41*(2), 64–72. doi:10.120715430421tip4102_2

Zimmerman, B. J. (2008). Investigating self-regulation and motivation: Historical background, methodological developments, and future prospects. *American Educational Research Journal*, *45*(1), 166–183. doi:10.3102/0002831207312909

Zimmerman, B. J., & Moylan, A. R. (2009). Self-regulation: where metacognition and motivation intersect. In D. J. Hacker, J. Dunlosky, & A. C. Graesser (Eds.), *Handbook of Metacognition in Education* (pp. 299–315). Routledge.

Zimmerman, B. J., & Schunk, D. H. (2018). *Handbook of self-regulation of learning and performance*. Routledge. doi:10.4324/978131569704

Zimmerman, B. J., & Schunk, D. H. (Eds.). (2001). *Self-regulated learning and academic achievement: Theoretical perspectives*. Routledge. https://www.routledge.com/Self-Regulated-Learning-and-Academic-Achievement-Theoretical-Perspectives/Zimmerman-Schunk/p/book/9780805835618

Zimmerman, B., & Campillo, M. (2003). Motivating Self-Regulated Problem Solvers. In J. Davidson & R. Sternberg (Eds.), *The Psychology of Problem Solving* (pp. 233–262). Cambridge University Press. doi:10.1017/CBO9780511615771.009

Zohar, A., & Barzilai, S. (2013). A review of research on metacognition in science education: Current and future directions. *Studies in Science Education*, *49*(2), 121–169. doi:10.1080/03057267.2013.847261

Zohar, A., & Ben-Ari, G. (2022). Teachers' knowledge and professional development for metacognitive instruction in the context of higher order thinking. *Metacognition and Learning*, *17*(3), 855–895. Advance online publication. doi:10.100711409-022-09310-1

Zumalt, C., & Williamson, V. (2016). Does the arrangement of embedded text versus linked text in homework systems make a difference in students' impressions, attitudes, and perceived learning? *Journal of Science Education and Technology*, *25*(5), 704–714. doi:10.100710956-016-9625-5

About the Contributors

Danny Glick has over 20 years of experience working in K-20 EdTech research and implementation. His expertise is in developing EdTech research and implementation strategy enabled by data engineering to inform product improvement and determine the efficacy of products and services. In his role as Academic Director at Edge, Center for EdTech Research and Innovation, Dr. Glick works on a range of EdTech research projects related to emerging technologies in education. In K-12 education, his team is studying the use of interactive geometry courses to support young children's STEM learning, embedding video-bots into English language classes, and examining the impact of 3D virtual learning and game-based learning environments on student achievement. In higher education, Danny's team is developing and studying the use of AI-powered virtual-human trainings to support student SRL strategy practice and use. Before his work at Edge, Dr. Glick established the pedagogical implementation strategy for Edusoft, a subsidiary of ETS. He led a team of EdTech implementation specialists specializing in designing, implementing and evaluating large-scale technology-enhanced learning and assessment solutions, serving K-20 institutions in over 30 countries worldwide. Dr. Glick is a former visiting scholar at the University of California, Irvine's Digital Learning Lab, where he examined the impact of technology-mediated language learning on student achievement and persistence in developing countries. He is the author and editor of a wide range of publications, including, most recently, "Early Warning Systems and Targeted Interventions for Student Success in Online Courses", "Predicting Success, Preventing Failure", and "Supporting Self-Regulated Learning and Student Success in Online Courses."

Jeff Bergin is the Vice President of Impact and Experience at General Assembly, where he leads the online design and delivery of accelerated technical training for job readiness. Previously, Jeff served as the Vice President of Learning Products and Experience at Universal Technical Institute where he launched a high-fidelity learning experience that drove improvements in learner performance and completion. Prior to that, Jeff served as the Vice President of Learning Research and Design at Macmillan Learning, where he led the R&D for a new active learning platform and the VP of Learning & Experience Design at Pearson, where he launched Pearson's flagship online learning product, CourseConnect. Jeff earned a Ph.D. from Arizona State University, where his research focused on the impact that learner-centered pedagogies make on student performance and persistence in online environments. He taught at Maricopa Community Colleges, facilitated design workshops through Northwestern University's Design for America, and served on the executive board of the Emerging Learning Design Conference and Journal at Montclair State University. He has published and presented on a wide range of topics related to online learning design and has been affiliated with i-NACOL, Quality Matters, U.S.D.L.A., and the American Council on Education.

* * *

Karin Avnit, PhD, is an Associate Professor at the Singapore Institute of Technology (SIT). She leads the team of Technology-Enhanced Learning at the Centre for Learning Environment and Assessment Development (CoLEAD), where she works with Educational Developers and Educational Technologies to support and develop educators in the adoption of technologies for teaching and learning. She is also a faculty member in the Infocomm Technology cluster and the recipient of the university's Teaching Excellence Award 2015, 2017 and 2019.

Matthew L. Bernacki is a Donald and Justeen Tarbet Distinguished Scholar and Associate Professor in the Learning Sciences and Psychological Studies program at the University of North Carolina at Chapel Hill in the United States of America. His scholarship on self-regulated learning includes specific lines of study on metacognitive and motivational processes as well as their involvement in complex and dynamic relationships that can be observed during learning. He designs digital interventions and personalized learning tools to build and leverage students' motivations and learning skills to improve their self-regulated learning in complex hybrid and digital environments. He uses learning analytics to understand, identify, and respond to students learning and has published over 60 peer-reviewed and invited works on self-regulated learning, personalized learning, motivation, learning analytics, and other topics. Matt is an Associate Editor of the Journal of Educational Psychology and an Editorial Board member for Contemporary Educational Psychology. He has previously edited special issues of Contemporary Educational Psychology, Metacognition and Learning, and the Journal of Research on Technology in Education. He completed postdoctoral training at LearnLab, a National Science Foundation Science of Learning Center spanning the Human Computer Interaction Institute at Carnegie Mellon University and the Learning Research and Development Center at the University of Pittsburgh. He holds a Ph.D. in Educational Psychology, as well as a Master's degree in Social Administration from Temple University in Philadelphia, PA, as well as a Master's degree in Experimental Psychology and a Bachelor's degree in Psychology from Saint Joseph's University in Philadelphia, PA.

Kelly Boden received her PhD in Cognitive Psychology from the University of Pittsburgh in 2022. Her research has focused on how motivation impacts learning, particularly the transfer of prior knowledge to new contexts. She was hired as a Research Scientist by Macmillan Learning where she continues researching issues around learning.

Jang Yuan Chao is a Communication Skills lecturer at the Centre for Life Skills, School of Humanities & Social Science, Temasek Polytechnic, Singapore. She is currently a doctoral candidate at the University of Sheffield, UK. Her research interests include curriculum design for ICT learning and contemporary debates in language and teaching.

Anat Cohen (PhD) is a senior academic staff at Tel Aviv University's School of Education, where she heads the Learning and Technology program in the Department of Education in Mathematics, Science and Technology. She is a deputy chair holder of technology and education affairs in the UNESCO Chair in Technology, Internationalization and Education; a research coordinator of Web-Supported Academic Instruction at Tel-Aviv University (Virtual TAU); and the PI of a research project funded by the Education Ministry's chief scientist: Integrating Mathematical Applets in the Teaching Sequence.

Dr. Cohen has vast research and teaching experience in the field of learning and cyber technologies. For the past 20 years she has been engaged in developing online learning materials, training academic staff and characterizing how to fit learning-management features to the university's needs. Her research activities focus on areas such as learning analytics and educational data-mining, social networks and privacy perception, ICT implementation in higher education, cost-effectiveness of online learning, open educational resources (learning object repositories & MOOCs) and mobile-assisted learning.

Qinnan Ding is a research associate in the National Institutes of Educational Policy Research of East China Normal University. Ding received her B.A. and M.D. in psychology from East China Normal University. Her research areas are student psychological health, student development and education policy evaluation. She has participated large-scale surveys include *2019 China College Teaching and Learning Survey, 2020 Shanghai Online Teaching and Learning Survey, 2021 Changjiang Delta education development survey*. Her current project is focus on the college graduates' job seeking process.

Linda Fang is a senior lecturer at Temasek Polytechnic, Singapore. Trained in TESOL, she has developed and taught many English language programmes for schools and tertiary institutions. She has trained teachers in language teaching, and lecturers and trainers in ICT. She has researched on e-Learning/ Blended learning, Simulation Based Learning, Serious Game-based learning, Virtual Reality, and Learning Analytics and has published widely. She received the best paper award for her paper at the IODL & ICEM International Joint Conference and Media Days, 2010, the AECT Robert de Kieffer International Fellowship Award in 2014 for her international work in ICT. She was one of the winners for the SIT Applied Learning Conference case study competition, 2022. She has been invited speaker at UNESCO Bangkok, Chulalongkorn University, IAL Adult Learning Symposium and ASTD -STADA conferences.

Ester Goh is a data developer at the School of Informatics and IT at Temasek Polytechnic while studying for her degree in Computer Science at Nanyang Technological University, Singapore. Her passion in developing cutting-edge solutions to improve daily life is what fuels her to blaze through the many technical challenges, including those from chatbots for personalised learning

Jiao Guo is an associate professor in the Institute of Higher Education of East China Normal University. Her research areas are economics of education, education policy evaluation, and survey design. The large-scale surveys she led include *2019 China College Teaching and Learning Survey* and *2020 Shanghai Online Teaching and Learning Survey*. Her scholarship explores the income effect of over-education and undereducation, the academic performance of first-generation college students, and the evolution of the digital divide. Guo recently released a new book *Reimagine Undergraduate Learning*. Her current projects include the behavior analysis on the online self-regulated learning of undergraduates. Guo received her B.A. in English and M.Ed. from Peking University and then her Ed.D. in Education Policy Analysis of Education from Harvard in 2012.

Kara McWilliams is the Associate Vice President of the ETS AI Research Laboratories. Kara develops the strategy for new product innovation and oversees the research and development of educational technology across four markets – K12, Higher Education, Languages, and the Workforce. She also leads the development of AI capabilities that are implemented in new products across portfolios and leveraged in ETS largest assessments. Most of Kara's work has focused on how to understand user needs from the perspective of their values, beliefs, and experiences and merge the research on how people learn most effectively with the application of innovative technology to build efficacious digital learning tools. She has conducted extensive work on the efficacy of educational technology, ethical use of AI, and communicating both to users in meaningful ways. Kara holds a doctorate in Educational Research, Measurement and Evaluation and a master's degree in Curriculum & Instruction from Boston College.

Shirley Miedijensky is a senior lecturer at the Faculty of Graduate Studies at Oranim Academic College. She received from the Technion- Israel Institute of Technology her B.Sc. in Biology, M.Sc. and Ph.D. in direct track in Science and Mathematics Education. As a Post-Doctoral fellow, she studied science learning environments for gifted students. She supervises graduate students and teaches graduate and undergraduate courses in the Department of Science and Mathematics Education and in the MTeach program. Dr. Miedijensky was the head of the Academic Portal System of Oranim Academic College and was a leading member in establishing the Unit for Online Studies in the college. Dr. Miedijensky received the Kaplan Award for outstanding researchers in the field of science education. Dr. Miedijensk's research interests include metacognition, self-regulation, online learning environment and educational technology, gifted education, STEAM education, assessment for learning, and interdisciplinary learning.

David Porcaro is currently the Vice President of Learning at Insight Partners, where he leads the development of online and blended learning for startup companies. He has led learning engineering, curriculum development, research, and learning design teams for large publishers, small education technology startups, international development organizations, and philanthropies in several countries. He has also taught at universities in the US and the Middle East. He holds a PhD in Learning, Design and Technology as well as degrees in Near Eastern studies and archaeology.

Richard. D. Roberts, Ph.D., is currently Co-Founder, Research & Assessment Design (RAD): Science Solution, Philadelphia, PA. A former Senior Lecturer at The University of Sydney (1998-2003), he has also been a Managing Principal Research Scientist at ETS (2003-2014), VP/Chief Scientist, at ProExam (2014-2017), and VP/Chief Scientist at ACT, Inc (2017-2018). During his career, Dr. Roberts has conducted research to enhance the quality of prominent existing cognitive assessments (e.g., Armed Services Vocational Aptitude Battery [ASVAB]) while also pioneering new approaches involving the use of psychometric models, cognitive paradigms, and multimedia IT platforms to measure individual differences in critically important constructs, including cross-cultural competence, cognitive biases (i.e., thinking fast, thinking slow), and processing speed. He has also been at the forefront of developing commercial products assessing behavioral, social, and emotional competencies, including the Mission Skills Assessment, ACT TesseraTM, and most recently, SELF+eTM. Over this career, Dr. Roberts has published over a dozen books with established publishing houses (e.g., OUP, MIT Press, Taylor & Francis), and more than 200 peer-review articles / book chapters on these topics in diverse sub-disciplines (including, education, psychology, business, medicine, health and economic policy, military science, and human and environmental engineering; see □Richard D Roberts - □Google Scholar). In addition to publication, he has presented his work nearly 400 times across the globe. Dr. Roberts has received grants and contracts as Principal Investigator from a diverse group of funders, a representative sample of which includes the Organisation for Economic Co-operation and Development (OECD), Army Research Institute (ARI), Intelligence Advanced Research Projects Activity (IARPA), Australian Research Council (ARC), Agencia de Calidad de la Educación, Chile, Employment and Social Development Canada (ESDC), and the

Bill and Melinda Gates Foundation. Among Dr. Roberts' professional honors are several editorships, two ETS Presidential Awards, two PROSE book awards, the University of Sydney H. Tasman Lovell Memorial Medal (for his doctoral dissertation), a National Research Council Fellowship, and various early (and then later) career awards.

Franklin M. Zaromb, Ph.D. is the Manager of the Department of Statistics and Research and Development at the National Authority for Measurement and Evaluation in Education in Ramat Gan, Israel, where he leads the development and implementation of statistical and psychometric analyses for national educational testing and research programs. From 2010 to 2015, Dr. Zaromb was a Research Scientist in the Research and Development division at Educational Testing Service (ETS) in Princeton, NJ, where he was Principal Investigator for a 4-year project to develop standardized assessments of judgment and decision-making biases for the U.S. Intelligence Advanced Research Project Activity (IARPA) Sirius Program. Other projects included directing research studies measuring longitudinal gains in college students' writing skills; and investigating the use of "no-stakes" educational testing to mitigate summer learning loss. Dr. Zaromb obtained his Ph.D. in Psychology from Washington University in St. Louis in 2010. His research interests include human learning and memory, judgment and decision-making, and educational and workforce applications of cognitive and educational psychology.

Huiyu Zhang has over a decade of experience training students and working adult learners in Artificial Intelligence and Analytics through Temasek Polytechnic (TP) full-time programmes and short courses. She received TP's Teaching Excellence Award in 2018. As Senior Academic Mentor, she coaches and supports colleagues in the School of Information Technology and IT to enhance teaching and learning experiences. To unleash the power of AI and Analytics in Education, she designs and implements pedagogical approaches in her own classes and then shares best practices with tutors. She is TP's Data Scientist representative in the Institutes of Higher Learning consortium that aims to produce a system to predict student outcomes for the Poly Foundational Programme. She recently published a paper on assessing the accuracy of AI enabled acoustic analytic technology on breath sounds in children, with her clinical collaborators from the KK Women's and Children's Hospital.

Index

F

G

H

I

L

M

N

O

P

R

S

T

U

V

Ensure Quality Research is Introduced to the Academic Community

Become an Evaluator for IGI Global Authored Book Projects

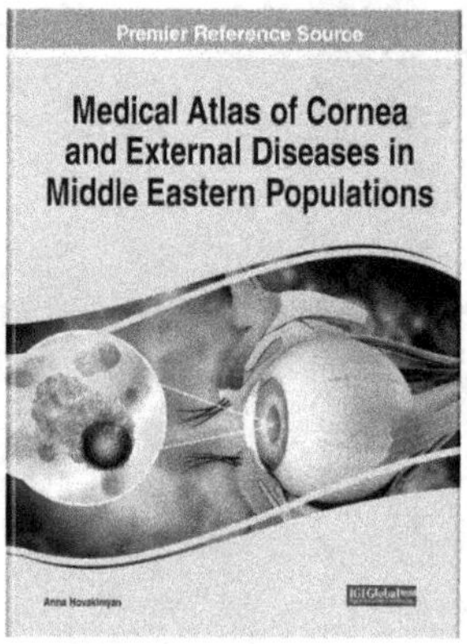

The overall success of an authored book project is dependent on quality and timely manuscript evaluations.

Applications and Inquiries may be sent to:
development@igi-global.com

Applicants must have a doctorate (or equivalent degree) as well as publishing, research, and reviewing experience. Authored Book Evaluators are appointed for one-year terms and are expected to complete at least three evaluations per term. Upon successful completion of this term, evaluators can be considered for an additional term.

If you have a colleague that may be interested in this opportunity, we encourage you to share this information with them.

CPSIA information can be obtained
at www.ICGtesting.com
Printed in the USA
LVHW051352210323
742129LV00007B/603